The Russian Patriotic War of 1812 tells the story that inspired Tolstoy's epic novel War and Peace and will appeal to those interested in Russian history, military history and wargamers alike. It is the only publicly available translation into English of Bogdanovich's official history of the Russian Forces involvement fighting against Napoleon and his allies in Russia in 1812. This translation also includes extracts from Ivan Liprandi's critique of Bogdanovich's work.

This final volume of the trilogy continues to cover operations from the Russian perspective; from Napoleon's abandoning of Moscow to the expulsion of the Grande Armée from the Russian Empire, including operations against the Prussian and Austro-Saxon auxiliary corps on the flanks. The author had full access to Russian state archives but also made extensive reference to published works by French and German historians in order to provide greater context. The maps show entire phases of the war, while the battle plans show locations of dominant terrain, according to detailed state surveys, while villages, forests and roads have been copied from previously published Russian plans. Appendices and footnotes also include detailed orders-of-battle, important correspondence, and a bibliography with Bogdanovich's and Liprandi's critical assessments of these sources.

Born in Sumy, Ukraine, in 1805, Bogdanovich was initially educated in the Noble Regiment, being commissioned into the artillery in 1823. Bogdanovich saw combat in the Polish campaign of 1831 and upon his return in 1833, he entered the Imperial Military Academy, becoming its Director of Operations until 1839. Thereafter, he served on committees of the General Staff. He died in August, 1882 in Oranienbaum. General Bogdanovich is famed for a number of major works, making an invaluable contribution to Russian military historiography. His *History of the Patriotic War of 1812* won the Demidov Prize for History in 1861.

Peter G.A. Phillips is a veteran of 27 years in the British Army Intelligence Corps, including working as a Russian, German, and Serbo-Croat linguist, thereafter spending five years as part of a Civil Service team training British Armed Forces personnel to serve in UK diplomatic missions. He is now retired and spends his time translating Russian military histories of the Coalition Wars. His published translations include: Mikhailovsky-Danilevsky's histories of the wars of 1805 and 1806-1807; a collaboration with renowned Napoleonic historian Dr Alexander Mikaberidze of Ilya Radozhitskii's trilogy of memoirs covering 1812-1814; and numerous articles for The Waterloo Association's website www.napoleon-series.org. Peter now lives in the Philippines with his Filipina wife of 34 years. They have two adult daughters.

The Russian Patriotic War Of 1812 Volume 3

The Russian Official History

Modest Ivanovich Bogdanovich

Translated by Peter G.A. Phillips

Helion & Company

Helion & Company Limited
Unit 8 Amherst Business Centre
Budbrooke Road
Warwick
CV34 5WE
England
Tel. 01926 499619
Email: info@helion.co.uk
Website: www.helion.co.uk
Twitter: @helionbooks
Visit our blog https://helionbooks.wordpress.com/

Published by Helion & Company 2025
Designed and typeset by Mach 3 Solutions (www.mach3solutions.co.uk)
Cover designed by Paul Hewitt, Battlefield Design (www.battlefield-design.co.uk)

Original text published as *History Of The Patriotic War Of 1812 According To Reliable Sources. Compiled in accordance with Supreme orders.*, St Petersburg, 1861
Translation © Peter Philips 2024
Maps and diagrams by George Anderson, Anderson Subtil © Helion & Company 2025

Cover: The Battle of Krasny by Peter von Hess (Public Domain)

Every reasonable effort has been made to trace copyright holders and to obtain their permission for the use of copyright material. The author and publisher apologise for any errors or omissions in this work, and would be grateful if notified of any corrections that should be incorporated in future reprints or editions of this book.

ISBN 978-1-804515-44-0

British Library Cataloguing-in-Publication Data.
A catalogue record for this book is available from the British Library.

All rights reserved. No part of this publication may be reproduced, stored in a retrieval system, or transmitted, in any form, or by any means, electronic, mechanical, photocopying, recording or otherwise, without the express written consent of Helion & Company Limited.

For details of other military history titles published by Helion & Company Limited, contact the above address, or visit our website: http://www.helion.co.uk

We always welcome receiving book proposals from prospective authors.

Contents

List of Maps		v
33	Napoleon's Departure From Moscow	7
34	Battle of Maloyaroslavets	28
35	The battle at Vyazma and Napoleon's retreat to Smolensk	53
36	The Battle of Krasny	80
37	The retreat of the enemy army from Krasny beyond the Dnieper	107
38	The Second Battle of Polotsk	117
39	The Battles of Chashniki and Smoliyantsy	135
40	Chichagov's movements from Brest to the Berezina	149
41	Napoleon's movements towards the Berezina	170
42	The Berezina crossing	186
43	The liberation of Vilna by Russian forces	210
44	Retreat of the remnants of the *Grande Armée* across the borders of Russia	233
45	The retreat of Schwarzenberg's and Reynier's Corps to the Russian frontier	248
46	The pursuit of MacDonald's Corps by Russian forces	257
47	Conclusions	274

Appendices
I	A return showing the approximate strength of Napoleon's force prior to the departure from Moscow	286
II	Prince Kutuzov's report to the Tsar, dated 16 (28) October 1812	287
III	The Viceroy's intercepted dispatches	289
IV	The strength of the French army between 8 to 14 November new style	291
V	Prince Kutuzov's report to Emperor Alexander I, dated 7 [19] November, No. 464	292
VI	Captain Seslavin's report, dated 8 [20] November	294
VII	Order of battle for the forces under Chichagov and Saken	296
VIII	*Situation de la place de Minsk à l'époque du 12 novembre* (new style) *1812*	300
IX	Details of Ertel's inaction	301
X	Yermolov's report to Wittgenstein, dated 11 [23] November, from Pogost	303
XI	The strength of Napoleon's forces	304
XII	Excerpts from General Bennigsen's letters to Emperor Alexander I	305
XIII	The composition of Chaplits' vanguard	306
XIV	The composition of the detachments at Berezina	307
XV	Declaration sent to Prince Kutuzov, under Supreme Orders, dated 6 [18] December 1812	308

XVI	Correspondence Regarding the Appointment of Chief of Artillery for all armies	309
XVII	Kutuzov's secret instructions regarding Schwarzenberg	310
XVIII	Listing of General Wintzingerode's detachment	311
XIX	Draft convention for an armistice between the Russian and Austrian forces	313
XX	Composition of Löwis' detachment	315
XXI	Yorck's letter to General Paulucci, dated 26 November (8 December)	316
XXII	Yorck's letter to MacDonald	317
XXIII	Massenbach's letter to MacDonald	318
XXIV	French forces on 5 January (new style)	319
XXV	Listing of troops under Count Wittgenstein, dated 31 December [12 January, 1813]	320
XXVI	Schedule of reinforcements joining the Russian Main Armies throughout the war of 1812	323
XXVII	Collection of Supreme Manifestos, Decrees and Rescripts. St Petersburg, 1816	324
XXVIII	Collection of Supreme Manifestos, Decrees and Rescripts. St Petersburg, 1816, page 69	326
XXIX	Ivan Liprandi's opinions on Clausewitz as Bogdanovich's 'reliable source' and an officer	327

Sources for the History of the War of 1812   329
Index   344

List of Maps

24	Plan of the Battle of Maloyaroslavets.	26
25	Map of Troop Movements from Maloyaroslavets to Smolensk.	43
26	Plan of the Battle of Vyazma, 22 October (3 November) 1812.	59
27a	Map of troop movements from Smolensk to Orsha.	79
27b	Plan of the Battle of Krasny.	89
28	Plan of the Battle of Polotsk 6 (18) October 1812.	116
29	Map showing troop movements of both sides towards the Berezina.	129
30	The Battle of Chashniki 19 (31) October 1812.	137
31	The action at Smoliyantsy, 2 (14) November 1812.	145
32	Plan of the action at Borisov.	166
33	Plan of the Berezina crossing.	192
34	Map of troop movements from the Berezina to Vilna.	209
35	Map of MacDonald's retreat to the Neman.	255

33

Napoleon's Departure From Moscow

The concentration of Napoleon's main force in the vicinity of Moscow. – Strength and composition of his forces. – Napoleon's operational plan. – Berthier's letter to Prince Kutuzov. – Occupation of the Kremlin by Mortier's detachment; instructions issued to him. – Instructions issued to Lariboisière. – The departure of Napoleon's army from Moscow; the slow movement of the force. – Their order of march. – Napoleon's orders for the march from Moscow to Borovsk.

Dorokhov's reports regarding the appearance of the enemy on the new Kaluga road. – Dokhturov's detachment towards Fominskoe. – The intelligence delivered by Seslavin regarding Napoleon's movement towards Borovsk. – Dokhturov's advance towards Maloyaroslavets. – Kutuzov's orders. – The departure of the Russian army from the Tarutino camp. – The strength of our force. – Construction of a monument on the fields of Tarutino.

Operations by Wintzingerode's detachment. – His and Captain Naryshkin's capture by the enemy. – The situation in Moscow during Mortier's departure. – The destruction of the Kremlin. – The suffering of the Muscovites. – The re-entry of Russian forces into Moscow. – The state of the capital. – The first solemn Mass. – Davydov's accomplishments near Vyazma.

In preparation for the campaign, Napoleon concentrated his forces: on 1 (13) October, Ney's *3e Corps* [Michel Ney], stationed in Bogorodskoe and the division under Delzons [Alexis Joseph Delzons] (from the Viceroy's *4e Corps* [Eugène Rose de Beauharnais]), which was in Dmitrov, received orders to return to Moscow; Davout's force [Louis Nicolas Davout], parts of which were located in the villages around Moscow, were also concentrated in the city; the *Vieille Garde* was ordered to be at immediate readiness to move. On 3 (15) October, the light cavalry and Broussier's infantry division [Jean-Baptiste Broussier] from *4e Corps*, which was on the road to Mozhaisk, near the village of Berezki, was switched to the new Kaluga road, towards Fominskoe, while the Viceroy's *cavalleria de la Guardia Reale Italiana* moved along the Mozhaisk road towards Sharapovo.[1] Napoleon made daily inspections of various units from his army. On 6 (18) October, at around noon, he inspected Ney's *3e Corps*, which had recently arrived in Moscow, in the Kremlin. From early morning, the thunder of a cannonade was heard from Murat's vanguard [Joachim Murat]. As the troops were marching past their Emperor, the aide de camp to the King of Naples, Béranger, rode up with news of the action on the Chernishnya.[2] Napoleon, visibly disconcerted by the transition of the Russian force from defensive to offensive operations, stopped the review and gave orders for an immediate departure. The Viceroy's *4e Corps* and Davout's *1er Corps* left the city in the evening of the same day and camped at the exits on the old Kaluga road; Ney's *3e Corps* and the *Garde* spent the night in Moscow.[3]

The French army, despite the losses inflicted on it by the operations of our partisans and peasant soldiers, was stronger than when it had entered Moscow. The number of recovered soldiers could not have been large, due to the very poor condition of the hospitals; consequently, the army owed its reconstitution almost exclusively to the arrival of replacements. Napoleon's force counted more than 100,000 men in its ranks, including with Murat's vanguard and Junot's *8e Corps* [Jean-Andoche Junot].[4] The infantry, made up of veteran, experienced soldiers, had managed to recover after a difficult campaign and was outstanding. The same can be said of the artillery crews, but their horses were exhausted in the extreme. The cavalry was in a very poor condition: of the 18,500 men who were enrolled on the lists, 4,000 did not have horses and had been reorganised into an infantry brigade; the rest, excluding 4,600 men of the *cavalerie de la Garde*, could not perform their proper duties of service due to the complete exhaustion of their horses. It follows from this that the infantry constituted the only reliable element of the French army.[5]

Napoleon, intending to envelope our army from the left flank, decided to head initially along the old Kaluga road, re-attaching Murat's vanguard to his force, and then, switching to the new Kaluga road, to take the route leading from Kaluga to Smolensk. In order to forestall our army located in the vicinity on this route, it was necessary that we remain in ignorance of the march of the French army for as long as possible. To that end, Napoleon resumed negotiations with Prince Kutuzov [Mikhail Illarionovich Golenishchev-Kutuzov]; Colonel Berthemy [Pierre-Augustin Berthemy] was sent to the headquarters of our army with a letter from Berthier

---

1   Chambray, *Histoire de l'expédition de Russie, 3e édit.* II, 206. Bernhardi, *Denkwürdigkeiten des Grafen v. Toll,* II, 232.
2   Fain claims that Moscow was aware of the attack on Murat's vanguard even before the arrival of his aide de camp (*On a entendu dans la matinée le canon gronder du côté des avant-postes du roi de Naples. Bientôt on apprend qu'il y a eu une surprise, qu l'alerte à été chaude, que Murat a payé de sa personne, qu'il a été blessé, que son aide-de-camp Dery a été tué… qu'enfin, après un engagement général en deçà de Vinkovo, l'ennemi repoussé est rentré dans ses lignes, mais que cette affaire nous coute un grand nombre de braves, entre autres le général polonais Fischer, une partie de nos bagages, et les pièces de canon, que, dans le premier désordre, les cosaques ont eu le temps d'enlever un parc de la division Sébastiani. L'officier Béranger vient confirmer ces nouvelles*). *Manuscrit de 1812,* II, 135.
3   Fezensac, *Journal de la campagne de Russie,* 64. Chambray, II, 212. Bernhardi, II, 233.
4   A schedule of Napoleon's force is at Appendix I.
5   Chambray, II, 313-316.

[Louis-Alexandre Berthier] expressing readiness; 'to take measures to give the war a character consistent with generally accepted rules and stop the needless devastation of the country, which is as harmful to Russia as it is regrettable to Emperor Napoleon.'[6]

Kutuzov replied to this letter as follows:

> Headquarters, 9 (21) October, 1812.
> Colonel Berthemy, having been received by me at my headquarters, has handed me your letter. Everything contained in it has already been presented to the Tsar, and, as you doubtless are aware, it was sent with Prince Volkonsky [Pëtr Mikhailovich Volkonsky]; but, owing to the distance and the poor condition of the roads at the present time of year, it has remained impossible to get an answer. And so, in relation to this matter, I can only refer to that which I said earlier to General Lauriston [Jacques Jean Alexandre Bernard Law, marquis de Lauriston]. But let me repeat the facts, the importance of which, of course, you will appreciate yourself: that it is difficult, even if one so wished, to keep a nation roused by everything that happens in their sight, a people who have not been subjected to enemy invasion for 200 years,[7] and are ready to sacrifice themselves for the Fatherland and are incapable of evaluating what is acceptable or what is not in conventional warfare. As for the armies entrusted to me, I flatter myself with the hope that everyone will recognise the principles characteristic of a brave, honest, generous people in the way in which they conduct themselves. I have never known any other principles during my long military service, and I can say that the enemies with whom I fought always did me justice in this respect.[8]

During Napoleon's departure from Moscow, as already mentioned above, Marshal Mortier [Adolphe Édouard Casimir Joseph Mortier] had been left in the Kremlin for the time being with a division of the *Jeune Garde* under General Delaborde [Henri François Delaborde], numbering 3,500 men, a brigade of dismounted cavalry under General Carrière [Louis Chrétien Carrière de Beaumont], numbering 4,000 men, two artillery companies and one of sappers, and several squadrons, in total some 8,000 men. He was ordered to publish a proclamation the next day to refute rumours of a final retreat by the French and to convince the inhabitants of Moscow that Napoleon's army was moving on Kaluga, Tula and Bryansk, in order to seize these important locations. At the same time, the Marshal was ordered to begin stocking the Kremlin with at least a month's worth of flour, potatoes, cabbage, vodka and other supplies by any means necessary, and to bake the flour into hard-tack. Each of the corps that were in Moscow (Davout's, Ney's and the Viceroy's) were ordered to leave detachments during the evacuation in order to occupy outposts in the city

---

6 Letter from *prince de Neuchâtel*. Chambray, II, 319.
7 Prince Kutuzov stated '300 years' in his letter.
8 A copy of Prince Kutuzov's letter is held in the Archive of the Ministry of Foreign Affairs [M.F.A.].

that were suitable for defence: the Viceroy's forces in the prison buildings on the St Petersburg road; while Ney's and Davout's were in the monasteries, which were to serve as redoubts; in particular, it was vital for the; 'prince d'Eckmühl to occupy the Monastery dominating the bridge over the Moskva river'[9] with a strong detachment.[10] General Lariboisière [Jean Ambroise Baston de Lariboisière] received orders to gather all ammunition caissons and other artillery carts in the Kremlin, as well as gunpowder, lead, charges and cartridges, while destroying only stocks of saltpetre and sulphur, and setting fire to magazines located outside the city, Russian ammunition caissons and, in general, everything that could not be removed to the Kremlin. Napoleon wrote: 'It is necessary to have as many charges as possible with the army, and therefore 400 horses must be transferred from the pontoon parks to ammunition caissons.' In the same instructions Napoleon stated: '*Il est possible que je revienne à Moscou*' (It is possible that I shall return to Moscow).[11]

Thus, Napoleon tried to mislead his closest associates about forthcoming operations, but he did not succeed: from general to soldier, no one considered it possible to return to Moscow; no one left behind either their own property or their acquired loot. This had a very disadvantageous effect on the French troops. Napoleon could only have forestalled our army on the road leading from Kaluga to Smolensk by moving quickly; but the huge wagon train pulled by exhausted horses that followed his force slowed down the march with every step; many carriages followed the army laden with luxuries of no use on campaign; instead of life saving supplies, the *Vivandières* were carrying booty looted from Moscow with which the artillery carts and infirmary wagons were also filled; the cavalry burdened their miserable horses beyond measure; the infantrymen were exhausted under the weight of their knapsacks.

The movement of the French army presented an extraordinary spectacle, similar to the migration of nations with all their property. Throughout entire stages, artillery pieces, ammunition caissons, infirmary and provisions wagons, carriages of every possible type and even *droshky*, loaded with various items, mainly food supplies and clothing, stretched in three or four files, meanwhile, no measures were taken for the timely resupply of the troops. Some elements of the army, during the hasty departure from Moscow, did not have chance to draw either hard tack or flour from the magazines; others did not have the means to take the supplies with them, and therefore on 7 (19) October in the morning, the significant grain stores in Moscow were torched. Large herds of cattle increased the length of the columns. The army crowded around the wagons, as if escorting a huge convoy. Many foreigners who left our capital at the time of the French exit, their families, women and children, made their way between artillery and troops, increasing the congestion and disorder. The wounded and sick, having left the hospitals voluntarily, gathered their strength in order to drag themselves after their regiments, but having said that, some 2,000 crippled patients were ruthlessly abandoned in the ruins of Moscow.

---

9 The convent, which was on the site of a newly built church with the name of Christ the Saviour.
10 Napoleon's orders, dated 18 October, new style.
11 Napoleon's orders to General Lariboisière, dated 18 October, new style.

At every bridge, at every bottleneck, carts and troops, crowding together, halted the movement of those elements of the column to the rear; the rearguard would close up before all the other wagons had chance to pass the defile; with every step, the enemy were forced to abandon them as a sacrifice to our partisans. Despite the warlike spirit of Napoleon's battle-hardened army, the chaotic and slow movement of troops disheartened the soldiers, tiring them as much as the most forced of marches, and presaged a gloomy future. Napoleon clearly saw the consequences of this state of affairs, but tolerated it out of necessity: not being able to guarantee life support to his army on the return march to the Dnieper, he allowed huge private convoys, in the hope that they would serve, at least in part, as a substitute for mobile magazines, of which he had a great shortage, and therefore could not satisfy the needs of 100,000 men moving collectively in one direction. In addition, these carriages and wagons might be used for the benefit of rescuing the wounded following the army. Napoleon in some ways had given rise himself to the increase in transport, having numbers of artillery pieces with his army disproportionate to its strength, as well as redundant carts. General Lariboisière, a former colleague of Napoleon's from the *Régiment d'artillerie de La Fère*, who enjoyed the right to express his opinions to him frankly, suggested leaving some of the artillery in Moscow, but Napoleon indignantly rejected this proposal. He hoped that the strength of his will would overcome the seemingly insurmountable difficulties. A similar conviction led him to burden the army with a special convoy of so-called 'trophies' i.e. with Turkish and Persian Colours stolen from the churches of our capital city.[12]

Napoleon's force adopted the following order of march: the Viceroy formed the vanguard; directly behind which was Ney's *3e Corps*; then the *Vieille Garde* and two divisions from Davout's *1er Corps*; General Roguet [François Roguet] with a division of *Jeune Garde*, escorted the *État-major général* [headquarters], the treasury and the convoy of trophies; finally, in the rear guard were Morand's division [Charles Antoine Louis Alexis Morand] (from Davout's corps) and Colbert's brigade [(Édouard) Pierre David de Colbert-Chabanais] of *cavalerie de la Garde*. The light cavalry brigades under Girardin [Alexandre Louis Robert de Girardin d'Ermenonville] and Beurmann [Frédéric Auguste de Beurmann], moving alongside the column, protected the army from the flanks. Both this force and the rearguard were ordered to burn every village they passed through on the way. Napoleon, having left Moscow himself on the morning of 7 (19) October, moved his *État-major général* to the village of Troitskoe at four o'clock in the afternoon. At the same time, the vanguard under the Viceroy reached the village of Vyatutinka.[13]

The next day, 8 (20) October, Napoleon ordered the evacuation of Moscow. Mortier was ordered to send all the convalescents remaining in the city to Mozhaisk immediately, and to set fire to the Kremlin Palace, barracks and all public buildings, except for the Orphanage, and blow up the Kremlin walls on 10 or 11 (22 or 23) October, at two o'clock in the morning. In addition to this, he was ordered to cut

---

12 Chambray, II, 316-318 & 475-476. Fain, II, 137-138. Fezensac, 69. Labaume, *Relation circonstanciée de la campagne de Russie en 1812, 4e édit*, 249. Comte de Ségur, *Histoire de Napoléon et de la grande armée pendant l'année 1812, 4e édit*, II, 112-113.
13 Chambray, II, 318. Fezensac, 70.

up the gun carriages and the wheels of ammunition caissons, to break the muskets that were impossible to take with him, and, having undermined the Kremlin towers, withdraw his troops along the Mozhaisk road, but to remain in Moscow himself until he had witnessed the blowing up of the Kremlin. He was also ordered to set fire to both of Rostopchin's houses [Fëdor Vasilievich Rostopchin] and the house of Count Razumovsky [Lev Kirillovich Razumovsky].[14]

The next day, 9 (21) October, Napoleon ordered Marshal Mortier, once he had fulfilled all orders in Moscow, to set out on 11 (23) October, at three o'clock in the morning along the road to Vereya (instead of the instructions where he had previously been directed towards Mozhaisk), and, having arrived at this city by 13 (25) October, to maintain communications between the Westphalian *8e Corps*, holding Mozhaisk, and the main body, which by that time should have passed Borovsk.[15] And, as if in order to demonstrate the hypocrisy common to human nature, Napoleon, who, only two days before, had ordered the burning and destruction of many Moscow buildings, not caring about the fate of the people who were to become victims of this cruelty, Napoleon touchingly expressed his concern for the salvation of the wounded and sick soldiers of his army.[16]

Following this, Marshal Junot was ordered to send all the march battalions and squadrons assembled in Mozhaisk to Vereya, as well as the *Artillerie de la Garde* and artillery of the army corps located there. The troops of *8e Corps*, which were under the direct command of the marshal, received orders, that having destroyed all the muskets and ammunition that could not be taken with them in Mozhaisk and

---

14 Napoleon's orders, dated 20 October, new style.
15 Napoleon's orders, dated 21 October, new style.
16 Napoleon's orders dated 21 October new style: '... *Je ne saurais trop lui (Mortier) recommander de charger sur les voitures de la jeune garde, sur celles de la cavalerie à pied, et sur toutes celles qu'on trouvera, les hommes qui restent encore aux hopitaux; que comme les Romains donnaient des couronnes civiques à ceux qui sauvaient des citoyens, le duc de Trévise en méritera autant qu'il sauvera de soldats; qu'il faut qu'il les fasse monter sur ses chevaux et sur ceux de tout son monde; que c'est ainsi que l'empereur a fait à Saint-Jean-d'Acre: qu'il doit d'autant plus prendre cette mesure, qu'à peine ce convoi aura rejoint l'armée, on trouvera à lui donner les chevaux et les voitures que la consommation aura rendus inutiles; que l'empereur espère qu'il aura sa satisfaction à témoigner au duc de Trévise pour lui avoir sauvé cinq-cents hommes;qu'il doit, comme de raison, commencer par les officiers, ensuite par les sous-officiers, et préférer les Français; qu'il assemble tous les généraux et officiers sous ses ordres, pour leur faire sentir l'importance de cette mesure, et combien ils meriteront de l'empereur d'avoir sauvé cinq-cents hommes.*' (I cannot recommend strongly enough to him (Mortier) to load the men who still remain in the hospitals onto the carts of the young guard, onto those of the dismounted cavalry, and onto any others which he might find; that just as the Romans gave civic wreaths to those who saved citizens, the Duke of Treviso will be rewarded with as many as the soldiers he saves; that he must make them ride on his horses and on those of all his men; that this is what the Emperor did at Saint-Jean-d'Acre: that he must take this measure all the more so, that as soon as this convoy might rejoin the army, we shall find ways to give him the horses and carriages which wear and tear will have rendered useless; that the Emperor hopes that he will have the satisfaction of witnessing the Duke of Treviso having saved five hundred men for him; that he must, of course, begin with the officers, then with the non-commissioned officers, and give preference to the French; let him assemble all the generals and officers under his orders, to make them understand the importance of this measure, and how much they will be rewarded by the Emperor for having saved five hundred men).

the Kolotsk monastery, to prepare for an immediate march on Vyazma and to take measures to evacuate the wounded from the hospitals that had been set up along the Mozhaisk road. The commander of French forces in Vyazma, General Teste [François Antoine Teste], was ordered to send *Général de brigade* Evers [Charles Joseph Evers], with a combined-arms detachment, numbering 4,000 or 5,000 men, to establish communications with the army via Yukhnov and to establish fortified outposts between Yukhnov and Vyazma, because, in abandoning the line of communications with Smolensk via Mozhaisk, it was necessary to secure a route leading thence via Yukhnov and Vyazma.[17]

On 8 (20) October, Napoleon remained in Troitskoe, while the Viceroy's corps, having reached Krasnaya Pakhra, headed along the country roads leading to the new Kaluga road, to Fominskoe, where Broussier had previously been sent ahead with his division and light cavalry of *4e Corps*. On that same day, Ney's *3e Corps* linked up with Murat's vanguard, which was stationed on the Mocha, while Poniatowski's *5e Corps* [Józef Antoni Poniatowski], moving back, followed the movement of the Viceroy, and was then sent to Vereya.

On 9 (21) October, Napoleon moved his *État-major général* to Pleskovo (near Ignatovo). The Viceroy arrived at Fominskoe; the *Vieille Garde*, Davout's *1er Corps* (which had been rejoined by the divisions under Friederichs [Jean-Parfait Friederichs] and Dufour [François Marie Dufour]), and behind them Roguet's division, crossed to Fominskoe via country roads, so that only Murat's cavalry, Ney's *3e Corps*, Claparède's division [Michel Marie Claparède], Morand's (from *1er Corps*) and Colbert's brigade remained on the old Kaluga road.[18]

On 10 (22) October, the Viceroy sent Broussier's division and the light cavalry from his corps ahead to the village of Kotovo and Delzons' division four *versts* [1 *verst* = 1,067 metres or ⅔ mile] further ahead, while he remained on the Nara river himself with the remaining troops. Napoleon's *État-major général*, the *Garde* and Davout's *1er Corps* moved to Fominskoe; Morand's division moved to link up with Davout's corps; Murat's cavalry was also directed on Fominskoe; Ney remained on the old Kaluga road with his *3e Corps*, Claparède's division, Latour-Maubourg's [Marie Victor Nicolas de Faÿ de Latour-Maubourg] *4e corps de cavalerie* and Davout's light cavalry. At this point the weather broke; the rains started and the roads became very poor, which, combined with crossings over many narrow and flimsy bridges,

---

17 Letter from the *chef d'état-major* of the *Grande Armée* (Berthier) to the *duc d'Abrantès* (Junot), dated 22 October new style: '... *L'intention de l'empereur étant qu'aussitôt que vous en recevrez l'ordre, vous vous portiez sur Viazma en reployant tous les postes et toutes le estafettes, et en communiquant avec Sa Majesté par Viazma et Iukhow... La communication avec Smolensk se fera par Viazma, après qu'on aura abandonné celle de Mojaisk...*' Napoleon's orders dated 23 October new style: '... *vous ferez connaître au général Teste que l'intention de l'empereur est que le général Evers, avec une colonne de trois à quatre mille hommes, infanterie, cavalerie, artillerie, en prenant spécialement les régiments de marche qui iraient rejoindre l'armée, se dirige de Viazma sur Iuchnow, à dix-huit lieues de Viazma, et de là pousse des postes jusqu'à d'intersection des routes à Znamenskoe. Le général menera avec lui les estaffetes qui seraient arrivées à Smolensk; il placera à chaque poste, c'est-à-dire à Sosowa, Troffimowa et Andreewka, des détachemens de cent hommes d'infanterie et d'un piquet de cavalerie, sous les ordres d'un commandant de place, qui se retrancheront dans les maisons pour être à l'abri des cosaques et des paysans...*'
18 Chambray, II, 322.

made it extremely difficult for the army to move, and especially for the transport. Napoleon, accompanied by Berthier, Murat and Davout, his entire staff and a small cavalry detachment, reconnoitred the area to the left of the road to Borovsk himself and encountered only a few Cossacks.[19]

As early as 7 (19) October, Major General Dorokhov [Ivan Semënovich Dorokhov], who was stationed near Kotovo with a detachment, reported the appearance of Broussier's division to our headquarters, numbering some 8,000 to 10,000 men with 16 guns across the Nara river near Fominskoe, and of his withdrawal to Koryakovo, as a result of which his detachment was reinforced by two regiments, 6th Jägers and 33rd Jägers, sent to him from Tarutino. Two days later [21 October new style], Dorokhov reported that the positioning of Broussier's division at Fominskoe was intended to maintain communications between Napoleon's main body (which, for some unknown reason, he considered to be at Voronovo), and Mozhaisk.

From Dorokhov's reports, it could be concluded that the occupation of Fominskoe by Broussier's force was the beginning of a general movement towards this location by the entire enemy army, and therefore the Field Marshal considered it necessary to detach General Dokhturov [Dmitry Sergeevich Dokhturov] in the direction of Fominskoe, with VI Corps under his direct command, Adjutant General Baron Meller-Zakomelsky's [Yegor Ivanovich Meller-Zakomelsky] I Cavalry Corps, two Lifeguard horse artillery batteries, Colonel Nikitin's [Alexey Petrovich Nikitin] horse artillery company, several Cossack regiments and part of the Tula mounted *opolchenie*. The detachments under Seslavin [Alexander Nikitich Seslavin] and Figner [Alexander Samoilovich Figner] were subordinated to him. The army Chief of Staff, General Yermolov [Alexey Petrovich Yermolov], was ordered to accompany Dokhturov. Kutuzov, having summoned Yermolov to him, told him that: 'I very much want our troops to take possession of Fominskoe' and concluded his instructions with the words: 'you are to go with Dokhturov; I shall be at peace; let me know very often about what is happening with you.'[20]

Dokhturov's force set out from the Tarutino camp on 10 (22) October in the morning. The poor country roads along which they had to pass were completely ruined by the persistent autumn drizzle that lasted almost the whole day. The movement was quite slow; the infantry had to stop in order to pull the heavy guns out of the mud in which they were incessantly bogging down; eventually, at Yermolov's suggestion, Dokhturov decided to leave them behind with a small escort and continued to advance with the light guns, which were with the troops in large numbers. From the intelligence delivered to Dokhturov's headquarters by General Dorokhov, it became apparent that the enemy, totalling 2,000 infantry, were advancing from Borovsk along the Maloyaroslavets road, that French bivouacs were seen near the village of

---

19 Chambray, II, 322-323.
20 Log of incoming and outgoing documents 1812 (archive of the M.T.D. No. 29,172). A.P. Yermolov's notes. [Liprandi comments: 'I know very well that Alexey Petrovich [Yermolov] never wrote to Kutuzov, because Dokhturov did very often, even if just in pencil while on horseback.' Adding that Yermolov's Notes actually state (page 216): '... Kutuzov ordered me to go with General Dokhturov, assuring me that he wished me well and that he would be at peace. Knowing Kutuzov well I did not to take this at face value'].

Kotovo, where there were approximately 4,000 men, and, finally, that enemy troops were stationed near Fominskoe in the forest and bivouac fires were visible, as was a battery at the bridge over the Nara river.

Our troops, having passed through Aristovo, halted for the night.[21] General Dokhturov, intending to attack the enemy by surprise at dawn near Kotovo, forbade the kindling of fires. Midnight had already long since passed and the time appointed for the approach march by the force was nearing, when intelligence was received that changed all our previous intentions:[22] the partisan Seslavin, galloping into Dokhturov's vanguard, reported that, concealed in the forest, about four *versts* short of Fominskoe, he had seen Napoleon with his entire retinue, as well as the French *Garde impériale* and other troops in significant strength. Having let them pass his detachment, Seslavin captured several straggling guardsmen, which he brought with him as irrefutable evidence of the presence of Napoleon himself in Borovsk, one of them, an intelligent non-commissioned officer, testified as follows:

> Four days have already passed since we left Moscow. Marshal Mortier was left in Moscow with a special detachment and blew up the Kremlin walls before rejoining the army. The heavy artillery, dismounted cavalry and all non-essential baggage was sent along the Mozhaisk road, under the protection of the Polish corps under Prince Poniatowski. Tomorrow the Emperor's *État-major général* will be in Borovsk. The onward direction of our army is towards Maloyaroslavets.

By delivering this intelligence, Seslavin rendered a significant service to the Fatherland: if he had not had chance to explain the current state of affairs, then Dokhturov's force, upon attacking the village of Fominskoe, would have suffered an inevitable defeat, and the enemy, having occupied Maloyaroslavets without hindrance, could have forestalled Prince Kutuzov in Kaluga and could have taken possession of all the supplies collected there for our army.

As soon as General Dokhturov had received this important intelligence delivered by Seslavin, he immediately sent Major Bologovsky [Dmitry Nikolaevich Bologovsky], the Duty Field Officer of VI Corps, to the Field Marshal with a report. It was easy to foresee that if Dokhturov had decided to wait for orders from headquarters regarding further operations, then the enemy would probably have forestalled him in Maloyaroslavets, and therefore General Yermolov proposed going back at dawn and, having recovered the heavy artillery left behind, to move towards Maloyaroslavets as quickly as possible.[23] General Dokhturov not only regarded

---

21 [Liprandi claims: 'The corps halted at Aristovo itself; before Aristovo, they split into two columns: 7th Division on the right side of the road, 24th Division on the left; their leading elements were level with the village... Only some cavalry units were moved forward in the direction of Dorokhov's detachment, located on the road to Borovsk'].
22 [Liprandi claims that Seslavin had passed this intelligence to Dokhturov well before midnight, before going on to find Yermolov].
23 [Liprandi comments: 'In A.P. Yermolov's Notes there is not a word about proposing to depart from Aristovo to Dokhturov before receiving orders from Kutuzov. On page 217 Alexey Petrovich suggested to Dokhturov that he should bring the heavy artillery six *versts* back,

this idea favourably, but also agreed to send Baron Meller-Zakomelsky on a reconnaissance in the direction of Borovsk, with his corps, Colonel Nikitin's horse-artillery company and the Cossack regiments. General Yermolov also went together with this force.[24] Although this reconnaissance was hampered by fog, nevertheless, our generals, approaching Borovsk, discovered the enemy in great strength; then, upon crossing the Protva, they saw the bivouacs of the Viceroy and Davout not far from them on the postal road and returned to the left bank of the Protva; meanwhile, a Cossack patrol from Sysoev's [Vasily Alexeevich Sysoev] regiment was sent along the far bank of the river to Maloyaroslavets, with orders to find out what was happening in the city and report about it to the detachment on their way back. An officer sent with the patrol reported to Yermolov just after midnight and brought intelligence that the bridge near Maloyaroslavets on the river Luzha had been partially dismantled by the locals, with whom he had spoken across the river downstream of the city, because three enemy battalions had been stationed opposite the bridge; that there was a Cossack patrol sent by Platov [Matvey Ivanovich Platov] in the city, and the mayor and other civil officials had left there that morning.

Meanwhile, as the detachment under Meller-Zakomelsky was moving all day and almost all night with short halts, Dokhturov's force, having departed from Aristovo in the morning of 11 (23) October,[25] headed for the village of Spasskoe [Spas-Zagorye], where they were intending to cross the Protva, and then move on to Maloyaroslavets. The roads along which the troops were intending to march ran through places extremely difficult for the movement of artillery and transport; the bridges had to be repaired constantly. Upon arrival at the crossing point at nine o'clock in the evening, it emerged that the inhabitants of Spasskoe, having learned about the French offensive and wanting to keep them away from their village, had destroyed the weirs on the Protva, from which the water level of the river rose and it was difficult for the troops to cross without a bridge: this misplaced precaution put Dokhturov in great quandary. The crossing was immediately resumed, and in

---

where there was a choke-point, and this proposal was made when there was still no question of going to Maloyaroslavets, but while operations were being planned for Kotovo… General Dokhturov, having received intelligence on the French army in Aristovo, reported everything to the Field Marshal and added: 'I have halted the corps in Aristovo and shall not go further,' describing the reasons for this and his orders. This report, dated 10 [22] October, was sent at nine o'clock in the evening. As a result, he received (from Kutuzov) order No. 216, dated 11 [23] October, 'to use all means for a rapid march from Aristovo to Maloyaroslavets'].

24 A.P. Yermolov's notes. According to General Mikhailovsky-Danilevsky, Dokhturov went from Aristovo to Maloyaroslavets, having received orders from Prince Kutuzov to go to this location. Liprandi writes the same (*Severnaya Pchela*, 1858, No. 46).

25 It is rather difficult to comment with any reliability about the timing of Dokhturov's departure: from A.P. Yermolov's notes it is apparent that our force departed Aristovo on 11 [23] October at dawn, while according to Liprandi (in *Severnaya Pchela*, 1858, No. 46), it was at 11 o'clock in the morning [Liprandi adds: 'Both statements are true. A.P. Yermolov set out with the cavalry under Meller-Zakomelsky for a reconnaissance towards Borovsk at dawn, while Dokhturov, having received orders from the Field Marshal, set off at 11 o'clock for Maloyaroslavets. A messenger (Ensign Count A.N. Panin) was sent to Yermolov with this news, and in the evening, having not reached Spasskoe, he rejoined the infantry. Had Dokhturov set out at dawn, he would have arrived at Spasskoe much earlier'].

the course of five hours two raft bridges had been built. Meanwhile, at 11 o'clock, Platov arrived with a strong Cossack detachment, sent by the Field Marshal from the Tarutino camp to Maloyaroslavets. The Cossacks found an opportunity to cross the Protva via a ford and transported some of the jägers across. While the Lifeguard *Équipage* were building bridges, it was discovered that the soil of the riverbed was firm and therefore it was decided to transport several guns via the ford. It was remarkable that although the ammunition caissons were more than half immersed in water during this crossing, nevertheless, the charges did not get wet. At dawn, a skirmish began at the brick factory and the rest of Dokhturov's force, crossing the bridges, moved towards Maloyaroslavets.

The news of Napoleon's abandonment of Moscow made Kutuzov very happy. It exposed the powerlessness of the conqueror; besides, Emperor Alexander, as already mentioned above, was urgently demanding the opening of offensive operations from the Field Marshal. Bologovsky states in his notes that Prince Kutuzov greeted him with the words: 'Tell me, my friend, what is the event about which you have brought intelligence to me? Has Napoleon really left Moscow and is retreating? Speak now; do not torment my heart; it is thumping.'

Bologovsky reported in detail to him about all the intelligence received at Aristovo, and as soon as he finished his story, the venerable old man, sobbing, turned to an image of the Saviour, saying: 'God, my Creator! Finally, You have heeded our prayers, and from this moment Russia is saved.'[26]

The initial orders from the Field Marshal, upon receiving the news of Napoleon's abandonment of Moscow, were as follows:

1. Platov was ordered to go to Maloyaroslavets immediately with all the Cossack regiments, with the exception of those in the vanguard under Miloradovich [Mikhail Andreevich Miloradovich], and with the Don Horse Artillery Company, and, upon reaching this location, to send a detachment to Borovsk.[27]
2. The Kaluga Governor Kaverin [Pavel Nikitich Kaverin] was to be informed: 'that the enemy is moving in the direction of Borovsk with some of his forces.' The Field Marshal, informing him that the Cossack regiments, under the personal leadership of the *Ataman* himself, had been sent to Maloyaroslavets, to protect the new Kaluga road, and that the whole army would march there, and ordered him 'to make all the necessary arrangements in advance.'[28]
3. General Dokhturov was ordered to make a flank march to Maloyaroslavets and to fix the enemy on the Borovsk road. He was also ordered to send four Cossack regiments on a forced march to forestall

---

26 Bologovsky's notes.
27 Orders dated 11 [23] October, No. 214. Since Platov arrived at Spasskoe at nine o'clock in the evening, it must be assumed that he left Tarutino no later than five or six o'clock in the afternoon.
28 Orders dated 11 [23] October, No. 215.

the French on the Borovsk road, in anticipation of Platov's arrival at Maloyaroslavets with 15 Cossack regiments.[29]
4. General Miloradovich received orders to make a reconnaissance in force along the old Kaluga road, in order to confirm the true direction of the troops facing him; in the event of a move by Murat's vanguard up the Nara, to rejoin Napoleon's main force, to detach the Cossacks and some of the cavalry in order to monitor the retreating enemy, while he was to follow the movement of the army through Tarutino with the remaining troops, i.e. with II Corps and IV Corps and the rest of the cavalry.[30]
5. The partisan Kudashev [Nikolay Danilovich Kudashev] was to go from the Tula road to the old Kaluga road.[31]
6. Major General Ivashev [Pëtr Nikiforovich Ivashev] was to repair the road leading from Letashevka [Letashovo] to Maloyaroslavets and to build a pontoon bridge over the Protva near Spasskoe.[32]

The main body of our army was ordered to prepare for an immediate tactical march, but their departure from the camp was postponed until the evening. The war diary of the Russian army states that the cavalry and artillery, after a three-week stay in the Tarutino camp by the force, were forced to forage 20 *versts* or more from the camp, and therefore on 11 (23) October the army remained in place awaiting the return of the foragers. But taking into account that they could catch up with the troops later, it is obvious that the Field Marshal did not dare to move over to the new Kaluga road for fear of exposing the route along the old road to Kaluga to the enemy. While our army remained in the Tarutino camp, a report was received from General Miloradovich, with news from Major General Karpov [Akim Akimovich Karpov], that at dawn on 11 [23] October, the retreat of French outposts from Voronovo had been noted. At the same time, Miloradovich wrote regarding the detachment by him of several officers from the Quartermaster's Department with Cossack patrols in order to reconnoitre the enemy.[33] General Miloradovich's aide de camp, Lieutenant Kiselev [Pavel Dmitryevich Kiselev], sent to Moscow to establish communications with Wintzingerode's [Ferdinand Fëdorovich Wintzingerode] detachment, entered the capital shortly after Mortier's departure from there: and thus, direct communications between the army and St Petersburg were restored.

This intelligence delivered by Miloradovich finally reassured Prince Kutuzov that the enemy had moved over to the new Kaluga road. On the evening of 11 (23) October, our troops set out from the Tarutino camp towards Spasskoe in two columns: the one on the right consisted of 20 squadrons from 2nd Cuirassier Division, tasked with

---

29 Orders dated 11 [23] October, No. 216 and 221. The Field Marshal, in issuing orders to protect the 'Borovsk' road, in all likelihood, meant the 'Kaluga' road.
30 Orders dated 11 [23] October, No. 218.
31 Orders dated 11 [23] October, No. 217.
32 Orders dated 11 [23] October, No. 220. A pontoon bridge at Spasskoe is mentioned in the war diary.
33 Miloradovich's report dated 11 [23] October, No. 42.

protecting the movement of the main body from the direction of the enemy, received orders to direct themselves from Letashevka via Polivanovka and Krivosheino, while that of the main body on the left was to move via Baev-Kolodez and the Ugodsky-Zavod ironworks. Both columns, uniting at Spasskoe, were intended to cross the Protva there and continue moving towards Maloyaroslavets. The transport, under escort from two Cossack regiments, was sent along the old Kaluga road to the village of Ovchinino, from where they were to rejoin the army on 15 (27) October.[34]

During the three-week stay in the Tarutino camp, our army had received significant reinforcements, including 26 Don Cossack regiments with six Cossack artillery pieces. These regiments, moving in several echelons at 26 *versts* per day, managed to arrive at the Tarutino camp in total by 11 (23) October.[35] The Russian army, upon entering this camp, counted no more than 60,000 regular troops in the ranks, which, by the time of its march to Maloyaroslavets had increased to 97,000, not including an additional 20,000 Cossacks, namely: 71,131 infantry, 5,498 *Opolchenie*, some incorporated as a third rank, 10,711 cavalry, 8,959 artillerymen, 813 pioneers, making a total of 97,112 men.

Comparing this total with that shown when the troops entered the Tarutino camp (Chapter XXVIII), at first glance it seems that our army (not including the 26 Cossack regiments that arrived from the Don) had increased by only 14,000 men, but, taking into account that, at the time of their arrival at Tarutino, among the infantry were: 15,530 warriors, partly pike armed, 7,690 untrained recruits and 40,000 soldiers, whereas, when we departed from the Tarutino camp, our infantry consisted of almost 5,500 warriors, therefore, more than 71,000 soldiers, it emerges that it had actually increased by 31,000 men. The number of men in the other arms of the military remained almost the same as at their time of arrival at Tarutino. The number of guns was still disproportionately large, namely: 216 heavy guns, 294 light guns, 112 horse artillery pieces, for a total of 622 guns.[36]

On the fields of Tarutino, where our army had rested and reconstituted itself, preparing for vengeance for the ruin of the Fatherland, there now stands a monument with the inscription: 'From this spot, the Russian army, led by Field Marshal Kutuzov, having reconstituted itself, saved Russia and Europe' [*На семъ мѣстѣ Российское воинство, предводительствуемое Фельдмаршалом Кутузовым, укрѣпясь, спасло Россию и Европу*]. This monument was erected by the Tarutino peasants, who, having been emancipated as freemen farmers by the owner of the village, the son of Field Marshal Count Rumyantsov-Zadunaisky, expressed their readiness to build a monument at their own expense, and, having received Supreme permission in memory of the late Emperor Nikolai Pavlovich for their request, erected a monument in 1834.[37]

---

34 Instructions issued to Lieutenant General Prince Golitsyn, dated 11 [23] October, No. 227. War diary.
35 Extracted from information stored in the archive of the M.T.D. No. 47,352 (Folder 2).
36 Army strength return dated 6 [18] October 1812. According to a statement by General Buturlin, the regular troops consisted of 78,840 men with 620 guns.
37 Correspondence on this subject is stored in the archive of the M.T.D. No. 47,352 (Folder 4).

While the main bodies of both sides were preparing for renewed bloody combat, General Wintzingerode, back in early [mid] October, having received intelligence regarding an offensive by the Viceroy of Italy's *4e Corps* towards Klin, which had the objective of masking the withdrawal of Delzons' division from Dmitrov to Moscow, moved on Dmitrov with two squadrons of Kazan Dragoons, two of Izyum Hussars, the Lifeguard Cossack and Stavropol Kalmyk regiments, intending to attack the enemy who occupied this city by surprise, but upon arrival there he learned that Dmitrov had already been abandoned by the troops under the Viceroy. On 5 and 6 (17 and 18) October, the Cossacks extended their searches as far as Moscow itself and captured several hundred prisoners, from whom intelligence was gleaned regarding Napoleon's departure and about the orders given to Marshal Mortier to blow up the Kremlin. On 10 (22) October, Wintzingerode, having temporarily relinquished command of the detachment entrusted to him, by then stationed in Chashnikovo, to Colonel Benkendorf [Alexander Khristoforovich Benkendorf], went to the village of Nikolskoe, to his vanguard commanded by Major General Ilovaisky 4th [Ivan Dmitryevich Ilovaisky], and ordered him to move forward to the Petrov Travel Palace; while he went into the city himself, taking Captain Naryshkin [Lev Alexandrovich Naryshkin] of the Izyum Hussars with him and announcing to Ilovaisky that he was going to Moscow to call for the surrender of any enemy troops remaining there.[38] Benkendorf's notes state that Wintzingerode, being carried away by enthusiasm, wanted to prevent the destruction of the Kremlin, but Naryshkin, who was with him at the time, stated that he wanted to open negotiations solely with the aim of lulling enemy vigilance and keeping them inactive, in order to be able to detach most of his force onto the Smolensk road and block the line of retreat of the detachment left in the Kremlin. Leaving the Cossack regiments stationed at the entrance to the suburbs, Wintzingerode and Naryshkin set off on horseback from the Tver checkpoint along Bolshaya Yamskaya [great coach-road] to the entrance to Tverskaya Ulitsa; ahead of them, instead of a trumpeter, whom they had forgotten to take with them, rode a Cossack with a white scarf tied to his lance. While they were moving forward, the peasants they met assured them that an enemy guard-room had been stationed at the governor-general's house. Indeed, an outpost of the *Jeune Garde* was posted there, who, after detaining our *parlementaires*, initially provided an escort for General Wintzingerode, and then for Naryshkin, to the Kremlin to Marshal Mortier. General Wintzingerode, upon being introduced to him, reproached the French for their perfidious violation of their rights sanctified by custom; Mortier, having calmly listened to all these criticisms, answered: 'I have sent a courier to the Emperor; your fate depends on him alone; meanwhile, hand over your swords and if you please, follow Baron Sicard [Joseph Victorien Sicard], who will show you to the rooms allocated to you.'[39]

The few inhabitants who remained in Moscow restlessly and fearfully awaited the final acts of the French, which might give rise to renewed looting and violence; rumours about mines arranged under the walls of the Kremlin spread ever more widely; after the evils suffered by Moscow, any atrocity seemed possible. No one

---

38 Major General Ilovaisky 4th's report to the Tsar dated 11 [23] October, No. 1,045.
39 Naryshkin's notes.

dared to leave their hiding place; many gates and doors were barricaded. On 11 (23) October, at noon, officials of the enemy-established police and almost all the French residents of Moscow rushed to the Kremlin gates in order to leave with the troops during their withdrawal; other foreigners, mostly Germans, left along the Smolensk road. The wagon train, accompanying the troops was as diverse as the one that had gone with Napoleon's army, was loaded with booty looted from Moscow, but, having said that, many bales of imported goods, shawls, tea, and so on, remained in the Kremlin. At six o'clock in the afternoon Mortier set out with all the troops of the Kremlin garrison; among the hand-picked gendarmes and the *Jeune Garde* were the prisoners, Wintzingerode and Naryshkin. Mortier's consolidated corps, made up of soldiers from almost every European nation, presented the spectacle on the march of a disorderly mob that had completely forgotten the concept of discipline.[40]

By midnight, once the enemy force had already withdrawn a considerable distance from Moscow, in the gloom of an unusually dark night, the Kremlin arsenal and other buildings were ablaze, doomed to destruction by reckless malice. There was a terrible explosion, followed by six more, one shortly after the other. These explosions were like an earthquake; the houses were shaken to their foundations; many walls were cracked to the full height of the building; huge chunks of masonry were thrown to a distance of several hundred paces by the force of the explosion; in every neighbouring building, doors were broken, windows were smashed, and furniture was splintered. Some of the towers and lengths of the walls of the Kremlin were blown up and the palace caught fire.[41] The ultimate disaster inflicted on Moscow by the enemy invasion had come to pass! The destruction of the Kremlin, utterly gratuitously by Napoleon, could have played to an eternal fury between the Russians and the French, had the mutual enmity of both nations not been tamed by the magnanimity of the man who repaid the evil inflicted on Moscow by sparing Paris.

The few inhabitants still remaining in Moscow, stricken with fear and stunned, left their shaken houses and rushed into the squares; some of them managed to get dressed and carry away the meagre remains of their possessions; all the rest, half naked, barefoot, wounded by shards of glass or fallen beams, rushed mindlessly, first in one direction, then in the other, crying out to the Heavens for vengeance. This terrible night was the last for many Muscovites, who up to that time had preserved their lives amidst all kinds of evil and hardship. As if to crown the despair of these unfortunates, a cold set in, unprecedented at this time of the year.[42] The sufferers, deprived of shelter, clothed in rags, exhausted by hunger and cold, wandered and died in the ruins of Moscow.

To all these disasters, which overcame all measure of misfortune that had befallen the Muscovites, were added the horrors of anarchy. Enemy marauders and even some Russians, taking advantage of the disorder, indulged in robbery and violence; shots rang out incessantly in the streets; fires broke out and there

---

40 Naryshkin's notes.
41 *Histoire de la destruction de Moscou en 1812*, 143-145.
42 [Liprandi comments: 'There is no reference for this… But what was this cold snap on 11 [23] October in Moscow, especially for the Russians, while the general consensus of French witnesses themselves was that the weather was beautiful at that time?'].

was no one to put them out.[43] Such was the situation in Moscow when Major General Ilovaisky 4th, the next senior officer in Wintzingerode's detachment, having learned about the capture of his commander and about the departure of Mortier, entered the city on the morning of 11 (23) October, with the Lifeguard Cossacks, his own Cossack regiment and the Perekop Tatar Regiment, wiped out or captured a significant number of French marauders and sent Denisov 7th's [Vasily Timofeevich Denisov] Cossacks, to monitor the retreating enemy force along the Kaluga road; Ilovaisky 12th's [Vasily Dmitryevich Ilovaisky] Cossacks along the Mozhaisk road and the Perekop Tatars along the Zvenigorod road. Chernozubov 8th's Cossacks were left, as before, between Gzhatsk [Gagarin] and Vyazma; while Moscow was occupied by the Lifeguard Cossacks, Ilovaisky 4th's Cossacks, Kazan Dragoons and Izyum Hussars.[44]

Moscow presented the sad vision of a desert, dotted with ruins, between which the gilded domes of the surviving churches shone, rising bell towers and buildings scorched by fire were occasionally visible; everything else, from one gate to another, through the whole city, presented an image of indescribable destruction to the eye, a kind of chaos in which it was difficult to identify the streets and squares. At every step there were corpses of humans and horses as if on a hotly contested battlefield, fragments of objects that had lost their identifying shape, entire piles of all sorts of rubble and debris. Here and there, among the ruins, half-naked barefoot shadows with dulled eyes wandered, ready to do anything to prolong their miserable existence.

The first objects of concern for General Ilovaisky 4th and those diligent well-meaning men, Colonel Benkendorf and Prince Shakhovsky [Alexander Alexandrovich Shakhovsky],[45] who was then serving in the Tver *opolchenie*, were the re-establishment of order in the city as much as possible and the supply of aid to its unfortunate inhabitants. In order to put a stop to the robberies and murders, guards were posted and patrols were sent out. Benkendorf went to the Orphanage, where women, orphans and many wounded, both ours and the enemy, were languishing without food, abandoned, during Mortier's departure, under the care of Tutolmin [Ivan Akinfievich Tutolmin], who had no resources to aid them. In the hospitals, rotting corpses lay next to the sick and maimed, barely able to move. It was not easy to clean out these repositories of humanitarian disaster. It was even more difficult to give the sufferers the aid they so urgently needed. There were almost no doctors or medicines; there was no bread to satisfy the hunger of these unfortunates. Of our wounded, 18 officers and some 700 lower ranks, for the most part, were placed in the Almshouse Hospital of Count Sheremetev [Nikolai Petrovich Sheremetev]; while four officers and more than 600 lower ranks remaining in the main hospital were treated there under the care of retired Lieutenant Colonel Kuris. The enemy wounded who were in the Orphanage were supplied, if possible, with everything they needed; the rest of the prisoners were sent, under the supervision of retired

---

43 *Histoire de la destruction de Moscou en 1812*, 147-152.
44 Major General Ilovaisky 4th's report to the Tsar dated 11 [23] October, No. 1,045.
45 The famous playwright and author.

Major Olenin, to those buildings of the Petrov Palace that had survived the fire, and later they were transferred to Tver.[46]

The destruction produced by the fire and explosions in the Kremlin was huge; the palace, the Faceted Palace, the extension to the bell tower of Ivan the Great, the arsenal, the Alekseevskaya tower were destroyed; the Nikolskaya tower and the Kremlin walls were damaged in many places. But the cathedrals in the Kremlin survived in a truly miraculous manner. The fire did not touch the houses of God, even though the ancient church of Spasana-Boru was blanketed with embers from buildings burning all around, and despite the outer doors of the Annunciation Cathedral being completely charred. Everything dedicated to God, with the exception of that which was plundered by blasphemers, remained intact. In the Uspensky [Dormition] Cathedral, otherwise cleaned out by looters, the silver plated reliquary in which the remains of the Sainted Metropolitan Jonah rested, was spared; the holy relics thrown onto the dais remained unharmed, and only the neck of a Saint had been cut up by an unholy hand. Near the relics lay a French sabre. The reliquary of the Sainted Metropolitan Peter could not be found at all, which gave the chance to discover his relics, which until then had been sealed; the tomb covering the relics of Metropolitan Philip, which were then still under cover, had been broken and the grave excavated. Of the tombstones over the graves of the Moscow archbishops, only one, Patriarch Yermolen's, had been smashed: the malice that pursued the worthy saint until the last day of his life was put to shame two hundred years later by vengeance on the plaque that covered his remains. At every step, to the horror of the Orthodox believers, there were signs of thoughtless contempt for the sacred: on the altar of the Kazan Cathedral a dead horse lay in place of the overturned throne. In the Archangel Cathedral, wine had been spilled from broken barrels and all the booty looted from the palaces and the Armoury had been scattered. In the Uspensky Cathedral, as in others, torn up icons lay on the floor. The presence of the enemy left traces of debauchery everywhere.

And at the same time, to the consolation of those faithful to the Holy Name of Christ, there remained signs of protection from above from the fire and the sword of the enemy. On the Spassky Gates, in the midst of the flames that had enveloped the Kremlin, as before, an icon in a golden robe remained, and even the iron canopy over the icon and the cord that held a lantern in front of it had been preserved in a perfect whole. No less wonderful was the preservation of the image on the Nikolsky Gates, the glass of the icon case and the lamp hanging in front of the icon on a thin chain, which remained untouched, despite the destruction of the upper part that was blown off from the explosion of the arsenal, almost as far as the image.[47]

The enemy, during the hasty evacuation of Moscow, could not remove the ancient Russian guns that stood around the arsenal. In addition, 14 of our guns and 28 of the enemy's, more than 200 ammunition caissons and more than 100 limbers and carts

---

46 Major General Ilovaisky 4th's reports to the Tsar dated 14 [26] October, No. 1,072 and 15 [27] October, No. 1,089.
47 Prince Shakovsky's notes.

were found in the ruins of the Kremlin. The hand-held firearms left by the French in Moscow were, as already mentioned above, destroyed on the orders of Napoleon.[48]

Upon the entry of Russian troops into Moscow, the robberies and arson were immediately stopped. The removal from the city of dead bodies, rubble and all the debris that lay in the squares and streets and filled the surviving buildings, took much time, because there were very few people, and even for those present, there were insufficient meagre supplies to be found in Moscow. This was alleviated by the industries around Moscow: from all directions, many carts with food supplies, flour, baked bread, oats, hay were assembled on the square facing the residence of the Commander in Chief; even samovars with hot drinks of spiced honey, and various footwear, were offered to those in need. Along with unemployed merchants, entrepreneurs of a different kind appeared, hoping to take advantage of the turmoil following the entry of our troops and to load their wagons with easily acquired property, but they were frustrated from their intentions:[49] Colonel Benkendorf ordered the corpses and carrion lying on the Moscow streets to be loaded onto their wagons, and sent them out of the city with this load.

Thus, little by little, order was re-established on the ruins of devastated Moscow. But the numerous churches that had adorned the capital city before its occupation by the French remained empty. Not until the third day after the entry of our troops into the city, was it possible to prepare the large church in the Strastnoy Monastery for a Divine Liturgy and thanksgiving service. The French, at the request of the elderly nuns who remained there, had not desecrated this house of God. Several priests were found; since there were no silver vessels, glass ones were found in their place. It had been intended to start tolling the bells at the same time from all the surviving bell towers of the city. Due to a shortage of bellringers, churchmen, peasants, and townspeople stood in. At nine o'clock the great bell of the Strastnoy Monastery was struck and the tolling was heard throughout the Moscow ruins. All of Moscow, as it were, was resurrected after a prolonged death. Not only the church, but the porch and courtyard of the monastery were filled with people. Perhaps the inhabitants of Moscow had never prayed with such enthusiasm as at the solemn moment when, at the end of the liturgy, a thanksgiving service was performed to God for strength and when everyone fell on their knees, it was not only Russians, but foreigners, even Bashkirs and Kalmyks. The general weeping, caused by the extraordinary triumph from the depths of their hearts, merged with the sounds of sacred hymns, the universal ringing of bells and the firing of cannon. It seemed that at that moment, the prayers of all those present united in the thought of boundless love for God, Tsar and Fatherland.[50]

The sacrifices made by our ancient capital had been great at that hour when the Blessed Monarch, appearing among the Muscovites, announced to them the dangers threatening Russia; but even greater were Moscow's losses during its

---

48 From the files of the Artillery Department.
49 [Liprandi notes that this allegation is not referenced: 'It should be in their (Benkendorf's) reports, which of course also exist in the archives; yet if there is no contemporaneous evidence, then why expose the inhabitants of the suburbs near Moscow so libellously as black-hearts?'].
50 Prince Shakovsky's notes.

occupation by the enemy army. It is believed that the destruction in the Moscow Governorate overall cost the people personally some 270 to 280 million roubles; the losses incurred by state and public departments cannot be estimated even with approximate precision. Several decades have passed: Moscow has risen from the ashes in greater beauty than before; the memory of past disasters has disappeared, but the firmness of spirit shown by Emperor Alexander and the self-sacrifice of the Russian people have remained forever as an example to future generations.

As Napoleon was leaving devastated Moscow, the Russian partisans exacted daily revenge on the enemy, striking and killing the uninvited guests. I have already had occasion to mention the most important raids by our detachments, during the army's encampment at Tarutino. To complete the picture of partisan operations in this period, it remains to describe the feat accomplished by Davydov [Denis Vasilevich Davydov] simultaneous with the emergence of the enemy from Moscow.

On the night of 7 (19) October, Lieutenant Colonel Davydov received intelligence from his informants about the arrival in Vyazma that evening of a huge convoy from Moscow, under escort from three regiments, of which the two of cavalry were in very poor condition. Despite this escorting force being disproportionate to his detachment, Davydov decided to attack the convoy during its departure from Vyazma and the next day, 8 (20) October, positioning his detachment between Vyazma and Semlevo, dividing it into three sections: the first, consisting of Popov 13th's Don Cossack Regiment, put the enemy to flight within sight of Vyazma; the second, of Bug Cossacks under Captain Chechenksy's [Alexander Nikolaevich Chechensky] command, charged at four large wagons, moving under the protection of a significant escort; the enemy hid in the forest, hoping to escape there, but were again attacked by dismounted Cossacks and almost completely wiped out. The third, consisting of hussars, under the command of Major Khrapovitsky [Yason Semënovich Khrapovitsky] of the Volhynia Hussar Regiment,[51] heading towards Semlevo, discovered a convoy with an escort of one of the Westphalian cavalry regiments in full uniform, attacked them and captured all the wagons with most of the escort. On this day the enemy lost: 375 men killed, including three officers; a field officer, four subalterns and 490 lower ranks taken prisoner; forty large wagons with hard-tack, oats and clothes and 140 yoke of oxen were captured; 66 of our prisoners were released, of whom the sick were sent to Yukhnov; while the rest, together with those who had fled from captivity, were armed with muskets taken from the enemy, to make up a full company. The casualties on our side did not exceed four killed and 38 wounded lower ranks.[52]

Let us pay tribute to each of the participants in the great work of saving our Fatherland: let us say with confidence worthy of the truth of our story that our partisans and national resistance greatly weakened Napoleon's army, both by daily blows inflicted on the enemy, and by depriving them of the opportunity to obtain essential supplies. But the French legions that set out from Moscow were still formidable, not so much in their actual strength, but from the glory of the victories they had won over the course of many years under the leadership of their brilliant commander.

---

51 [Liprandi remarks: 'Who are they? I have not heard that there was ever an hussar regiment of this name in the Russian army'].
52 Lieutenant Colonel Davydov's reports dated 7 and 8 [19 and 20] October.

26 THE RUSSIAN PATRIOTIC WAR OF 1812 VOLUME 3

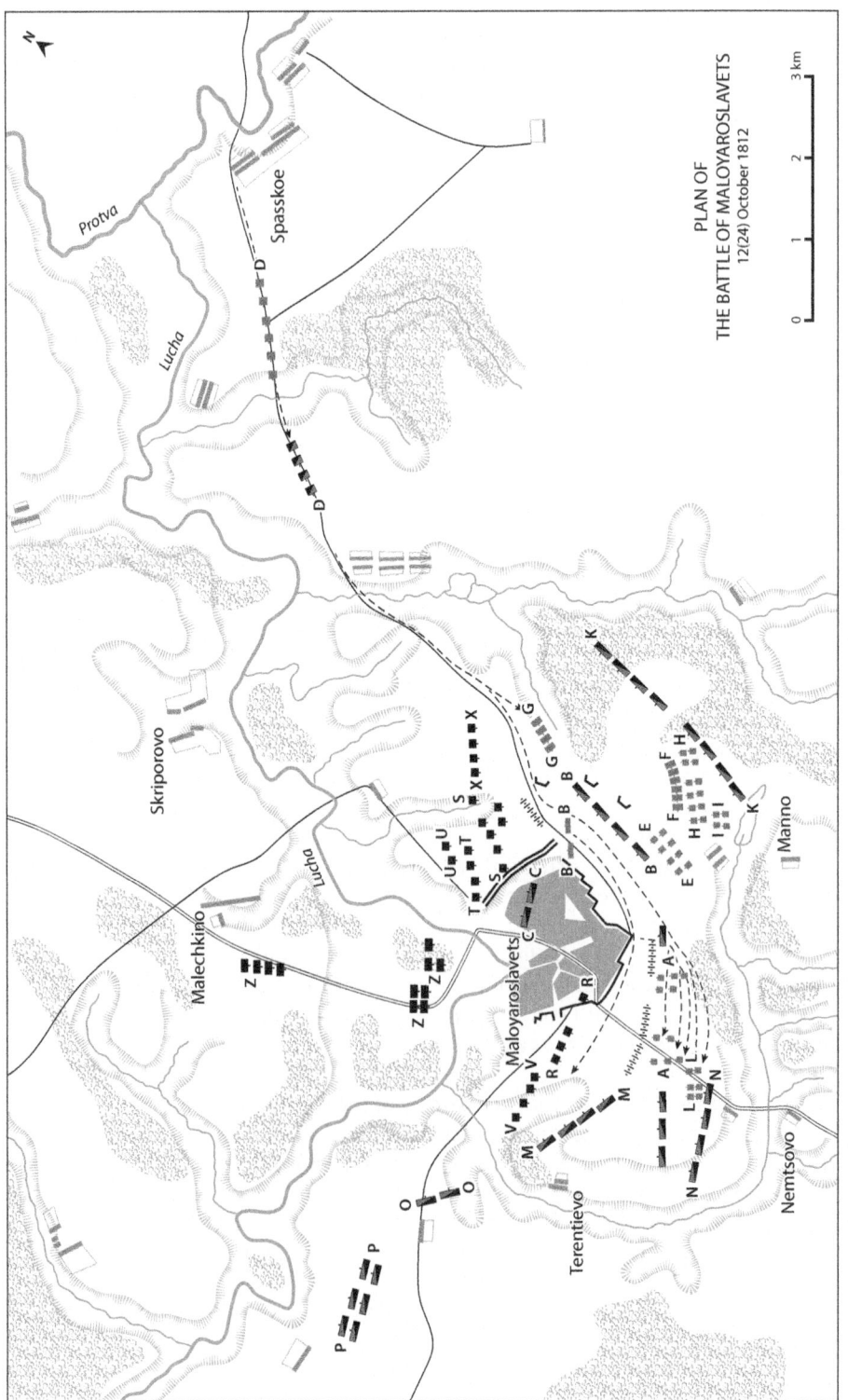

PLAN OF
THE BATTLE OF MALOYAROSLAVETS
12(24) October 1812

Plan of the Battle of Maloyaroslavets.

Legend:
Russian Forces
AA. Dokhturov's Corps
BB. Chevalier Guard & Dorokhov
CC. 6th Jägers & 33rd Jägers
DD. Approach march of the army to Maloyaroslavets
EE. VII Corps
FF. VIII Corps
GG. 3rd Division
HH. II Corps & IV Corps
II. 1st Grenadier Division
KK. II Cavalry Corps & IV Cavalry Corps
LL. V Corps
MM. I Cavalry Corps (second position)
NN. Cuirassier Divisions
OO. Dorokhov's Detachment (second position)
PP. Platov's Cossacks

French Forces
RR. Delzons' Division
SS. Broussier's Division
TT. Pino's Division
UU. *Guardia Reale Italiana*
VV. Gérard's Division
XX. Compans' Division
ZZ. Reserves

34

Battle of Maloyaroslavets

Location of the battlefield. – The Viceroy's advance followed by the other elements of Napoleon's army towards Maloyaroslavets and Medyn. – The battle of Maloyaroslavets. – The detachment of Ilovaisky 9th towards Medyn, while Platov went along the Borovsk road. – Kutuzov's and Napoleon's intentions. – Situation of the French army at that time. – Platov's sweep. – The state of the troops. – The retreat to the Smolensk highway. – Kutuzov's retreat to Goncharovo. – The detachment of Paskevich towards Medyn and the march of the Russian army along the Medyn road. – The transfer of Miloradovich to this location with the vanguard. – The offensive by the Cossack detachments under Platov and Orlov-Denisov.

Napoleon's arrival in Vereya. – Napoleon and Wintzingerode. – The arrival of the French army on the Smolensk highway and Napoleon's march towards Vyazma. – The situation of his forces. – The pursuit of the enemy by Russian forces.

The small town of Maloyaroslavets is where the limit of Napoleon's offensive was set and from where the reverse campaign of the *Grande Armée*, replete with disasters, began. This town lies on the edge of a plateau between the right bank of the Luzha river and its tributary, enveloping the plateau from the south and west. The northern side of the plateau, facing the Luzha, is formed of rather steep slopes; on the opposite bank of the river, the terrain is flat, rising imperceptibly as one moves away from the bank. The river Luzha forms a loop in the direction of the town. A little above the base of this loop there was a bridge, partly dismantled by the inhabitants of the town following the withdrawal of the Cossacks to the right bank of the Luzha.[1]

On 11 (23) October, having assessed from a reconnaissance he had made the day before and reports received that the Russian army was still in the camp at Tarutino, Napoleon decided to continue moving towards Kaluga. After occupying this city, he intended to move through Yelnya towards Smolensk; in the event of being unable to reach Kaluga, he could still reach the Yelnya road from Maloyaroslavets via Medyn and Yukhnov. The Viceroy, moving with his *4e Corps* in the vanguard of the army,

---

1   See Plan of the Battle of Maloyaroslavets.

passed Borovsk and placed three divisions in front of this city (Broussier's, Pino's [Domenico Pino] and the *Guardia Reale Italiana*), sending a fourth (Delzons') forward along the Kaluga road. At dusk, Delzons reached the banks of the Luzha, repaired the dilapidated bridge, and having sent two battalions to occupy Maloyaroslavets, stationed the rest of his force in bivouacs facing the town. On the same day, 11 (23) October, Poniatowski established communications with the troops stationed in Mozhaisk and Borovsk and sent his vanguard towards Medyn, having occupied Vereya the previous day.[2]

The enemy, having entered Maloyaroslavets without resistance,[3] hoped to continue moving towards Kaluga without a break the next day. But Dokhturov's force had arrived at Maloyaroslavets by dawn on 12 (24) October and was stationed on both sides of the Kaluga road. In order to prevent the enemy from establishing themselves in the town, Dokhturov immediately sent in 6th Jägers and 33rd Jägers from General Dorokhov's detachment, followed by 11th Jägers in reserve. The infantry of VI Corps were positioned facing the town, while the cavalry, both from the Lifeguard and Dorokhov's, were stationed to the right, to guard the crossing at Spasskoe and in order to prevent the enemy from crossing the Luzha, on which there are many fords downstream of Maloyaroslavets. As the enemy, at that time, had not yet completed the repairs to the bridge, the horse artillery, placed on our left wing, opened fire on their labourers.[4]

At five o'clock in the morning, our troops went on the attack. The 33rd Jäger Regiment was the first to enter the town and drove the enemy out of there almost up to the bridge itself. The Viceroy, having heard the firefight, mounted his horse and galloped to Maloyaroslavets with his entire staff, and at the entrance to the town was met by Delzons, who explained the state of affairs to him. Delzons' entire division was ordered to cross the river and enter the town. The enemy numbers were constantly building up and they managed to transport two guns over the bridge, across the masonry piers. From our side, 6th Jägers and 19th Jägers, under the command of Colonel Vuich [Nikolai Vasilevich Vuich] were sent to assist 33rd Jägers. The troops

---

2   Chambray, *Histoire de l'expédition de Russie*, II, 326-327. Labaume, *Relation circonstanciée de la campagne de Russie en 1812, 4e édit*, 255. Sołtyk writes that Poniatowski occupied Vereya on 11 (23) October, not on 10 (22) October.
3   Liprandi, who was serving as Chief Quartermaster of VI Corps, wrote that Maloyaroslavets was only occupied by a small number of enemy. *Severnaya Pchela*, 1858, No. 45 [Liprandi's article claims that the Russians came under fire from a single volley of about 100 muskets immediately upon their arrival in the town and that the enemy then fled towards the bridge]. But this is contradicted in Labaume (p. 256) by Delzons' verbal report to the Viceroy: '*Hier au soir en arrivant, je m'emparai de la position, et rien ne semblait me la disputer, mais, vers les quatre heures du matin, j'ai été attaqué par une nombreuse infanterie; aussitôt deux bataillons ont pris les armes; repoussés par des forces de beaucoup supérieures, ils ont été obligés de descendre du plateau et d'abandonner Malo-Jaroslavetz.*' (Yesterday evening on arriving, I seized the position, and nobody seemed to dispute it with me, but, at around four o'clock in the morning, I was attacked by numerous infantry; two battalions immediately stood to arms; repulsed by much superior numbers, they were forced to descend from the plateau and abandon Maloyaroslavets).
4   Description of the battle of Maloyaroslavets from the War Diary. A.P. Yermolov's notes.

that entered the town were placed at the disposal of General Yermolov.[5] His orders, quickly transmitted to all points of the battlefield, were carried out with extraordinary precision. Our regiments, animated by the determination of their commander, fought fearlessly. A bitter battle ensued.[6] General Delzons, seeing that his troops were edging back towards the bridge under pressure from ours, rushed forward to encourage them, and at that very moment as he was stubbornly defending the exit from the town, he was mortally wounded by a bullet to the head; his brother [Benoît Delzons], who had raced to his aid, perished with him. The Chief of Staff of *4e Corps*, *Général de brigade* Guilleminot [Armand Charles Guilleminot?], took command of Delzons' force. The positions they occupied were unfavourable in that our artillery, placed on the dominant plateau, could strike the columns crossing the bridge over the Luzha, while the Russian troops located behind Maloyaroslavets were shielded by the crest of the high ground. General Guilleminot, in spite of this, exploited the numerical superiority of his infantry and drove our jägers out of the town, from where we managed to extract out artillery with great difficulty. Wanting to hold out in Maloyaroslavets until the arrival of the Viceroy's remaining divisions in support, he occupied the church and two houses with marksmen, dominating the valley along which the highway runs. The troops stationed in these buildings were ordered to remain in them even if their parent division were forced to evacuate the town.[7]

At half-past eleven, Broussier's division crossed the bridge, which, after passing through the town, began to form up in the gardens at a range of about 500 paces from our position, but the operations of Russian batteries with canister forced the enemy to take refuge in Maloyaroslavets so hastily that our artillerymen only managed to fire a single salvo.[8] General Dokhturov reinforced the jägers with the Libau Infantry and Sofia Infantry regiments, under the command of Major General Talyzin [Fëdor Ivanovich Talyzin] and Colonel Khalyapin [Vasily Mikhailovich

---

5   [Pointing out the confusion of Russian units in Bogdanovich's narrative, Liprandi briefly explains: '6th Jägers and 33rd Jägers, who had joined Dokhturov at Aristovo, were sent towards the town not from the position facing Maloyaroslavets, but from Spasskoe, crossing the Protva on rafts of logs that were being prepared for the bridges (therefore, it was impossible to send artillery with them, which was sent at the first opportunity. Dokhturov was in a hurry to seize Maloyaroslavets as quickly as possible, and thus, as soon as the opportunity presented itself, he sent the aforementioned regiments), and were directed to the town, which they entered a quarter of an hour before dawn, without going on the attack in this case. Once the bridges at Spasskoe were ready, Dokhturov crossed and learned of the situation in Maloyaroslavets, whereupon Vuich was sent with 19th and 40th Jägers (it should be noted here that these regiments, having suffered enormous losses at Borodino, were reduced to a single weak regiment designated 19th) with Devel's light artillery company, following 6th and 33rd Jägers].
6   Yermolov's notes. According to Liprandi, 6th Jägers under Colonel Glebov entered the town first; while Colonel Bistrom's 33rd Jägers; 'stopped at the entrance to the town, as if in reserve.' When Dokhturov learned that our jägers had reached the bridge, he then ordered Vuich to move at the double with 19th Jägers and 40th Jägers from 24th Division and with Devel's Light Artillery Company, to assist Glebov. *Severnaya Pchela*, No. 45.
7   Yermolov's notes. Chambray, II, 330. Labaume, 257. Comte Ségur, *Histoire de Napoléon et de la grande armée pendant l'année 1812*, II, 120-121.
8   Yermolov's notes. Labaume, 257-258. The disposition of Broussier's division is shown on Labaume's battle plan.

Kahlyapin]. By order of Yermolov, these regiments moved forward with unloaded muskets and without the customary shout of 'Hurrah!' Both regiments fought very bravely and suffered heavy losses, especially the Sofia Infantry. Under the thunder of a strong bombardment by our batteries, all the jäger regiments were committed to action. The enemy, driven from the high ground, was pushed back to the bridge, but the buildings occupied at the entrance to Maloyaroslavets by Guilleminot's hand-picked companies, afforded the French a stronghold in the form of a redoubt. Russian troops broke into the town several times, but as soon as they left these posts to their rear, the enemy marksmen opened fire on the from behind, throwing them into disorder and assisting their columns in pushing our regiments back to the main square. But eventually the French, having suffered considerable losses, were forced to cede the majority of the town to us. Colonel Nikitin, in occupying the high ground near the cemetery with his horse guns, struck the enemy troops, who could not counter us with equivalent artillery, because operations for the battery on the left bank were rather difficult, and the Viceroy did not dare to move it to our side, for fear of losing the guns in the event of a retreat.[9]

The considerable number of French wounded leaving the battlefield, and the obvious impossibility of driving our troops out of the town using the divisions under Delzons and Broussier already fighting there, forced the Viceroy to reinforce them with fresh forces. Pino's division, which had not yet been in action during the whole campaign, rushed into battle with extraordinary fervour; at the heads of the regiments were officers of the general staff, belonging to the noblest Italian families. The enemy troops, with shouts of: *'Vive l'Empereur!'* ascended the slopes at the double; but this success came at a high price: many Italians fell victim to the competitiveness that motivated them; General Levié [Joseph Marie Levié] fell here as did the the brother of General Pino, who was himself wounded. At one o'clock in the afternoon, the *Reggimento Granatieri* and *cacciatori* of *La Guardia Reale Italiana* arrived at the scene of the battle; as at this time Pino's division, located along with the troops under Broussier on the left wing of *4e Corps*, had already been repulsed, the *cacciatori* of *La Guardia Reale* moved into the front line and advanced against our columns, but, being greeted with canister fire, suffered terrible casualties.[10] On our side,

---

9 Yermolov's notes. Labaume, 258. Chambray, II, 330-331.
10 Labaume, 259 states: '... *la quinzième division (Pino) ayant été repoussée, ils s'avancèrent pour l'appuier à l'instant où l'ennemi faisant des progrés rapides, marchait vers le pont et menaçait de culbuter dans la rivière les troupes qui l'avaient franchie. Voyant qu'ils n'avaient pas un moment à perdre, ils attaquerent les Russes et leur reprirent la position, d'où la division italienne avait été chassée. L'acharnement des deux partis était extrême, lorsque l'ennemi ayant demasqué deux grandes redoutes, fit plusieurs decharges à mitraille, qui detruisirent les chasseurs.*' (... they advanced in support of Fifteenth Division (Pino's) which had been repulsed, just as the enemy, making rapid progress, marched towards the bridge and threatened to drive the troops who had already crossed it into the river. Seeing that they had not a moment to lose, they attacked the Russians and recaptured the position from which the Italian division had been driven. The fury of the two parties was extreme, whereupon the enemy, having unmasked two great redoubts, fired several salvos of canister, which destroyed the *cacciatori*). The fortifications shown on Labaume's battle plan had already been built by the arrival of Prince Kutuzov at Maloyaroslavets.

the Wilmanstrand Infantry and 11th Jägers,[11] brought into Maloyaroslavets by order of Yermolov, helped us to hold out in the town for a long time, but the original advantageous position was lost by us, which forced us to withdraw some of the artillery.[12] Until our troops could be ejected from Maloyaroslavets, the enemy could not deploy their forces, because in order to do this they would have to bypass the town, which lies on steep sided high ground and is intersected by ravines. As soon as the French reached the crest of the high ground, they were greeted with heavy fire from artillery located in the fields facing the city, and were unable to counteract this with equivalent batteries, because it was necessary to drag them through the town in order to do this. Our troops also could not get around Maloyaroslavets, in order to operate against the bridge that served as a line of communications for the enemy: as soon as Dokhturov's regiments appeared in the Luzha valley, they were exposed to the fire of the batteries stationed on the opposite side of the river. As a result, the battlefield, during the whole day, was restricted to the town, which had been on fire throughout the morning; the troops could engage each other in no other way than by advancing over the corpses with which all the streets were littered.[13]

Meanwhile, Davout's troops and the *Garde impériale* had arrived on the Luzha. From our positions strong columns could be seen covering the opposite bank of the river. General Yermolov, having asked Dokhturov's permission, instructed Adjutant General Count Orlov-Denisov [Vasily Vasilevich Orlov-Denisov] to report to the Field Marshal on the state of affairs and the need to speed up the advance of the army. Count Orlov-Denisov found Prince Kutuzov with the main body near the village of Spasskoe, where Kutuzov, having crossed the Protva, had halted the troops five *versts* from the battlefield and was giving them a break. The cautious Kutuzov would not willingly decide to move towards Maloyaroslavets, which might lead to a general battle, but, having received the news of Dokhturov's predicament for a second time, sent VII Corps to assist him and instructed Konovnitsyn [Pëtr Petrovich Konovnitsyn] to go and get a feel for the course of the battle. Konovnitsyn struck the enemy with the first battalions he came across, those of the Orël Infantry.[14] After that came the timely arrival of Raevsky [Nikolai Nikolaevich Raevsky] with his corps on the right flank of our position, by three o'clock in the afternoon, placing 12th Division to the right of the town, he sent 26th Division to join the troops of VI Corps in support of the left wing, and brought part of 12th Division into the town.[15] The enemy was ejected almost entirely from Maloyaroslavets once more; the *Guardia Reale Italiana* had suffered terrible casualties; generals Guylain and

---

11 [Liprandi states that the Wilmanstrand Infantry were not present at this time, having been returned to the main army from Dorokhov's detachment on 29 September (11 October)].
12 Yermolov's notes. Labaume, 260.
13 Chambray, II, 332-333.
14 [A.P. Yermolov's notes state that Konovnitsyn's visit was fleeting and only to make a reconnaissance. Liprandi also doubts the account of Konovnitsyn leading the Orël Infantry into action, as they only arrived later, with VII Corps].
15 Raevsky's letter to General Jomini (archive of the M.T.D. No. 47,352, folio II). In this letter, among other things, Raevsky stated that he did not remember the detachment of 6th Jägers from 12th Division (to Dorokhov's detachment).

Fontane [Jacques Fontane] were wounded.[16] Napoleon, having arrived about noon on the high ground on the left bank of the Luzha himself, confirmed that our army was in fact concentrated at Maloyaroslavets; but this did not force him to abandon his intended move on Kaluga. Having received a verbal report on the predicament of *4e Corps*, he responded to the messenger: 'Return to the Viceroy and tell him that since he has begun to drink the cup, he must drain it; I have ordered Davout to support him.'[17]

Two divisions from Davout's *1er Corps* were ordered to cross to the right bank of the Luzha via a trestle bridge built half a *verst* upstream of the permanent bridge; whereupon the troops under the Viceroy took possession of the town after a stubborn battle. Exploiting this success, the enemy artillery passed through the conflagration of Maloyaroslavets over piles of corpses and the wounded, with which every street was littered. Davout's troops were located on the flanks of *4e Corps*: Compans' *5e Division* [Jean Dominique Compans] was stationed on their left, while Gérard's *3e Division* [Étienne Maurice Gérard], not immediately able to take part in the battle, was on the right wing.[18] The regiments under Dokhturov and Raevsky, having retreated to long cannon range from the town, set up strong batteries.[19] The enemy repeatedly attempted to attack our positions, but each time their dense columns, engaged with canister, were forced to retreat and were pursued by our troops, who broke into the town on their heels, which, it has been claimed, changed hands eight times in the course of the battle.[20] Colonel Kozen [Pëtr Andreevich Kozen], who commanded the Lifeguard Horse Artillery Batteries, galloped up to the Kaluga gate with four guns loaded with canister, where the guns were emplaced with difficulty because of the corpses and wounded lying in heaps, and lashed the enemy, preventing them from exiting the town into the open.[21]

The day was already advancing toward nightfall when the Field Marshal arrived at Maloyaroslavets with the rest of the corps that had come up from Tarutino. These troops were stationed on the high ground, on both sides of the Kaluga road, two and a half *versts* from the town.[22] The Field Marshal went up to the fighting troops himself and remained under fire, paying no attention to the pleas from General

---

16 Description of the battle of Maloyaroslavets from the War Diary. Labaume, 260 & 262.
17 Sołtyk, *Napoléon en 1812*, 356: 'Retournez auprès du viceroi et dites lui, que puisqu'il a commencé à boire la coupe, il faut qu'il l'avale; j'ai ordonnè à Davoust de le soutenir.'
18 Chambray, II, 333-334.
19 [Liprandi contends that this is misleading: 'Raevsky, having arrived with his VII Corps, halted on the right flank of VI Corps, therefore, simply in continuation of the original positions taken up by Dokhturov at dawn. From this position, both corps began to send reinforcements to those fighting in the town, which changed hands several times, while our position remained in the same place as it had originally occupied the whole time'].
20 Description of the battle of Maloyaroslavets from the War Diary.
21 Kozen's notes on operations by the Lifeguard Horse Artillery in the battle of Maloyaroslavets.
22 [Liprandi comments: 'Kutuzov, upon arrival at Maloyaroslavets, placed all his and Miloradovich's troops, not as General Bogdanovich says, but to the right of Dokhturov and Raevsky, which is also correctly shown on the plan, in a word, facing the town, having the Nemtsovo ravine behind, and protected the frontage with three fortifications, constructed with astonishing speed by General Förster, at half cannon range from the town...' Positions 2½ *versts* from the town were taken up, but not until the morning of 25 October, new style].

Tormasov [Alexander Petrovich Tormasov] and Quartermaster General Lanskoy [Vasily Sergeevich Lanskoy], who were with him at the time.[23] He followed the course of the battle for some time and, eventually, ordered Lieutenant General Borozdin 1st [Mikhail Mikhailovich Borozdin] to relieve the battle-weary regiments of VI Corps with those of VIII Corps; at the same time, the construction of several redoubts within cannon range of the town was started. The French continued to fight with great tenacity, which forced the Field Marshal to support Borozdin's under pressure corps with the grenadier regiments from Prince Shakhovsky's 3rd Division [Ivan Leontevich Shakhovsky]. Kutuzov turned to Konovnitsyn: 'You know how much I care about you and always beg you not to throw yourself into the fire, but now I am asking you to clear this town out.'[24]

Konovnitsyn led the grenadiers, directing their operations until the very end of the battle, rousing the courage of the troops with his composure, and was one of the last to leave the town. Overall, some 24,000 men were committed into combat from each side.[25] The enemy, having finally seized control of Maloyaroslavets, placed strong batteries on the outskirts of the town. With the onset of darkness, the forces on both sides, having halted the desperate struggle, remained in their positions, the French in Maloyaroslavets, and the Russians at a range of less than a *verst* from the town; but the cannonade and musketry continued almost until midnight.[26] Dokhturov, approaching 7th Battery Artillery Company, called for two volunteers. They were supplied with gunpowder and fuses and sent into the town, with orders to set the last surviving buildings ablaze, which was carried out. The fires, brightly illuminating the area, helped us to track all the movements of the French as they exited the town. Our artillery directed their fire to wherever the enemy was assembling to extinguish the flames. At the end of the battle, Miloradovich's force arrived, having made a forced march of 50 *versts*. Delighted by his unexpected arrival, the Field Marshal said to him: 'You march swifter than the flight of angels.' In this way, in order to block the enemy advance, we had managed to concentrate, in addition to VI Corps, VII Corps and VIII Corps, also II Corps, III Corps, IV Corps and V Corps and all our cavalry, with the exception of a few regiments that were with the partisan detachments.[27] On Napoleon's side, the Viceroy's *4e Corps*, Davout's *1er Corps*, the *Réserve de cavalerie* and *Garde impériale* were concentrated around Maloyaroslavets.[28] In the battle of Maloyaroslavets, which lasted fully 18 hours, the

---

23 *Denkwürdigkeiten eines Livländers*, I, 257 (partisan Löwenstern's notes).
24 [Liprandi bemoans the lack of a source for this quote, as it makes no sense].
25 Yermolov's notes. Bernhardi, *Denkwürdigkeiten des Grafen v. Toll*, II, 249. *Denkwürdigkeiten eines Livländers*, I, 259.
26 Yermolov's notes. According to Chambray, the fighting continued until 11 o'clock at night, II, 334. In Löwenstern it states, until ten o'clock, I, 259. And in Labaume, until nine o'clock, 260. [Liprandi comments: 'Here the word ferocious would be more appropriate. Once our entire army had already approached, the desperation can only have applied to the French'].
27 [Liprandi comments: 'the entire army was ordered to cross the Nemtsovo ravine and take up another position, which was done in the early hours of 13 [25] October. But even then, the position originally held by Dokhturov remained occupied by Miloradovich until ten o'clock in the morning of 13 [25] October with the vanguard, in which, by chance, there were also three regiments from VI Corps'].
28 Description of the battle of Maloyaroslavets from the War Diary. Chambray, II, 332.

losses on each side in killed and wounded reached 6,000 men.[29] On our side, the valiant General Dorokhov was seriously wounded by a bullet to the heel.[30] Among the missing were many who perished in the flames of Maloyaroslavets; in contrast, very few prisoners were taken, because on both sides they fought with unusual bitterness and gave no quarter.[31]

This town that served as the site of a massacre presented a spectacle of utter destruction. The course of the streets was discernible only by the piles of corpses with which they were littered; mutilated bodies lay everywhere, crushed by the guns that had been driven over them. Every building had been turned into smoking ruins, under which charred skeletons smouldered; many of the wounded who had taken refuge in the buildings of the town, instead of being rescued, died in the fires, or screamed for help as they were being completely disfigured and burned.[32]

Experienced military men, including some participants in the war of 1812, believe that the Field Marshal, upon the arrival of the army at Maloyaroslavets, should have ordered the town to be evacuated immediately, because the objective of our operations, blocking the French route to Kaluga, had already been achieved, and if the enemy dared to move out into the open, then, judging by the relative strengths of both sides, they would have been completely defeated. In contrast, all further efforts to hold out in Maloyaroslavets by our army, without bringing us any benefit, were associated with a pointless loss of life.[33] The validity of this opinion was convincingly proved by subsequent events. Prince Kutuzov, remaining with the main body of the army two and a half *versts* from Maloyaroslavets, ceased his attempts to capture the town. In order to monitor the enemy in the direction of Medyn, Colonel Ilovaisky 9th [Grigory Dmitryevich Ilovaisky] was sent there, with three Cossack regiments, his own, Ilovaisky 11th's and Bykhalov 1st's [Vasily Andreevich Bykhalov]; meanwhile, Platov received orders to conduct a sweep behind enemy lines with the Cossack regiments located at Maloyaroslavets and 20th Jägers.

At the end of the battle, when Prince Kutuzov had already arrived at the bivouacs prepared for him, Quartermaster General Toll [Karl Fëdorovich Tol or Karl Wilhelm von Toll], as his appointment required, suggested that he attack Napoleon with our

---

29 According to the returns signed by Colonel Kikin, it appears that we lost: 1,282 men killed, 3,130 wounded and 2,253 missing; for a total of 6,665 men. The French casualties are reported as 6,000 in Chambray, II, 338.
30 Dorokhov was seriously wounded by a bullet to the heel right at the end of the fighting, suffered with this wound for more than two years and died in Tula on 25 April [7 May], 1815. His remains, according to his expressed desire shortly before his death, rest in the city of Vereya, liberated from the enemy by him. Emperor Alexander I and His contemporaries in 1812, 1813, 1814 and 1815, Volume I.
31 Buturlin, *Histoire militaire de la campagne de Russie en 1812*, II, 163.
32 Labaume, 263.
33 Extract from Yermolov's notes: 'Was it unnecessary to start building redoubts, which seemed inappropriate to everyone, and not simply to commit fresh forces in large numbers to hold the town, rather, on the contrary, it was better to withdraw those whose stubborn defence had been essential before the arrival of the army. This would have reduced the loss of more than one thousand men and is attested to by the fact that Napoleon, having the town under his control and seeing the withdrawal of our army, did not dare to do anything and did not even make any preparations for offensive operations.'

entire force, and, pushing the enemy back behind the Luzha, pursue them if they begin to retreat further. Kutuzov did not agree with Toll's opinion, challenging his protege's arguments and trying to moderate the vehemence of his recommendations. In the midst of this conversation, Bennigsen [Leonty Leontevich Bennigsen] appeared. He remarked to the Field Marshal: 'I wish Your Grace success in a second battle of Eylau. The French apparently want to hold out in Maloyaroslavets at all costs and to attack you tomorrow.'

Kutuzov continued, turning to Toll: 'You heard that, an experienced general reports to me that the enemy wants to attack me tomorrow, and you suggest that I act like a wild hussar. No! No! We had better get ready to engage them.'

After that, lightly patting Toll on the shoulder, the Field Marshal bade him farewell: 'Go, my dear general, and prepare everything as I have told you.'[34]

After the battle of Maloyaroslavets, Napoleon, returning to spend the night at Gorodnya, where one of the peasant houses had been cleared for him, summoned Berthier, Murat and Bessières [Jean-Baptiste Bessières] to meet him immediately. Having explained to them that the arrival of the Russian army on the Kaluga road had changed the situation, Napoleon suddenly clutched his head with both hands and, leaning on the table on which lay a map of the theatre of operations, fixed his gaze upon it in absolute silence. The marshals looked with surprise at their sovereign; never before had he shown such obvious perplexity. Eventually, once more than an hour had already passed, Napoleon dismissed his associates without saying a word to them about future operations.[35] But he had already decided them in his mind, in accordance with his usual way of waging war: intending to launch into a general battle, he ordered Marshal Davout to change places with the Viceroy's corps, with the troops entrusted to him; the *Garde impériale* was intended to head towards Maloyaroslavets once more, at dawn; Ney was issued orders to settle down between Borovsk and Maloyaroslavets, leaving Claparède's division in Borovsk to guard the parks and transport, while Marchand's division [Jean Gabriel Marchand], which at that time consisted of only a few hundred Württembergers, was to stay behind Borovsk.[36]

On 13 (25) October, at five o'clock in the morning, (*officier d'ordonnance*) Gourgaud [Gaspard Gourgaud] returned to Napoleon from Maloyaroslavets with a report that the Russians remained in the positions they had occupied the previous evening and that in the night the movement of cavalry to the right of the highway had been heard, which, in all likelihood, was moving towards Medyn. Having received this intelligence, Napoleon ordered firstly Murat, then Bessières, and eventually Mouton [Georges Mouton] (comte de Lobau) to be summoned. He said to them: 'It appears that the enemy will hold on to the positions they have occupied, and that we shall have to give battle. Would this be to our advantage, or would it not be better to avoid a battle?'

---

34 *Denkwürdigkeiten eines Livländers*, I, 259-260.
35 Chambray, II, 334. Fain said nothing about this conference, except to suggest that Napoleon wanted to attack Kutuzov and make his way to Kaluga by force, but abandoned this intention on the advice of his entourage. *Manuscrit de 1812*, II, 208-209.
36 Chambray, II, 334-335.

Bessières and Murat, mistakenly believing that our army consisted of untrained *opolchenie*, did not doubt a victory, but noted that even after a battle won, their forces would be in disarray; that the cavalry and artillery horses were exhausted from lack of forage, and that their losses could not be made good; finally, that all the wounded would perish: in this situation, the success of an offensive on Kaluga was very doubtful, and, in their opinion, it was necessary to retreat to Smolensk. 'And you, what are your thoughts?' asked Napoleon turning to Mouton. Mouton repeated his reply several times: 'Retreat along the shortest and best known route to Mozhaisk, towards the Neman, and, as swiftly as possible.'

Napoleon, after listening to these points of view, said that he wanted to inspect the battlefield before deciding on the matter, and immediately set off for Maloyaroslavets.[37]

Meanwhile, Platov, executing the orders issued to him, crossed the Luzha during the night after the battle via a dam and bridge at a mill about five *versts* upstream of Maloyaroslavets with six Cossack regiments commanded by Major General Ilovaisky 3rd [Alexey Vasilevich Ilovaisky]; 20th Jägers also followed them across and occupied the forest in order to cover the detachment's return crossing. Before dawn had even broken, the Cossacks raced off in three different directions to the Borovsk road, captured the park of the *Artillerie de la Garde* near Gorodnya including 40 guns of which only 11 could be dragged away, and captured a Colour.[38]

During this raid, Napoleon himself was in great danger. Having left Gorodnya with his staff and with three platoons from the *Garde*, he was moving at pace along the road to Maloyaroslavets and had already ascended the high ground dominating the village of Gorodnya, when suddenly the *Chasseurs à cheval de la Garde* platoon, riding some distance ahead of his retinue, noticed a large number of horsemen to their right, approaching the highway in loose order. By this time, dawn was barely breaking, and therefore it was difficult to identify these horsemen, but as soon as it was discovered that these were in fact Cossacks, the *Chasseurs à cheval* turned back to notify the imperial suite of the presence of the enemy. Napoleon immediately turned his horse around and galloped towards his escort, which consisted of three squadrons of *Garde*, while the generals and officers accompanying him, along with the platoons from the *Garde*, raced towards the Cossacks; during the melee, the escort arrived quickly, and thereafter the entire *cavalerie de la Garde* came up. Napoleon ordered Bessières to pursue the Cossacks, but they managed to escape under the protection of the jägers, concealed in the scrub near the banks of the Luzha.[39] At the same time, Major General Kuteinikov [Dmitry Yefimovich Kuteinikov] raided the rear areas of the enemy army, taking a number of prisoners and liberating a convoy loaded with church silver. Among the documents seized

---

37 Gourgaud, *Examen critique de l'ouvrage de M-r le C-te de Ségur*.
38 War Diary entry signed by Prince Kutuzov. Yermolov's notes. Chambray, II, 336.
39 War Diary. Gourgaud, *Examen critique de l'ouvrage de M-r le C-te de Ségur*. Sołtyk, 360-362. Chambray, II, 335-336. Sołtyk claims that Bessières' cavalry scattered the Cossacks and captured several hundred jägers. In contrast, according to Chambray; 'the *cavalerie de la Garde*, advancing at a trot in order to maintain close order, were unable to catch up with the Cossacks.'

here was the following handwritten note from Marshal Berthier to the head of the topographic depot, General Sanson [Nicolas-Antoine Sanson]: 'Try to collect intelligence on the old road from Moscow through Borovsk, Maloyaroslavets and Peski, from Peski to Medyn, from Medyn to Vyazma, from Vyazma and Kaluga to Mosalsk, from Mosalsk to Yelnya and Smolensk.'

This note, sent to our headquarters, served to shed light on Napoleon's plans to retreat to Smolensk along roads that provided more resources for the army than the devastated route through Mozhaisk.

The detachment under Ilovaisky 9th, sent to Medyn, as mentioned above, having learned from Colonel Bykhalov's leading elements about an advance from Kremenskoe to Medyn by the vanguard of *5e Corps* (Poniatowski's), under the command of General Lefebvre-Desnouettes [Charles Lefebvre-Desnouettes], moved towards this detachment and set up an ambush six *versts* from Medyn, letting the enemy pass closer to the town, attacking them by surprise with his three Cossack regiments. The enemy detachment was totally routed, losing five guns and many prisoners, including General Tyszkiewicz [Tadeusz Tyszkiewicz], and was driven back to Kremenskoe.[40]

After the alarm caused by the appearance of Cossacks on the Borovsk road, Napoleon returned to Gorodnya, departing from there again for Maloyaroslavets at ten o'clock in the morning and, having carefully examined the battlefield, returned to his *État-major général* by five o'clock in the afternoon. All that day his troops were preparing for battle. The Russian army remained two and a half *versts* from Maloyaroslavets, while the enemy were deployed in the sector between Maloyaroslavets and Mozhaisk: Davout's *1er Corps* and two of the cavalry corps were forwards of Maloyaroslavets; the Viceroy's *4e Corps* held the town and the Luzha valley; the *Garde* and two cavalry corps were located between Maloyaroslavets and Gorodnya; Ney was between Gorodnya and Borovsk with two divisions; Claparède's division was in Borovsk; Marchand's division was behind this town; Poniatowski's *5e Corps* was in Vereya; Mortier's combined corps was en route between Kubinka and Vereya; Junot's *8e Corps* was in Mozhaisk; the artillery parks and transport were in Borovsk, Gorodnya and behind Maloyaroslavets.[41] As early as 12 (24) October, on the day of the battle of Maloyaroslavets, Napoleon wrote to Marshal Victor [Claude-Victor Perrin] such that, in the event that Gérard's division had not yet received any particular mission, he was to move through Yelnya with the troops of this division and with a light cavalry brigade, towards the army, which was heading for Yukhnov and Yelnya towards Smolensk. Once Napoleon had decided to retreat along the Mozhaisk road, then word was sent to Victor regarding the new direction taken

---

40 War Diary. In Buturlin it states that the Cossacks took 500 prisoners, II, 166. In *Napoléon en 1812*, 369, Sołtyk wrote: '*Le prince s'y trouvait depuis le 23 d'après ses instructions, et avait poussé le 24 une reconnaissance, sous les ordres de Lefevre-Desnouettes, sur Medynn. Elle fut repoussée avec perte par les cosaques de Ielovaysky et le général Tyszkiewicz fut fait prisonnier.*' (The prince (Poniatowski) had been there since 23 October (new style) in accordance with his instructions, and on 24 October (new style), had pushed a reconnaissance out towards Medyn under the orders of Lefebvre-Desnouettes. It was repulsed with losses by Ilovaisky's Cossacks and General Tyszkiewicz was taken prisoner).

41 War Diary. Chambray, II, 337-338.

by the main force and he was ordered to send as much food as possible towards the army, to Vyazma and Dorogobuzh.[42]

On our side, more than 90,000 men were concentrated at Maloyaroslavets; on the part of the enemy, subtracting the casualties suffered in the battle of Maloyaroslavets from the total number of men, as well as the troops under Junot, Mortier, Poniatowski, Marchand and 4,000 men who were escorting the baggage, stragglers, and so on, it emerges that the strength of Napoleon's army near Maloyaroslavets was no more than 70,000 men. The number of regular cavalry on each side extended to 10,000 men. There were more than 600 guns with our army, while the French had only 360. Thus, numerical superiority in troops was in our favour. The French infantry, made up of veteran soldiers, surpassed ours in tactical training and combat experience, in contrast, Napoleon's cavalry, with the exception of the *cavalerie de la Garde*, was in very poor condition; the artillery similarly, due to the complete exhaustion of their horses, was incapable of rapid movement, moreover, the artillery and infantry were supplied with ammunition only in such quantities as would be exhausted in one great battle.[43]

As regards the state of the French army, in relation to the morale and discipline of the troops, I have already had occasion to state what harmful effects firstly the long, hard campaign, and then the halt in Moscow, had on them. From intercepted letters by many persons from the enemy army, one can clearly see the hopelessness and despondency that then prevailed among the French forces. The sole thought of each and every one, from general to soldier, was to return to their homeland.

'*Notre grand homme nous promet un prompt retour dans notre patrie; nous le desirons tous ardemment...*' (Our great man promises us a speedy return to our homeland; this we all crave).

That was the subject of most of these letters:

> We are on the verge of leaving the unfortunate city of Moscow; if it were not for the fodder we could have spent the winter here... When will this campaign end? We don't know, we all yearn for France, but we are more than 800 leagues away.[44]

> My dear glutton, you are probably eating choice grapes from Fontainebleau, or rather from your garden, you store away your apples, your winter pears, and we here, we calculate for how much longer we shall have potatoes and cabbage...[45]

---

42 Napoleon's instructions to *chef d'état-major*, Berthier, dated 24 and 26 October, new style.
43 Chambray, II, 338-339. Bernhardi, 251-252.
44 '*Nous sommes à la veille de quitter la malheureuse ville d Moscou; excepté les fourrages nous aurions pu y passer l'hyver... Quand cette campagne finira-t-elle? Nous l'ignorons, nous soupirons tous après la France, mais nous en sommes à plus de 800 lieues.*' Lettre de M-r Lemestre à sa femme. 16 October, new style (archive of the Ministry of Foreign Affairs).
45 '*Tu manges probablement, ma bonne gloutonne, du bon raisin d fontainebleau, ou plutôt de ton jardin, tu ranges tes pommes, tes poires d'hyver, et nous ici, nous calculons combien de temps encore nous aurons des pommes de terre et des choux...*' Lettre d'un officier français, dated 15 October, new style, from the Kremlin (archive of the M.F.A.).

We are going to Kaluga: another 40 leagues to go at noon. What will become of us if it is the same there as here; my faith, there will be enough to die for. When you learn, my worthy friend, the details of our existence, of our deprivations, of our needs, of our filth, of our illnesses, you will not be able to imagine how I could have endured them...[46]

Such letters are compelling evidence that the morale of the French troops, at the very moment they left Moscow, had already been weakened and therefore Napoleon, to whom this circumstance could not have remained unknown,[47] no longer hoping to deliver a decisive blow to our army, was in need of evading a general battle.

The retreat along the Mozhaisk road to Vyazma and Smolensk, through utterly devastated country, also presented extraordinary difficulties. Napoleon wavered in indecision and, it seemed, still had not abandoned his intention of opening the route to Kaluga by force. On 14 (26) October, he again headed for Maloyaroslavets with the *Garde, 2e corps de cavalerie* and *4e corps de cavalerie*, but halted at the bivouac fires before reaching the valley of the Luzha. There he received intelligence, at nine o'clock in the morning, regarding a withdrawal by our forward troops, but instead of taking advantage of this circumstance to move on towards Kaluga, Napoleon, believing that the honour of his armed forces had been preserved by Kutuzov's deliberate avoidance of battle, decided to retreat to Mozhaisk. The *Garde* and the cavalry corps that had accompanied them were immediately withdrawn to Borovsk; the Viceroy followed them with *4e Corps*; while Davout's *1er Corps* remained as the rearguard together with *1er corps de cavalerie* and *3e corps de cavalerie*. At the same time, the following orders were issued: Ney was to move to Vereya that same day with *3e Corps* and all the transport located in Borovsk, and on to Mozhaisk the following day; Poniatowski was to deploy at Yegorievskoe, to protect the movement of the army from the flank, and then move along country roads to Gzhatsk; Marshal Mortier, who was expected to arrive at Vereya in the evening, was to accelerate his march to Mozhaisk and Vyazma; Claparède's division was to link up with Mortier's corps; Junot was to move quickly to Vyazma, in order to link up with Mortier in Mozhaisk; General Evers, currently on the march from Vyazma to Yukhnov, was to return to Vyazma. Davout was ordered to set off from Maloyaroslavets with the rearguard at ten o'clock that night.[48]

---

46 '*Nous allons à Kalouga: encore 40 lieues à faire au midi. Comment serons-nous si c'est là comme ici; ma foi, il y aura de quoi mourir. Quand vous connâitrez, mon digne ami, le detail de notre existence, de nos privations, de nos besoins, de notre saleté, de nos maladies, vous ne pourrez concevoir comment j'avais pû y tenir...*' *Lettre d'un officier français*, dated 15th October, new style, from Moscow (archive of the M.F.A.).
47 By his own orders, all private correspondence was opened and read by the post office.
48 Chambray, II, 339-340. Fain, II, 214, wrote: '*nous marchions pour attaquer l'ennemi, fait-il écrire par le prince de Neufchâtel à tous les commandans qui sont en arrière, mais Koutousoff s'est mis en retraite. Le prince d'Eckmuhl s'est d'abord porté à sa poursuite, mais le froid et la nécessité de se debarrasser des blessés qui sont avec l'armée, décident l'empereur à revenir sur Mojaisk, et de là sur Viasma.*' (we were marching to attack the enemy, he had the Prince of Neufchâtel write to all the commanders in the rear, but Kutuzov had retired. The Prince of Eckmuhl (Davout) initially set off in pursuit, but the cold and the need to evacuate the

Thus, Napoleon, having undertaken a movement to Kaluga, abandoned his intentions for no good reason when, in all likelihood, Kutuzov was already prepared to open the way for him to this city.[49] If Napoleon would not continue the advance he had begun, not wanting to fight under disadvantageous circumstances, then why did he choose a direction in which he was bound to encounter Kutuzov? Did he really hope to reach Kaluga, by outflanking our army? It is true that he nearly succeeded; but was it practical to base the success of one's own operations on the slowness and inaction of the enemy? Wouldn't it have been better to retreat from Moscow directly along the Mozhaisk road than to reach it by a roundabout route, wasting several days pointlessly, and, more importantly, exhausting the supplies taken from Moscow, with which the army could have been fed all the way to Vyazma and beyond?

On 12 (24) October, in the evening, after the battle of Maloyaroslavets, the Field Marshal wrote to the Tsar: 'Tomorrow, I believe there will be a general battle, no-one, under any circumstances, will allow the enemy into Kaluga.'[50]

But the next day [25 October, new style], news was received of the success won near Medyn by Ilovaisky 9th over the vanguard under Prince Poniatowski, and Kutuzov, from the appearance of the enemy on the Medyn road, concluded that Napoleon intended to attack our army, enveloping it from the left flank. This assessment made our Commander in Chief concerned for Kaluga. It is easy to imagine the terror felt by the inhabitants of Kaluga for a continuation of the bloody battle at Maloyaroslavets, which had raged all day 57 *versts* from their city. Having been notified by Prince Kutuzov about the advance of the enemy army towards Maloyaroslavets, the population of Kaluga moved beyond the Oka and, crowding around the fires laid out on the hills of the right bank of this river, dejectedly watched the transportation of provisions, ammunition and other state property through it, and the departure of the sick and wounded to Belëv and Odoev. Nobody wanted to remain in the city.[51]

Kutuzov, despite our numerical superiority and the advantages of his location, doubted the possibility of winning a general battle himself and preferred to retreat. As there was no position on the route to Kaluga that could equal the advantages of the area occupied by our troops near Maloyaroslavets, then a retreat by Prince Kutuzov from this town clearly shows that, in the event of Napoleon's offensive, he could not have blocked his route to Kaluga, but would have to retreat beyond the Oka.

---

wounded who were with the army, convinced the emperor to return to Mozhaisk, and from there to Vyazma).

49 [Liprandi comments: 'Kutuzov left his strong position two and a half *versts* away, occupied by him on the night after the action at Maloyaroslavets, as a result of intelligence on the appearance of the enemy on the road to Medyn; because it was still impossible to determine with certainty whether Napoleon would break straight for Kaluga from Medyn or turn towards Yukhnov, whereupon, without leaving the Kaluga road, Kutuzov went to Detchino in order to be able to cut across Napoleon's path in the event that he might advance from Medyn and there is no reason to assume that Kutuzov, after informing the Tsar that he would not let the enemy into Kaluga, had changed his intention'].

50 From Prince Kutuzov's report to Emperor Alexander I, dated 13 [25] October [*sic*].

51 Mikhailovsky-Danilevsky. Description of the Patriotic War of 1812, III, 109.

The Field Marshal, concerned about being outflanked from the left and cut off from the southern *Oblasts* of the Empire, set out to close up to Kaluga. General Yermolov and Colonel Toll, summoned in succession to a meeting with Prince Kutuzov, tried to convince him to remain in the position he currently occupied. The former remarked to him that there was no evidence of preparations for offensive operations on the part of the enemy; according to Yermolov, it was impossible to expect Napoleon to attack our army in this advantageous position, having a built up area to his rear, awkward slopes to the river and bridges, over which, in the event of a reverse, he would have to retreat under fire from our artillery; an entire day was not enough for the enemy to move the whole army through the town and to reform the force into battle order; besides, numerical superiority was on our side, and in particular due to the detachment to Medyn of Poniatowski's *5e Corps*; a significant part of the enemy artillery remained in the rear; while Napoleon's cavalry was in a sorry state.[52] Colonel Toll, for his part, believed that we should not lose contact with the French army, and that by retreating from Maloyaroslavets along the Kaluga road, we would provide the enemy with a route leading to Medyn and Yukhnov.[53] Berthier's note to Sanson, sent to our headquarters on the night of 13 to 14 (25 to 26) October, revealed the enemy intention of making their way via a roundabout route to the Smolensk road. Nevertheless, on 14 (26) October, on the very day when Napoleon began to retreat towards Mozhaisk, the Russian army was withdrawn back along the new Kaluga road, leaving Miloradovich's rearguard near Maloyaroslavets, composed of II Corps and IV Corps, II Cavalry Corps and a number of Cossack regiments under Major General Karpov.[54] Our remaining troops moved towards Goncharovo in three columns, while Prince Kutuzov's headquarters moved to Detchino.[55]

Thus both armies retreated in opposite directions at the same time. By retreating to Goncharovo, Kutuzov gave the enemy the opportunity to head, through Medyn, Yukhnov and Yelnya, to Smolensk, or to Krasny, as the countryside had not yet been depleted and offered some resources for the troops, while Napoleon, probably not knowing about our retreat, was moving towards Borovsk to get to the devastated Smolensk highway.[56]

---

52 Yermolov's notes.
53 Bernhardi, II, 255.
54 War Diary. *Journal du 2me Corps d'infanterie, rédigé par le prince Eugène de Württemberg* (archive of the M.T.D, No. 47,344).
55 See Map showing Movements From Maloyaroslavets to Smolensk.
56 [Liprandi comments: 'The map shows otherwise. Goncharovo and Detchino, being on the Kaluga road, shielded it, and if Napoleon were to go to Medyn, then it would be easier to block his path and threaten the left flank of his movement from either of these locations… I think that no matter how much Napoleon was at a loss after the outcome of the action at Maloyaroslavets, he was at such close proximity to our entire army that he would not have dared to open his left flank to us on the long stretch via Medyn and Yukhnov, all the more so because, given the mindset of our population at that time, they would not have profited much from the unspoiled nature of the region, along country roads and bridges which were not always suitable, especially for such a large army, so burdened with transport pulled by exhausted horses and closely harassed by our army; the Cossacks, on the other hand, would

BATTLE OF MALOYAROSLAVETS   43

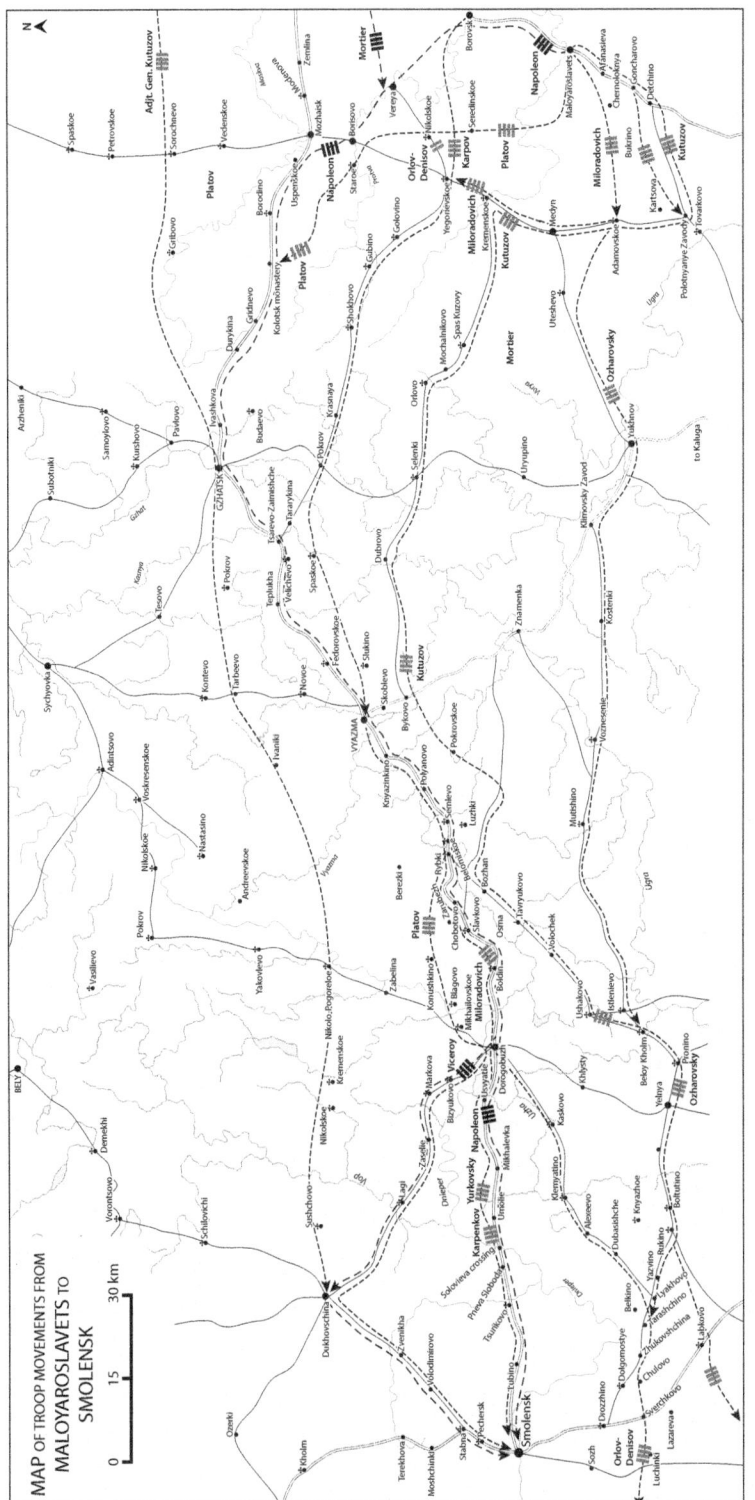

Map of Troop Movements from Maloyaroslavets to Smolensk.

The vanguards from both sides remained in contact with one another for two days, exchanging a few cannon shots from time to time, and then proceeded after their armies, in opposite directions: on the night of 14 to 15 (26 to 27) October, wanting to close up to the main body, Miloradovich withdrew his force from Maloyaroslavets to Afanasieva, leaving 4th Division under Prinz Eugen von Württemberg with some of the cavalry to monitor the enemy. At the same time, Davout, having evacuated Maloyaroslavets, moved to the left bank of the Luzha and marched towards Borovsk. At dawn on 15 (27) October, our forward outposts, and after them the force under Prinz Eugen, reoccupied Maloyaroslavets.[57]

Kutuzov, having received intelligence on the enemy retreat along the Borovsk road, entrusted their pursuit to Platov with the Cossack regiments and other light detachments, while he remained with the main body at Goncharovo and Detchino himself. 'Having meanwhile received intelligence on the enemy movement from Borovsk and Vereya to Medyn on the morning of 15 (27) October, the Field Marshal detached General Paskevich [Ivan Fëdorovich Paskevich] towards the Medyn road with 26th Division, the Nezhin Dragoons and 18 guns, via Polotnyanye Zavody, towards Adamovskoe, and set out after them with the army on the night of 15 to 16 (27 to 28) October, in two columns: the left consisted of III Corps and V Corps and both cuirassier divisions, under the command of Prince Golitsyn [Dmitry Vladimirovich Golitsyn], and marched along the highway from Goncharovo, via Detchino, initially towards Polotnyanye Zavody; while the right, of VI Corps and VIII Corps, 12th Division (from VII Corps) and I Cavalry Corps, under the command of Dokhturov, was directed via Bukrino, Kartsova and Luki, also towards Polotnyanye Zavody. Miloradovich, having received the Field Marshal's orders to leave an infantry brigade with three Cossack regiments at Maloyaroslavets,[58] to protect his march, and to march directly on Medyn with the rest of the vanguard force, having been misled about the movement of the enemy army from Borovsk to Medyn by poor intelligence, did not go to this town, but turned left towards Adamovskoe (halfway between Polotnyanye Zavody and Medyn) and only managed to reach Chernoloknya (ten *versts* from Maloyaroslavets), where he spent the night of 15 to 16 (27 to 28) October.[59]

The next day, Kutuzov remained at Polotnyanye Zavody with the army; Miloradovich's vanguard arrived in Adamovskoe; 26th Division passed Medyn, and Paskevich reached Kremenskoe himself, with the cavalry attached to his formation, where Count Orlov-Denisov was already located, with the detachment under Colonel Ilovaisky 9th, reinforced by three more Cossack regiments; finally, Platov, with another Cossack detachment, was heading along the left bank of the Luzha and camped at Seredinskoe, between the roads leading from Vereya to Medyn and Borovsk.[60]

---

have found the opportunity not only to threaten their flanks, but to destroy supplies and shelter ahead of Napoleon's vanguard'].

57 Prinz Eugen von Württemberg's diary.
58 This detachment followed the movement of Miloradovich's vanguard as soon as Napoleon's intention to move over to the Smolensk highway was discovered.
59 War Diary. Prince Kutuzov's report to the Tsar, dated 16 [28] October, No. 251, from Polotnyanye Zavody. For the text of this report, see Appendix II
60 War Diary. Platov's letter to Duty General Konovnitsyn, dated 17 [29] October.

Kutuzov, informing Count Wittgenstein about the battle of Maloyaroslavets, wrote to him: 'The enemy has suffered a great loss of manpower. The results of this action were very significant: we captured 11 cannon, and the next day five more, and captured General Tyszkiewicz, several field officers and subalterns and some 300 lower ranks, General Lefebvre was killed (*sic*). 10,000 Cossacks, under the command of General Platov and three detachments of partisans, harass the enemy rear and right flank, burn their carts and force them to blow up their own ammunition caissons. Such was the situation that compelled them to retreat before dawn yesterday. Our cavalry, under the command of General Miloradovich, is pursuing them relentlessly. They have apparently taken the direction back towards Borovsk, making their way for a flanking march towards Gzhatsk. I believe it will cause the greatest harm to them by moving parallel and eventually to operate against their line of operations...'[61]

From these instructions it is clear that Kutuzov, while still in Polotnyanye Zavody, had already appreciated the benefits of a flanking pursuit and, if he did not immediately carry this out, then it was only because of his instinctive caution, which would later prevent him from striving resolutely towards the operational objective.

Having received the official report of the reoccupation of Moscow by our troops on 11 (23) October by Major General Ilovaisky 4th while in Polotnyanye Zavody on 16 (28) October, Kutuzov informed the Tsar about this and ordered the commander of the Vladimir *Opolchenie*, Prince Golitsyn [Boris Andreevich Golitsyn], to move out to Moscow with his regiments and establish an administration there, pending the arrival of military and civil authorities.[62]

While our main body remained at Polotnyanye Zavody, the French had reached the Smolensk highway.

On 15 (27) October, the day after Napoleon's withdrawal from Maloyaroslavets to Borovsk with the *Garde*, his *État-major général* moved to Vereya. There, Poniatowski's *5e Corps*, which had been in the vicinity of Vereya since 11 (23) October, and Mortier's Combined Corps, which had arrived from Moscow, rejoined the enemy army.[63] Napoleon expressed a desire to see the prisoners he had caught, General Wintzingerode and Captain Naryshkin. By the time they were introduced to Napoleon, he had travelled around the neighbourhood of Vereya, enquiring about everything he encountered during this inspection from one of the town's residents, who served under duress as a guide to the French. As the prisoners were brought to him, Napoleon turned away in the opposite direction and continued his inspection; and then a few minutes later, he dismounted from his horse, as did his entire retinue: Berthier, Murat, Caulaincourt [Armand Augustin Louis de Caulaincourt], Lauriston, Rapp [Jean Rapp] and others. All of them stood, along with *l'escadron de service auprès de l'Empereur*, a few paces behind their sovereign. On his orders, the gendarmes brought the prisoners forwards.

'You are in the service of the Russian Emperor?' Napoleon enquired of General Wintzingerode.

---

61 Instructions for Count Wittgenstein, dated 16 [28] October, No. 255.
62 Instructions for Prince Golitsyn, dated 16 [28] October, No. 259.
63 Chambray, II, 354. Sołtyk, 369.

'Yes, Sire!' he replied.

'And who gave you permission? ... *Miserable*! I have encountered you everywhere. Why did you come to Moscow? ... To find out what had happened there?'

'No! I placed my trust in the integrity of your troops.'

'What do you care about my troops? Unworthy man! Take a look at what Moscow is like. It has been driven to this by fifty *miserables* like yourself! You persuaded Emperor Alexander to fight against me in alliance with Austria. Caulaincourt told me this. You bandits kill my soldiers on the roads. Oh! Your fate is sealed. Gendarmes! Take him away and shoot him; deliver me from him! I am not so easy to get rid of; in six weeks I shall be in St Petersburg. Shoot him now, or, better yet, put him on trial; if he is a Saxon, or a Bavarian, then he is my subject; if not, that's another matter.'

Throughout this tirade, Wintzingerode, although not expecting such a reception, seemed to swell up the more that Napoleon tried to humiliate him. To the threat of being shot, he replied: 'For twenty-five years I have been awaiting death from a French bullet and I am ready for whatever comes; my wife and children are safe; Emperor Alexander will not abandon them.'

Napoleon, repeated himself several more times: 'If he is a Bavarian or Saxon subject, let him be shot!'

And on approaching the second prisoner, said to him: 'You are Mr Naryshkin, the son of the *Ober Kammerger* [Master Chamberlain]. You do your duty as a nobleman; but what are you doing serving with such a *miserable*? You should be serving with Russians.'

Both prisoners were taken to a hut, where Rapp, Narbonne [Louis-Marie-Jacques-Amalric de Narbonne-Lara] and Berthier continued interrogating General Wintzingerode, while Naryshkin was ordered to report to the Assistant Chief of Staff, General Monthion [François Gédéon Bailly de Monthion], and was then invited to dine with Napoleon. Since Wintzingerode was not a subject of any of the sovereigns of the Confederation of the Rhine, but had been born in Prussia, the matter ended with idle threats, and orders were issued to take him to Metz along with Naryshkin.[64]

Emperor Alexander I, having received a report on the capture of Wintzingerode, wrote to Prince Kutuzov:

---

64 The details regarding Wintzingerode and Naryshkin, as well as everything Napoleon said to them, were extracted from Naryshkin's handwritten notes (archive of the M.T.D. No. 47,352, folio IV). In Napoleon's letter to Berthier, dated 3 November, new style, it states: 'Let General Wintzingerode know that you have reported to me in regard to his letter in which he declares that he has never been a subject of any of the rulers of the Confederation of the Rhine, and that I have ordered him to be considered a prisoner of war... Order the duc de Trévise (Mortier) to send Count Wintzingerode to the duc d'Abrantès corps (Junot), who will send him, together with his aide de camp, to Smolensk, and on to Vilna, by *poste chaise*, under escort and accompanied by two gendarmes. Oblige them to sign their parole (*on leur faira signer leur parole d'honneur*). From Vilna direct them to Metz... Point out to the duc d'Abrantès and General Charpentier the necessity of ridding the army of the presence of these officers as quickly as possible, and of transporting them with all possible speed.'

Prince Mikhail Ilarionovich! You should, of course, have already been informed about the unfortunate experience that has befallen Adjutant General Baron Wintzingerode, according to reports from Major General Ilovaisky 4th. Even Turks and Asiatic peoples know how to respect those who come out to negotiate. But it seems that all the rules, hitherto revered as sacred and observed throughout most of the revolutionary wars, are now held in contempt and have given way to the arbitrary cruelty of Napoleon. If you, before receiving this order, have not already demanded the repatriation of General Wintzingerode, who was captured, regardless of the sign of truce he had in his hands, I order you to send a dedicated *parlementaire* with the explanation that he has been taken against all the recognised rules of war and that he should be returned. If, regardless of justice, he is to be considered a prisoner, then offer to exchange him at the outposts at an appropriate time for General Ferrier [Gratien-Ferrier]. But if, despite expectations, Napoleon's anger has extended to a death sentence for General Wintzingerode, then announce that the life of General Ferrier shall be hostage to his preservation, whom you must shoot in front of the outposts if you learn from your *parlementaire* that General Wintzingerode is already no longer alive, and then let the enemy camp know that henceforth five Frenchmen will be hostage for every man wearing Russian uniform who is deprived of life, starting always with the senior ranks of the prisoners we hold. Issue also a demand, or, at least, an exchange for Captain Naryshkin of the Izyum Hussar Regiment, who was captured along with Baron Wintzingerode. St Petersburg, 18 [30] October 1812.

Kutuzov, having received this Supreme Rescript, sent to Berthier with a demand for the release of General Wintzingerode and Captain Naryshkin,[65] but by that time they had already passed through Smolensk.

Napoleon, who had repeatedly violated the time-honoured customs that moderated the cruelty of wars, spared Wintzingerode; but if he had acted differently, then Emperor Alexander I, despite the magnanimity and mercy inherent in Him, would have punished the criminal murder of His warrior and forced the enemy to respect the rights recognised by all civilised nations.

On the night of 15 to 16 (27 to 28) October, there were some four degrees of frost. The weather was clear, which greatly favoured the French retreat, but in the bivouacs, at night, they were already suffering from the cold.[66] On 16 (28) October, Napoleon emerged onto the Smolensk highway with the *Garde*, leaving Mozhaisk to the right and stopped for the night in Uspenskoe. On that day, one of our officers was captured by a patrol from the rearguard of Davout's *1er Corps*, who, when asked about the location of the main body under Kutuzov, announced that the Russian army was

---

65 Prince Kutuzov's letter to the Chief of Staff of the French army, dated 29 October [10 November] (archive of the M.T.D. No. 46,692, folio IV).
66 Chambray, II, 334. Denniée, in contrast, wrote that on 26 October, new style, there was a fine cold rain, which badly ruined the roads, *Itinéraire de l'empereur Napoléon pendant la campagne de 1812*, 114.

marching directly on Smolensk. The following night, a report from Marshal Davout arrived at Napoleon's *État-major général*, which had been sent at four o'clock that afternoon: the Marshal, sending the captive officer to Napoleon, wrote that the rearguard had retreated no farther than Borovsk and that he was being pursued by Cossacks alone, who had appeared at nine o'clock in the morning. This information, which confirmed the claims made by the prisoner, made Napoleon concerned that Kutuzov would actually get across the lines of communication of the French army by the shortest route to Vyazma, or to Smolensk. Napoleon tried to suggest that the statement by our officer did not deserve any attention and even ordered his Chief of Staff to write in this respect to Marshal Davout,[67] but nevertheless considered it necessary to hasten the retreat of his *Garde*.[68]

At dawn on 17 (29) October, Napoleon passed through the battlefield of Borodino with the *Garde* and with part of Murat's *Réserve de cavalerie*. Fifty-two days had already passed since the battle, but the field still presented a frightful picture of death in every possible form. There were corpses at every step; the fields were strewn with fragments of weapons, torn clothing, harness and ammunition. After that, passing by the Kolotsk Monastery, where an extensive hospital had been established since the battle of Borodino, Napoleon ordered the use of all the wagons that the troops had, and even his own carriages, for the wounded, some 500 of whom still remained in the monastery. But these unfortunates, for the most part, became victims of the inhumanity of the drivers who were in the wagon train, or soldiers who had become rich with loot, who, at the first opportunity, threw the wounded onto the road, where they died of hunger and cold, in the most severe agonies. By nightfall on 17 (29) October, Napoleon had arrived in Gzhatsk with the *Garde* and *Réserve de cavalerie*, pushing Junot's Westphalian *8e Corps* further along the Smolensk road. On the following day, 18 (30) October, the *État-major général* of the French army was located in the ruins of the village of Velichevo, in a small hut without glass in the windows or doors, and on 19 (31) October, Napoleon arrived in Vyazma. During this stage, for the first time since the departure from Moscow, he rode in a carriage, dressed in fur clothing Polish-style.[69]

On the day of the arrival of Napoleon's *État-major général* in Vyazma (where Evers' detachment linked up with the army), the enemy forces occupied the following location: the *Vieille Garde* and Murat's *Réserve de cavalerie* were eight *versts* from Vyazma; Mortier and Junot had not reached Vyazma. Ney was in Velichevo, between

---

67 Berthier's letter to Davout, dated 29 October, new style: '... *Le prisonnier que vous avez envoyé ignore la marche de l'ennemi, puisqu'il en est separé du 25 au soir, et qu'il a été pris le 26 à onze heures du matin, c'est-à-dire trois heures après que les avantpostes de l'ennemi avaient pris connaissance de notre mouvement rétrograde. Si l'ennemi se dirige sur Smolensk, tant mieux; tous nos moyens sont réunis, et nous tomberons sur ses derrières avec une armée plus forte que celle que nous lui aurions présentée il y a huit jours, mais il est fâcheux que des bruits pareils se propagent, que des aides-de-camp en parient; cela donné à l'armée des idées de la force de l'armée ennemie, bien loin de la vérité. Il faut que votre interprète se soit trompé s'il a cru trouver cela dans les réponses du prisonnier. Il est hors de doute que, si cela était, un officier subalterne n'aurait pu en être instruit.*'
68 Chambray, II, 354-355.
69 Chambray, II, 355-357. Fain, II, 217-218. Sołtyk, 369-370.

Gzhatsk and Vyazma; the Viceroy and Poniatowski were around Gzhatsk; Davout was at Gridnevo; being in the rearguard, he was committed, by order of Napoleon, to burn every village or isolated building that remained on his route. He was subsequently criticised for retreating too slowly, step by step, unnecessarily taking up positions against the Cossacks pursuing him and wasting time solely to save a few guns and ammunition caissons, barely mobile with emaciated, exhausted horses, which would soon have to be abandoned.[70] But remembering the words of the unforgettable Bagration [Pëtr Ivanovich Bagration], during the retreat to Preußisch Eylau: 'that is why we are in the rearguard, so as not to gift anything to the enemy' one cannot agree with the opinion of the Marshal's detractors.

During the movement of the French to Mozhaisk and Vyazma, the temperature consistently dropped to four or five degrees below freezing at night: the despondency and discouragement of the troops gradually increased; and at the same time the number of sick men multiplied; the physical strength of the soldiers weakened to the point that many of the men considered their weapons a burden and threw them away; at every step crowds of unarmed infantrymen could be seen as well as horseless cavalrymen who had abandoned the colours, wandering along the sides of the highway in order to find a means of salvation from starvation, and often paying for it with their lives. The decline in discipline, which had emerged during the extended stay in Moscow, fell ever lower; hunger suppressed both the sense of honour and subordination; the soldiers would not listen to their officers and showed open disrespect towards them.[71] Although the troops still had some stores and the cold was moderate, nevertheless, everyone was aware of the onset of unheard-of disasters. The Westphalian *8e Corps*, on the first two stages from Mozhaisk to Gzhatsk, at the head of the army, out of contact with the Russian forces, lost some 400 stragglers out of 5,690 men. The transports of a Westphalian division got mixed up with one from the *Jeune Garde* and presented a spectacle of turmoil and disorder; ration wagons and herds of cattle belonging to the Westphalians were robbed by soldiers from the *Garde*; there were repeated bloody clashes between the French and their allies.[72] Napoleon had ordered that the army was not to leave any wagons behind, but from the very first stages along the Smolensk highway, the troops, seeing the obvious impossibility of taking away all the baggage that accompanied them, began to burn the wagons and blow up ammunition caissons. As the transport decreased, the resources for provisioning the troops were destroyed. In particular, the plight of our prisoners was disastrous, forced to follow the French during their rapid retreat. When these unfortunates, having not received any food to maintain their strength, fell from fatigue, the enemy finished them off with musket butts.[73]

---

70 Chambray, II, 358-359.
71 Lemazurier. *Medicinische Geschichte*.
72 Lossberg, *Briefe in der Heimath*, 237.
73 The French themselves confess to the murder of their captive prisoners, attributing this cruel measure to their allies. Comte de Ségur, *Histoire de Napoléon et de la grande armée pendant l'année 1812*, 4e édit, II, 164. According to Gourgaud, only a few men were killed. But in *Journal de la campagne de Russie en 1812*, 74, Fezensac wrote: 'une colonne des prisonniers russes marchait en avant de nous, conduite par des troupes de la confédération du Rhin. On leur distribuait à peine un peu de chair de cheval, et les soldats chargés de les conduire massacraient

As has already been stated above, on 16 (28) October (on the very day when Napoleon emerged onto the Smolensk highway with the greater part of his army), our troops occupied the following locations: Kutuzov remained in Polotnyanye Zavody with the main body; Miloradovich's vanguard was in Adamovskoe; Paskevich was beyond Medyn; Orlov-Denisov was in Kremenskoe on the river Luzha; Platov was in Seredinskoe; Karpov, having ejected Davout's rearguard from Borovsk, turned towards Yegorievskoe. At the same time, partisan detachments were chasing after the enemy from various directions: Colonel Kaisarov [Paisy Sergeevich Kaisarov] and Prince Kudashev were located around Borovsk; Colonel Yefremov [Ivan Yefremovich Yefremov] was between Mozhaisk and Moscow; Captains Seslavin and Figner were between the Medyn and Smolensk roads, at the village of Kuprovo; Lieutenant Colonel Davydov was between Gzhatsk and Vyazma.[74]

On the following day, 17 (29) October, Prince Kutuzov, moving along the Medyn road with the main body, marched to Adamovskoe; Miloradovich's vanguard, proceeding through places where the inhabitants had not abandoned their homes and where the troops found everything they needed, arrived at Yegorievskoe and linked up with the detachments under Paskevich and Karpov there; Count Orlov-Denisov formed the lead element of the vanguard with five Cossack regiments on the road to Vereya; Platov was located near Borisovo at Staroe. In addition, a newly formed detachment from the main body, of 19th Jägers, Mariupol Hussars and four Cossack regiments, with six guns, under the command of Adjutant General Count Ozharovsky [Adam Petrovich Ozharovsky], was directed to Yukhnov and Yelnya, directly towards Smolensk.[75] On 18 (30) October, at the time when the main body of the enemy army was hastily retreating to Vyazma and had already passed Gzhatsk,

---

ceux qui ne pouvaient plus marcher. Nous rencontrions sur la route leurs cadavres qui tous avaient la tête fracassée. Je dois aux soldats de mon régiment la justice de dire qu'ils en furent indignés...' (a column of Russian prisoners marched in front of us, led by troops from the Confederation of the Rhine. They were barely given a bit of horse flesh, and the soldiers in charge of leading them massacred those who could no longer walk. We encountered their corpses on the road, all of whom had their skulls shattered. I owe justice to the soldiers of my regiment to say that they were outraged...)[Liprandi comments: 'the beating to death of our prisoners was a general policy adopted by the French, as can be seen from the book: Fiftieth Anniversary Of The Battle Of Borodino, Moscow, 1866'].

74 The force composition was: Kutuzov's main body of III Corps, V Corps, VI Corps, elements of VII Corps (12th Division), VIII Corps, I Cavalry Corps and both cuirassier divisions; Miloradovich's vanguard of II Corps, IV Corps, II Cavalry Corps and IV Cavalry Corps; Paskevich's detachment of 26th Division, Nezhin Dragoons and 18 guns; Count Orlov-Denisov's detachment of Colonel Yagodin 2nd's Cossacks and *Starshina* Troilin's Cossacks, supported by Ilovaisky 9th's detachment of his own Cossacks, Ilovaisky 11th's Cossacks and Bykhalov 1st's Cossacks; Platov's detachment of 15 Cossack regiments; Karpov's detachment of seven Cossack regiments.

75 The 19th Jägers and six horse artillery pieces, as well as two newly arrived Poltava Cossack Regiments were donated by the army; the Mariupol Hussars came from the vanguard, and two Don regiments from Platov's Cossack detachment. In addition to these troops, 25 mounted warriors from the Smolensk *Opolchenie* were given to the detachment under Count Ozharovsky, equipped with entrenching tools (orders from Prince Kutuzov to generals: Miloradovich, Dokhturov, Platov, Ozharovsky, Löwenstern and Ivashev, dated 16 and 17 [28 and 29] October, archive of the M.T.D. No. 29,172).

Kutuzov continued to move in the same old direction to the right with the main body and stopped for the night in Kremenskoe. The reason for this was the lack of accurate intelligence on the enemy: from the official correspondence of Prince Kutuzov and Konovnitsyn with Platov, it is clear that for a whole day in our headquarters there was no intelligence from the vanguard.[76] The Field Marshal, sharing the prevailing opinion among us of that time, believed that Napoleon would retreat to Gzhatsk, Sychyovka and Bely to the Dvina [Daugava], and therefore, in paying attention mainly to this route, did not turn left towards Vyazma. But it is rather difficult to explain why he remained at Polotnyanye Zavody for almost two days and why he subsequently moved from there to Medyn, in such a direction that would not allow him to cross the enemy's path, even in the event that they were actually retreating towards Sychyovka. Meanwhile, Miloradovich, having reached Yegorievskoe 18 (30) October, turned towards Gzhatsk the next day, having Count Orlov-Denisov in the lead, while Platov, having reached the Smolensk highway with 20 Cossack regiments, attacked the enemy at dawn on 19 (31) October, at the Kolotsk monastery, taking 20 (according to other sources 25) guns, and wiped out two battalions, taking their Colours. The disorder of the enemy, forced by the relentless pursuit of the Cossacks to speed up the retreat, increased more and more: at every step they were blowing up ammunition caissons and abandoned many men who were unable to keep up with the troops.[77]

The Field Marshal received intelligence on this from General Yermolov, who was with Miloradovich's vanguard, and wrote to him from Yegorievskoe on 18 (30) October that the army could shorten its route and go directly towards Vyazma, being perfectly protected by the movements of the vanguard. This forced Kutuzov to undertake the flanking pursuit which would cause great harm to the enemy army.[78] On 19 (31) October, the army set out from Kremenskoe to Spas-Kuzovy and the next day [1 November, new style] arrived in Selenki (on the road from Gzhatsk to Yukhnov). Preparing to move in this new direction, Kutuzov ordered Miloradovich: 'March to the left of the Smolensk highway with the vanguard entrusted to you (so long as the enemy continue their march towards Vyazma), maintaining communications with the main body of the army.'

But even before receiving this order, Miloradovich's vanguard was headed to the left of this road, towards Nikolskoe at the same time as Platov's arrival on the Smolensk highway.[79]

Thus, on 20 October (1 November), at the same time as Napoleon's army was between Gridnevo and Vyazma, moving in several echelons stretched over a distance of 90 *versts*, our troops were pursuing the enemy from the rear and flanks: Kutuzov's main body was moving towards Vyazma, in order to sever the French line of retreat; Miloradovich's vanguard, which at that time included Pakevich's 26th Division, was in the interval between our main body and the Smolensk highway, towards Gzhatsk

---

76 Instructions dated 19 [31] October (archive of the M.T.D. No. 29,172).
77 War Diary [With reference to the 20, or 25 guns captured, Liprandi asks who were the sources?].
78 Yermolov's notes.
79 Orders for Miloradovich, dated 19 [31] October, No. 290 (archive of the M.T.D. No. 29,172).

and Tsarevo-Zaimishche; the Cossack detachment under Count Orlov-Denisov was ahead of the vanguard. Platov was following the enemy from behind; the partisan detachments under Davydov, Seslavin and Figner made raids from the flank and on the French line of retreat;[80] Colonel Yefremov was ordered to operate along the axis Gzhatsk to Sychyovka, and then to lunge at the right flank of the retreating enemy, trying to forestall them on the march.[81] The detachment under Adjutant General Count Ozharovsky was ordered to head to the town of Yelnya towards Smolensk to destroy enemy detachments and magazines. A similar mission was received by General Wintzingerode's former corps, which Kutuzov entrusted to the command of Count Saint-Priest [Guillaume Emmanuel Guignard de Saint-Priest], who had just recovered from his wounds and arrived at the headquarters of the army. But Adjutant General P.V. Kutuzov was appointed by Supreme Command to occupy this position while Saint-Priest was on the way to Moscow in order to take command of the detachment.[82]

Despite the loss of time after the battle of Maloyaroslavets and the speed of the enemy retreat, we still had the opportunity to block the path and deliver a decisive blow to Napoleon's army. This was the objective of our subsequent operations, because to base our successes solely on the influence of the coming winter would be very unreasonable. Some foreign historians have attributed the destruction of the *Grande Armée* to the frosts. In acknowledging that the severity of the winter of 1812 had a disastrous effect on the soldiers of Napoleon, unaccustomed to the cold and poorly dressed and shod, I shall confine myself, this time, to the remark that the Russians, who were used to the frosts and had sheepskin coats, nevertheless, suffered a great deal from the cold. The existence of a military man is a continuous chain of tasks, deprivation and suffering, and woe betide that warrior who cannot endure them. If in 1812, the Russian troops, relying to a greater extent on the assistance of winter, had left the enemy alone, then they would have been able to spread a considerable distance away from the Smolensk highway, to obtain food supplies without difficulty, to retreat with impunity into Lithuania and settle down there in winter quarters. But the French did not succeed, because we did not allow them to stop or leave the devastated Smolensk road, and meanwhile, at every bloody encounter, the enemy, no longer dared to think of victory, but restricted themselves to the business of retreating with the fewest casualties. Let us pay tribute to Napoleon's battle-hardened soldiers; they did not die until such time as their terrible struggle with disaster had exceeded human endurance; but the elements alone did not destroy a half-million man army. This required the efforts of the entire Russian people, who, at the behest of their Monarch, had accomplished the great feat of liberating their Fatherland.

---

80 War Diary.
81 Orders for Colonel Yefremov, dated 19 [31] October, No. 289.
82 Prince Kutuzov's orders for Ozharovsky, dated 17 [29] October, No. 279 and to Count Saint-Priest dated 18 [30] October, No. 280. Adjutant General Kutuzov's report to Emperor Alexander I, dated 19 [31] October.

35

The battle at Vyazma and Napoleon's retreat to Smolensk

The situation during Napoleon's halt in Vyazma. – Napoleon's instructions to: Victor, Baraguey d'Hilliers, Charpentier. – Comparison of forces on both sides assembled in the vicinity of Vyazma. – The situation of French forces. – The circumstances preventing the Russian vanguard from exploiting the disorder in the enemy army. – The deployments of both sides before the battle of Vyazma. – The battle of Vyazma.

The situation of Napoleon's forces after the battle of Vyazma. – The circumstances preventing Kutuzov from taking full advantage of the attrition of the enemy army. – The continuing French retreat. – Prince Kutuzov's orders. – Napoleon's arrival in Smolensk. – The action at Dorogobuzh. – The pursuit to Smolensk. – Action at Lyakhovo. – The Viceroy's retreat. – The crossing of the Vop. – The Viceroy's arrival in Smolensk. – Ney's retreat over the Solovieva crossing towards Smolensk and his arrival and the pursuit of the French by our light detachments. – The offensive by the main body of the Russian army during Napoleon's halt in Smolensk. – Composition of the Russian forces.

On 19 (31) October, on the day that Napoleon arrived in Vyazma, the French army was moving along the highway in several echelons, in the sector between Vyazma and Gridnevo, while our vanguard and Kutuzov's main body were on the side roads to Gzhatsk and Vyazma; Cossack detachments pursued the enemy from the rear and flanks and strove to cut the lines of communication of the French army.

On the following day [1 November, new style], Napoleon remained in Vyazma in order to issue instructions to individual formations of his army, while his troops continued to retreat, loading all the wounded who remained at the city hospitals onto the wagons that were with them.[1] In Vyazma, reports were received from: Saint-Cyr [Laurent de Gouvion-Saint-Cyr] about his evacuation of Polotsk, Victor about his move from Smolensk to the Dvina, and from the duc de Bassano (Maret [Hugues-Bernard Maret]) from Vilna [Vilnius], about the successes achieved by Chichagov [Pavel

---

1   Chambray, *Histoire de l'expédition de Russie*, II, 358-359.

Vasilevich Chichagov] over Schwarzenberg [Karl Philipp Fürst zu Schwarzenberg]. This intelligence revealed our intention to sever the lines of communication of his army to this experienced commander, but Napoleon still had not lost hope of getting out of the difficult situation in which he found himself. Believing that the co-operation between the corps under Victor and Saint-Cyr and the imminent arrival of the *Grande Armée* in Smolensk would rectify the matter, he hoped that Chichagov would be delayed by a pursuit by Schwarzenberg along a difficult route through the forests of Lithuania, which would prevent our troops from moving with the necessary speed. In addition, the vastness of the distance separating our armies and the inevitable influence of chance in such extensive movements as Wittgenstein, and especially Chichagov had to make, offered the probability of success to Napoleon.[2] General Charpentier [Henri François Marie Charpentier] (Governor of Smolensk) was ordered to send a statement of essential supplies, artillery, and regarding all resources that were in Smolensk in general, to Dorogobuzh by 3 November (new style). He was also ordered to write to the Governor of Mogilev and Commandant of Vitebsk about arranging the largest possible stocks of grain for the army and to notify them: 'that the movement of the army is voluntary, that it is a movement of manoeuvre to be a hundred leagues closer to the armies which form our wings; that, since we left the environs of Moscow, we no longer have any intelligence on the enemy except through a few Cossacks.'[3]

General Baraguey d'Hilliers [Louis Baraguey d'Hilliers], who had set out from Smolensk along the Kaluga road with a detachment to meet the *Grande Armée*, was informed of the new direction in which it was moving and was ordered to take appropriate precautions.[4] Finally, Marshal Victor was informed that the army was on its way, as had already been written to him previously; that the purpose of such a march was to close up to the troops operating on the flanks for the winter, and that, in all likelihood, the main body, located between the Dvina and the Dnieper, would establish communications with the corps under his command.[5]

Meanwhile, the French army, exhausted by hunger, moved almost without rest, with the exception of the troops that had managed to reach Vyazma; Davout, who was following the army in the rearguard, having passed through Gzhatsk on 20 October (1 November), continued to retreat further, wanting to bypass the defile at Tsarevo-Zaimishche. Platov's Cossacks were constantly harassing the enemy on the march and forced them to abandon guns and wagons. Paskevich was moving directly behind Davout's force with 26th Division; while Miloradovich's vanguard advanced to the left of the highway. Prinz Eugen von Württemberg's 4th Division was the lead formation of the vanguard.[6]

---

2   Fain, *Manuscrit de 1812*, II, 228-229.
3   'que le mouvement de l'armée est volontaire, que c'est un mouvement de manoeuvre pour être à cent lieues plus rapproché des armées qui forment nos ailes; que, depuis que nous avont quitté les environs de Moscou, nous n'avons plus de nouvelles de l'ennemi que par quelques cosaques.'
4   Berthier's letter to General Charpentier, from Vyazma, dated 1 November, new style: '... Faites connaître au général Baraguay-d'Hilliers le mouvement de l'armée etc. Je vous ai déjà fait connaître que ce général ne devait pas se compromettre: renouvellez-lui de ma part cette disposition...'
5   Chambray, II, 363.
6   Prinz Eugen von Württemberg, *Erinnerungen aus dem Feldzuge des Jahres 1812*, 128.

General Miloradovich was very well aware that he could not cut the line of retreat of Napoleon's entire army with his vanguard alone, without exposing it to the danger of being overwhelmed by superior numbers, and therefore decided, having allowed the bulk of the French force to pass by, to go to Tsarevo-Zaimishche, where (as we knew) the terrain was advantageous for isolating the columns of the enemy rearguard. Indeed, although the number of Napoleon's troops decreased noticeably every day and the leading formations of his army (the *Garde*, Westphalians, *2e corps de cavalerie* and *4e corps de cavalerie*), continuing to retreat non-stop, could not take part in the battle along with the remaining corps, nevertheless, the enemy had 37,500 armed men in the vicinity of Tsarevo-Zaimishche at the time,[7] against whom Miloradovich and Platov could operate with no more than 25,000 men.[8] It is true that our troops were in incomparably better condition than the enemy corps moving past them (*1er Corps, 3e Corps, 4e Corps, 5e Corps, 1er corps de cavalerie* and *3e corps de cavalerie*), which, having set out from Moscow numbering 73,000 men, and having lost no more than 7,000 men in the battles at Maloyaroslavets and Medyn, had weakened by almost half, due to the many unarmed stragglers, or those following the army in disarray who had dispersed in all directions to find food. Of the entire enemy army, only Ney's *3e Corps* was still in a fairly good state; in contrast the corps under Davout and the Viceroy, formerly noted for their observance of good order and discipline, were in a pitiful state. The addition of fresh fighting units to the army, the Westphalian *8e régiment d'infanterie de ligne* in Gzhatsk and the 4,000 man detachment under Evers in Vyazma, did not improve the situation of the French army at all, because these troops, carried away by the example of others, indulged in marauding with them and diminished markedly.[9]

Having said that, Napoleon's forces were incomparably more numerous than our vanguard, and the disorder in the enemy army was not fully known to us. The speed of the French retreat, removing the ability to pursue in contact with the enemy, prevented us from having accurate intelligence about their situation and strength. 'The enemy is running like no army has ever run' Platov wrote in one of his reports.[10] For this very reason, at the time of start of the pursuit, we were operating in the dark. Miloradovich, fearless, level-headed, invariably cheerful in the midst of dangers, possessed many of the qualities of a vanguard commander, but did not pay attention to precision in the orders for the troops entrusted to him at all. His orders in 1812, sometimes incomprehensible, placed all those who were directed to carry them out in difficulties. Indeed, there was generally no order in his headquarters; it was not even always possible to find him, yet at the first shots he would appear in

---

7   According to the approximated statement by Chambray (II, 371) consisted of: *1er Corps* – 13,000 men; *3e Corps* – 6,000 men; *4e Corps* – 12,000 men; *5e Corps* – 3,500 men; *1er corps de cavalerie* & *3e corps de cavalerie* plus cavalry from the corps – 3,000 men; total: 37,500 men.
8   According to estimates, consisted of: II Corps – 7,000 men; IV Corps – 7,000 men; II Cavalry Corps & IV Cavalry Corps – 3,500 men; total for Miloradovich: 17,500 men. 26th Division – 4,000 men; Cossack regiments – 3,000 men; total for Platov: 7,000 men. Consequently, some 25,000 men were assembled with us in the vicinity of Vyazma. Prinz Eugen von Württemberg, 132-133.
9   Bernhardi, *Denkwürdigkeiten des Grafen v. Toll*, II, 277-278.
10 Platov's report dated 20 October [1 November].

his customary place, in front of everyone, wherever the greatest danger threatened. There he would rouse the troops to be contemptuous of death through his own example; beyond that, he did not seem to care. 'Operate as you please' he used to say to the unit commanders of the force: 'I am your guest.' Nevertheless, however, from time to time, he would interfere with the orders issued by unit commanders subordinate to him, not informing them of his orders, which often led to misunderstandings. Each of the generals in Miloradovich's vanguard operated in their own way, not being sure either of the coordination or cooperation with other units, or of their consistent direction towards a common objective.[11]

Miloradovich, intending to attack the enemy army's rearguard around Tsarevo-Zaimishche on the morning of 21 October (2 November), wanted, firstly, to assemble his force there, and therefore, on the last stage to this village, it was confirmed to the commanders of the vanguard's leading units specifically that they settle down for the night covertly and prohibited bivouac fires from being lit.[12] But Prinz Eugen von Württemberg, swept along by his customary valour, not only did not conceal the movements of his division, but, by passing through the village of Vorontsovo with them, came so close to the highway, along which the enemy was then negligently stretched, that skirmishers were deployed by both sides and a rather fierce firefight ensued. Thus Miloradovich's intention was compromised. Prinz Eugen, noticing the disorder of the French troops and wanting to take advantage of this, formed his 4th Division into battalion columns, positioned them for battle and advanced artillery into the intervals of the front line; Paskevich attached his 26th Division to the right flank of 4th Division; as there was almost no cavalry at all with this force, Prinz Eugen invited Adjutant General Korf [Fëdor Karlovich Korf], who had arrived at the village of Vorontsovo with II Cavalry Corps, to close up to the infantry and stand behind it in reserve. In anticipation of his arrival, the regiments of 4th Division moved forward; but, after that, Korf, leaving his corps in place, visited Prince Eugen and made it clear to him that in the disposition for the vanguard issued to the force, it was forbidden to move further than Vorontsovo. Darkness fell during this engagement, and our troops were forced to stop, which facilitated the enemy passing them along the highway and to the right of it.[13] Had the French not been alarmed by the untimely appearance of the head of our vanguard, then at dusk on 20 October (1 November) they would have stopped for the night in the vicinity of our troops and the next day they would have been attacked and defeated by superior numbers. Miloradovich's vanguard, setting off at dawn on 21 October (2 November) towards Tsarevo-Zaimishche, arrived at the long embankment lined with poplars located near this village, along which the muddy road ran. It is easy to imagine the difficulties that the enemy had to overcome, forced to cross it at night. In many places

---

11 A.P. Yermolov's notes. Prinz Eugen von Württemberg, 126-127 [Liprandi complains that there is no indication of which source provided which parts of this appraisal, unsupported by any examples, adding; 'Miloradovich, who always commanded powerful vanguards, rearguards and in the line of battle with nothing less than brilliant success, could he really be so insubstantial as he is portrayed here!'].
12 Yermolov's notes.
13 Herzog Eugen von Württemberg, 129.

there were guns, ammunition caissons and wagons left in the mud or shoved off the embankment to clear the way for the troops. Ségur [Philippe Paul de Ségur] states that Davout passed through the swamps and Tsarevo-Zaimishche so close to our bivouacs that their fires illuminated the workers who were repairing a bridge on the causeway.[14]

The enemy army, having passed the defile at Tsarevo-Zaimishche, on the evening of 21 October (2 November) were located as follows: the Westphalians at Semlevo (at a distance of about 30 *versts* beyond Vyazma on the road to Smolensk); the *Garde* and part of the *Réserve de cavalerie*, together with Napoleon's *État-major général*, in Semlevo; Ney, having received orders to let all other troops past him and to proceed as the rearguard, remained in Vyazma; the troops under the Viceroy and Poniatowski, having passed about a *verst* beyond Fedorovskoe, stopped to support Davout's corps, which, having made a forced march the day before, settled down near Fedorovskoe on this day. A shortage of cavalry made it impossible for the enemy to obtain accurate intelligence about our forces.[15]

On that same day [2 November, new style], Prince Kutuzov reached Dubrovo (27 *versts* from Vyazma) with the main body of the army. Ahead of him was Raevsky's vanguard. The raiding detachment under Adjutant General Count Orlov-Denisov, having raided enemy troops near Vyazma, captured a gun, the chancellery of Napoleon himself and more than 100 lower ranks. Platov was halted between Tsarevo-Zaimishche and Fedorovskoe with his Cossack detachment reinforced by regiments from Paskevich's 26th Division; General Yermolov was also with this detachment. Miloradovich, moving between the main body under Kutuzov and Platov's detachment, spent the night of 21 to 22 October (2 to 3 November) near the village of Spaskoe less than a day's march from Vyazma.[16]

On 22 October (3 November), Miloradovich and Platov agreed to attack the enemy with all their might. In support of this attack, the Commander in Chief detached General Uvarov [Fëdor Petrovich Uvarov], with both cuirassier divisions, the Tula Cossack Regiment and two Lifeguard Horse Artillery Batteries, while he moved from Dubrovo to the village of Bykovo himself, on the road from Yukhnov to Vyazma, ten *versts* from this city, with the main body of the army and halted there. Miloradovich set out from the overnight halt with his vanguard at four o'clock in the morning: II Cavalry Corps, IV Cavalry Corps and five Cossack regiments were in the lead; the infantry proceeded at some distance behind them. On this day, Platov began the pursuit later than usual, wanting to give Miloradovich's force time to reach the highway at the appointed place and calculating that they would not arrive there before eleven o'clock. Hoping to arrive in time to deliver the final blow to the retreating enemy, Platov sent forward several regiments with a Don [horse artillery] company at dawn, under the command of major generals Ilovaisky 5th [Nikolai Vasilevich Ilovaisky] and Kuteinikov, giving them 300 men from 5th

---

14 Yermolov's notes. Ségur, *Histoire de Napoléon et de la grande armée pendant l'année 1812*, 4e édit, II, 170.
15 Chambray, II, 360. Yermolov's notes.
16 War Diary of the Russian Army. Yermolov's notes. *Journal milit. des opérations du II corps*, rédigé par le prince Eug. de Württemb. (archive of the M.T.D. No. 47,344).

Jägers, mounted on Cossack horses; while he set out from his overnight stay himself at seven o'clock in the morning with the remaining Cossacks and with Paskevich's infantry division. A little later, a cannonade was heard from the left side of the road and the Cossack regiments sent forward returned with the news that the enemy were in large numbers, holding back the movement of the vanguard. Whereupon Platov instructed Yermolov to deploy all the regular troops from his detachment,[17] and sending them several Cossack regiments. The jägers, mounted on horseback, arrived immediately on the battlefield; they were quickly followed by Paskevich's division.[18]

Meanwhile, the vanguard was approaching the highway in three columns:[19] on the right, under the personal command of Miloradovich, were II Cavalry Corps, IV Cavalry Corps and Lieutenant General Olsufiev's [Zakhar Dmitryevich Olsufiev] 17th Division; in the centre, commanded by Prinz Eugen von Württemberg, were 4th Division and the jäger brigade from 11th Division; on the left, under Count Osterman-Tolstoy [Alexander Ivanovich Osterman-Tolstoy], was IV Corps.[20] Generals Korf and Vasilchikov [Ilarion Vasilevich Vasilchikov], passing through the village of Maksimovo, at about eight o'clock in the morning, deployed their cavalry on the high ground dominating the highway between the villages of Fedorovskoe and Myasoedovo; 17th Division proceeded behind them, at some distance. At that very moment, Ney's *3e Corps* was located at Krapivna, south of Vyazma; the Viceroy's *4e Corps* and Poniatowski's *5e Corps*, having passed through Myasoedovo, were moving towards Vyazma; while Davout's *1er Corps*, pursued from behind by Platov's Cossacks, was approaching Federovskoe. The strength of this force (as already mentioned above) reached 37,000, while the strength of Miloradovich's and Platov's force was 25,000 men; having said that, the enemy had no more than 3,000 inferior cavalry, while on our side there were some 3,500 regular and 3,000 irregular cavalry, subsequently reinforced by 2,000 cuirassiers.

As soon as the men of II Cavalry Corps and IV Cavalry Corps had deployed parallel to the highway, Miloradovich ordered Vasilchikov to attack the enemy.

---

17 Ladoga Infantry, Poltava Infantry, Nizhegorod Infantry, Orël Infantry, 5th Jägers, Courland Dragoons, Nezhin Dragoons and two foot artillery companies.
18 Yermolov's notes.
19 See Plan of the Battle of Vyazma, inset.
20 Column composition: Right: II Cavalry Corps, commanded by Adjutant General Korf; Moscow Dragoons, Pskov Dragoons, Kargopol Dragoons, Ingermanland Dragoons, Yelisavetgrad Hussars, one horse artillery company (24 squadrons); IV Cavalry Corps, commanded by Adjutant General Vasilchikov; Kharkov Dragoons, Chernigov Dragoons, Kiev Dragoons, Belorussia Dragoons, Akhtyrka Hussars, one horse artillery company (24 squadrons); 17th Division, Lieutenant General Olsufiev; Ryazan Infantry, Belozersk Infantry, Brest Infantry, Wilmanstrand Infantry, one foot artillery company (8 battalions).
Centre: 4th Division, Prince Eugene of Württemberg; Tobolsk Infantry, Volhynia Infantry, Kremenchug Infantry and 4th Jägers; 11th Division, 1st Jägers and 33rd Jägers, one light artillery company (12 battalions).   Left: 11th Division, Major General Choglokov; Kexholm Infantry, Pernov Infantry and Yelets Infantry; 23rd Division, Major General Laptev, Rylsk Infantry, Yekaterinburg Infantry, Alexopol Infantry and three foot companies (12 battalions). In total, under the direct command of Miloradovich, there were 32 battalions (of which some had been merged, two into one), and 48 squadrons, with 84 guns.

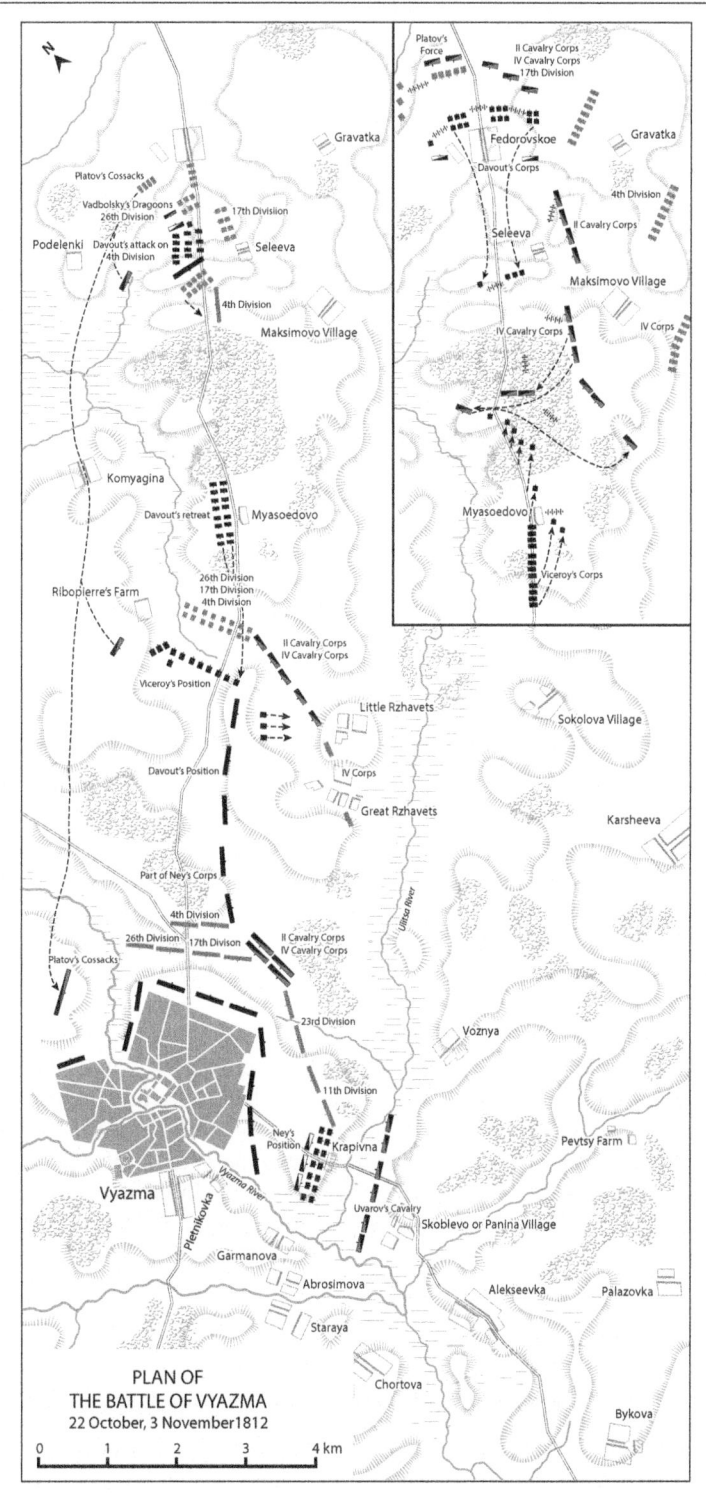

THE BATTLE AT VYAZMA AND NAPOLEON'S RETREAT TO SMOLENSK 59

Plan of the Battle of Vyazma, 22 October (3 November) 1812.

Colonel Emmanuel [Georgy Arsenievich Emmanuel], with four squadrons of Akhtyrka Hussars and with the Kiev Dragoon Regiment, despite terrain unfavourable for cavalry operations, it being covered with scrub, made a very successful attack, cutting off one of the enemy brigades,[21] scattering it and capturing many. Colonel Yuzefovich [Dmitry Mikhailovich Yuzefovich], with the Kharkov Dragoon Regiment, having moved a little to the left, crossed the highway and struck the enemy who had turned to the right off the road. Meanwhile, Miloradovich, having posted three horse artillery batteries on the high ground, in order to fire into the flank of the retreating troops, left Vasilchikov's and Korf's remaining regiments, along with artillery, in anticipation of the arrival of 17th Division. The enemy, taking advantage of the pause before our infantry could arrive on the battlefield, attacked the regiments blocking their route to Vyazma and forced them to get off the highway. Davout's columns, quickly pressing forwards, isolated the Kharkov Dragoons from our other cavalry. But this regiment galloped at full speed past the enemy, astonished by their audacity, and joined their own (as they say), without losing a single man. Following that, 17th Division arrived. Davout's situation became extremely perilous. Separated from Poniatowski and the Viceroy by a long queue of wagons and stragglers stretching along the road to Vyazma, in the meantime the carts and crowds of unarmed men slowed down the troop movements, Davout tried to speed up the retreat of his columns, concerned at being cut off by our infantry approaching the highway. At the same time, Yermolov was already catching him up from behind.[22]

At about ten o'clock, Prinz Eugen von Württemberg, having arrived on the battlefield with his division, went around the right flank of Davout's position, which had turned to face General Miloradovich, settled down along the highway and severed the enemy line of retreat.[23] General Yermolov, for his part, pushed forward the dragoon regiments, under the command of Prince Vadbolsky [Ivan Mikhailovich Vadbolsky], and opened a cannonade against the high ground held by the French. The enemy sent some of their infantry back against our force, which, being attacked by the Courland Dragoons, were scattered by them, despite coming under fierce canister fire from a battery. At that very moment, the regiments of 26th Division ran up in support of the dragoons.[24]

As soon as the Viceroy noticed the movements of our cavalry across Davout's line of retreat, he deployed his columns and formed them up for battle at Myasoedovo while behind him, moving up in the second echelon, were Poniatowski's force returning from Vyazma and the remnants of the *Réserve de cavalerie*. Miloradovich, noticing their advance, sent orders to Prinz Eugen von Württemberg to suspend his attack, because the enemy, moving from the direction of Vyazma, was heading into his rear. Shortly afterwards, a second, similar, instruction was sent to the prince also

---

21 The war diary says that this brigade, under the command of General Nagle, belonged to Viceroy's corps. In Labaume, 288, it states: '*1er Brigade, 13e Division*, under the command of General Nagle, marching in our rearguard, was attacked on their left flank, six *versts* (*à une lieue et demie*) from Vyazma.'
22 Chambray, II, 369.
23 See Plan of the Battle of Vyazma, main map.
24 Yermolov's notes. Prinz Eugen von Württemberg, 141.

giving orders to get off the highway and redeploy the force parallel to it. This order was untimely: if Prinz Eugen von Württemberg, with the assistance of Korf's and Vasilchikov's cavalry as well as Platov's force, had attacked the enemy, then, in all likelihood, Davout's corps would have been destroyed before the Viceroy could arrive to assist him, as his artillery could hardly move and impeded the infantry advance. As the enemy troops concentrated near Vyazma were not collectively subordinate to any of the corps commanders, the Viceroy, Poniatowski and Davout, having met to confer, decided most emphatically not to enter into a decisive battle, but to retreat with all possible haste. Meanwhile, the jägers of 4th Division, having left the highway, occupied the scrub alongside it, while the Kremenchug Infantry, Volhynia Infantry and Tobolsk Infantry were located to their right; a battery was established in front of the latter in order to fire on the road. The enemy, encouraged by the withdrawal of our troops and wishing to secure their route to Vyazma, directed an intensive assault on our battery, which, being showered with bullets from enemy marksmen and having shot off almost all of its ammunition, was already preparing to withdraw from the position, but was rescued by the prince's aide de camp, Wachten, who raced up to engage the enemy with one of the battalions of the Tobolsk Infantry. Davout's columns, moving along the road and to the right of it, past the frontage of the entire 4th Division, ran the gauntlet of battalion volleys, inflicting a severe defeat. Our troops also suffered significant casualties: in the Kremenchug Infantry alone, 13 officers were killed or wounded. Miloradovich, not seeing an opportunity to cut off the enemy retreat, decided to attack them from the flank with his full force: 17th Division moved forward to the right of 4th Division and, at around noon, linked up with Paskevich's 26th Division, which was pressing the enemy from behind; IV Corps headed for the village of Rzhavets; the cavalry corps followed 4th Division and 17th Division, while Platov's Cossacks raced to the right of the main road, to bypass the French from their left flank.

The Viceroy's force, without waiting for Davout's corps to join them, retreated hastily, but having received Razout's division [Louis-Nicolas de Razout] as reinforcements from Ney's corps, they halted and took up positions between Ribopierre's farm and Rzhavets. The enemy attempted to eject the men of 23rd Division from Rzhavets, but, being greeted with canister fire, were forced to retreat with casualties. Meanwhile, Davout, scattering marksmen in the scrub to cover his columns from the left flank, continued to retreat without pause. The stragglers and carts that accompanied his corps rushed to the right and, having bypassed the Viceroy and Poniatowski to their left, went along the Chernogryazhya river into Vyazma and beyond; Davout's force headed to the left of the highway in order to form up on the right of *4e Corps*, but, at the same time, being struck by the enfilade fire of our batteries, and attacked from the flanks and rear, they were thrown into disorder and barely managed to take the positions indicated for them. Here, the Kargopol Dragoons particularly distinguished themselves, driving off a strong enemy column. By one o'clock in the afternoon, the French troops were positioned as follows: the Viceroy's corps stood on the highway near Ribopierre's farm, refusing the tip of their left wing to prevent the Cossacks outflanking them; while Davout's corps, having anchored their left flank to the Viceroy's position, formed up at a very acute angle to the highway. Poniatowski's force and the cavalry remained in the second echelon.

General Miloradovich attacked this position with the full force of the vanguard and Platov's detachment, which were preceded by more than 80 foot and horse artillery pieces. Half of IV Corps (23rd Division) marched on Rzhavets, while the other half (11th Division) moved to their left, to face Davout's corps. The enemy, after a very short resistance, withdrew from their positions and fell back to Vyazma. Meanwhile, Uvarov, with both cuirassier divisions (excluding the Chevalier Guard and Lifeguard Horse regiments), and with the Lifeguard Ulans, appeared in sight of Ney's corps, on the left bank of the swampy river Ulitsa, and was forced to confine himself to a cannonade from long range.

Upon the retreat to Vyazma, the enemy settled on the high ground in front of the city, revealing an intention to defend this position stubbornly; but our superiority in artillery, the location of our cuirassiers near Krapivna, and the crossing of the Ulitsa by Seslavin's and Figner's raiding detachments, on the right flank of the French, which they had considered inaccessible, forced the enemy to retreat. The rearguard left in the city was ordered to burn the surviving buildings, and especially those in which there were ammunition and other military stores, while, in the meantime, the remaining French troops retreated through the city and along its flanks. The daylight was already fading and it was hoped that the enemy would retreat further during the night, but Miloradovich, not limiting himself to the successes already won, ordered the storming of the city, already engulfed in flames. The divisions located on the flanks of the vanguard, Paskevich's 26th Division and Choglokov's [Pavel Nikolaevich Choglokov] 11th Division, moved up for the assault. At the head of the latter, the Pernov Infantry and Kexholm Infantry, supported by the Belozersk Infantry from 17th Division, entered Vyazma ceremoniously, with unfurled Colours, announcing their presence with drums beating and bands playing; ahead of them, Yermolov's aide de camp, Lieutenant Grabbe [Pavel Khristoforovich Grabbe], who was with Miloradovich, was the first to enter the city with two horse artillery pieces and marksmen. The partisans Seslavin and Figner broke into Vyazma from the opposite side. The Russian troops quickly passed through the city in the midst of clouds of smoke and flame enveloping most of the buildings, which even included hospitals filled with wounded and sick Frenchmen, crossed the Vyazma river and occupied the city limits and the Smolensk gate. Platov, bypassing the city on the right side with his Cossack detachment, also crossed the river and stood on the far bank in order to continue the pursuit at dawn. The troops under Miloradovich, following the occupation of Vyazma, spread out in bivouacs between the city and the village of Krapivna. The fighting had ceased by six o'clock in the evening. The enemy, retreating along the road to Smolensk, left Ney's corps near Vyazma in the rearguard; the rest of the corps, having moved a few *versts* from the city, settled down in the vast forest.[25]

French losses in the actions around Vyazma, extended to 4,000 killed or wounded, 3,000 prisoners (including General Pelletier [Jean-Baptiste Pelletier] and more than 30 field officers and subalterns), one Colour and three guns. Losses on our side of

---

25 Labaume, 288-293. Chambray, II, 368-372. Prinz Eugen von Württemberg, 138-145. War Diary.

killed or wounded were 1,800 men.[26] But the manpower losses suffered in this battle by Napoleon's army were incomparably less disastrous for it than the disorder and discouragement that seized the French troops after their defeat. Fezensac [Raymond Aymeric Philippe Joseph de Montesquiou-Fezensac], who commanded one of the regiments in Ney's corps, describing the retreat of the French after the battle of Vyazma, stated: '... *4e Corps* and *1er Corps* passed through our lines in the greatest disarray. It never occurred to me that they could suffer and be disordered to such an extent. Only the *Guardia Italiana* was still in good condition; the rest of the troops appeared numbed and exhausted from fatigue. A myriad of stragglers wandered about, for the most part also unarmed; many of them spent the night, together with us, in the forest near Vyazma. I tried to persuade them to move on before the rearguard turned up; they had to withdraw as far as possible, and besides, we could not allow them to rush into our lines and sow disorder in them. Thus their own salvation was in harmony with the exigencies of the service; but fatigue and indolence made them indifferent to the impending danger. As soon as dawn began to break, *3e Corps* set out from their overnight halt. At that very moment, all the stragglers, leaving their bivouacs, joined the troops. Only the sick and wounded, crowding around the fires, begged us not to leave them at the mercy of the enemy; but we did not have any means to evacuate them from the army, and therefore we pretended that we did not hear their pleas. I gave orders to drive away the scoundrels who, despite being able to fight, had deserted the Colours, using musket butts and warned that, in the event of an enemy attack, I would order them to be shot if they interfered with the activities of my soldiers...'[27]

The day after the battle of Vyazma [4 November, new style], Napoleon received a report from Ney, in which, *inter alia*, it stated: 'If we had been better deployed, we might have expected a most advantageous outcome. The most irritating thing is that my soldiers witnessed the collapse of *1er Corps*. Such a disastrous example shook their morale, etc.'[28]

Despite the fact that the French, after the actions at Vyazma, were in desperate need of a rest, the Viceroy considered it necessary to leave the bivouacs at one o'clock in the morning in order to take advantage of the darkness to get away from our forces, against whom the enemy, exhausted from hunger and fatigue no longer dared to fight. Napoleon's troops made their way through the darkness, along a road cluttered with guns and carts; men and horses could barely move their feet, and as soon as a horse fell, the nearest soldiers rushed to it, sharing the horse meat among themselves, which had served as their only food for several days, and had soon roasted it; others, poorly clothed and shod, suffering from cold and damp almost as much as from hunger, kindled fires, lay down by them and remained in place, in anticipation of death or captivity, which seemed to them more tolerable than the efforts and hardships of the campaign.[29]

---

26 War Diary, In Chambray's *Histoire de l'expédition de Russie*, II, 372, it states: 'l'armée perdit environ quatre mille hommes, tués ou blessés, beaucoup de bagages, quelques canons, et l'ennemi lui fit plusieurs milliers de prisonniers, la plupart traineurs.'
27 Fezensac, *Journal de la campagne de Russie en 1812*, 79-80.
28 Ney's report, dated 4 November, new style.
29 Labaume, 294.

Such was the state of Napoleon's army immediately after the battle of Vyazma. Gourgaud, and other French historians after him, out of a desire to prove that the Russian armed forces had no influence on the demise of the *Grande Armée*, claim, in defiance of the truth, that not the slightest disorder was found among the French troops in this action, and even for a few days afterwards, and that it was only the onset of a premature winter, having upset all Napoleon's calculations, which burdened his army with unprecedented disasters and had prevented it from reaching Smolensk as a cohesive force.[30] An impartial, fact-based study of the reasons for the destruction of this army leaves no doubt that the French forces, being surrounded on all sides by our light detachments and not being able to obtain essential supplies, were already very weakened upon reaching Vyazma, and that the actions at Vyazma dealt the remnants of the *Grande Armée* such a blow, following which it could no longer recover. The consequences of this battle prove that if Kutuzov having retreated this time due to his customary caution, and instead of turning onto the Yukhnov road, towards Bykovo, and remaining there in complete inaction, had sent his main force towards Vyazma, he would have destroyed Davout's corps, and perhaps other corps from Napoleon's army close by. But Kutuzov did not dare to block the enemy's path, being unaware of their debilitation, which had not been completely exposed before the actions near Vyazma. And Napoleon, for all his decisiveness, would not enter into a general battle before having collected accurate intelligence about everything concerning the enemy army. It is impossible not to admit that, in Kutuzov's place, he would not have built a 'golden bridge' for the enemy,[31] but would have fought a general battle near Vyazma, and judging by the relative strengths of both sides, he would have won a decisive victory. But our commander, who had already reached advanced years, was weighing up the odds and, by acting cautiously, hoped to achieve a less brilliant, but, on the other hand, more likely success. Moving across friendly territory with the army, receiving vital supplies in abundance for his troops from all the surrounding provinces,[32] encircling Napoleon's army with raiding detachments that gave the enemy neither rest nor the opportunity to get food, Kutuzov hoped to spare his force and subject Napoleon's tired, weakened army to blows from Chichagov and Wittgenstein. He was so sure of the infallibility of this course of action that neither the proposals from Konovnitsyn and Toll, who were with him, nor the note he received from Yermolov, about the need to move the army to Vyazma, prompted him to block Napoleon's path. It subsequently emerged that the old Field Marshal's calculations were erroneous: our army, pursuing the enemy in the harsh season, although being better supplied with food and infinitely better clothed and shod than the enemy, nevertheless suffered such a loss in manpower that it could hardly have endured a general battle. Napoleon's army was almost completely destroyed, but he himself, all his marshals and cadres of the enemy corps managed to get

---

30 Gourgaud, *Examen critique de l'ouvrage de M-r le C-te de Ségur*, Livre 9e, Chap XI: '... C'est en effet de ce jour fatal, mais seulement de ce jour, que data l'hyver prématuré, qui trompa tous les calculs et accable l'armée de tant de maux. Encore trois jours, et elle arrivait intacte à Smolensk.'
31 One of Prince Kutuzov's favourite expressions. Description of the war of 1812, Vol III.
32 The War Diary mentions that, as the army moved from Maloyaroslavets to Vyazma, supplies were brought to the troops in abundance.

beyond the Neman, and this was enough for the ingenious war-administrator to form new armies and to stubbornly resist the new coalition over the course of three campaigns. And so, it is recognised that Kutuzov was mistaken in his calculations; but it is noted that other loudly celebrated generals have made similar mistakes. Some military historians have attributed the slowness of Kutuzov's operations to the ambiguity of his intentions, basing this judgment about him from his official correspondence. Indeed, his reports to the Tsar, for the most part, are obscure and vague: this describes exactly the report on the reasons that prevented his main force from taking part in the battle of Vyazma,[33] but such reports served the Field Marshal to deflect the accusations against him, while he went straight for the operational objectives in his own way, being in no hurry to reach them, but without losing sight of them. The dispatching of Uvarov with the cuirassiers to Vyazma, simultaneously with the movement of the army away from the battlefield towards Bykovo, was also done to satisfy the prevailing general view at the time, simply to be able write in a report that the reserves had been committed to battle.

On 21 October (2 November), Napoleon, on the eve of the battle of Vyazma, having left this city at noon, arrived in Semlevo at about four o'clock in the afternoon and stopped in a small church, which had been turned into a posting stage and was surrounded by palisades.[34] The next day [3 November, new style], upon reaching Slavkovo, where the *Garde* also arrived, he received news of the actions at Vyazma, which forced him to move on 23 October (4 November). Napoleon was mistaken about the state of his army to the extent that he made plans to set up an ambush between Slavkovo and Dorogobuzh, for a simultaneous attack with all his forces on our troops pursuing him, but subsequently abandoned this intention, convinced that it did not present any probability of success.[35]

On 24 October (5 November), Napoleon's *État-major général*, together with the *Vieille Garde*, arrived in Dorogobuzh; the Westphalian detachment, the *Jeune Garde* and the remnants of *2e corps de cavalerie* and *4e corps de cavalerie*, having passed through Dorogobuzh, settled down on the road to Smolensk; Poniatowski, the Viceroy and Davout were between Slavkovo and Dorogobuzh, while Ney had passed through Semlevo with the rearguard. Snow had fallen the night before, and continued over the succeeding days; the temperature gradually fell to 12 degrees of frost; the roads were covered with ice, on which the horses slid and fell. The French, who had not forged spiked shoes for them, lost most of the rest of their cavalry and were forced to abandon many wagons and several guns. Having no food, no winter clothing or footwear, the enemy suffered extremely from the cold, wrapping themselves up in anything and could hardly move. Physical suffering led to a decline in morale: discipline had evaporated; all ties of friendship and loyalty had given way to the instinct for self-preservation; each person cared only about themselves, paying no attention to the tragedies of those close by. Some of the soldiers robbed their comrades who had

---

33 Prince Kutuzov's report to the Tsar, regarding the battle of Vyazma, dated 28 October [9 November], from Yelnya.
34 See Map Showing Movements From Maloyaroslavets to Smolensk.
35 Chambray, II, 373-374. Denniée, 191. Fain does not mention this proposal by Napoleon, *Manuscrit de 1812, de 1812*, II, 233-236.

become exhausted by disease or wounds; every evening, at the bivouacs, these unfortunates, who wandered like shadows behind the force, approached the campfires, begging for permission to warm their numbed extremities; but they were often driven off with musket butts, demanding that they bring firewood. In the morning, as camp was broken, the army's sites were marked by corpses, like a battlefield. According to Roos [Heinrich Ulrich Ludwig von Roos], on the night of 8 to 9 November (new style), up to 300 men froze to death in one of the bivouacs. Despite the prohibition on executing prisoners, many of them, unable to follow the enemy army, were shot, and this was repeated at every stage.[36] The excuse for such atrocities was the fear that released prisoners might reveal the plight of the remnants of the *Grande Armée*. But by now it could no longer remain a secret. The Russian bivouacs were constantly surrounded by crowds of unarmed enemy, whom our soldiers often treated to hard tack and porridge. Little effort was made to capture these unfortunates, no attention was paid to them, leaving them to roam freely, which for many enemy who fell into the hands of embittered peasants had disastrous consequences.[37]

Smolensk, where, by order of Napoleon, it had been necessary to collect vast stocks for the army, seemed like a promised land to the unfortunate French troops; they hoped to find everything there that they needed to overwinter and rest after their strenuous efforts and hardships. Napoleon shared this conviction himself, or at least wanted to convince others of it, and continued to move directly towards Smolensk, making no attempt to detour from the Smolensk highway to places not yet devastated. Some of our generals, including Toll, believed that Napoleon, being unable to hold in Smolensk, would try to get off the devastated highway by any means and retreat in another direction. To that end, he could use the road from Dorogobuzh, through Yelnya and Mstislavl, to Mogilev, along which the division under Baraguey d'Hilliers was already stationed at Yelnya. In Toll's opinion, we had to prevent the enemy from using this route, and the surest way to do this seemed to be an advance by our army from Bykovo to Yelnya. If Napoleon had turned towards Mogilev from Krasny, or, along the right bank of the Dnieper, from Orsha, then, by moving from Yelnya directly towards Mogilev, we would still have the opportunity to drive the enemy army back onto the devastated highway.

Accordingly, the main force under Prince Kutuzov was directed towards Yelnya, while Miloradovich, Platov and the raiding detachments harassed the enemy from the rear and left flank.[38] Intending to block the routes leading south, the Field Marshal ordered: the Governor of Tula, Bogdanov [Nikolay Ivanovich Bogdanov], to go to Roslavl with the *Opolchenie* under his command;[39] the Kaluga *Opolchenie*, supported by two Don regiments and some regular cavalry, were to move to Yelnya, link up with the Smolensk *Opolchenie* there and move towards Mstislavl;[40] subsequently,

---

36 Chambray, II, 382-384. Roos, *Ein Jahr aus meinem Leben*, 187. Lemazurier, *Medicinische Geschichte des Russischen Felzugs von 1812*.
37 Bernhardi, II, 292.
38 Orders dated 23 October [4 November]: to Platov, No. 320; to Count Orlov-Denisov, No. 321; to Miloradovich, No. 326 (archive of the M.T.D. No. 29,172).
39 Orders dated 21 October [2 November], No. 304.
40 Orders dated 21 October [2 November], No. 305 and dated 28 October [9 November], No. 362.

the Smolensk *Opolchenie* was sent to Dorogobuzh;[41] Count Gudovich [Nikolay Vasilievich Gudovich], with the Chernigov *Opolchenie* and Poltava *Opolchenie*, was ordered to advance on Belorussia;[42] while General Ertel [Fëdor Fëdorovich Ertel], who was in Mozyr with his detachment, was to move to Bobruisk, unless there were contrary orders from Chichagov.[43] It was suggested to Admiral Chichagov, that having left an observation corps facing Schwarzenberg, he make for Minsk and Borisov with all possible haste.[44] Prince Kutuzov ordered Count Wittgenstein, from whom a report had arrived about the victory he had won on 6 to 7 (18 to 19) October at Polotsk, in the event of an enemy retreat through Lepel [Lyepyel] towards Borisov, to pursue them in this direction, and then, leaving them under observation by Count Steinheil's corps [Fabian Gotthard von Steinheil], to close up to the Dnieper; in the event of Saint-Cyr retreating to link up with Napoleon's army (through Senno to Orsha), having left a detachment in an advantageous position on the road leading from Dokshitsy [Dokšycy] to Beshankovichi [Bieszenkowicze] to protect himself from behind, Count Wittgenstein was to persistently pursue the enemy and not allow them to join the main force under Napoleon.[45] Upon reaching the environs of Yelnya, Kutuzov, setting out his intent in orders to Miloradovich, wrote:

> At the present time, the operations of the main army are such that, having cut the road from Yelnya to Dorogobuzh, this leaves the route from Yelnya to Smolensk, while afterwards, leaving Smolensk to the right, runs towards Krasny and Orsha. By choosing this route, we gain the following benefits: firstly, we can reach the city of Orsha by the shortest route while crossing the Dnieper at this city just once, while the enemy will be forced to cross three times, namely: at Solovieva, Smolensk and Orsha; secondly, by moving in this direction, we close up to the regions from which supplies come to our troops…[46]

On 25 October (6 November), the *État-major général* of the French army was moved to Mikhalevka. Having received a report from Marshal Victor there, dated 21 October (2 November), about the battle of Chashniki and the French retreat to Senno, Napoleon finally decided to inform him, albeit not completely, about the plight of his army. Berthier wrote:

> His Majesty would like you, having concentrated your six divisions, to immediately attack the enemy, throw them back behind the Dvina and capture Polotsk.[47] This movement is very important: in a few days, the entire country behind your lines may be flooded with Cossacks. The army

---

41 Orders dated 29 October [10 November], No. 374.
42 Orders dated 21 October [2 November], No. 306.
43 Orders dated 29 October [10 November], No. 368.
44 Orders for Chichagov, dated 23 October [4 November], No. 324.
45 Orders for Count Wittgenstein, dated 22 October [3 November], No. 315.
46 Orders for Miloradovich, dated 26 October [7 November], No. 347.
47 The rest of this document was encrypted.

and *État-major général* will arrive in Smolensk tomorrow, but we are very tired from a non-stop march of 500 *versts (cent vingt lieues)*. Be aggressive; the salvation of the army depends on this; every day lost is a disaster. Our cavalry is dismounted. All the horses have fallen from the cold...[48]

The following day [7 November, new style], just before Napoleon's departure from Mikhalevka, news was received from Paris of the attempted coup by General Malet [Claude-François de Malet]. Napoleon was most struck by the fact that the rumours of his death had almost destroyed the government created through his many years of effort in one day. 'And Napoleon II; we could not even consider it!' he said.[49] Having moved to the right bank of the Dnieper at around noon on 26 October (7 November), he stopped with the *Garde* at a manor outside Solovieva; the army continued to move along the Smolensk highway in the same order, except for the Viceroy's *4e Corps*, who headed from Dorogobuzh towards Smolensk via Dukhovshchina, in order to establish communications with the troops operating on the Dvina through Vitebsk; on that same day, Baraguey d'Hilliers' division withdrew from Yelnya in the direction of Smolensk. On 28 October (9 November), Napoleon's *État-major général* was moved to Smolensk. Twelve degrees of frost and strong winds on the last stage into Smolensk forced Napoleon and his entire retinue to dismount from their horses and walk several *versts*.[50] The troops were ordered to halt before reaching the city, or to bypass it and wait for food to be delivered to them from the Smolensk magazines; but there was insufficient strength to hold back the discordant crowds of unarmed stragglers, the city was soon filled with hungry, ragged marauders; these unfortunates, barely retaining their humanity, rushed at anything that might satisfy the hunger that tormented them. In the course of one night, from 28 to 29 October (9 to 10 November), the soldiers slaughtered and ate 215 cart horses. The distribution of provisions was most irregular: Napoleon ordered that the *Garde* be issued two-weeks of rations, while the rest of the troops were to be issued six-days' worth, and as this was issued to the regiments of the *Garde* in full before any of the others, thereafter the corps under Davout and the Viceroy were forced to live without bread for two full days; meanwhile, the stragglers flooded in, and although orders had been given not to issue anything, nevertheless these unfortunates besieged the magazines, and having been driven off with musket butts and ruthlessly beaten, threw themselves with terrible cries at anyone who had a piece of bread or other food, and carried off their booty, killing those who resisted their frenzied efforts. Hour by hour, the officials of the commissariat were in danger of dying at the hands of the starving, driven to despair. Hand mills sent from Paris had been delivered to Smolensk. Napoleon ordered a test of their action for himself, and they

---

48 Napoleon's orders dated 26 October (7 November), from Mikhalevka. Chambray, II, 379-380. In Fain's work, Napoleon's orders to Victor are presented, in which not a word is said about the plight of the army, *Lettres du major-général au duc de Bellune, de Mikalevka, le 6 et 7 novembre, et 9 novembre*.
49 '*Et Napoléon II; on n'y pensait donc pas!*' Fain, II, 239-240.
50 Chambray, II, 381. Fain, 241. Denniée, *Itinéraire de l'empereur Napoléon pendant la campagne de 1812*, 191.

turned out to be most suitable; but they did not bring any benefit, because it was no longer possible to get grain for bread-making anywhere.

During the four-day halt of Napoleon's *État-major général* in Smolensk, preparations were made for mines to blow up the city's fortifications. The lack of draft horses forced the abandonment of some of the artillery, the burning of gun limbers, ammunition caissons, carriages and many luxury items; everyone cared only about obtaining food supplies. The lightly wounded were provided with rations and evacuated from the city; all the other wounded and sick, some 5,000 in total, were abandoned without any supervision, because the doctors and orderlies who had been in the hospitals left after the troops. A few hard-won sacks of flour for these sufferers could not provide them security from hunger. The distribution to the troops, which had constituted the only means of supplying the army, provided new pretexts for rioting, robbery and waste of supplies.[51]

On the very day that Napoleon arrived in Smolensk, 28 October (9 November), the French forces suffered significant defeats on the Dukhovshchina and Yelnya roads.

After the action at Vyazma, Platov had set off after the enemy immediately, catching up with them several times, inflicting heavy casualties on them and capturing many prisoners. General Miloradovich followed Platov to Semlevo with the vanguard, and then took over the pursuit from behind, while Platov headed towards Dorogobuzh to the right of the highway. On 26 October (7 November), Miloradovich, having caught up with the enemy during their crossing of the Osma, attacked them with an advance detachment under Major General Yurkovsky [Anastasy Antonovich Yurkovsky] (composed of 1st Jägers, 4th Jägers and Yelisavetgrad Hussars) and drove the French back to Dorogobuzh with losses. Marshal Ney, wishing to gain time for the main body to cross the Dnieper at Solovieva, decided to make a stand at Dorogobuzh. Razout's division, assigned to the defence of the city was deployed as follows: two guns were positioned at the town's exit, protected by *4e régiment d'infanterie de ligne*; to their left, by the bridge over the Dnieper was a company from *18e régiment d'infanterie de ligne*, while to their right, on a rise in front of the church, were some 100 men from *4e ligne*; Razout was himself on the same rise with the remainder of his division, in a fortification surrounded by palisades; finally, Ledru's division [François Roch Ledru des Essarts] was behind the town in reserve. Approaching Dorogobuzh, Miloradovich ordered 30th Jägers and 48th Jägers to attack the enemy settled there; but the French defended themselves very stubbornly, which forced Miloradovich to send Prinz Eugen von Württemberg to the left with the troops of his 4th Division, to envelope the enemy position from the flank. After a rather stubborn resistance, the French were forced to evacuate the town. General Yurkovsky pursued the enemy doggedly; 4th Jägers, who were under the command of Major Rusanov [Vasily Mikhailovich Rusanov?] at the time, particularly distinguished themselves. They captured six guns, of which two were captured by jägers and two by Cossacks; the remaining two were abandoned by the enemy during their retreat. As they were leaving Dorogobuzh, the French set fire to the town, but heavy snow prevented the fire from spreading, and helped our soldiers to extinguish it.

---

51 Puybusque, *Lettres sur la guerre de Russie*, 122-132.

The weather was stormy; the men had the blizzard at their backs, and therefore, having entrusted the initial pursuit of the enemy, along the routes to Smolensk and Dukhovshchina, to the detachments under General Yurkovsky and Colonel Vasilchikov 2nd [Dmitry Vasilevich Vasilchikov], composed of Cossacks with some regular cavalry, General Miloradovich placed the vanguard in Dorogobuzh for the night, appointed a commandant for the town and sent patrols in all directions to notify the scattered inhabitants of the expulsion of the enemy and invite them to return to their homes. A few hours later the townspeople began to gather; their joy at meeting their liberators, was indescribable. The elderly priest, in tears, threw himself at Miloradovich's feet, invoking the blessings of the Lord on the soldiers who had wrenched their ancestral remains from the hands of the enemy.[52]

Upon the occupation of Dorogobuzh by our troops, intelligence was received regarding the retreat by the Viceroy along the Dukhovshchina road. For their pursuit, Platov moved towards Dukhovshchina, with six Cossack regiments, 20th Jägers and the Don horse artillery, detaching Major General Grekov 1st [Dmitry Yevdokimovich Grekov] towards Smolensk with five Cossack regiments.[53] Meanwhile, having received orders from Prince Kutuzov, to turn to the left of the highway with the vanguard, in order to stay close to the main body, Miloradovich directed the pursuit of the enemy from behind to a light detachment and sent Major General Yurkovsky to the Solovieva crossing with several Cossack regiments under the command of Major General Karpov, supported by the Novorossia Dragoons, Chernigov Dragoons and 1st Jägers, with four heavy guns: Miloradovich moved to Kaskovo himself, with II Corps and IV Corps and with the rest of the vanguard cavalry, and arrived at Alexeevo on 28 October (9 November). The main force under Kutuzov, departing from Bykovo on 24 October (5 November), headed via Beloy Kholm to Yelnya and having reached this town on 27 October (8 November), remained there for a rest day on 28 October (9 November). The raiding detachment under Count Ozharovsky, moving ahead of the army, passed through Boltutino onto the Roslavl road on 27 October (8 November), while Count Orlov-Denisov and the partisans Davydov, Seslavin and Figner were in front of the vanguard between Alexeevo and the Yelnya road.[54]

Major General Prince Iashvili (Vladimir Mikhailovich) was in Yelnya with elements of the *opolchenie* from Kaluga Governorate a few days before the arrival of our army there. Having learned about an offensive against him by General Augereau [Jean-Pierre Augereau] with a powerful formation of recruits, he left the town, but was caught and forced to accept an unequal battle, during which Count

---

52 War Diary. *Journal militaire des opérations du 2me Corps, redigé par le prince Eugène de Württemberg* (archive of the M.T.D. No. 47,344). Fezensac, 82-83. Mikhailovsky-Danilevsky, Description of the War of 1812.
53 Platov's report to Prince Kutuzov dated 29 October [9 November], No. 174. In Platov's report dated 3 [15] November, No. 185, it states that on the highway from Dorogobuzh to Smolensk the enemy were pursued by Major General Grekov 1st with four Don regiments, the Simferopol Tatars, 1st Jägers and six squadrons of dragoons, and that he captured two guns at the Solovieva crossing.
54 War Diary.

Orlov-Denisov arrived on the scene and rescued him.[55] Following which, General Augereau, having retreated along the Smolensk road, halted at Lyakhovo, 15 *versts* from Boltutino, with one of the infantry brigades from Baraguey d'Hilliers' division and with some cavalry. The poor condition of the French cavalry did not allow the enemy to guard his disposition through proper patrols; the French were also unaware of the movement past their detachment by Count Ozharovsky, and of the arrival of our partisans in the area. Meanwhile, on the night of 26 to 27 October (8 to 9 November), patrols sent out by Davydov reported to him on the location of a strong enemy detachment in Lyakhovo and Yazvino, which was also confirmed by a statement from a prisoner captured by the Cossacks, who confirmed that General Augereau was actually in the former village with 2,000 infantry and some cavalry. Based on this intelligence, Davydov, Seslavin and Figner decided to attack the detachment stationed in Lyakhovo. But as there were no more than 1,200 cavalry and 80 infantry from 20th Jägers, with four guns in their units combined, Lieutenant Colonel Davydov suggested that his comrades invite Count Orlov-Denisov to assist, who was nearby with six Cossack regiments and the Nezhin Dragoons.

On 27 October (8 November), our partisans, on the march to Belkino, had received news from Orlov-Denisov about his move towards them to assist their detachments. The next day [9 November, new style], in the morning, Seslavin, Davydov and Figner arrived at a village occupied by Chechensky's Cossacks, about two *versts* from Belkino. Davydov recalled; 'Lyakhovo was visible in the distance; bivouac fires were smoking around the village; several infantry and cavalry soldiers were observed between the cottages and huts; nothing more could be seen. Half an hour later, we saw enemy foragers, numbering 40 men, riding in the direction of Tarashchino without the slightest caution.' Having captured most of these foragers, together with one of General Augereau's aides de camp, the partisans were convinced of the reliability of the intelligence they had collected. Shortly thereafter, Davydov's group arrived; the regiments under Orlov-Denisov and the other two groups also arrived, except for 80 of Seslavin's jägers. In order to replace them, Cossacks who had muskets were nominated for dismounted action.

The enemy were still unaware of the danger that threatened them. In order to sever communications between Baraguey d'Hilliers' other force and Augereau's brigade, our troops were directed to the Yelnya road. Davydov's detachment was marching at their head. As soon as they approached Lyakhovo, confusion was noticed in the enemy bivouacs and in the village occupied by the French, and drum signals were heard; the troops hurriedly stood to arms; the skirmishers detached by them them ran out from behind the huts towards our detachment. Davydov, urging on the Cossacks, immediately went into action. His partisans and Popov 13th's Cossacks formed up on the left flank of the dismounted men of the Don, while Chechensky's Cossacks were detached even further to the left, outflanking the Yelnya road, to disrupt enemy communications with Yazvino, where the French were also present. Seslavin, riding up to our marksmen with four horse guns, pushed the artillery forward, screened by his hussars, and opened fire on the columns leaving Lyakhovo;

---

55 A.P. Yermolov's notes.

Figner's group stood in reserve, while Count Orlov-Denisov, placing his detachment to the right of Seslavin's and Figner's, sent patrols along the road to Dolgomostye. The enemy, despite the fire of our guns, reinforced their skirmishers in the forest adjacent to the village and led an attack on Orlov-Denisov's regiments. Seslavin replaced the dismounted Cossacks with jägers from his group who had arrived on the battlefield, and at that moment, French cavalry raced towards our marksmen, Captain Gorstkin drove them off with the Akhtyrka Hussars and cleared the forest with the help of the jägers. Taking advantage of this, Seslavin moved the guns to the crest of the high ground closer to the village, while Lieutenant Lizogub [Alexander Ivanovich Lizogub] attacked the French marksmen leaving the forest onto open ground to the right flank of his detachment with the Lithuania Ulans. About a hundred Frenchmen, who were holding out in sheds separate from the village and continued to shoot at the Cossacks from there, were burned out along with the sheds.

During these actions, Count Orlov-Denisov, having learned of the appearance of an enemy column from the direction of Dolgomostye, sent Colonel Bykhalov with two Cossack regiments to hold them up along the Smolensk road; but the Cossacks, encountering superior numbers, were forced to retreat; it emerged that 2,000 cuirassiers were moving into our rear. Whereupon Orlov-Denisov turned to face the cuirassiers with his entire detachment, attacked them with the Nezhin Dragoons and two Cossack regiments, supported by the fire of six horse guns, and put them to flight. Seven hundred cuirasses taken from the enemy dead were subsequently given to the Pskov Dragoon Regiment. Having entrusted the pursuit of the French to Colonel Bykhalov with two Don regiments, the count returned to the partisans near Lyakhovo. Had Augereau taken advantage of his absence and moved towards Dolgomostye, then our small groups would not have been able to hold him back. But he remained inactive, content to refuse a surrender demand from the *parlementaire* Staff Captain Chemodanov. Once the cuirassiers had been forced to retreat, Count Orlov-Denisov sent Figner to Augereau with a repeated demand to lay down their weapons. The negotiations lasted no more than an hour. The outcome was the surrender of General Augereau with 19 officers and 1,650 lower ranks. Our troops captured a significant enemy magazine in Lyakhovo; but some of them died in a fire in the village, which was ignited during the battle.[56] The Field Marshal, reporting to the Tsar about the action at Lyakhovo, added: 'This victory is all the more notable because for the first time in the course of the present campaign, an enemy corps laid their weapons down before us.'[57]

On 28 October (9 November), on the very day that Augereau's brigade was captured by our partisans, the Viceroy's *4e Corps* suffered heavy losses at the crossing over the river Vop.

In sending this corps to Vitebsk, to assist a force under General Pouget [François René Cailloux, *dit* Pouget], which was garrisoned there, Napoleon had previously

---

56 D.V. Davydov's memoirs, 472-478. Prince Kutuzov's report to the Tsar dated 1 [13] November. Davydov wrote that 60 officers and 2,000 men were taken prisoner in the action at Lyakhovo.
57 Kutuzov's reports to the Tsar dated 31 October [12 November] and 1 [13] November. Artillery Captain Figner, sent to St Petersburg with the report on the capture of General Augereau by his detachment, was promoted to lieutenant colonel, with a transfer to the Lifeguard Artillery.

sent General Sanson, with three officers (*ingénieurs-géographes*) and a small detachment, to survey the routes leading there and especially the banks of the Vop, but as soon as they reached the outskirts of Dukhovshchina, they were captured by a Cossack patrol from the vanguard under Major General Ilovaisky 12th, marching from Moscow ahead of Adjutant General Kutuzov's detachment. At the same time, we acquired a large collection of maps and plans.[58] On 26 October (7 November), the Viceroy's force crossed to the right side of the Dnieper at Dorogobuzh, over a bridge of rafts; but the ascent of the steep bank, which had become very slippery from the icy conditions, presented such difficulties that 12 or even 16 horses had to be harnessed to each gun. Much of the transport was abandoned, and the contents were looted by the soldiery. The area through which the corps was moving was littered with baggage, clothing, and various booty removed from Moscow. That night the looting continued; men and horses were dying of hunger and cold. Platov, having confirmed that the Viceroy was retreating along the Dukhovshchina road, set off after him. On 27 October (8 November), constantly prowling on the flanks of the French columns, the Cossacks carried off enemy foragers, while several Don guns fired on the retreating columns; General d'Anthouard [Charles Nicolas d'Anthouard de Vraincourt] halted his batteries several times and opened fire in order to hold off the Cossack raids and was seriously wounded by round shot that crushed his leg. The Viceroy sent two officers to Smolensk, reporting on the difficulties he had encountered, but both of his couriers were intercepted by Ilovaisky's Cossacks.[59]

As the French were to cross the Vop the next day, 28 October (9 November), the Viceroy had sent General Poitevin [Jean Étienne Casimir Poitevin de Maureilhan] to this river the day before with a sapper squad, instructing him to build a bridge. On the morning of 28 October (9 November), the troops arrived at the river, but could not cross, because suddenly rising water levels had torn the bridge apart and there were no materials to repair it. The Don men, noticing a crowd of enemy troops and vehicles on the bank, opened a bombardment on them and began to press in on the French from behind, while strong Cossack patrols, having crossed the Vop, appeared on the opposite side of the river. The Viceroy, concerned about being encircled by our troops, immediately set about crossing, Broussier's division, left in the rearguard, were instructed to hold back the Cossacks pressing in from the rear. At the head of the corps, the Viceroy's aide de camp, Bataille [Jean Pierre Bataille?], and Delfanti [Cosimo Damiano Del Fante], who was with him, rushed into the ford, waist-deep in water; they were followed by the *Guardia Reale*; whereupon the Viceroy, having crossed the river with all his staff, ordered the carts to be transferred. The first carts and guns were transported safely, but soon deep ruts formed in the riverbed, into which artillery bogged down, blocking the only available ford, because in other locations the steep and slippery banks required approach ramps to be prepared.

Meanwhile, the Cossacks put more and more pressure on the rearguard. The enemy, horrified, despairing of escape, decided to abandon the artillery and carts

---

58 Platov's report to Prince Kutuzov dated 27 October [8 November], No. 173. A.P. Yermolov's notes.
59 The Viceroy's intercepted dispatches are at Appendix III.

that had not yet crossed. Everyone abandoned their carriages and wagons, hastening to load their most valuable items onto horses and cross the river; those who did not have horses were forced to cross to the other bank almost up to their necks in water, and froze from the cold. At the same time, the bank deserted by the enemy presented a spectacle of indescribable chaos: marauders robbed their own, looking mainly for flour and vodka in the convoy; gunners tried to spike their guns; soldiers rushed in disorder into the river choked with wagons and corpses. The Viceroy's force, with the exception of Broussier's division left in the rearguard, managed to cross over to the right bank of the Vop by evening and settled down to rest close to the water. Throughout the night, desperate cries from those crossing the river could be heard. The troops spent that night on bare snow, under the open sky; the soldiers, barefoot, half naked, exhausted from hunger and fatigue, disturbed hourly by the Cossacks, dozed while sitting, or, having taken a log from the dismantled houses of the nearby village, tried to dry their wet clothes and roast horse meat.

At dawn on 29 October (10 November), Broussier's division crossed, leaving 64 guns and almost all the corps' transport on the left bank of the Vop. Many soldiers, after crossing the river, having exhausted the last of their strength, abandoned their weapons. It is difficult to say how great *4e Corps* losses in men were, but their enormity can be inferred from the fact that after crossing the Vop, the Viceroy had no more than 6,000 men under arms.[60]

As soon as Platov noticed the retreat of the enemy rearguard, he crossed the Vop after them, caught up with them and captured another 23 guns. The Viceroy, entrusting the 12 guns remaining with the corps to Broussier's division for the protection of his continuing retreat, tried to gather the scattered soldiery, but hunger was stronger than any sense of military duty, and all the efforts to restore order in units by their commanders were in vain.

The troops under the Viceroy, relentlessly pursued and harassed from all sides by the men of the Don under Platov, on approaching Dukhovshchina, were suddenly halted by a Cossack detachment that blocked their route to this town. These were two regiments under Major General Ilovaisky 12th, marching in the vanguard of Adjutant General Kutuzov's detachment (formerly Wintzingerode's detachment), who, departing from Moscow on 22 October (3 November), had moved via Zvenigorod, Ruza and Gzhatsk, to the village of Nikolo-Pogoreloe, on the Dnieper. The appearance of Ilovaisky on the French line of retreat sowed consternation in the disordered *4e Corps*, but the Viceroy, maintaining his usual presence of mind, formed the Italian *Guardia Reale* into square and sent them to face Ilovaisky, along with the Bavarian cavalry; they were followed by unruly crowds of unarmed men, jostling around the enemy columns. The force under Ilovaisky managed to capture some 500 prisoners, but were forced away from the road to Dukhovshchina. The Viceroy, seeing the need to hasten the retreat, ordered the repair of a very poor bridge on the road to this town, and in order to raise the enthusiasm of the soldiers, he set an example for them himself through his personal participation in the task.

---

60 War Diary. Labaume, 313-322. Chambray, II, 388-390.

The town of Dukhovshchina, although it had been abandoned by the inhabitants, was nevertheless completely intact, presenting the French with some means of subsistence, and in particular for the accommodation of the troops in substantial buildings, which served as a refuge from the chill and blustery wind for the shivering enemy. Taking full advantage of this, the Viceroy granted a rest day to the remnants of the corps, detaching his aide de camp Batal, with *15e Division d'Infanterie*, to Smolensk to notify Napoleon of the losses from the crossing of the Vop. As news about the Russian liberation of Vitebsk had arrived in the meantime, the Viceroy decided, without waiting for orders from *État-major général*, to march on Smolensk on the night of 30 to 31 October (11 to 12 November). But then at ten o'clock in the evening, as the weary French were resting in anticipation of their departure, Platov's Cossacks appeared in front of the town. Several shots from the Don artillery alarmed the enemy and struck the forward outposts of *106e régiment d'infanterie*, posted in front of the church. At two o'clock in the morning, the French left the town, putting both the town and all surrounding villages to the torch. The night march by the enemy columns was illuminated by the ominous reflection of flames. Only those villages that were located at a considerable distance from the road were spared. Throughout the entire march, Cossacks constantly accompanied the enemy, capturing foragers who left from their columns to get food. The next day, the French, believing that Smolensk would be the end of their disasters and wanting to get there as quickly as possible, set out from their overnight stay long before dawn; but, on the approach to Stabna, they encountered great difficulties in climbing a steep icy slope; at every step, men and horses fell and rolled one on top of the other. Having overcome this obstacle, the French were now only four *versts* from Smolensk; the tallest belfry was already visible; each strained with the last of their strength, striving to reach the city as quickly as possible. But as soon as the leading troops entered the suburbs, they learned that *9e Corps* had gone to assist the troops operating on the Dvina, that they would have to move on without stopping and that all supplies had already been used up. This news dumbfounded the French; no one wanted to believe it, but soon, seeing soldiers of the Smolensk garrison throwing themselves upon fallen horses and greedily devouring horse flesh, everyone became convinced of the bitter truth. The Viceroy brought the remnants of his corps into the city, except for Broussier's division, left on high ground on the right bank of the Dnieper with several guns, facing Platov, while the *Guardia Reale* was stationed behind Broussier's force in reserve. Platov's detachment, persistently pursuing the enemy all the way from Dukhovshchina to Smolensk, had captured many prisoners, taking two more guns, and closed up to Smolensk on 31 October (12 November), on the very day that all Napoleon's corps were assembled there. The losses in the Viceroy's force were incalculable; on our part, the casualties could not have been great, judging by the following words from Platov's report: 'I have not reported on our dead and wounded, which, thanks to God, are few; these will be in the administrative account.'[61]

---

61 Labaume, 322-332. Platov's report to Prince Kutuzov, dated 29 October [10 November].

The Field Marshal, in Army Orders, dated 29 October (10 November), informing the troops of Platov's victories, wrote: 'After such extraordinary successes, gained by us daily and everywhere over the enemy, all that remains is to swiftly pursue them, and perhaps thereafter, the Russian countryside which they dreamed of enslaving, would instead be littered with their bones. And so – we shall pursue tirelessly. Winter is coming, blizzards and frosts: should you fear them, sons of the north? Your iron chests fear neither the severity of the weather nor the malice of your foes; they are the dependable wall of the Fatherland, against which everything shall be crushed. You will also be able to tolerate temporary shortages, should they occur. Good soldiers are resilient and patient; old veterans will set the example for the youngsters. Let everyone recall Suvorov: he taught that when it was a matter of victory or the glory of the Russian people, both hunger and cold were to be endured. Onwards! God is with us; before us is a defeated enemy; may peace and tranquillity follow us.'

On 1 (13) November, the frost intensified to minus 17 degrees (to minus 22 degrees, according to other sources); the enemy troops gathered in Smolensk could not find shelter from the cold in the few buildings that had survived, and besides, hunger forced them to crowd around the magazines for days at a time; some returned without having managed to obtain anything; others obtained supplies by force, breaking into the storehouses, taking bags of flour, hard-tack and barrels of vodka with them, and forcing their way back at bayonet or sabre point.[62]

During his stay in Smolensk, Napoleon tried to reorganise his army, wherever possible. The remnants of the four *corps de cavalerie* were merged into a formation under the command of Latour-Maubourg; orders were issued seeking to attract marauders back to the colours with a distribution of supplies together with firearms; a total of 50 cartridges per pouch were completed for each of the soldiers and handmills were distributed to the regiments.

Napoleon, convinced of the impossibility of holding out in Smolensk, had the intention of setting out from there on 30 October (11 November) with the *Garde*; but the slow pace of the proper distribution of supplies and the need to wait for the Viceroy to rejoin made it necessary to postpone the departure of the *État-major général* until 2 (14) November. Despite the loss of Vitebsk and the disorder in the once *Grande Armée*, Napoleon still considered positioning his forces between the Dnieper and the Dvina, and to that end he issued written orders to Marshal Victor, instructing him to attack Count Wittgenstein and expressed concern that Kutuzov, moving towards Vitebsk, should not be allowed to link up with him on the Dvina, 'which, according to Napoleon, would force the French army to settle in winter quarters, leaving the Russians along the course of the Dvina and partly in Lithuania.'[63]

Having in mind to wait for the Viceroy to rejoin, Napoleon ordered Ney, who was at the Solovieva crossing with the rear guard, to retreat step by step, and hold our forces up on the road to Smolensk for as long as possible. Major General Yurkovsky, pursuing Ney from Dorogobuzh to the Solovieva crossing, captured three guns.

---

62 Labaume, 337-338. Fain, II, 250-251.
63 '... *nous serions donc obligés de prendre des quartiers d'hiver, en laissant la Dwina à l'ennemi et une partie dela Lithuanie...*' Berthier's letter to Marshal Victor, dated 11 October, new style.

Having received orders to link up with Miloradovich, who was moving to the left of the Smolensk highway, Yurkovsky assigned the further pursuit of Ney to Colonel Karpenko [Moisey Ivanovich Karpenko], with the 1st Jägers, Moscow Dragoons, a Cossack regiment and four guns. On 28 October (9 November), Karpenko closed up to the Solovieva crossing. Our jägers, having driven the enemy skirmishers from the left bank, settled down in cover and tried to prevent the French from dismantling the bridge; meanwhile, our guns were brought up and opened fire on the enemy labourers. The French responded with a bombardment from the earthworks they had built on the opposite bank and with fire from the skirmishers until they had broken the bridge, and then retreated along the Smolensk highway. The next day [10 November, new style], our troops crossed the Dnieper on very thin ice, took about 1,000 prisoners and found 18 guns, 60 ammunition caissons and many carts on the other side of the river. Most of the booty was left to the peasants, who emerged from all sides in the wake of the French. En route to Smolensk, Karpenko joined up with Grekov and upon arrival at Valutina Gora established communications with Platov's Cossack formation.

During Napoleon's four-day halt in Smolensk, our main forces advanced parallel to the Smolensk highway. On 29 October (10 November), Prince Kutuzov passed from Yelnya to Boltutino, while Miloradovich went from Alexeevo to Lyakhovo. The next day [11 November, new style] our headquarters, together with the III Corps, V Corps and VI Corps and both cuirassier divisions, were moved to Labkovo on the Roslavl road; ahead of these formations, Miloradovich was stationed on the same road, near Sverchkovo, with a new vanguard, composed of II Corps, VII Corps and IV Cavalry Corps, while IV Corps, VIII Corps and II Cavalry Corps were left near Zhukovshchina and Chulovo in order to monitor the Yelnya road. On that same day, 30 October (11 November), Colonel K.I. Bistrom [Karl Ivanovich Bistrom], with his detachment of two battalions of Lifeguard Jägers, a squadron of His Majesty's Cuirassiers and a *Sotnia* of Tula Cossacks, captured a large enemy magazine and 1,300 prisoners in the village of Klementyev (Klemyatino). Another magazine was captured in the village of Knyazhoe.

On 1 (13) November, on the eve of the departure of Napoleon's *État-major général* from Smolensk, Kutuzov moved to the Mstislavl road, to the village of Shchelkanovo, in the vicinity of which III Corps, V Corps, VI Corps, VII Corps and VIII Corps and both cuirassier divisions were located. IV Corps and II Cavalry Corps stood near the village of Luchinki, in order to cover the army from the direction of Smolensk; while Miloradovich's vanguard of II Corps and I Cavalry Corps went to Chervonoe. Count Orlov-Denisov and Seslavin, moving ahead of the vanguard, captured more than 1,000 men, and, even more importantly at that time, captured 1,000 artillery horses marching to Smolensk, four hundred wagons of provisions and wine and 200 head of cattle. Afterwards, Count Orlov-Denisov attacked part of the Polish corps, under the command of General Zajączek [Józef Zajączek] in Chervonoe, who, along with other troops from *5e Corps* under Prince Poniatowski, had received orders to go to Mogilev for reconstitution.[64] Zajączek, having lost several hundred

---

64 War Diary. Buturlin, II, 202-204.

men and having no hope of reaching the location to which he had been directed, diverted along country roads to Volkovo towards Krasny. The detachment under Count Ozharovsky went ahead of our main forces directly towards Krasny, while the detachment under Adjutant General Kutuzov went to Dukhovshchina.

On 2 (14) November, Kutuzov's main forces moved towards Yurovo; 23rd Division and IV Cavalry Corps were in Luchinki; Count Osterman, moved towards Kobyzevo with 11th Division and II Cavalry Corps, while Miloradovich was ordered to go to Rogailovo with the vanguard, reinforced by the troops of VII Corps, and on the following day, to reach the highway at the village of Rzhavka and cut the enemy line of retreat; on 3 (15) November, our main forces remained at Yurovo, while Osterman (whose detachment was joined by 23rd Division and IV Cavalry Corps) was at Kobyzevo.[65]

Thus, the necessary loss of four days by Napoleon in Smolensk made it possible for our main forces, moving as if in peacetime, with rest days and even partly settling down in quarters, to draw level with the enemy once more and to overtake his leading columns with light detachments. Taking into account that our troops had to complete stages of 25 *versts* or more, along country roads blanketed in deep snow, in the bitter cold, Moreover, the ox-drawn mobile magazines lagged behind the troops,[66] let us not be surprised at the enormous losses suffered by the Russian army in the sector from Vyazma to the outskirts of Smolensk. Despite our soldiers being accustomed to enduring the cold and despite the fact that, in accordance with the prescient, personal order from Emperor Alexander, they were equipped with sheepskin coats,[67] the army, which had marched from the Tarutino camp about 100,000 strong, having lost no more than 10,000 in combat, counted only 50,000 men in its ranks three weeks later. But most of our losses consisted of the sick, who would subsequently recover and rejoin the army, and, more importantly, the extraordinary decline in manpower did not affect the morale of our troops, who, pressing on the heels of the enemy, forgot both hunger and cold, caring only about overtaking the French.

---

65 War Diary. Buturlin, II, 206-210. Orders for General Miloradovich, dated 2 [14] November (Archive of the M.T.D. No. 29,172).
66 Prince A.B. Golitsyn's notes, as Prince Kutuzov's permanent orderly.
67 Emperor Alexander I's Supreme Orders, announced in a note from Count Arakcheev to Prince A.I. Gorchakov, dated 28 August [9 September] (Archive of the M.T.D. No. 46,692, in book No. 7).

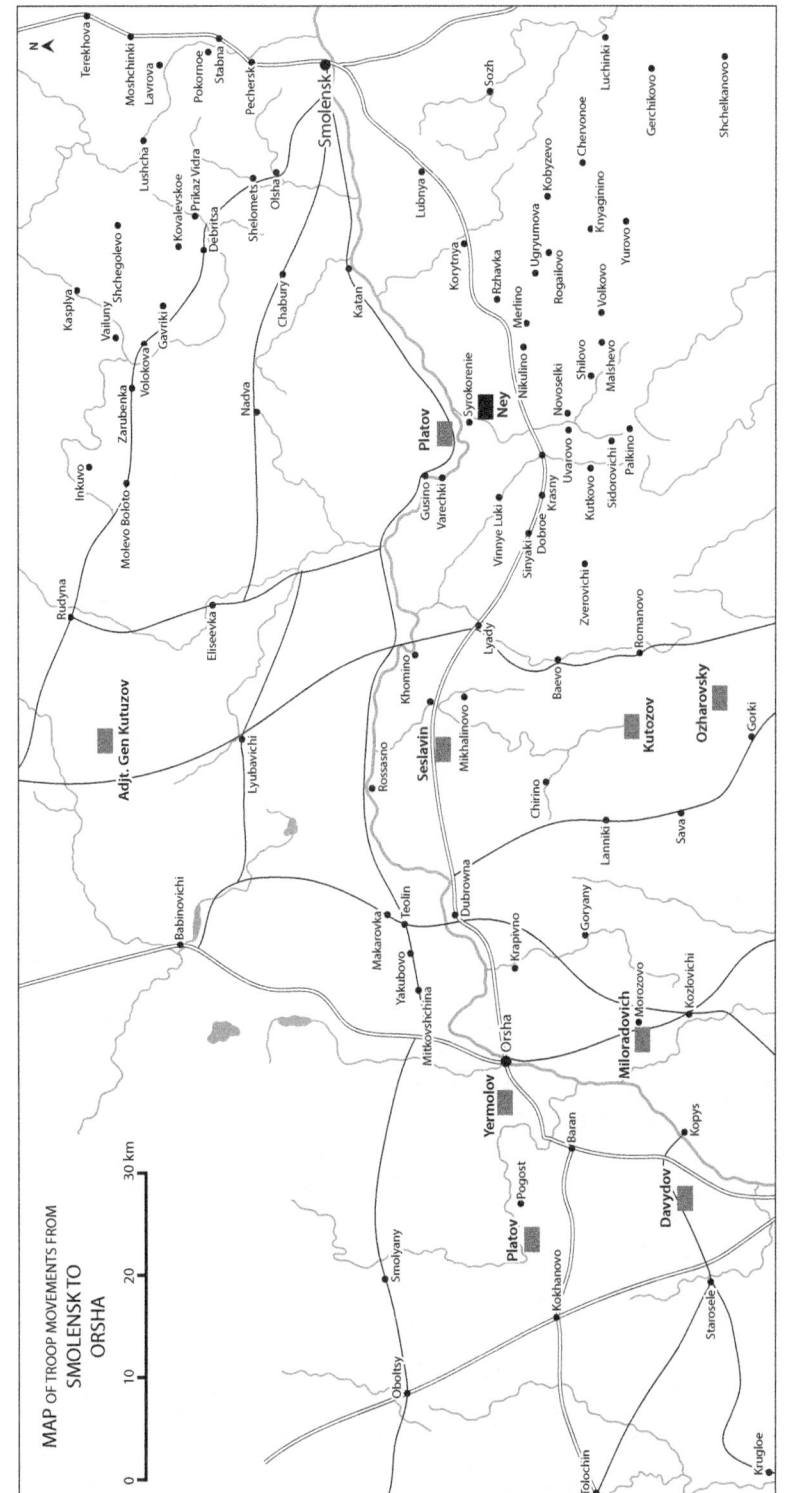

THE BATTLE AT VYAZMA AND NAPOLEON'S RETREAT TO SMOLENSK 79

Map of troop movements from Smolensk to Orsha.

36

The Battle of Krasny

The reasons that prompted Napoleon to bring forward the departure from Smolensk. – Strength and composition of the *Grande Armée*. – Napoleon's orders for the continuation of the campaign. – Napoleon's intentions.

Order of departure of Napoleon's forces from Smolensk. – Action at Kobyzevo. – The defeat of the French *Garde* at Rzhavka. – Action at Kutikovo. – The defeat of the Viceroy at Merlino. – Action at Uvarovo. – The dispositions of the forces of both sides after this action. – Ney's departure from Smolensk and the reoccupation of the city by Russian forces. – Action on the Losmina against Ney. – Ney's retreat towards Orsha. – Enemy losses in the actions around Krasny. – Assessment of the operations by Kutuzov around Krasny.

Upon the arrival of the Viceroy's force in Smolensk, although Napoleon had concentrated the remnants of the *Grande Armée* near this city, except for Ney's corps, which formed the rear guard on the Moscow road, he could not halt and rest his troops. Kutuzov, heading to intersect the routes leading from Smolensk, had already reached the Mstislavl road and threatened the enemy's line of communications with Orsha. On the other hand, the offensive operations by Count Wittgenstein and Chichagov, who were moving to link up with each other to the rear of the *Grande Armée*, prompted the enemy to accelerate their march to the Berezina in order to cross this obstacle before the Russian forces could occupy it. In addition, the Smolensk magazines were insufficient to provide the French army with supplies. All these factors forced Napoleon to begin his march from Smolensk as soon as the troops of the Viceroy had closed up, without waiting for Ney to rejoin with the rearguard.[1]

The extent the enemy army was disordered upon reaching Smolensk has already been mentioned above. The number of fighting men in it did not exceed 50,000 overall,[2] of which the 5,000 cavalry were in the worst condition. The artillery had diminished by 350 guns, including those abandoned in Smolensk. Those remaining

---

1 Chambray, *Histoire de l'expédition de Russie, 3e édit*. II, 427. Buturlin, *Histoire militaire de la campagne de Russie en 1812*, II, 207-208.
2 According to Chambray, II, 435, who calculated the strength of the French army between 8 to 14 November new style. For details see Appendix IV.

could accompany the force only on level ground; if the batteries had to cross ravines to get themselves into firing positions, then the crews, shouldering the wheels, pushed them forward to help the horses, who could barely lift their hooves.[3]

Napoleon further weakened his disordered army, sending it from Smolensk towards Orsha in several groups (echelons), which departed piecemeal, at one day intervals, one after the other. It is difficult to explain the reasons for such orders: neither the food supply for the force, nor the march itself could be alleviated by dividing the corps into entire stages (for the convenience of which it was enough to leave small intervals between the echelons), which exposed the army to defeat in detail. It is even more difficult to answer why the French army, or at least most of it, was not sent from Smolensk along the right bank of the Dnieper, where it would encounter only Platov's detachment. Perhaps Napoleon, still hoping for the blessings of Fortune, which had already betrayed him, believed that the Russians would not have chance to intercept him on the way to Orsha. All orders for the onward movement of the French force were made as if they were in danger only from the rear: the echelons that left Smolensk first were weaker than the others; the baggage of every corps moved ahead of the force. It was easy to foresee what fate awaited the miserable remnants of the *Grande Armée*, slowed down by wagon trains and cannon that could hardly drag themselves along, and surrounded by crowds of unarmed men who, at each encounter with our troops, rushed into the ranks of the French columns and brought them into confusion and disorder.

On our part, based on the intelligence received at headquarters, it was believed that Napoleon's army would head from Smolensk along three roads leading towards: Vitebsk via Kasilla, Babinovichi via Lyubavichi and Orsha via Krasny. The Field Marshal, in notifying Count Wittgenstein of this, remarked, however, that this intelligence required confirmation. In the event that the enemy actually began to retreat in three different directions, Kutuzov hoped to break the column closest to him, cross the Dnieper at Orsha, or at some other place, and move towards Senno or Lepel, in order to defeat Napoleon's army between the Dnieper, the Berezina and the Dvina, with the assistance of Wittgenstein's force. Two days later, the Field Marshal, having received a report from Chichagov about the impending arrival of his army in Minsk by 7 (19) November, concluded from this that Napoleon would be forced to head from Orsha, via Senno and Lepel, to Dokshitsy, and would move towards Wittgenstein with his entire force. Kutuzov, concerned that our troops operating on the Dvina could be suppressed by superior forces, suggested that Count Wittgenstein take a strong position on the route to Dokshitsy and halt the enemy army.[4]

On 31 October (12 November), the lead echelon of Napoleon's army, consisting of Polish troops, totalling 800 men (not including those without weapons), commanded by General Zajączek due to the illness of Prince Poniatowski, set out from Smolensk for Mogilev.[5] Zajączek was ordered to reorganise *5e Corps* in Orsha, adding the

---

3 Chambray, II, 436.
4 Orders for Count Wittgenstein, dated 1 [13] November, log of outgoing documents, No. 402, and dated 3 [15] November, No 426 (Archive of the M.T.D. No. 29,172.
5 See the Map of Operations Between Smolensk and Orsha.

march-regiments that belonged to him there.[6] But, as mentioned previously, these orders could not be carried out; the Polish force, having been engaged by our light detachments, was forced to divert along country roads leading from Chervonoe to Volkovo, to the town of Krasny.[7] On that same day, 31 October (12 November), Junot set out from Smolensk along the high road to Orsha with the Westphalians, totalling 700 men, a large artillery park and 500 dismounted cavalrymen. An eyewitness (Lossberg [Friedrich Wilhelm von Lossberg]) commented that the cuirassiers, without cuirasses, in long, heavy riding boots, lugging their valises, presented a miserable sight. This detachment, of little overall combat capability, moved in short stages.

On 1 (13) November, Claparède's division set out from Smolensk with the so-called trophies, the treasury and the *État-major général* transport. Davout crossed the Dnieper with four divisions from his corps and stationed these troops in the Smolensk suburbs and surrounding villages; while Ricard's division [Étienne Pierre Sylvestre Ricard] (formerly Friant's [Louis Friant]) was left on the right bank of the Dnieper, in order to support Ney, who was 15 *versts* from Smolensk. On that same day [13 November, new style], the Viceroy arrived in the city (as already mentioned), leaving Broussier's division and the Italian *Guardia Reale* on the St. Petersburg road facing Platov.[8]

On 2 (14) November, Claparède overtook the Westphalians, who were moving slowly along the highway, and closed up to Krasny. Meanwhile at dawn, Count Ozharovsky ejected a French battalion, which had been garrisoning the town since August, and captured a huge variety of booty;[9] but upon being attacked by a superior force under Claparède, they retreated to the village of Kutkovo, three *versts* from Krasny. The Westphalians closed up to the town. Mortier, with two divisions of the *Jeune Garde* (Roguet and Delaborde), set out from Smolensk at dawn on 2 (14) November, while Napoleon set off himself with the *Vieille Garde* at nine o'clock in the morning. The entire *Garde*, having assembled at Korytnya in the evening, spent the night there together with the *État-major général*; the *Artillerie de la Garde*, which had set out as early as three o'clock in the morning, arrived at the overnight halt after midnight, having abandoned many wagons along the way. On our side, the main body of the army moved towards the village of Volkovo, the vanguard under Miloradovich to Knyaginino; while Count Osterman, having set off for Kobyzevo with 11th Division and II Cavalry Corps, encountered an enemy detachment there (Zajączek's force?), attacked them with the Poland Ulans, Kargopol Dragoons, Pskov Dragoons and Cossacks, and captured five officers and 590 lower ranks.[10] On this day, there were 19 degrees of frost.[11] Upon leaving Smolensk, Napoleon had

---

6 Napoleon's orders dated 11 November, new style.
7 Chambray, II, 427.
8 Chambray, II, 427.
9 Count Ozharovsky's detachment consisted of the 19th Jägers, Mariupol Hussars and four Cossack regiments, with six horse artillery pieces.
10 War Diary, signed off by Prince Kutuzov. Count Osterman's letter to Duty General Konovnitsyn, dated 3 [15] November. Log of Outgoing Documents, No. 499.
11 War Diary. Chambray, II, 427-428 & 436. Fain, *Manuscrit de 1812*, II, 251-253 & 255. Deniée, *Itinéraire de l'empereur Napoléon pendant la campagne de 1812*, 191. Bernhardi, *Denkwürdigkeiten des Grafen v. Toll*, II, 298.

instructed Davout to support Ney, who was with the rearguard, and to march out of the city, with the fighting men of *1er Corps* and *3e Corps* and with the Smolensk garrison under General Charpentier, on 16 or 17 November (new style), having blown up the towers on the city wall, destroying military supplies and ammunition caissons and breaking any muskets which could not be taken away with them. Orders were also given to saw the trunnions off the guns, which turned out to be impossible due to a lack of time and of the tools needed for the job. Finally, both marshals received orders to round up all the stragglers and evacuate any sick who remained in the city hospitals.[12]

On 3 (15) November, having passed Krasny, Zajączek reached Lyady with the remnants of the Polish corps. Claparède arrived in Krasny; Napoleon, having overtaken the Westphalians, also moved with the *Garde* to this town.[13] On our side, on this day, the main body remained in Volkovo and Yurovo on a rest day, with the exception of III Corps and the cuirassiers who were detached to Malshevo, while Miloradovich, Osterman and the light detachments emerged onto the highway, in the vicinity of the enemy line of retreat.[14]

General Miloradovich, with VII Corps, having let Napoleon's *Garde* pass through the village of Rzhavka, turned his troops to the left, parallel to the highway, and limited himself to bombarding the retreating columns. The number of enemy troops moving past our vanguard did not exceed 12,000 to 13,000; while Miloradovich had 16,000 men in II Corps, VII Corps, I Cavalry Corps and II Cavalry Corps, which had joined the vanguard; but part of our force still remained behind, which prevented us from standing astride the French line of retreat. Only once the majority of the retreating column had passed the position occupied by the vanguard under Miloradovich, were several squadrons of Lifeguard Hussars and Colonel Gogel [Fëdor Grigorievich Gogel] sent to the highway with the 5th Jägers, where they captured five guns (six, according to other sources) and several hundred prisoners. At the same time, Prinz Eugen von Württemberg, advancing to the right of VII Corps with 4th Division at the head of II Corps, noticing the progress of a huge enemy convoy, under the protection of a column surrounded by crowds of unarmed men and stragglers, pushed forward 28 guns, opened a bombardment on the retreating French and, taking advantage of the enemy disorder, attacked and scattered them; but as our infantry could not catch up with the retreating troops, then General Yurkovsky raced after them with the Yelisavetgrad Hussars and Sumy Hussars and took six more guns. Overall, on this day [15 November, new style], 2,000 prisoners and 11 guns were taken. By nightfall, having left the Cossack detachment under Major General Yurkovsky on the highway, Miloradovich redeployed his force four *versts* from the main road at the village of Ugryumova.[15] General Yermolov, informing the Field Marshal of the outcome of the action on 3 (15) November, wrote:

---
12 Orders for the *prince d'Eckmühl* (Davout) and the *duc d'Elchingen* (Ney), dated 14 November, new style. Further instructions to them of the same date.
13 Bernhardi, II, 298.
14 War Diary.
15 War Diary. General Miloradovich's report to Prince Kutuzov, dated 7 [19] November. *Journal militaire du 2me Corps, redigé par le prince de Württemberg* (Archive of the M.T.D. No.

Your Grace, I have the honour to most humbly report that General Miloradovich's vanguard, on the highway from Smolensk near the village of Rzhavka, attacked the enemy who are now fleeing in disorder. Resistance was minimal; all of them ran in terror and fear; several cannon were taken; one column surrendered, having been attacked by Adjutant General Baron Meller-Zakomelsky; many officials were detained; the prisoners claim that 25,000 men remain in Smolensk with Marshal Davout. These must all be wiped out or be taken into our possession. Today, it was possible to drive the enemy off the highway with batteries alone, and they were forced to move across country and were completely dispersed, where one cold night should be enough for their demise even without a pursuit.

If the enemy *Garde* is still in Krasny, then there is no doubt that, having learned about today's events, they will not stay there. Your Grace will complete their defeat if our army arrives at Krasny tomorrow and halts in position two *versts* from the highway. The enemy has no other options for retreat than via Krasny, or the right bank of the Dnieper. It is impossible towards Mstislavl, or Gorki. Today's movements rob them of all hope, and it will be impossible to undertake this without complete destruction. Your Grace, do not refuse this advance on Krasny. Tomorrow, success will be complete. It is up to us not to expose ourselves to danger. 3 [15] November, 1812.

On that same day, 3 (15) November, Napoleon arrived in Krasny and deployed his *Garde*, totalling around 15,000 men, in bivouacs around this town. Here he learned of the location of Russians close by, at Kutkovo, and decided to attack them. General Roguet, with one of the divisions of the *Jeune Garde*, attacked the detachment under Count Ozharovsky during the night of 3 to 4 (15 to 16) November and pushed them back to the village of Palkino.[16] Napoleon, having extracted intelligence from the prisoners on the location of Prince Kutuzov just one stage from Krasny, remained there with the *Garde* in order to assist the corps under the Viceroy, Davout and Ney, who were to follow. Roguet's and Delaborde's divisions were stationed in front of the town; Latour-Maubourg's cavalry were to their right, while the *Vieille Garde* were in the town itself.

Meanwhile, in Smolensk, on 2 (14) November, the Viceroy and his suite, hearing cannon fire, visited the rear guard, Broussier's division, left on the high ground of the right bank of the Dnieper, and took command of the reserve, which consisted of the Italian *Guardia Reale*. The frost was so severe that, while forming the detachment up for battle, 30 grenadiers fell, their arms and legs completely frozen. A counterattack by the *Guardia Reale* helped Broussier's force, ousted by the Cossacks from the village they had been holding, to hold on to the high ground and cover the movement of *4e Corps* trains across the bridge. The following day, 3 (15) November,

---

47,344). Prinz Eugen von Württemberg, *Erinnerungen aus dem Feldzuge des Jahres 1812 in Russland*, 152.
16 War Diary. French historians claim that Ozharovsky lost many men. Chambray, II, 437. Fain, II, 256. Sołtyk, *Napoléon en 1812*, 406.

the Viceroy set out along the road to Krasny, with his entire force, some 5,000 men in total, and reached Lubnya. Platov's Cossacks, following in the wake of the French, occupied the St. Petersburg suburbs, but were driven out of there by Ney's corps.[17] The Viceroy's fighting men, continuing their march from Smolensk to Krasny, encountered the sight of the destruction of the *Grande Armée* at every step; an overwhelming number of guns had been abandoned near the city; further on, the entire road was choked with wagons; muskets, helmets, shakos, cuirasses and valises were scattered everywhere along the soldiers route. Numerous corpses surrounded the extinguished bivouac fires; gullies and ditches were also filled with bodies piled up to make improvised culverts across them for the wagon trains.[18]

On 4 (16) November, the viceroy set out from his overnight halt on the road to Krasny; Napoleon remained forwards of Krasny with the *Garde*; Junot reached Lyady, with the Westphalians, the main artillery park and dismounted cuirassiers, while Zajączek arrived in Dubrowna with the Polish formation.[19] On our side, the vanguard under Miloradovich, reinforced by II Cavalry Corps (from the formation under Count Osterman), made a flanking movement, parallel to the highway, from Rzhavka to the village of Merlino; Osterman remained at Kobyzevo with IV Corps and IV Cavalry Corps, in order to protect the convoys heading towards the army, and more importantly, Kutuzov's force, moving from Shchelkanovo to Krasny, in two columns,[20] settled down in the evening between Novoselki and Shilovo, as follows: III Corps forwards and somewhat to the right of the village of Novoselki; 2nd Cuirassier Division behind them; VI Corps and VIII Corps between Novoselki and Shilovo, on both sides of the Roslavl road; the Lifeguard and 1st Cuirassier Division forwards of Shilovo, where Kutuzov's headquarters were located. The detachment under Lieutenant Colonel Davydov was ordered to move directly towards Orsha; Count Ozharovsky was to get to the highway between Krasny and Lyady; Seslavin remained near Krasny. The first two were informed that Napoleon's escort consisted of Dutch red light horse [*2e régiment de chevau-légers lanciers de la Garde*] at that time, not more than 300 strong.[21]

On the morning of 4 (16) November, Miloradovich, approaching the highway near the village of Merlino with the vanguard, some 17,000 strong, halted there until four o'clock in the afternoon, waiting for the enemy troops to emerge from Smolensk.[22] At that moment, Cossacks appeared on the road and along the verges, having over-

---

17 Chambray, II, 440. Buturlin, II, 224.
18 Labaume, *Relation circonstanciée de la campagne de Russie en 1812*, 344-345.
19 Bernhardi, II 302.
20 Constitution of the columns: the right, under General Lavrov's command, with V Corps (Lifeguard), moving to Volkovo and Malyshevo (where III Corps and 1st Cuirassier Division, which were part of the vanguard of the column, joined them), thence to Novoselki; the left, under General Dokhturov's command, with VI Corps and VIII Corps, moved to Britovo and Vasilyevo to Bryukhanovo, where 2nd Cuirassier Division, which was part of the vanguard of this column, joined, and thence to Shilovo.
21 Orders dated 3 [15] November: for Davydov, No. 420, and for Count Ozharovsky, No. 422 (Archive of the M.T.D. No. 29,172). Bernhardi, II, 302-303.
22 In the War Diary it states that the Viceroy's corps came within sight of our forces at three o'clock in the afternoon.

taken the Viceroy's corps but held at some distance from the enemy by musket fire. Behind them came the columns under the Viceroy, accompanied by many unarmed men. At every step, the enemy were ditching guns and wagons, men and horses were falling constantly. Prinz Eugen von Württemberg, who was marching with 4th Division at the head of II Corps, without waiting for orders, pushed 44 guns forwards, his own and Göring's [P.Kh. Göring] horse artillery company, and placing them across the road, behind a ravine, opened a strong bombardment on the French; behind the artillery was 4th Division, and behind them at 1,000 paces was II Corps; in the meantime, Paskevich had arrived with 26th Division, which, together with 12th Division, which made their timely arrival a little later, formed up to the right of the regiments under Prinz Eugen.[23] With our first shots, the enemy lead column scattered. All that remained was to exploit the disorder of the French force, but instead, Miloradovich, galloping onto the battlefield, halted Prinz Eugen von Württemberg's infantry enroute and ordered the cavalry to get off the road; Prinz Eugen had only the Volhynia Infantry and Kremenchug Infantry, a total of 700 men to protect the artillery on the road. Several squadrons of hussars, also remaining on the road, launched a charge and captured many prisoners. Hoping to induce the enemy to surrender, Miloradovich sent Colonel Prince Kudashev to the Viceroy as a *parlementaire*. General Guyon [Claude-Raymond Guyon], having met with him, asked why had he been summoned. Prince Kudashev replied

> General Miloradovich has ordered me to announce to you that yesterday we defeated Napoleon with his *Garde*, and today the Viceroy is surrounded by 20,000 men, and therefore, if he agrees to lay down his arms, then he is offered the most favourable terms.

Guyon answered 'Go back and tell the man who sent you that if you have 20,000 men, that we have 18,000.'[24] Meanwhile, the Viceroy, having reached the vanguard

---

23 The sources for the fighting on 4 (16) November are highly inconsistent with each other. In the War Diary it states that VII Corps was placed across the highway facing Smolensk; II Corps were also on the highway facing Krasny, while all the cavalry, under Uvarov's command, was supposedly in support of these corps; General Buturlin wrote that II Corps were stationed across the highway, while VII Corps were parallel to the road; in the works of General Mikhailovsky-Danilevsky, that II Corps and I Cavalry Corps were stationed across, while VII Corps were parallel to the road. In the Memoirs of Prinz Eugen von Württemberg, it is said that only one brigade of 4th Division and a small part of the cavalry blocked the enemy route, and that Paskevich's 26th Division was attached to the right flank of this brigade in line (and not at an acute angle); in Raevsky's Notes, that II Corps and 12th Division stood across the highway; while 26th Division were parallel to the road. Finally, from A.P. Yermolov's, it is evident that along with 4th Division, the Belozersk Infantry (17th Division) were also in action.
24 General Raevsky wrote that, noticing the enemy disorder, he sent Prince Kudashev with a demand to lay down their weapons. Kudashev returned with the answer that the French general in command at this point could not comply with our demand without permission from the Viceroy, to whom an officer had been sent for orders. Meanwhile night was falling and the enemy, taking advantage of the twilight, managed to slip away from the danger that threatened them. The War Diary also says that the proposal for surrender was made to the Viceroy at the end of the action, once his force had been disordered. Labaume, on the other hand, states emphatically that our *parlementaire* came to the French force even before the start of the fighting.

and having learned about the offer made to him, decided to break through our forces towards Smolensk. If Miloradovich had blocked the road with all the forces that were in the area of Merlino, then the French would have suffered a total defeat. But he had orders from the Field Marshal to avoid a decisive encounter with the enemy. Despite the intelligence sent to the headquarters by General Yermolov, who wrote that the Viceroy had no more than 3,000 or 4,000 men with him,[25] Kutuzov stubbornly followed the operational principles adopted by him, even when enemy impotence was beyond doubt.

The Viceroy, preparing to break out by force, ordered General Broussier to attack along the highway with the remnants of *14e Division*, numbering 1,000 men, with two guns; several hundred of our infantry, who had moved forward to pursue the leading enemy column, fell back and drew the French squares towards our batteries. The enemy, caught in a crossfire of canister, was driven off once more. General d'Ornano [Philippe Antoine d'Ornano] rushed to assist Broussier's force with the remnants of *13e Division*, but, having suffered a severe contusion, fell unconscious from his horse. The Viceroy, aware of the perilous situation of *35e ligne* (*14e division*), under attack by hussars, sent (*officier d'ordonnance*) Colonel Delfanti to their rescue, with a battalion of 200 men; but this outstanding officer was wounded twice and eventually mortally wounded by round shot, which decapitated the former quartermaster of Smolensk, Villeblanche, who had rushed to his aid. The battalion entrusted to Delfanti, left leaderless, charged as a mob into the square of *35e ligne* and disordered them; exploiting this opportunity, Colonel Davydov (Nikolai Vladimirovich) cut into the enemy column with the Moscow Dragoons and captured some 2,000 men, including General Heyligers [Ghisbert Martin Cort Heyligers], who was leading this regiment. The Eagle of this regiment was among the trophies taken, one of the most famous in the French army. Colonel Poll [Ivan Lavrentievich Poll] captured four guns with the Kargopol dragoons. According to an eyewitness, the horses in Davydov's regiment were exhausted to the point that the dragoons, crashing into the centre of one of the enemy columns, were halted and could not push to its tail. But the Viceroy's infantry, exhausted by hunger and fatigue, not only did not defend themselves, they did not even move from their positions and laid down their weapons.[26]

Meanwhile, the Viceroy, wishing to force our troops to move to the right flank and then force their way along the highway, ordered *15e Division* to attack: the right hand column raced along the road; the centre one attacked the forest in front of the centre of Paskevich's division; the left hand column enveloped his right flank. This forced Miloradovich to withdraw the infantry brigade that was straddling the road, to the right; the regiments of 1st Brigade of 26th Division, attacked from the right flank, were forced to pull back; but then, having been reinforced by the Moscow Dragoons and Kargopol Dragoons, they isolated the French left column. The centre column was defeated by the 5th Jägers, while the right hand column, engaged with canister fire from 24 guns and the 6th Jägers, retreated in complete disorder. The

---

25 General Yermolov's reports (log of incoming documents, Archive of the M.T.D. No. 29,172. Report No. 519).
26 General Yermolov's notes.

enemy, driven back at all points, raced off down the road to their right and, taking advantage of the encroaching darkness, made their way to the town, losing on this day [16 November, new style] more than 2,000 prisoner alone (1,500 according to other sources), mostly stragglers, one colour[27] and all the artillery they had with them, a total of 17 guns. On our side, the casualties did not exceed 800 men.[28]

Despite the fact that the Viceroy managed to reach Krasny with the remnants of *4e Corps*, a total of 3,500 men, and join up with the *Garde* there, the situation of the French corps following on behind was very dangerous, and therefore Napoleon, whose courage was bolstered through the caution of his adversary, decided go on the offensive in order to divert our forces from the highway and facilitate the arrival of Davout's and Ney's corps in Krasny. Having deciphered the character and methodology of warfare by Prince Kutuzov completely, he took advantage of the weaknesses of his operational system. Indeed, although Kutuzov understood the utterly disastrous situation of the enemy army, nonetheless, instead of completing the destruction of its remnants with a decisive blow, he hoped just as surely to achieve the war objectives without a battle, conserving his own forces and leaving the annihilation of the enemy to the destructive effects of the environment itself, which indeed turned out to be the case. Kutuzov believed that the French troops, in the event of being cut off from their line of retreat, with a courage born of desperation, would sell themselves dearly, yet whose destruction, in the opinion of the old Field Marshal, and without any effort on our part, was beyond doubt. Our commander, despite the obvious superiority of the Russian army over the enemy, remained apprehensive about engaging Napoleon, who on more than one occasion had made up for a lack of strength through his operational art. Unable to come up with some sort of precise plan to neutralise the inspired acts of a brilliant enemy, Kutuzov exaggerated their resources. At a time when our commander's colleagues were convinced of the success of operations at each encounter with the French, and when he, carried away by the general mood, was preparing to attack the enemy with the main body of the army himself, Count Ozharovsky received orders from the headquarters: to discover if the enemy army had stopped in Krasny, or was continuing to move onwards; and also, the precise location of the French *Garde*. The partisan Seslavin was also ordered: to seize informants (prisoners), in order to obtain intelligence about which troops are in Krasny and which ones have departed from there, 'because the Field Marshal does not intend to attack the enemy without this.'[29] The intelligence delivered by Seslavin regarding Napoleon's departure from Krasny towards Lyady with the *Garde* dispelled the concerns of the Field Marshal,[30] and convinced him to

---

27 In the War Diary, it states that Colonel Davydov took a colour, while a private from the Nizhegorod Regiment took an Eagle.
28 General Miloradovich's report to Prince Kutuzov, dated 7 [19] November. War Diary. *Journal du 2me Corps, rédigé par le prince de Württemberg* (archive of the M.T.D, No. 47,344). Prinz Eugen von Württemberg, *Erinnerungen,* 153-155. Labaume, 347-355. Buturlin, II, 213-214.
29 Orders dated 4 [16] November: for Count Ozharovsky, No. 438, and to Lifeguard Captain Seslavin, No. 442 (Log of outgoing documents, Archive of the M.T.D. No. 29,172).
30 Orders for Seslavin, dated 5 [17] November, No. 444 (Archive of the M.T.D. No. 29,172). The intelligence delivered to General Konovnitsyn by Seslavin was as follows: 'As God is my judge, Y.E. In Krasny there is also inaction and the same indecision as in Vyazma. The third

THE BATTLE OF KRASNY 89

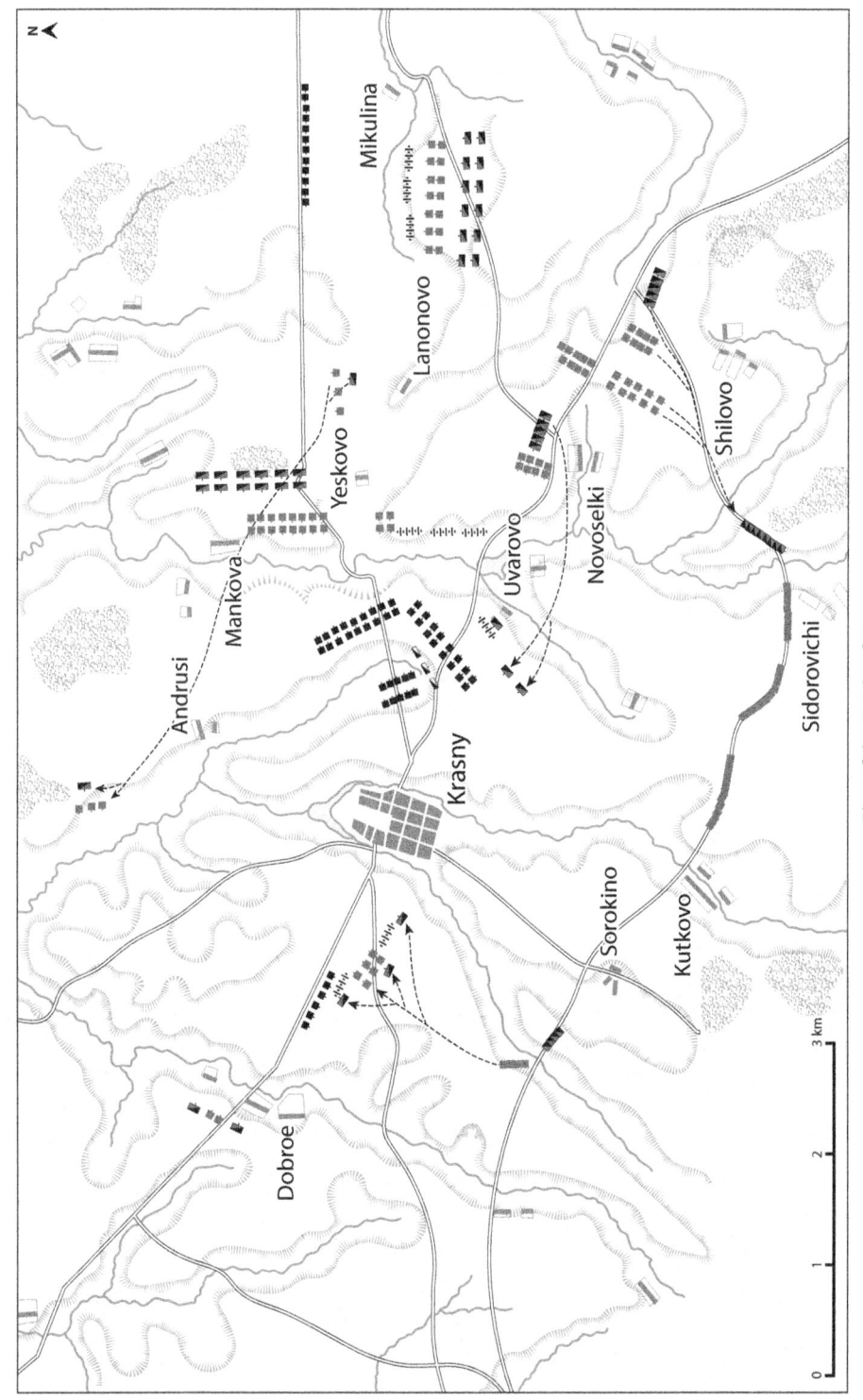

Plan of the Battle of Krasny.

attack the French on 5 (17) November; but it was easy to foresee that this attack, undertaken against his principles, would not be carried out with the decisive aim of getting across the path of the retreating enemy.

Thus, both Napoleon and Kutuzov prepared for battle, but neither one nor the other had the intention of the battle becoming general: Napoleon simply wanted to facilitate the retreat by Davout and Ney, who, on the basis of the orders issued to them, were to set out from Smolensk and proceed to Krasny together; while Kutuzov limited the objective of his operations to inflicting attrition on the remnants of the *Grande Armée*. Yielding to the proposals of those closest to him, Konovnitsyn and Toll, he agreed that our main body, under the command of General Tormasov, masked from the enemy point of view by III Corps and 2nd Cuirassier Division stationed at Novoselki,[31] made a flank march to the road leading from Krasny to Orsha, and having occupied it, they completely cut off the only line of retreat for the French army. The force stationed at Novoselki were assigned to fix the enemy frontally and maintain communications between the main body with the vanguard under Miloradovich, who was ordered: 'upon the approach of the French to Krasny, do not harass them on the march, but once they have passed the vanguard, pursue them from the rear in order to put the enemy between two fires.'

The disposition for the upcoming operations, for 5 (17) November, compiled by Toll, contained the following orders: Tormasov's vanguard, under the command of Major General Baron Rosen, consisting of the Lifeguard Jägers, Lifeguard Finland Regiment, His Majesty's Cuirassiers, Her Majesty's Cuirassiers, a light company of Lifeguard Artillery and a Cossack regiment, at six o'clock in the morning, is to set off from Sidorovichi and move up the highway to Dobroe, half a *verst* ahead of the main column, made up of VI Corps, VIII Corps and V Corps and the other three regiments of 1st Cuirassier Division. This column is intended to set off at seven o'clock from Shilovo, to Zunikovo, Sidorovichi, Kutkovo and Sorokino, to Dobroe. Upon reaching Sorokino, the force is to deploy parallel to the highway: the infantry in regimental column, in three echelons; while the cuirassiers are to be on the left wing, and in this combat formation they are to proceed behind the advance by Rosen's vanguard onto the highway. The troops stationed at Novoselki, namely III Corps and 2nd Cuirassier Division, under the command of Prince Golitsyn, were ordered to move, an hour and a half after the departure of the column under General Tormasov, through the village of Uvarovo, directly towards Krasny. The vanguard under Miloradovich, consisting of II Corps, VII Corps, I Cavalry Corps and II Cavalry Corps, together with the detachment under Major General Borozdin 2nd [Nikolai Mikhailovich Borozdin],[32] was to go out onto the highway, attack the enemy on the march, push them into Krasny and link their left flank to the right

---

day since Smolensk was abandoned by the enemy. They left there on 2 [14] November, had a rest day in Krasny; the *Garde* came to Lyady this day with Napoleon. According to statements by the prisoners, Napoleon, riding along the road, was attacked by Cossacks, but escaped unharmed. A march from Lyady along the highway to Orsha is scheduled for tomorrow...' (Archive of the M.T.D. No. 29,172. Log of incoming documents, No. 511).
31 See Plan of the Battle of Krasny, 5 (17) November.
32 Major General Borozdin 2nd, due to the illness of Count Orlov-Denisov, commanded his detachment, which consisted of seven Cossack regiments with six horse artillery pieces.

flank of Prince Golitsyn's detachment. Count Ozharovsky was to go out onto the highway between Krasny and Lyady with his raiding detachment as soon as the fighting began, towards the village of Sinyaki. Finally, Count Osterman was ordered to close up to the highway near Korytnya with IV Corps and III Cavalry Corps, sending Cossack patrols to the roads leading from Smolensk to Mstislavl and Roslavl and, after allowing the enemy to pass by, to press them from behind.[33]

If these orders had been executed, then, in all likelihood, Napoleon would not have been able to break through to Orsha, which would have forced him to dash off the highway to the right, where he had no resources to construct a crossing on the Dnieper. In such circumstances, he could only have escaped with a small part of his force and the French army would have been utterly destroyed.[34]

On that same day, Napoleon intended to move against Kutuzov with 15,000 men of the *Garde* under his direct command. Kutuzov had twice their strength, not including the troops under Miloradovich and Osterman, and more than three times their strength with them. There is no doubt that Napoleon, basing the success of his plans on the excessive caution of his adversary, hoped that Kutuzov, being, attacked by French forces beyond all expectation, would bring Miloradovich closer to the main body of the Russian army and thereby enable Marshal Davout to pass along the highway to Krasny. In accordance with these plans, on the night of 4 to 5 (16 to 17) November, the following orders were issued: Mortier, with the remnants of two divisions of the *Jeune Garde*, was to move along the Smolensk highway; he was to be followed by the *Vieille Garde* with 30 guns; while the *cavalerie de la Garde* and Latour-Maubourg were in reserve. The defence of the town of Krasny was entrusted to Claparède, with his division, various straggling regiments and several guns from the *Garde*. All these troops did not exceed 13,000 infantry and 2,200 cavalry (1,800 from the *Garde* and 400 under Latour-Maubourg), with 50 guns. Only the artillery attached to the *Jeune Garde* was capable of moving along with the troops; the rest could not make a single step away from the road, even with each gun being harnessed to 12 or more horses, barely lifting their hooves.[35] The Viceroy set out for Lyady with the remnants of his corps even before dawn, because his troops, completely disorganised and having lost all their artillery, were no longer battle-worthy.[36]

Marshal Davout, having set out from Smolensk on 4 (16) November, settled in the evening with the leading division from his corps in bivouacs four *versts* beyond the village of Korytnya; the other three, following one after another at intervals of

---

33 Disposition for 5 [17] November. Orders dated 5 [17] November: for General Miloradovich, No. 445; for Count Ozharovsky, No. 446, and for Count Osterman, No. 443. Subsequently, once the battle was already underway, Osterman was ordered to go along the very route along which the army was moving towards Krasny, and take post near the village of Tolstyakovo. Orders dated 5 [17] November No. 447 (Archive of the M.T.D. No. 29,172). Yermolov's notes.
34 Bernhardi, II, 307.
35 Chambray, II, 444-445.
36 'Son combat de la veille et sa marche nocturne avaient achevé son corps d'armée: ses divisions avaient encore quelque ensemble, mais pour se trainer, pour mourir, et non, pour combattre.' Ségur, II, 263-264. (Their fight the day before and their night march had finished off this army corps: its divisions still had some strength, just enough to drag themselves along, and to die, but not to fight).

about two *versts* (*à des intervalles d'une demi-lieue*), in order to protect the artillery and carts from the incessant Cossack attacks and halted along the road in the same order in which they had marched. Shortly after arriving at the overnight halt, Davout received news of the unsuccessful action involving the Viceroy and of the location of Miloradovich's force on the route to Krasny. Clearly, it was necessary to speed up the retreat in order to deny the Russians time to build up strength: having informed Ney of the impossibility of waiting for the arrival of his corps, at three o'clock in the morning on 5 (17) November, Davout set off, and, preparing for battle, ordered his divisions to proceed one immediately after another. At dawn, the French crossed the area where the Viceroy had fought the day before, not encountering any Russian troops on the way, except for Cossacks, because Miloradovich had made a flanking movement towards the village of Larionovo in the night and settled there in the vicinity of the highway.[37]

As early as about nine o'clock in the morning, the lead column under Davout, who that day had 7,500 men with 15 guns, caught up with our vanguard, II Corps, with 52 guns pushed forwards into the front line, lunging at the enemy. Our first shots scattered the enemy column, the remnants of which dashed to the right of the road. The nearest Cossack regiments pursued them and took many prisoners. The situation was all the more dangerous for the French because in order to reach Krasny they still had to cross the rather deep ravine of the Losmina [Losvinka] river, which cuts across the highway, three *versts* short of the town. But no sooner had II Corps managed to fire a few rounds, than they were stopped by Miloradovich, who, having approached Prinz Eugen von Württemberg, announced to him that the Field Marshal had forbidden becoming entangled in combat. Indeed, as has already been mentioned, the vanguard was forbidden from severing the enemy line of retreat, but had been ordered to pursue them persistently as soon as they had passed by. This was not done, and the vanguard force remained inactive almost until evening.[38]

Meanwhile, Tormasov, with VI Corps, VIII Corps and V Corps and with 1st Cuirassier Division, preceded by Rosen's vanguard, moved in the direction assigned to them; while Prince Golitsyn, having placed the Chernigov Infantry regiment in the village of Uvarovo, behind the Losmina, was preparing to cross the river and attack the enemy with his entire force. But Napoleon prevented our attack and sent the *Jeune Garde* and a combined cavalry detachment under Latour-Maubourg to the village of Uvarovo: the right flank of this force was in front of Krasny, while the left adjoined the rather steep Losminka ravine; the line stretched almost parallel to the Smolensk highway behind the French positions, and a battery had been pushed forwards opposite the village of Uvarovo. The *Vieille Garde* stood in regimental columns in the second line on the road with 12 guns from the *artillerie à cheval de la Garde*, whose crews had long since been dismounted. Napoleon was here himself, in his winter outfit, on foot, leaning on a birch stave. Berthier and several officers of the *État-major général* were with him, also on foot; the rest, on horseback, stood a short way off. At this point, one of the generals close by the Emperor of the French, brought to his notice that he was in great danger, due to the disproportionate strength of the

---

37 Chambray, II, 446-447.
38 Prinz Eugen von Württemberg, 155.

enemy forces. Napoleon said in reply: 'I have been the emperor enough; now is the time to be the general.'[39]

As the *Jeune Garde* could not occupy the entire length of their position, the Dutch Grenadier Regiment [*3e régiment de grenadiers à pied de la Garde*] were ordered to be brought into the front line. Once the leading division of Davout's corps had crossed to the left bank of the Losmina, Napoleon ordered it to squeeze into the front line facing the village of Uvarovo. In the meantime, his force had burst into this village, with four Hessen-Darmstadt battalions distinguishing themselves in particular; whereupon Prince Golitsyn sent the Selenginsk Infantry to assist the Chernigov Infantry,[40] and supported them with fire from all the light artillery and the battery company under Colonel Taube [Karl Karlovich Taube], located on the right bank of the Losmina. Our troops not only managed to hold out in the part of the village of Uvarovo closest to the river, but occupied the nearby high ground, which dominates the surrounding area. Major General Duka [Ilya Mikhailovich Duka], bypassing the village on the left side, placed the Novgorod Cuirassiers and Malorussia Cuirassiers behind the skirmisher screen, which covered the advance of our foot artillery onto the left bank of the river. At the same time, Colonel Nikitin, moving his horse artillery company along the right bank of the Losmina, within musket range of the highway, struck Davout's retreating columns with canister fire. Prince Golitsyn, trusting that the vanguard under Miloradovich was approaching the troops fighting on the Losmina and would completely secure them from the right flank, decided to go on the offensive. Adjutant General Count Stroganov [Pavel Alexandrovich Stroganov] was ordered to line the opposite bank of the river with artillery and transfer the entire III Corps there, except for one brigade of the grenadier division, which was assigned to remain in reserve on the right bank of the Losmina. At the head of the corps moving across the river were the Reval Infantry and Murom Infantry from Prince Shakhovsky's 3rd Division, with 20 guns. The enemy, wanting to get a foothold in the village, resumed the attack with the *1er régiment de Voltigeurs de la Garde*, who, forming up in column, moved swiftly towards our batteries. Genera Duka charged at the enemy with the Novgorod Cuirassiers and Malorussia Cuirassiers, but the French managed to form up in square and repelled several attacks by our cuirassiers.[41]

Meanwhile, General Tormasov was moving to sever the enemy line of retreat with a significant part of the army, but Kutuzov, having received intelligence about Napoleon being present himself with the *Vieille Garde*, sent orders to Tormasov to halt: thus the enemy was able to retreat along the road to Orsha.[42]

---

39 'J'ai assez fait l'empereur; il est tems de faire le général.' Chambray, II, 447-448 & 491.
40 In Prince Golitysn's report on the action of 5 [17] November, and in Buturlin, it states that the Selenginsk Infantry (IV Corps) were sent to assist the Chernigov Infantry.
41 Lieutenant General Prince Golitsyn 5th's report to General Tormasov, dated 12 [24] November, No. 251.
42 Buturlin, II, 220-221. Bernhardi, II, 310. One of the eyewitnesses of the fighting at Krasny wrote that Kutuzov, at the suggestion of Konovnytyn and Toll, agreed to send General Tormasov to sever the enemy line of retreat with part of the army, only in the event that Napoleon himself were not in command of forces at Krasny. During the action, a captured Bavarian captain was brought in. The Field Marshal, who still doubted whether Napoleon

As Davout's divisions passed over the Losmina ravine, Napoleon immediately sent them on to Krasny, and further along the road to Lyady. Two divisions had already crossed the battlefield when he learned about Russian movements on the Orsha road. At the same time, our troops were advancing from the direction of Uvarovo and Cossacks appeared on the flank and in the rear of the French between Krasny and the Dnieper. Under these circumstances, not yet having intelligence about orders issued to Tormasov to halt enroute to Dobroe, Napoleon decided to continue the retreat to Orsha, after waiting for the last of Davout's divisions to arrive. As soon as this division, which was under the command of General Friederichs, crossed the Losmina, the division which had been pushed forwards to Uvarovo was withdrawn and proceeded behind the troops sent through Krasny along the Orsha road; behind them firstly the *Vieille Garde*, then the *Jeune Garde*, and finally Friederichs' division began to withdraw to Krasny, the latter, forming the rear guard, received orders to hold out in the town.[43]

As soon as Napoleon's troops fell back from the Losmina, Prince Golitsyn attacked them once more with the cuirassier brigade, under the personal command of Duka, and sent the Reval Infantry and Murom Infantry into action. A small rise protected the French from the effects of our artillery, but once Ensign Panaev, having taken this high ground with two guns from the light artillery company under Lieutenant Colonel Dietrichs 6th, fired two rounds of canister at the enemy and disrupted a square of the *1er régiment de Voltigeurs de la Garde*, whereupon the Reval Infantry and Murom Infantry, under the personal command of Prince Shakhovsky, assaulted them with bayonets fixed, while Duka's Novgorod Cuirassiers and Malorussia Cuirassiers broke into the square and completed the destruction of the voltigeurs, of whom only the captured regimental commander, Lieutenant Colonel Pion, wounded in the head, and several officers were spared. It has been claimed that one old Wachtmeister [Sergeant-Major] of the Novgorod Cuirassiers, his patience exhausted by the failure of several previous charges, was first to race straight at the bayonets, saying: 'When is someone going to end this!' The brave warrior was killed, but paved the way for his comrades.[44] At around noon, the force under Prince Golitsyn, having driven the enemy from the position they had occupied in front of Krasny completely, pursued their forces, who had been put to flight by cavalry alone. Colonel Nikitin, 'whose activity, courage and skill (in the words of Prince Golitsyn), exceeded all praise' having crossed to the left bank of the river, drove up to very close range from the left wing of the French position with his company, and

---

was facing him, began to ask the prisoner about this in German, about which he spoke quite freely. It turned out that the captain did not know who was in command of the French force, although he had seen him during the fighting. Kutuzov began to describe the indicators of Napoleon's presence, and when the captain answered yes to several such questions, Kutuzov, turning to face his staff standing behind him, said: *c'est lui* (it's him). When, in answer to the question: *ist er klein* (is he short)? he replied: *nein, er ist sehr gross* (no, he's very tall), Kutuzov said, confidently, he was probably speaking of Mortier: *non ce n'est pas lui* (no, that's not him). But soon after that he received other intelligence, which removed all doubt about the presence of Napoleon (Alexander Andreevich Shcherbinin's notes).

43   Bernhardi, II, 311.
44   War Diary. Prince Golitsyn's report dated 12 [24] November, No. 251. Bernhardi, II, 312.

scattered them with canister and, having formed his gunners into a squadron ahead of the cavalry pursuing the enemy, relentlessly drove the routed troops through the streets through the entire town and captured three guns. The cuirassiers completed the dispersing of the enemy. One of their columns, which had been unable to pass through the town, was cut off by Major General Kretov [Nikolai Vasilievich Kretov], with the Military Order Cuirassiers and Yekaterinoslav Cuirassiers, and suffered heavy losses.

The defeat of the enemy by the force under of Prince Golitsyn, having dispelled the Field Marshal's concerns, urge him to send orders to Tormasov to continue moving towards Dobroe. But it was already too late: our fighting men, having stood still for about three hours, could not make up for lost time with a forced march, because they were forced to string themselves out in one long column along a country lane blanketed with snow. Only Tormasov's vanguard, under Rosen's command, emerged onto the highway at Dobroe, and even then only at dusk. By this time, Napoleon had already passed on towards Lyady with most of Davout's corps and with the *Garde*, and only the remnants of Friederichs' division remained between Krasny and Dobroe; their situation was most grave, especially since Prince Golitsyn had already taken possession of Krasny. General Rosen, for his part, attacked the enemy with the cuirassiers in his detachment, blocked their line of retreat with the Lifeguard Jägers and Lifeguard Finland Regiment and drove them back towards Krasny. Two regiments from this French division were disordered and driven back into the forests extending towards the Dnieper, while the *33e légère*, which was at the tail of the column, was completely wiped out. The raiding detachments under Count Ozharovsky and Borozdin 2nd, pursuing the French from the flank and rear, also inflicted heavy casualties on them. Had Rosen's detachment been sent after the enemy immediately, strengthened with reinforcements, they could have caught up with them, or at least shadowed them, but they were ordered to remain in the town.[45]

Overall, on this day [17 November, new style], the enemy lost more than 6,000 men in prisoners alone (or according to other sources more than 9,000), 45 guns (or according to other sources 70), two colours and a large number of carts, in which Marshal Davout's baton and part of Napoleon's *Chancellerie* were found.[46] On our side, the casualties did not exceed 700 men.

Napoleon arrived in Lyady at three o'clock in the afternoon, where, during the night the remnants of the *Garde* and Davout's corps gathered, and moved towards Dubrowna on the following day [18 November, new style].

---

45 War Diary, signed off by Prince Kutuzov. Lieutenant General Prince Golitsyn 5th's report to General Tormasov, dated 12 [24] November, No. 251. Tormasov's report to Prince Kutuzov, dated 7 [19] November, No. 39. Kutuzov's report to the Tsar, dated 8 [20] November. A.P. Yermolov's notes. Chapuis, *Observations sur les historiens de la campagne de Russie*. Chambray, II, 444-450. Buturlin, II, 217-223.
46 Sources on losses of both sides in the actions of 5th [17th] November are highly imprecise. Enemy losses are given as follows: In the War Diary: two generals, 57 field officers and subalterns, 6,170 lower ranks taken prisoner. 45 guns captured; two colours, four standards and icons; a marshal's baton.   In Kutuzov's report to the Tsar: two generals, 134 field officers and subalterns; 9,170 lower ranks; 70 guns captured; two colours and standards; Davout's marshal's baton.

On the evening of 5 (17) November, Tormasov's force settled in bivouacs between Krasny and Dobroe, facing towards Orsha. Prince Golitsyn, having occupied Krasny with 3rd Division, halted, with 1st Grenadier Division and 2nd Cuirassier Division, just short of the town. Some of Miloradovich's troops overtook the grenadiers: 17th Division reaching Dobroe; 4th Division and I Cavalry Corps remained at Krasny; II Cavalry Corps were around Uvarovo; VII Corps were located in bivouacs behind the force under Prince Golitsyn, near the Losmina, south of the highway. Most of Miloradovich's artillery, totalling some 60 guns, having crossed the Losmina, were halted near the river. At the same time, by order of the Tsar, who had decided to unite both grenadier divisions into a corps, under the command of Count Stroganov, 2nd Grenadier Division was transferred to III Corps (Grenadier); 3rd Division, together with 4th Division, formed II Corps, under the command of Prinz Eugen von Württemberg (promoted to lieutenant general); while 17th Division moved into VIII Corps, entrusted to Lieutenant General Prince Dolgorukov [Sergei Nikolaievich Dolgorukov] in place of General Borozdin 1st.[47] Count Osterman, with IV Corps and IV Cavalry Corps, moved from Kobyzevo to Tolstiki, on the road from Yelnya to Krasny.[48]

Kutuzov moved his headquarters to Dobroe in the evening. On the way, he encountered thousands of enemy prisoners, including officers and soldiers of Napoleon's *Garde*, many guns, some abandoned by the French, others captured in combat; at every step he saw undoubted evidence of our victory and the disorder of the enemy army. The Field Marshal, evidently amazed at the outcome of the action, appeared rejuvenated. Here, for the first time since his arrival in the army, he set off at a gallop on his white horse, cantering up to the column of the Preobrazhensky Regiment and, pointing to the captured trophies, exclaimed loudly: 'Hurrah!' echoed several times, first by the giants of the guard, and then by all the troops nearby.[49]

Ney's corps, which formed the rearguard of Napoleon's forces, entered Smolensk after all the other corps, namely on the afternoon of 3 (15) November. The force under Davout, who held the city in the morning, plundered all the stores remaining in the magazines, even those that were reserved for Ney's corps. At around noon, Platov, with his raiding corps, closing up to the city, ordered Colonel Kaisarov, with the 20th Jägers and a *Sotnia* of dismounted Cossacks scattered as skirmishers to attack the Petersburg suburb in order to distract the attention of the enemy, while Lieutenant General Martynov [Andrei Dmitrievich Martynov] was directed to lead an attack on the Moscow suburb with four Cossack regiments. The enemy dashed back to the gates, but having received reinforcements and becoming aware of how small the numbers of our infantry were, pushed Kaisarov back and placed a battery of eight guns on the high ground closest to the suburb. Thereupon Platov,

---

47 Army Orders dated 3 [15] November, No. 62. Archive of the Military Topographic Depot, No. 36,749. Chambray, II, 450-451. Eugen von Württemberg, 162. Bernhardi, II, 312-313. 2nd Grenadier Division did not link up with 1st Grenadier Division until 10 [22] November. Orders for Prince Karl von Mecklenburg, dated 9 [21] November, No. 475.
48 Orders for Count Osterman, dated 5 [17] November No. 447.
49 Scherbinin's notes [Liprandi points out that Mikhailovky-Danilevsky's description of this event, sourced from eyewitnesses, differs markedly].

having pushed the artillery that was attached to his formation forwards, reinforced Kaisarov with the 1st Jägers, most of the dismounted Cossacks, the Chernigov Dragoons and Novorossia Dragoons, while Major General Kuteinikov 2nd was ordered to repeat the attack on the Moscow suburb with the Cossacks. This decisive attack was a total success: the enemy were driven off the high ground, with the loss of all eight guns, and were pushed back to the far side of the Dnieper, from where our jägers continued the firefight until nightfall.[50] On the following day, 4 (16) November, many buildings in various parts of the city were in flames; the chaos that reigned in Smolensk had increased. In addition to the Ney's corps, there were many soldiers from a variety of formations and some 5,000 sick and wounded fleeing the fires and crowded in the streets cluttered with abandoned guns and carts, littered with corpses and strewn with muskets and munitions. At eight o'clock in the evening, a dispatch was received in which Davout, informing Ney of the defeat of the Viceroy, let him know of the danger of his situation, urging him to bring forward the march to Krasny; but Ney was permitted to postpone the departure from Smolensk until 5 (17) November, in this case, because he had not been able to make all the necessary preparations for the destruction of Smolensk's walls and to render the abandoned artillery unserviceable the night before, whereupon the brave marshal, having received a response from his comrade, told those around him that 'Cossacks could not force him to deviate from the orders he had received' and he decided to stay in the city until the next morning.[51]

On 5 (17) November, at two o'clock in the morning, Ney set out from Smolensk with the remnants of his corps and Ricard's division, totalling some 8,000 infantry and 300 cavalry, with 12 guns; in Smolensk these troops had been issued greatcoats, shoes, cartridges and a three-day supply of rations;[52] some 7,000 unarmed men and stragglers, accompanying the troops, made their movements very awkward.[53] No sooner had the rearguard withdrawn about two *versts*, than an explosion was heard in the city; soon followed by others. Many of the hospitals were destroyed; the sick and wounded of the French army who were in them died victims of the insane vengeance of a conqueror embittered by failure.[54] But his revenge appeared impotent. Although the enemy laid mines under all the towers, they only blew up eight towers and the royal fortress. Many marauders who remained in burning Smolensk in the hope of robbery, did not find victims but found death at the hands of the

---

50 Platov's report to Prince Kutuzov, dated 5 [17] November, No. 190.
51 Fezensac, 96-98. Chambray, II, 463-464.
52 Ney's infantry consisted of three divisions: Ricard's (*1er Corps*); Razout's and Ledru's, reorganised from the remnants of *3e Corps*, 500 men who had arrived in Smolensk from France and the Smolensk garrison (*129e régiment d'infanterie de ligne* and one of the *régiment d'Illyrie*). The Württemberg division under Marchand had ceased to exist. Fezensac, 95. Chambray, II, 464. According to other sources, Ney's corps still had one Württemberg battalion (*3e provisoire*). Miller, *Darstellung des Fedzugs der französischen verbündeten Armee gegen die Russen im Jahr 1812, mit besonderer Rücksicht auf die Theilnahme der Königlich-Württembergischen Truppen*, II, 39. According to the author of the work: *Das Buch vom Jahr 1812*, Ney had 7,000 infantry, 80 cavalrymen and 16 guns, III, 172.
53 See Map of Movements From Smolensk to Orsha.
54 Chambray, II, 464-465.

inhabitants, hiding in basements and other shelters and ruthlessly taking revenge on their oppressors. Some of the enemy were thrown into the flames of burning buildings; others were drowned under the ice on the Dnieper. But as soon as Major Gorikhvostov [Alexander Zakharievich Gorikhvostov] entered the city, with the 20th Jägers, these killings were stopped and all possible assistance was provided to the French sick and wounded.[55]

In Smolensk, 17 Russian and 140 enemy guns were found, as well as some 600 wagons and carts of various types and more than 4,000 enemy sick and stragglers. Leaving the commandant, Major Gorikhvostov in Smolensk with the 20th Jägers and a *Sotnia* of Cossacks, Platov moved along the right bank of the Dnieper to Katan, with 1st Jägers, 12 Cossack regiments and the Don artillery; while major generals Grekov 1st and Denisov were sent to pursue the enemy along the road to Krasny and in the area between this road and the Dnieper, with six Cossack regiments, six squadrons of dragoons and four heavy guns.[56]

By the evening of 5 (17) November, Ney had arrived at the village of Korytnya without encountering any resistance. Only occasionally would Cossacks appear, and in the distance, from the direction of Krasny, a cannonade could be heard. The French, not knowing about the locations of our forces near Krasny, considered this gunfire to be a sign of the approach of Victor's corps.[57] The next day, 6 (18) November, Ney's troops, having set out from the overnight halt at around noon, encountered Cossacks in greater numbers and with guns, which forced the enemy to move tactically.

Meanwhile, the Cossacks sent to the highway were constantly snatching prisoners, from some of whom it was claimed that Ney was marching from Smolensk with the rearguard of the French army, made up of his own men, lagging units from other corps, 900 cavalry from a variety of regiments and quite a significant amount of artillery, with a total of some 15,000 men. On our part, orders to engage the enemy corps were not issued in time, and Ney's troops appeared on the Losmina before our generals had chance to bring the artillery into position and deploy the regiments assigned to protect the battery for battle. At three o'clock in the afternoon, Ney's vanguard, consisting of Ricard's division, under cover of thick fog, crossed the Losmina, stumbled upon the nearest guns and even passed them, but other artillery, having driven a short distance, managed to open fire on the advancing column and the individuals who were with it; whereupon, 12th Division dashed forwards and defended those guns under attack; while Paskevich opened fire with 26th Division and struck the left flank of the French. General Ricard was wounded and his division was forced to retreat in disorder towards the troops from Ney's Corps following

---

55 '… any wounded or sick enemy that might be found in Smolensk are to be fed in accordance with humanity, inasmuch as the prisoners are mostly German nationals and Italians, and in order to show them through this that the Russian government treats prisoners of war in a completely different way than they had imagined. Russian sick and wounded, if there are any, should be given special care…' Platov's orders to Major Gorikhvostov of 20th Jägers, dated 5 [17] November, No. 186.
56 Platov's reports to Prince Kutuzov, dated 5 [17] November, No. 190, and dated 7 [19] November, No. 193.
57 Fezensac, 101.

them. Meanwhile, Miloradovich's nearest troops had just arrived on the Losmina: initially, three regiments from 1st Grenadier Division and the Lifeguard Ulans (I Cavalry Corps), then II Cavalry Corps, which crossed the Losmina near Uvarovo, in order to envelope the enemy from the flank, while II Corps arrived from Krasny. Our force stood astride the highway: on the right wing was VII Corps formed in a single echelon;[58] on the left was III Grenadier Corps, in two echelons; II Corps was in reserve; I Cavalry Corps was assigned to support VII Corps; while 2nd Cuirassier Division was stationed behind the grenadiers. Miloradovich directed the operations of the force personally. Noticing the utter disorder of the routed French division, he sent Major Rennenkampf [Astafy Astafievich Renenkampf] of the Smolensk Infantry as a *parlementaire* to Ney, demanding that he lay down his arms; our representative assured the marshal that the respect inspired in them by his courage and abilities would not allow us to offer any conditions inconsistent with his dignity; that an army of 80,000 stood before him and that he could verify the truth of what was said by instructing any one of his officers to check for himself. At the time this offer was made to Ney, he had no more than 6,000 men under arms; his entire artillery consisted of 12 guns, and the cavalry, a single platoon, was with him as his escort. The Marshal only then managed to withdraw Ricard's division from being under fire; nevertheless, however, instead of answering, he ordered Major Rennenkampf to be detained, under the pretext that several cannon shots were fired by us in the course of the negotiations; the real reason for this was the worry that our officer might pass on intelligence about the miserable state of the French force. Razout's division was ordered to attack our positions, while the enemy battery of six guns, having been pushed forward, opened fire, but was quickly silenced by a bombardment from our 40 guns. In spite of this, however, the enemy, under the protection of a larger number of skirmishers, pushed back our screen, repaired the crossing over the river and emerged in front of our guns; in the lead was Colonel Bouvier with two sapper companies; they were followed in regimental column by *4e régiment d'infanterie de ligne, 18e régiment d'infanterie de ligne*, the *régiment d'Illyrie* and the Württemberg battalion, the last remnant of Marchand's division. Enemy files fell under our canister fire, but the French advanced without hesitation. Fezensac, a participant in this action, stated; 'Eventually, we came so close to the Russians that the entire leading division [pair of companies] of my regiment, lashed by canister, was driven back upon the division following us and disordered them.' At that very moment, as the French, advancing in the fog, without a shot being fired and maintaining a profound silence, were already almost within reach of our guns, Miloradovich ordered the artillery to be pulled back, and the troops closest to the enemy to move to engage them. The fearless Paskevich, with the Orël Infantry and 5th Jägers, struck the left column advancing along the highway and scattered them. Miloradovich rode up to our left wing himself, where the 1st Grenadier Division was stationed, and pointed out the *régiment d'Illyrie* closest to the Pavlov Grenadiers saying: 'My lads, I present to you! This column!' And the enemy was driven back here and chased into the ravine with heavy losses. *18e régiment d'infanterie de ligne*,

---

58 General Raevsky's notes.

advancing along with five guns in the centre column, was attacked by the Lifeguard Ulans, lost their artillery and their Eagle, but repulsed all subsequent attacks with musketry. *Général de division* Razout and Colonel Pelleport [Pierre de Pelleport] were wounded here, and *Général de brigade* Lanchantin [Louis François Lanchantin] was captured. Ledru's division moved into the front line with six guns, and meanwhile, Ney, having withdrawn the remnants of Razout's division two *versts* (*demi-lieue*) along the Smolensk road, directed them to the left towards the Dnieper; this force were followed a little later by Ledru's men with the rest of the guns and baggage, and finally all the sick and stragglers (*soldats isolés*) who were still able to move. On our side, the troops were returned to quarters, and even the cavalry, sent to monitor the retreating French, completely lost sight of them. The reason for such casual behaviour was a belief in the total disintegration of Ney's corps. By dawn of the following day [19 November, new style], an enemy deputation had arrived in Krasny, where Miloradovich was located at the time, they had been gathering in the surrounding forests, and now offered to surrender as prisoners of war. The total of these mostly unarmed men reached 6,000; by this time, none of us cared about capturing prisoners, considering the exhausted French doomed to certain death. With the exception of a small number of enemy soldiers who remained under arms, who retained a vestige of military morale, of a sense of national pride, the remainder wandered like shadows around our bivouacs, and were ready to willingly sacrifice their freedom for a crust of bread. Raevsky wrote that after repulsing Ney's force, he went to the quarters allocated to him in the nearest village and lay down to rest, he was awakened by an orderly, saying that two officers had arrived with 5,000 Frenchmen who did not want to surrender to anyone except General Raevsky. It turned out that one of these officers, who had previously served as a page with Raevsky's brother, having learned from a captured Lifeguard Hussar that the corps under our general, with whom he was acquainted, was in the vicinity of the French column, convinced his colleagues to surrender to him and went to look for Raevsky with a French surgeon, taking the captive Lifeguard Hussar as a guide. Raevsky commented; 'Thus, I took 5,000 prisoners without leaving my bed.' Colonel Gundius [Vilim Antonovich Gundius], with three squadrons of Lifeguard Ulans, having been detached to pursue the enemy column that had been attacking Krasny, blocked their line of retreat and captured some 2,500 men, that is, ten times more than the number of his lancers present.[59] Such was the state of the enemy force, which inspired in us a carelessness, which Ney took advantage of to save the remnants of his corps.

In the twilight following the action on 6 (18) November, he moved along a country road and, for a stretch, across country, without guides with 3,000 men, leading them himself in order to break through to Orsha along a route leading through Krasny, he decided to cross to the right bank of the Dnieper and led his soldiers down any streams he came across, in the hope that they flowed into the Dnieper, and that, by heading downstream, the troops would reach the river bank. Upon arrival at a village abandoned by its inhabitants (Danilovka?), Ney assembled all his divisional generals and senior officers of the corps headquarters for a meeting, while the detachment

---

59 General Raevsky's notes. Adjutant General Meller-Zakomelsky's report to General Konovnitsyn, dated 7 [19] November.

settled down to rest around their bivouac fires. Having fully explained the gravity of their situation, the fearless marshal said that the only means of saving the remnants of the corps was a forced march to the Dnieper and a crossing of this river. Orders were issued to build large fires and to leave a few men to maintain them, while, in the meantime the force moved on, taking with them a lame peasant they had captured as a guide. To the questions: is it far to the Dnieper and is it possible to cross the river on the ice, the peasant answered that four *versts* from there, near the village of Syrokorenie, the river, in all likelihood, would be frozen solid. Heavy snow blinded the men in the darkness of the night; the moderate cold following severe frosts foreshadowed a thaw, diminishing hopes of a successful crossing. In spite of this, however, the troops marched with good fortune but, upon arrival at the Dnieper, found that, at the places where it was possible to cross the ice on foot, access to the river channel was restricted by rather steep banks. While some of the soldiers were looking for the most convenient places to climb down to the river, the wounded went to the huts of a neighbouring village, where the surgeons tried to give them aid and change their initial dressings; others busied themselves getting food. Meanwhile, a most advantageous place was found for crossing on the ice between the villages of Syrokorenie and Gusino (near the village of Varechki). At about midnight they were ordered to stand to arms for the crossing; artillery, carts, the wounded who did not have the strength to move with the force, were left behind. Due to the fragility of the ice, only a few horses were able to be brought across the river, and when the men crowded together, they fell through and perished; many of them were forced to crawl across the creaking ice on all fours. Having made this dangerous crossing, the French moved on towards Orsha, along scarcely detectable paths hidden in deep snow through the forest, constantly driven astray by the heavy blizzard, and after a three-hour march arrived at a village, where they managed to find a small amount of flour and potatoes. Fires were kindled and the soldiers, encouraged by the hope of salvation, although they trembled from the cold and damp, reminisced about their emperor, saying: 'Bah! he would know how to get us out of this dog of a country.'[60] The blizzard continued all night, but it did Ney's detachment a favour, concealing their presence from the Cossacks in pursuit. At dawn on 7 (19) November, having already passed the village of Gusino, abandoned by the inhabitants, but having delivered some scraps of food for the detachment, the French headed along the road to Lyubavichi. Along this route, the enemy found food supplies in all the villages and, having replenished their strength, hoped for salvation, but Platov's Cossacks soon caught them up.

If Ney had been pursued persistently after the action on the Losmina on 6 (18) November, and been attacked on the Dnieper by even a small element of the regular force, while Platov, moving along the other bank of this river, could have engaged them from the front, then the French detachment would have been subjected to total destruction. It has been claimed that on the evening of 6 (18) November, after Ney's defeat, General Opperman [Karl Ivanovich Opperman], who knew the surrounding area well, brought to Konovnitsyn's attention that, at one of the bends of the Dnieper

---

60 'Bah! il saura bien nous tirer de ce chien de pays.'

near Syrokorenie, the river between its high banks was always frozen over earlier than in other places, and that Ney could conveniently get away in this direction. The orders preserved in the archives issued in the name of the Commander-in-Chief to generals Golitsyn and Miloradovich, in which, among other things, they were instructed: 'monitor the enemy with redoubled vigilance, and try to forestall them at Syrokorenie' but since these papers were only sent after the arrival of Prince Kutuzov's headquarters in Dobroe, it is very doubtful that the orders contained in them could have been executed in a timely manner.[61]

It is impossible not to admit that Ney owed much of the salvation of the remnants of his corps to the poor perseverance of our pursuit. Although our men were in an incomparably better condition than the enemy's, they were extremely exhausted by the efforts and hardships of a winter campaign. In such circumstances, extraordinary energy was required of the commanders in order to subject their own troops to even more hard work and hardships for the final destruction of the enemy army, whose demise seemed inevitable even without a relentless pursuit.

French historians rightly praise Ney's courage, who not only retained his presence of mind in the most difficult of situations, but knew how to use it to inspire his soldiers. For three days, he moved through unfamiliar countryside, with the remnants of his corps, without artillery, surrounded by Cossacks, who cut off his retreat several times. On the evening of 7 (19) November, he was forced to divert off the road leading to Lyubavichi, heading to the left through the forests along the Dnieper; but even here the Cossacks were waiting for him. It was necessary to break through by force and, after giving the detachment a rest in the night, he set out at dawn on 8 (20) November, because it was still more than 30 *versts* (*huit lieues*) to Orsha; as soon as the French came out into the open, the Cossacks reappeared. Several guns of the Don artillery, mounted on sleds, drove up to the retreating column and opened fire with canister; then, getting carried away by the utter disarray of the enemy, Platov ordered the Cossacks to 'charge with the lance.' Whereupon Ney, having formed the remnants of his divisions into two squares, forcibly placed all the unattached men who still had their muskets into their ranks and sent skirmishers to keep the Cossacks at long range from the squares, but the men of the Don, herding a crowd of marauders in front of them, closed up to the

---

61 Log of outgoing documents, 1812 (Archive of the M.T.D. No. 29,172. Orders for Lieutenant General Prince Golitsyn 5th: '6 [18] November, Dobryanka (Dobroe?). According to various intelligence reports from prisoners, it appears that Ney's corps of 3,000 is stretched out from Smolensk to Krasny. It is probable that the enemy, desiring to clear a route, will dash to the right or to the left in order to evade us, as a result of which His Grace has ordered that your troops redouble their vigilance, sending patrols out as often as possible in order to discover their actual direction and to forestall them. Syrokorenie is a convenient crossing over the Dnieper, thus it would be best to keep Syrokorenie in mind.' General Miloradovich received similar orders with the following supplement: 'The Cossack regiments that were in the lead, under the command of Major General Karpov, and belonging to elements of IV Corps, are preferably to again rejoin those regiments. This would be absolutely essential to prevent the enemy from racing to the right through Kobyzevo.' These orders and some others immediately following them in the Log of Outgoing Documents are entered without serial numbers, in contrast, as all other documents are numbered, this gives reason to doubt that they were dispatched in a timely manner.

French force and showered them with canister. Several times the enemy, driven to despair, seemed ready to scatter and seek salvation in flight; but the presence of Marshal Ney, *le brave de braves* (the bravest of the brave), as the French called him, his calmness and steadfastness kept the detachment in order and helped the enemy reach the village of Yakubovo at around noon. Here, having occupied the houses and the surrounding forest with skirmishers, the marshal decided to defend himself to the bitter end and kept his word: 'holding on with ferocious stubbornness' as Platov wrote in his report. Meanwhile, in the morning, a Polish officer Przebendowski had been sent to the *État-major général* with a report from Ney about the perilous situation of the French detachment. At the moment this news arrived in Orsha, Napoleon had already left from there on the road to Borisov, but the forces under the Viceroy and Davout were still holding the city. The Viceroy immediately moved himself to assist Ney with some of the remnant of his corps, while Ney, having set out from Yakubovo at nine o'clock in the evening, took the shortest route to Orsha. His small detachment were ordered to maintain perfect silence and quicken their pace. After covering about ten *versts*, Ney linked up with the Viceroy's vanguard and, under escort of the men of *4e Corps* who formed the rearguard, continued the onward retreat to Orsha, where he led in some 800 to 900 men.[62] The feat accomplished by Ney is worthy of astonishment, even though he only managed to save a small part of the force under his command in the action at Krasny.

The battle of Krasny, from 3 to 6 (15 to 18) November, completed the atrophy of the already very disordered enemy army: more than 26,000 prisoners,[63] including seven generals and 300 officers, several Eagles, 116 guns (not counting 112 abandoned by the enemy along the highway within 17 *versts* of Smolensk and found by *Sotnik* Nazkin), and the baton of Marshal Davout captured in his baggage, were the trophies of the actions around Krasny; the enemy losses in killed and wounded cannot be determined exactly, but, judging by the estimated information collected, it reaches at least 6,000 men. On our side, some 2,000 were killed or wounded.[64] But no matter how great the results of the actions at Krasny, there is no doubt that they could even have been much greater if we had acted more aggressively. Gourgaud, with a speculative explanation for the slowness of the advance by the Russian army, believed that 'Kutuzov did not want to attack the French because the real Russian army had died in the battle of Borodino, and the newly formed one had been defeated at Maloyaroslavets and Vyazma, despite their five-fold superiority

---

62 Fezensac, 106-119. Labaume, 373. Platov's report to Prince Kutuzov, dated 8 [20] November, No. 194, from the village of Makarovka (near Yakubovo). An intercepted letter from one of the officers of the French *État-major général* dated 22 November new style from Orsha. Ségur, 297-308. *Das Buch vom Jahr 1812*, III, 183-194. The description of Ney's retreat from Krasny to Orsha found in the latter work, contains some details that are contradicted by the testimony of the eyewitnesses; Fezensac's and the French officer's from the *État-major général*.
63 Prisoners captured by the forces: under Tormasov – 4,000; under Miloradovich from 3 to 5 [15 to 17] November – 5,170; under Miloradovich on 6 [18] November – 12,000; under Count Osterman – 4,000; in pursuit of Ney – 1,000; total: 26,170. From the War Diary and formation after-action reports.
64 War Diary. The total of prisoners taken by our troops includes not only those who were in the ranks, but also marauders and unarmed men.

in numbers of troops.' An impartial account of events, based on evidence from both sides, persuades us of the groundlessness of such conclusions: neither at Maloyaroslavets, nor at Vyazma, did the number of Russian troops actually fighting exceed the strength of the enemy operating against them; it is even stranger to read that we were defeated in these battles, one of which resulted in the disastrous retreat of the *Grande Armée* back to the devastated Smolensk road against the will of Napoleon, and in the other, our men took trophies and many prisoners from the battle. Consequently, Kutuzov acted hesitantly at Krasny, not so much out of distrust of the quality of his troops (although there were many recruits among them), but rather having a dread of engaging with a brilliant opponent face to face, whose superiority was instinctively acknowledged by all of Napoleon's contemporaries.[65] This de facto predominance of Napoleon was so powerful that despite the fact that the weakening of his army was already obvious to everyone by this time, and even more so to the experienced Kutuzov, our commander, instead of taking advantage of this situation to end the war with a decisive blow, left the completion of the destruction of the enemy army to the effects of hunger, cold and the collapse of discipline. Kutuzov was fully aware that many of our most worthy generals did not approve of his modus operandi, and therefore, wanting to justify himself to public opinion, he guaranteed that Napoleon's forces would be subjected to complete destruction. Prinz Eugen von Württemberg wrote that the Field Marshal, meeting with him in one of the villages between Krasny and Orsha, said to him: 'Our young men are hotly annoyed with me for reining in their elan. They do not realise that the environment itself is more effective than our weapons. We must not arrive at the border, like a crowd of vagabonds!'[66] It is also claimed that when the British General Wilson [Robert Thomas Wilson], who was at our headquarters, urged Kutuzov to take decisive action, he replied: 'I do not believe that the destruction of Napoleon's regime would be at all advantageous for Europe; this would lead to the predominance of Britain, instead of the present predominance of France.'

Indeed, after the actions at Krasny, the French *Grande Armée* had completely lost its combat capability. But the moral effect of our success was diminished by the fact that not only our enemies, but also those nations which owed their liberation to Russia, would (as later happened) attribute the demise of Napoleon's army in 1812 solely to the effects of the climate. And the material results of our Patriotic War, for all their immensity, could have been much greater: none of the French marshals were

---

65 [Liprandi comments: 'What dread could Kutuzov have regarding his force while their main mass remained spectators and elements of it consistently defeated each enemy corps coming from Smolensk to Krasny on successive days? He witnessed that the total losses were negligible for us and enormous for the enemy, to the extent that it was impossible to count them, as we saw above.' Adding: 'This is an obvious libel against our Field Marshal. Kutuzov had not been afraid to face this brilliant man in the field at Borodino, with weaker numbers than the enemy, when that man was still at the height of his glory, while here, at Krasny, he dreaded to come face to face, being stronger, fresher than the forces of the genius, troops that had already lost a significant part of their artillery, half had discarded their weapons, without cavalry, hungry, half-naked, exhausted, who were taken prisoner in their thousands within sight of Kutuzov himself, yet he was afraid! No'].
66 Eugen von Württemberg, 171-172.

captured; although only a tenth of the 500,000 enemy troops returned from Russia, however, it included many officers and a cadre which gave Napoleon the opportunity to form a new army by next spring and successfully resist the Russo-Prussian army. That which later required the participation of Germany in the continuation of the bloody campaigns of 1813 and 1814, the same results, in all likelihood, could have been accomplished in 1812 by Russian troops alone, with fewer losses and with greater glory. But for Kutuzov, invested with full authority by Emperor Alexander I in the fateful year of the struggle of our Fatherland with Napoleon, it was difficult to decide on operations whose outcome were not so obvious then as they are now, and this made him prefer a less brilliant, but surer, modus operandi. Kutuzov himself, setting out in a report to the Tsar the reasons for the slow pursuit of the French by our troops, confessed his mistakes and attributed them to the impossibility of obtaining accurate intelligence about the enemy at every moment of operations, which quite often forces one to base military assessments on conjecture and hearsay.[67] Was it possible to demand from the sixty-seven-year-old commander, who was already standing with one foot in the grave, that he act otherwise than cautiously?

So thought the overall leader of the Patriotic War, Emperor Alexander I. Having assessed, with His characteristic faithful vision, what had been achieved at Krasny, He repeatedly expressed regret about the hesitancy of our operations during the enemy army's retreat to the Dnieper; but he rewarded Prince Kutuzov for the victory at Krasny and across the Smolensk Governorate in general, ordering him to be titled Prince of Smolensk. Miloradovich, as the main perpetrator in the defeat inflicted on the enemy at Vyazma and Krasny, was awarded the Order of St George, 2nd class; Platov was elevated to the dignity of a count.

Once Smolensk had been reoccupied by our troops, work was immediately begun establishing the central magazine in this city and transporting supplies there from Tver, Vyshny Volochyok and the surrounding areas.[68] But the non-stop offensive by the Russian armies did not allow these stores to be distributed and the troops had to be fed through regional resources supplemented by magazines recaptured from the enemy.

Upon entering the Mogilev Governorate, the Field Marshal issued the following orders: 'On entering Belorussia with the army, into that region where, during the invasion by the enemy, some of those with ill intentions, taking advantage of the confusion at that time, tried to mislead the peaceful inhabitants and to divert them from their sacred duties sealed by an oath to their lawful Sovereign, I find it necessary in all the armies led by me to strictly forbid any spirit of vengeance or reproach for anything done by the inhabitants of Belorussia, and even less any infliction of insults or harassment on them; but on the contrary, let them see us as brothers, as compatriots and subjects of our Most Merciful Tsar, protectors from a common enemy and comforters in all that they have suffered in their short occupation under the yoke of an alien and violent power, and with our coming, let peace and tranquillity be established among them.

---

67 Prince Kutuzov's report to Emperor Alexander I, dated 7 [19] November, No. 464. For the full text, see Appendix V.
68 Prince Kutuzov's letter addressed to the Minister of War, dated 7 [19] November.

To the population of Belorussia, it is announced: not to offer any advantage to the enemy, either directly or indirectly, nor to provide them with information, and whoever acts contrary to this from now on will be condemned to suffer execution according to martial law; but through good behaviour and obedience to these orders, they can also erase the perception that some of them have given about themselves through their actions. These orders are to be announced both in the army and in both Belorussian governorates.'[69]

Emperor Alexander I honoured the Field Marshal with the following Rescript:

> Prince Mikhail Ilarionovich. I note with particular pleasure the precise and speedy fulfilment of My will, expressed to you upon your departure from the capital, in the orders issued by you upon the entry of the army into Belorussia. I give thanks to you for taking timely measures to preserve mutual cooperation between the population and the troops and to forget past delusions, in which the former were carried away by false promises from the common enemy regarding the restoration of their Fatherland, I am sure that you will extend the execution of the aforementioned orders to the other armies, and that, with your well-known concern for the common cause, you will not neglect to observe the execution of it in full force, both in the military and in the civilian departments.[70]

---

69 Army Orders dated 9 [21] November 1812, No. 68 (Archive of the M.T.D. No. 36,749).
70 Supreme Rescript to General Field Marshal G.-Kutuzov-Smolensky, dated 19 November [1 December], No. 337 (Log of Outgoing Directed Supreme Decrees and Rescripts, 1812. Archive of the M.T.D. No. 46,692).

37

The retreat of the enemy army from Krasny beyond the Dnieper

Composition of the enemy army after the actions at Krasny. – Napoleon's plans. – Orders issued to: Dąbrowski, Bronikowski, Oudinot and Victor. – Measures taken by Kutuzov for the pursuit of the enemy army. – Napoleon's orders in order to restore good order into the *Grande Armée*. – The composition of his forces enroute to Borisov. – The crossing of the Dnieper by our raiding detachments and General Yermolov's vanguard. – The pursuit to the Berezina river.

Having evacuated the town of Krasny of enemy troops, Napoleon, having spent the night, of 5 to 6 (17 to 18) November, in Lyady, set out from there with the *Garde* before dawn, on the route to Orsha. At this time, after freezing cold that had lasted for several consecutive days, a thaw set in; the road became muddy, which was extremely tiring for the troops. Napoleon, wanting to encourage them, got out of his carriage several times and accompanied his soldiers on foot. At five o'clock in the afternoon he arrived at Dubrowna with the remnants of the *Vieille Garde*, at an estate that belonged to Princess Lubomirskaya [Maria Lvovna Naryshkina], and stayed at her house; Davout with his corps and Mortier with the *Jeune Garde* remained in the rearguard. The troops under Zajączek and Junot reached Orsha that day, while the Viceroy was between Orsha and Dubrowna.[1] The French found a small magazine in Dubrowna; villages in the Mogilev Governorate had not been abandoned by their inhabitants and offered some means for providing the troops with supplies. But nothing could restore the order and structure of the former *Grande Armée*, the strength of which, together with dismounted cavalrymen and other elements of the force incapable of combat, after the actions at Krasny, did not exceed 25,000, in which there were almost no cavalry or artillery, because, with the exception of a few guns that remained with the force, all the others had been lost in the actions at Krasny, abandoned on the road, or were buried in cellars during the evacuation of the town. To crown Napoleon's precarious situation, news arrived in Dubrowna regarding the liberation of Vitebsk by the Russians, about Victor's

---

1 Denniée, *Itinéraire de l'empereur Napoléon*, 191. Fain, *Manuscit de 1812*, II, 276-268. Chambray, *Histoire de l'expédition de Russie,* II, 451.

unsuccessful battle at Chashniki (Smoliyantsy), on 2 (14) November, and about the occupation of Minsk on 4 (16) November, by our Army of the Danube.[2]

Having received this information, Napoleon decided to march on Minsk, take possession of this city and settle in winter quarters behind the Berezina river. In all likelihood, he was not deceiving himself regarding the difficulties that awaited him in such operations, but was trying to show self-confidence to others, which in previous wars had been constantly justified by success. To that end, orders were issued: to General Dąbrowski [Jan Henryk Dąbrowski] to assemble the troops of his division in Borisov and defend the bridgehead built opposite this town; to the governor of Minsk, Bronikowski, to retreat to link up with Dąbrowski and with the men of the main army towards Borisov; to Marshal Oudinot [Nicolas Charles Marie Oudinot], also to go immediately with his corps to Borisov, to assimilate Dąbrowski's division and Bronikowski's formation into his force and move as the vanguard of the army towards Minsk in order to capture this city; he was also ordered to prepare 30 guns for transfer to other corps, which had an extreme shortage of artillery. Finally, Marshal Victor was ordered to protect Borisov, Vilna and Orsha through the disposition of his troops, such that by the time that the army, upon reaching Minsk, was settled on the Berezina, he could move to the Upper Berezina, secure the Vilna road and establish communications with *6e Corps* (withdrawn into Lithuania at the time); he was also ordered to send a return of the artillery that was attached to his corps, in order to redistribute the guns to the corps of the former *Grande Armée*.[3]

The situation of the enemy forces, after the casualties they had suffered at Krasny, was desperate. Not only were almost all the guns lost, but also the most essential transport. The number of individuals, throwing down their weapons and straggling in disarray after the force, constantly increased. Many of the soldiers who remained under arms, were emaciated, with overgrown beards, almost completely blinded from bivouac smoke, with frostbitten hands and feet, could not recognise each other and were completely discouraged. On 7 (19) November, before dawn, Napoleon's *État-major général* was suddenly alarmed by cries of: *aux armes!* The *Garde* formed up for battle, but it emerged that the cause of this panic was the appearance of a handful of Cossacks.[4]

Napoleon, witnessing the complete disorder of his force, which had spread even among the *Garde*, set off from Dubrowna with them, at dawn on 7 (19) November, halting the infantry of the *Vieille Garde*, forming them into square, dismounted from his horse and standing in the middle of the square, turned to the soldiers with with the following speech: 'Grenadiers of my *Garde*! you see the disorder of the army; many of the soldiers, with disastrous short-sightedness, have discarded their weapons. If you follow this destructive example, then there is no hope left for us. The salvation of the army depends upon you; you will justify the regard in which I have always held you. It is not enough that the officers concern themselves with maintaining strict discipline; you yourselves must mind one another and punish

---

2 Fain, 268-269.
3 Orders for the *chef d'état-major*, Berthier, dated 18 November new style. Orders for Marshal Victor, dated 19 November new style, from Dubrowna. Chambray, II, 451-452.
4 Chambray, II, 454.

those who leave the ranks.'5 On that same day, at about one o'clock in the afternoon, Napoleon arrived in Orsha and settled down together with the *État-major général* in the Jesuit monastery.6

Meanwhile, on 5 (17) November, on the day of the fight against Napoleon's *Garde* at Krasny, the partisan Seslavin had proposed sending elements of the army to Zverovichi, Baevo and Chirino, towards Dubrowna, such that the enemy could be overtaken in the event of them crossing over the Dnieper at the latter point; according to Seslavin, it was essential to move our main forces there following the defeat of the French at Krasny, detaching only a small part of the force along the highway to Lyady.7 But this proposal from the valiant partisan was not executed, and only the detachment under Baron Rosen (consisting of the Lifeguard infantry with two cuirassier and three Cossack regiments) received permission to move along the highway, but no further than Lyady.8 Even before their arrival there, Major General Borozdin had driven the enemy out of this town at dawn on 7 (19) November, captured five guns and several prisoners, pursued the French to the village of Bolshaya-Kolotovka and settled down alongside the detachment under Count Ozharovsky at Mikhalinovo; while Rosen's force arrived at Lyady in the evening.9 On that same day, 7 (19) November, General Yermolov proposed to the Field Marshal that he be entrusted with command of Rosen's detachment, supported by part of the army. Kutuzov agreed to this proposal. The following units formed Yermolov's vanguard: the Lifeguard Jägers, Lifeguard Finland Regiment, His Majesty's Cuirassiers, Her Majesty's Cuirassiers, Lifeguard Foot Artillery, a horse- artillery battery, six battalions from VI Corps and two Cossack regiments.10 The Field Marshal ordered him to go to Dubrowna and transfer some of his infantry to the right bank of the Dnieper to assist Platov, who intended to fix the enemy at the crossing point at Dubrowna or Orsha, but did not manage to forestall them. The detachment under General Borozdin moved towards Dubrowna ahead of Yermolov; Count Ozharovsky turned left towards Gorki, where, according to intelligence provided by Seslavin, there were enemy magazines and depots, while Davydov headed towards Kopys.11 The Field Marshal, having received intelligence that significant stores had also been collected in Mogilev for the French army, guarded by a small number of troops, ordered Count Ozharovsky to go to Mogilev, take possession of the magazines and disband the

---

5 Chambray, II, 455.
6 Deniée. 191. Fain, II, 272.
7 Captain Seslavin's letter to General Konovnitsyn, dated 5 [17] November. Log of Incoming Documents, No. 530.
8 A.P. Yermolov's notes.
9 Borozdin's report, dated 7 [19] November. Log of Incoming Documents, No. 546. Baron Rosen's report, dated 7 [19] November. Log of Incoming Documents, No. 566.
10 A.P. Yermolov's notes. In the orders for General Yermolov (Log of Outgoing Documents, No. 460), it states that 'his detachment consisted of 12 battalions and two Cossack regiments, with artillery.' Buturlin, II, 226.
11 A.P. Yermolov's notes. Borozdin's report, dated 8 [20] November, from Dubrowna (Log of Incoming Documents, No. 582). Count Ozharovsky's report, dated 8 [20] November, from Gorki (Log of Incoming Docs. No. 581). Davydov's report, dated 7 [19] November from Lanniki (Log of incoming Docs, No. 576). For an extract from Captain Seslavin's report, dated 8 [20] November (Log of Incoming Docs. No. 580), see Appendix VI.

enemy established administration. Lieutenant General Shepelev [Vasily Fëdorovich Shepelev] was sent there with the Kaluga *Opolchenie*, while Count Gudovich, in order to assist Ozharovsky and Shepelev, was assigned to cross the Dnieper and move between Mogilev and Belynichi [Białynicze], on the Minsk road with the Malorussia *Opolchenie*.[12]

The Field Marshal, informing Count Wittgenstein of the enemy defeat at Krasny, wrote to him that, in accordance with the circumstances, the formations of our main army were deployed as follows:

> General of Cavalry Platov is operating on the right bank of the Dnieper with 15 Cossack regiments, the Don artillery and 1st Jägers. He has been ordered not only to constantly harass the enemy from the flank, but also to get ahead of their leading column. Adjutant General Golenishchev-Kutuzov is operating to his right and has already reached Dubrowna in cooperation with Platov. Three partisans are escorting the enemy on the left bank,[13] constantly harassing the enemy on the march, one of whom is near Orsha. Our vanguard is pressing on their rearguard. The army is making a swift flank march towards Kopys, where, after crossing the Dnieper, they will take directions in accordance with the movements of the enemy army. From this you can see that your operations against the enemy on our right flank are helpful and will be supported by Platov and Adjutant General Kutuzov, who have been given the instructions below.[14]

The Field Marshal, hoping that Count Wittgenstein, with the assistance of the detachments marching on the right bank of the Dnieper, would prevent Napoleon from heading for the Dvina, focussed most of his attention on blocking the enemy routes to the left of the highway, moving along which Napoleon could (as seemed likely then) establish communications with the Austrian corps under Schwarzenberg. Having remained in the vicinity of Krasny for the duration of 7 (19) November, on the following day, the main body of the Russian army moved in two columns to Romanovo,[15] while on 9 (21) November they moved to Lanniki, where they stopped in anticipation of the crossing of the Dnieper at Kopys by General Miloradovich, with the vanguard of II Corps, VII Corps, II Cavalry Corps and four Cossack regi-

---

12 Orders dated 9 [21] November, to Count Ozharovsky, No. 469, to Count Gudovich, No. 470, and to General Shepelev, No. 471 (Log of Outgoing Documents).
13 Davydov, Borozdin and Count Ozharovsky.
14 Orders dated 7 [19] November (Log of Outgoing Documents, No. 466).
15 The right hand column, under General Dokhturov's command, moving to Zverovichi towards Romanovo, comprising I Cavalry Corps, 1st Cuirassier Division, V Corps and VI Corps; the left hand column, under Count Osterman's command, moving to Polyanka to Starosele, comprised IV Cavalry Corps, IV Corps and 27th Division. General Miloradovich proceeding behind the right hand column with II Cavalry Corps, II Corps, III Corps, VII Corps and 2nd Cuirassier Division. The headquarters was relocated to Romanovo, while the troops settled down in quarters in the surrounding villages. The following were left to round up enemy marauders who were wandering between Krasny and the Dnieper: 2nd Grenadier Division with one Cossack regiment at Syrokorenie, and a brigade from 27th Division with another Cossack regiment at Krasny. Buturlin, II, 233-234.

ments. Meanwhile, Platov and the partisans dashed towards the Dnieper in order to defeat the enemy at the river crossing points, but they had retreated so quickly that there was no way to overtake them.[16]

Upon Napoleon's arrival at Orsha, he immediately set about reorganising and restructuring the remnants of his army. The troops received provisions and weapons from the stores there; in order to reincorporate marauders, collection points were assigned in Orsha, Barany and Kokhanovo. In Orsha there were 36 guns and two pontoon parks. Napoleon decided to sacrifice the pontoons in order to provide the artillery with horses: of the six newly formed batteries, two were given to the Viceroy, who had lost all his artillery, two batteries went to Davout's corps, which had only eight guns left, and two were handed over to Latour-Maubourg's cavalry. The pontoon parks and all the surplus carts were burned. The soldiers were permitted to carry only bread, linen and footwear.[17] All these measures, which, had they been enforced upon leaving Moscow, would have had undoubted benefits, could no longer improve matters when retreating from the Dnieper to the Berezina.

On the following day, 8 (20) November, Napoleon, preparing to move out of Orsha, ordered Marshal Victor to station himself at Chereya with his corps, initially to cover the army's march from Orsha to Borisov from the flank, and then to move behind them, as the rearguard.[18] As in the meantime, there was still no word about Ney, Napoleon decided to move on without waiting for him, ordering the marshal and the Viceroy to stay only a few hours in Orsha, and departing on 8 (20) November at noon, arrived in Barany in the evening. Gourgaud rode there after him with a report that Ney was just a short stage from Orsha and that the Viceroy had gone to meet him with 4,000 men. Napoleon, who had thought Ney was dead, upon learning of his salvation, said: *'J'ai deux cents millions dans mes caves de Tuilleries, je les aurais donné pour sauver le maréchal Ney...'* (I have two hundred million in my vaults at Tuileries, I would have donated them to save Marshal Ney).[19] Over the following days, the enemy troops continued to move without pause along the road to Borisov. Their situation was somewhat improved by the fact that, on the occasion of the thaw, which began on 6 (18) November, the nights in the bivouacs were more tolerable than before; but when it began to rain on 8 (20) November, which continued intermittently for several days in succession, then the movement of the men through deep, softened snow and through mud became very onerous, especially since the soldiers, having completely worn out their shoes, had wrapped their feet in all sorts of rags that did not protect against the sludge and damp at all. The villages, which for the most part had remained intact, provided dry wood for campfires; the magazines found in Dubrowna and Orsha served to supply the army with foodstuffs, and in general, beyond the Dnieper, there were some sources of food for the troops. But having said that, the soldiers, and especially the marauders, who did not receive provisions from the magazines, ate a stew of flour, or cereals, and horse meat. The incessant marches by the troops, who were in dire need of rest, and

---

16 War Diary.
17 Orders for the Army, dated 19 November new style.
18 Orders for Victor, dated 20 November new style.
19 Fain, II, 275.

lodging for the night in bivouacs, in ragged, damp clothing, completed the disorder of the *Grande Armée*. Physical suffering was accompanied by discouragement; insubordination and the nomadic life thinned the ranks of the troops: on the first stage from Orsha towards Borisov, the detachment under Latour-Maubourg was reduced to 200 men; the cavalry attached to the infantry corps were even fewer; while the *cavalerie de la Garde*, which provided the escort for Napoleon's *État-major général*, did not exceed 1,600 men.[20] The insignificant reinforcements that joined the army could not compensate for its losses.[21] The French army was in these positions when Napoleon, approaching Tolochin [Tołoczyn], on 10 (22) November, received a report from Marshal Oudinot about the capture of the Borisov bridgehead by Russian forces. This news was so unexpected for Napoleon that he, unable to hide his dismay, said: 'it is therefore decided that we shall achieve nothing but follies!'[22]

Meanwhile, the leading formation under Major General Borozdin 2nd had occupied Dubrowna on 8 (20) November; but General Borozdin, not bothering to repair the bridge destroyed there by the French, moved further on to Orsha. When Yermolov arrived in Dubrowna with his vanguard [21 November new style] and, following the order given to him, wanted to establish communications with Platov, who was on the right bank of the Dnieper, he was forced to halt, awaiting the reconstruction of the crossing. General Yermolov, having learned that the previous bridge in Dubrowna had been built by one of the inhabitants of the town under the guidance of a French officer, forced him to repair this bridge once more, and supplied him with chains and ropes from the artillery and regimental transport necessary for the reconstruction, and remained at work almost incessantly for a day and a half. Upon the restoration of the bridge, the infantry crossed over without stopping; the guns were manhandled on thick planks laid along the bridge; it was incomparably more difficult to move the horses, because the bridge under them wobbled and threatened to collapse at any minute. The horses of both cuirassier regiments could only be transported by binding their legs, laying them on their sides and dragging them along the planks; the Cossack horses were driven across the river by swimming. As soon as the force was across, General Yermolov hurried to link up with Platov, while floating ice thickened on the Dnieper and destroyed the bridge, as a result of which, all the carts, some of the cartridge caissons and all the ration wagons remained on the highway, on the other side of the river and were subsequently sent directly to Orsha.[23]

On 9 (21) November, on the same day that Yermolov's detachment arrived in Dubrowna, General Platov, approaching Orsha, attacked the enemy and forced them to evacuate the city, which had been set on fire during the retreat by the French. Colonel Kaisarov, having entered Orsha, immediately set about extinguishing fires and was made aware of the military booty left by the enemy. Sixteen guns and a small magazine were found in the city. During the pursuit to Orsha, many prisoners

---

20 Chambray, III, 10-12.
21 These reinforcements consisted of: the Orsha garrison, a cavalry depot set up in Gorki, and the Mogilev garrison, heading for the highway at Bobr. Chambray, III, 13.
22 *'il est donc decidé que nous ne ferons que des sottises!'* Chambray, III, 15.
23 A.P. Yermolov's notes.

were captured by the Cossacks, and among them was one of the chief officials of the enemy army, from the commissariat (*commissaire-ordonnateur-général*), Puybusque [Louis-Guillaume de Puybusque], the author of Letters on the War in Russia.[24]

At the same time as Orsha was being liberated, our other leading formations also reached the Dnieper. Adjutant General Count Ozharovsky, having arrived in Gorki on 8 (20) November, found no enemy there, as they had, in the meantime, retreated along the road to Kopys. Count Ozharovsky, having detached Major Rzhevsky [Pavel Alexeevich Rzhevsky] after them, with Shamshev's [Ivan Karpovich Shamshev?] Don Cossacks and two squadrons of hussars, gave his detachment a rest day, and then on 10 (22) November arrived at Shklov [Szkłów], where Major Rzhevsky, who had caught up with the French on the way to Kopys, rejoined him, moreover, many vehicles and 250 prisoners were captured by our forces.[25] Having received orders on 11 (23) November to go to Mogilev, Count Ozharovsky set out the next day [24 November new style], in two columns, along the highway and to the town of Knyazhitsy (towards where, according to intelligence received, the Polish troops that had set out from Mogilev were moving at the time). On the way to Mogilev, Count Ozharovsky was informed by several residents who had come out to meet our detachment that the enemy who remained in the city had threatened to burn it down. Taking the necessary horses from the Poltava Cossacks who were part of the detachment, Ozharovsky put some jägers on horseback, and, having galloped with the jägers and cavalry to the city, scattered the enemy who were there. Meanwhile, Staff Captain Nashchokin [Fëdor Alexandrovich Nashchokin] of the Lifeguard Hussars, moving with the second column through Knayzhitsy, drove off the enemy detachment retreating through this place and put them to flight, while some 100 men were captured. Magazines were found in Mogilev and bakeries were immediately set up to make bread and hardtack.[26]

Lieutenant Colonel Davydov, on the march from Lanniki to Gorki, having intercepted a courier sent by *chef d'état-major* Berthier to the commander of the depot in Gorki, with a duplicate of the order to retreat to Kopys immediately, decided to divert to this latter location, attacked the enemy there on the morning of 9 (21) November, and took 285 men prisoner and captured a large number of wagons. Following that, Davydov and Seslavin, having received orders; 'to establish communications, if possible, with Admiral Chichagov, who should be in Borisov with his army, on or about 10 [22] November' headed for the Berezina river via forced marches.[27] On the other side of the French army's line of retreat, Adjutant General Kutuzov, having travelled 540 *versts* in 14 days since departing Moscow, arrived in Babinovichi on

---

24 Platov's report to Prince Kutuzov, dated 7 [19] November, No. 193 (Log of Incoming Documents No. 586); *Lettres sur la guerre de Russie*.
25 Count Ozharovsky's report to General Konovnitsyn, dated 11 [23] November, No. 28 (Log of Incoming Documents No. 600).
26 Count Ozharovsky's report to General Konovnitsyn, dated 13 [25] November, No. 29 (Log of Incoming Documents No. 610).
27 Orders for Lieutenant Colonel Davydov, dated 9 [21] November (Log of Outgoing Documents No. 473). Lieutenant Colonel Davydov's letter to General Konovnitsyn, dated 12 [24] November (Log of Incoming Documents No. 615). Orders for Captain Seslavin, dated 11 [22] November (Log of Outgoing Documents No. 490).

9 (21) November, sent patrols towards Tolochin in order to block the route to the enemy, and established communications with Count Wittgenstein.[28] The Field Marshal, intending to head along country roads to the left of the Orsha highway towards Kopys, where it was possible to quarter the army in villages that had not been devastated and find some sources of food for the force, ordered Miloradovich to set out on 10 (22) November from the outskirts of Krasny and move to Kopys with II Corps, VII Corps and II Cavalry Corps, sending patrols out to the Dnieper as often as possible and maintaining liaison with Yermolov's vanguard.[29] General Miloradovich, having arranged a crossing for the army at Kopys, was supposed to head from there to the Borisov road at Tolochin and assimilate Yermolov's vanguard, who had received orders to halt in Tolochin and wait for the arrival of Miloradovich there.[30] Following the unification of both formations, they were assigned to move together following the enemy along the highway to Borisov.[31] But General Yermolov, having learned from a report sent to the Field Marshal from Count Wittgenstein that Marshal Victor remained in his former positions near the town of Chereya,[32] shielding the highway and Oudinot's corps from Wittgenstein's force, he considered it necessary to continue moving without halting and reported to Prince Kutuzov that the order to wait for Miloradovich's vanguard in Tolochin had only been received after the detachment had passed this location,[33] and they were now a full stage from Tolochin. Platov confirmed his agreement with this report and, for his part, commented that, upon entering the vast forests of the Minsk Governorate, he would need infantry, which is why he suggested that General Yermolov proceed behind his detachment.[34]

The Field Marshal, intending to establish communications with Chichagov, on 10 (22) November, sent *Flügel-adjutant* [equerry], Lieutenant Orlov [Mikhail Fëdorovich Orlov] to him, with orders informing the admiral of the directions given to the leading formations and the main army, in which he wrote:

> It may simply be that Napoleon, seeing the impossibility of clearing his route via Borisov to Minsk, will divert from Tolochin, or Bobr, to Igumen [Chervyen], and wants to make his way to Volhynia, to which end it would

---

28 Adjutant General Kutuzov's report to Prince Kutuzov, dated 9 [21] November, No. 142 (Log of Incoming Documents No. 614).
29 Orders for General Miloradovich, dated 9 [21] November (Log of Outgoing Documents No. 476).
30 Orders for General Yermolov, dated 11 [22] November (Log of Outgoing Documents No. 493).
31 Orders for General Miloradovich, dated 11 [22] November (Log of Outgoing Documents No. 494).
32 General Yermolov, during his absence from the headquarters, in order to fulfil the Field Marshal's special assignments, was ordered to open reports sent to the Commander-in-Chief, attaching supplementary information to them, or annotating: 'read by the Chief of Staff.' A.P. Yermolov's notes.
33 Yermolov's report to General Konovnitsyn, dated 13 [25] November (Log of Incoming Documents No. 629).
34 A.P. Yermolov's notes.

not be superfluous to monitor him with partisans in order to be notified in advance of his movement and to forestall him.[35]

In another order, sent to Chichagov three days later, Kutuzov wrote:

> If Borisov has been occupied by the enemy, then it is likely that, having crossed the Berezina, they will go by the most direct route to Vilna, going through Zembin, Pleshchenitsa [Pliešcanicy] and Vileyka [Wilejka]. To prevent this, it is necessary that Your Excellency holds the defile at Zembin with a detachment, where it is convenient to detain a much more numerous enemy.[36]

Such were the measures taken by Prince Kutuzov to block Napoleon's route. But before describing further events, I shall outline the preceding operations by Count Wittgenstein and Admiral Chichagov before their arrival in the main theatre of war.

---

35 Instructions for Admiral Chichagov, dated 10 [22] November, from Lanniki (Log of Outgoing Documents No. 485). According to Chichagov himself, these orders were delivered to him by Orlov on the night of 15 to 16 [27 to 28] November, just after his return to Borisov from Shabashevichi with the army. *Mémoires inedits de l'amiral Tchitchagoff*, 74.
36 Instructions for Admiral Chichagov, dated 13 [25] November, from Kopys (Log of Outgoing Documents No. 502). Chichagov wrote that he received this document on 18 [30] November, in Zembin, after the enemy had already crossed the Berezina, and that it was allegedly sent from the Field Marshal's headquarters retroactively. *Mémoires inedits de l'amiral Tchitchagoff*, 81-82. In any case, even if it was actually sent from Kopys on 13 [25] November, Chichagov could not have received it before the 14 or 15 [26 or 27 November], therefore, the warning about the defile at Zembin was too late.

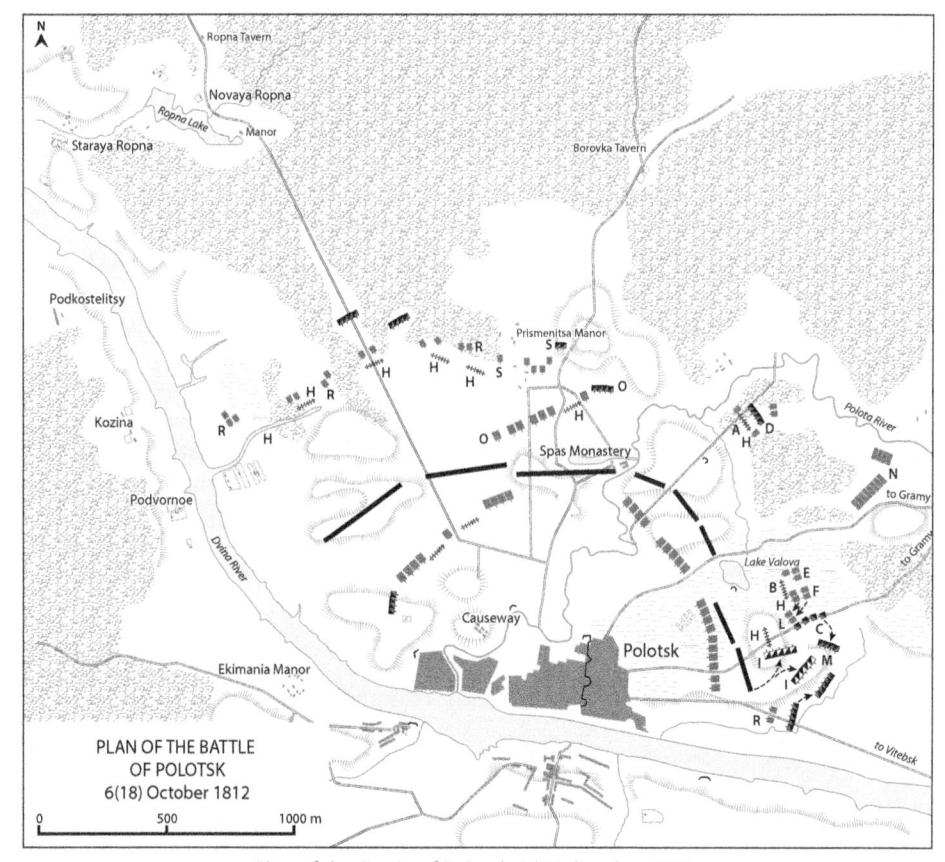

Plan of the Battle of Polotsk 6 (18) October 1812.

Legend:
Movements by both sides on 6 (18) October 1812:
A. 26th Jaeger Regiment and two squadrons of Grodno Hussars with 12 guns.
B. A battalion of 25th Jaegers and the Replacement Battalion of the Kexholm Infantry.
C. Two squadrons of Grodno Hussars and Rodionov's Cossack Regiment.
D. Sevsk Infantry Regiment.
E. Perm Infantry Regiment.
F. Mogilev Infantry Regiment.
H.H.H. Russian batteries.
I.I. French cavalry attacks.
K. Kaluga Infantry Regiment and Lifeguard Combined Cavalry Regiment.
L. Advance by the Mogilev Infantry Regiment and 6th Group, St Petersburg Opolchenie.
M. Attack by the Lifeguard Combined Regiment and Grodno Hussars.
N. Movements of the Reserve.
R.R. Initial locations of Prince Iashvili's force.
S.S. Subsequent locations of Prince Iashvili's force.
O.O. General advance by Russian forces.

38

The Second Battle of Polotsk

Count Wittgenstein's forces in early [mid] October 1812. – His plans. – The deployment of Russian troops for offensive operations. – Measures taken by Saint-Cyr. – The strength of Saint-Cyr's forces and their locations. – The advance by Wittgenstein's main force. – The deployment of Saint-Cyr's forces for the defence of the position at Polotsk. – The approach march of Russian troops to Polotsk. – The fighting on 6 (18) October. – Count Steinheil's move to Polotsk. – Wittgenstein's intent for an all-out attack on the enemy position at Polotsk. – Saint-Cyr's detachment of some of his force to face Steinheil. – The precarious situation of the French. – Saint-Cyr's retreat to the left bank of the Dvina and the assault of Polotsk on the night of 7 to 8 (19 to 20) October. – The losses on both sides. – Count Wittgenstein's orders for the troops.

Saint-Cyr's operations against Steinheil. – The defeat of the vanguard of the Finland Corps. – Steinheil's retreat to Disna and his crossing to the right bank of the Dvina. – Orders by Wittgenstein and Saint-Cyr. – The construction of a bridge and the crossing by Russian troops in Polotsk. – The retreat to Chashniki by the French *2e Corps*, while the (Bavarian) *6e Corps* took the Vilna road. – Their pursuit by Russian forces. – The unification of the Russian I Corps with the Finland Corps at Lepel. – The separation of Russian forces. – The link up between the French *2e Corps* and *9e Corps* at Chashniki.

Following the arrival of most of the reinforcements assigned to Count Wittgenstein's corps and the approach of the corps under Count Steinheil, the strength of our forces in the vicinity of Polotsk had increased significantly. In early [mid] October, there were about 40,000 men (including 9,000 *opolchenie*), with 152 guns under Wittgenstein's direct command,[1] while some 10,000 men with 18 guns were under Steinheil's command. In accordance with the general plan of operations outlined by Emperor Alexander, Count Wittgenstein decided to start crossing the Dvina. As

---

1 Combatant return on the composition of I Corps, dated 4 [16] October 1812. *Tableau des forces disponibles aux ordres du comte Wittgenstein le 4 octobre 1812* (Archive of the M.T.D. No. 29,200). Combatant return on the composition of Finland Corps, dated 22 September [4 October].

the corps did not have pontoons, engineer Colonel Count Sievers [Yegor Karlovich Sievers] was ordered to collect materials needed to build two bridges on the Dvina from Sivoshina, and carts to transport them to the place assigned for the crossing, upstream of Polotsk, near the village of Goryany; meanwhile, on their own initiative, pioneers completed the construction of a bridge of rafts at Pridruisk [Piedruja], for a crossing by Steinheil's corps, and materials were being prepared for the construction of a similar bridge in the vicinity of Disna [Dzisna], in order to have, just in case, the closest communications between both corps. In order to guard the crossing points downstream of Polotsk, Count Sievers was entrusted with a detachment under Major Bellingshausen, of two combined infantry regiments with four guns from 23rd Horse Artillery Company, numbering about 1,600 men. Upon the arrival at Disna of the Combined Hussar Regiment under Lieutenant Colonel Bedryaga, these forces were intended to link up and proceed up the left bank of the Dvina, as the vanguard of Steinheil's corps.[2] Major General Begichev [Ivan Matveevich Begichev], who had arrived on the Dvina with elements of the St Petersburg *Opolchenie*, received orders, upon reaching Nevel, to detach Major General Alekseev [Ilya Ivanovich Alekseev], with the Mittau Dragoons, 1st Marines, 15th Group of the *opolchenie* and six guns from 49th Light Artillery Company, numbering about 2,600 men, through Gorodok and Kozyany, to the village of Goryany, near the mouth of the Obol river, to protect the construction of bridges there and to clear the countryside of enemy marauders who had devastated it. The remainder of Begichev's force moved to Krasnopolye, where they joined the detachment under Major General Diebitsch [Ivan Ivanovich Dibich or Hans Karl Friedrich Anton von Diebitsch und Narten], who, upon being reinforced with six guns, on 2 (14) October headed towards Lipova as the vanguard of the column.

On 3 (15) October, all the troops under the direct command of Count Wittgenstein, were divided into three columns for the offensive on Polotsk, of which two, the centre and left, made up the first corps, under the personal command of Wittgenstein, while the third, right column, the second corps, entrusted to Lieutenant General Prince Iashvili [Levan Mikhailovich Iashvili]. The centre column, Lieutenant General Berg's [Grigory Maksimovich Berg], which was assigned to move from Sivoshina to Yurovichi, consisted of Rodionov 2nd's [Mark Ivanovich Rodionov] Cossack regiment, 16 squadrons and 18 battalions, with 56 guns, numbering about 12,000 men;[3] the left column, Major General Begichev's, directed from Krasnopolye towards Yurovichi, in cooperation with the centre column, consisted of a *Sotnia* of Cossacks,

---

2   War Diary of I Corps (Archive of the M.T.D. No. 29,200).
3   The composition of the centre column was: vanguard, under Major General Balk; four battalions from 25th Jägers and 26th Jägers, replacement battalion of the Kexholm Infantry, four squadrons of Grodno Hussars, Rodionov 2nd's Cossacks, six guns from 3rd Horse Artillery Company. *Corps de bataille*; eight battalions of infantry from 5th Division, Combined Grenadier Regiment with two squadrons of Poland Ulans (five squadrons in total), three squadrons of Riga Dragoons, 5th Battery Artillery Company, 27th Light Artillery Company and six guns from 3rd Horse Artillery Company. Reserve, under Major General Kakhovsky's command; three grenadier battalions, two Lifeguard reserve battalions, Combined Cuirassier Regiment (four squadrons), 14th Battery Artillery Company and eight guns from 23rd Horse Artillery Company.

four squadrons, eight battalions, eight Groups of *opolchenie*, and 18 guns, for a total of 9,000 men;[4] the right column, Lieutenant General Prince Iashvili's, assigned to advance along the right bank of the river Polota, in order to divert the attention of the enemy while the other two columns crossed over to the left bank of the Dvina, consisted of Platov 4th's Cossacks, seven squadrons, 14 battalions, six Groups, with 68 guns, for a total of 11,000 men.[5] Subsequently, on 5 (17) October, once our force had already closed up to Polotsk, almost all the Groups were attached to infantry regiments and the combined battalions from 5th Division and 14th Division and made up their reserves, located in the second echelon and formed in column exclusively for the assault: this combination of *opolchenie* with regular troops gave our warriors combat experience and gave them the opportunity to distinguish themselves brilliantly in several engagements against enemy forces.[6]

During the time that Count Wittgenstein was preparing for offensive operations, Marshal Saint-Cyr, knowing about the build up of Russian forces and having no hope of receiving any assistance, tried to fortify the position he had taken at Polotsk. Due to the low numerical strength in both *2e Corps* and *6e Corps*, he was forced to confine himself to a defence of the city and the construction of several fortifications in front of the city walls. However, despite the activities of the Chief of Engineers, General Dode de la Brunerie [Guillaume Dode de la Brunerie], it was impossible to complete the planned works earlier than 8 or 10 (20 or 22) October.[7]

While Wittgenstein's corps had been significantly strengthened by newly arrived reinforcements, the enemy force assembled at Polotsk, although they had been reinforced by several thousand convalescent soldiers, nevertheless counted no more than 27,000 men in the ranks, of whom 22,000 were in *2e Corps*, and 5,000 in *6e Corps*.[8]

The provisioning of these troops was fraught with extreme difficulties. By late September [early October], foraging had become onerous and dangerous, due both

---

4 The composition of the left column was: vanguard, under Major General Baron Diebitsch; four combined grenadier battalions from 5th Division and 14th Division, three battalions of the Combined Jäger Regiment, two squadrons Yamburg Dragoons, one squadron each from the Riga Dragoons and Ingermanland Dragoons, a Cossack *Sotnia* and six guns from 49th Light Artillery Company. *Corps de bataille*; replacement battalion of the Polotsk Infantry, 4th, 5th, 6th, 10th, 11th and 12th Groups of the St Petersburg *Opolchenie*, 35th Light Artillery Company. Reserve; 13th and 14th Groups of the St Petersburg *Opolochenie*.
5 The composition of the right column was: vanguard under Major General Vlastov; 23rd Jägers, 24th Jägers (four battalions), 9th and 1st Groups of the St Petersburg *Opolchenie*, four squadrons of Grodno Hussars, Platov 4th's Cossacks, and six guns from 1st Horse Artillery Company. *Corps de bataille*, under Lieutenant General Sazonov; four regiments from 14th Division (eight battalions), 2nd, 3rd, 7th and 8th Groups, Mogilev Infantry (two battalions), Combined Dragoon Regiment (three squadrons), six guns from 27th Battery Artillery Company, 28th Battery Artillery Company (11 guns), 50th Battery Artillery Company, 26th Light Artillery Company, 27th Light Artillery Company, six guns from 9th Light Artillery Company, and three guns from 1st Horse Artillery Company.
6 Buturlin, II, 257.
7 Saint-Cyr, *Memoires*, III, 120-121 & 125.
8 Chambray, II, 173. According to Saint-Cyr, in *2e Corps* there were 15,500, while in *6e Corps*, there were 2,600 men. Saint-Cyr, III, 129-130, *Situation du 6e corps à l'époque du 15 octobre* (new style).

to the devastation of the surrounding countryside and the activities of our patrols, while the delivery of provisions from Vilna was insufficient to supply the troops assembled at Polotsk. Getting forage was even more difficult. Saint-Cyr, aware of the total impossibility of feeding the cavalry and artillery horses in his corps, found it necessary to send them across the Dvina to locations where there were still stocks of oats and hay, and in the event of a general battle that would require the return of horses to the position at Polotsk, the commanders of cavalry regiments and batteries were ordered to have forage supplies in Polotsk for two days. But Count Wittgenstein launched offensive operations before these orders could be carried out, which forced Saint-Cyr to prioritise his attention exclusively on the defence of the positions he was holding.[9]

The offensive by the Russian force began on 4 (16) October. The main body of the right column under Prince Iashvili closed up to Beloe from Sivoshina and deployed behind Vlastov's [Yegor Ivanovich Vlastov] vanguard, which remained in its previous position. The vanguard of the centre column, commanded by Balk [Mikhail Dmitrievich Balk], moved from Sivoshina to Zhartsy; while General Berg went to Arteikovichi, with the main body of the column. The vanguard of the left column, under Diebitsch's command, reached the village of Mikulichi, while General Begichev reached Dretun with the *opolchenie*. The offensive by our troops, together with the flanking march by Alekseev's detachment to Gorodok, forced General Maison [Nicolas-Joseph Maison], sent to Kozyany with 2,000 men to protect foragers, to retreat and fall back on Polotsk. On the opposite side, the construction of a bridge and the location of the detachment under Colonel Sievers at Disna made the enemy concerned at being outflanked and attacked from the rear by part of our force. Saint-Cyr, intending to hold out in Polotsk while Wittgenstein crossed the Dvina with significant forces, while then moving to the left bank of the river and protecting the line of retreat of Napoleon's main army, on 4 (16) October, beyond the Dvina, detached all his cavalry to provide the most reliable monitoring of our attempted offensive, except for five squadrons left in the position.[10] General Doumerc [Jean-Pierre Doumerc], with *3e division de cuirassiers*, was instructed to guard the left bank of the river, upstream, as far as Beshankovichi, while General Corbineau [Jean-Baptiste Juvénal Corbineau], with a light cavalry brigade and three Bavarian battalions, was to monitor the bank from Polotsk to Drissa, and beyond. On that same day, the city hospitals were completely evacuated and vehicles were sent across the Dvina.[11]

The troops under Saint-Cyr, assigned to the defence of Polotsk, were deployed as follows:[12] the remnants of *6e Corps* (Bavarian), commanded by Wrede [Carl Philipp von Wrede], were entrusted with the defence of the redoubts in front of the city and

---

9 Saint-Cyr, III, 123-124.
10 Although Saint-Cyr claimed that only five squadrons were left in position, nevertheless, from the description of the subsequent action at Polotsk, it emerged that Saint-Cyr had at least eight squadrons remaining.
11 War Diary of I Corps (Archive of the M.T.D. No. 29,200). Saint-Cyr, III, 130-132. Chambray, II, 175.
12 See Plan of the Battle of Polotsk 6 (18) October 1812.

a bridgehead, protecting a bridge of rafts, built on the Dvina, near the village of Strunya, three *versts* upstream of the city; Legrand's [Claude Juste Alexandre Louis Legrand] and Maison's divisions of *2e Corps* were stationed on the left bank of the Polota between the city and earthwork No. 7; while Merle's [Pierre Hugues Victoire Merle] division (also *2e Corps*) was astride the St Petersburg road, forwards of earthworks No. 4 and No. 5. The cavalry was on the right wing close to the Dvina.[13]

On 5 (17) October, General Balk's vanguard moved from Zhartsy to the village of Yurovichi and attacked the enemy there, who were holding the left bank of Polota and part of the village lying on it. Marksmen from the 26th Jägers, scattered behind the fences and in the buildings on the left bank, opened a very rapid fire; once Diebitsch began to support the leading troops under Balk with Cossacks from his vanguard, having also arrived at Yurovichi, our jägers immediately dashed across the bridge to the left bank of the Polota. The enemy, already disordered by effective fire from 3rd Horse Artillery Company, were forced to evacuate the village and retreat to Polotsk. Afterwards, Count Wittgenstein, having arrived in Yurovichi with the main body of the corps, ordered Balk to pursue the enemy along the left bank of the Polota, while Lieutenant Colonel Stolypin [Nikolai Alekseevich Stolypin] was to clear the right bank as far as the Lazovka tavern with a special detachment, which was done.[14] At the same time, orders were sent to Prince Iashvili to push back the French forward detachments stationed on the St Petersburg and Riga roads. His vanguard, under Vlastov's command, by early afternoon had moved from Beloe to the chapel near Ropna and at four o'clock drove out the leading detachment from Merle's division; in the evening, the French, having been reinforced by one battalion of the *1er régiment suisse*, again occupied the chapel, but at night they were forced out once more by the 23rd Jägers and 24th Jägers. Meanwhile, seven *opolchenie* Groups, from among those under General Begichev's command, were attached to four infantry regiments from 5th Division and three replacement grenadier battalions,[15] while Begichev was entrusted with command of General Kakhovsky's reserve [Mikhail Ivanovich Kakhovsky], reinforced by three combined grenadier battalions and 35th Light Artillery Company.

On the morning of 6 (18) October, the force under Prince Iashvili, having established communications with Stolypin's detachment, reached the Prismenitsa manor.[16]

Count Wittgenstein, intending to attack Saint-Cyr's position decisively, both in order to ensure the construction of bridges at Goryany, and to distract the enemy from the corps under Count Steinheil (which at that time was in the vicinity of

---

13 Saint-Cyr, III, 137. Chambray, II, 175-176.
14 One combined grenadier battalion from 5th Division with 12th Group, two squadrons of Yamburg Dragoons and one squadron of Ingermanland Dragoons.
15 The groups attached were: 5th to the Perm Infantry, 4th to the Mogilev Infantry, 10th to the Sevsk Infantry, 11th to the Kaluga Infantry, 13th to 1st Replacement Grenadier Battalion (Leib Grenadiers and Count Arakcheev's Grenadiers), 14th to 2nd Replacement Grenadier Battalion (St Petersburg Grenadiers and Tauride Grenadiers), 6th to 3rd Replacement Grenadier Battalion (Yekaterinoslav Grenadiers and Pavlov Grenadiers).
16 War Diary of I Corps. Prince Iashvili's report to Count Wittgenstein, dated 6 [18] October (Archive of the M.T.D. No. 44,585, Log of Incoming Documents No. 431).

Disna), instructed Balk's vanguard, reinforced with six more guns from 3rd Horse Artillery Company, to force the enemy out of the forest on the left bank of the Polota, and followed him himself with the main body of the corps, ordering Prince Iashvili to advance along the right bank of the Polota. The leading French detachment, occupying the village of Gromy, attempted to halt the advance by our troops, but were forced to retreat. Whereupon General Balk sent Colonel Roth [Loggin Osipovich Roth], with the 26th Jägers, 12 guns of the 3rd Horse Artillery Company and two squadrons of Grodno Hussars, down the left bank of the Polota; the 25th Jägers, replacement battalion of the Kexholm Infantry and four guns from 49th Light Artillery Company were sent to the left of Valova lake, while two squadrons of the Grodno Hussars and Rodinov 2nd's Cossacks, went even further to the left through the scrub. Colonel Rüdiger [Fëdor Vasilievich Ridiger or Friedrich Alexander Graf von Rüdiger] charged towards the enemy cavalry with the hussars, but being struck in the flank by fire from Bavarian guns positioned in the bridgehead at Strunya, was forced to veer to the right. Enemy cavalry pursued them, but were halted by the Combined Lifeguard Cavalry Regiment sent to assist Rüdiger. At the same time, Count Wittgenstein supported the 26th Jägers with the Sevsk Infantry, while the Mogilev Infantry and Perm Infantry were in support of the 25th Jägers. The 5th Battery Artillery Company was advanced in the centre, while the 27th Light Artillery Company was placed on high ground in front of the left wing.[17]

As soon as Saint-Cyr noticed the advance by our troops on the left bank of the Polota, threatening to envelope the French divisions stationed along the left bank of this river, he ordered them to change front in such a manner that Legrand's division stood behind redoubt No. 7, between the Polota and Valova lake, while Maison's division was to the right and somewhat behind Legrand's force; some of the artillery and troops that had previously held this area were left to defend the left bank of the Polota.[18]

At about 11 o'clock in the morning, at the very moment that the enemy forces were moving to the locations assigned to them, Count Wittgenstein, wanting to inspect the right wing of Saint-Cyr's position, moved towards the Vitebsk road with the Kaluga Infantry and Combined Lifeguard Cavalry Regiment and onwards towards the city along the banks of the Dvina. The enemy, noticing that this force were separated from the others by a fairly considerable distance, hoped to break through our line, and raced into the attack with several squadrons,[19] striking the flank of the light company from one direction, and the Combined Lifeguard Cavalry from the other, they threatened to drive our left-flank detachment into the Dvina. The Commander-in-Chief himself was in danger of being captured by the French horsemen who surrounded him. At this decisive moment, the replacement squadrons of the

---

17 War Diary of I Corps.
18 Saint-Cyr, III, 143.
19 Saint-Cyr claims that this brave attack was led by Captain (*chef d'escadron*) Curély, with two squadrons of the *8e Chevau-Légers Lanciers* and *20e Chasseurs à Cheval*, while the remaining cavalry was located at other points in the position. *Mémoires*, III, 143-145. In fact, Saint-Cyr's entire cavalry (5-8 squadrons) stood on the right flank and, in all likelihood, participated in this attack.

Combined Lifeguard Cavalry, Colonel Albrecht's Lifeguard Dragoons [Alexander Ivanovich Albrecht] and Captain Skobeltsin's Lifeguard Hussars [Vladimir Nikolaievich Skobeltsin?], charged towards the enemy, while Major Nabel [Andrei Andreevich Nabel] with a battalion of Grodno Hussars struck them in the flank and drove off the French; another unit of enemy cavalry, having captured the guns of 27th Light Artillery Company, charged at the marksmen from 6th Group and began to cut them down, but were engaged by the Mogilev Infantry and 4th Group, which gave the Grodno Hussars chance to race to assist the battery captured by the enemy and rescue the guns. The enemy cavalry were forced to retreat with significant casualties. The St Petersburg *Opolchenie* fought very bravely, hitting the enemy with musket butts and hatchets. The skirmishers, going out to the marksmen, dashed towards the enemy screen and pushed it right back to the fortifications.[20]

During these actions, General Begichev arrived on the battlefield with the reserve. Count Wittgenstein ordered him to support the centre with two combined grenadier battalions from 14th Division, the replacement battalion of the Tauride Grenadiers and St Petersburg Grenadiers, 14th Group and the Combined Cuirassier Regiment, under the command of Major General Gamen [Alexey Yuryevich Gamen]; the replacement battalion of Leib Grenadiers and Pavlov Grenadiers with 13th Group were then sent to help Roth on the right wing; two Lifeguard reserve battalions went to assist Rüdiger, who was with the 25th Jägers, the replacement battalion of the Kexholm Infantry and two squadrons of Grodno Hussars between the centre and the right wing; the replacement battalion of Pavlov Grenadiers and Yekaterinoslav Grenadiers was left behind the forest in reserve. Meanwhile, our marksmen, the skirmishers of the St Petersburg *Opolchenie* in their midst, quickly pressed forwards, driving the enemy out of their advanced fortifications. The regiments of Legrand's division, *26e régiment d'infanterie légère, 19e régiment d'infanterie de ligne* and *56e régiment d'infanterie de ligne*, forced the warriors to evacuate the fortifications; but the Perm Infantry and the reserve battalion of Tauride Grenadiers and St Petersburg Grenadiers, with 5th Group and 14th Group, charged into redoubt No. 9 at the brick works and recaptured it, while the commander of 5th Group, Chamberlain Mordvinov [Alexander Nikolayevich Mordvinov], had his leg shattered by canister shot. At the same time, Colonel Rüdiger, with the 25th Jägers and Lifeguard reserve battalions, pushed the enemy back beyond Valova lake. The Lifeguard battalions, which consisted for the most part of recruits, having asked permission to assault with fixed bayonets, fought like veteran, experienced soldiers. Marshal Saint-Cyr galloped towards Valova lake, wanting to get a feel for the course of the battle, and was wounded by a bullet in the leg, but gave orders for the bullet to be quickly removed and a first dressing applied, and continued to control the operations of the force.

Simultaneously with the attack by our centre, Lieutenant General Berg, bringing the Kaluga Infantry and the cavalry of the left wing closer to the advancing troops, contributed to their success; while Major General Begichev supported the force in the centre with combined grenadiers and artillery from the reserve, the effective fire from which forced the enemy to retreat to the city itself. French cavalry

---

20 Communique on the battle of Polotsk, from the War Diary of I Corps.

moved towards the flank of our marksmen, scattered in front of the fortifications behind Valova lake, but being attacked initially by the Riga Dragoons, and then by the Combined Cuirassiers and Combined Lifeguard Cavalry, were also forced to retreat to the city. Following this, heavy fire from enemy artillery, which was falling back, prompted Count Wittgenstein to evacuate the fortification at the brick works captured by our troops and withdraw the main body somewhat to the rear. At about four o'clock in the afternoon, our Commander-in-Chief, having called a halt to the fighting, ordered Major General Diebitsch (who had taken over command of the vanguard, in place of Balk, who had been wounded at the beginning of the battle), to extend a screen of skirmishers facing the enemy advanced fortifications and to take up positions behind.[21]

Meanwhile, as fighting on the left bank of the Polota died down and was limited to a bombardment at fairly long range, Prince Iashvili received orders to attack the enemy. Starting at dawn, Lieutenant Colonel Stolypin, pushing back the enemy outposts located at the exits from the forest, had taken possession of the Prismenitsa manor, which had been completely devastated by the enemy. Vlastov's vanguard also attacked the troops pushed forwards to the forest along the Disna and Sebezh roads, drove them off and deployed within cannon range of the forward enemy fortifications, behind which Merle's division had retreated, in accordance with previously issued orders from Saint-Cyr. The forces on both sides remained in these positions until Iashvili received a second order to attack the French. As soon as Vlastov's infantry, with 1st Group and 9th Group attached to it, moved forward, the enemy began to retreat to the city; but the *1er régiment suisse* and *2e régiment suisse* (general Candras' brigade [Jacques Lazare Savettier de Candras]), without orders, went to engage our force, dragging *3e régiment croates* and *4e régiment suisses* (Amey's brigade [François-Pierre Joseph, baron Amey]) behind them and pushed Vlastov back. The regiments that came to help him, commanded by Sazonov [Ivan Terentyevich Sazonov], held the enemy back; while the Grodno Hussars, charging into the flank of the advancing infantry, isolated the Croats and forced them to lay down their weapons. Merle's men were forced to retreat hastily behind forward fortifications No. 4 and No. 5, and to the city itself, while ours, in pursuing them, were subjected to enfilade fire from the guns emplaced in the fortifications and frontal fire from the direction of the city; at the same time, Bavarian batteries, emplaced on the left bank of the Dvina, hit the force under General Helffreich [Bogdan Borisovich Gelfreikh or Gotthard August von Helffreich], directed along the Disna road. However, despite the destructive effect of the enemy artillery, Prince Iashvili, deploying his batteries to face them, attempted to break into the city twice, but, not being able to do so, he pulled the troops back, leaving vedettes up close to the city and placing Vlastov's vanguard at Prismenitsa, alongside Stolypin's detachment; while

---

21 Major General Diebitsch's vanguard consisted of: four battalions of 25th Jägers and 26th Jägers, replacement battalion of the Kexholm Infantry, 1st Replacement Grenadier Battalion (Leib Grenadiers and Count Arakcheev's Grenadiers), two combined grenadier battalions from 14th Division, Combined Lifeguard Cavalry, four squadrons of Grodno Hussars, 3rd Horse Artillery Company (Rodionov 2nd's Cossacks were left to monitor the enemy holding the bridgehead at Strunye).

a small element of the corps, under Helffreich's command, was close to the Disna road. Count Wittgenstein, also wanting to give the troops some rest, left Diebitsch in sight of the enemy with the vanguard, while taking his remaining forces to Gromy, where the headquarters had also relocated.[22]

The Finland Corps, by the evening of that same day, was positioned at Polyudovichi (25 *versts* from Polotsk); their vanguard had reached the river Ushacha. Count Steinheil informed Wittgenstein that the Finland Corps could attack Polotsk the next day [19 October new style] from the left bank of the Dvina, while Count Wittgenstein, aware that the lack of pontoons and the impossibility of delivering materials collected from Sivoshina to Goryany, along the very poor road from Beloe to Yurovichi, prevented a bridge being built upstream of Polotsk, let Steinheil know about the outcome of the fighting and proposed that he attack the enemy in Polotsk simultaneously with an attack by I Corps.[23]

Saint-Cyr was waiting for intelligence from the cavalry detachments sent by him to the left bank of the Dvina; while Count Wittgenstein intended to attack the enemy on both banks of the Polota not before Count Steinheil had closed up to Polotsk. At ten o'clock in the morning, General Corbineau's aide de camp came to Saint-Cyr, with a report of an advance from Desna, down the left bank of the Dvina, by a Russian corps, totalling some 5,000 infantry with 12 squadrons and 12 guns, and with a request to send reinforcements. Despite the low numbers of the force defending Polotsk, Saint-Cyr was forced to weaken himself by detaching three regiments from *2e Corps*. The command of this detachment was entrusted to General Amey, which was joined by the *7e régiment de cuirassiers* under General Lhéritier [Samuel François Lhéritier de Chézelles], stationed on the left bank of the Dvina, between Polotsk and Ulla. Wittgenstein's preparations for an attack became noticeable as the cannonade intensified on the left bank of the river. But Saint-Cyr still hoped that the force he had detached would be able to hold the Russians on the Ushacha until nightfall, when suddenly, at about two o'clock in the afternoon, General Corbineau's aide de camp galloped up again, with intelligence that the detachment advancing against the French on the left bank of the Dvina, had a total of 12,000 infantry, that they had many guns with them, and that the reinforcements sent would be unable to hold them back. A few minutes later, the *vivandières* from the detachment under General Amey appeared along with wagons with the wounded: all this was visible to the Russian troops on the right flank; we also noticed that the Bavarian batteries, emplaced across the river to provide flank defence for the Polotsk fortifications, were taken from the locations occupied by them and positioned so that they could cover Corbineau's retreat with their fire and operate against Steinheil's men as they came out of the forest and into open ground close to the city.[24]

Such was the situation of Saint-Cyr's corps at three o'clock in the afternoon; on the one hand, an attack was threatened by the superior forces under Wittgenstein and Iashvili; on the other, Steinheil's corps was moving towards the French line

---

22 Communique on the battle of Polotsk, from the War Diary of I Corps. Saint-Cyr, III, 150-156. Chambray, II, 177-178.
23 War Diary of I Corps.
24 Saint-Cyr, III, 160-162.

of retreat. Many of the generals surrounding the marshal pleaded with him to retreat. But Saint-Cyr refused, believing that his first step back, once noticed by the Russians, would give them the signal to attack and induce Steinheil to pursue the troops left facing him relentlessly, which would have resulted in his taking the exits from the bridges laid by the French in Polotsk. The unexpected arrival of the hostile Finland Corps had upset all Saint-Cyr's calculations; he had no choice but to move back across the river; but he wanted to retreat by night, slowly and maintaining silence in order to completely conceal his intentions and transfer the troops to the left bank of the Dvina before we could discover this crossing. Fortunately for the French, thick fog hastened the onset of darkness, which forced Count Steinheil to halt four *versts* from Polotsk. The cannonade and musketry on the left bank of the Dvina died down, and Saint-Cyr immediately ordered General Aubry [Claude Charles Aubry de La Boucharderie] to remove the artillery from the batteries. But the execution of this order presented many difficulties: the number of guns with the force were disproportionately large; poor roads and the steep climb up the left bank of the Dvina required doubling the number of horses in harness: all these factors slowed down the French retreat. Prince Iashvili, who had received orders from the Commander-in-Chief, to open a bombardment of the enemy fortifications and city, as soon as the approach of the Finland Corps was apparent, having observed the retreat of the enemy columns along the left bank of the Dvina, from the direction of Disna, opened fire from all the batteries emplaced opposite Spas manor. According to Saint-Cyr, one of the generals from Legrand's division, out of inconceivable stupidity (*par un excès inconcevable de stupidité*), ordered the barracks to be set on fire so that the Russians could not use them; with the speed of lightning, the flames spread throughout the camp, which unveiled the marshal's intent to abandon the position he had occupied. From our side, the bombardment of the city was intensified. The many shells lobbed there set fires at several points, but the prudent orders from Saint-Cyr prevented confusion and helped the French to make the difficult retreat with the numerous vehicles that were with the force. They were ordered to retreat, ignoring our attempts to break into the city. Legrand's division was assigned to retreat first of all; they were to be followed by Maison's division and, finally, Merle with his force and with the Bavarians occupying the forward fortifications No. 4 and No. 5, on the Sebezh road. To avoid confusion, troops were directed to one of the bridges, while artillery was directed to the other.[25]

During the heavy bombardment of the city, the detachment under Major General Alekseev, having arrived at Strunya, attacked the enemy holding the bridgehead there and pushed them back beyond the Dvina. The force under the immediate command of Count Wittgenstein, attempted several times to break into the earthworks arranged to protect the city on the left bank of the Polota. Eventually, at two o'clock in the morning, the assault was ordered. By the light of the fires that enveloped the city, Vlastov burst into them from one side, while Rüdiger came in from the other. Russian soldiers, under fire from enemy marksmen occupying the earthworks, hacked down the palisades and fell dead or covered with wounds; others

---

25 Communique on the battle of Polotsk, from the War Diary of I Corps. Saint-Cyr, III, 165-167.

followed them, striving voraciously to be greeted by certain death. On the western side, in addition to a double palisade surrounded by a moat, it was necessary to cross the Polota river, flowing in a deep ravine, over which a wooden bridge had been laid, as if hanging over the abyss, adjoining the city entrance, cut through a very high hill, strongly held by the enemy. When 12th Group under State Councillor Nikolev, approached the bridge ahead of the other troops, the commander of the Group ordered governorate secretary Petrov to dash into the ravine with the skirmishers, wade across the river and shout Hurrah! as the signal for a general assault. The fearless Petrov, executing the mission assigned to him precisely, crossed the Polota and struck the enemy with fixed bayonets, who, finding themselves outflanked and not being able to see in the dark how many troops had appeared to their rear, retreated. Our warriors (*les hommes à grandes barbes*, as the French referred to them) took possession of the bridge, which the enemy had no chance to destroy, pushed off the *cheval de frise* blocking it and were the first to appear on the left bank of the Polota. According to Saint-Cyr himself, they fought with extraordinary ferocity and fearlessness.[26] General Helffreich, with 2nd Reserve Grenadier Battalion (from the St Petersburg Grenadiers and Tauride Grenadiers), and with 14th Group, captured fortification No. 10 (and was wounded); after that, his detachment, having forded the Polota, on the lower reaches of its course, also entered the city, on the side of the upper castle, and captured one gun. The enemy, having destroyed the bridges on the Dvina at three o'clock in the morning, opened heavy fire on the city from batteries placed on the left bank of the river. The cannonade was stopped on our side as soon as the troops under Saint-Cyr had retreated beyond the Dvina. The enemy losses from both days of the battle at Polotsk, on 6 and 7 (18 and 19) October, in prisoners alone, reached 2,000 men; many projectiles and large stocks of food and fodder collected by Saint-Cyr, went to the victors. The number of men lost to the enemy ranks ranged from 6,000 to 7,000.[27] On our side, some 8,000 men were killed or wounded; among the wounded, in addition to Balk, were generals Prince Sibirsky [Alexander Vasilievich Sibirsky] and Gamen, and Colonel Roth.[28]

Just before dawn, Count Wittgenstein entered the city, snatched from the hands of the enemy through the courage of Russian troops. In the morning, our soldiers entered Polotsk in triumph, but as the whole city presented a spectacle of utter ruin and was littered with corpses, Count Wittgenstein ordered that almost all the troops be withdrawn to the camp formerly occupied by the French, and accommodated in bivouacs.

---

26 '... *Ce fut un des points sur le quel les hommes à grandes barbes (comme les nommaient nos soldats), c'est à dire les milices de St Petersbourg combattirent avec le plus d'acharnement et celui de tous où les Russes montrèrent le plus d'intrépidité...*' (This was one of the locations at which the men with big beards (as our soldiers called them), that is to say the militia from St. Petersburg, fought most fiercely and that of all where the Russians showed the greatest courage). Saint-Cyr, III, 170.
27 Saint-Cyr does not say a word about the casualties suffered by his force in the battle of Polotsk, but these can be inferred from the fact that after the battle only 12,000 men remained in both of his corps. Saint-Cyr, III, 179. According to Chambray, the French lost 6,000 and the Russians 12,000. Chambray, II, 180.
28 War Diary of I Corps (Archive of the M.T.D. No. 29,200).

On that same day [20 October new style], the following order was issued in the name of the Commander-in-Chief:

> Heroes! The Almighty has heeded our prayers and Polotsk is liberated! You have harvested new laurels on the field of Mars even in the midst of the fiercest combat facing a million deaths shot from hellish fortifications, you have proved in practice that true faith and love for the Fatherland can prevail, and that which may be achieved through ardour for glory and sense of honour. The corps commander has the most agreeable delight in expressing his sincere gratitude, both to all the regular troops of the former, and especially to the Groups of the St Petersburg *Opolchenie*,who, having been removed from their rural occupations and having taken up arms for the first time, displayed miracles of valour and courage; who, within sight of his excellency, have justified the hopes of their compatriots and deserve the honourable title of defenders of Russia. His Excellency finds himself with the most pleasant duty of bringing the outstanding feats of his colleagues to the attention of our Most Gracious Tsar, and to petition for awards commensurate with the merits of each. Meanwhile, my friends, let us fulfil our primary duty and, with poignant hearts, bring the most fervent prayers of thanksgiving to God, who has blessed our arms with victory; yes, with His help and blessings, those enemy who escaped our blows here will soon find their graves where, in their arrogant pride, they dreamed of earning laurels.

The next morning, 9 (21) October, prayers of thanksgiving for the victory and a memorial service for the fallen soldiers were performed in the cathedral. No sooner had the rumble of the gun salute subsided, than a courier arrived from St Petersburg with a rescript, which, by Supreme will, granted Count Wittgenstein permission to publish, following the recapture of Polotsk. Having won the right to do so as the concluding reward for this feat, the Commander-in-Chief learned of his promotion to the rank of general of cavalry.

Meanwhile, Count Wittgenstein tried to speed up the construction of a bridge of rafts across the Dvina at Polotsk by every means possible, both to pursue the enemy and to establish communications with Count Steinheil, who was in danger of being attacked by superior enemy numbers. But despite the diligence of our sappers, who worked vigilantly under the guidance of engineer Colonel Count Sievers, the construction of the bridge could not be completed before 11 (23) October.

Saint-Cyr took advantage of Count Wittgenstein's involuntary inaction. The appearance of the Finland Corps on the enemy line of retreat prompted the marshal to attack Steinheil as a matter of urgency, despite the extreme fatigue of the Franco-Bavarians after the two-day battle at Polotsk. Only part of Legrand's division, which had crossed the Dvina ahead of all the other troops and had rested for several hours, was able to participate in the proposed attack. Saint-Cyr, suffering from his wound and not being able to personally direct the troops assigned to operate against the Finland Corps, entrusted them to General Wrede. The detachment entrusted to him consisted of three infantry regiments and one of cavalry, under the command

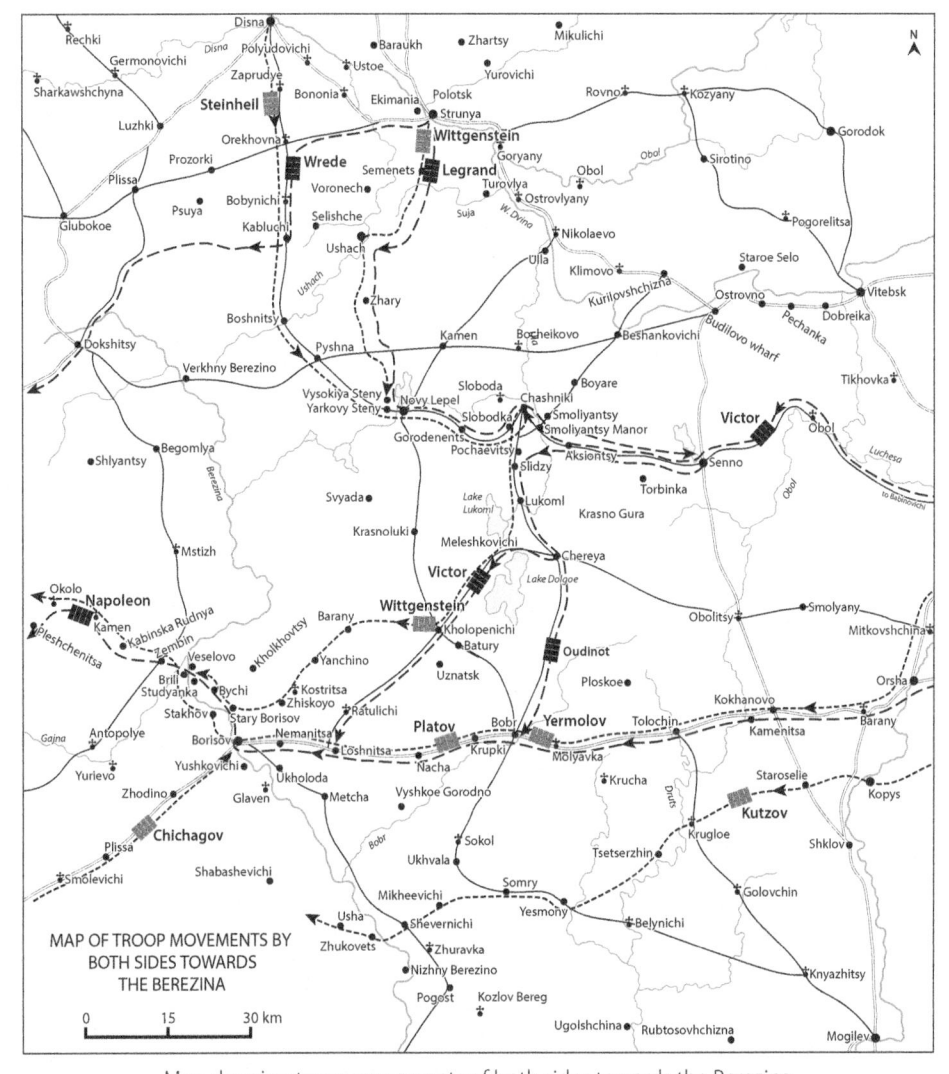

Map showing troop movements of both sides towards the Berezina.

of General Amey, and the cavalry brigade under General Corbineau, reinforced by cadres from the Bavarian *6e Corps* under General Ströhl [Alois Johann Nepomuk Franz Xaver Joseph Max Freiherr von Ströhl], and the *2e régiment suisse*.[29]

On the morning of 8 (20) October, at the same time as Wrede, having assembled his force, was moving against Count Steinheil, the main body of Finland Corps was at Bononia on the Ushacha river, while Colonel Turchaninov [Andrey Petrovich

---

29 Wrede's formation consisted of: *19e régiment de ligne, 37e régiment de ligne* and *124e régiment de ligne, 2e régiment suisse*, a Bavarian regiment, Corbineau's light cavalry brigade and *7e régiment de cuirassiers*: for a total of 16 battalions and 15 squadrons, all in all 3,000 infantry and 1,200 cavalry, with 18 guns. Saint-Cyr, III, 177.

Turchaninov] was deployed forwards of the defile near the village of Ekimania, with the vanguard, consisting of 2nd Jägers and 3rd Jägers.[30] At five o'clock in the morning the enemy force set out towards our vanguard in three columns, of which one, under Wrede's personal command, moved along the Disna highway, while the others, enveloping the flanks, went towards Rudnya and Ustie. Turchaninov, having not taken any timely measures to protect his force from an unexpected attack, was taken by surprise in the forest choke-point and pushed back behind the Ushacha, with the loss of 1,800 men taken prisoner alone, among whom was the famous Willoughby [Nesbit Josiah Willoughby], later a British admiral who, in 1812, was serving as a volunteer in our army, with the rank of colonel, wounded more than 70 times in the course of his military career and known in the British Royal Navy as 'the man who cannot die.'[31] Count Steinheil, unaware of the true strength of Wrede's formation and believing that Saint-Cyr was following up, with the full force of the Franco-Bavarian corps, retreated to Disna and crossed over the bridge built there onto the right bank of the Dvina on 9 (21) October.

As soon as Count Wittgenstein learned of the defeat of Finland Corps, he sent General Sazonov down the right bank of the Dvina with 12,000 men in order to assist him. Marshal Saint-Cyr, concerned that Wrede might be defeated in detail, ordered him to halt on the Ushacha and return the regiments detached to him the day before to *2e Corps*. Wanting to maintain communications with the *Grande Armée*, Saint-Cyr decided, in the event of Wittgenstein crossing to the left bank of the Dvina, to retreat to the Ulla river, to link up with Victor moving from Smolensk. In addition, the troops of the French *2e Corps* suffered from a shortage of artillery ammunition, and therefore had to avoid an engagement with Russian troops.[32]

Nevertheless, it was imperative that Saint-Cyr slow down our crossing of the Dvina as much as possible. On the morning of 8 (20) October, the enemy occupied the left bank of this river facing Polotsk and had a toehold on the right, in the bridgehead at Strunya, but the Bavarian detachment under Colonel Lamotte [Peter de La Motte?], who had been entrusted with the defence of this point, evacuated it as soon as the force under General Alekseev appeared opposite him, and destroyed the bridge, which deprived the French of the opportunity to threaten us with a crossing of the Dvina and contributed to future offensive operations by Count Wittgenstein. On that same day, Saint-Cyr, exhausted from the wound he had suffered, handed over command of the force to Legrand.[33]

The next morning [21 October new style], Colonel Rüdiger crossed the Dvina, near Polotsk with two squadrons of Grodno Hussars and Rodionov 2nd's Cossacks, which initially forced the enemy to withdraw their outposts, and thereafter to move away from Polotsk for a full stage and deploy *2e Corps* between the Dvina and Ushacha rivers, from Turovlya to the village of Voronech. General Wrede, who had

---

30 See the Map of the Advance to the Berezina river.
31 Willoughby had seventy wounds; from firearms, three from shell splinters, and many cuts from sabres and the tomahawks of savages. Having been exchanged from captivity, he lost an arm in the battle of Leipzig in 1813.
32 Saint-Cyr, III, 183-186.
33 Saint-Cyr, III, 187-188.

no desire to serve under Legrand, instead of maintaining communications with *2e Corps*, stayed on the road to Orekhovna. Offended by this overt insubordination, Legrand refused command of the force, which Merle accepted, but on condition, however, that he would not issue any orders to the Bavarian *6e Corps*. Saint-Cyr, despite his injury, was forced to send orders to General Wrede and to control the movements of his corps, but Wrede continued to operate at his own discretion, completely independently from *2e Corps*, and instead of maintaining communications with them, he sought only to close up to Vilna and the Neman, hoping to save, at least, the remnants of the Bavarian *6e Corps*.[34]

Meanwhile, the construction of the bridge at Polotsk was completed by Count Sievers on the night of 10 to 11 (22 to 23) October, and Count Wittgenstein, on the very next day, sent his main body across the Dvina and reached the village of Semenets, pushing the vanguard, under Rüdiger's command, on to the river Suja.[35] A garrison of 3,500 men was left in Polotsk, which included two Groups of Novgorod *Opolchenie* and the Teptyar Cossack Regiment, which had just arrived.[36] On that same day, 11 (23) October, Count Steinheil, having assimilated Sazonov's detachment into his corps at Disna, crossed again to the left bank of the river and reached Zaprudye. Major General Vlastov, was sent to Druya with an independent detachment of some 5,000 men with 14 guns,[37] this location was quickly put into a defensible state and was intended, together with Polotsk, to serve as a base for future operations by the corps; in addition, Vlastov's detachment was assigned to monitor MacDonald's [Étienne Jacques-Joseph-Alexandre Macdonald] force.[38] The offensive by our troops had forced the enemy corps to retreat: *2e Corps* to the village of Ushach, while *6e Corps* went to Bobynichi, from where it was vital for them to move to Selishche and cross the river flowing through there the next day, 12 (24) October. Indeed, Wrede sent his carts along the shortest route to Ushach, but being attacked by Count Steinheil's vanguard, under the command of Major General Helffreich, he turned right towards Kabluchi in order to secure the route to Vilna, leaving the carts practically without an escort. General Helffreich, having caught up with this convoy, sent Colonel Albrecht to take possession of it with three squadrons, and having scattered the escort, captured many wagons, including the treasury and a wagon with 22 colours belonging to regiments of *6e Corps*. Steinheil's corps stopped at Dmitrovshchina, near Bobynichi, while Wittgenstein's corps arrived at Ushach,

---

34 Saint-Cyr, III, 189-192. ButurlinButurlin, *Histoire militaire de la campagne de Russie en 1812*, II, 163., II, 278.
35 Colonel Rüdiger's report, dated 11 [23] October.
36 The composition of the Polotsk garrison under the nominated city commandant, State Councillor Nikolev, was: two Lifeguard reserve battalions, a squadron of the Combined Dragoon Regiment, 12th Group, St Petersburg *Opolchenie*, a brigade (two Groups) of Novgorod *Opolchenie*, Teptyar Cossack Regiment, 50th Battery Artillery Company and 49th Light Artillery Company (War Diary of I Corps).
37 Vlastov's detachment consisted of: 24th Jägers, one battalion from 23rd Jägers, two combined infantry regiments, Finland Dragoons, Loshchilin's Cossack Regiment, eight guns from 23rd Horse Artillery Company and six guns from 28th Battery Artillery Company (War Diary of I Corps).
38 War Diary of I Corps.

where on 13 (25) October the men were given a rest day. The bad roads along which our troops were moving forced the Commander-in-Chief to leave three artillery companies (27th Battery, 35th Light and 57th Light) in Ushach, under the protection of the Tula Infantry and 7th Group of the St Petersburg *Opolchenie*, under the command of Major General Harpe [Vasily Ivanovich Garpe or Otto Wilhelm Harpe], who received orders to send this artillery to Polotsk, with a small escort, as soon as the enemy had retired to a safer distance.[39]

Meanwhile, as the main body under Count Wittgenstein were resting in front of Ushach, having pushed Rüdiger's vanguard out to the village of Voron, the vanguard of Steinheil's corps caught up with the Bavarians at Kabluchi on 13 (25) October and pursued them along the road to Glubokoe, moreover, eight guns were captured from the enemy.[40] On the following day, 14 (26) October, Wittgenstein's vanguard, reinforced by several battalions and placed under the command of Major General Alekseev, attacked the enemy near the village of Vysokiya-Steny, but, having run into superior forces, returned to Voron; on our side Lieutenant Colonel Kotzebue of the General Staff, son of the famous German author, was mortally wounded.[41]

General Wrede, retreating along the Vilna road with the remnants of the Bavarian *6e Corps*, towards Glubokoye, taking Corbineau's light cavalry brigade with him, which, by order of Saint-Cyr, was to remain in Pyshna, on the left flank of *2e Corps*.

On 16 (28) October, the vanguard of I Corps under Prince Iashvili's command, occupied the village of Vysokiya-Steny, and on 17 (29) October, having forced the enemy to evacuate Lepel, pursued them along the road towards Chashniki. Once both Russian corps had linked up in Lepel on this day, Count Wittgenstein divided his force, which (with the exception of Vlastov's detachment and the Polotsk garrison) consisted of a total of 30,000 men, into four fighting formations.

The Vanguard, under the command of Prince Iashvili: Regular infantry; Mogilev Infantry, Polotsk Infantry, Navaginsk Infantry, 2nd Jägers, 3rd Jägers, 25th Jägers, one battalion of 23rd Jägers; a total of 13 battalions. Regular cavalry; Grodno Hussars, Combined Dragoon Regiment; a total of 15 squadrons. Irregular cavalry; Rodionov 2nd's Cossacks, Platov 4th's Cossacks. Militia; three Groups of St Petersburg *Opolchenie*. Artillery; 1st Company (ten guns), 26th Light Company, six guns from 14th Battery Company; a total of 28 guns.

Right Flank Corps, under the command of Lieutenant General Count Steinheil (the lead echelon commanded by Lieutenant General Sazonov, the second echelon by Major General Adadurov [Vasily Vasilievich Adadurov]): Regular infantry; Tenginsk Infantry, Tula Infantry,[42] Estland Infantry, Voronezh Infantry, Neva Infantry, Petrovsk Infantry, Lithuania Infantry and 26th Jägers; a total of 16 battalions. Regular cavalry; Mittau Dragoons, Riga Dragoons; a total of eight squadrons. Militia; three Groups of St Petersburg *Opolchenie*. Artillery; 6th Battery Company

---

39 Major General Harpe's report to Major General Dovre, dated 17 [29] October, No. 1,679.
40 War Diary of I Corps.
41 Major General Alekseev's report dated 14 [26] October. War Diary of I Corps.
42 Left in Ushach for the time being, in order to protect the artillery designated to depart for Polotsk.

(recently arrived in the corps), 11th Light Company, four guns from 28th Battery Company; a total of 28 guns.

Left Flank Corps, under the command of Lieutenant General Berg (the lead echelon commanded by Privy Councillor Bibikov [Alexander Alexandrovich Bibikov], the second echelon by Major General Kulnev [Ivan Petrovich Kulnev][43]): Regular infantry; Perm Infantry, Sevsk Infantry, Kaluga Infantry, Azov Infantry, Combined Jäger Regiment; a total of 11 battalions. Regular cavalry; Combined Lifeguard Cavalry Regiment, Yamburg Dragoons; a total of seven squadrons. Militia; three Groups of St Petersburg *Opolchenie*. Artillery; 5th Battery Company, 27th Light Company; a total of 24 guns.

Reserve, under the command of Major General Foch [Alexander Borisovich Foch]: Regular infantry; Nizov Infantry, 1st Marines, three replacement grenadier battalions, four combined grenadier battalions from 5th Division and 14th Division; a total of 11 battalions. Regular cavalry; Combined Cuirassier Regiment; four squadrons. Artillery; 21st Battery Company, 3rd Horse Artillery Company, six guns from 14th Battery Company, four guns from 23rd Horse Artillery Company; a total of 34 guns.

Overall, the force under Count Wittgenstein comprised: 51 battalions, 34 squadrons, two Cossack Regiments, 13 Groups, attached to regular units, and 11 artillery companies, a total of 20,000 regular infantry, 7,000 *opolchenie* and 3,500 cavalry, all in all some 30,000 men, with 114 guns.[44]

On the following day, 18 (30) October, the enemy *2e Corps* and *9e Corps* linked up at Chashniki, a total of 36,000 men.[45]

Victor's corps, consisting of 54 battalions and 16 squadrons on its original formation, for a total of 33,000 men, during the crossing of the Neman and advance to Smolensk by the *Grande Armée*, had been in fortresses along the lower reaches of the Oder and Vistula. On 28 July (9 August), Marshal Victor's corps headquarters was moved to Tilsit [Sovetsk], where his force was assembled (leaving some units behind), consisting of 41 battalions and 15 squadrons, numbering some 26,000 men. After a three-week stay at Tilsit, the corps set out on the onward campaign with a huge train, the size of which can be judged from the fact that there were 42 peasant carts with each battalion for the carriage of twenty-days' worth of provisions and fodder. This force, passing through Kovno [Kaunas], Vilna and Minsk, and leaving a fairly significant number of sick and some of the artillery in these cities, arrived in Smolensk on 16 (28) September. The cavalry and horse artillery were located at a distance of one stage from the city to provide them with forage; the infantry and foot artillery stationed in the city, received a meagre issue of provisions from the magazines, which very often consisted of stale flour, and having no means of baking it into bread or hard-tack, suffered hunger and were subjected to debilitating disease.

As the force under Count Wittgenstein had, in the meantime, been strengthened through significant reinforcements, then Marshal Victor, foreseeing their offensive

---

43 Brother of the late renowned vanguard commander.
44 War Diary of I Corps.
45 Saint-Cyr wrote that there were 25,000 men in Victor's corps, while Chambray stated that there were 36,000 men in both corps. Saint-Cyr, III, 198. Chambray, II, 186.

against Saint-Cyr, considered it necessary to bring part of *9e Corps* closer to the Dvina. To that end, on 3 (15) October, Daendels' [Herman Willem Daendels] division was transferred to Babinovichi; Partouneaux's [Louis de Partouneaux] force, together with Fournier's [François Louis Fournier-Sarlovèze] cavalry, were stationed in Mstislavl as most convenient for the provision of rations and fodder. Such was the situation of Victor's corps, during the period when the French *2e Corps*, having been ejected from Polotsk and deprived of assistance from the Bavarians, was retreating from the Dvina. Marshal Victor immediately sent Daendels' division to assist them (of which one Berg battalion with two guns was left in Vitebsk), and thereafter, the remaining troops of *9e Corps*. Although the French corps had established communications with each other on 17 (29) October, nevertheless, Victor's force was unable to assemble on the Ulla until the night of 19 to 20 October (31 October to 1 November).[46]

Thus, Count Wittgenstein, due to the impossibility of building bridges and crossing the Dvina upstream of Polotsk, failed to accomplish the mission assigned to his force on the basis of the general operational plan: the enemy corps operating in the vicinity of Polotsk had not been kept separate from Napoleon's army or been driven back towards the Neman, but, on the contrary, the forces under Oudinot and Victor, united with each other, had the opportunity to protect the line of retreat of the *Grande Armée*. To counteract this, our commander decided to attack the enemy, not yet knowing about the arrival of significant reinforcements to assist them, and did not change his intentions, despite subsequent exaggerated intelligence indicating that Victor's corps was incomparably stronger than it actually was.

---

46 *Beitrag zu der Geschichte des neunten Korps der Französischen verbündeten Armee im Feldzug gegen Russland 1812*, Oestr. Militärische Zeitschrift, 1812, Drittes Heft, 245-259.

39

The Battles of Chashniki and Smoliyantsy

The unification of Oudinot's and Victor's corps. – The composition of these forces. – The deployment of Count Wittgenstein's army near Chashniki. – The deployment of the French corps on both banks of the Lukomka. – The battle of Chashniki. – Saint-Cyr's departure.

Count Wittgenstein's deployments and those of the detachments sent out by him after the battle of Chashniki. – The liberation of Vitebsk by General Harpe's detachment. – The expedition towards Borisov. – Prince Volkonsky's detachment.

The situation of the French forces after their retreat to Senno. – The French movement towards Chereya. – The deployment of Count Wittgenstein's detachments. – Our system of mobile magazines. – The French offensive. – The deployment of Russian forces near Chashniki. – The battle at Smoliyantsy. – Napoleon's orders for Marshal Victor. – The deployments by both sides during the arrival of the remnants of the Grande Armée at Orsha.

During the period from 17 to 19 (29 to 31) October, the French *2e Corps* and *9e Corps* linked up on the Ulla river, namely: Merle's and Maison's divisions were of the right bank of the river Lukomka at its confluence with the Ulla with the main body of Victor's corps, while Legrand's division was on the road from Beshankovichi to Chashniki with Daendels' division. This concentration of French troops raised their morale: the soldiers under Oudinot hoped to avenge the defeats they had suffered with the assistance of the significant reinforcements which had arrived; while the troops under Victor, who had not yet had a chance to fight, wanted to prove that they were not inferior in courage to their colleagues in other corps of the *Grande Armée*. Victor's corps were in excellent condition, in relation to the health, appearance and clothing of the soldiers, who represented a completely contrasting spectacle to the troops under Oudinot, exhausted from hardship and deprivation, blackened from bivouac smoke and covered with rags; but these warriors had been tested in combat and had endured hunger, bad weather and fatigue, and formed the most reliable element of the army.[1]

---
1   Saint-Cyr, *Mémoires*, III, 199-200.

On 18 (30) October, on the same day that almost all of Victor's force had just arrived to assist *2e Corps*, General Merle withdrew along the right bank of the Ulla river to Chashniki and halted there, anchoring his right flank on this river forwards of the town. Prince Iashvili positioned himself within sight of the French with Count Wittgenstein's vanguard, and reported on the readiness of the enemy to accept battle to headquarters. Indeed, Victor, having managed to concentrate the majority of both corps at Chashniki, decided to take advantage of his superiority to put a stop to Count Wittgenstein's success. To that end, orders were sent to Daendels, under whose command the divisions were marching from Beshankovichi to Chashniki, to bring them up as soon as possible, to join the main force. The cavalry, which was one stage away from the main force, also received orders to hurry to Chashniki. Daendels arrived on the Lukomka river on the night of 18 to 19 (30 to 31) October, but with only one of his divisions, having sent Legrand to Bocheikovo through a misunderstanding. The cavalry, however, did not set out from their overnight halt before daylight on 19 (31) October. Thus Victor, deprived of the assistance of 4,000 infantry and 2,000 cavalry, postponed his proposed attack until his entire force could be assembled. Whereas, in the meantime, Count Wittgenstein, not knowing about the arrival of *9e Corps*, had decided, on that same day, 19 (31) October, to attack the enemy, and to that end he stationed his army at the village of Sloboda the evening before, three *versts* behind the vanguard under Prince Iashvili.[2]

Enemy troops were located on both banks of the Lukomka river:[3] Merle's and Maison's divisions were stationed in the front line, forwards of the town of Chashniki, with their right flank on the Ulla, while Victor's corps was on the high ground on the right bank of the river. A weir at Smoliyantsy manor served to allow liaison between the French corps, at a distance of about two *versts* from Chashniki. The right wing of Oudinot's force was covered by the stream, while the left wing leaned into the forest occupied by French infantry. There were some 10,000 men in this position.

At dawn on 19 (31) October, Prince Iashvili, having received orders to attack the enemy, advanced against the French with his entire vanguard, consisting of 13 battalions with three groups of *opolchenie* attached to them, 15 squadrons and two Cossack regiments, with 28 guns.[4] The Cossack regiments drove the enemy outposts back across the river, and after that, at about seven o'clock in the morning, Prince Iashvili crossed the river with five battalions (2nd Jägers, 3rd Jägers and 23rd Jägers) and attacked the French troops occupying the town, but, having encountered fierce resistance, was forced to withdraw his infantry. Soon after, Wittgenstein's main force came up: Steinheil's corps deployed to the right of the vanguard, while Berg's corps remained in reserve. Whereupon Iashvili resumed his attack on the town

---

2   Chambray, II, 186-187. War Diary of I Corps (Archive of the M.T.D. No. 29,200).
3   See the Plan of the Battle of Chashniki.
4   The vanguard comprised: 2nd Jägers, 3rd Jägers, 25th Jägers and a battalion from 23rd Jägers, three groups of St Petersburg *Opolchenie*, the Grodno Hussars, Combined Hussar Regiment, Combined Dragoon Regiment, Rodionov 2nd's Cossacks, Platov 4th's Cossacks, 1st Horse Artillery Company (ten guns), 26th Light Artillery Company and six guns from 14th Battery Artillery Company.

THE BATTLES OF CHASHNIKI AND SMOLIYANTSY 137

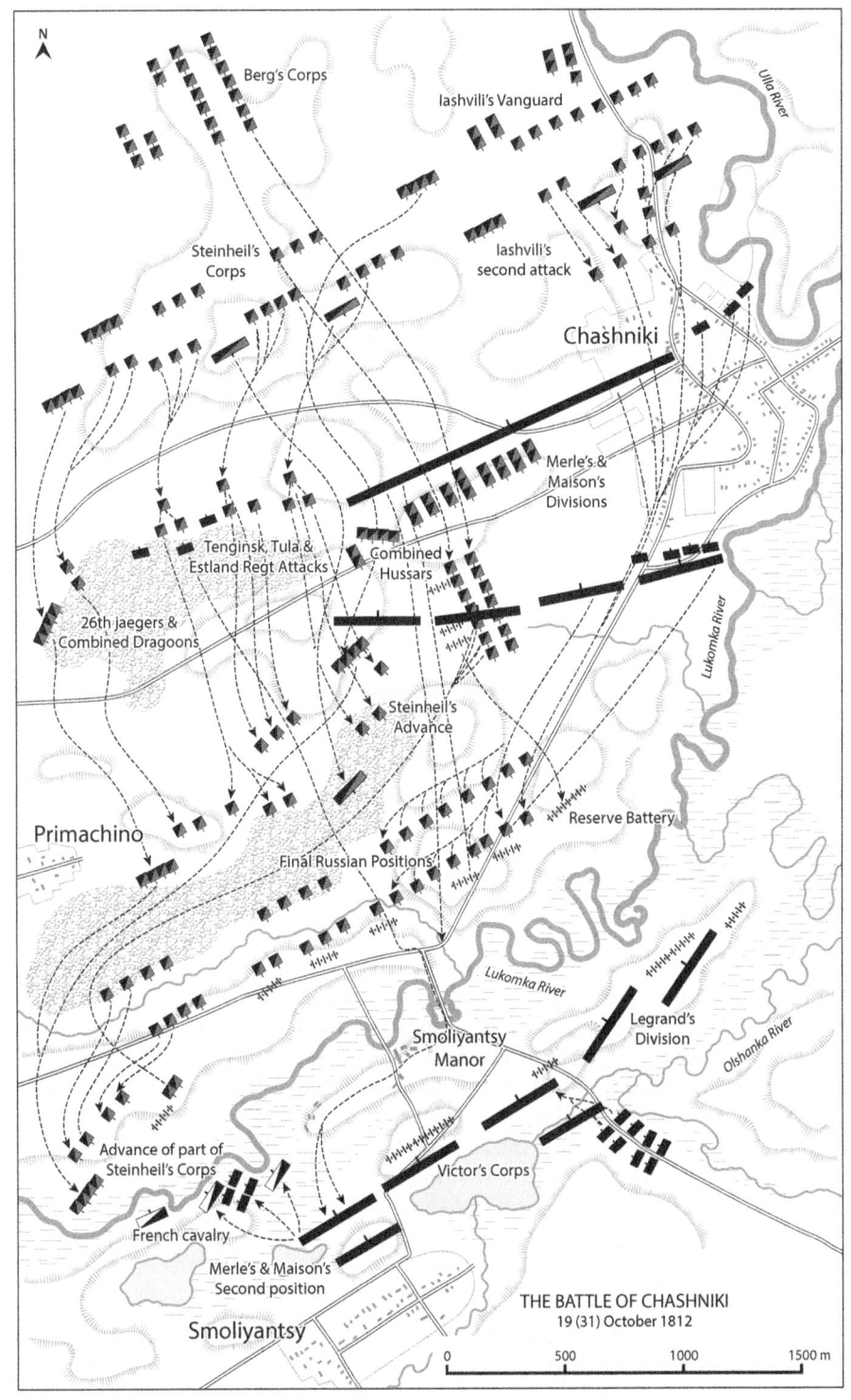

The Battle of Chashniki 19 (31) October 1812.

of Chashniki and drove the French out of the place, who refused their right wing rearwards, leaving the left in the forest, in front of Smoliyantsy manor as before. Simultaneously with the advance of the vanguard infantry, the Grodno Hussars, marching on our right flank, drove off the enemy cavalry. Meanwhile, Count Steinheil attacked the enemy in the forest and was repulsed, but repeated the attack with a line of six battalions (Tenginsk Infantry, Tula Infantry and Estland Infantry), sending the 26th Jägers and Combined Dragoon Regiment around the forest against the left flank of the enemy force, while the Combined Hussars enveloped their right flank. At the same time, Count Wittgenstein reinforced the artillery of the vanguard with battery companies, initially 6th Battery Company under Lieutenant Colonel Shulman [Fëdor Maksimovich Shulman], and later with 5th Battery Company. The French, being forced to evacuate the forest, were pursued by our vanguard, and in particular by the Combined Dragoons and Combined Hussars, who distinguished themselves here, and were forced to retreat across the Lukomka river, where the troops of the enemy right wing had also retreated.

It was at this point that our Commander-in-Chief became aware of the arrival of Marshal Victor to assist *2e Corps* from prisoners, and therefore, without undertaking a decisive offensive, he limited himself to occupying the left bank of the Lukomka. Only Colonel Gerngross [Rodion (Ilarion) Fëdorovich Gerngross or Renatus Samuel August von Gerngroß], with the Combined Dragoon Regiment, crossed the river, upstream of the position occupied by the enemy, threatening their left flank, but was ordered to return to the left bank.

Upon retreating behind the Lukomka, the troops of the French *2e Corps* took post to the left of Victor's divisions stationed behind the river, while Steinheil's infantry and the vanguard under Iashvili stood facing them, pushing their batteries onto the high ground on the left bank of the Lukomka; Berg's force and all the cavalry were placed in reserve. Subsequent activity was limited to a cannonade. In the evening, Legrand's division moved up to assist the enemy along the road from Beshankovichi, which, located to the right of the rest of the force, set up batteries facing our left wing. Count Wittgenstein reinforced this point with four guns from 5th Battery Company, which, together with the artillery under Prince Iashvili, forced the enemy batteries and cuirassiers, which constituted their escort, to retreat into the forest behind the Roganovichi manor. At the same time, the French batteries, stationed on commanding high ground facing Count Steinheil's right wing, inflicted painful damage on his force, but once our artillery had been reinforced by 3rd Horse Artillery Company, the enemy guns were forced into silence. Meanwhile, 6th Battery Company and 14th Battery Company with 26th Light Company and 27th Light Company worked against the batteries located facing the Smoliyantsy manor with a similar outcome. The enemy, wishing to force our artillery to retreat, sent out cavalry from their left wing, which indicated their intention to cross the river, but by order of Count Steinheil, were engaged by four battalions and six squadrons,[5]

---

5   The report by Count Steinheil stated that reinforcements sent to our right wing were: the Combined Hussar Regiment, a squadron of Riga Dragoons and two squadrons of Mittau Dragoons, with one horse artillery piece, one combined grenadier battalion from 5th Division, one battalion of 26th Jägers and the Lithuania Infantry Regiment. Count Steinheil's

and were forced to take cover in the forest. The enemy force, having no success with their attempted attacks, retreated from the Lukomka in the evening and retreated the next day [1 November new style], along with Legrand's divisions and Fournier's cavalry that had joined them, along the road to Senno.[6]

In the battle of Chashniki, the casualties in our force did not exceed 400 men overall. Among the wounded was Colonel Silin [Vasily Mikhailovich Silin] of the Grodno Hussars, whose arm was severed by round shot. The enemy lost 23 officers and some 800 lower ranks taken prisoners alone.[7] The St Petersburg *Opolchenie*, on this day, fought as courageously as they had at Polotsk. The enemy, amazed at the courage of the 'foot Cossacks' (*cosaques à pied*), as they called these warriors, asked: 'from where did these fearless people with crosses on their caps come, who have come to harm us?'[8]

Marshal Saint-Cyr, whose wound suffered in the battle of Polotsk prevented him from participating in the battle of Chashniki, believed that Victor should have moved the troops of *9e Corps* across to the left bank of the Lukomka to assist *2e Corps* and to attack Wittgenstein with the full force of both French corps. Dissatisfied with the actions of his colleague, Saint-Cyr left for Orsha, from where he went on to Vilna.[9]

After the battle of Chashniki, Count Wittgenstein transferred his main body to the left bank of the Ulla and placed them facing Chashniki in order to rest his force and to wait for Chichagov's army to draw closer. The headquarters was in the town. Some elements of the force were in bivouacs; others were accommodated in the surrounding villages. General Alekseev, who took command of the vanguard once more, settled initially at Smoliyantsy, and later at Aksentsy, sending part of the cavalry to monitor the retreating enemy corps.[10] Victor's retreat gifted our Commander-in-Chief the same benefits that a decisive victory in a pitched battle would have given him. Being at Chashniki, he could send detachments to Borisov, Minsk or Vitebsk. In addition, the lack of activity did him a favour, weakening the enemy forces, who were poorly clothed and obtaining provisions with the greatest of difficulties.[11] Count Wittgenstein, having thus far been unable to establish communications with either Prince Kutuzov or Admiral Chichagov, was forced to confine himself to monitoring the enemy corps standing facing him, because if he lost contact with them, then they, having united with the remnants of the *Grande*

---

report to Count Wittgenstein, dated 28 October [9 November], No. 231. In the War Diary of I Corps (Archive of the M.T.D. No. 29,200), it claims that four battalions, six squadrons and 12 guns were sent to assist the right wing.
6   *Oestreichische militärische Zeitschrift, 1821, Drittes Heft.*
7   War Diary of I Corps.
8   From Notes on the St Petersburg *Opolchenie*.
9   Saint-Cyr, *Mémoires*, III, 202-204.
10 On 23 October [4 November], the vanguard was split into two detachments: the first, under the direct command of Major General Alekseev, was in the village of Aksiontsy and consisted of: Rodionov 2nd's Cossacks, Combined Lifeguards, Mittau Dragoons, 25th Jägers, a battalion of 23rd Jägers and six guns from 3rd Horse Artillery Company; the second, commanded by Major General Helffreich, was stationed at Boyare on the Beshankovichi road, and consisted of: Platov 4th's Cossacks, Combined Dragoons, 2nd Jägers, 3rd Jägers and six guns from 3rd Horse Artillery Company.
11 Saint-Cyr, III, 204-205. Chambray, II, 188.

Armée, could turn against the independent I Corps and defeat them before the rest of our troops could arrive in time to assist.[12]

The main body of Count Wittgenstein's army remained in the locations they occupied until 1 (13) November, and meanwhile the detachments sent from them exploited the influence of the victories won at Polotsk and Chashniki, clearing the entire surrounding country of the enemy. The vanguard under General Alekseev was located forwards of the Lukomka river at Aksiontsy and Boyare, on the roads to Senno and Vitebsk; a detachment under Major General Harpe, consisting of two battalions and two squadrons with two guns,[13] was sent via Bocheikovo towards Beshankovichi, to monitor the sector to the left of the vanguard as far as the Dvina; while the Combined Hussar Regiment was sent to Lepel, to protect the positions of the main body from the direction of Glubokoe, where the remnants of the Bavarian *6e Corps* had retreated.[14]

On the basis of the general plan of action for the Russian armies, Count Wittgenstein, after pushing the enemy corps back from the Dvina, had been ordered to seize Vitebsk, to that end the detachment under Major General Harpe was assigned this mission, reinforced with two battalions, two squadrons, four guns and a *Sotnia* of Cossacks.[15] General Harpe arrived at Staroe Selo on 25 October (6 November) and would move towards Vitebsk on the following day, along the right bank of the Dvina, detaching Lieutenant Colonel Stolypin along the left bank with two squadrons of Yamburg Dragoons. Both detachments closed in on the city at dawn on 26 October (7 November). Although the enemy was taken by surprise, nevertheless, the guard stationed at the Polotsk gate, having crossed the bridge to the left bank of the Dvina, managed to set it alight. Whereupon a squadron of Poland Ulans and skirmishers from the entire detachment, led by the commander of 7th Group of the St Petersburg *Opolchenie*, Colonel Shemiot [Pavel Leontievich Shemiot or Szemiot], hot on the heels of the French, dashed to the bridge and started a firefight with the enemy occupying the opposite bank. Shortly thereafter, Harpe arrived himself in time to help the skirmishers, with 26th Jägers and with a platoon from 1st Horse Artillery Company under Sub Lieutenant Sukhozanet 2nd [Nikolai Onufrievich Sukhozanet]. As soon as the effects of our guns firing canister had forced the enemy marksmen to evacuate the buildings closest to the bank, the skirmishers of 26th Jägers and 7th Group, together with the dismounted ulans, ran across the burning bridge to the left bank and pursued the French through the streets of the city, while our other soldiers extinguished the flames that threatened the complete destruction of the crossing with the help of the inhabitants. General Harpe, leaving one battalion of the Navaginsk Infantry to repair the bridge, sent another, under the regimental commander, Major Winter [Karl Fëdorovich Winter], with two squadrons of Poland Ulans and Riga Dragoons, to attack the enemy who had managed to settle across the river.

---

12 Count Wittgenstein's report to the Tsar, dated 30 October [11 November].
13 The Navaginsk Infantry Regiment with a squadron each of Riga Dragoons and Poland Ulans, 7th Group of the St Petersburg *Opolchenie* and two guns from 1st Horse Artillery Company.
14 War Diary of I Corps.
15 26th Jägers and two squadrons of Yamburg Dragoons.

These men, supported by the other two squadrons and warriors, drove off a French column, forced them out of the city and captured many prisoners. Meanwhile, Lieutenant Colonel Stolypin, with two squadrons of Riga Dragoons and a Kalmyk sub-unit, attacked the enemy as they left the city, racing to pursue them along the Smolensk road and caught up with them 15 *versts* from Vitebsk, where the French, numbering several hundred men, with two guns,[16] recovering from their defeat, took up very advantageous positions. But this did not stop our brave dragoons, who, having charged at the enemy infantry, scattered them and took both guns. Among the 400 prisoners captured by our troops were the governor of Vitebsk, *général de brigade* Pouget and ten field officers and subalterns.[17] On our side, 44 men were lost. Large stockpiles were found in Vitebsk, that the enemy did not have chance to destroy, in particular, a huge amount of salt, 750 *Chetvert* [one *Chetvert* = 5¾ bushels] of rye and flour, 250 *Chetvert* of oats and 40 *Chetvert* of cereals, 4,000 *Pud* [one *Pud* = 36 pounds] of hay, etc.[18] General Harpe, leaving Colonel Pahlen [Matvei Ivanovich Palen or Carl Magnus von der Pahlen] in Vitebsk, with the 26th Jägers, two guns and a Cossack sub-unit, moved to Beshankovichi with the rest of the force, in order to close up to the main body.

Together with the initial report on the liberation of Vitebsk, General Harpe also delivered the joyful news of the liberation of Moscow from the enemy and the beginning of the retreat of Napoleon's *Grande Armée*, obtained from captured French officers, to Count Wittgenstein's headquarters.[19] Russian dreams had come true! No one then could have foreseen that this rebuff of the enemy invasion would lead us all the way to Paris; but the whole of Russia was already rejoicing in the triumph of its deliverance.

In order to protect the main body under Count Wittgenstein from the direction of Glubokoe, to where the remnants of the Bavarian *6e Corps* had retreated after the battle of Chashniki (as mentioned above), Colonel Gerngross had been sent to Lepel with the Combined Hussar Regiment, while a squadron of Poland Ulans had been sent on to Plissa for close monitoring of the enemy. Colonel Gerngross, who also had the mission of establishing communications with Chichagov's army, made his way via country lanes to Kholopenichi and from there towards Borisov, catching an enemy outpost stationed there by surprise and captured the town, but was subsequently driven out by troops arriving from the right bank of the Berezina

---

16 In General Harpe's report it states: over 1,000 men with two guns.
17 [Liprandi comments: 'What is most remarkable here is that neither the commander of the 26th Jäger Regiment, the commander of the 7th Group, nor the brave leaders of the skirmishers from these units or the dismounted ulans, dashing across a burning bridge, pursuing the French and taking prisoners, are named, yet the commander of a mere platoon of artillery, a sub-lieutenant is named! Where is the uniformity, the systematic proportionality in the narrative? Impartiality should guide those describing events, especially when there are still living witnesses to them. General Bogdanovich acknowledged this himself, in his preface, and solemnly promised to be impartial'].
18 Major General Harpe's report to Count Wittgenstein, dated 28 October [9 November], No. 45. War Diary of I Corps.
19 Major General Harpe's report to Count Wittgenstein, dated 26 October [7 November], No. 35. Emperor Alexander I and His Colleagues, Vol. IV. Biography of General Harpe.

and returned to Lepel on 27 October (8 November) without having been able to get any information on Chichagov.[20]

At the same time as Vitebsk was being liberated by Harpe's force, the detachment under Adjutant General Volkonsky was moving there. Back in early [mid] October, Lieutenant Colonel Diebitsch [Wilhelm Friedrich von Diebitsch], who was in the Bely *Oblast*, Smolensk Governorate, with a partisan detachment,[21] reported directly to the Tsar on the movements of enemy troops from Smolensk in three directions, towards Toropets, Bely and Sychyovka. Having received this report, Emperor Alexander ordered Prince Volkonsky to assemble a detachment of three Ural Cossack regiments between Toropets and Bely, moving thereafter from Vyshny Volochyok to Ostashkov to Count Wittgenstein's corps. The Sychyovka *Opolchenie*, Bely *Opolchenie* and Toropets *Opolchenie* and Diebitsch's partisans were also assigned to this detachment; while the force under Prince Volkonsky was reinforced with a detachment under Major General Novak [Ivan Ivanovich Novak?], located in Novgorod, consisting of 2nd Marine Regiment and 6,000 warriors of the St Petersburg *Opolchenie* and Novgorod *Opolchenie* with 18 guns.[22] Upon arriving in Ostashkov, Prince Volkonsky became convinced that the report by Lieutenant Colonel Diebitsch had been based on false rumours; at the same time, it emerged that his partisan detachment had inflicted humiliation and harassment on the population. In order to put a stop these abuses, Volkonsky assimilated all the Russian soldiers and Cossacks who were in Diebitsch's detachment into his force, and disarmed the foreign prisoners of war, sending them on to Novgorod. Emperor Alexander I, having received the report from Prince Volkonsky, did not approve of the disarming of the German volunteers and ordered them to be returned, as before, under the command of Lieutenant Colonel Diebitsch; at the same time, a Supreme Order was issued to the head of the Ministry of War, to supply Diebitsch with a delivery of winter clothing in an amount appropriate to those in need in this detachment.[23] Prince Volkonsky, having received Supreme Orders to attach the troops entrusted to him to the independent I Corps under Count Wittgenstein, assembled them in Vitebsk, in mid [late] November, and returned to St Petersburg.[24]

Upon the arrival of the French *2e Corps* and *9e Corps* at Senno, they were given a two-day rest; but this did not work in the troops' favour, due to the lack of food supplies and the most essential materials for building shelters. The onset of winter,

---

20 War Diary of I Corps. Colonel Gerngross' report to Count Wittgenstein, dated 27 October [8 November], No. 10, from Lepel.
21 This detachment was formed by Lieutenant Colonel Diebitsch from 60 dragoons and Cossacks who had escaped from captivity, and more than 300 mixed prisoners of war taken by us, who had voluntarily armed themselves against the French. Prince Volkonsky's report to the Tsar, dated 31 October [12 November].
22 Supreme Orders for Prince Volkonsky, dated 15 [27] October.
23 Prince Volkonsky's report to the Tsar, dated 31 October [12 November]. Supreme Orders for Prince Volkonsky, dated 28 October [9 November], No. 255, and dated 31 October [12 November], No. 274. The latter was issued following a complaint from Lieutenant Colonel Diebitsch.
24 Supreme Orders for Prince Volkonsky, dated 3 [15] November. Prince Volkonsky's report to the Tsar, dated 13 [25] November.

under such unfavourable circumstances, had a very harmful effect on the health of the men, and since there was no way to establish permanent hospitals, each of the sick was inevitably condemned to die. A few days later, all the sick were taken to Chereya, but due to a lack of resources due to the evacuation of this place by the French soon after, all the measures taken to alleviate the plight of the suffering soldiers failed to bring the slightest benefit. On 23 October (4 November), both corps moved to Torbinka, and the next day [5 November new style], to Chereya. From there, Legrand's division and the light cavalry with four Badenese horse artillery pieces were advanced to Lukoml in order to form a vanguard for both corps. Colonel Rüdiger was stationed facing them, with an independent detachment, in the village of Slidzy.[25]

MacDonald's inaction prompted Count Wittgenstein to transfer Vlastov's detachment from Druya to Luzhki (except for one squadron of Yamburg Dragoons and a Cossack troop left on the Dvina). General Vlastov was instructed to fix the force under Wrede, who, meanwhile, had moved from Glubokoe to Dokshitsy. To that same end, General Foch, who was stationed near the town of Kamen with the reserve, received orders to take up positions at Lepel.[26]

In order to provision our troops stationed in Chashniki and in the vicinity of this location, a mobile magazine of 3,000 peasant carts was formed, under the care of the Pskov civil governor, Prince Shakhovsky [Pëtr Ivanovich Shakhovsky], divided evenly into six sections located in Sebezh, Osyno, Klyastitsy, Beloe, Polotsk and Ushach, at a distance of 20 to 35 *versts* from one another. From Ushach, supplies were assigned to be transported to the town of Kamen, and from there delivered to the troops on regimental carts. Each section of the mobile magazine was divided into two convoys, which departed daily by turns. It was intended to carry 15 *Pud* of hard-tack or cereals on each cart, or three *Chetvert* of oats, therefore, in the course of two days it was possible to deliver 3,750 *Pud* of provisions and 750 *Chetvert* of oats to the army.[27]

Meanwhile, Marshal Oudinot, although not yet fully recovered from his wound, nevertheless took command of *2e Corps*. Victor, as the senior by rank, had the right to control the operations by both corps, to the extent that the compliance of his comrade permitted. During their stay at Chereya, having received orders from Napoleon to attack Wittgenstein and push him as far as possible from the line of retreat of the *Grande Armée*,[28] the French military commanders could not agree among themselves on future operations: Oudinot believed that it was necessary to attack the Russians in their positions, while Victor, considering these to be too strong, and wanted to move around it towards Bocheikovo in order to distract Wittgenstein away from the Orsha road. On 30 October (11 November), Victor

---

25 *Oestreich. milit. Zeitschrift*, 1821, Drittes Heft. *Précis de la campagne du 1er corps de la 1er armée d'Occident pendant l'année 1812* (Archive of the M.T.D. No. 29,200). Rüdiger's detachment comprised: four combined grenadier battalions, the Grodno Hussars and four guns.
26 Colonel Valstov's and Major General Foch's reports, dated 31 October [12 November].
27 Regulations on the mobile magazine, signed by the ruling Intendant General Zhukovsky.
28 These orders were sent from Mikhailovka. *Lettres du major-général au duc de Belluno de Mikalewka, le 6 et 7 novembre, et de Smolensk, le 9 novembre* (new style). See Chapter 35.

moved from Chereya to Lukoml with his corps. Oudinot proceeded behind him. Count Wittgenstein, having received intelligence on the French offensive, ordered General Alekseev to concentrate the vanguard force from Aksiontsy and Boyare to Meleshkovichi, on the Lukoml lake; on the following day, 31 October (12 November), Alekseev and Helffreich moved towards this village, but having learned of its seizure by significant enemy forces, they linked up before reaching the indicated location on the road from Chereya to Lukoml. Count Wittgenstein, wanting to support them with his main body, transferred his force to the right bank of the Ulla and stationed Steinheil's corps at Smoliyantsy, while Berg was at Chashniki.

On 1 (13) November, Partouneaux's division with all the cavalry from *9e Corps*, having crossed the road leading from Senno to Chashniki, attacked the vanguard under General Alekseev near Aksiontsy at about ten o'clock in the morning. After a two-hour battle, our troops were forced to retreat, but being supported by three regiments (Tenginsk Infantry, Voronezh Infantry and Neva Infantry) sent by Count Steinheil, they halted the enemy once more, three *versts* from Smoliyantsy, and held them until nightfall. On our side, the casualties reached 500 men; among the seriously wounded were the Colonel-in-Chief of the Podolsk Infantry Regiment, Colonel Maslov [Andrei Timofeevich Maslov], and the commander of the 25th Jäger Regiment, Colonel Vetoshkin [Mikhail Mikhailovich Vetoshkin].[29] Colonel Rüdiger, having advanced on Lukoml with the lead detachment stationed at Slidzy, drove the enemy out of Lukoml and captured some 300 prisoners, but after learning of the retreat by the vanguard, he retreated to Pochaevitsy.[30]

During that night of 1 to 2 (13 to 14) November, Count Wittgenstein ordered Lieutenant General Prince Iashvili to go to the vanguard under General Alekseev and, having taken command of it, withdraw the entire force, except for two foot regiments – Mogilev Infantry and Podolsk Infantry, the Mittau Dragoons and six guns from 3rd Horse Artillery Company, to reinforce Steinheil, who was holding a position at Smoliyantsy, and arrange the artillery to defend this position at his own discretion. General Foch, who was stationed at Lepel with the reserve, was ordered to come to Chashniki and stand on the left bank of the Ulla; four bridges were laid for communications between the corps' fighting lines.[31]

The force under Count Wittgenstein, in anticipation of an enemy attack on 2 (14) November, were located as follows:[32] the infantry regiments of 14th Division (Tula Infantry, Navaginsk Infantry, Tenginsk Infantry and Estland Infantry) and Neva Infantry, on the right bank of the river Lukomka, partly on the high ground, partly on the reverse slope; several squadrons on the left wing of the infantry; two guns from 14th Battery Company and six guns from 11th Light Company on the very favourable high ground at the Smoliyantsy manor. 6th Battery Company and six guns from 11th Light Company were positioned in order to bombard the front line from the right flank, on the left bank of the Lukomka, upstream of the manor, while

---

29 Communique on military operations by the independent I Corps. *Oestreich. milit. Zeitschrift*, 1821, *Drittes Heft*.
30 *Précis de la campagne du 1er corps* etc.
31 *Précis de la campagne du 1er corps* etc.
32 See the Plan of the Battle of Smoliyantsy.

THE BATTLES OF CHASHNIKI AND SMOLIYANTSY   145

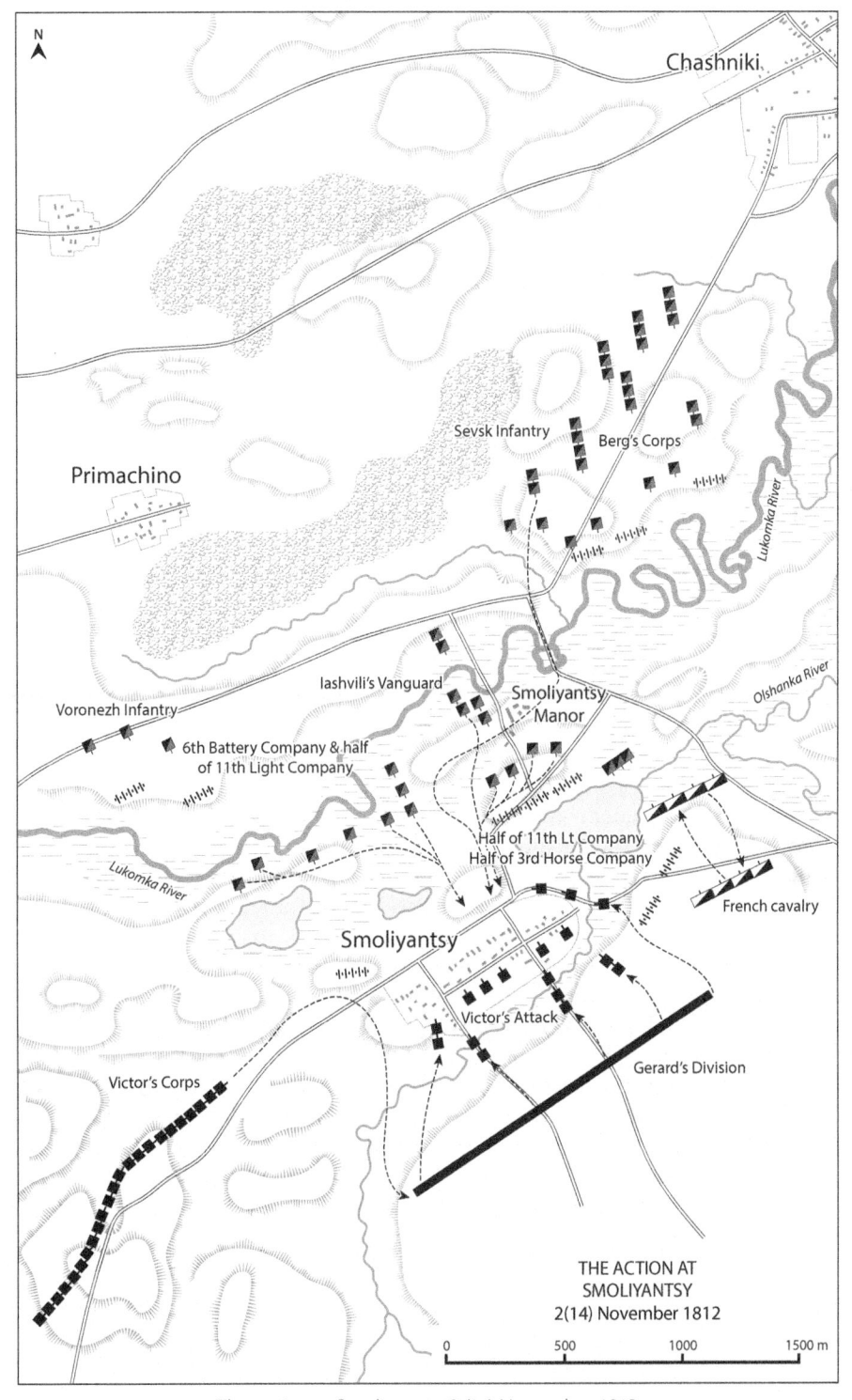

The action at Smoliyantsy, 2 (14) November 1812.

their protection was entrusted to the Voronezh Infantry Regiment, located on the reverse slope. Berg's corps was also on the left bank of the river, downstream of the manor, pushing batteries forwards in order to fire on the troops of the front line from the left flank. The village of Smoliyantsy in front of the position was occupied by our jägers. The detachment under Rüdiger, still located at Pochaevitsy, was shielding the corps forces from being enveloped from the direction of Chereya, while the Lithuania Infantry Regiment was placed near Dubrovo in order to liaise with them.

At 11 o'clock in the morning, Gérard's division attacked the vanguard under Prince Iashvili, which consisted of four battalions and four squadrons, with six horse artillery pieces. Our troops, giving way to the significantly superior enemy numbers, withdrew slowly, in the greatest order, and having passed through the battle line, they became its reserve, while the six guns from 3rd Horse Artillery Company were attached to the batteries that were already in position. The village of Smoliyantsy, assaulted by the French, changed hands several times and, finally, remained with the enemy. Meanwhile, Marshal Victor, gradually forming up his other divisions to the left of Smoliyantsy, led an attack on our right wing, but, being engaged in crossfire from batteries located on the right bank of the Lukomka river and from 6th Battery Company under Lieutenant Colonel Shulman, which was stationed on the left bank, his troops were thrown into disorder several times, which finally forced the marshal to withdraw his artillery. During these attacks, the French columns, repulsed by the cannonade, gradually shuffled to their right and settled facing our centre, out of range of the fire, while those who followed them in turn were committed to action and then joined the others who had previously retreated from Steinheil's position. Thus, Victor's entire corps ended up at a distance of half a *verst* beyond the village of Smoliyantsy.

Following this, the enemy cavalry, forming up on the right wing of their infantry, moved to attack our left wing, but being engaged by artillery fire from Berg's corps, were forced to retreat. Marshal Victor, witnessing the failure of his attempts against the flanks of the front line, flanked by the batteries on the left bank of the Lukomka, decided to attack the centre and, having withdrawn strong columns from the village of Smoliyantsy, directed them against our batteries stationed in front of the manor. Several battalions from Steinheil's corps moved towards the enemy; bitter hand-to-hand combat ensued, during which, first ours, then the French broke into Smoliyantsy; the entire Russian force stationed on the right bank of the river took part in this fight, and eventually, the Sevsk Infantry Regiment, sent from the left bank, repulsed the French for the last time and seized the village. The enemy, moving out of range of our fire, settled down for the night on the right flank towards the Beshankovichi road. The next morning [15 November new style], Marshal Victor retreated down the road to Chereya with his corps. During the entire action at Smoliyantsy, Oudinot, having formed his force up facing Rüdiger's detachment, at Pochaevitsy, opened a strong cannonade, but also retreated to Chereya the next day.[33]

---

33 Chambray, II, 417.

The Battle of Smoliyantsy cost the French about 3,000 men, including some 800 prisoners. On our side, the casualties were almost the same, including the losses to the vanguard under General Alekseev during the retreat on 1 (13) November.[34]

Napoleon, concerned that the force under Count Wittgenstein could get astride the line of retreat of the remnants of the *Grande Armée*, from Smolensk, ordered Marshal Victor to attack and push Wittgenstein back; in the event that our troops were holding a strong position, Victor was ordered to envelope the army under Count Wittgenstein from a flank, threatening to cut us off from the Dvina, because it was said that 'Wittgenstein could not allow his line of communications to be severed.'[35] Indeed, Count Wittgenstein considered it vital to guard his line of retreat to the Dvina and, in all likelihood, would have moved away from the Orsha road if Victor had gone around the left flank of our force.[36] But Victor did not dare to make this move. Concerned about being driven back to the Dvina and losing the opportunity to reopen communications with Napoleon's force, he remained at Chereya until 10 (22) November; while Wittgenstein, for his part, stationed himself at Chashniki waiting for the main body under Kutuzov and Chichagov's army, limited himself to monitoring the enemy corps.[37] General Harpe, whose detachment had rejoined the force under Wittgenstein on 3 (15) November, the day after the action at Smoliyantsy, was advanced to the village of Aksiontsy with a new vanguard, some 4,000 men in total.[38] Lieutenant Colonel Stolypin, with a detachment of about 1,000 men with two guns,[39] was stationed at Pochaevitsy, to relieve the detachment under Rüdiger, who were incorporated into Harpe's vanguard, and protected the communications between this vanguard and the detachment under General Vlastov, who shifted from Luzhki to Lepel. Rodionov's Cossack Regiment was to the left of the vanguard,

---

34 Communique on military operations by the independent I Corps (Archive of the M.T.D. No. 44,585, Annex 7). Count Wittgenstein's report to the Tsar on the battle at Smoliyantsy, dated 5 [17] November, No. 66.
35 '... *il devient d'autant plus urgent que vous attaquiez Wittgenstein. Si ce général a choisi un camp et une position avantageuse, où il soit difficile de livrer bataille, il vous est facile de manoeuvrer de manière à lui couper sa retraite et ses communications sur la Dwina. Vous devez partir du principe que Wittgenstein ne peut se laisser couper sur cette rivière.*' Napoleon's orders to Marshal Victor, dated 11 November new style, from Smolensk. These orders were received by Victor in Chereya on or about 4 (16) November.
36 Count Wittgenstein, reporting to the Tsar on his attempt to collect information about the movements of Admiral Chichagov towards the Berezina and about the reoccupation of Minsk by enemy troops, wrote; '... my position at Chashniki became dangerous; the corps under Victor and Saint-Cyr were in superior strength; general Wrede, retreating through Glubokoe towards Vilna, could link up with the Polish army (probably the troops forming up in Lithuania), and having pressured Major General Vlastov across the Dvina, in cooperation with most of McDonald's corps, would be able to move quickly on Polotsk to threaten my right flank and cut off communications with Polotsk, and more particularly with Disna.' Count Wittgenstein's report to Emperor Alexander I, dated 30 October [11 November], No. 62.
37 *Précis de la campagne du 1er corps* etc. (Archive of the M.T.D. No. 29,200).
38 The vanguard consisted of: Navaginsk Infantry, Petrovsk Infantry, four combined grenadier battalions, the Grodno Hussars, Combined Dragoon Regiment, Platov 4th's Cossacks, 12 horse artillery pieces and six foot artillery pieces.
39 Two battalions, two squadrons of Yamburg Dragoons.

between Aksiontsy and the Dvina, at Boyare, and maintained communications between the force under Harpe and the Vitebsk garrison. Overall, our advanced detachments were monitoring the entire sector from Lepel through Chashniki to the Dvina. This were the dispositions of the troops of the independent I Corps until 10 (22) November, that is, until the time when Oudinot and Victor moved towards the Orsha road in order to protect the remnants of the *Grande Armée* from the front and rear. Count Wittgenstein, being unable to drive the enemy troops operating on the Dvina back towards Vilna and away from the main body under Napoleon, to occupy the course of the Ulla and establish communications with Chichagov on the right bank of the Berezina (as should have happened on the basis of the overall plan), and could not stand on the line of retreat of the French army towards Borisov, which would have exposed him to the danger of being driven back into the swamps of the Berezina, while being forced to limit the objective of his operations to pursuing the enemy from the rear and isolating part of their army. Instead of engaging Napoleon on his line of retreat with the armies under Wittgenstein and Chichagov, who, having established communications between themselves, would have presented an insurmountable barrier to the enemy, this important operation was left to the army of Admiral Chichagov alone.

Let us turn to his operations from the position at Brest until his arrival on the Berezina.

40

Chichagov's movements from Brest to the Berezina

Chichagov's deployment at Brest and Schwarzenberg's at Drohiczyn. – The division of Chichagov's army into two formations; the composition of each. – Chichagov's advance to Slonim; the movement of the Austro-Saxon army behind him to Wołkowysk and Slonim. – Saken's movement to the rear of Schwarzenberg and Reynier.

Chernyshev's expeditions from Slonim to the Neman and Berezina.

Saken's advance through the Białowieska forest to Wołkowysk. – Reynier's deployment at Wołkowysk. – The battle of Wołkowysk. – Saken's plans for future operations. – Schwarzenberg's movement into Saken's rear. – Saken's retreat. – The pursuit by the enemy corps. – Comments on the operations by both sides.

The advance by Chichagov's army from Slonim to Minsk. – Orders issued by the Governor of Minsk, Bronikowski. – Dąbrowski's movements to assist him. – Actions at Novo-Sverzhen and Kojdanów. – Dąbrowski's and Bronikowski's retreat to the Berezina. The liberation of Minsk by Russian forces. – The link-up with Liders. – Ertel's inactivity in Mozyr and his replacement by Tuchkov. – The deployment of Chichagov's force for the occupation of Minsk. – Count Lambert's rapid advance to the Berezina river and the capture of the Borisov bridgehead. – The outcome of Lambert's operations. – Chichagov's advance to the Berezina. – The Supreme Rescript on prisoners and orders for their subsistence.

Following the action at Biała, on 6 (18) October, the main body under Admiral Chichagov was still in the sector between Brest and Kamieniec, while the corps under Schwarzenberg and Reynier were at Drohiczyn. The troops of the Army of the Danube remained in the positions they occupied until 15 (27) October, in anticipation of the collection of provisions, as well as to confirm the ongoing moves by Schwarzenberg. Chichagov, preoccupied with securing the army from the rear during the advance to the Berezina, initially proposed pushing the enemy corps back to Warsaw, and then proceeding with the implementation of the overall operational plan, but subsequently discarded this intent. Schwarzenberg and Reynier, in anticipation of reinforcements moving towards them from Warsaw, remained at Drohiczyn even longer. The strength of our force reached over 60,000 men; the enemy had about 38,000, excluding Durutte's [Pierre François Joseph Durutte] division (*11e Corps*), which was moving to assist them, with a strength of 9,000 to 10,000 men.[1]

Admiral Chichagov, having completed all preparations for the impending campaign and having provided rations for his troops through requisitioning in the surrounding countryside, divided his army into two formations; he would go to the Berezina with one himself, leaving Lieutenant General Saken [Fabian Wilhelmovich Osten-Saken or Fabian Gottlieb von der Osten-Saken], with the other, to monitor the corps under Schwarzenberg and Reynier. The force assigned to march to the main theatre of war consisted of a vanguard, under Count Lambert's [Karl Osipovich de Lambert or Charles de Lambert] command, a corps under Lieutenant General Voinov [Alexander Lvovich Voinov] and a reserve under Lieutenant General Sabaneev [Ivan Vasilievich Sabaneev]. The corps under Major Generals Bulatov [Mikhail Leontievich Bulatov] and Lieven [Ivan Andreevich Lieven] were under Lieutenant General Saken's command at Brest; the corps under Lieutenant General Essen 3rd [Pëtr Kirillovich Essen] was left for the time being at Chernavchitsy, to join whichever formation of the army had greatest need of reinforcements; but no sooner had the main body of the Army of the Danube started moving, than Admiral Chichagov saw fit to reinforce Saken with Essen troops. The force that marched to the Berezina, under Chichagov's command, consisted of 48 battalions, 64 squadrons, 14 artillery companies and one of pioneers and ten Cossack regiments; during the march to Slonim, the men of Chaplits' [Yefim Ignatievich Chaplits] detachment were to join them, consisting of four battalions, 12 squadrons and three Cossack regiments, with one horse artillery company; overall, the army marching on the Berezina consisted of about 30,000 men with 180 guns. In addition, in support of this army, a detachment under Major General Liders [Nikolai Ivanovich Liders], numbering 3,500 men, was to come up from Moldavia, via Pinsk, while the reserve corps under Lieutenant General Ertel, with a strength of 15,000 men, was to go from Mozyr towards Minsk. Under General Saken's command, there were 47 battalions, 36 squadrons, six Cossack regiments, eight artillery companies and one of pioneers, numbering 27,000 men, with 92 guns. The remainder of Chichagov's force, consisting of several battalions and squadrons, were located near Vladimir, on the upper Bug, in order to defend Volhynia, along with the Ukrainian Cossack regiments under Colonel Count de Witt [Ivan Osipovich de Witt], who were supposed to arrive there soon.[2]

---

1 Strength returns on the composition of the corps of the Army of the Danube.
2 Information on the composition of the forces under Chichagov and Saken was extracted from the returns placed in the War Diary of the Army of the Danube, following its renaming as Third Army, in 1812, compiled by Lieutenant Colonel Malinovsky of the Suite of His Imperial Majesty's Quartermaster Department (Archive of the M.T.D. No. 32,417, notebook 15), and War Diary of General Saken's Corps in 1812, 1813 and 1814, compiled by Lieutenant Colonel Gotovsky (Archive of the M.T.D. No. 16,643). For the full order of battle, see Appendix VII.

On 18 (30) October, Chichagov's army set out from its locations for Pruzhany. The force marched in two columns: the vanguard under Count Lambert and Lieutenant General Sabaneev's reserve were on the right with army headquarters, while Lieutenant General Voinov's corps was on the left. On 25 October (6 November), both columns arrived in the vicinity of Slonim, where the headquarters were established.[3]

Chichagov's advance towards the Berezina could not be concealed from the enemy commanders stationed at Drohiczyn. Schwarzenberg, having received intelligence on this and believing that our entire army guarding Volhynia had moved towards Slonim, went after them in order to halt, or at least slow down their movement. Upon the arrival of some reinforcements to the Austro-Saxons, of which the most important were the troops from Durutte's division, consisting of 15 battalions,[4] Schwarzenberg launched a feint offensive towards Biała, and then moved his army to the right bank of the Bug at Drohiczyn and Siemiatycze, on 18 (30) October, advanced through Boćki and Bielsk, directing Reynier's corps and part of the Austrian force to Kleszczele, and crossed the Narew at Narewka and Ploski on 23 October (4 November). Thereafter, having left Reynier's corps on this river in order to protect his advance, he continued to Wołkowysk and on towards Slonim.

As soon as Saken learned of the crossing of the Bug by significant enemy forces in the vicinity of Drohiczyn, he ignored Schwarzenberg's feints at Biała and decided to follow in the footsteps of the Austro-Saxon army. According to all the available intelligence, the enemy force was twice as strong as the Russian corps, but our commander, intending to contribute to the success of the overall operational plan, was determined to pursue and halt Schwarzenberg, even though he could be defeated himself.[5] On 22 October (3 November), Saken's force departed from Brest: with Major General Melissino [Alexey Petrovich Melissino] in the vanguard, with Chikilev's Cossacks, Lubny Hussars, Vladimir Dragoons, 37th Jägers and with two guns from 15th Horse Artillery Company, marching to Wysokie Litewskie and on towards Kleszczele; they were followed by the main body in two columns: Lieutenant General Essen's on the right, consisting of his corps and Count Lieven's reserve which, having crossed the river Lesna, marched in the direction of Wysokie Litewskie, while Major General Bulatov's corps, which formed the left column crossing at Terebun, was directed on Wołczyn. The Bialystok Infantry Regiment was left to guard Brest, under the command of Colonel Zass [Alexander Pavlovich Zass or Christoph Alexander Freiherr von Saß].[6]

Meanwhile on 26 October (7 November), during a rest-day granted to the troops in Slonim and its surroundings, Admiral Chichagov, having received intelligence about the emergence of the enemy from Wołkowysk and Grodno, instructed *Flügel-adjutant*

---

3   War Diary of the Army of the Danube (Third Army), compiled by Lieutenant Colonel Malinovsky.
4   Durutte's division consisted of 18 battalions, although one regiment was left in Warsaw.
5   *Journal militaire des opérations du Corps sous les ordres de lieutenant-général baron de Saken, par le comte de Venançon quartier-maître de ce Corps* (Archive of the M.T.D. No. 29,180).
6   War Diary of Saken's Corps, compiled by Colonel Gotovsky (Archive of the M.T.D. No. 16,643).

Colonel Chernyshev [Alexander Ivanovich Chernyshev] to reconnoitre the direction taken by the enemy force with Panteleev's Cossack Regiment. On 27 October (8 November), upon arrival in Dereczyn, Chernyshev learned of the movements of an Austrian detachment, under the command of General Mohr [Johann Friedrich Freiherr von Mohr], from Grodno to the town of Mosty on the Neman, in order to construct a crossing there and to establish communications with Schwarzenberg's force marching towards Wołkowysk. Colonel Chernyshev, intending to prevent a concentration of enemy forces, immediately sent a Cossack raiding party to Mosty, which destroyed all the materials for crossing the Neman collected by Mohr's leading detachment. Just at that moment, intelligence was received from a patrol sent to Wołkowysk about the occupation of this town by the enemy, Chernyshev quickly marched over to Zelwa, destroyed the bridges on the Zelvyanka river, close to Zelwa and Ivashkovichi, and, having interrogated the prisoners, became convinced of the occupation of Wołkowysk and Izabelin by 12,000 Austro-Saxons. In the meantime, having received orders from the Commander-in-Chief to march from Dereczyn, via Zdzięcioł, to Novogrudok and onwards, on the morning of 28 October (9 November), in order to establish communications with Count Wittgenstein, following a forced march, Chernyshev arrived in Novogrudok and raced along the indicated direction, across territory occupied by the enemy, where most of the inhabitants were sympathetic to them, along country lanes, and for the most part, a very awkward route. Having swum their horses across the Neman at Kolodzina, Chernyshev continued to advance via Nalibaki and Kamen to Dubrovo, captured an enemy picket there, from whom he learned about the retreat by the French *Grande Armée* to Smolensk, and reached the highway between Minsk and Vilna, near the town of Radoszkowicze. He managed to capture three enemy couriers here with important dispatches and liberated several of our prisoners, who were being escorted by French gendarmes: Among the released officers were: Adjutant General Wintzingerode, Izyum Hussars Captain Naryshkin, who had been captured with him, Major General Svechin, among others.[7] Shortly thereafter, having closed up to the town of Verkhny-Berezino, Colonel Chernyshev met Cornet Demidov, sent from Count Wittgenstein's headquarters to the Army of the Danube, and sent him on with a report for Admiral Chichagov about the success of his expedition and arrived in Lepel, having covered more than 350 *versts* in five days. During this bold march, Chernyshev destroyed several French magazines and captured many prisoners, but since he did not have the means to transport them with his detachment, he let them go, content with taking away and destroying their weapons.[8] Although Chernyshev could not deliver definitive information to Count Wittgenstein on the timing of Chichagov's arrival in Minsk, he nevertheless gave assurance that, in all probability, the Army of the Danube should reach this location by 5 (17) November. Panteleev's Cossack Regiment became part of Vlastov's detachment stationed at Lepel.[9]

---

7   In a letter to General Mikhailovsky-Danilevsky, Naryshkin wrote that he, along with his comrades in captivity, had been liberated by *Sotnik* Dudkin, who had been sent on patrol by Colonel Chernyshev.
8   Colonel Chernyshev's report to Count Wittgenstein, dated 5 [17] November, from Lepel.
9   *Précis de la campagne du 1er corps* etc. (Archive of the M.T.D. No. 29,200).

As has already been stated above, the force under General Saken, at the first news of the enemy movement towards Wołkowysk, went to intercept them in two columns, towards Wysokie Litewskie and Wołczyn. On 22 October (3 November), Chikilev's Cossacks and the Ural Cossack regiments, encountering two squadrons of Austrian hussars four *versts* from Wysokie Litewskie, on the road to Kleszczele, drove them back to Telatycze, and captured 75 men. General Melissino, having received intelligence that the enemy was holding Kleszczele, moved there with his vanguard and learned from the inhabitants that the Saxon corps had set out from Kleszczele towards Orla the day before, quickly pursued them, catching up with the enemy rearguard, on 27 October (8 November), behind the Narew, at Rudnia, near the village of Krinki, he took some 100 men prisoner and captured some of their vehicles. At the same time, intelligence was received on the retreat by the main body of Reynier's corps to Porozów, which forced Saken to divert through the Białowieska forest, to Białowieża, towards Porozów. Reynier attempted to isolate our vanguard from the force pursuing him under Saken, but Melissino evaded being drawn into combat, and in the meantime our remaining troops closed up to assist him. So the Saxons retreated, on 1 (13) November, via Izabelin, towards Wołkowysk. On that same day, Saken, having assembled his corps at Gornostaevichi, forced the enemy rearguard under General Gablenz [Heinrich Adolph von Gablenz] to retreat to Wołkowysk, on the night of 1 to 2 (13 to 14) November. The following day [14 November new style], our entire corps was located at Izabelin. There, intelligence was received on Reynier's intention to halt at Wołkowysk and about the movement from there, three days previously, by Schwarzenberg with the Austrian corps towards Slonim, from where Chichagov had set out, on 27 October (8 November), onwards towards the Berezina.[10]

Indeed, Schwarzenberg, not paying proper attention to the reports by Reynier concerning the danger that threatened him, continued to proceed behind the Army of the Danube, while Reynier was forced to stay at Wołkowysk, both to protect the transports that were with his corps, and in order to give his weary troops some rest. The positions occupied by the Saxons, outside the town, on high ground, presented defensive advantages. But as there were no convenient buildings for the corps headquarters behind it, Reynier and all the other Saxon generals occupied quarters in the town, forwards of the troops.[11]

General Saken, intending to take advantage of this enemy lapse, decided to attack them the very same night, and to that end he issued dispositions at nine o'clock in the evening, on the basis of which three detachments, each of three battalions with 100 light cavalrymen, were to break into the town from the front and from the flanks; Colonel Belokopytov [Ivan Petrovich Belokopytov?], with one of the battalions of the 39th Jägers, had the mission of going around the town on the right side, 'to go directly to the house where the French General Reynier is lodging.' All three detachments were ordered to move through the town without noise and without

---

10 *Journal militaire des opérations du Corps de Saken*. Saken's War Diary, compiled by Gotovksy. War Diary of the Army of the Danube (Third Army), compiled by Lieutenant Colonel Malinovsky.
11 Chambray, II, 405-407.

firing; they were to be followed by our remaining troops. The transports were assigned to go from Izabelin, via Yasenovitsa and Blankitni [Błękitni], to Gniezna [Hniezna], and so on.[12] The entire corps, leaving their places at ten o'clock, closed up to the town. The weather was bad, stormy; a blizzard prevented the Saxons from seeing the advance by our troops, which facilitated the lead battalion of 39th Jägers approaching the outposts completely unnoticed, but shuffling noises during the removal of a *cheval de frise* aroused the attention of the sentries stationed near the bridge over the river; an enemy picket began to shoot and sounded the alarm, while Colonel Belokopytov, ignoring the Saxons assembling at various points, went directly to the house where he hoped to capture General Reynier; but as he had moved to another house shortly before, our jägers could not immediately find him. Reynier managed to jump out of a window and leave the town for the bivouacs; one of his aides de camp was killed; *Général de division* Durutte was wounded; a Saxon regiment which raced to the rescue of the headquarters in the town, lost its colour, captured by soldiers from the Vyatka Infantry Regiment; all the carriages from the corps headquarters and Reynier's chancellery were captured. The chaos and confusion of the enemy in the town reached its peak when a fire broke out in the town, spread by the stormy wind. Saken's remaining troops, following our leading detachments, closed in; but they were forced to confine themselves to seizing the town. The firefight went on all night; while at dawn [on 15 November new style] the enemy opened a powerful bombardment of the town, trying re-take it from time to time. General Melissino was sent from our side to attack the high ground held by the Saxons; but by evening both sides remained in their original positions: Reynier on the high ground behind Wołkowysk; while Saken was on this side of the river, holding the town with a small part of the infantry. Despite the superior numbers of our force, Saken postponed the attack on the enemy position, having received intelligence the day before that Schwarzenberg was marching back from Slonim to Wołkowysk, to assist the Saxon corps. But at about five o'clock in the evening, Cossacks sent out on patrols returned with more than 20 prisoners, who unanimously swore that Schwarzenberg had turned back towards Slonim. General Saken, convinced of the superiority of his force over the enemy corps standing facing him, issued orders to attack the next morning [16 November new style], while Reynier, noticing our preparations and knowing that Schwarzenberg was moving up to assist him, had no doubt of success. 'Wołkowysk and Victory:' this was the challenge and response he issued to the men of the Saxon corps.

On 4 (16) November, at ten o'clock in the morning, skirmishing and a bombardment ensued at the town. General Saken, wanting to envelope the enemy on their left flank and thereby deprive them of the opportunity to retreat to link up with Schwarzenberg, ordered Major General Bulatov to cross the river upstream of the town with the Staro-Oskol Infantry and with 45th Jägers and 29th Jägers, when they suddenly heard two cannon shots to the right of the location of our force: this was a signal to the Saxon corps from Schwarzenberg. After that, at about one o'clock in the afternoon, Saken received word that an enemy detachment, of infantry and

---

12 Force Dispositions, dated 2 [14] November.

cavalry with guns, having occupied Izabelin in the rear of the corps, had captured our carts and sick there, who, according to the disposition, were supposed to have been transported to Gniezna, on the road to Białowieża. The situation of our corps was very grave: Reynier stood facing them frontally, while the Austrian vanguard, commanded by Fröhlich [Franz Freiherr von Fröhlich], was located several *versts* behind our right flank, by making a small flank movement towards Blankitni, could take our only crossing over the river Ross.[13] To crown this difficult situation, General Saken, believing that all our carts and sick had already been taken to Gniezna in accordance with the issued orders, called for the Serpukhov Dragoon Regiment, located in Izabelin, to come to Wołkowysk, but after learning about the mistake that had occurred, he sent this regiment to Izabelin. Our dragoons, having encountered several Austrian squadrons on the way, drove them off, saving some of the captured carts and pursued the enemy to Izabelin, but could not force them out of there, because Izabelin was being held by a strong Austrian detachment under General Fröhlich.[14] The reserve, under the command of Major General Count Lieven, was ordered to go to Gniezna and attack the enemy if they had seized the bridge on the Ross; while several battalions were sent to Wołkowysk, where only a few of our marksmen remained at that time, in order to conceal this movement from the Saxon troops standing within sight of us. Meanwhile, it emerged that the enemy had not yet managed to reach the village of Blankitni (on the road to Porozów), and that it was held by part of our reserve; Taking advantage of this, General Saken sent Essen's corps along this road, and ordered Bulatov's force to cover the retreat of the other corps.

General Reynier, finding his left flank secured by the arrival of Schwarzenberg, sent part of his force across the Ross, on his right flank, enveloping Bulatov's left, arriving at Blankitni at the very moment that Essen's men, as soon as they had arrived there, were repairing the bridge that had collapsed under the artillery. But Reynier, instead of supporting the advance by this force sent by him, remained on the high ground behind Wołkowysk, and thus gave our corps time not only to fix the collapsed bridge, but to retreat to Gniezna, rest there for several hours and retreat onwards to Świsłocz on the night of 4 to 5 (16 to 17) November, without further loss. Upon arrival there, on 5 (17) November, at two o'clock in the afternoon, General Saken deployed his corps near the town, leaving Major General Melissino two *versts* ahead with the Lubny Hussars and Cossack regiments.[15]

It is difficult to say anything conclusive about the losses to both sides in the Wołkowysk action: on the basis of our data, the enemy lost 500 prisoners between 2 to 4 (14 to 16) November; while some 100 men were killed on our side. Foreign historians have claimed that we lost more than 2,000 prisoners alone in the fighting and during the retreat, while casualties overall were some 10,000 men, which is obviously an exaggeration.[16]

---

13 *Journal militaire des opérations du Corps de Saken*.
14 *Journal militaire des opérations du Corps de Saken*. War Diary of Lieutenant General Essen 3rd's corps, in 1812, maintained by Lieutenant Colonel Freigang.
15 *Journal militaire des opérations du Corps de Saken*. War Diary of Essen 3rd's corps.
16 War Diary of Essen 3rd's corps.

Simultaneously with Saken's retreat from Wołkowysk to Świsłocz, the Austrian corps made a flank movement via Porozów towards Berniki, from where the enemy could reach the bridge at Rudnia before our troops, who were much further from there and had no other crossing over the Narew (because the bridge at Ploski had been burned on Saken's orders, by General Gamper [Yermolai Yermolaevich Gamper] on 27 October (8 November), and even if this bridge had remained intact, Saken could not get there without exposing himself to the risk of being cut off from Volhynia). But the Austrians did not take the opportunity to inflict a decisive defeat on our corps, and the force under Schwarzenberg, exhausted by marches along difficult country lanes, halted at Berniki for the night of 4 to 5 (16 to 17) November and did not arrive at Rudnia before 6 (18) November, after Saken's entire force had already passed through. The enemy, before reaching Rudnia, made their way along forest paths and attacked our transport; but were repulsed by the rearguard under General Melissino, supported by the Schlüsselburg Infantry and 37th Jägers; thereafter, at five o'clock in the afternoon, our jägers, having occupied the village of Rudnia, held out there, and at seven o'clock set fire to several houses in order to stop the advancing enemy, and destroyed the bridges on the river Rudavka and on the river Narew.[17] On 7 (19) November, General Saken retreated to Białowieża. The enemy did not dare to follow our force into the Białowieska forest, but went around in two columns: to Shereshov and Pruzhany. Saken, who was not yet aware of this, not wanting to lose contact with the enemy and to divert them even further south, detached Colonel Prince Zhevakhov [Ivan Semënovich Zhevakhov] to Shereshov, with the Serpukhov Dragoons and Ural Cossack regiments; while sending Major General Berdyaev [Alexander Nikolaevich Berdyaev] to Kamieniec, on the direct route to Brest, with a squadron of Tver Dragoons and one Cossack regiment; after that, General Melissino also set out for Shereshov with the Lubny Hussars, two guns from 15th Light Company and all the Cossack regiments, where they were joined by Zhevakhov's leading detachment and the 3rd Ukrainian Cossack Regiment, sent there by Count de Witt via Brest towards Pruzhany. On the morning of 9 (21) November, the enemy, appearing at Shereshov from the direction of Velikoe Selo, opened a bombardment, but then pulled back and made for Pruzhany. On that same day, General Melissino was sent to Kobrin with the Lubny Hussar Regiment in order to protect the *Wagenburg* stationed there; all Saken's remaining troops withdrew along the road to Brest-Litovsk and deployed, during the night of 11 to 12 (23 to 24) November, behind the river Mukhavets, their right flank on the Kamyanitsa Zhyravyetskaya manor, and the left was on Brest, while the Saxon corps, following our troops, closed up towards Brest, and Schwarzenberg enveloped Saken from the right flank from Pruzhany to Kobrin with the Austrian corps.[18] On 13 (25) November, there was a rather sharp clash at Kamyanitsa Zhyravyetskaya in which the brave and skilled artillery Colonel Bastian was killed.[19]

---

17 War Diary of Saken's Corps, compiled by Gotovsky. *Journal militaire des opérations du Corps de Saken.*
18 *Journal militaire des opérations du Corps de Saken.* War Diary of Essen 3rd's corps. Chambray, II, 410.
19 War Diary of the Army of the Danube (Third Army), compiled by Lieutenant Colonel Malinovsky.

General Saken, upon reaching Brest, and wanting to secure a supply of provisions for his corps and, if possible, maintain communications with Chichagov, ordered the force under Essen 3rd to head via Ruda and Mokrany to Ratno, and make their way through Kamień Koszyrski to Pinsk; upon Essen's arrival in Ratno, General Saken received Chichagov's orders to detach Essen's corps to join the Army of the Danube via Minsk, however, the occupation of Pinsk by the enemy and the loss of our magazines located there prevented Essen from fulfilling these orders and on 18 (30) November, forced him to divert via Datin and Kovel in Volhynia; the rest of Saken's force, reinforced by the Ukrainian Cossack regiments under Count de Witt, withdrew to Matseiv and Lyuboml and held advanced outposts in the sector facing Kobrin and Brest and the course of the Bug.[20]

Meanwhile, Schwarzenberg, on the occupation of Kobrin, on 13 (25) November, received a letter there from Maret in Vilna, in which the necessity for a quick advance by the Austro-Saxon army to Minsk was put to him. This obliged him, after a rest-day granted to the troops on 14 (26) November, to march back to Pruzhany; but he did not go beyond Slonim, while Reynier remained at Brest with his corps until 19 November (1 December). Removing them from the line of retreat of the remnants of the *Grande Armée* prevented them from taking part in operations in the main theatre of war.[21]

Saken's operations speak for themselves: being left facing an enemy who had almost double his strength, he showed the ability of an independent military commander in full, pursuing Reynier persistently, forcing Schwarzenberg, threatening the Army of the Danube with an attack from the rear, to turn back, knowing how to evade defeat, having been outflanked by the significant forces of the Austrian corps, and how to draw an enemy off to a significant distance without losing contact with them, but avoiding a decisive battle with the superior numbers of the Austro-Saxon army. Foreign historians have exaggerated the casualties suffered by our forces in the action at Wołkowysk and during the retreat to Brest. If Saken had really lost 10,000 men, almost all of his transport and much of the artillery,[22] then, leaving Reynier's corps to pursue him and monitor him (which in this case would have been almost as strong as our corps), Schwarzenberg could have turned from Wołkowysk to Slonim and on to Minsk and covered the retreat by the remnants of Napoleon's army. But there is no doubt that the force under Saken, despite the losses suffered, was superior in strength to the Saxons, and besides, Schwarzenberg was not so much concerned about the fate of the *Grande Armée*, than about the preservation of the force entrusted to him, which he could better achieve by staying facing Saken and closing up to the border of Galicia, rather than delving deeper into our *Oblasti* and working in cooperation with the *Grande Armée*.[23]

Let us turn to the operations by the Army of the Danube after its departure from Slonim. Admiral Chichagov, upon arrival in Slonim on 25 October (6 November), having received the news there that Moscow had been evacuated by the enemy and

---

20 *Journal militaire des opérations du Corps de Saken*.
21 Chambray, II, 410.
22 Chambray, II, 410.
23 Chambray, II, 412. Beitzke, *Geschichte des russischen Krieges im Jahre 1812*, 319-320.

that Napoleon's army was retreating, and seeing the obvious need to hasten to the Berezina, on the following day [7 November new style], in the vicinity of Slonim, he assembled all the troops that had straggled, while Count Lambert was pushed forwards to Nesvizh with the vanguard.[24] To protect the army from the left flank, Chaplits' detachment was initially assigned to go from Slonim, via Novogrudok and Mir, to Novy-Sverzhen, but was replaced by Voinov's corps. General Chaplits' force formed the rearguard, shielding the army from Schwarzenberg. Ahead of Voinov's column was a vanguard under Major General Count O'Rourke [Iosif Kornilovich Orurk or Joseph Cornelius O'Rourke].[25] As cold, wet weather had already set in by this time, the corps commanders were ordered to accommodate the troops in quarters, or at least in sheds, observing: firstly, to establish outposts and patrols to secure themselves against surprise attack, and secondly, appointing stand-to positions in case of alarm.[26]

On 30 October (11 November), Count Lambert set out from the village of Torchitsy (near the town of Stalavichi) for Nesvizh with the vanguard, such that, having driven the enemy out of there, they were to pursue them relentlessly to Novy-Sverzhen and not give them chance to destroy the bridge over the Neman there. Upon reaching Snov, intelligence was received that the enemy had evacuated Nesvizh and marched to Novy-Sverzhen, where preparations had already been made to burn the bridge. In order to prevent the achievement of this intention and to seize this crossing on the direct route to Minsk, Lambert decided to go to Novy-Sverzhen immediately, detaching part of his vanguard to Nesvizh (namely, 7th Jägers, Alexandria Hussars and Starodub Dragoons), under the command of Colonel Knorring [Karl Bogdanovich Knorring]. The remainder of the force under Count Lambert (10th Jägers, 14th Jägers, 38th Jägers, Tatar Ulans, Zhitomir Dragoons, Barabanshchikov's Cossacks with 12 horse artillery pieces) set out along country lanes by forced march towards Novy-Sverzhen and halted at dusk at the village of Golovenchitsy, four *versts* from the town.[27]

---

24 Count Lambert's vanguard consisted of: 7th Jägers, 14th Jägers, 38th Jägers, Alexandria Hussars, Starodub Dragoons, Tatar Ulans and 12th Horse Artillery Company. War Diary of the vanguard of Third Army in 1812, compiled by Lieutenant Colonel Baron Üxküll (Archive of the M.T.D. No. 32,417).
25 Count O'Rourke's vanguard consisted of: Apsheron Infantry, 10th Jägers, Livland Dragoons, Kireev's Don Cossacks, 3rd Ural Cossacks and 16th Light Artillery Company. Four battalions, four squadrons, two Cossack regiments with 12 guns in total. War Diary of the Army of the Danube (Third Army), compiled by Lieutenant Colonel Malinovsky.
26 Orders for generals Count Langéron and Voinov, dated 19 [31] October, and for Count Lambert, dated 27 October [8 November]. Log of Outgoing Documents of the Commander-in-Chief, Army of the Danube and Third Army, Admiral Chichagov. Archive of the M.T.D. No. 44,585.
27 War Diary of the vanguard of Third Army in 1812. This diary states that the regiments sent to Nesvizh were: 7th Jägers, Alexandria Hussars, Starodub Dragoons, while those sent to Novy-Svezhen with Lambert himself were: 14th Jägers, 38th Jägers, Tatar Ulans, Zhitomir Dragoons, Barabanshchikov's Cossacks with 12th Horse Artillery Company. In General Krasovsky's notes it states that Count Lamber, having sent Colonel Knorring to Nesvizh with a cavalry detachment, went to Novy-Sverzhen with 10th Jägers and 14th Jägers and with some of the cavalry. From the Diary of the vanguard of Third Army, it can be seen that, in addition to the

At the same time as the vanguard under Count Lambert, and behind them the main body of the Army of the Danube, were moving towards Minsk, this city, so important due to its position on one of the main lines of communications for the French army and the significant magazines located there, was occupied by a very small force, consisting of the Württemberg *Infanterie-Regiment Nr. 7*, various depots of French, Polish and other foreign regiments, and a small element of the newly raised troops from Lithuania. The number of men in all these units did not exceed 2,000 veteran soldiers and 3,600 recruits.[28] Napoleon, while still in Moscow, had ordered Victor to hold the Württemberg *Infanterie-Regiment Nr. 7* in Minsk, on the march from Danzig [Gdańsk] to Gzhatsk at the time, and the sixth battalions of *22e légère* and *46e de ligne* and *93e de ligne*, and to form a reserve Minsk brigade from them, consisting of five battalions.[29] Later, having captured Slonim, as Chaplits was striking terror throughout the French administration in Lithuania, General Bronikowski, the governor of Minsk at the time, reported the danger that threatened him to *chef d'état-major* Berthier. As at that time Victor's corps had already gone to assist Saint-Cyr, Napoleon could assign only two divisions from Augereau's [Charles Pierre François Augereau] *11e Corps* to secure Lithuania: of these, Durutte's division had been sent (as mentioned above) to assist the Saxon corps under Reynier, while Loison's [Louis-Henri Loison] division, which was stationed at Königsberg [Kaliningrad], had received orders to move to Vilna, but could arrive there no earlier than 9 (21) November.

General Dąbrowski was also unable to get to Minsk in time. Back in September, the defeat of his detachments by the force under of General Ertel, at Glusk on 2 (14) September and at Gorbatsevichi on 3 (15) November, and the occupation of Pinsk on 4 (16) November by Major General Zapolsky [Andrei Vasilievich Zapolsky] forced Dąbrowski to abandon offensive operations in Polesia and focus his entire attention on protecting Minsk. To that end, *17 Pułk Piechoty* [infantry] and *15 Pułk Ułanów* [lancers] were left between the Dnieper and the Berezina, to protect Mogilev from the troops under Ertel (who, at that time, had retreated to Mozyr), and two battalions of *14 Pułk Piechoty*, at Svislach in order to monitor Bobruisk, while a small detachment under Captain Zwoliński was at Glusk, in order to liaise with the main body of the Polish division located at Slutsk. Having received only one battalion from *14 Pułk Piechoty* stationed in Grodno as reinforcements, Dąbrowski had assembled no more than 5,000 men, with whom he was supposed to protect a sector of four hundred *versts*, which forced him to increase the number of observation detachments and to form them from cavalry and skirmishers mounted on horseback. Such was the state of affairs in Polesia when, on 16 (28) October, General Dąbrowski received orders from Marshal Victor to concentrate his entire division on the Berezina. But as soon as the Polish troops began to assemble, orders came to divert to Minsk. The execution of this order was very dangerous, because the

---

above-mentioned troops, it also included Grekov 8th's Cossacks, Grekov 11th's Cossacks and the Yevpatoria Tatars.
28 *Situation de la place de Minsk à l'époque du 12 novembre* (new style) *1812* (Archive of the M.F.A.). For a breakdown of numbers, see Appendix VIII.
29 Orders for Marshal Victor, dated 16 October 1812 new style.

troops of the Army of the Danube, already approaching this city, were incomparably stronger than Dąbrowski's division.[30]

General Bronikowski, forced to defend Minsk with the insignificant garrison stationed there, sent General Kosiecki to Novy-Sverzhen with five battalions and several squadrons, numbering some 3,500 men in total, in order to defend the crossing over the Neman.[31] Kosiecki, instead of destroying the bridge and deploying on the left bank of the Neman, crossed the river and positioned his detachment beyond the Neman.

On 1 (13) November, Count Lambert, approaching Novy-Sverzhen two hours before dawn, sent the 10th Jäger Regiment under Colonel Ivanov [Ivan Dmitrievich Ivanov] to the right of the town to cut the road leading to Nesvizh, while Colonel Krasovsky's [Afanasy Ivanovich Krasovsky] 14th Jägers were ordered to attack the enemy frontally. Having formed his regiment into two battalion columns, Krasovsky quickly burst into the town and, without a shot, struck a battalion stationed in the square with fixed bayonets. The enemy, stunned by the onslaught of our infantry, fired only one volley and, having no time to reload their muskets, surrendered. Meanwhile, the 10th Jägers, having encountered another Lithuanian battalion on the Nesvizh road, drove them into the town and pursued them so relentlessly that Kosiecki did not have chance to destroy the bridge over the Neman, the protection of which had been entrusted to him. On that same day, the detachment under Count O'Rourke, with the assistance of Major Vietinghoff, sent by Count Lambert from Novy-Sverzhen towards Mir with two squadrons of Tatar Ulans and two companies of jägers, ejected the enemy from this town and forced a total of 400 men to surrender.[32] Overall, on this day, Count Lambert's force captured: one field officer, 12 subalterns and 760 lower ranks. The enemy losses in killed reached 500, while on our side seven privates were killed and two officers and 35 lower ranks were wounded.[33] The most important of our successes was the capture of the bridge over the Neman, which was vital for the future movements by the army towards Minsk and the Berezina. At dusk, Count Lambert received a report from Colonel Knorring about his seizure of Nesvizh, where more than a million diamonds and pearls looted by the enemy from Moscow were found.[34]

On the following day, 2 (14) November, the Cossacks, moving ahead of the vanguard, with the assistance of two squadrons of Arzamas Dragoons, destroyed an enemy detachment, including 100 cavalry and 200 infantry.[35]

On 3 (15) November, Count Lambert's forward detachment, approaching Kaidanovo [Dzerzhinsk], discovered a Lithuanian force, who immediately began to

---

30 *Mémoire concernant les opérations de la 17me division sous les ordres de général Dombrowsky en 1812*, Archive of the M.T.D. No. 32,417.
31 The strength of Kosiecki's force is shown in Chambray as 2,600 men, but as Kosiecki's detachment had five battalions and 300 cavalry men, in all probability his troops strength reached 3,500 men. Chambray, II, 403-404.
32 War Diary of the Army of the Danube (Third Army), compiled by Lieutenant Colonel Malinovsky. War Diary of the vanguard of Third Army. Krasovsky's notes. Chambray, II, 404.
33 War Diary of the vanguard of Third Army.
34 Admiral Chichagov's report to the Tsar, dated 6 [18] November.
35 War Diary of the vanguard of Third Army.

retreat on sight along the road to Minsk. Count Lambert, intending to completely surround the enemy, sent four squadrons of Alexandria Hussars, with the two Cossack regiments under Grekov 8th [Pëtr Matveevich Grekov] and Grekov 11th, enveloping the Lithuanians from the left flank, while Knorring would envelope the right flank with the Starodub Dragoons, Tatar Ulans, Barabanshchikov's Don Cossacks and the Yevpatoria Tatars. The rest of the vanguard troops pursued the enemy from behind along the highway. Kosiecki, having marched more than ten *versts* from Kaidanovo and seeing only cavalry behind him, sent two Lithuanian battalions along the road to Minsk and covered their retreat with two French battalions and all the cavalry that remained with him.[36] The Zhitomir Dragoons attacked the Lithuanian cavalry, drove them off and captured a gun; while Major General Grekov pursued the enemy onwards as far as Priluki and captured all the remaining lancers, except for 100 men who escorted Kosiecki to Minsk. After this brilliant attack, the Zhitomir Dragoons turned to face the French regiment and blocked their line of retreat. The French, surrounded on all sides, continued to return fire and repulsed several attacks. But once Colonel Apushkin, having circled the enemy with four guns, engaged them with canister, this excellent infantry, staring at certain death and having suffered terrible casualties, laid down their arms.

After that, Knorring, before reaching the village of Grechin, caught up with one of the columns of Lithuanian infantry, blocked the enemy's path with the Yevpatoria Tatars and Barabanshchikov's Cossacks and attacked them with the Starodub Dragoons and Tatar Ulans so swiftly that the Lithuanians laid down their weapons almost without firing a single shot. The other column was surrounded and captured by Grekov, and another gun was taken. As both field officers from this battalion, Colonel Czapski and Major Szymanowski, fled without waiting for the attack by our cavalry, the senior captain, having been discouraged by the superior numbers of troops that had cut him off, ordered the battalion to lay down their weapons. Thus, the detachment that had sortied from Minsk was completely destroyed, with the exception of 100 cavalrymen who fled with Kosiecki. On both days, 1 and 3 (13 and 15) November, the enemy lost some 3,000 men taken prisoner alone, two colours and two guns. Our casualties were negligible.[37]

The return of Kosiecki to Minsk, after defeats in the actions at Novy-Sverzhen and Kaidanovo, spread terror in the city; but the inhabitants of Minsk still hoped for the arrival of Dąbrowski, whose strength had been exaggerated by a hundred rumours. Having passed Smilavichi and leaving his leading troops on the way to the Sinelo post station, he went to Minsk to personally familiarise himself with the situation. There he learned of Chichagov's offensive, whose vanguard was just 20 *versts* from the city. Dąbrowski could muster no more than 2,300 men with 12

---

36 In the War Diary of the vanguard of Third Army it states that Kosiecki 'left the *46e demi-brigade* of French troops and his cavalry to cover his retreat.'
37 War Diary of the vanguard of Third Army. In the diary compiled by Malinovsky, it states that on both days 1 and 3 [13 and 15] November, our troops took: two colours, two guns ten artillery and cartridge caissons, 65 field officers and subalterns and 3,870 lower ranks, and that the enemy lost more than 1,000 killed. In Chambray, II, 404, it states that the Lithuanian recruits, finding themselves surrounded, lay down on the ground and surrendered without resistance.

guns; the remainder of his force was far behind, and therefore, fearing the same fate that had befallen Kosiecki, he returned to his division and led them to Igumen and Nizhny-Berezino towards Borisov. Bronikowski, who had about 1,000 men left, set out with them from Minsk for Borisov on 4 (16) November, at two o'clock in the afternoon. Many officers with no troops to command and civilian officials went to Vilna, where the arrival of these fugitives, who spread exaggerated rumours, spread fear and doubt about the success of operations by the French army.

On the same day, 4 (16) November, Count Lambert, after a skirmish with Bronikowski's troops evacuating Minsk, liberated the city, where he captured 45 field officers and subalterns and over 2,000 lower ranks, mostly wounded and sick, as well as huge magazines with provisions and fodder, and freed 110 of our men who were being held captive by the enemy.[38]

On the following day, 5 (17) November, the infantry of the vanguard, the reserve and Chichagov's headquarters arrived in Minsk; the rest of our troops were stationed in the vicinity of this city. Colonel Paradovsky, sent out by Major General Count O'Rourke, from Raków along the Vilna road to Radoszkowicze with the Livland Dragoons and Kireev's Cossacks, captured many vehicles and delivered more than 2,000 prisoners to Minsk. At the same time, two regiments from the detachment under General Liders, marching from Serbia via Pinsk, joined the army.[39] Chichagov hoped to reinforce his army with the much larger corps under General Ertel, who had been ordered to go via Igumen to Minsk with all the troops entrusted to him, some 15,000 men. The arrival of this corps would swell the Army of the Danube's ranks to around 45,000 men, and would allow Chichagov to operate with complete independence against Napoleon's retreating army. But Ertel did not comply with these orders repeated several times, initially pleading the need to protect the magazines established in Mozyr, while later citing the difficulty in supplying troops on the march to Minsk and the inability to set up a mobile magazine, on the pretext of cattle. When, eventually, the Commander-in-Chief sent orders to go to Igumen without fail, Ertel reported that there were more than 2,000 sick in his corps, that General Ignatiev [Gavriil Alexandrovich Ignatiev] had demanded that 5,000 *Chetvert* of bread be sent to Bobruisk, and that the Field Marshal himself had ordered the Mozyr detachment to dispatch this convoy. Based on this, General Ertel asked for guidance (for a march route) and reported to Chichagov that the lack of a bridge over the Pripyat prevented immediate operations by his corps, and even if he managed to build a bridge in Mozyr, then the river Sluch would delay him and would not allow him to round up all the minor detachments.[40]

Admiral Chichagov, rightly dissatisfied with Ertel's procrastination, reported to the Tsar, on 5 (17) November, that, in pursuance of the Supreme Will, before

---

38 War Diary of the vanguard of Third Army. War Diary of the Army of the Danube (Third Army), compiled by Lieutenant Colonel Malinovsky. According to Chambray, our troops found more than 2,000,000 rations in Minsk and captured 4,700 men in hospitals. Chambray, II, 404-405.
39 Volhynia Ulans and 22nd Jägers. War Diary of the Army of the Danube (Third Army), compiled by Lieutenant Colonel Malinovsky.
40 For full details of Ertel's inaction, see Appendix IX.

leaving the headquarters of the Army of the Danube in Brest, he had ordered Liders, who was marching with 3,500 men from Moldavia, and Ertel, who was stationed in Mozyr with 14,000 to 16,000 men, to join the army, the former via Pinsk to Nesvizh, and the latter via Igumen to Minsk. According to the admiral, by moving in this manner, they would not only clear the entire sector between the Pripyat and the Berezina of the enemy, but would capture, as if in a net, every enemy unit that might be too slow to retreat. 'Major General Liders has carried out the orders issued to him precisely; in contrast, General Ertel did not move from Mozyr, seeking insignificant pretexts and asking irrelevant questions.' Chichagov wrote on, 'Such defiance could, and might still, have grievous consequences.' Mentioning the advantages that the assimilation of Ertel's corps into the Army of the Danube would bring, the admiral remarked that 'General Ertel judged otherwise, and as defiance very often goes unpunished in our country, he set out to test this.'

After that, informing the Tsar of the departure of Major General Tuchkov [Sergei Alekseevich Tuchkov] to relieve General Ertel of command of the corps, and to proceed to Rogachev, to join the Army of the Danube, Chichagov wrote that Dąbrowski owed his salvation to Ertel.[41]

On 7 (19) November, as he was preparing to march from Minsk to the Berezina, Chichagov received Ertel's final report, from which it emerged that he remained in Mozyr with the main body, having sent only six weak replacement battalions, four squadrons and one Cossack regiment to join the Army of the Danube.[42] Chichagov immediately sent the Duty General of his army, Major General Tuchkov 2nd, to replace Ertel, who was also under investigation at the time,[43] and ordered Saken to send Essen 3rd's Corps via Pinsk to join the army to replace the missing troops.[44] Emperor Alexander instructed Prince Kutuzov to examine Chichagov's correspondence with Ertel, and subsequently, once Chichagov had reported to the Field Marshal himself that General Ertel had acted mistakenly, more from excessive caution than from negligence in service, Kutuzov reassigned him as *generalpolizeimeister* [Provost Marshal] of all active armies.[45]

Following the liberation of Minsk, Chichagov's force remained in this city and its environs until 8 (20) November, in order to rest and resupply itself with provisions, with the exception of the vanguard under Adjutant General Count Lambert (reinforced by the 13th Jägers, Vitebsk Infantry and 34th Battery Artillery Company from Langéron's Corps [Alexander Fëdorovich Lanzheron or Louis Alexandre Andrault de Langéron]), which had been pushed forwards to the village of Yukhnovka, on the road to Borisov, on 7 (19) November. Count Lambert received orders, upon the

---

41 Extract from Admiral Chichagov's report to the Tsar, dated 5 [17] November (Archive of the M.T.D. No. 46,692, Folio 2).
42 Six replacement battalions from 2nd Grenadier Division, two squadrons each from the Pavlograd Hussars and Olviopol Hussars, and Isaev 2nd's Cossacks. War Diary of the Army of the Danube (Third Army), compiled by Lieutenant Colonel Malinovsky.
43 Chichagov's orders for generals Ertel and Tuchkov 2nd, archive of the M.T.D. No. 44,585. Log of Outgoing Documents of the Army of the Danube.
44 War Diary of Essen's Corps.
45 Prince Kutuzov's reports to the Tsar, dated 24 December [5 January 1813], No. 1,417 and No. 1,445.

occupation of this town, to establish communications with Wittgenstein immediately. Colonel Lukovkin [Gavriil Amvrosievich Lukovkin] was sent to Igumen with his Cossack regiment, in order to monitor the Polish detachment under Dąbrowski, which had retreated in this direction.[46] The detachment under Major General Chaplits was sent to the town of Zembin.[47] Colonel Knorring was assigned with the protection of Minsk and the stores that remained there, with the Tatar Ulans and one battalion of 27th Jägers, following the departure of the army.[48]

On 8 (20) November, Count Lambert's vanguard moved on to Zhodino, where Count Langéron's reserve also arrived behind him; the headquarters, together with Voinov's corps, moved to the left of the Borisov highway, towards Antopolye; Chaplits' detachment reached Zembin, while Lukovkin, arriving in Igumen at dawn, found the detachment sent from Mozyr to Minsk there and learned of the movement by Dąbrowski towards Borisov and the retreat by the Polish force monitoring the Bobruisk fortress, via Nizhny-Berezino.[49]

Adjutant General Count Lambert, upon arrival in Zhodino, with the vanguard of Chichagov's army, consisting of ten battalions, eight squadrons, one battery artillery company and two of horse artillery,[50] some 4,500 men in total,[51] sent to the Berezina river for a reconnaissance of the enemy, the patrols, having captured several prisoners, delivered intelligence that the Borisov bridgehead was to be occupied by a contingent from Württemberg and other allied units and that not only was Dąbrowski's detachment expected to arrive in Borisov, but also Victor's entire corps. Having received this intelligence, Count Lambert decided to immediately march on Borisov in order to seize the fortifications there before the enemy could concentrate their forces. Despite the fact that the vanguard had made a forced march of 35 *versts* from Yukhnovka to Zhodino on this day along poor roads, the troops were given only a few hours rest, after which they continued to move through the darkness of the night, and an hour before dawn they emerged from the forest into a clearing at a range of two *versts* from the bridge fortification, without being discovered by the enemy. The infantry was very tired from marching more than 50 *versts* in one day, but there was no time to rest; Count Lambert immediately issued orders to attack the Borisov bridgehead, having very detailed information on the fortifications, which he had obtained from an engineering officer who had been at work there in the spring. 14th Jäger Regiment was assigned to attack the right flank of the

---

46 War Diary compiled by Malinovsky.
47 Chaplits' detachment comprised: 28th Jägers, 32nd Jägers, Pavlograd Hussars, Tver Dragoons, Dyachkin's Cossacks, the Kalmyks, some Bashkirs and 13th Horse Artillery Company. War Diary compiled by Malinovsky.
48 Admiral Chichagov's orders for General Liders and Colonel Knorring, dated 6 [18] November.
49 War Diary of the vanguard of Third Army. War Diary compiled by Malinovsky.
50 For the move out to Borisov, the vanguard consisted of: the Vitebsk Infantry, 7th Jägers, 13th Jägers, 14th Jägers, 38th Jägers, four squadrons each of Arzamas Dragoons and Alexandria Hussars, 34th Battery Artillery Company, 11th Horse Artillery Company and 12th Horse Artillery Company.
51 In the War Diary of the vanguard of Third Army (compiled by Colonel Baron Üxküll) the number of infantry with Count Lambert is given as 3,200 men; there were no more than 1,300 men in the eight squadrons and three artillery companies making up the vanguard.

bridgehead, while 38th Jägers faced the left flank; 7th Jägers were ordered, to wait for the attacks by these regiments to start, and then to assault the centre vigorously; 11th Horse Artillery Company and 34th Battery Artillery Company were to open fire on enemy fortifications from positions to the sides of the assaulting troops; all other troops remained in reserve.[52]

Meanwhile, as the vanguard under Count Lambert was advancing towards Borisov, Bronikowski had arrived there on 6 (18) November with the remnants of the Minsk garrison and assimilated the units already located in Borisov; but, instead of taking care to bring the bridgehead into a defensible state, he remained for the next two days, 7 and 8 (19 and 20) November, not only in complete inactivity, but scattered his already weak detachment, leaving all in all only two battalions to protect the Borisov fortifications and sending all the rest of the force to Veselovo, to observe the upper reaches of the Berezina. On 8 (20) November, at nine o'clock in the evening, Dąbrowski's detachment arrived at Borisov. Bronikowski, mindful of the fatigue of the Polish troops, persuaded their commander to give them a rest, giving assurances that all approaches to the bridge were guarded by forward outposts and that patrols had been sent in all directions to reconnoitre the movements of the Russian forces. Dąbrowski, trusting in his comrade's discretion and believing that the Russians could not reach Borisov until the next day, left four regimental guns and six battalions that had arrived with him in the bridgehead, while he stationed himself on the other side of the river in the town with all the cavalry and eight guns. Thus, all the troops that had come from Igumen were gathered at Borisov, except for one infantry regiment and two squadrons, under the command of General Pakosz [Czesław Karol Pakosz], who were still a half-stage away, in anticipation of the arrival of whom, Dąbrowski would have 5,500 men with 20 guns.

At three o'clock in the morning, Dąbrowski, a veteran, experienced warrior, rode to his troops on the right bank of the Berezina on horseback. Exhausted from the rigours of the campaign, the soldiers lay around large campfires in their bivouacs in the fortification. Only the regiment of another veteran of the Italian campaigns, Colonel Małachowski [Kazimierz Małachowski] (*1 Pułk Piechoty*) was ordered to stand to arms after midnight at full combat readiness. There were no indications of an attack by our troops; everything was calm, and Dąbrowski returned to Borisov.

But the Russians were already close. Bronikowski's forward outposts, caught by surprise, were taken prisoner without having had chance to fire a single shot. Taking advantage of this, at about six o'clock in the morning, our troops closed up to within musket range of the fortifications unnoticed.[53] Suddenly there were shouts of Hurrah! The 14th Jägers and 38th Jägers, formed up in battalion columns, dashed at the flanks of the bridgehead towards the redoubts and captured them. The chaos and confusion of the enemy was extreme, particularly since any movement by troops was hampered by the timber heaped in the fortifications from the time of their construction and not cleared away by the French. Colonel Małachowski charged at the 38th Jägers with his regiment, drove them out of the left [south] redoubt and pursued them as far as a ravine. Noticing the enemy success, Count Lambert ordered the 7th

---

52 War Diary of the vanguard of Third Army.
53 See Plan of the Assault of the Borisov Bridgehead.

166 THE RUSSIAN PATRIOTIC WAR OF 1812 VOLUME 3

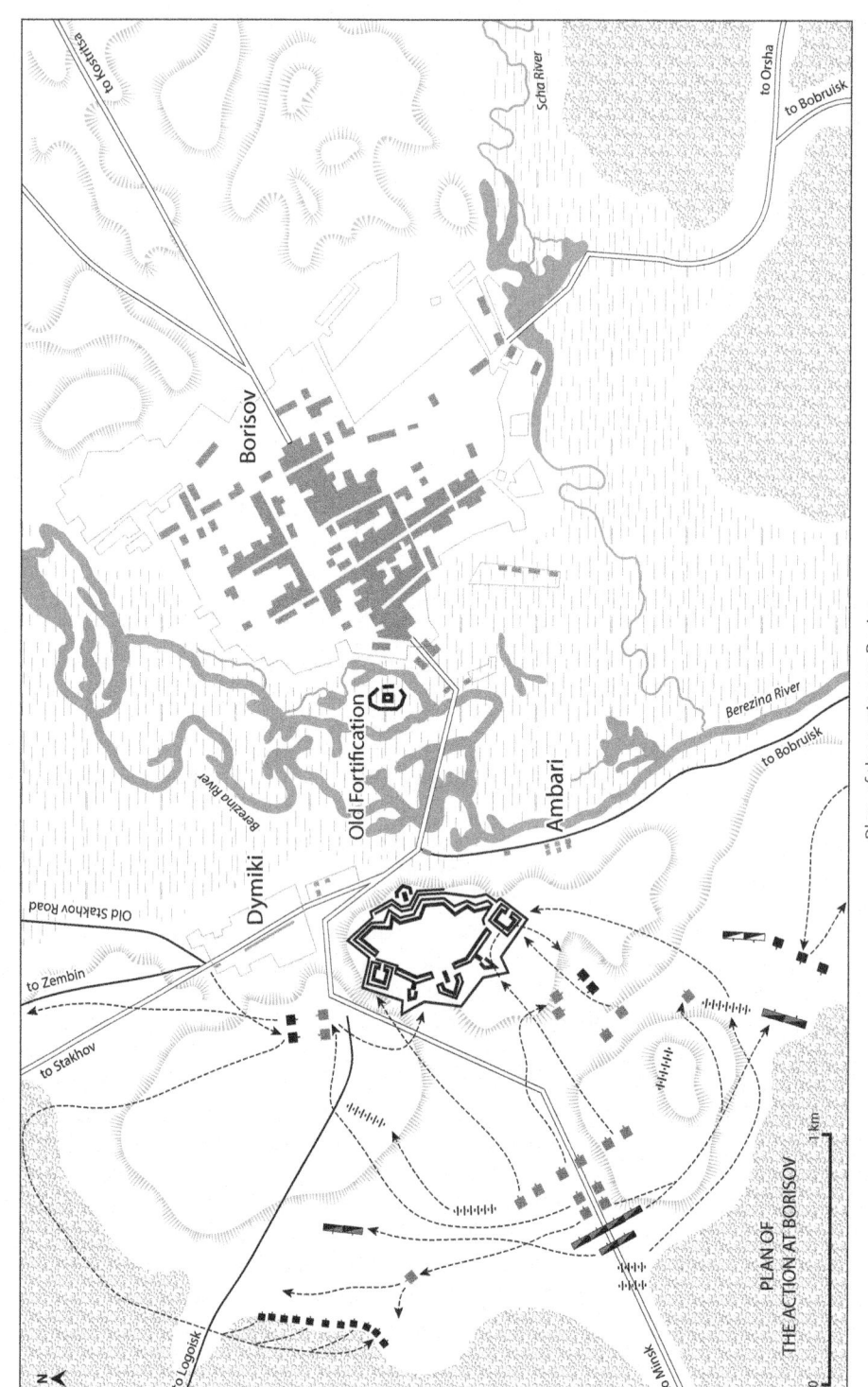

Plan of the action at Borisov.

Jäger Regiment, advancing towards the centre, to turn to their right and take possession of the redoubt once more. Major General Engelhardt, at the head of the jägers, struck the flank of the enemy column, drove them off and took the redoubt a second time, but was killed while accomplishing this glorious feat.

On the other side, two battalions of 6 *Pułk Piechoty*, under the command of Colonel Sierawski [Jan Kanty Julian Sierawski], having left the bridgehead along the Zembin road, returned from the village of Dymki towards the right [north] redoubt occupied by our 14th Jäger Regiment, but once Count Lambert had sent the 13th Jägers from the reserve to engage these flanking columns, the enemy were driven back, and being cut off from the bridge fortifications, they took refuge in the forest in the direction of Zembin.

Meanwhile, at ten o'clock in the morning, the remainder of Dąbrowski's force, under the command of Pakosz, who had reached the battlefield just at that moment, appeared on our right flank, from the direction of the village of Yushkovichi; at the same time, the cut off columns under Sierawski were moving along the edge of the forest behind the flank of our formation. Count Lambert's situation was awkward: enveloped by superior numbers, he was forced to consider saving his force; as the only infantry remaining in the reserve were the weak Vitebsk Infantry, he resorted to increased support from the artillery, and they justified his hopes. The 12th Horse Artillery Company was directed against the columns advancing from Yushkovichi, with one battalion of the Vitebsk Infantry and with the Alexandria Hussars. The artillery fire halted the enemy; thereafter, the Poles, having been attacked by infantry and hussars, turned back along the Bobruisk road in utter disarray and, crossing the Berezina on the ice, joined the troops under Dąbrowski in Borisov. At the same time, the other battalion of the Vitebsk Infantry and the Arzamas Dragoons halted the enemy who were trying to get through the forest into the rear of our force. Thus, having secured his flanks, Count Lambert decided to complete the seizure of the bridgehead. The order was given to open fire on the enemy infantry occupying the fortifications from all guns; following which, the 13th Jägers and 38th Jägers went into the assault, but were repulsed. Lambert rode up to these men himself in order to encourage them with his presence, and was badly wounded by a bullet in the knee. Then the 12th Horse Artillery Company, stationed in the left redoubt, showered the troops defending the bridgehead with canister and sowed confusion in their ranks. Several of our guns fired round shot and shells across the bridge and made it difficult for the Polish troops to liaise with the left bank of the river to such an extent that Dąbrowski, with his headquarters staff, who were in Borisov, tried to cross the bridge several times without success and, eventually, were forced to abandon this intention. On his orders, eight guns were placed on the left bank to provide counter-battery fire, but the fire of their six-pounder guns, which stood about a *verst* from our men, could inflict no significant damage on us, while our guns were smashing the enemy at close range.

At three o'clock in the afternoon, Colonel Krasovsky, with the 7th Jägers and 38th Jägers, resumed the assault and, despite stubborn resistance from the enemy, drove them out of the bridgehead entirely, which was also facilitated by the 14th Jägers, who descended from the right redoubt onto the flood-plain near the bridge and threatened to cut the line of retreat of the bridgehead defenders. The enemy troops, driven back at all points, abandoned six guns in the fortifications and dashed across the bridge into the town; the 14th Jägers, pursuing the Poles, crossed with them to the left bank of the Berezina and captured one of the guns being aimed along the bridge; following the jägers, the Arzamas Dragoons and Alexandria Hussars crossed with six guns from 11th Horse Artillery Company. The enemy, forced out of the town and put to flight, were pursued up the Orsha road by our hussars and dragoons. Count Langéron arrived on the Berezina with his corps as the action was ending, but did not have chance to take part in it. Meanwhile, Sierawski, pushed back into the forest on the Vilna road, decided to cross the river upstream of Borisov, and as the ice was very thin due to the onset of a thaw, the Poles laid straw and boards across it, over which they crossed to the opposite bank with great difficulty and, via a roundabout route through forest, rejoined the remnants of Dąbrowski's force on 10 (22) November.

Enemy casualties in the action at Borisov ranged from 1,500 to 2,000 killed, and from 2,000 to 2,500 taken prisoner; among the latter were more than 40 field officers and subalterns; while General Dziewanowski [Dominik Jan Chryzostom Dziewanowski], the commander of the cavalry in Dąbrowski's formation, was among those mortally wounded. Eight guns and two colours went to the victors. Chichagov's Notes give the enemy losses as 700 killed and 2,300 prisoners, six guns, an Eagle and two colours. On our side, the casualties were also very significant: out of the 3,200 infantry that were in Count Lambert's vanguard, between 1,500 and 2,000 men were killed or wounded, therefore half of the total number of men present.[54]

In the course of ten days, the vanguard under Count Lambert had destroyed Kosiecki's detachment, numbering 3,500 men, inflicted a severe defeat on Dąbrowski's formation, captured some 5,000 men and seized the bridge at Borisov, Napoleon's most important crossing point on the Berezina.

The day after the action at Borisov, on 10 (22) November, Chichagov's main body concentrated near this town. The infantry from the corps under Voinov and Langéron, with all the transport that was with them, having passed through Borisov, settled down in the direction of the town of Bobr, while the headquarters had moved into Borisov the previous evening. The flanking formations of the Army of the Danube closed up to the main body: Chaplits' detachment moved from Zembin to Borisov and settled down on the left bank of the Berezina; while Lukovkin arrived at Shabashevichi, having driven off one of Dąbrowski's columns the day before at Usha.

In this way, our forces drew closer and closer to each other, like menacing storm clouds surrounding the enemy. Chichagov would have the honour of putting an end

---

54 War Diary of the vanguard of Third Army, compiled by Baron Üxküll. War Diary of the Army of the Danube (Third Army), compiled by Lieutenant Colonel Malinovsky. General Dąbrowski's report to the prince de Neuchâtel (Berthier), dated 24 November new style. Sołtyk, *Napoléon en 1812*, 422-430. Chambray, III, 17-19. *Mémoires inedits de l'amiral Tchitchagoff*, 1855, p. 53. Dąbrowski claimed that he had only 2,500 men at Borisov (probably not including either Bronikowski's detachment or the Borisov garrison), of whom he lost 1,800.

to the existence of the remnants of the *Grande Armée*, while Napoleon, it seemed, could not avoid death or captivity. Our partisans dreamed of capturing him, and Chichagov shared their hopes himself. During the march by the Army of the Danube from Minsk to the Berezina, the following orders were sent to all corps and formation commanders: 'Napoleon's army is fleeing. And the author of Europe's disasters with it. We stand in his way. It might easily be that the Almighty would be pleased to cease His wrath by delivering him to us. Which is why I wish that the appearance of this person be known to everyone: he is short, stocky, pale, has a short and thick neck, a large head, and black hair. For greater reliability, seize and bring to me all the shorter men. I shall not comment on a reward for this prisoner. The famous generosity of our Monarch will respond to this.'[55]

Simultaneously with this operational endgame, prepared by the far-sighted orders of the main wartime leader, Emperor Alexander I, this benevolent Monarch, even in the midst of a thunder of criticism, kept in mind the relief of the plight of those suffering. On 7 (19) November, as the forces of His arrogant adversary were already being crushed at Krasny, Imperial Rescripts were issued, addressed to Field Marshal Kutuzov and Count Wittgenstein.

The Tsar wrote:

> I have repeatedly received information on the plight of prisoners sent from the army, via the provincial authorities, for onward transmission. The latest notification I received from His Highness, the Governor General of Novgorod, Tver and Yaroslavl, of which a copy is attached, indicates that the condition of the captives is an appeal to humanity itself.
>
> Convinced of their misfortune, I instruct you to confirm to whomever it is necessary that prisoners taken by the army led by you are sent in perfect order, while also observing en route, not only with regard to sufficient provisions and clothing for the current season, ordering the governor of the relevant province into which from the very beginning each time a party of prisoners enters, immutably demanding his orders, such that these men should not go on their way otherwise than in accordance with a copy, which would save them from further need, especially in the present winter time.[56]

Despite the difficult situation of our finances in 1812, the subsistence for prisoners was improved and they were all provided with clothing at a cost of about 50 Roubles each,[57] which all together amounted to several millions.

---

55 Admiral Chichagov's orders: to Lieutenant General Count Lambert, Lieutenant General Voinov, etc. Archive of the M.T.D. No. 44,585. Log of Outgoing Documents of the Army of the Danube, under Chichagov's signature.
56 Archive of the M.T.D. No. 46,692. Outgoing Log of Directed Supreme Decrees and Rescripts, No. 302 and No. 303.
57 Most Humble Report by the Minister of Police, 16 [28] November, 1812.

41

Napoleon's movements towards the Berezina

> Napoleon's departure from Orsha; the order of march of his forces. – The Russian advance. – The composition of the enemy army after the actions at Krasny. – Napoleon's assessments. – Measures taken by him in anticipation of the crossing of the Berezina.
>
> Chichagov's situation upon his arrival on the Berezina; the intelligence he received. – The offensive by Pahlen 2nd's vanguard along the Orsha road. – The action at Loshnitsa. – The withdrawal of Russian troops from Borisov behind the Berezina. – The deployment of the Army of the Danube. – Concurrent operations by Count Wittgenstein and the Main Army under Prince Kutuzov. – Napoleon's orders. – The link up of his army with the forces under Oudinot and Victor.
>
> Oudinot's arrival at Borisov. – Reconnaissance of the banks of the Berezina and the selection of a crossing point. – Description of the ground near the village of Studyanka. – Feint crossings at various points. – Napoleon's arrival at Borisov. – Circumstances behind the misleading of Chichagov. – The deployment of his forces on the morning of 13 (25) November. – His movement from the Borisov bridgehead down the Berezina. – Oudinot's movement from Borisov to Studyanka. – The move by Chaplits' detachment from Brili (opposite Studyanka) to Stakhava. – The situation of both sides at the beginning of the French crossing of the Berezina.

Upon Napoleon's departure from Orsha towards Borisov with the remnants of the *Grande Armée*, on 8 (20) November, in addition to the Orsha garrison, he was joined by the troops under the Viceroy and several hundred men from Ney's corps, the cavalry depot from Gorki and the Mogilev garrison, which had moved up the highway towards Bobr.[1] The troops under Junot and Zajączek proceeded as the vanguard; followed by the *Garde*, Ney, the Viceroy, and finally, Davout's corps as the rearguard.[2]

---

1 See Map of Movements to the Berezina.
2 Chambray, *Histoire de l'expHistoire de l'expédition de Russie,édition de Russie*, III, 13.

On 9 (21) November, on the same day that Dąbrowski was marching towards the French army with the remnants of his detachment after the action at Borisov, Oudinot's corps, having reached the main road, took up positions at Bobr, Victor, who was still stationed at Chereya, was preparing to close up to the same road, while Napoleon's *État-major général* was in Kamenitsa, near the village of Kokhanovo, 35 *versts* from Orsha and 100 *versts* from Borisov.[3] At the same time, Count Platov, pursuing the enemy from behind, liberated Orsha;[4] General Yermolov, having crossed to the right bank of the Dnieper, at Dubrowna, upstream of Orsha, went to link up with Platov.[5] Kutuzov's main body (III Corps, IV Corps, V Corps, VI Corps and IV Cavalry Corps) was located to the left of the Borisov road, in the vicinity of Lanniki; Miloradovich was on the Kopys road with the vanguard (II Corps, VII Corps, I Cavalry Corps and II Cavalry Corps), at the village of Goryany, while Lieutenant Colonel Davydov was in Kopys with his partisan detachment. Part of VIII Corps was marching on Romanovo; while Count Ozharovsky was on the way to the town of Gorki.[6] The army under Count Wittgenstein, was stationed at Chashniki, while the detachment under Adjutant General Kutuzov, who had arrived in Babinovichi, was preparing to pressure the enemy from the north, towards the highway. Thus, Napoleon's army, as it was moving towards the Berezina, was surrounded on all sides by the superior numbers of our armies.

After the fighting at Krasny, a thaw set in; it sometimes rained at night; the French, forced to bivouac constantly, suffered from the damp; at this time, eye disease was very widespread among the troops, both from the smoke from camp fires, and from the brightness of the reflected light on the vast plains covered with snow.[7] It has already been mentioned previously that, upon reaching the Mogilev Governorate, the troops could get some supplies, but as it was impossible to contemplate how to distribute it correctly, many of the men, and especially those who had abandoned the colours had, unwillingly, to put up with horse meat; the usual diet of those soldiers who remained under arms was a stew of rye flour with horse meat. Incessant marches, with barely any rest-days, weakened the troops at every step; regiments melted away extremely swiftly; it was hard to recognise these ragged, tattered, semi-armed men as warriors; all the disasters that had befallen Napoleon's army and their inevitable consequences, were now joined by discouragement and sometimes even madness. Many of the sufferers, turning their blank gaze in the direction of their fatherland, picked up the pace and, having exhausted the last of their strength, fell, unconsciously waiting for the end of the torment they had endured, or, having begged for permission from their comrades to warm their frostbitten limbs by the fire, deteriorated from life and died a cruel death. Among these thousands of men, no voices were heard, except for the groans of suffering: the movement of the former

---

3   Chambray, III, 21. Denniée, *Itinéraire de l'empereur Napoléon*, 191.
4   Count Platov's report to Prince Kutuzov, dated 9 [21] November, No. 195.
5   Yermolov's handwritten notes. Yermolov's report to Prince Kutuzov, dated 9 [21] November, from Dubrowna. Archive of the M.T.D. No. 29,172. Log of Incoming Documents for November, No. 591.
6   War Diary from 2 [14] September 1812 to 1 [13] October 1813, Archive of the M.T.D. No. 46,692.
7   Roos. Lemazurier.

Grande Armée was like a funeral procession. Almost all the artillery that had been with them was already lost. The cavalry, exhausted from the lack of forage, badly shod and slithering over the ice, had diminished even more than the infantry.[8]

Such was the situation in Napoleon's army when, while moving from Kamenitsa, on 10 (22) November, he received the fatal news that the Russians had seized the Borisov bridgehead and the town of Borisov. This news was a blow to Napoleon all the more because he was now obliged to cross the Berezina within sight of the Army of the Danube, and he must also perform this operation with all possible speed so as not to be caught at the crossing site by the forces under Kutuzov and Wittgenstein; the quick construction of a bridge was impossible due to the lack of pontoons, which had been burned, some by Marshal Mortier during the evacuation of Moscow, some by order of Napoleon himself during the French army's departure from Orsha.

General Dode de la Brunerie, who had joined Napoleon from Oudinot and Victor, on being summoned by him to a meeting on the choice of a crossing point on the Berezina, believed that there was no way to cross in either Borisov, where an entire army blocked the French route, or anywhere downstream of Borisov, where impenetrable forests and swamps stretch along the Berezina; on the other hand, the upper reaches of the river, in the vicinity of Lepel, where it flows through sandy terrain, having a depth of no more than two and a half feet, had never been an obstacle to the movements of *2e Corps*, which had repeatedly crossed over the Berezina in these places. And therefore, General Dode proposed a move to the right of the highway, to attach Oudinot's and Victor's corps to the army and, having driven back Wittgenstein's force, head for Vilna via Glubokoe. Napoleon, on the contrary, intended to turn left along the road to Minsk, where he hoped to find better resources for provisioning the army and also to assimilate the corps under Schwarzenberg and Reynier into his force, in addition to Oudinot and Victor, who would already be with him. According to Napoleon, the direction proposed by Dode exposed the army to a clash with Wittgenstein's significant force and obliged them to take a very roundabout route, during which the Russians, moving along the direct path, could take Vilna. Meanwhile, as Napoleon was talking with Dode and examining a map of Russia unfolded in front of him, and it is said, was repeating distractedly: 'Poltava! Poltava!' Murat, the Viceroy, Berthier, and General Jomini [Antoine Henri de Jomini] were also summoned to him, the latter had been the governor of this part of the country for a while and had access to very detailed information about the nature of the ground around the Berezina. General Jomini, opposing Dode's view completely, at the expense of the inconvenience of moving to the Lower Berezina, believed that a detour to the source of this river would be extremely draining for the army, weakened by the hardships of the campaign, and therefore suggested going straight to Borisov, crossing a little upstream of this location and moving towards Vilna via Smorgon, along the shortest and least devastated route. Napoleon, without reacting to this proposal at all, said that if everyone had not been overwhelmed by the collapse of morale, then, not being restricted to a crossing, it might have been possible to attack Wittgenstein and take his army prisoner. General Jomini

---

8   Chambray, III, 10-12.

remarked that this might have been achievable in Germany, where supplies of food for the army could be found everywhere, and, moreover, with troops that had not been exhausted by prolonged hardship. Eventually, after listening to these opinions, Napoleon decided to go straight towards Borisov.[9] But in order to cross in the vicinity of this location, it would be essential to seize the Borisov bridge, or build bridges, using the very limited resources that could be found at any place chosen for the crossing.

Napoleon's initial orders were instructions issued: to Marshal Oudinot, regarding the seizure of the ford at Veselovo, the laying of bridges there and of their fortification.[10] To Marshal Victor, regarding the securing of the Lepel road in order to protect Oudinot's corps from Wittgenstein.[11] Thereafter, at half-past-four in the morning on 12 (24) November, the *chef des équipages de pont*, General Éblé [Jean-Baptiste Éblé], and the *commandant du génie*, General Chasseloup [François Charles Louis de Chasseloup-Laubat], were immediately ordered to go with all possible haste to Marshal Oudinot in Borisov and begin building several bridges on the Berezina. General Jomini was sent with them in order to assist in surveying the course of the Berezina. At the same time, all the pontoniers, sappers and miners were ordered to go to Borisov via forced marches.[12] Upon the arrival of Napoleon's *État-major général* in Bobr, the formations under Zajączek, Junot and Claparède, moving at the head of the army, were ordered to burn half of the unit transport and give all the horses (*chevaux et cognats*) from the destroyed carts to General Sorbier [Jean Barthélemot de Sorbier]. The other corps were also ordered to burn all surplus wagons and carriages, such that no officer, up to and including colonels, had more than one wagon.[13]

Meanwhile, Oudinot's troops had encountered the vanguard of Admiral Chichagov's army.

If in 1812 our troops, fighting against the battle-hardened phalanx under Napoleon, generally showed themselves worthy of their opponents, then how much more could be expected from the Army of the Danube, seasoned from a six-year war, of an army made up of veteran soldiers, led by many generals worthy of renown? And indeed, since the time of their departure from Brest to the occupation of the line of the Berezina river, each engagement with the enemy was a victory for our troops. Although Chichagov's army had not been reinforced with Ertel's troops, it was still able to present Napoleon with an insurmountable barrier, because the 33,000 men in it should have been enough to delay a French crossing until the leading elements under Prince Kutuzov and Wittgenstein could arrive behind them.[14] The

---

9 Thiers, *Histoire du Consulat et l'Empire*, Edit. de Brux, XIV, 658-663.
10 Orders for Marshal Oudinot, dated 23rd November new style.
11 Orders for Marshal Victor, dated 23rd November new style.
12 Orders for General Éblé dated 24th November new style. Chambray, III, 32.
13 Orders dated 24th November new style.
14 In Lieutenant Colonel Malinovsky's notes On the Crossing of the Berezina, it seems that on 9 [21] November Chichagov's army consisted of 59 battalions, 88 squadrons and 13 Cossack regiments, with 180 guns, and that, calculating at least 350 men per battalion, 100 per squadron, 250 per Cossack regiment and 1,000 in the artillery, the number of troops in the army was 32,800. Indeed, on departing Brest, Chichagov had some 30,000 men, and en route

soldiers who had come up from the banks of the Danube, fresh, vigorous, supplied in abundance with provisions from the Minsk magazines, had a great advantage over the enemy, who, according to the most optimistic statements, had no more than 40,000 to 45,000 men under arms and a similar number of unarmed men; the majority of this enemy force were the remnants of the *Grande Armée* and the corps under Oudinot, exhausted by hunger, fatigue and the effects of the harsh season; the unarmed, following the troops at random, due to their physical and moral condition, were considered a hindrance and could not be used to reinforce the army. The defence of the course of the Berezina was fraught with the difficulties that any long linear defence presents; but Chichagov's operations were greatly facilitated by the locations of our other forces, Wittgenstein's and Prince Kutuzov's, at that time, which prevented Napoleon from heading either via Chereya and Lepel to Vilna, or via Igumen to Minsk: consequently, Chichagov needed to guard the course of the Berezina for about 50 *versts* from Veselovo to Usha. As for the intelligence from Prince Kutuzov and Count Wittgenstein, which, according to Chichagov himself, forced him to divert from the Orsha road,[15] indeed Kutuzov sent Lifeguard Lieutenant Orlov to the admiral on 10 (22) November (not 11 (23) November as stated in Chichagov's notes), with orders in which, mentioning the possibility of Napoleon moving towards Igumen, the Field Marshal proposed monitoring him with partisans.[16] Count Wittgenstein, for his part, wrote to Chichagov about the impossibility of providing any reliable intelligence on Napoleon's *Grande Armée*, expressing the opinion that, in all likelihood, they had turned towards Bobruisk, because if Napoleon had continued to move towards Borisov, then Marshal Victor would have held at Chereya in order to cover the flank of their retreat.[17] This intelligence, together with a report from Colonel Knorring in Minsk, regarding the appearance of advanced elements of Schwarzenberg's corps near Smorgon, Novy-Sverzhen and Svislach, made Chichagov assume that the movement by the Austrian troops towards Svislach revealed the intention of their Commander-in-Chief to establish communications with Napoleon and facilitate the *Grande Armée's* crossing of the Berezina downstream of Borisov.[18]

Meanwhile, having seized the Borisov bridgehead, on 9 (21) November, Count Lambert, seriously wounded, went to Stakhov. The vanguard force, which had crossed to the left bank of the Berezina and occupied Borisov, remained without a

---

to Borisov, some 8,000 joined from the detachments under Chaplits, Liders and Ertel, and after deducting combat losses from Novy-Sverzhen, Kaidanovo and Borisov, as well as the men of Colonel Knorring's detachment, left in Minsk, and Panteleev's Cossacks, sent under Chernyshev's command, to open communications with Count Wittgenstein, the number of troops in Chichagov's army turns out to be very close to that shown in Malinovsky's Notes. In Chichagov's notes (*Mémoires inedits de Tchitchagoff*, 59) it states, that he departed Brest with 25,000 men and had only 20,000 to guard the crossings over the Berezina, of which no more than 11,000 were infantry: consequently, there were fewer than 200 men per battalion, which seems highly doubtful.

15 *Mémoires inedits de Tchitchagoff*, 61-62.
16 Orders for Admiral Chichagov from Lanniki, dated 10 [22] November, No. 485.
17 Count Wittgenstein's report to Chichagov, dated 11 [23] November.
18 *Mémoires inedits de Tchitchagoff*, 60-62.

commander for almost the entire next day; no reconnaissance patrols were sent out. Count Langéron had also moved into Borisov with some of his corps and with the heavy baggage;[19] the main body of the army remained on the right bank of the river, in the bridge fortifications; Chaplits' detachment was at Zembin, while Lukovkin was at Usha.[20]

On 10 (22) November, Chichagov transferred his infantry with all their carts to the left bank of the river and placed them in bivouacs in front of Borisov, facing in the direction of Orsha; Chaplits' detachment had arrived in the Borisov bridgehead from Zembin, while all the cavalry remained on the right bank of the river, while Lukovkin's detachment went over to Shabashevichi. The admiral, in preparing to cross all his other troops over the Berezina and move along the Orsha road, in order to open communications with Wittgenstein, sent the vanguard out on 11 (23) November, in order to make contact with the enemy, about whom there was no intelligence. Chichagov had intended to entrust the command of the vanguard to Count O'Rourke, but O'Rourke offered this mission to his senior in rank, Major General Count Pahlen (Pavel Petrovich [Paul Carl Ernst Wilhelm Philipp von der Pahlen]) himself, who, having barely accepted the mission and not yet having had time to make an assessment of the situation, set out from Borisov at six o'clock in the morning along the Orsha road; the main body was ordered to set out at ten o'clock.[21] During the occupation of Borisov two letters had been found in the quarters formerly occupied by Bronikowski from Napoleon's aide de camp, Prince Sułkowski [Antoni Paweł Sułkowski], from Orsha, with news of the imminent arrival of the French *État-major général de la Grande Armée* in Bobr on 9 (21) November, and in Borisov on 10 (22) November, and although the content of these letters was known to Chichagov, he did not give them any credibility:[22] Some 3,000 cavalrymen were sent out for foraging and (just as is done when out of contact with the enemy) the quartermasters moved ahead of the vanguard with a small escort in order to occupy camp sites near the village of Loshnitsa. These quartermasters, on reaching Loshnitsa, managed to take two prisoners, who revealed that the entire French army was one stage away. Staff Captain Malinovsky [Sylvester Sigismundovich Malinovsky] immediately let Count Pahlen know about this,[23] who, informing the admiral about the imminent contact with the enemy, asked for reinforcements to be sent, because he had few

---

19 Chichagov wrote that he ordered the carts to be transferred back to the right bank of the Berezina, but this order was carried out so slowly that he found it necessary to repeat it. *Mémoires inedits de Tchitchagoff*, 55.
20 War Diary of the Army of the Danube (Third Army), compiled by Lieutenant Colonel Malinovsky.
21 Malinovsky's notes.
22 '... *On trouva dans le logement qu'avait occupé le Général Bronikowsky deux lettres à lui adressées par le prince Soulkofsky, aide-de-camp de Buonaparte dans les quelles il lui mandait d'Orscha: que le quartier-général serait le 9 à Bobr et le 10 à Borissof... Première nouvelle et indice certain que Buonaparte se dirigeait sur Borissof. Le matin, l'amiral étant arrivé à Borissof, lut les deux lettres susdites. Cependant il établit son quartier-général dans cette ville et envoya l'avant-garde que commandait le Comte Pahlen 2 sur Loschnitsa...*' From Count Lambert's notes.
23 Malinovsky was an officer of the Quartermaster's Department (General Staff) and later became a lieutenant general.

infantry, while the cavalry could not operate at all due to the nature of the terrain, intersected with ravines at every step. But Chichagov did not believe these statements from the prisoners were credible and, neglecting to reinforce Pahlen, ordered him to take up his appointed post without fail. The troops located at Borisov were ordered to cook porridge, while the cavalry remained out foraging.[24]

At this point in time, when our vanguard, numbering no more than 2,800 men, following the orders issued to them, were on the way to Loshnitsa, the vanguard of Oudinot's corps continued to move towards Borisov, having linked up with the remnants of Dąbrowski's detachment, still in Bobr on 9 (21) November; these troops, under the command of General Castex [Bertrand Pierre Castex], numbering 2,500 infantry and 1,100 cavalry, with 12 guns, having passed Loshnitsa, encountered Pahlen's vanguard three *versts* from this village. The enemy, being constantly reinforced, drove our troops back (the Polish *2 Pułk Ułanów* and *7 Pułk Ułanów* distinguished themselves in particular). Count Pahlen, finding it impossible to hold the numerous enemy up, ordered the infantry to retreat into the forest to the left (north) of the road, while several horse artillery pieces, under cavalry escort, moving with the carts along the road, struck at the enemy with round shot and canister. Eventually Castex, shrugging off the effective musket fire from our infantry operating on the flank of the advancing enemy columns, forced our guns to leave, drove off the cavalry escorting them once more, and having driven the regiments operating in the forest (7th Jägers, 14th Jägers and 38th Jägers) off the road, reached Borisov at two o'clock in the afternoon.[25]

Only then did Chichagov become convinced of the danger that threatened him. The ground at the town of Borisov and its environs was very unfavourable for defence against an enemy advancing from Orsha, in particular because in the event of a reverse, they would have to retreat across a bridge 200 *sazhen* [one *sazhen* = 2.1 metres or seven feet] long. All this notwithstanding, however, there was no reason to hasten the withdrawal: even if Napoleon actually had 100,000 men left (as the prisoners claimed), he still could not extract these troops from the forest defile in one go, nor form them up for battle before Chichagov's army withdrew behind the Berezina, shielded by some of the force left as a rearguard. But, unfortunately, the unreasonable over-confidence that reigned in Chichagov's headquarters led to equally unreasonable chaos. The order was given to retreat, but no measures were taken to retreat in good order. Only Major General Prince Shcherbatov [Alexei Grigorievich Shcherbatov], having received orders to form a rearguard from the troops holding the town, managed to place a battery on the Orsha road, beyond the Scha river. Orders were then issued to recall the foragers sent to collect hay on the left bank of the Berezina. An extraordinary turmoil was noticeable at every stage in the town itself; the Commander-in-Chief crossed the bridge to the other side of the river with all his staff; horses were saddled in a hurry, carriages were harnessed, transport was sent off, but the enemy, relentlessly pursuing Pahlen's force, were

---

24 Malinovsky's notes.
25 War Diary of the Army of the Danube (Third Army), compiled by Malinovsky. Sołtyk, 433. His claims regarding the capture of 2,000 men from Count Pahlen's vanguard by the troops under Castex are a huge exaggeration.

already close. The cavalry and horse artillery from our vanguard, racing down the highway, missed the dyke defended by Shcherbatov, and dashed to the right, crossing the swampy river Scha via a ford. Behind them charged the Polish lancers, supported by the rapidly moving infantry under Castex. Prince Shcherbatov, threatened with envelopment from the left flank, led his troops back to the bridge, but encountered extreme difficulties as they were crossing it from the congestion of artillery and transport crowding in from all sides and barely had chance, having got his detachment across, to set fire to the bridge. Meanwhile, the cavalrymen sent out to forage, having received orders to return to the regiments from which they had been detached as quickly as possible, jettisoned bales of hay and arrived in Borisov, formed up in column, but the enemy had already seized the town, which had caught fire in several places, and the bridge was in flames: thus, the foragers, finding themselves completely cut off, turned towards Stary-Borisov, joined in the vicinity of this manor by the three jäger regiments which had been driven away from the rest of the vanguard force, and moved upstream in order to seek out a crossing point somewhere. On the way they came across a peasant who volunteered to serve as a guide, who suggested a ford opposite the village of Brili. Our troops crossed there and rejoined the army in the Borisov bridgehead at dawn on 12 (24) November.[26]

During the retreat by Chichagov's force from Borisov to the right bank of the Berezina, we lost much of the regimental transport in the town, the office of the Commander-in-Chief, most of the private carriages, including the covered wagon containing Chichagov's table service, and all our sick and wounded, some of whom died in the fires that devastated the town. Our losses this day, 11 (23) November, in killed and taken prisoner, is shown overall in the War Diary as some 1,000 men.[27]

On 12 (24) November, Chichagov's army remained in the Borisov bridgehead. The detachment under Major General Chaplits was ordered to move to the village of Brili and hold the town of Zembin, placing strong observation posts upstream along the Berezina; while Major General Count O'Rourke was sent to the village of Yushkovichi (downstream of Borisov), in order to take over command of the detachment under Colonel Lukovkin, with the Volhynia Ulan Regiment, 12th Horse Artillery Company and a pontoon half-company attached. He was ordered to make a feint crossing of the Berezina and to hold the enemy if they attempted to cross at the town of Nizhny-Berezino.[28]

Simultaneously with the arrival of the Army of the Danube on the Berezina, Count Wittgenstein began to put pressure upon Victor's corps once more. He had received intelligence regarding Victor's retreat to Chereya on the previous night, in

---

26 War Diary of the Army of the Danube (Third Army), compiled by Malinovsky.
27 '... l'avant-garde traversa Borissof avec une perte de six cents hommes et d'une grande quantité de bagages. Un de mes fourgons, contenant de la vaisselle et des provisions, tomba au pourvoir de l'ennemi.   ... Cet échec d'avant-garde, le premier qu'eût éprouvé mon armée jusqu'alors victorieuse, fut représenté à Petersbourg comme une défaite totale. J'avais eu, disait-on, quatre mille hommes, tués ou blessés; tous mes équipages, ma chancellerie, ma correspondance secrète, étaient tombés au pouvoir de l'ennemi. Les bulletins français portèrent ma perte à deux mille hommes; les rapports russes, plus mensongers encore ne la portaient à rien du tout.' Mémoires de Tchitchagoff, 57.
28 War Diary of the Army of the Danube (Third Army), compiled by Malinovsky.

the direction of Borisov, as early as the morning of 10 (22) November, and decided to pursue the enemy, without losing contact with them, in order to be able to attack them as soon as they halted upon encountering Chichagov. On 10 (22) November, Victor evacuated Chereya, and on the following day, 11 (23) November, retreated behind Kholopenichi, after a rather heated clash, in which our Combined Hussar Regiment, under the command of Colonel Gerngross, with the assistance of Loshchilin's Cossacks and Panteleev's Cossacks, drove off the *2e régiment chevau-légers de Berg*, broke a square of the *126e régiment d'infanterie de ligne*, killing some 200 men and capturing 27 officers and more than 300 lower ranks.[29] Following that, on 12 (24) November, General Harpe, with the vanguard of Count Wittgenstein's army, caught up with Daendels' division moving as Victor's rearguard, which, located forwards of Batury, attempted to end the pursuit by our force, but was driven back and retreated towards Bobr with the loss of several hundred men killed or captured. General Vlastov, having arrived at Batury with his detachment on the night of 12 to 13 (24 to 25) November, took command of the vanguard. Wittgenstein's main body was concentrated at Kholopenichi.[30]

Meanwhile, Count Wittgenstein had received news that forced him to divert from the direct pursuit of Victor and move straight towards Borisov. Admiral Chichagov had written to him about the liberation of Borisov by our troops, Count Pahlen 2nd's encounter with superior enemy forces, and the retreat of the Army of the Danube to the right bank of the Berezina. Having invited Count Wittgenstein to link up with him via Borisov, Chichagov wanted, in this instance, to build a pontoon bridge.[31] At the same time, General Yermolov, reporting on the arrival of his vanguard in Pogost [17 kilometres west of Orsha] and regarding Platov moving ahead of him at a considerable distance with a strong Cossack formation, was stressing the need to pursue the enemy army as swiftly as possible.[32] Indeed, on 11 (23) November, having passed Tolochin, Platov was putting pressure upon Napoleon's rearguard along the highway; but the main body under Kutuzov was only then approaching Kopys; while Miloradovich, with their vanguard, had not yet managed to build a bridge over the Dnieper at this town.[33]

Meanwhile, Napoleon was preparing for a desperate act, to cross a significant river in the midst of Russian forces surrounding him on all sides. As early as 11 (23) November, upon arriving in Bobr, he ordered the Eagles of all regiments to be brought to him and burned. The dismounted *cavalerie de la Garde*, numbering 1,800 men, of whom about a third did not have firearms, were reorganised into two battalions. The *réserve de cavalerie* of the *Grande Armée*, under the command of Latour-Maubourg,

---

29 Major General Vlastov's report to Count Wittgenstein, dated 11 [23] November, No. 326.
30 *Précis de la campagne du 1er corps de la 1er armée d'Occident pendant l'année 1812* (Archive of the M.T.D. No. 29,200).
31 Chichagov's memo, dated 11 [23] November.
32 Yermolov's report to Wittgenstein, dated 11 [23] November, from Pogost. For the full text see Appendix X.
33 '... I have the honour to inform Your Excellency that there is no crossing yet. As soon as it is done, I shall hasten to fulfil the will of His Grace...' from Miloradovich's letter to Duty General Konovnitsyn, dated 12 [24] November, from Kopys. Log of Incoming Documents for November 1812, Archive of the M.T.D., No. 29,172.

in which only 150 men remained, was reinforced by 500 cavalry officers who still had riding horses; the command of this detachment, which received the name *l'escadron sacré* [the Sacred Squadron] from Napoleon, was entrusted to Generals Grouchy [Emmanuel de Grouchy] and Sébastiani [Horace François Bastien Sébastiani]; and in which *généraux de brigade* commanded platoons.[34] Having the preservation of the artillery in mind, at least until the crossing of the Berezina, Napoleon repeated the order to burn all surplus transport and pass their horses to the artillery.[35]

The success won by Marshal Oudinot over the vanguard of the Army of the Danube, after the string of failures suffered by Napoleon's forces, raised their hopes. Despite the weakness of Oudinot's corps, which could only be supported during the crossing of the Berezina by the nearest troops of the *Garde*, and even then not until the next day, Napoleon believed that Oudinot, having driven off our vanguard, could construct bridges by evening, or at least by the next night. But no sooner had the *État-major général* of the French army managed to arrive in Loshnitsa, on 12 (24) November, at about six o'clock in the afternoon, than one of its members, *officier d'ordonnance* Mortemart [Casimir-Louis-Victurnien de Rochechouart de Mortemart], rode up to Napoleon, having been sent by him the day before to Oudinot and had now returned with a report from the marshal that Chichagov's army was much stronger than he perceived, and that, in his opinion, the extraordinary difficulties in arranging the crossing required the personal orders of the emperor himself. Napoleon said; 'Go back to Oudinot at once and reassure him that he is mistaken on the strength of the enemy force; oblige him to hasten to build bridges on the Berezina; under the present circumstances, I cannot leave the army.'[36]

But in the meantime, although Napoleon had expressed himself with such self-confidence, his troops, in the course of the march from Bobr to Loshnitsa, heard the rumble of a cannonade to the right of the highway, which made them concerned about bumping into Wittgenstein's army: at the same time, ominous rumours were spreading about the advance by Kutuzov's army behind the French. Anxiety and doubt dominated Napoleon's troops. Suddenly loud cheers were heard: these were the regiments under Victor, who were greeting their master and his army with the usual cries. The unprecedented disasters that had befallen the *Grande Armée* had remained unknown to the soldiers who had been fighting on the Dvina; none of them imagined that, instead of the formidable legions that had conquered Moscow, having been masters of victory for so many years, would appear as miserable shadows, barely covered with tatters of mixed costume, ladies' *salop* coats, priestly vestments, carpets and matting, dragging their feet with great effort, wrapped in leather, linen and felt. Their pale, emaciated faces, overgrown with dishevelled hair and beards, expressed all the hardships they had endured; many officers, and even generals, walked alongside unarmed soldiers who paid no attention to them; discipline had vanished: both superiors and subordinates had been equally overwhelmed by the disaster. Small sub-units, the remnants of what had once been corps and divisions,

---

34 Chambray, III, 34. Ségur, *Histoire de Napoléon et de la grande armée pendant l'année 1812*, II, 330.
35 Chambray, III, 32-33.
36 Chambray, III, 34-35.

surrounded by a crowd of unarmed vagabonds, constituted the entire army. None of Oudinot's or Victor's soldiers wanted to believe what they were seeing with their own eyes. The good order that had prevailed among these troops was destroyed on the very first day of their reunion with the remnants of the *Grande Armée*.[37]

Such was the situation of the enemy force at the time of Napoleon's arrival in Loshnitsa, just a short march from Borisov. Had Chichagov and Wittgenstein been fully aware of the extent to which the strong Napoleonic hordes had been diminished in recent days, then the French army would have been subjected to its inevitable demise. It can be positively stated that Napoleon, in this case, owed his salvation solely to the influence of his previous victories, which forced his opponents to operate too cautiously and lose the opportunity to inflict a total defeat on him.

Oudinot himself (as has already been said) doubted the success of the mission assigned to him. During the night of 11 to 12 (23 to 24) November, on his orders, a reconnaissance of the course of the Berezina upstream and downstream of Borisov was carried out. It emerged that the nearest crossing point downstream of Borisov was about 12 *versts* from this town, near the village of Ukholoda, lying on the left bank of the river, but the road to this village was only passable for artillery during severe frosts. More suitable crossing points were found upstream of Borisov: firstly, at Stakhov, six *versts* from the town; secondly, at the village of Studyanka, 16 *versts* from Borisov, and thirdly, at Veselovo, four *versts* beyond Studyanka. With regard to the area around Studyanka, which later served as the crossing point for the French, information had been obtained quite by accident. General Corbineau, who had been with the Bavarian corps under Wrede with his light cavalry brigade, during their retreat from Polotsk, having received orders on 27 October (8 November) to join Victor's corps, headed from Danilovichi [DunilaviČy] to Borisov, via Dokshitsy and Zembin, arriving on the evening of 9 (21) November opposite Studyanka and, having discovered that Chichagov's entire army had been concentrated in the vicinity of Borisov, crossed the Berezina via a ford shown to them by a peasant from one of the nearby villages. The next day, 10 (22) November, having reached Oudinot at Loshnitsa with his detachment, Corbineau informed him that the road from Borisov to Zembin passed less than two *versts* from Studyanka, that on 9 (21) November the ford had been half a *sazhen* deep and that a swamp stretched along the right bank of the river, unsuitable for the passage of wagons in the event of a thaw. On 12 (24) November, a frost set in, but the river did not ice over. The success of a crossing at Stakhov was subject to great doubt, due to the proximity of this location to the main body under Chichagov, which was stationed in the Borisov bridgehead; at Veselovo, the river was deeper than at Studyanka. The ground at the latter point was well-known, and although the movement of artillery and transport was hampered by the swamps lying on the right bank of the river, nevertheless, the state of the temperature gave hope that it might be made passable by filling the swamps with fascines.[38]

All these factors forced Oudinot to choose the area near Studyanka for the crossing.[39] The Chief of Artillery of *2e Corps*, *Général de brigade* Aubry, was ordered to go

---

37 Ségur, III, 332-333. Sołtyk, *Napoléon en 1812*, 439.
38 Chambray, III, 36-38.
39 See Plan of the Crossing of the Berezina.

there immediately and prepare the materials necessary for building bridges, being careful not to be seen from the opposite bank. On the evening of 12 (24) November, Aubry reported to the marshal that the river at Studyanka was from 30 to 35 *sazhen* wide, that the ford, which three days before had not been more than half a *sazhen* deep, was now deeper, as far as can be judged from statements by the locals, and that on the opposite side of the river, the road leads through a swamp passable only in severe frosts. General Aubry also reported that the right bank was occupied by our [Russian] troops with artillery, and that the corps stationed opposite Borisov had been reinforced by 8,000 men who had arrived from Lepel. At the same time, General Aubry reported that by nine o'clock in the evening the trestles and timbers would be ready for laying the proposed bridge.[40]

The village of Studyanka sits atop bluffs on the left bank of the Berezina, 150 paces from the river. The height of these bluffs dominate the right bank, where there are swamps and water meadows, frozen from the deep cold that had come on 12 (24) November (as mentioned above), and facilitated the concentration of troops under the protection of a battery located at Studyanka. The ridge of high ground stretching along the left bank of the Berezina, conceals the road going from the town of Borisov, past Stary-Borisov, and onwards through the village of Bychi, to Studyanka. On the right bank of the river, there is a wide country road leading from Bobruisk past the Borisov bridgehead, and onwards to the village of Bolshy-Stakhov and the Stakhov Forest; after passing through this forest and leaving the village of Brili on its right, the road turns almost at a right angle from this village for four *versts*, and crosses a large forest and awkward defiles formed by the swampy river Gajna, to the towns of Zembin and Molodechno, where it joins the main road to Vilna.

Oudinot, having received the report from Aubry, remained in Borisov and sent a report to the *État-major général* on 12 (24) November, at a quarter to six in the afternoon, in which he asked for reinforcements from other forces for his corps, informing them of the appearance of Steinheil's force near Studyanka, which had arrived there via the Upper Berezina (*sic*). This report was received by Napoleon in Loshnitsa at midnight, and at one o'clock in the morning on 13 (25) November, *chef d'état-major* Berthier's aide de camp, Flahaut [Auguste Charles Joseph de Flahaut de La Billarderie], went to Borisov with orders in which Napoleon, informing the marshal of the immediate movement of two *Garde* divisions to assist him, wrote: '... if you have not crossed over this night, it becomes very urgent, in the present circumstances, to cross over today.'[41]

Meanwhile, Oudinot, having occupied Borisov, Novy-Stakhov and Ukholoda with detachments, collected materials for bridge construction and made preparations for a crossing at these locations in order to divert attention away from Studyanka, where preparations were being made in total secrecy, from our forces stationed opposite

---

40 General Aubry's report to Marshal duc de Reggio (Oudinot), dated 24 November new style, from Borisov.
41 Oudinot's report dated 24 November new style, from Borisov. '... *si vous n'avez pas passè cette nuit, il devient très urgent, dans les circonstances actuelles, de passer aujourd'hui*.' Orders for Marshal Oudinot, dated 25 November new style, at one o'clock in the morning, from Loshnitsa.

them. At the same time, troops showed themselves in various places along the river bank, and especially downstream of Borisov. Not content with this, the French collected intelligence on the routes leading south of this town, towards Igumen and Minsk, displaying an intention to move in this direction, promising generous rewards to any guides who could point out the most suitable route and demanding a pledge from the Jews gathered in Borisov that all this would be kept in deepest secrecy. The marshal very much hoped that they would let our troops know about his plans and involve us in unwittingly making a false assumption.[42]

On 13 (25) November, at eight o'clock in the morning, Napoleon rode to Borisov on horseback; on the way, he received several reports from the Berezina. On several occasions, the severe cold forced him to dismount from his horse and walk; he stopped on the road often, letting troops past him, accompanied by crowds of unarmed men. Upon arrival in Borisov, at five o'clock in the afternoon, he stayed there until 11 o'clock, and then moved to the Stary-Borisov manor, which belonged to Prince Radziwill.[43] On that same day, at about five o'clock in the morning, generals Éblé and Chasseloup arrived in Borisov and, having left some of the pontoniers there, most likely in order to make a feint of a crossing being carried out at this point, went on to Studyanka arriving there an hour before dusk to find that the trestles prepared for the construction of the bridge were very rickety: Thus, all that day, General Aubry had not made any preparations for the impending crossing at Studyanka.[44]

Fortunately for the French, at the very moment as Oudinot was preparing to head for Studyanka, Chichagov had turned his attention exclusively in the opposite direction, towards the lower Berezina; while Count Wittgenstein, instead of establishing communications with Chichagov, in accordance with the general operational plan, ferrying his army, or at least one of the corps, across the upper Berezina, had been distracted in Chereya by the pursuit of Victor, who was retreating before him.

Everything tended towards misleading Chichagov: the materials collected by the enemy and the preparations for a crossing downstream of Borisov; movements down the river by French detachments, whose true strength was difficult for our troops to assess, being separated from the enemy by a significant obstacle; finally, according to him, all the intelligence received regarding the direction of Napoleon's army, from Prince Kutuzov, Count Wittgenstein and Colonel Knorring. However, this intelligence did not contain any definitive notification of Napoleon's movements south of Borisov; moreover, as far as can be judged from the report by *Flügel-Adjutant* Orlov, sent on 11 (23) November, with the field marshal's orders for the admiral, these were received by Chichagov no earlier than 14 (26) November, that is, after he had shifted down the Berezina with his main body, and therefore these orders could not be the cause of the false assumption he had made.[45] Chichagov himself, in orders to Count

---

42 Notes by active State Councillor Khrapovitsky, who was serving in Chichagov's army in 1812. Chambray, III, 39. Ségur, II, 338-339.
43 Denniée, 191. Chambray, III, 40-41. Fain, *Manuscrit de 1812*, II, 314-315.
44 Chambray, III, 41-42. Fain, 311.
45 *Flügel-Adjutant* Orlov, in his report dated 12 [24] November, reported on his arrival in the town of Kruglae, on this date, from where there were still more than 80 *versts* to the Berezina.

Langéron, outlining the reasons that prompted him to move down the Berezina, mentions only the intelligence he received from Count Wittgenstein.[46]

As has already been mentioned, that on 12 (24) November, following the action at Loshnitsa, Chichagov's army was located in the Borisov bridgehead, while the flank detachments under Chaplits and O'Rourke were upstream and downstream on the Berezina: General Chaplits was on high ground at the village of Brili, having detached Major General Umanets [Andrei Semënovich Umanets] to Zembin with the Kinburn Dragoons and Major General Kornilov [Pëtr Yakovlevich Kornilov] to Veselovo, with the 28th Jägers, two Cossack regiments and four horse artillery pieces;[47] while Count O'Rourke, who had received orders to monitor the course of the lower Berezina, spent the night of 12 to 13 (24 to 25) November in the village of Yushkovichi.[48]

By remaining in these positions, Chichagov could conveniently guard the course of the river upstream and downstream of Borisov. Were the enemy army to head north of Zembin, they would encounter the army under Count Wittgenstein across their route; while getting around Chichagov south of Borisov, would involve Napoleon taking a roundabout route, to Usha, or to Nizhny-Berezino, towards Minsk.

Such a move would be appropriate only in the event of a coincidence of two circumstances very favourable to the enemy army, namely: a slow advance of the Main Army under Kutuzov, and the onset of freezing weather, as a result of which the swamps downstream of Borisov would become passable for troops and vehicles. As Napoleon could get neither timely intelligence on the slowness of Kutuzov's advance, nor forecast the onset of frost, he very roundly preferred to cross upstream of Borisov.

Meanwhile, instead of staying at Borisov on the main route leading to Minsk and within reach of the route running to Vilna via Zembin, Chichagov paid exclusive attention to blocking the route to Minsk via Igumen. To that end, having left Count Langéron at the Borisov bridgehead with one infantry division and its organic artillery, and two dragoon regiments,[49] the admiral moved down the river on the afternoon of 13 (25) November, with all the remainder of the force, and had already arrived at the town of Shabashevichi during the night of 13 to 14 (25 to 26) November. The admiral's orders as he was departing from Borisov were as follows: Count Langéron was instructed to defend the Berezina crossing at Borisov, while General Chaplits initially received orders to leave only observation posts at Brili and opposite Veselovo

---

46 Admiral Chichagov's orders to General-of-Infantry Count Langéron, dated 13 [25] November, No. 1,166.
47 *Remarques sur la campagne de 1812, par le général Czaplitz.* Archive of the M.T.D. No. 44,712.
48 War Diary of the Army of the Danube (Third Army), compiled by Malinovsky.
49 Chichagov wrote that he had ordered Langéron to guard the Borisov bridgehead, while Chaplits was to defend the crossing at Veselovo, and had decided to move to Shabashevichi with Voinov's division. From this it might be concluded that the bulk of the army had been left in the bridgehead, but in orders to Count Langéron, dated 13 [25] November, No. 1,166, it states: 'All the regiments of the corps entrusted to you remain in your formation, that is, 15th Infantry Division with its artillery, eight heavy guns from 38th Battery Artillery Company, the Zhitomir Dragoons and Arzamas Dragoons.' Consequently, Langéron was left with eight to ten battalions and eight squadrons.

and to go to the Borisov bridgehead himself with a detachment, and if there was no intelligence on the enemy from the outposts, then to go on to Shabashevichi; later, once the admiral had received a report from Count Wittgenstein about his approach to the Berezina, Chaplits was ordered to liaise with him, and to that end, to return to Zembin and in general to the very locations that had been occupied by his detachment previously. The Commander-in-Chief, wanting to give Chaplits the resources to hold the enemy on the upper Berezina, ordered Langéron to reinforce him with one infantry regiment and 38th Battery Artillery Company.[50]

On 13 (25) November, on the very day that Chichagov set off down the right bank of the Berezina, towards Shabashevichi, Oudinot moved at dusk from Borisov, up the left bank of the river to Studyanka, with *2e Corps* and the rest of Dąbrowski's detachment, totalling 7,000 men:[51] thus, the forces under Napoleon and Chichagov headed in opposite directions simultaneously. Not yet aware that the materials collected for the construction of the bridges had turned out to be unsuitable, Napoleon ordered work to begin at ten o'clock in the evening, but the French were forced to spend the whole night collecting timber, in the shape of logs from dismantled houses from nearby villages, and building trestles. Oudinot and Murat, who had arrived at Studyanka before first light, surveyed the surrounding area and tried to speed up the process. It was intended that Éblé and Chasseloup would build two bridges through their combined efforts. While Chaplits' force remained in the locations they had previously occupied, opposite Studyanka and Veselovo throughout almost the entire night, the huge fires blazing in their bivouacs aroused enemy concerns, believing they would encounter the entire Army of the Danube beyond the Berezina.[52]

Although Chaplits, like our other generals, did not have accurate intelligence on the enemy, nevertheless, on 12 (24) November, by approaching through an area screened by scrub up to the river bank opposite Studyanka, he observed several officers who were carrying out a reconnaissance of the ground around this location, under the guise of seeking watering places for horses. This obliged him to stay in his positions at Brili, opposite Studyanka, all day of 13 (25) November and part of the next night despite having received orders to go to the Borisov bridgehead. By the evening of 13 (25) November, observing troop movements and large fires on the opposite bank, and wanting to ascertain the intentions of the enemy, Chaplits ordered Melnikov's Cossack Regiment to swim across to the other side of the river after dark and take prisoners, or bring back one of the inhabitants who could provide the necessary intelligence. Colonel Melnikov returned with several prisoners and the steward of one of the villages lying in the direction of Veselovo. The prisoners revealed that their entire army was concentrated between the town of Borisov and the Stary-Borisov manor, but they did not know exactly where the crossing would take place; the steward, for his part, let slip that the enemy had begun the construction of two bridges, and that, in all probability, they would be laid at Brili or at

---

50 Orders to Count Langéron, dated 13 [25] November, No. 1,166 and No. 1,171, and to General Chaplits, dated 13 [25] November, No. 1,165 and No. 1,170.
51 War Diary of the Army of the Danube (Third Army), compiled by Malinovsky.
52 Chambray, III, 42, 45 & 47.

Veselovo. Such explicit intelligence should have prompted Chaplits to guard Brili and the upper Berezina, but instead of that, he not only withdrew the detachments stationed at Veselovo and Zembin back to himself, but fell back to Stakhov at dawn on 14 (26) November, leaving Colonel Kornilov at Brili with part of his detachment, and only Cossack outposts along the river upstream, and then withdrew even further, almost to the bridgehead itself.[53]

On the evening of 13 (25) November, at the time when Oudinot was marching from Borisov to Studyanka, Napoleon's main force, in anticipation of the construction of the bridges on the Berezina, were partly in Borisov, where the *Garde*, Junot's troops and Ney's corps, made up of the remnants of Dąbrowski's detachment, Poniatowski's corps and the Mogilev garrison were located; partly on the march to Borisov along the Orsha road, in the vicinity of Loshnitsa;[54] Victor's corps remained north of the highway at Ratulichi in order to shield the army from Wittgenstein.[55] On our side, the Army of the Danube was stationed (as was mentioned above), at Shabashevichi and Borisov; Count O'Rourke reached Usha in the evening and sent the cavalry from his detachment on towards Nizhny-Berezino; Count Wittgenstein's army was located at Barany, where they were joined by Vlastov's vanguard during the night, while the other vanguard, under Colonel Albrecht's command,[56] had been pushed on towards Borisov and had halted at Yanchino. Count Platov, pressing in on the enemy from the rear, had reached Nacha; Yermolov's detachment was in the village of Molyavka; Miloradovich had arrived in Tolochin from Kopys, via Staroselie, with II Corps, VII Corps and II Cavalry Corps; the detachment under Count Ozharovsky (as already mentioned above) had liberated Mogilev, where large enemy magazines were captured; finally, the Field Marshal remained at Kopys with the rest of his army.[57]

Such were the dispositions of the forces on both sides at the start of the French crossing of the Berezina.

---

53 Chaplits, *Remarques sur la campagne de 1812*. Archive of the M.T.D. No. 44,712. War Diary of the Army of the Danube, compiled by Malinovsky. In his notes Regarding the Berezina Crossing, General Arnoldi, in 1812 commander of 13th Horse Artillery Company in Chichagov's army, stated that the detachment in Brili was commanded by Major General Kornilov.
54 See the Map of the Advance to the Berezina river.
55 Chambray, III, 43.
56 Colonel Albrecht's vanguard consisted of the Combined Lifeguard Regiment, Combined Dragoon Regiment and 25th Jägers.
57 War Diary, signed off by Prince Kutuzov. Buturlin, *Histoire militaire de la campagne de Russie en 1812*, II, 364 & 365.

42

The Berezina crossing

The first day of crossing, 14 (26) November. Constructing the bridges; Oudinot's force crosses the Berezina. – Chichagov's orders. – The offensive by Count Wittgenstein and the detachments dispatched from our main army. – The deployment of the enemy corps.

The second day of crossing, 15 (27) November. The crossing by Napoleon with the *Garde* and part of Victor's corps; the contemporaneous locations of the enemy troops remaining on the left bank of the Berezina. – Chichagov's orders. – Inaction. – The crossing by Davout and the Viceroy. – Move by Count Wittgenstein to Stary-Borisov; while Seslavin and Platov head for the town of Borisov. – The capitulation of Partouneaux's division. – The repair of Borisov bridge by Chichagov's men.

The third day of crossing, 16 (28) November. The deployment of enemy forces in order to defend the crossing point on both banks of the Berezina. – Operations by the Army of the Danube. – Operations by the troops under Count Wittgenstein.

The destruction of the bridges and Napoleon's retreat to Zembin, along the Vilna road. – Enemy troop losses.

Prince Kutuzov's crossing of the Dnieper at Kopys. – His orders at this time. – The advance of our main army from the Dnieper to the Berezina. – The deployment of Napoleon's forces on the first stage following the crossing. – Measures taken on our part for the initial pursuit of the remnants of the enemy army.

Analysis of operations by both sides.

Before dawn on 14 (26) November, Napoleon set off on horseback from Stary-Borisov for the site chosen for the crossing at Studyanka.[1] The vast swamps lying along the Berezina had frozen from the cold that had set in at the time; although the

---

1 Fain, *Manuscrit de 1812*, II, 315.

river had not yet had time to freeze, it was choked with ice floes, which made it very difficult to build the bridges. At eight o'clock in the morning, as soon as the workers had managed to prepare all the necessary materials, Napoleon ordered General Corbineau to swim across to the opposite shore with one of the squadrons from his brigade; several small rafts, each of which could carry ten men, were provided to transfer 400 light infantry from Dąbrowski's detachment.[2] At the same time, all the artillery from Oudinot's corps and the *Garde*, a total of 40 guns (or 56 guns, according to other sources), were emplaced on the high ground at Studyanka.[3] We had only one horse artillery company to counteract this powerful battery consisting mostly of heavy guns, and besides, the swamps extending along the right bank stopped our guns from closing up to the river and prevented them not only from firing at the enemy battery, but also from firing on the workers constructing the bridges. General Kornilov attempted to drive the troops that had crossed over back to the river, but the French battery hammered our small detachment with round shot and forced them to retreat to the forest.[4] Exploiting this opportunity, the enemy began to lay two bridges, at a distance of about 200 *sazhen* from one another: the right hand bridge (from the French point of view) was assigned exclusively for infantry and cavalry, while the left, of more robust construction, was not only for the troops, but also for artillery and vehicles. Having destroyed the pontoon park in Orsha, the construction of these bridges would have been completely impossible had General Éblé not saved two mobile forges, two wagons loaded with coal and six wagons with nails, iron and various tools, just in case.[5] All this notwithstanding, however, the French encountered extreme difficulties as they were building the bridges on the Berezina. Due to the rains and thaw that had happened earlier, the width of the river opposite Studyanka had increased to 50 *sazhen*, and the depth to 60 feet in many places. But none of this could stop the courageous pontoniers and sappers. Along with all their other colleagues, they were exhausted from the strenuous campaigning and every kind of hardship, but invigorated by the presence of Napoleon, they threw themselves into the water between ice floes up to their chests, and worked day and night and died to save the army.[6]

By one o'clock in the afternoon, the right hand bridge had just been completed, and Napoleon, who was constantly with the builders, ordered the troops under Oudinot to cross the river, consisting of the remnants of *2e Corps*, Dąbrowski's detachment and Doumerc's *3e division de cuirassiers*, totalling 5,600 infantry and 1,400 cavalry: this force, passing Napoleon in the best order, greeted him with loud cheers. Although this bridge reserved for the crossing of infantry was fragile and very narrow, the French nevertheless managed to pass two guns with ammunition caissons and several cartridge caissons over it. Meanwhile, Chaplits, who had gone

---

2   Fain, II, 316-317. Sołtyk, *Napoléon en 1812*, 442.
3   [Liprandi complains that the conflicting sources are not identified].
4   General Arnoldi's notes, commander of 13th Horse Artillery Company in Kornilov's detachment.
5   Chambray, *Histoire de l'expédition de Russie*, III, 195.
6   Chambray, III, 49-51. Gourgaud, *Examen critique de l'ouvrage de M. le comte de Ségur*, Livre XI, Chap. V. Fain, II, 306.

to Stakhov at just the wrong time, was leading his detachment back to Brili, but the march of 12 *versts* would take about three hours. Upon arrival at Brili, Chaplits could not attack the enemy decisively without exposing his troops to fire from the battery stationed on the high ground of the left bank, and limited himself to occupying the edge of the Stakhov forest. This made it possible for Marshal Oudinot to consolidate himself on the right bank of the river and, forming his front line to face Stakhov, shielded the crossing of the remaining French corps; at the same time, Oudinot sent a small detachment towards Zembin, in order to seize the long bridges and causeways leading through the swamps of the river Gajna. The Cossack outpost, stationed in Zembin, withdrew through the forest to Stakhov, having been unable to destroy the bridges: thus the onward route to Vilna was open to the enemy. Oudinot, wanting to deny the initiative to Chaplits, attacked him in the forest and, taking advantage of his superiority in infantry, pushed our force back almost as far as Stakhov.[7]

During the course of these actions, the other bridge designated for the crossing of vehicles was completed by four o'clock in the afternoon;[8] the artillery was directed over it – first from *2e Corps*, and then from the *Garde*. Although the swamp on the other side of the river, through which the guns were intending to pass, was frozen, they nevertheless broke through in many places, which greatly delayed the crossing.[9]

All that day, 14 (26) November, the Commander-in-Chief of the Army of the Danube remained at Shabashevichi with the majority of his force, having detached Major General Rudzevich [Alexander Yakovlevich Rudzevich], with two regiments of jägers, one of hussars and one light artillery company, along the road to Borisov, to the town of Glaven, to advance from there (as Chichagov's orders stated) 'in whichever direction circumstances demand.'[10] Meanwhile, Count O'Rourke, having been sent to Nizhny-Berezino with a detachment, for a reconnaissance of

---

[7] Chambray, III, 51-53. Sołtyk, 443. Chaplits, *Remarques sur la campagne de 1812* (Archive of the M.T.D. No. 44,712). On the outcome of leaving the bridges to Zembin intact, Chichagov wrote (*Mémoires inedits*, 68) that: 'the detachment stationed there did not burn them, although the orders issued to Chaplits gave instructions to destroy them. However, this omission did not carry the consequences that were attributed to it. Indeed – if there had been no frosts, then the destruction of these bridges would have trapped the French in impenetrable swamps; on the contrary, frosts had set in during the crossing, whereupon the enemy would have been able to pass the destroyed bridges just as I passed them during the pursuit, which was not delayed in the least even though the bridges had been destroyed by the French...'

[8] In the construction of each of these bridges, 23 trestles were provided, from three to ten feet in height; they were constructed from rough-cut logs. The decking of the larger bridge consisted of timbers in the round, about 15 feet long, and three to four inches thick; the decking of the bridge for the infantry was made of three layers of thin boards taken from the roofs of peasant houses, and in addition, both bridges were strewn with hemp and hay. Had the French kept the pontoon park with them, then 15 pontoons would have been sufficient to build a bridge, and the work itself would have required no more than two hours. Chambray, III, 196-197.

[9] Chambray, III, 54.

[10] Chichagov's orders dated 14 [26] November, to Count Langéron, No. 1,177, and to General Rudzevich, No. 1,178. Archive of the M.T.D. No. 44,585. Log of Outgoing Documents from the Commander-in-Chief of the Army of the Danube.

the enemy and to distract their attention with feint crossings, sent out patrols in all directions on the opposite side of the river, who extracted reliable intelligence from prisoners taken by them and from the inhabitants regarding movements by the enemy army towards Borisov, in order to cross the Berezina in the vicinity of this location. Count O'Rourke immediately reported this to the Commander-in-Chief,[11] and at the same time sent to him an enemy squadron commander taken prisoner by the Cossacks, who revealed that: 'he belongs to the corps under Marshal Victor, which is moving towards Studyanka, where a crossing is already being established, and he believes that the bridges are probably already completed.' In the meantime, Count O'Rourke received orders from the admiral: 'to send a reliable officer over the Berezina in order to locate any detachment belonging to our Main Army, to announce to the commander of said detachment that intelligence has been received of an enemy crossing at Studyanka, and give him orders, in the name of the Commander-in-Chief of the Army of the Danube, to bring this to the attention of Prince Kutuzov immediately.' Count O'Rourke entrusted this important task to Major Khrapovitsky, from his detachment, who crossed the Berezina, made his way to the town of Pogost and, chancing upon Count Ozharovsky's raiding detachment on the march from Mogilev to the Berezina, handed the admiral's orders to him. Count Ozharovsky initially doubted the accuracy of the intelligence delivered by Khrapovitsky, but then, having become convinced of its reliability, he sent an officer of the Lifeguard Horse, Palitsyn, to Prince Kutuzov with the report on Napoleon's crossing at Studyanka.[12] The Field Marshal, who was in Kopys, only received this report once the entire enemy army had already managed to cross the Berezina.

On 14 (26) November, Count Wittgenstein, having set up a new vanguard under the command of General Vlastov, consisting of six battalions with two groups of *opolchenie*, seven squadrons, four Don regiments and one of Bashkirs, some 5,000 men in total with six guns,[13] pushed them forwards to Zhiskovo while moving to Kostritsa himself. On that same day, Count Platov moved to Loshnitsa, Yermolov to Krupki, Miloradovich to Molyavka.

While the force under Oudinot, numbering some 7,000 to 9,000 men, having crossed the Berezina, was fighting against the 5,000 strong detachment under Chaplits, Ney arrived at Studyanka, where Claparède's division was to join him the next morning: there were some 5,000 to 6,000 men in total, under Ney's command; the *Vieille Garde* and *Jeune Garde*, with the exception of Claparède's division, numbering 7,000, were also stationed at Studyanka; Victor, having set out

---

11 War Diary of the Army of the Danube, compiled by Malinovsky.
12 Notes on the crossing of the Berezina by the active state councillor Khrapovitsky (serving as a major in 1812). Count Ozharovsky's report to Duty General Konovnitsyn, dated 16 [28] November, from Kozlov-Bereg, No. 38 (Archive of the M.T.D. No. 29,172).
13 The vanguard comprised: the 25th Jägers, Combined Jäger Regiment, Azov Infantry, Combined Hussar Regiment, Finland Dragoons, Platov's Cossacks, Rodionov's Cossacks, Loshchilin's Cossacks, Chernozubov's Cossacks (the latter from Adjutant General Kutuzov's detachment), 5th Bashkir Regiment (from Adjutant General Prince Volkonsky's former detachment), two groups of Novgorod *Opolchenie* (newly arrived), and six guns from 9th Light Artillery Company. *Précis de la campagne du I Corps* etc. Archive of the M.T.D. No. 29,200.

from Ratulichi on the morning of 14 (26) November, emerged onto the highway and remained in Loshnitsa as the rearguard in place of Davout, Partouneaux's division and Delaitre's cavalry brigade [Antoine Charles Bernard Delaitre], some 5,000 men, and arrived in Borisov by nightfall with the rest of his force, some 10,000 men in total; finally, the remnants of the corps under the Viceroy, Davout and Junot, in which no more than 2,400 men remained, were located between Borisov and Loshnitsa.[14]

During the night of 14 to 15 (26 to 27) November, the bridge designated for artillery and vehicles partially collapsed twice; at eight o'clock in the evening and at two o'clock in the morning; repairing it required three hours on the first occasion, and four hours on the second. This caused extraordinary congestion on the left bank at Studyanka. In order to preserve order among the troops as much as possible and to speed up the crossing, Napoleon himself spent the night near the bridges in one of the surviving huts from this village, observing the execution of the orders issued by him; whenever he took a break, he was replaced by Murat, Berthier, or Lauriston. Ney's troops and the *Jeune Garde* crossed during the night. Strenuous efforts were made to encourage the unarmed men and stragglers to cross, but nothing could induce these unfortunates to soldier on, who preferred to wander about in the vicinity of Borisov, hoping to find a crust of bread somewhere. On the morning of 15 (27) November, Victor's corps came up to the bridges, with the exception of Partouneaux's division, which had been left at Borisov as the rearguard; the arrival of this corps secured the crossing from Wittgenstein's direction, and therefore, at one o'clock in the afternoon, Napoleon moved the *Vieille Garde* across and crossed the Berezina himself. Following them, the Baden brigade and artillery from Daendels' division were to cross, as well as the remnants of the corps under the Viceroy, Davout and Junot: thus, only Gérard's division and one of Daendels' brigades, Fournier's cavalry division and the reserve artillery from *9e Corps* would be located at Studyanka; Partouneaux's division and Delaitre's brigade remained at Borisov (as mentioned above), while the remnants of the corps under the Viceroy, Junot and Davout were on the march from Borisov to Studyanka.[15]

As Napoleon's troops crossed, they formed up in battle formation facing the Stakhov forest. Ney's force formed the second line behind Oudinot's *2e Corps*; while the *Jeune Garde*, under Mortier's command were in reserve behind Ney. Doumerc's cuirassiers and the light cavalry under Corbineau and Castex supported the infantry: Overall, on this day, some 15,000 men were formed up for battle on the right bank of the Berezina, including some 2,000 cavalry.

On our side, the troops under Chaplits, who were stationed near Stakhov, were reinforced on the orders of Chichagov with two infantry regiments from the forces under Langéron, who had received orders: 'in the event of notification from General Chaplits that the enemy has crossed anywhere in the sector he is holding, leave no more than one battalion with some of the artillery in the bridgehead, and go to the enemy crossing point with all other forces without waiting for confirmation.' General Rudzevich, who was stationed in the village of Glaven, was ordered: 'return

---

14 For an analysis of French manpower strength, see Appendix XI.
15 Chambray, III, 55-57. Fain, II, 320-323.

to the bridgehead, and if Count Langéron sets off to assist Chaplits, you are also to move up the Berezina, leaving one battalion with two cannon in the bridgehead.' Chichagov himself set off from Shabashevichi for Stakhov with his main body. But the attack on the enemy was postponed until the following day, because the admiral could not get his troops back from the lower Berezina to the Borisov bridgehead before the evening of 15 (27) November.[16] One of the main participants in the operations by Chaplits' detachment, in describing the action on 14 (26) November, stated:

> Nightfall stopped the fighting, while the dawn lit up both forces within sight of each other and well within musket range. Thus, the whole day of 15 [27] November passed; neither side was willing to re-start the action: we were too weak for that, although some regiments had come up to us at night from Borisov, while the French were in a hurry to cross, and for that reason they were content simply not to be harassed.[17]

If our forces had indeed attacked the enemy on 15 (27) November, then they would have been placed in a most precarious position. Up to this point, some order had been maintained at the crossing, and the movement of troops was delayed only by damage to the larger bridge, which gave way for a third time at about four o'clock and was not repaired before six o'clock. At that moment, the stragglers and walking wounded surged forwards in a mob, leading many horses and wagons behind them; the entire area between Studyanka and the riverbank was smothered by them to such an extent that there was no way to get to the bridges without being exposed to the greatest peril.[18]

Count Wittgenstein had intended to move to Veselovo or Studyanka that day, but as the road leading from Kostritsa (where our troops had spent the night of 14 to 15 (26 to 27) November) to Veselovo turned out to be impassable, it was decided to head for Borisov. In the morning, the vanguard set out from Zhiskovo, under Vlastov's command; they were followed by the corps under Berg and Steinheil. The reserves were ordered to halt once they had reached Zhiskovo; while Seslavin, whose partisans had joined the corps, and Chernozubov 8th's Cossack Regiment were ordered to go straight to Borisov and establish communications with Platov's Cossack detachment. At about three o'clock in the afternoon, Vlastov, as he was emerging from the forest near the Stary-Borisov manor, encountered a French column. These were the leading elements of Partouneaux's division, who, having arrived in the town of Borisov at around noon, had wanted to continue their retreat to Studyanka immediately, but were ordered to hold in Borisov until the next morning. By evening, Seslavin's Cossacks had appeared in front of the town, along the Orsha road; thereafter – the thunder of guns from Stary-Borisov and a large number of wagons and men returning from there in disorder towards the town left General Partouneaux

---

16 War Diary of the Army of the Danube (Third Army), compiled by Malinovsky. Chichagov's orders to Count Langéron, dated 14 [26] November, No. 1,181, and to General Rudzevich, dated 14 [26] November, No. 1,183. *Mémoires inedits de Tchitchagoff*, 71-73.
17 From General Arnoldi's notes regarding the Berezina crossing.
18 Chambray, III, 57-58.

Plan of the Berezina crossing.

in no doubt that he was surrounded by Russian forces.[19] Having decided to break out towards Studyanka, Partouneaux set out for Stary-Borisov with his division and Delaitre's light cavalry brigade, some 4,000 men; this force moved off in perfect order, but a multitude of wagons and unarmed men dragged along in between the columns and all around them.[20]

Meanwhile, Vlastov, having encountered a French column at the Stary-Borisov manor, positioned the vanguard for battle and placing the 9th Light Artillery Company and 27th Battery Artillery Company on the high ground, opened fire on the enemy, threw them into disorder and having taken possession of the manor, he forced the French to retreat, partly along the road towards Veselovo, partly towards the town of Borisov: Cossacks, supported by the Consolidated Hussar Regiment, pursued the enemy in the first of these directions, while the Grodno Hussar Regiment, who had arrived to reinforce the vanguard, took the route to Borisov. This cavalry force captured a gun and much of the baggage train and took a significant number of prisoners, who revealed that Partouneaux's division, which was proceeding as the rear guard to Victor's corps, had not yet managed to pass Stary-Borisov.

Having received this intelligence, Count Wittgenstein issued the following instructions in order to block the route of the enemy: the vanguard under Vlastov, positioned behind the manor, strongly held by our marksmen, were to attach their right flank to the road leading from the town of Borisov to Veselovo, forming the right wing; Count Steinheil's corps were to occupy the centre and left wing, while Berg's corps were to remain in reserve. After that, having sent a *parlementaire* to the commander of the enemy force, demanding that they lay down their arms, Wittgenstein remained waiting for a response. But night had fallen in the meantime; Partouneaux detained our *parlementaire* and, taking advantage of the darkness, decided to make his way to Studyanka.[21] Having pushed the Grodno Hussars and the Cossacks back, the French lined up parallel to our position and simultaneously attacked Count Wittgenstein's right wing and centre. The left wing of the enemy line swiftly moved forward in several columns; the French took possession of the manor in spite of the heavy fire from our batteries. In order to hold them, General Vlastov sent the 25th Jägers and Azov Infantry into the attack; meanwhile – in the centre, the Navaginsk Infantry with two groups of Novgorod *Opolchenie*, driving back the advancing enemy, moved to their right and, together with the Azov Infantry and 25th Jägers, ejected the French from the manor, which forced Partouneaux to retreat towards the town of Borisov.[22] But at the same time, Captain Seslavin broke into the town with his partisan detachment, where he captured more than 3,000 prisoners, mostly marauders, and established communications with the

---

19 See the Plan of the Berezina Crossing.
20 Extracted from Count Wittgenstein's reports to the Tsar. Archive of the M.T.D. No. 44,585. Chambray, III, 60-61.
21 [Liprandi tells us: 'The *parlementaire* was Captain Kochubey (later a Member of the State Council, who died in 1859)'].
22 *Précis de la campagne du I Corps de l'armée d'Occident pendant l'année 1812*. Archive of the M.T.D. No. 29,200.

Army of the Danube.[23] General Partouneaux, blocked from the front and rear by Russian troops, offered to surrender in capitulation and, during the negotiations, attempted to break through with several hundred men to join forces with Victor, but when they encountered Chernozubov's Cossack Regiment, they were forced to lay down their arms; the remaining two infantry brigades of this division and the cavalry under Delaitre retreated into the town itself, where, being surrounded on all sides by the troops under Wittgenstein and Platov, they surrendered the next morning, along with all the stragglers who were with them; in all, we captured 240 field officers and subalterns, 7,800 lower ranks, two colours and three guns; among the prisoners were generals Partouneaux, Billard [Pierre Joseph Billard], Camus [Louis Camus de Moulignon], Blanmont [Marie Pierre Isidore de Blanmont] and Delaitre.[24] Of the entire division, only a single battalion managed to escape, numbering 120 men, who, having moved along a country road right on the bank of the Berezina, rejoined Victor's corps.[25]

Meanwhile, upon arrival at the Borisov bridgehead, Chichagov ordered a pontoon bridge to be built and established communications with both Count Wittgenstein and the force under Count Platov, which had arrived in Borisov, and with General Yermolov, who was stationed 17 *versts* from Borisov during the night of 15 to 16 (27 to 28) November. Count Wittgenstein sent Captain Seslavin to Chichagov to inquire about his orders; the admiral sent orders to Wittgenstein informing him that he [Chichagov] would be attacking the enemy on the right bank of the Berezina at dawn, and, as, in all likelihood, the French had four times the strength of the Army of the Danube, he proposed [that Wittgenstein launch] an attack on them on the left bank of the river also. At the same time, Chichagov asked Wittgenstein to reinforce the Army of the Danube with two infantry divisions. Count Wittgenstein gave his word that he would attack the enemy; but gave no response to the request for

---

23 Captain Seslavin's report to General Konovnitsyn, dated 17 [29] November, from Borisov: 'On 15 [27] November, at Kruchaya, I attacked the corps under Count Tyszkiewicz. One column was ordered to surrender; they obeyed; the other was cut down for resisting.   On 16 [28] November, at Loshnitsa, I ordered the Cossacks to attack the bivouacs. On 16 [28] November, on the orders of Count Wittgenstein to take the town of Borisov at all costs and establish communications with the army under Admiral Chichagov, after desperate efforts on the part of the enemy, I occupied the town of Borisov and established communications with Admiral Chichagov. The outcome of this action was the capture of more than 3,000 men. Your Excellency! Having taken the town, I established communications with Chichagov, who put infantry at my disposal, and as I was feeding the horses outside the town, Denisov bypassed the town with Cossacks from Platov and reported to Platov that he had taken the town. Platov gave orders for all the prisoners to be sent to himself and to take over the occupation of the town. Thus the glory of this action was taken from our detachment. In order not to yield, one must be a general oneself. Ask Chichagov about all this. I will not stand for this.' (Archive of the M.T.D. No. 29,172. Log of Incoming Documents, No. 666). Admiral Chichagov's report to Prince Kutuzov, dated 22 November [4 December], No. 1,944 (Archive of the M.T.D. No. 29,172. Log of Incoming Documents, No. 698).
24 Count Wittgenstein's report to the Tsar, dated 16 [28] November, No. 75. *Précis de la campagne du I Corps*. Chambray, III, 61-62. Fain, II, 341-342.
25 Chambray, III, 62. Gourgaud wrote that this was a battalion of *55e régiment d'infanterie de ligne*; but since this regiment was in Spain at the time, it must be assumed that the aforementioned battalion was from a provisional regiment (*régiment provisoire*).

reinforcements.[26] Count Platov and Yermolov, at the admiral's request, were tasked to cross the Berezina and to support the Army of the Danube.[27]

During the night of 15 to 16 (27 to 28) November, the enemy continued to move artillery, vehicles and men separated from their units across, but very slowly due to the disorder and congestion at the bridges. The most disorganised corps (the Viceroy's, Davout's, and probably Junot's, if there were still remnants of his by this point) were ordered, immediately after crossing the Berezina, to retreat further, taking with them all the vehicles they could find and all the unarmed men and sick, via Zembin, in order to link up with Wrede's Bavarian corps, which had been ordered to take up positions at Vileyka at this point, in order to guard the crossing over the Viliya [Neris], and to collect rations for the army.[28] Napoleon, intending to keep the bridges open until 17 (29) November and concerned that Victor, who had only Gérard's division on the left bank of the Berezina, might be crushed by Wittgenstein's superior numbers, ordered the Baden brigade (from Daendels' division), numbering 2,240 men, to re-cross the river to Studyanka, leaving their artillery on the right bank: in total, there were some 5,000 men in Gérard's division (composed of Polish troops), the Baden brigade and Fournier's cavalry brigade, which had just 300 horses, for the defence of the crossing point on the left bank of the river.[29] This force were in fighting positions on a plateau, protected from the direction of Stary-Borisov by a stream, easily fordable and not an obstacle to troop movements: the Baden brigade stood on the right wing with a battery attached from Gérard's division, resting their right flank on the Berezina, while on their left, the Berg contingent (also from Daendels' division) were in the nearest houses of the village of Studyanka; Victor's left wing consisted of Gérard's division, which, due to their low numbers, could not occupy the entire plateau as far as the nearby forest, and therefore, in order to protect the infantry of the left flank, Fournier's cavalry (regiments from Baden and Hessen) were located behind them. The force had moved down the reverse slope of the high ground such that it was impossible to see them from the slope on the other side of the stream; while the base of the high ground was guarded by a screen of skirmishers. A total of 14 artillery pieces covered the approaches to the left wing. Finally, several batteries of *artillerie de la Garde* were located on the right bank of the Berezina on the frozen swamps, in order to defend the position from the flank.[30]

In order to protect the crossing point on the right bank of the river facing Chichagov, the forces were located as follows: Oudinot's and Ney's corps, numbering 10,000 men,[31] including some 1,500 cavalry, resting their right flank on the dense forest

---

26 *Mémoires inedits de Tchitchagoff*, 73-74.
27 General Yermolov's manuscript notes. *Précis de la campagne du I Corps*. Buturlin, II, 374-375.
28 Orders dated 27 and 28 November new style. Fain, II, 333.
29 Chambray, III, 63. According to Fain and Sołtyk, there were 10,000 men under Victor's command on the left bank of the Berezina. Fain, II, 334. Sołtyk, 445.
30 *Beitrag zu der Geschichte des neunten Corps der französischen Armee im Feldzug gegen Russland, 1812. Oesterreich. milit. Zeitschrift, 1821, Drittes Heft*, 277. Chambray, III, 63. In the first of these works, the author erroneously mentions Veselovo instead of Studyanka.
31 According to Sołtyk, Ney and Oudinot had 18,000 men, while according to Fain, there were 14,700. Sołtyk, 445. Fain, II, 334.

through which the road from Borisov runs: Oudinot's men held the right wing and centre, while Ney held positions on the left, extending overall to a frontage of two *versts*. The *Garde* were in reserve under Napoleon's personal command, totalling 7,000 men, including 1,400 cavalry.[32] The battlefield was, for the most part, wooded, which did not allow our cavalry to be brought into action in significant numbers; across the whole area of the Stakhov forest, through which the Russian troops were intending to pass, artillery could only be positioned on the Borisov road.[33]

On 16 (28) November, our forces attacked the enemy on both banks of the Berezina.

Chaplits was ordered to advance from the direction of Stakhov, having been reinforced with several regiments from Pahlen's former vanguard; meanwhile, Chichagov, who had managed to concentrate his forces in the night and absorb O'Rourke's detachment, was preparing to support Chaplits. In anticipation of his arrival, Chaplits sent his force off in four columns, of which one, under the command of General Rudzevich, was to drive in the advanced screen of enemy outposts; two others, under generals Kornilov and Meshcherinov [Vasily Dmitrievich Meshcherinov], supported the first, while the final column, entrusted to Colonel Krasovsky, was directed to the right of the others along the river bank. Due to the restricted width of the road, Arnoldi's [Ivan Karlovich Arnoldi] 13th Horse Artillery Company, which was marching in platoon column at the head of Chaplits' force until first contact with the enemy, could provide fire support to the screen from just two guns. The action began at dawn, at the very place where our troops had stopped on the evening of 14 (26) November, in the forest near Stakhov. Our jägers pushed the enemy back, covering themselves with glory.[34] The skirmishing in the forest was very bloody; Oudinot was wounded at the very beginning of the fighting, and therefore Ney commanded the entire action on the right bank of the Berezina alone. Our troops, in anticipation of being reinforced, moved forward, but as they approached Brili, they encountered increasing resistance and, upon exiting the forest, were engaged with round shot, which, shattering trees and splintering branches, caused great harm to our jägers. At about nine o'clock in the morning, Chichagov, having arrived in Stakhov, sent the 9th Division and 18th Division into action, under the command of his chief of staff, General Sabaneev, who, being extremely fond of open-order formations, had deployed a significant portion of his infantry before reaching the battlefield. This cloud of skirmishers, who could not be controlled in the forest, dashed forward with loud cheers and opened fire into the rear of Chaplits' vanguard. At the same time, Ney, taking advantage of the more open terrain onto which Chaplits' marksmen had entered, ordered his cavalry to attack them. Doumerc's cuirassiers, striking at our jägers with the speed of lightning, broke through the skirmishing screen, and the enemy was able to take some 600 prisoner, but the intrepidity of our generals restored

---

32 Chambray, III, 50. Fain, II, 334. According to Sołtyk, there were 10,000 men in the *Garde*. *Napoléon en 1812*, 445.
33 Chambray, III, 63-64.
34 12th Jägers, 22nd Jägers, 27th Jägers, 7th Jägers, 14th Jägers, 28th Jägers and 32nd Jägers. Malinovsky's notes regarding the Berezina crossing.

the situation: Chaplits himself, with two squadrons of Pavlograd Hussars, charged to engage the French cavalry and rescued Prince Shcherbatov, who had already been surrounded by enemy dragging him from his horse. After that, the stubborn skirmishing action continued until 11 o'clock at night; as one screen weakened, it was replaced by another; our artillery, as before, only had space to work two guns, while the enemy bombarded the exits to the open ground with the fire of a powerful battery: our guns could not endure this for more than half an hour and, having lost all their crews and horses, were replaced by others. Following the elimination of Arnoldi's company, it was replaced eventually by three others:[35] all of them, working in the same manner, suffered heavy casualties.[36] The losses to our force in this action extended to 2,000 men overall. Chaplits himself was among the wounded. The enemy lost around 5,000 men. In addition to Marshal Oudinot, the following generals were wounded: Legrand, Zajączek, whose leg was shattered by round shot, Claparède, Dąbrowski and Kniaziewicz [Karol Otto Kniaziewicz].[37]

On that same day, 16 (28) November, Count Wittgenstein, having detached the corps under Count Steinheil from Stary-Borisov along the road to the town of Borisov, in order to disarm Partouneaux's division that had surrendered at dawn (as already mentioned), sent his remaining troops towards Studyanka. The vanguard under General Vlastov, having set off at five o'clock in the morning, encountered Victor's forward outposts near the village of Bychi, drove them back and took up positions on the high ground facing the enemy at about eight o'clock, at the same time as the bitter fighting in Stakhov forest began. Behind the vanguard, Berg's corps, under the command of General Foch, arrived at seven o'clock. Count Wittgenstein himself went to Admiral Chichagov for a meeting regarding future operations.

As soon as the vanguard troops had formed up parallel to Victor's position, facing the stream, then General Vlastov, deciding to attack the enemy position on their left flank, detached the Combined Hussar Regiment and Rodionov's Cossacks for the envelopment; in order to divert the attention of the enemy, 1st Horse Artillery Company under Colonel Sukhozanet [Ivan Onufrievich Sukhozanet] was pushed forward opposite their right wing, and their fire, directed at the bridges and at the enemy troops gathered on the left bank of the river, caused chaos among the wagon trains huddled together in anticipation of crossing. The people surrounding them stampeded in disorder towards the bridges; those on horseback trampled down those on foot blocking their way; people were being crushed by carriages and wagons. Everyone was mixed into a discordant mass, subject to the destructive action of our artillery. In this turmoil, many people died suffocated in the crush between retreating wagons; others, shoved into the river, tried to escape by swimming between the ice floes. Horses forced into the river drowned; others, having

---

35 Pashchenko's, de-Bobrish's and Prebsting's companies. Arnoldi's notes regarding the Berezina crossing.
36 Arnoldi's notes.
37 War Diary of the Army of the Danube (Third Army), compiled by Malinovsky. According to Chambray, the Russians lost 1,500 in prisoners alone, while, according to Fain, it was 1,800 men. Chambray, III, 67. Fain, II, 338-339. Sołtyk, 451. Buturlin, *Histoire militaire de la campagne de Russie en 1812.*

gathered in huge herds, blocked the approaches to the bridges already congested with people and vehicles moving across them. Meanwhile, on our right wing, Rodionov's Cossacks had been driven back by Fournier's cavalry; but Gerngross struck the enemy in the flank with the Combined Hussar Regiment, and drove them back to their starting positions. Victor, seeing the impossibility of continuing to cross under the deadly fire of our guns, ordered the troops of his centre to cross the stream and attack the hill occupied by the Russians. This attack was repelled by canister fire from 1st Horse Artillery Company and 27th Battery Artillery Company. The enemy repeated the attack with fresh forces; a dense screen of their skirmishers, passing through the scrub lining the banks of the stream, had already appeared at the foot of the slope near our batteries: at this moment, the 24th Jäger Regiment, marching at the head of Berg's corps, struck the enemy screen with fixed bayonets, scattered them and pursued them with their own marksmen. Whereupon Victor ordered his right wing to move forward, under covering fire from the *artillerie de la Garde* battery, which was stationed across the river and brought the troops of our left wing under enfilade fire. But already by this time, other troops from the front line of Berg's corps were gradually approaching, which allowed us to reinforce the left wing with the Sevsk Infantry, 1st Marine Regiment, 10th Group of the St Petersburg *Opolchenie* and a little later the Perm Infantry Regiment. The enemy, being repulsed by these troops, suffered significant casualties during their retreat due to the actions of 9th Light Artillery Company and 14th Battery Artillery Company. During these actions, our reserve closed up. Major General Foch directed the 23rd Horse Artillery Company under Markov [Alexander Ivanovich Markov] and part of the Combined Cuirassier Regiment to support the right wing. Meanwhile, the enemy in the centre pressed forwards again; in order to hold them, the Nizov Infantry and Voronezh Infantry were sent up, who, having driven the columns advancing against them back across the stream, captured a battery, but, upon being counter-attacked by Victor's reserve, retreated across the stream and were relentlessly pursued by the enemy, who managed to break through our centre. General Foch halted them by opening fire with canister from the guns of 11th Artillery Company; while a swift attack by two squadrons of the Combined Cuirassier Regiment (replacement squadrons from the Chevalier Garde and Lifeguard Horse) and an assault by the Pavlov Grenadiers' replacement battalion forced Victor to retreat to the position across the stream once more. Exploiting this success, General Foch enveloped the enemy left flank with the Mogilev Infantry and Combined Cuirassier Regiment, which forced Victor to refuse his left wing, at an angle with the other troops, in order to protect the village of Studyanka and bridges on the Berezina. Nightfall brought an end to the fighting. The Russian troops bivouacked on the very spots where they had been fighting at the end of the action. The part of Berg's corps, which through a misunderstanding had remained at Stary-Borisov, arrived on the battlefield in the evening, while Steinheil's corps came up at night: thus, of the 28,000 or 30,000 men who were under Count Wittgenstein's command, only 14,000 participated in the battle at Studyanka; namely, 4,000 in Vlastov's vanguard, 4,000 in Berg's corps and 6,000 in Foch's reserve. Casualties in I Corps, over the two days of 15 and 16 (27 and 28) November, reached 4,000 men out of action overall. The enemy lost some 13,000 men taken prisoner alone, including Partouneaux's division, but most of these consisted of stragglers and unarmed men who did not belong to Victor's corps. In addition, we took four guns and two colours (from Partouneaux's division). General Candras was among the dead, while the wounded included Victor himself and generals: Fournier, Gérard and Damas [François-Étienne Damas].[38]

During the night of 16 to 17 (28 to 29) November, Victor, having left a small rearguard at Studyanka, to cover the retreat of the stragglers and wagons, crossed to the right bank of the river. As the bridge approaches had become completely impassible due to being choked with vehicles, General Éblé ordered his pontoniers to clear a passage resembling a trench with the assistance of the *artillerie de la Garde*. Horses left unattended were herded to the right bank, while carts abandoned on the route were dragged to the bridge and pushed into the water; but corpses could not be removed and lay in multitudes along the sides of the cleared passage to the crossing point.[39]

The fighting on 16 (28) November had been very bloody; the enemy army in particular had suffered innumerable losses, and were forced to abandon all the wounded and most of their vehicles. The end of the existence of the *Grande Armée* took place on the banks of the Berezina. The subsequent retreat of its remnants was nothing more than a rout. The corps under Oudinot and Victor, who had rations for several days with them at the time of their arrival at the Berezina, retained their strength, and therefore suffered less from the cold than the men who had come from Moscow; all this notwithstanding, however, on 17 (29) November, in these corps there were not even half the number of men that had been counted in their ranks upon reaching the Berezina. In the course of three days, from 14 to 17 (26 to 29) November, the *Vieille Garde* which did not participate in the fighting at all, lost 1,500 men out of 3,500, while the *Jeune Garde* lost 700 out of 1,500 men. The remainder of the *Garde* (2,800 men) were, for the most part, sick and could no longer bear the privations of further campaigning.[40]

It is truly remarkable that among Napoleon's troops that fought on the Berezina, more than three-quarters consisted of foreigners: one of Victor's infantry divisions was Polish, while another was German; his cavalry consisted of Germans; there were only 300 Frenchmen serving under Ney's command, among whom officers were seen carrying muskets and fighting in the ranks with the soldiers; the remainder of his troops were Polish; finally, Marshal Oudinot had one division consisting of Poles, another of Croats and Swiss, and only the other two were of Frenchmen. According to Sołtyk [Roman Sołtyk], half of Napoleon's army fighting on 16 (28) November was made up of Polish troops.[41]

---

38 *Précis de la campagne du I Corps*. Archive of the M.T.D. No. 29,200. Chambray, III, 67. Fain, II, 336-339. Sołtyk, 451.
39 Chambray, III, 69-70. Fain, II, 339. *Oesterreich. milit. Zeitschr. 1821, Drittes Heft*, 283-284. The author of this article mentions the defeat of the Russian 34th Jäger Regiment, on the right flank of the force under Count Wittgenstein, on 16 (28) November; this regiment had never been in Wittgenstein's corps at all; 34th Jäger Regiment were part of II Corps in Prince Kutuzov's main army. Furthermore, no one has written about the defeat of any of the regiments under Count Wittgenstein, except for the author of this article.
40 Chambray, III, 68.
41 Chambray, III, 68-69. Sołtyk, 451.

Throughout the action on 16 (28) November, the Viceroy, Davout and the majority of officers and soldiers made their way to Zembin. Napoleon himself spent that night in a hut, which had remained intact except for the roof, dismantled to feed bivouac fires. Nevertheless, the other buildings in the village, which contained the *État-major général de la Grande Armée*,[42] were razed to the ground, and even those wretched huts in which the wounded were seeking refuge were not spared. A host of sick and wounded officers, soldiers, officials, servants, and sutlers remained on the left bank of the river, at Studyanka; there were also women and children who had followed the army from Moscow. Some of the stragglers might have crossed over during the night of 16 to 17 (28 to 29) November by abandoning their wagons and horses, but they remained in place in the hope of saving them; still others, wounded or sick, lay exhausted; finally, there were those who, having managed to kindle a fire, warmed themselves, immersed in total reverie. Victor and the other French generals vainly tried to convince the men separated from their units to look out for their own salvation. At five o'clock in the morning the abandoned vehicles were set on fire, which forced many to cross over to the right bank; at half past seven, Victor moved the rearguard across and withdrew his forward outposts. Whereupon all the stragglers rushed in a mob towards the bridges and choked the approaches to them once more. General Éblé had been ordered to torch the bridges at eight o'clock, but since the Russians had not yet appeared, he hesitated to carry out the mission assigned to him, wanting to give the people who remained on the left bank of the river a chance to save themselves. At half past nine, on the high ground at Studyanka, the men of the Don appeared, fearsome to the retreating enemy; the bridges were set alight in order to delay them. Thousands of sick and wounded, women and children, had been abandoned. Those who still had any strength wandered along the waterline, in despair, begging the heavens and humanity for help, or rushed in a mob towards the flaming bridges, which collapsed under their weight; others attempted to cross to the far side on the ice that had formed between the bridges, or by swimming, downstream of the bridges, and drowned, or perished, crushed between the ice floes.[43]

An extraordinary vista opened up to the troops under Count Wittgenstein as they appeared at Studyanka: an area almost a *verst* square was full of abandoned carriages, wagons, carts, between which, among the looted booty, lay piles of corpses, remnants of the enemy crawled and the dying wandered hungry and half-frozen.[44] With 20 degrees of frost, the situation of these unfortunates, and especially the women and children who wandered among them, was horrifying.[45] In the

---

42 Chambray and Fain refer to this village as Zanivki. It no longer exists.
43 Chambray, III, 70-71. Ségur, *Histoire de Napoléon et de la grande armée pendant l'année 1812*, II, 369-373.
44 '... various vehicles, both state-owned and private, were in such great numbers that more than half a *verst* square was chock-full of them, in such a way that it was impossible to move or pass through, and three *opolchenie* groups were sent just to clear a path for the passage of troops...' Extracted from Count Wittgenstein's report to the Tsar, dated 17 [29] November, No. 76.
45 [Liprandi comments: 'a thaw set in on 7 [19] November, which continued until the crossing of the Berezina itself, which was not yet frozen, allowing some units to cross by fording, and although the next day, as Napoleon was approaching, a light frost occurred, nevertheless,

midst of the many luxury items taken from Moscow by the enemy, men and women, barely covered with dirty rags, asked our soldiers for the mercy of a crust of bread. Russian hard-tack, about which foreigners have spoken so unfavourably, were sold at a high price to our unwelcome guests; officers who had managed to hang on to their watches, rings and money offered them for a hunk of bread; but many of our soldiers, prompted by the feelings of compassion inherent in the Russian people, did not think about profiting, but shared their last crumbs with the enemy, and with women and children in particular.[46] The overall number of prisoners taken at Studyanka by Count Wittgenstein's troops reached 5,000; in addition, we took 12 guns, a large number of ammunition and cartridge caissons and a huge train of booty, which was divided up among the soldiers and warriors, with the exception of church property, which was sent to the Commander-in-Chief of Moscow, by order of Count Wittgenstein.[47]

Napoleon left the banks of the Berezina himself at six o'clock in the morning and rode in a carriage to Zembin, accompanied by the remnants of his *Garde*; he was followed by Victor's force; while Ney led the rearguard, which was forced to halt at the place where the country lane leading to Zembin forks, and to cover the retreat of the troops and trains jammed along the narrow causeway and bridges over the Gajna river.[48] This circumstance leaves no doubt that if the bridges on the Gajna had been destroyed in advance by our troops, then Napoleon would have encountered even greater difficulties at the crossing of the Berezina.[49]

It is difficult to make a definitive statement of the overall losses suffered by the enemy at the Berezina crossing. Fain [Agathon Jean François Fain] confesses that

---

it was not enough to freeze the swamps, while the ice that formed on the Berezina was so thin that it did not interfere with the construction of the trestle bridges, therefore, under no circumstances could there have been 20 degrees of frost on any known thermometer on the day that Wittgenstein closed up to Studyanka; as on that same day, according to Chambray (Vol. 3, page 69), some routed French fled across the Berezina by swimming'].

46 General Mikhailovsky-Danilevsky's Description of the Patriotic War of 1812, IV. Verbal testimony from eyewitnesses.

47 According to Chambray, 5,000 were captured by Russian troops at Studyanka, including women and children. This calculation almost aligns with that of the War Diary of I Corps (*Précis des opérations du I Corps*. Archive of the M.T.D. No. 29,200), where we find that the number of prisoners taken on 16 [28] November by the troops under Count Wittgenstein reached 13,000 men (including Partouneaux's division). According to Chambray, the Russians took three guns, while in the War Diary, Count Wittgenstein claims 12. Count Wittgenstein's report to the Tsar, dated 17 [29] November, No. 76.

48 Chambray, III, 71-72.

49 Chichagov wrote that, on the occasion of the onset of frost, it was possible to cross through the swamps away from the bridges, and that he himself proceeded in this manner, in pursuit of the French. *Mémoires inédits de Tchitchagoff*, 68. But why did the French not do this to avoid congestion during the retreat? An eyewitness to the events of the 1812 campaign, Dr. Bourgeois, stated that during the retreat from the Berezina, some, trying to make their way through the swamps away from the bridges, fell through the ice and perished. *Un grand nombre d'hommes et de chevaux furent précipités dans les fossés latéraux, et se noyèrent dans les boues dont ils étaient remplis; d'autres, ayant voulu se frayer un passage au travers des marais qu'ils croyaient assez fortement gelés pour les soutenir, s'enfoncèrent jusqu'à mi-corps dans la fange, et ne purent s'en retirer. Tableau de la campagne de Moscou*, 158.

the French lost some 12,000 to 15,000 men taken prisoner alone (including stragglers). Ségur believed that the overall losses among Napoleon's troops were 20,000 men. Gourgaud argued that this crossing was not as disastrous as many historians had described it, having exaggerated the disasters of the French army in their accounts. In contrast, Chambray [Georges, marquis de Chambray] believes that they had suffered immense damage and had been placed in a most horrific situation. Fezensac wrote that more than 15,000 men were lost on the final day of the crossing.[50] With the exception of Chambray's vague statement, albeit consistent with the truth, all other French historians have tried to hide the damage suffered by the *Grande Armée*, which, in all likelihood, reached half of the total enemy numbers who had made it as far as the Berezina: this can be seen by comparing Napoleon's strength as they were moving up to the Berezina with those remaining with him after the crossing. According to the very conservative statements by Chambray and Fain, the actual number of these troops, excluding those men separated from their units, on 14 (26) November, ranged from 30,000 to 40,000 men, and three days after the crossing was less than 9,000.[51] Consequently, the losses of Napoleon's army on the Berezina, in armed men, were at least 20,000 or 25,000 men, and as the casualties among the stragglers and unarmed men were at least equal to the loss of men in the ranks, then Napoleon lost from 45,000 to 50,000 men overall. Only 24 guns were captured or found by Russian troops, of which seven were abandoned by the enemy after the crossing in the village of Brili.[52] But, in addition, many guns had been ditched in the river, which was completely choked with the bodies of enemy dead, corpses of horses and vehicles.[53]

Meanwhile, Prince Kutuzov upon arrival in Kopys with the main body of the army, on 12 (24) November, granted a rest day to his troops, whereupon he crossed the Dnieper on 14 (26) November, leaving the Lifeguard light cavalry in quarters in the vicinity of Kopys, in order to be reconstituted with manpower and remounts; ten artillery companies were left in Kopys for a similar purpose, from which some of the crews and horses were sent to replenish other artillery.[54] Then, on the occasion of the arrival of Grand Duke Konstantin Pavlovich in the army, the Field Marshal entrusted the Lifeguard, the Grenadier Corps and both cuirassier divisions to the command of His Highness.[55]

---

50 '… *Plus de 15,000 hommes périrent ou furent pris dans cette affreuse journée*.' Fezensac, *Journal de la campagne de Russie en 1812*, 134.
51 Chambray, III, 49-50 & 93-94. Fain, II, 334. Fezensac wrote that Napoleon, upon linking up with 2e Corps and 9e Corps, had 50,000 men under arms. Fezensac, 126.
52 *Précis des opérations du I Corps*. Admiral Chichagov's report to Prince Kutuzov, dated 19 November [1 December], No. 1,191.
53 Engineer Major General Förster's report to Lieutenant General Oppermann, who had been sent to Borisov, by order of the Field Marshal, to collect information on operations that had taken place on the Berezina… 'that between the bridges built by the enemy and for a distance of 500 *sazhen*, the fields and the river were so littered with dead bodies and horses that in places it was possible to walk across the river on them…'
54 Orders for Major General Löwenstern, dated 12 [24] November (Outgoing Log, No. 496), and to Adjutant General Uvarov, dated 15 [27] November (Outgoing Log, No. 527). Archive of the M.T.D. No. 29,172.
55 Army Orders, dated 15 [27] November, No. 72.

Kutuzov's orders included the remarkable expulsion of Bennigsen from the army. Back in October, having learned about the disagreements that had arisen in the Field Marshal's headquarters, Emperor Alexander had sent him the following Rescript:

> Prince Mikhail Ilarionovich! Information has reached me that you have just cause to be dissatisfied with the behaviour of General Bennigsen. If these rumours are true, then tell him to leave the army and wait for a new assignment from Me in Vladimir.
> St Petersburg, 9 [21] October 1812.

The Field Marshal, highly dissatisfied with Bennigsen's constant opposition, and even more with his views on the course of the war, which he had reported to Count Arakcheev [Alexey Andreevich Arakcheev] and other persons, had ordered him to go to Kaluga and await an appointment from His Imperial Majesty there, all of which he reported to the Tsar.[56] A few days before his removal from the army, Bennigsen had sent a letter to Emperor Alexander in which he complained about Prince Kutuzov, attributing his personal dislike of Bennigsen to the intrigues of Toll and presented Toll as an upstart, whose inexperience would endanger the success of our operations. Once the Field Marshal had ordered him to go to Kaluga, Bennigsen wrote to the Tsar once more that he had been removed from the army in the event of an imminent end to the war, during which he had constantly been on the front line, and so on.[57]

Emperor Alexander I, although he knew that Bennigsen had incurred the personal dislike of the Field Marshal, nevertheless, as a consolation to the renowned general, honoured him with the following Rescript:

> General, I have received your letters; I very much regret everything that has happened between you and the Field Marshal. I Myself am leaving soon for the army, I invite you to wait for me on My route, where I intend to meet you and inform you of my intentions with regard to your future...[58]

After crossing the Dnieper at Kopys, on 14 (26) November, Prince Kutuzov moved to Krugloe with the main body of the army, towards the village of Mikheevichi,[59] where he arrived on 17 (29) November and where his troops spent the following day

---

56 'On the occasion of General Bennigsen's painful seizures and various other factors, I have ordered him to go to Kaluga and await a further appointment from Your Imperial Majesty there.' Report dated 15 [27] November, Log of Outgoing Documents, No. 531. Archive of the M.T.D. No. 29,172. A copy of the handwritten Rescript by Emperor Alexander I is held in the Archive of the General Staff Department.
57 Excerpts from General Bennigsen's letters are at Appendix XII.
58 'J'ai reçu, Général, voslettres; Je regrette beaucoup tout ce qui s'est passé entre vous et le Maréchal. Partant Moi-même ces jours-ci pour l'armée, Je vous invite à m'attendre sur la route, où Je compte m'aboucher avec vous et vous faire part de mes intentions a votre égard...' Rescript dated 1 [13] December, No. 402 (Archive of the M.T.D. No. 46,692).
59 War Diary. In the Log of Outgoing Documents it states that the Field Marshal's headquarters was at the village of Somry on 17 to 18 (29 to 30) November.

resting. Due to the significant distance of Miloradovich's vanguard from the axis of advance being followed by the main body, a new vanguard was sent out, under the command of Adjutant General Vasilchikov, consisting of IV Cavalry Corps, 33rd Jäger Regiment, Denisov's Cossack Regiment and six horse artillery pieces.[60] On 17 (29) November, having crossed the Berezina, Napoleon set out across Zembin towards the town of Kamen and stopped there for the night with his *Garde*. The Viceroy and Davout managed to retreat to Pleshchenitsa. Victor halted at Zembin; while Ney held positions just short of this location.[61]

On our side, as early as 16 (28) November, while the fighting in the Stakhov forest was still ongoing, Chichagov detached Major General Lanskoy [Sergei Nikolaevich Lanskoy] to pursue the enemy with the Belorussia Hussars, Alexandria Hussars, Livland Dragoons and three Ural regiments, ordering him to get around the enemy, ahead of the lead units of the remnants of the enemy army at Pleshchenitsa and, make it difficult for them to retreat.[62] For the pursuit from behind, a vanguard was set up, under the command of Major General Chaplits, consisting of eight infantry regiments, four of cavalry and eight more of Cossacks, with three horse artillery companies.[63] The cavalry of this detachment came under the command of Major General O'Rourke.

On that same day, 17 (29) November, at around noon, the Cossacks forming as the lead element of the detachment under General Lanskoy, having cut the line of retreat of the enemy force, at Pleshchenitsa, captured General Kamieński [Michał Ignacy Kamieński] and a mobile hospital. Oudinot himself was almost captured.[64] And so began the pursuit of the French by our troops. Meanwhile, having no pontoons with his corps, Count Wittgenstein remained waiting for their arrival from Chichagov's army at Studyanka, having sent Vlastov's vanguard right up to the water's edge of the Berezina, to open a bombardment of the enemy troops and vehicles stationed on the far side of the river. At a council of war, convened on 17 (29) November, it was proposed: Chichagov pursue the enemy along the route via Smorgon to Vilna; that Platov, who had crossed the Berezina the day before, at Borisov, was to move to the left of Chichagov, so as to prevent Napoleon from moving towards Minsk, while Wittgenstein was to proceed ahead of Chichagov, towards Niemenczyn.[65]

The crossing of the Berezina had dealt the final blow to Napoleon's army, which not only had lost what remained of its fighting strength here, but became incapable of retreating in good order. The pitiful remnants of this army, already unable to either protect the multitude of stragglers following them, or to defend themselves, could only flee, accompanied by all the tribulations of hunger and extreme cold. Napoleon,

---

60 Orders for Adjutant General Vasilchikov, dated 14 [26] November, Log of Outgoing Documents, No. 513.
61 Chambray, III, 73. Napoleon's strength return, filed three days after the Berezina crossing: *Vieille Garde*; 2,000 infantry, 1,200 cavalry. *Jeune Garde*; 800 infantry. Ney's & Oudinot's forces; 1,800 infantry, 500 cavalry. Victor's corps; 2,00 infantry, 100 cavalry. *1er Corps* & *4e Corps*; 400 infantry. Totalling: 7,000 infantry, 1,800 cavalry. Chambray, III, 94.
62 War Diary of the Army of the Danube (Third Army), compiled by Malinovsky.
63 For the full composition of the vanguard, see Appendix XIII.
64 Buturlin, *Hist. milit. de la campagne de 1812*, II, 383. Fain, II, 345-346.
65 *Précis des opérations du I Corps*. Archive of the M.T.D. No. 29,200.

however, managed not only to depart himself, but also to take the remnants of his corps with him: all his marshals, many generals and a significant number of officers and old, reliable non-commissioned officers escaped a death which had seemed inevitable. At the end of the campaign, about 2,500 officers from the French *Garde* and the corps under Davout, Ney and the Viceroy crossed the Neman, of whom more than 1,800 would again return to service. Had Napoleon not succeeded in saving them, then he would hardly have been able to form a new army from conscripts in four months, capable of operating successfully against the superior forces of Russia and Prussia. This army owed much of its military prowess to the outstanding cadres from the former *Grande Armée*.[66] If destiny had decreed that Napoleon end his career on the banks of the Berezina, then, in all likelihood, in 1813, 1814 and 1815, the fields of Germany and France would not have been stained with the blood of every European nation. And that is why the crossing of the Berezina, despite the enormous success we gained and the extraordinary losses suffered by Napoleon, was rightly considered in the eyes of the people in 1812 as the kind of event that, having not fulfilled our hopes, did more honour to the vanquished than to the victors. It remains to be investigated to whom the failure of the general operational plan of the Russian armies should be attributed, the main objective of which was the intent: 'to wipe out Napoleon with his main forces to the last man.' Contemporaries of our Patriotic War blamed Chichagov alone for this. And it could not have been otherwise: Prince Kutuzov, the liberator of Russia from the invasion by Napoleon and his hordes, Count Wittgenstein, the defender of our northern capital, who consoled the Russians with his victories at a difficult time, when news of our misfortunes was coming in from all sides: both of them stood so high in popular opinion that no one dared to doubt the infallibility of their actions. No one thought that military science, being based for the most part on unknowable factors, is fraught with errors that even a genius cannot avoid. Chichagov was subjected to general criticism, because, firstly, the position occupied by his army gave him the best chance of blocking Napoleon's route; secondly, by the fact that, commanding land forces for the first time in the Patriotic War, he had not yet managed to earn the laurels of a skilled military commander. Moreover, he made an important error by diverting from the axis along which Napoleon's army was retreating.

Due to the nature of the roads in this theatre of operations between the Dnieper and the Berezina, Napoleon could only retreat towards Minsk. Movement in any other direction would be fatal for him, lengthening the line of his retreat and forcing him to move through the native Russian regions, in which the population was so hostile to him, for longer. In addition, by heading towards Minsk or Vilna, he could make use of the stores collected in the local magazines and assimilate his reserves. In order to block these lines of retreat for Napoleon, it was necessary for our flank armies to hold the courses of the Ula and Berezina rivers (as stated in the general operational plan). The latter, over which Napoleon, by moving towards Minsk, absolutely had to cross, presents a number of forests and swamps throughout the entire length of its course from its sources to the town of Svislach. The most convenient crossing points

---

66 Bernhardi, *Denkwürdigkeiten des Grafen v. Toll*, II, 319.

on the route between Smolensk and Minsk are in Veselovo, Studyanka, Borisov, Ukholoda (all four are close to each other), Usha and Nizhny-Berezino. As their army moved towards whichever of the first four crossing points, it must certainly go along the highway through Tolochin and Bobr; while moving from Smolensk towards Usha, or towards Nizhny-Berezino, it is possible to take either the direct route via Krugloe and Mikheevichi, or turn off the Smolensk highway at Bobr towards Nizhny-Berezino. The course of the Ula, which crossed the direct line of retreat for the French towards Vilna, presents incomparably fewer obstacles to the movements of an army than the course of the Berezina, and therefore we had to hold it with strong forces in order to block Napoleon if he moved towards any of the many crossing points over this river. But Count Wittgenstein, distracted from the direction indicated to him by the enemy, did not establish communications with Chichagov: thus, not only was the upper Berezina not held by Russian forces, where they were supposed to link up with each other, but even the monitoring of this sector of its course was most haphazard.

Admiral Chichagov, for his part, having not yet managed to open communications with Count Wittgenstein, and therefore having no sound reason to hope for the assistance of I Corps in the defence of the Berezina, had to assume that the main army under Prince Kutuzov or, at least, part of it, was moving up behind Napoleon, which, if the French army diverted to the left of the highway, could catch up with them on the Berezina. Consequently, Chichagov was left, not concerning himself with diversionary movements by enemy forces, which would expose Napoleon to the risk of encountering the troops under Count Wittgenstein, or being overtaken by the main body under the Field Marshal, and was mainly guarding the sector between Veselovo and Usha, no more than 50 *versts* in total. To that end, it was necessary for Chichagov to remain in the Borisov bridgehead with his main force, holding the most convenient crossing points opposite Veselovo or Studyanka with small detachments, as well as those at Borisov, Ukholoda and Usha, and to destroy the bridges on the Gajna river, because it was impossible to predict the onset of severe frosts, which would make the swamps around the Gajna passable for troops and vehicles. With regard to the intelligence received by the admiral on the movements of the armies under Napoleon and Schwarzenberg, and having, according to him, a decisive influence on his subsequent actions, I have already had the opportunity to say that: firstly, the Field Marshal, in orders from Lanniki, dated 10 (22) November, had already expressed his opinion to the admiral that Napoleon, having lost hope of making his way via Borisov, might turn towards Pogost and Igumen from Tolochin, or Bobr, and had advised Chichagov: 'monitor these with partisan detachments in order to be notified in advance of their movements and forestall them.' Such orders were not intended to divert Chichagov from the objective of his operations, and besides, they were only received after the Army of the Danube had set off for Shabashevichi. Secondly, Count Wittgenstein had also written to the admiral from Chereya that; 'I cannot say anything definitive about the intentions of the enemy, and although it is claimed that they are heading for Borisov, it must nevertheless be concluded from it all that they have turned towards Bobruisk' etcetera. Thirdly and finally, Colonel Knorring reported on appearances of the French at Smorgon, 150 *versts* from Borisov, at Nesvizh and Novy-Sverzhen to Chichagov; while the locals were saying that an enemy detachment of 2,000 had arrived in the town of Svislach, at a distance of about 100 *versts* from Borisov.[67] Did such intelligence justify diverting from the main axis of Napoleon's army? This mistake by Chichagov is all the more astonishing because when Chaplits later sent him intelligence about enemy preparations for a crossing at Studyanka, Chichagov, instead of going there with the troops that were immediately to hand, lost a whole day concentrating his main force. Count Langéron and Chaplits were no less culpable in that, being closer than the Commander-in-Chief to the location at which the action would be decided, they confined themselves to the literal execution of orders issued to them; rather than immediately attacking the enemy. If Chaplits, having noticed French preparations for a crossing, had not retreated to Stakhov, but deployed his detachment to engage the crossing troops, while Langéron, reacting to the first notification from Chaplits, had immediately come to his aid, then Napoleon would hardly have been able to complete his bold enterprise.

As for the criticism made of Prince Kutuzov that he had lagged behind at a considerable distance with the main body of the army and completely halted the pursuit of Napoleon, it should be noted that although the Field Marshal had halted at Kopys with most of the army at the very moment that the enemy was approaching the Berezina, nevertheless, he had also sent General Miloradovich after the retreating troops, with one cavalry corps and two more of infantry, which consisted of 54 battalions and 20 squadrons, together with the detachments under Platov and Yermolov, in which there were 16 battalions, 17 Cossack regiments and two artillery companies: consequently, 70 battalions, numbering at least 20,000 infantry, had been detached from the main army. The remainder of the force under Prince Kutuzov moved slowly, due to taking rest-days in order to preserve the men's strength and in order to allow for the delivery of supplies, which were lagging several marches behind.[68] It is impossible not to admit that we had enough troops to block the path of Napoleon: there were 30,000 men each in both the Army of the Danube and in the corps under Count Wittgenstein, according to the most conservative calculations; Platov, Yermolov and Seslavin had some 10,000 men, followed by Miloradovich, one

---

67 Prince Kutuzov's orders for Admiral Chichagov, dated 10 [22] November, from Lanniki, Log of Outgoing Documents, No. 485. *Mémoires inédits de l'amiral Tchitchagoff*, 60-61.
68 Prince Kutuzov's Army Orders, dated 17 [29] November, No. 74. Headquarters, Somry. 'This is this reason why, during the rapid marches by the army in order to pursue and exterminate the remnants of the fleeing enemy force, convoys with rations prepared for the army cannot keep up with the troops, the provisions do not always reach the men in good time or are in smaller amounts than that which the situation demands. In respect of this and to make up for deficiencies, I have decided on a general issue of cash for six days worth of provisions to all regiments, artillery companies and other independent commands, at a rate of ten roubles and 50 kopecks for a *chetvert* of flour and 16 roubles for a *chetvert* of cereals, from which each soldier is to receive ten kopecks for daily rations of the indicated provisions; and therefore, having issued my orders to Senator Lanskoy, the chief manager of food supply for the army, I order the gentlemen corps commanders, and independent commanders to send representatives as soon as possible from their corps and commands, in order to collect the cash for this intent of mine, and upon receipt, to distribute it immediately to the soldiers, under strict supervision, such that the money is guaranteed to reach their hands; it is my pleasure to report this.' The original Army Orders for 1812. Archive of the M.T.D. No. 36,749.

stage behind with 15,000 men. Consequently, the French army was surrounded by forces twice as strong, not to mention the fact that the enemy were exhausted in the extreme and that they, in fighting with our troops, were forced to protect their huge convoys and a myriad of enfeebled and unarmed men. But these troops were commanded by Napoleon; rumours inflated their strength to 60,000, and even to 80,000 men; neither Wittgenstein nor Chichagov had an accurate understanding of the unprecedented weakening of the *Grande Armée*, considering all the intelligence they received from Prince Kutuzov to be exaggerated, and therefore both of them, wherever possible, intended to avoid engaging Napoleon. Without any doubt, had Wittgenstein arrived on the Berezina one or two days earlier, he would have put the enemy in a very difficult position; but one should not be surprised at his caution, as by operating completely independently of our other forces, he could have been defeated by Napoleon: he did not wish to diminish the glory he had acquired through constant success; Chichagov was concerned about being subjected to a defeat similar to that which his vanguard had suffered, while Kutuzov did not want to exhaust his army in the end through forced marches and had no intention of engaging in a decisive battle with a brilliant adversary and his army, which, being placed in a desperate situation, would sell their lives dearly. The Field Marshal hoped to achieve the war aims of destroying the enemy forces, while preserving his own, without resorting to that. These considerations saved many thousands of our soldiers, but helped Napoleon to carry out one of his most brilliant feats. On the banks of the Berezina, he had to overcome both the superior numbers of our troops and the difficulties of crossing a large river with a lack of bridge-building resources; but the moral influence of his previous victories was on the side of the great commander, and this was enough for him to achieve what he alone could have achieved – the salvation of himself and the remnants of his army.

Kutuzov was much more thoroughly criticised for not arriving on the Berezina himself at the decisive moment of Napoleon's crossing.[69] The presence of the venerable military commander would have given the operations by our troops that unity, that liaison, without which the best of plans cannot lead to the intended objective. And yet he was aware of the disarray in the former *Grande Armée*. He alone could take responsibility for the consequences of an engagement with Napoleon, and perhaps on the banks of the Berezina, the glory awaited him of defeating the man whom all of Europe had been accustomed to consider invincible for many years.

---

69 Chambray, III, 78.

THE BEREZINA CROSSING 209

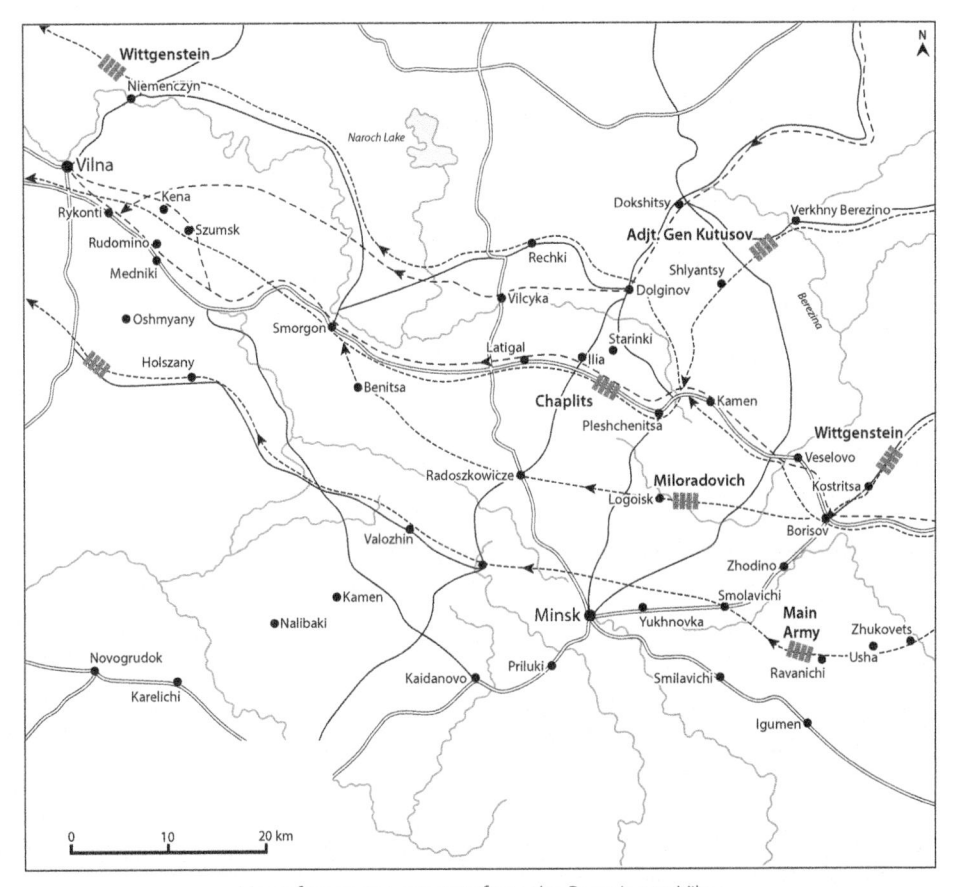

Map of troop movements from the Berezina to Vilna.

43

The liberation of Vilna by Russian forces

The pursuit of the enemy by Russian forces following the Berezina crossing. – Prince Kutuzov's orders. – Napoleon's orders. – The composition of his army. – The advances by Chaplits and Platov. – The action at Molodechno. – The advances by other Russian formations. – *Le 29e Bulletin de la Grande Armée*. – Napoleon's departure from the army. – His final orders. – The further enemy retreat towards Vilna. – Operations around Vilna and the liberation of this city by Russian forces. – Prince Kutuzov's arrival in Vilna. – His orders for the pursuit of the remnants of the enemy army. – The strength of the Russian forces and their composition upon reaching Vilna.

Upon the retreat of Napoleon's forces from the Berezina along the Vilna road, at a Council of War by Russian military commanders it was decided that the Army of the Danube would pursue the enemy relentlessly along a route towards Smorgon and Vilna, while Platov would move to the left and prevent the remnants of the *Grande Armée* from turning towards Minsk, while Count Wittgenstein would move to the right of the Vilna highway towards Niemenczyn. The direct pursuit of the enemy was entrusted by Chichagov to the detachment under Lanskoy and the vanguard under Chaplits;[1] the main body of the Army of the Danube, after the troops were granted a rest-day on 17 (29) November, were to follow the vanguard. General Vlastov, having passed the devastated village of Studyanka on the morning of 17 [29] November and reaching the river bank with the vanguard of I Corps, opened a heavy bombardment on the army retreating on the far bank, but could not go further, and was waiting for a pontoon bridge to be built. Count Wittgenstein, remaining on the left bank of the Berezina, initially due to the impossibility of crossing, and then, in order to give time for the trains of the Army of the Danube to cross the Zembin swamps, instructed two detachments to directly pursue the enemy:

1. Adjutant General Kutuzov's,[2] located in Lepel and directed towards Dokshitsy.

---

1 The compositions of the detachments under Chaplits and Lanskoy are given in Chapter XLII and Appendix XIII.
2 Adjutant General Kutuzov's detachment consisted of five Cossack regiments, including the Lifeguard Cossacks, one Kalmuk regiment and another of Tatars, the Izyum Hussars and part

2. General Orlov-Denisov's, having been sent forward from the main army, was reinforced with troops from various regiments of I Corps,[3] crossed the Berezina upstream of Krichev [Krichino] and moved towards the town of Kamen.

The Podolsk Infantry Regiment, a group of St Petersburg *Opolchenie*, with 4th Bashkir and 5th Bashkir regiments were directed towards Vitebsk as escort to the 13,000 prisoners taken on the Berezina by the troops of I Corps.[4] General Miloradovich, upon arrival in Borisov on 17 (29) November with II Corps and VII Corps, granted his troops a rest day in order to give them a much needed chance to recover, to give the ration wagons loaded with hard-tack chance to catch up and generally stock up with provisions for the detachment entrusted to him on its march to Vilna.[5] Of all our formations that had arrived at the Berezina, the corps under Count Wittgenstein was in the best condition, in which there were 22,000 infantry and 3,000 cavalry, with 133 guns, not including the detachments under Adjutant General Kutuzov, Major General Novak, Colonels Zhemchuzhnikov [Apollon Stepanovich Zhemchuzhnikov] and Baron [M.I.] Pahlen, or the units left to guard the magazines, in total more than 14,000 men with 16 guns.[6]

Meanwhile, Prince Kutuzov, on the final stage of the Main Army's march to the Berezina river, having learned of Napoleon's crossing from Captain Palitsyn (sent to him by Count Ozharovsky), at first doubted the truth of this news and demanded an explanation from Admiral Chichagov of how this could have happened and what measures and route had been taken by him after the enemy crossing?[7] The Field Marshal, remaining ignorant of whether Napoleon had actually managed to cross, asked the admiral to inform him definitively about this, and, in anticipation of his report, did not dare to go beyond the Berezina, as he wrote, 'so as not to leave Count Wittgenstein alone against the entire enemy force.'[8] Thereafter, having received intelligence that confirmed Ozharovsky's report, Kutuzov initially showed annoyance and displeasure; but later he did not even give it a thought, but then just once, when already in Vilna, in response to a toast: 'to the health of the victor!' he said at his dinner, 'Ah, not all was done! But for the admiral, simple Pskov noblemen could now be saying: Europe may breathe freely.'[9]

The Field Marshal, having approved all the measures taken for the immediate pursuit of the enemy force, for his part, issued the following orders:

---

of the Kazan Dragoon Regiment, with two horse artillery pieces, for a total of 3,300 men.
3   Rodionov 2nd's Cossacks, Chernozubov's Cossacks, Lishchilin's Cossacks, the Grodno Hussars, one battalion of 23rd Jägers, mounted on draught horses captured from the enemy on the Berezina, and 1st Horse Artillery Company.
4   *Précis des opérations du I Corps de l'armée d'Occident*. Archive of the M.T.D. No. 29,200.
5   General Miloradovich's report to Prince Kutuzov, dated 17 [29] November, from Borisov.
6   For the composition of these various detachments, see Appendix XIV.
7   Prince Kutuzov's orders for Admiral Chichagov, dated 17 [29] November, No. 539. Archive of the M.T.D. No. 29,172.
8   Prince Kutuzov's orders for Admiral Chichagov, dated 18 [30] November, No. 548. Archive of the M.T.D. No. 29,172.
9   Shcherbinin's notes.

1. Admiral Chichagov was to move quickly in the footsteps of the fleeing enemy.
2. Count Platov was to get ahead of their lead columns and block their retreat.
3. Count Wittgenstein was to march to the right of Chichagov, towards Vileyka and Niemenczyn.
4. The Main Army, having crossed the Berezina at the village of Zhukovets, was to march on Novy-Troky via Smolevichi, Raków and Valozhin; while General Miloradovich was to head towards Logoisk and Radoszkowicze, and on to Holszany with the corps entrusted to him.

According to the Field Marshal, our troops, by moving along these four axes, would find provisions along them and block any link up between Napoleon and the corps under Schwarzenberg and MacDonald.[10] The detachment under Adjutant General Count Ozharovsky was directed towards Novogrudok, to the left of the main army, to protect its left flank from Schwarzenberg.[11] The partisans Davydov and Seslavin were ordered to go directly towards Kovno and to destroy the enemy stores there.[12] Major General Tuchkov, who was on the march with Ertel's former corps to Bobruisk from Rogachev at the time,[13] received orders to move to Minsk by the shortest route in order to join Chichagov's army.[14] Major General Prince Urusov [Alexander Petrovich Urusov], who was nearing Kopys with the men of the division entrusted to him, was ordered to move towards Minsk.[15] The 20th Jäger Regiment, which had remained in Smolensk since enemy forces had departed from there, was ordered to follow the movements of the army.[16] The commandant of the Bobruisk fortress, Major General Ignatiev, was ordered to send a convoy with provisions, following the army to Minsk, under escort by four battalions with four guns, and was then ordered to send six more battalions also to Minsk in order to form a

---

10 Prince Kutuzov's report to Emperor Alexander I, dated 19 November [1 December], No. 568. Archive of the M.T.D. No. 29,172.
11 Orders for Count Ozharovsky, dated 17 [29] November, No. 540, and dated 21 November [3 December], No. 585. Archive of the M.T.D. No. 29,172.
12 Orders dated 19 November [1 December], No. 560 and No. 561. Archive of the M.T.D. No. 29,172.
13 Tuchkov's corps consisted of: 15 battalions, 14 squadrons, two Cossack regiments and two heavy artillery companies. Major General Tuchkov's report to Prince Kutuzov, dated 15 [27] November, No. 19. Archive of the M.T.D. No. 29,172. Log of Outgoing Documents, No. 678. In a subsequent strength return by Tuchkov, it is shown that his detachment had: 25 battalions (active, replacement, recruit and 75th Navy Crew), 24 squadrons (active and replacement), two irregular regiments and four irregular units, two heavy artillery companies a light artillery half-company and two light guns, one Austrian gun, for a total of 10,000 men with 33 guns. Strength return dated 11 [23] December. Archive of the M.T.D. No. 29,172.
14 Orders for Major General Tuchkov, dated 18 [30] November, No. 549. Archive of the M.T.D. No. 29,172.
15 Orders for Major General Prince Urusov, dated 17 [29] November, No. 541. Archive of the M.T.D. No. 29,172.
16 Orders dated 16 [28] November, No. 538. Archive of the M.T.D. No. 29,172.

garrison there.[17] Count Gudovich was ordered to deploy the Malorussia *Opolchenie* in the Chernigov Governorate and Poltava Governorate, as well as in Volhynia and Belorussia.[18] Three foot regiments of the Moscow *Opolchenie* were to be located in Borisov and Orsha.[19] Part of the Kaluga *Opolchenie* and Tula *Opolchenie* were used to form garrisons in Bobruisk and Minsk.[20] The Ryazan *Opolchenie* was left for the time being in the Ryazan Governorate; while the Vladimir *Opolchenie* remained in Moscow.[21] Major General Lebedev [Nikolai Petrovich Lebedev] had previously been ordered to deploy the entire Smolensk *Opolchenie* in the vicinity of Smolensk.[22] At the same time, in order to provide rations for the Army of the Danube on the march from the Berezina to Vilna, Chichagov ordered Colonel Knorring to send provisions from the Minsk magazines, on peasant carts, under escort by troops, and to attempt to collect as many supplies as possible from the surrounding countryside.[23]

Napoleon, still positive of halting in Vilna in order to give his troops time to at least rest and recover after the forced pace of the retreat, ordered Wrede, who was stationed at Dokshitsy with the remnants of the Bavarian corps, to go to Vileyka, secure the river crossing there, collect as many provisions for the army as possible and open communications with the Smorgon commandant (*adjudant-commandant*) d'Albignac [Philippe François Maurice d'Albignac], who was also ordered to supply the magazines in Smorgon and Oshmyany with provisions, to send some of the supplies to meet the retreating troops and to send all the remaining oxen to Vilna so that they could not be taken by Cossacks.[24] Napoleon, wanting to hide his failure from that part of Europe oppressed by him for as long as possible, gave orders to send a message to Schwarzenberg that the arrival of Chichagov on the Berezina had changed the direction of the Emperor, and that the army, having crossed this river through brute force and defeated the Russians several times, was moving towards Vilna. At the same time, it was suggested that Schwarzenberg move closer to the upper Neman and to the right flank of the army, at Schwarzenberg's discretion, should he consider this advantageous.[25] MacDonald, who was still stationed in

---

17 Orders for Major General Ignatiev, dated 17 [29] November, No. 543, and dated 21 November [3 December], No. 577. Archive of the M.T.D. No. 29,172. Of these ten battalions, eight came under the command of Major General Radt, and two went to the garrison of the city of Minsk.
18 Orders dated 19 November [1 December] No. 558. Archive of the M.T.D. No. 29,172.
19 Prince Kutuzov's report to the Tsar, dated 21 November [3 December], No. 989.
20 Orders for Lieutenant General Shepelev, dated 21 November [3 December], No. 578, and for Major General Bogdanov, dated 19 November [1 December], No. 564. Archive of the M.T.D. No. 29,172.
21 Prince Kutuzov's report to the Tsar, dated 21 November [3 December], No. 989.
22 Orders for Major General Lebedev, dated 12 [24] November, No. 498. Archive of the M.T.D. No. 29,172.
23 Orders for Colonel Knorring, dated 16 [28] November, No. 1,168. Archive of the M.T.D. No. 44,585. Log of Outgoing Documents of the Commander-in-Chief of the Army of the Danube.
24 Orders for General Wrede, dated 28 November new style, and to the Smorgon Commandant d'Albignac, dated 3 December new style.
25 Letter from the duc de Bassano (Maret) in Vilna to Prince Schwarzenberg, dated 2 December 1812 new style: '*L'arivée de l'amiral de Tchitchagoff sur la Bérésina a changé les dispositions de Sa Majesté; toute l'armée, après avoir forcé le passage de cette rivière et battu plusieurs fois l'ennemi, marche dans la direction de Wilna. L'empereur sera probablement ici de Sa personne*

Courland, had been sent no information about the movements of the remnants of the *Grande Armée* towards Vilna.[26]

But the general blindness would not last long: the French army no longer existed. A few days after crossing the Berezina, the temperature dropped to more than 27 degrees of frost and completed the catastrophe for our enemy. The distinction between the troops arriving from Moscow and the corps under Oudinot and Victor vanished; almost no one remained in the ranks, no one issued orders, and there was no one to give them to; every unit in the force, every arm of service, were mixed into a disorderly mob; at every step, the men, dragging along on foot, were in danger of falling under the wheels of artillery or wagons. The riders and drivers, like everyone else, caring only to get out as quickly as possible, paid not the slightest attention to the wounded and feeble, crushing anyone who happened to get in their way and moving on. Many men and wagons, crowded on the narrow bridges on the Gajna, were shunted into the ditches and swamps and were suffocated in the mud, which had not yet completely frozen. Men and horses stopped and fell incessantly, cannon and wagons got stuck in the mud; weapons themselves became a burden to the soldiers: many of them discarded their muskets and cartridges. Compared to most, happy was the man who had a chunk of bread left in his bag, or a few potatoes, which he would stealthily consume, away from his comrades. Both silver and gold lost their value: everyone was ready to sacrifice anything in order to somehow alleviate this unbearable torture.

The men had completely lost their former military bearing: it was impossible to identify them either as soldiers or officers. Thousands of beggars, wrapped in dirty rags, barely dragging their feet wrapped in woollen blankets or furs, tied with string, bast fibre, or whatever was to hand. Each of these unfortunates had frost-bitten ears, hands, or feet. The only treatment available was rubbing the chilled parts with alcohol or snow. Those who inadvisedly warmed themselves by bivouac fires perished in absolute agony. Others, stricken with insensibility, fell into an eternal sleep. The predominant diseases were rheumatism, chest infections and bloody diarrhoea. There were not enough doctors for the thousands of sick men, and there were no medical facilities. It was every man for himself. Many, already doomed to death, still retained enough awareness to be able to feel their comrades, not even waiting for the end of their fatal languor, stripping them naked and dividing the miserable rags that had covered the victim among themselves. Men known for their courage, crushed by this unprecedented disaster, became cowardly; almost no one thought of resisting the enemy; everyone sought refuge in flight yet no one was able to escape from the utter exhaustion. As soon as Cossacks appeared nearby, or even peasants armed with clubs, an unreasoning fear gripped the thousands of hungry, half-frozen warriors. It was as if every true concept of humanity had disappeared in this multitude of men doomed to torment and death. Almost every one of them was

---

avant six ou huit jours. Je n'ai pas reçu d'ordres à transmettre à votre excellence; mais j'ai dû sentir l'importance de vous informer promptement de cette nouvelle direction des opérations militaires. A defaut d'instructions, votre excellence jugera ce qu'elle doit faire; elle considérera s'il ne conviendrait pas qu'elle se rapprochât du Haut-Niémen et du flanc droit de l'armée...'

26 Fain, *Manuscrit de 1812*, II, 351-352.

prepared to rob or kill anyone, no matter who, for a chunk of bread; many men set houses on fire just to keep warm.[27]

In this situation, the main effort on our part was to pursue the enemy without giving them rest; our troops were obliged to make forced marches, being subjected to both hunger and cold almost in equal measure with the enemy. During the twelve-day march from the Berezina to Vilna, the Russian armies, and especially the leading detachments, suffered a great shortage of rations and lost many men to straggling and sickness, but were incomparably better off than the French, due to the fact that they were better dressed and shod, and due to a greater dispersal of troops away from the main roads, which allowed some of the men to be accommodated in quarters, while the enemy were forced to remain on the march and constantly in bivouacs. And therefore, despite the heavy losses among the Russian troops, they moved briskly and caught up with the enemy at every stage.

On 18 (30) November, on the very day that Napoleon reached the town of Pleshchenitsa with his *État-major général* and the *Garde*, General Chaplits, moving through the frozen swamps of the Gajna river, past bridges burned by the French, caught up with the enemy rearguard beyond Zembin and captured some to 400 prisoners and seven guns.[28] On the following day, 19 November (1 December), Chaplits' vanguard, together with Platov's Cossack detachment, having driven Victor out of Pleshchenitsa with the remnants of *9e Corps*, pursued them to Khotavich, captured six guns and took more than 1,400 prisoners. On 20 and 21 November (2 and 3 December), the enemy rearguard, pursued by Platov and Chaplits beyond Latigal, via Starinki and Ilia, lost 1,900 taken prisoner, ten guns and two standards, one of which was inscribed: Austerlitz, Eylau, Wagram. Among the prisoners was General Preysing [Maximilian Graf von Preysing-Moos].[29] The main body of the Army of the Danube had a rest-day in Pleshchenitsa on 21 November (3 December). On that same day, Napoleon's *État-major général* arrived in Molodechno, on the Vilna highway.[30] On our side, the vanguard of I Corps, under Vlastov's command, numbering 3,500 men, with 14 guns arrived in Kamen, while behind them came the main body under Count Wittgenstein.[31] The leading elements of Adjutant General Kutuzov's force, under the command of Lieutenant Colonel Tettenborn [Friedrich Karl von Tettenborn], having caught up with the rearguard of Wrede's Bavarian corps at Dolginov, on 20 November (2 December), as they were retreating from Dokshitsy to

---

27 Bourgeois. *Tableau de la campagne de Moscou en 1812*, 156-169. Lemazurier. *Medizinische Geschichte des russischen Felzugs von 1812.*
28 '... et quoique je trouvasse le pont de Zembin détruit, la difficulté du passage ne m'arreta point; je poussai ma marche jusqu'au de là de Zembin...' *Remarques sur la campagne de 1812, par le général Czaplitz.* Archive of the M.T.D. No. 44,712. War Diary, signed off by Prince Kutuzov. War Diary of the Army of the Danube, compiled by Malinovsky.
29 *Remarques sur la campagne de 1812, par le général Czaplitz.* War Diary, signed off by Prince Kutuzov. War Diary of the Army of the Danube. Count Platov's report to Prince Kutuzov, dated 22 November [4 December], No. 215.
30 Denniée. *Itinéraire de l'empereur Napoléon,* 191.
31 Vlastov's vanguard consisted of: 24th Jägers, a battalion of 23rd Jägers, the Lithuania Infantry Regiment, the Combined Dragoon Regiment and Finland Dragoons, Platov 4th's Cossacks, eight guns from 28th Battery Artillery Company and six guns from 11th Light Artillery Company. *Précis des opérations du I Corps.* Archive of the M.T.D. No. 29,200.

Vileyka, defeated the enemy and took some 700 prisoners. On the same day, Adjutant General Kutuzov moved from Verkhny-Berezino to the town of Shlyantsy.[32]

On 22 November (4 December), Napoleon arrived in Benitsa, and arrived in Smorgon the following day [5 December]. His rearguard, under Victor's command, having been driven back to Molodechno by Platov and Chaplits with the loss of 500 men taken prisoner alone, and eight guns, dismantled the bridges on the Usha and attempted to hold back the offensive by our formations which, in the meantime, had arrived in time to assist Yermolov's force and the main body under Chichagov. During the night of 22 to 23 November (4 to 5 December), a causeway was found in the forest by our troops, three *versts* downstream of Molodechno, the bridges on it were repaired, and at four o'clock in the morning Chichagov's cavalry, having crossed the river, cut off part of the enemy rearguard and seized Molodechno, where by dawn the bridges had also been restored and the entire Army of the Danube began to cross. The enemy did not defend themselves at all, throwing down their muskets and fleeing, or surrendering in droves. The number of prisoners taken by our troops reached 2,500; 24 guns were also taken.[33] On the final stage into Molodechno, Napoleon had issued orders to smash the Eagles and poles and bury them; at the same time, the officers were also ordered to arm themselves with muskets; but this order could not be executed, because everyone, officers and soldiers alike, having lost what remained of their strength, had become incapable of using weapons of whatever kind.[34]

At the same time as the arrival of the Army of the Danube Army in Molodechno, Wittgenstein's main body moved towards Dolginov. Meanwhile, Miloradovich had reached the town of Logoisk; while Prince Kutuzov, having crossed the Berezina near the village of Zhukovets with the Main Army, had arrived in Ravanichi. Count Orlov-Denisov, having received orders to join the Main Army, left the troops attached to his formation from I Corps under the command of General Borozdin 2nd.[35]

As our troops were rapidly moving towards Vilna, Napoleon, having lost hope of restoring order in the decayed legions of the *Grande Armée*, had decided to depart for Paris. But just two days before his departure, he issued *le 29e Bulletin de la Grande Armée* on 21 November (3 December), from Molodechno, in which he outlined quite openly the plight of his troops. Until this point, he had never hesitated to distort the truth in the news of military operations, considering such deviation from the truth to be one of the best means of influencing public opinion. He was not alone in using this tool, but hardly anyone else exaggerated their successes or hid their failures in the way that Napoleon did in his bulletins: '*il ment comme un bulletin*' (he lies like a bulletin) had become proverbial. The victories of the French

---

32 Adjutant General Kutuzov's report to Count Wittgenstein, dated 21 November [3 December], No. 182, from the village of Shlyantsy.
33 War Diary of the Army of the Danube, compiled by Malinovsky.
34 Fezensac, *Journal de la campagne de Russie en 1812*, 139.
35 One battalion of 23rd Jägers mounted on peasant horses, the Grodno Hussars, three Cossack regiments and 1st Horse Artillery Company. *Précis des opérations du I Corps*. In Count Wittgenstein's report to the Tsar, it states that the following were also with this force: the Combined Hussar Regiment. Archive of the M.T.D. No. 44,585. Reports on military operations by I Corps.

were glorified and the brilliant situation of the *Grande Armée* was painted in the brightest colours in every news item on the course of the war sent from Russia. Such as the penultimate *28e Bulletin* issued on 30 October (11 November) from Smolensk for the general consumption of Europe. True, it did mentioned the onset of winter and the loss of 3,000 draught horses; thereafter the battles at Vyazma and (second) Polotsk were presented as brilliant victories, such that the retreat by Saint-Cyr looked like an advance towards Victor, with the aim of re-crossing the Dvina, and so on. But no matter how much Napoleon masked the actual state of affairs, it could no longer remain a secret once the miserable remnants of the *Grande Armée* returned to Lithuania.

In *29e Bulletin*, after repeating everything that had been said in *28e Bulletin* about the onset of freezing weather and announcing the loss of many cavalry and artillery horses, Napoleon wrote: '… Our right departed from the axis of operations towards Minsk, and took the axis towards Warsaw as the pivot of its operations. The Emperor, learning on 9 November at Smolensk of this change of axis of operations, assessed what the enemy would do. Hard as it seemed to him to set off in such a cruel season, the new state of affairs necessitated it. He had hoped to reach Minsk, or at least the Berezina, before the enemy; he left Smolensk on 13 November; on 16 November he slept at Krasny. The frosts which had begun on 7 November suddenly increased and from 14 to 15 and 16 November the thermometer recorded 16 and 18 degrees below freezing.[36] The roads were covered with ice; cavalry, artillery, and draught horses perished every night, not by hundreds but by thousands, especially horses from France and Germany. More than 30,000 horses perished in a few days; our cavalry was all dismounted; our artillery and our vehicles were without teams. It was necessary to abandon and destroy a good part of our artillery, ammunition and war materiel. This army, so fine on 6 November was very different on 14 November, without cavalry, without artillery, without vehicles. Without cavalry, we could not reconnoitre beyond a quarter of a league (*à un quart de lieue*); moreover, without artillery, we could not risk a battle or make a stand; we had to march in order not to be forced into a battle, which the lack of ammunition prevented us from offering; it was necessary to hold a large frontage in order not to be outflanked, and this without cavalry, which should have reconnoitred and secured communications between the columns. This disadvantage, added to the sudden excessive cold, made our situation untenable. Men whom nature has not tempered strongly enough to be above all the vicissitudes of fate and fortune seemed shaken, lost their gaiety, their good humour, and dwelt only on misfortune and catastrophe; the enemy, seeing the traces of this frightful calamity which had struck the French army along the roads, sought to exploit it. They surrounded each of the columns with their Cossacks, who carried off those wagons and carriages which deviated, like Arabs in the desert. This contemptible cavalry, which makes only noise and is incapable of riding down a company of *voltigeurs*, had made itself formidable through favourable circumstances.' After that, having described the actions at Krasny and the crossing of the Berezina in a manner

---

36 [Liprandi comments: 'Severe frosts had begun immediately after the crossing of the Berezina, and by Molodechno temperatures had dropped to minus 20 degrees Réaumur and decreased daily'].

at complete odds with the truth, Napoleon revealed that his troops needed to restore discipline, to recover, to provide remounts for the cavalry and artillery, and that rest was the main need for the army.

This *bulletin* was drafted by dictation from Napoleon in Molodechno, as already mentioned above, where Napoleon spent the night in the palace of Prince Ogiński [Michał Kleofas Ogiński]. On the following day, 22 November (4 December), he moved his *État-major général* to Benitsa, ordering Loison's division (Augereau's *11e Corps*) to march from Vilna to Oshmyany to meet the army; detachments had also been positioned in Smorgon and Medniki.[37] Having thus secured his route to Vilna, Napoleon moved to Smorgon on 23 November (5 December). Here, having summoned Murat, the Viceroy, Berthier and all the marshals who were with the army,[38] he announced to them his intention to leave for Paris and entrusted the command of the forces to Murat, as his lieutenant (*lieutenant-général*); he told his companions '... I am leaving you in order to fetch 300,000 soldiers. It is necessary to put ourselves in such a position that we can conduct a second campaign, because for the first time a war has not ended in a single campaign.' After that, in a lengthy monologue, reviewing the course of the entire war, Napoleon concluded that the reasons for his failure were: the burning of Moscow, the extreme cold, squalid intrigues, mistakes and, possibly, treason (this was an allusion to Schwarzenberg's deviation from the axis of operations of the *Grande Armée*).[39]

On the morning of 23 November (5 December), Napoleon issued instructions to Murat that included the following orders:

> Concentrate the army in Vilna, hold out in this city and take up winter quarters: the Austrians on the Neman are covering Brest, Grodno and Warsaw, while the remaining forces are near Vilna and Kovno. In the event of an offensive by the Russians or if it proves impossible to remain forward of the Neman, then protect Warsaw with the right wing, and Grodno if possible, while the rest of the troops stand along the left bank of the Neman, holding Kovno in the role of a fortified bridgehead. Establish large ration stores in Königsberg, Danzig, Warsaw and Thorn [Toruń]; evacuate everything from Vilna and Kovno in order to facilitate the movement of troops; send the most valuable items to Danzig.

Berthier stated in these orders that the King of Naples (Murat) was permitted to make any amendments to these instructions as dictated by the situation. According to Napoleon, it was necessary to reform: the Lithuanian militia in Kovno; *5e Corps* in Warsaw; *6e Corps* in Grodno; *8e Corps* in Olita [Alytus], to set up small depots in Merecz [Merkinė] and Olita and to send the dismounted cavalrymen and transport units that have no horses to Warsaw and Königsberg for remounts. The diplomatic corps were ordered to move from Vilna to Warsaw immediately; all wounded generals and officers were to go to Königsberg and Warsaw to make room for the

---
37 Sołtyk, *Napoléon en 1812*, 456. Chambray, III, 106.
38 Ney, Davout, Lefebvre, Mortier and Bessières. Chambray, III, 106.
39 Fain, II, 354-357.

forces assembling in Vilna. The military treasury was also ordered to be sent to Warsaw and Königsberg.[40]

On that same day, 23 November (5 December), at 11 o'clock at night, Napoleon set off from Smorgon, along the Vilna road, in a carriage with Caulaincourt; Captain Vonsovich [Wąsowicz?] of the *1er régiment de chevau-légers lanciers polonais de la Garde impériale* and the Mameluke Roustam [Roustam Raza] sat on trestles; *Grand maréchal du palais* Duroc [Géraud Christophe de Michel du Roc] and aide-de-camp General Mouton were in a sleigh, behind the carriage; the escort consisted of small detachments of cavalry replacing one another on the way to Vilna. There were 20 degrees of frost that night. Napoleon, wanting to pass through Germany anonymously, intended to travel under the title of Duc de Vicence (Caulaincourt's). Berthier was instructed to issue Army Orders for the appointment of Murat as commander of the forces and to spread rumours about the movement of the Emperor of the French to Warsaw, with the Austrian and Saxon corps. Orders were given that his departure for Paris be announced no sooner than five or six days hence.[41]

But the departure of Napoleon, who could not be replaced by any of his associates, did not remain a secret for long, and as soon as it was learned about, the last link that held the wreckage of the *Grande Armée* together collapsed. The men, embittered by unprecedented disasters, cursing Napoleon shouted: 'he is fleeing as he fled from Egypt; he is abandoning us, condemning us to death.' But these calls were pointless. Napoleon, combining commander and ruler of a powerful Empire in his person, could not turn his attention exclusively on the troops, whose fate was already irrevocably sealed. He had to prepare the resources needed to continue the war, and even if he abandoned his power-hungry plans and decided to make peace with Emperor Alexander, then even in that event he would still have to return to France. Malet's attempted coup showed what danger his regime was exposed to following the unsuccessful campaign in Russia; while his unwilling allies eagerly wished to be free from the yoke imposed by the conqueror.

On the very day of Napoleon's departure from the army, 23 November (5 December), in the afternoon, Loison arrived in Oshmyany with the division entrusted to him and placed his frozen soldiers in quarters in the city. Colonel Seslavin, moving along a country lane to the left of the Vilna highway, also arrived at Oshmyany in the evening and broke into the city, but was forced out and stationed himself at Taborishki [Tabariškės]. Napoleon passed through Oshmyany the following night, where he halted just to change horses. If Seslavin, who was bivouacking five or six *versts* from the highway, had known about Napoleon's journey, he could have captured him, especially since the loyalty of the troops stationed in Oshmyany was very doubtful. Loison's division consisted almost entirely of troops from the Confederation of the Rhine and Italians. As soon as Napoleon arrived in the city, a guard of honour was posted at the house he occupied, made up of men from the grenadier companies of German regiments. It should be noted that Loison's division, which had set out from Vilna with 10,000 men, having completed

---

40 *Chef d'état-major* Berthier's orders with instructions for Murat, dated 5 December new style.
41 Sołtyk, 457-458. Chambray, III, 106-107. Orders for *Chef d'état-major* Berthier, dated 5 December new style.

the march to Oshmyany in the bitter cold, counted no more than 3,000 in its ranks; while the Neapolitan *Veliti della Guardia Reale* had almost all perished.[42] Both officers and soldiers, embittered by their suffering, did not hide the disillusionment that prevailed in the countries oppressed by the French at the time. It is claimed that one Lapie, a major from a regiment (*113e régiment d'infanterie de ligne*), which consisted of Tuscans,[43] turning to several officers among his fellow soldiers, said: '*Maintenant, messieurs, ce serait le moment.*' (Gentlemen, now would be a good time). They all seemed to understand what was being spoken about. Surrounding the major on all sides, the officers conferred with him in low voices about methods for executing their plot. It was decided that the senior of the captains, breaking into the house with his company, would kill anyone who might offer any resistance. Thereafter, the German regiments intended to defect to the Russians; there was no doubt about the willingness of the *113e régiment de ligne*. Of all the captains who were present, the commander of the Saxe-Weimar Grenadier Company [*Rheinbund Regiment Nr. 4*] was the senior commander. Only once he had the opportunity to begin the execution of the conspiracy did he realize that the job entrusted to him was consistent neither with the principles of a nobleman, nor with the duties of an honest soldier. And therefore, having refused direct participation in the attempt on the life of Napoleon, he believed that role belonged to the man who proposed it. Major Lapie, for his part, did not want to be the main protagonist, indicating that there were no men from companies under his command present, and that therefore he did not have men on whom he could completely rely. While the major and the captain were excusing themselves from the execution of their planned undertaking, Caulaincourt, coming out onto the porch, shouted: '*Eh bien! Pourquoi ne partons-nous pas?*' (Well! Shall we not be on our way?). Following which, the carriage and sleigh were brought up, and Napoleon and his entourage rode on, unaware of the danger that had threatened them.[44]

In Medniki, Napoleon was met by the French *ministre des Relations extérieures* [minister of foreign affairs], Maret, who had received orders to move there from Vilna. Napoleon installed Maret in the carriage with him, while Caulaincourt continued the journey in Maret's carriage. From Medniki, the escort consisted of fifty Neapolitan cavalrymen, under the command of the duca di Roccaromana [Lucio Caracciolo], who, on this stage, had several fingers on his left hand frostbitten. Napoleon arrived in Vilna on 24 November (6 December) at about ten o'clock in the morning. A few hours previously, Bignon [Louis Pierre Édouard Bignon] had announced the impending arrival of the Emperor in Vilna to all officials, not knowing about his intention to slip into the Duchy of Warsaw unnoticed; but no sooner had they started to make preparations for his reception, than word came that he had passed through the city and set off along the Kovno road. Indeed, Napoleon,

---

42 *Rückzug der Franzosen bis zum Niemen. Vermehrte Ausgabe*, 39.
43 *Histoire de l'armée et de tous les régiments*, IV, *Tableau de l'organisation de l'armée française*, p. XXXVII.
44 Perhaps, in this case, the eyewitness account does not quite match the truth, but it gives a fairly accurate idea of the disillusionment with Napoleon that prevailed among his foreign troops. Bernhardi, *Denkwürdigkeiten des Grafen v. Toll*, II, 343-344.

having bypassed the city through the suburbs, paused at the Kovno gate in an empty house, around which all the buildings had been destroyed in a fire. In conversation with Maret, he explained the reasons that prompted him to return to France. He commented:

> As for the army, it no longer exists: one cannot call disorderly crowds wandering hopefully in search of food and shelter an army. It might still be possible to form an army out of them, if we managed to find food, footwear and clothing at any of the nearby locations for hungry men who cannot continue the campaign on frozen ground, in frosts of more than 20 degrees. But my commissariat anticipated none of this; my orders were not carried out.

In response to this criticism, Maret presented Napoleon with a return on the state of the Vilna magazines, in which there were forty days of provisions for 100,000 men, not including bread expected from Zhmud [Samogitia]. In the city and its environs there were cattle on the hoof for thirty-six days, also for 100,000 men, and a large supply of vodka and beer; while there were 30,000 pairs of shoes, a large amount of munitions and 27,000 muskets in Vilna warehouses.[45] Napoleon, who was apparently unaware of this, was extremely pleased with the report from his minister. He remarked; 'You have given me my life back. Stay here until the arrival of Murat and order him, in my name, to remain in Vilna for at least a week, in order to reorganise the army by whatever means, and continue the retreat in a less miserable state.' After this conversation, at around noon, Napoleon carried on towards Kovno and returned to the Russian border at dawn on 26 November (8 December), on the feast of St George the Victorious.

Two days later, Napoleon arrived in Warsaw, where he stayed at the Hôtel d'Angleterre and invited his envoy Pradt [Dominique Frédéric Dufour de Pradt], President of the Council of Ministers Potocki [Stanisław Kostka Potocki], Minister of Finance Matuszewicz [Tadeusz Wiktoryn Matuszewicz] and several other dignitaries of the Polish government to his residence. He said to them; 'You are curious at seeing me here; I was unable to fight the elements. I have lost all my cavalry, almost all my artillery and my entire train; in two nights, 3,000 horses dropped dead... I was convinced that the French could still fight in seven degrees of frost; The Germans cannot endure more than five. I shall be judged by posterity. I made a mistake staying two weeks too long in Moscow. I was led astray by assurances that the *boyars* would take my side and that the peasants would turn to me in order to escape from serfdom. All this was a lie: I found the villagers, and especially the Courlanders (*sic*), very loyal to the Tsar, while the nobility were full of enthusiasm for the Government. These are wild superstitious people, with whom nothing can be done. *Les cosaques ont le diable au corps...* I have entrusted command to the King of Naples, while I myself am going to Paris to prepare for another campaign... I have heard nothing of Prince Schwarzenberg; I had hoped to find him here, believing that

---

45 Chambray, III, 107-109 & 218-219.

he was guarding the Duchy of Warsaw. But you yourselves must contribute to the restoration of your Fatherland' he continued, turning to the Poles.

> It is essential to make a final effort, to recruit troops once more, and in particular as much light cavalry as possible... If we cannot conclude a peace, then I shall return to you in the spring with a new army. I shall have sufficient men to protect you. Moreover, I hope that Prussia and Austria will embrace my cause more positively (*plus positivement*).

Thereafter, having issued orders for the raising of 10,000 Cossacks in the Duchy of Warsaw and having rested for several hours, Napoleon continued his journey towards Dresden and Mainz, and on to Paris, where he appeared on the night of 7 (19) December, two days after the publication of the *29e bulletin* there.[46]

Following the failed campaign in Russia, while Napoleon returned to his capital, the men of the once *Grande Armée* were retreating to the Russian border.

After the action at Molodechno, on 22 November (4 December), Marshal Victor reported to the *chef d'état-major* that the combat endured by him was the final effort of which his rearguard was capable. He wrote:

> My troops are in such a pitiful condition that I am forced to avoid any kind of engagement with the Russians... Our vedettes are within sight of the Russians; I shall probably be pursued as keenly today as yesterday; and I think it proper for His Majesty to distance himself a little from us...[47]

On 24 November (6 December), the remnants of the enemy army moved from Smorgon towards Oshmyany, under the protection of Victor's rearguard, retreating via Benitsa towards Smorgon, which, on being caught by Chaplits, was pursued to Rudzich, with the loss of 1,200 prisoners and seven guns.[48] Meanwhile, the main body under Chichagov, close behind Chaplits' vanguard, reached Benitsa, while the corps under Count Wittgenstein reached the town of Rechki. On the following day, 25 November (7 December), Murat's headquarters, having passed through Oshmyany, arrived in Medniki. The enemy had hoped to draw rations in Oshmyany, which had not been distributed to them since their departure from Orsha, but the Oshmyany magazines had been destroyed on the night of 23 to 24 (5 to 6 December), immediately after Napoleon's departure from Oshmyany, by Kaisarov's partisan detachment, which had captured an Eagle and some 500 prisoners the day before. General Chaplits, pursuing Victor's rearguard, completely dispersed it, took 25 guns

---

46 Humboldt's letter to the King of Prussia, form Vienna, dated 19 December new style. Chambray, III, 109-110.
47 'Le combat que l'arrière-garde a soutenu le 4 est le dernier effort qu'elle pourrait faire contre les ennemis; les troupes qui la composent sont aujourd'hui tellement réduites et le peu qui en reste est si misérable, que je suis obligé de les soustraire aux poursuites de l'ennemi et d'éviter toute espèce d'engagement... Les vedettes des ennemis et les nôtres se voient; je serai vraisemblablement suivi aussi vivement aujourd'hui qu'hier, et je crois qu'il convient que Sa Majesté s'éloigne un peu de nous...' Report dated 5 December new style.
48 War Diary of the Army of the Danube, compiled by Malinovsky.

and 3,000 prisoners and seized Smorgon. The enemy, as they were leaving the town, set it ablaze it in several places, but our troops extinguished the fires. The Army of the Danube also arrived in Smorgon; Count Wittgenstein's corps spent the day in Rechki.[49]

At the same time as our forces were approaching Vilna, the Field Marshal, wanting to directly control their operations, on 24 November (6 December) had moved his headquarters, to Radoszkowicze, where the vanguard of Miloradovich's detachment was located at the time; during the absence of Prince Kutuzov, the command of the main army, moving in its assigned direction, towards Valozhin, was entrusted to General Tormasov.[50]

Upon arrival in Radoszkowicze, Prince Kutuzov reported to the Tsar on 25 November (7 December) on his proposal to halt the main bodies of the armies entrusted to him in the vicinity of Vilna in order to enable them to gather in stragglers and convalescents and to assimilate Urusov's division. It was intended to entrust the further pursuit of the enemy to the leading detachments of the formations under Count Wittgenstein and Chichagov, who, in the opinion of the Field Marshal, were only intended to follow Schwarzenberg as far as the Austrian border. Kutuzov asked for authority from the Tsar with regard to operations on Prussian territory.[51]

On 26 November (8 December), while pursuing the enemy to Oshmyany, who were already retreating without a rearguard, Chaplits captured 61 guns and 2,000 (according to other sources, around 4,000) prisoners, including Marshal Davout's aide de camp, de Castries.[52] On this same day, Murat arrived in Vilna.

On 27 November (9 December), a new rearguard, formed from Loison's division, under Victor's command, while being pursued by Chaplits towards Medniki, lost 16 guns and 1,300 men taken prisoner alone. After which, retreating to Rykonti [Rukainiai], Victor linked up with the Bavarian corps under General Wrede there, in which there were still 2,000 men and several guns, and received orders from Murat to hold out as long as possible in the positions he now held. But upon being attacked by Seslavin's detachment (accompanied by several guns mounted on sleds), Victor, with the loss of six cannon, retreated into Vilna. At two o'clock in the afternoon, cannon fire could already be heard in the city. The rearguard, recently formed from the remnants of Loison's division (commanded by General Gratien [Pierre Guillaume Gratien] due to Loison's illness), and Wrede's corps, under Ney's overall command, were driven back by Seslavin, who broke into the suburbs, but having no

---

49 War Diary of all Russian armies, signed off by Prince Kutuzov. Count Platov's report dated 23 November [5 December], No. 217. Colonel Kaisarov's report to General Konovnitsyn, dated 27 November [9 December], with a postscript by Count Platov (Archive of the M.T.D. No. 29,172. Log of Incoming Documents). War Diary of the Army of the Danube, compiled by Malinovsky. *Précis des opérations du I Corps*.
50 Prince Kutuzov's orders for General Tormasov, dated 21 November [3 December], No. 584. Archive of the M.T.D. No. 29,172.
51 Prince Kutuzov's report to the Tsar, dated 25 November [7 December], No. 599. Archive of the M.T.D. No. 29,172.
52 Admiral Chichagov's report to Prince Kutuzov, dated 26 November [8 December], No. 1,978, from Oshmyany.

infantry, was forced out by the enemy and, having retreated a short distance, made camp, waiting for the vanguard of the Army of the Danube. In this action, Seslavin suffered a serious gunshot wound to the arm. Afterwards, Ney's force settled down on the high ground dominating the city from the direction of the Minsk gate.[53] On that same day, Major General Laskin [Alexei Andreevich Laskin] pursued the enemy who had fled from Oshmyany along the so-called Black Road, to Szumsk [Šumskas] and Kena with the Volhynia Ulans and Melnikov 5th's Cossack brigade. Major General Borozdin reached Chervonny Dvor [Raudondvaris?], Adjutant General Kutuzov, who had taken more than 1,000 prisoners from the Bavarian corps on the march from Dolginov, arrived at Niemenczyn, while Count Platov reached the town of Rudomino.[54]

The appearance in Vilna of Napoleon's pitiful force shocked the population, who just the day before had no reason to doubt the continuing existence of the *Grande Armée*. Even the abandonment of Moscow by the enemy, thanks to rumours spread by French agents, had long been considered a manoeuvre to withdraw to Smolensk with the objective of moving closer to St Petersburg in order to open the next campaign by conquering our northern capital. Despite Napoleon's retreat to Vilna, there remained, as before, many depots, huge magazines and a treasury amounting to about 11,000,000 francs,[55] furthermore, no preparations of any kind were made for the removal of the depots right up until the arrival of the remnants of the army. Napoleon's feigned self-confidence, who did not want to reveal his failure, had blinded his associates to the truth. On 25 November (7 December), as the French army, approaching Vilna, and had already descended into a disorderly rabble that had lost both military bearing and any concept of discipline, Berthier wrote to the governor of Lithuania, General Hogendorp [Diderik van Hogendorp], about preparing quarters for the *Garde impériale* and *cavalerie de la Garde*, about the movement of the corps under the Viceroy and Davout to Vilna, and so on.[56] After all of that, it is easy to imagine how surprised everyone was by the arrival of these ragged ogres, barely recognisable as humans. Their passage through the city, which lasted several days, might be compared to a macabre masquerade, had these victims not presented such a striking image of every kind of misfortune. Large numbers of them fell down and died from exhaustion and cold within a few minutes as they were passing through the streets; others broke into houses and fell into eternal sleep. Some of the Vilna population, who had been subjected to oppression during the French occupation, greeted them with ridicule; others, rightly fearing robbery, hid in their houses and locked up their businesses. Under such circumstances, many of the enemy were in a hurry to leave the city as soon as possible, so as not to fall into the hands of the Cossacks, and did not manage to stock up on rations; others, in contrast, refused to go any further. Despite the abundance of provisions in the

---

53 Colonel Seslavin's report dated 27 November [9 December].
54 War Diary, signed off by Prince Kutuzov. War Diary of the Army of the Danube, compiled by Malinovsky. *Précis des opérations du I Corps*. Chambray, III, 125-126.
55 More than 2,500,000 roubles.
56 *Chef d'état-major* Berthier's instructions for General Hogendorp, dated 7 December new style, from Medniki.

magazines, not everyone was lucky enough to get some, because of inefficiencies in the distribution, inevitable in such general turmoil. Meanwhile, the Russians were already closing in from several directions. It was essential to hold them back, in order to gain time to evacuate at least some of the stores stockpiled in the city; while only the remnants of the *Garde* and divisions under Loison and Wrede, numbering 4,000 men, were battle-worthy. Just 300 fighting men remained in the other five corps; all the rest, no longer thinking about resisting our forces, cared only about keeping warm and satisfying the hunger that gnawed at them.[57]

Murat was himself a cause of alarm and disorder by leaving the city as soon as Seslavin's force appeared, taking his entire headquarters with him to a coffee house at Pogulianka on 27 November (9 December). The remnants of the *Garde* settled down in bivouacs, in the vicinity of the Kovno gate. In this extraordinary situation, Murat not only did not care about the execution of the duties of a Commander-in-Chief, but lost heart. On the evening of the same day, Ney was ordered to cover the retreat of men and convoys leaving Vilna with a rearguard made up of Wrede's and Loison's divisions, attaching any individual capable of bearing arms. He was also instructed to send the artillery and treasury out of the city, to blow up all the ammunition caissons that could not be evacuated, and smash the muskets. At the same time, he was informed of the plans for the next day, that at four o'clock in the morning, the King of Naples would depart for Kovno, where it was intended to rally the scattered men and take up positions.[58] Whereupon Comte Daru [Pierre-Antoine-Noël-Mathieu Bruno Daru] received orders to use all possible means to save the treasury, to distribute rations, clothing and footwear to all those who require them without slow administrative formalities and with a generous hand (because, as was stated in the orders, the enemy situation prevents us from staying in Vilna). Finally, orders were issued to take everything possible to Kovno.[59] In the name of Napoleon, Schwarzenberg was ordered to go to Bialystok, in order to secure the Duchy of Warsaw; while MacDonald was to close up to Tilsit in order to shield Königsberg and Danzig. Both of them were given the vital responsibility of retreating as slowly as possible, unless they were close to overwhelming numbers of Russian troops.[60]

On 28 November (10 December), at four o'clock in the morning, Murat set off along the Kovno road in a carriage with the *chef d'état-major* of the French army; the Viceroy, Davout, Lefebvre [François Joseph Lefebvre], Mortier and Bessières accompanied them on horseback, while the *Garde* provided the escort for the *État-major général*; with the exception of several Polish units sent via Novy-Troky to Olita, the remaining fighting men still under arms as well as the unarmed mob stretched along the road to Kovno.[61] Ney's rear guard, despite the efforts of their commander,

---

57 Chambray, III, 131. Strength return for Napoleon's forces upon reaching Vilna: *Vieille Garde* – 600 infantry, 800 Cavalry. *Jeune Garde* – 100 infantry. Bavarian corps & Loison's division – 2,300 infantry, 200 cavalry. *1er Corps, 2e Corps, 3e Corps, 4e Corps & 9e Corps* – 300 infantry. Total – 3,300 infantry, 1,000 cavalry.
58 *Chef d'état-major* Berthier's letter to Marshal Ney, dated 9 December new style.
59 *Chef d'état-major* Berthier's letter to *Comte* Daru, dated 9 December new style.
60 *Chef d'état-major* Berthier's letters to Schwarzenberg and MacDonald, dated 9 December new style.
61 Chambray, III, 130-131.

were unable to expel all the stragglers from the city. Many of the inhabitants, most of whom were Jews who had been hiding in houses and cellars before the departure of the French, poured out from there, pushing the enemy out into the streets and even killing some; they went for the *Garde* in particular, who had oppressed the population of Vilna more than any others.[62] Count Orlov-Denisov's detachment appeared on the Kovno road at dawn. His Cossacks raided the road several times and carried off more than a thousand men as prisoners. Meanwhile, Platov, having managed to reach the same location, ordered Colonel Prince Kudashev to open fire on the retreating enemy with canister from six Don Cossack artillery pieces, and four horse artillery pieces from Orlov-Denisov's detachment; followed by a general attack. The enemy columns, having been overwhelmed, lost more than a thousand men taken prisoner alone, two colours and two standards. The remainder of Murat's force were pursued, from the rear and along both sides of the highway, by Major General Ilovaisky 5th and Kuteinikov 2nd with eight Cossack regiments,[63] Colonel Prince Kasatkin-Rostovsky, with the Ataman's Regiment, and Major General Dekhterev [Nikolai Vasilievich Dekhterev], with the Olviopol Hussars, Arzamas Dragoons and Zhitomir Dragoons. Having closed up to the Ponary hills [Aukštieji Paneriai], six *versts* from Vilna, the enemy were forced to climb the steep, icy slopes. In order to protect the retreating personnel and convoys, Ney placed a rearguard in columns at the foot of these hills, each of which consisted of several hundred men, earlier, Murat had arrived there at about five o'clock in the morning with his retinue and the *Garde* who were accompanying him, in a hurry to move further on. But the exhausted horses, unable to climb the slopes, slipped and fell; many wagons and men crowded and congested the route, preventing even individuals from moving. Murat himself and all the marshals were forced to abandon their carriages and dismount their horses and make their way through the forest on foot, away from the road, ordering that their carts be burned and for the treasury, Napoleon's own silver and other highly valuable items, to be loaded onto the horses. But the enemy only managed to get away with a little before shots rang out from the Cossack guns. Murat and the other French commanders rode off along the Kovno road; behind them went Ney's rearguard. The stragglers, marauders and drivers, seeing the obvious impossibility of saving the treasury, rushed to the barrels of gold and silver, broke them open and carried away huge sums of money; others opened the baggage and pulled out gold-embroidered court uniforms or rich furs; but everyone was greedily searching for edible supplies, and when any were found in the abandoned carriages, they rushed there, abandoning the treasure. All in all, money had lost its customary value: on occasion, some men were offered ten five-franc coins for a glass of vodka, or they exchanged whole heaps of silver for several *napoléon d'or*. Many of Ney's rearguard threw down their muskets and filled their pockets with gold. In the midst of this turmoil, the men of the Don swooped in and completed the looting of rich booty. Of this entire treasury, which reached some 11,000,000 francs, little more

---

62 Labaume, *Relation circonstanciée de la campagne de Russie en 1812*, 422. Bourgeois, 178 & 180.
63 Ilovaisky 5th's Cossacks, Ilovaisky 10th's Cossacks, Sysoev 3rd's Cossacks, Grekov 18th's Cossacks, Zhirov's Cossacks, Kharitonov 7th's Cossacks, Vlasov 3rd's Cossacks and Sulin 9th's Cossacks.

than 4,000,000 were saved; while 6,800,000 francs were plundered.[64] In addition, the enemy were forced to abandon the rest of their artillery, including twenty-eight guns, their so-called trophies, almost all their carts, many wagons with wounded and sick officers, and Napoleon's own carriage.[65]

On that same day, 28 November (10 December), Russian forces liberated Vilna. At the same time as the actions under Platov were taking place at the Ponary hills, Chaplits, having assimilated the detachments under generals Lanskoy and Laskin into his force, closed up to Vilna. The Ostrobram gate, barricaded with wagons, guns and logs, was defended by some enemy who had settled in neighbouring houses during the retreat of the rearguard. General Chaplits, not wanting to lose men to no purpose, pulled his troops back out of range and sent the 28th Jägers and 32nd Jägers to the right of the gate, who, on approaching Subotskaya Street, pulled down several barricades. As soon as the enemy saw our jägers, they began to retreat, and Chaplits' troops, following them, eventually took the city.[66] At the same time, the leading detachments under General Borozdin and Adjutant General Kutuzov, under the command of Colonel Sukhozanet and Lieutenant Colonel Tettenborn, each of two Cossack regiments with two squadrons, entered Vilna, the first through the Zarechye gate, and the second through the Zamok Gate.[67] The prudent orders issued by Chaplits and the rapid occupation of the city from several directions by our troops saved the inhabitants of Vilna from robbery and arson, to which almost all of our cities were sacrificed as the enemy abandoned them. The French did not even have time to burn the huge stores in Vilna. During the occupation of the city, in addition to more than 100 guns abandoned in the streets and on the road to Ponary by the enemy, 41 guns were found in the arsenal. Seven generals,[68] 242 field officers and subalterns and more than 14,000 lower ranks were captured, of whom 5,000 were sick in the hospitals. 14,000 *chetvert* of rye, 5,000 *chetvert* of flour, vast stores of commissariat items, and so on, were found in the magazines. Over the following days, large stores were found in the vicinity of the city and many prisoners were rounded up.[69]

On the day Vilna was liberated by Russian forces, the enemy retreated to Jewie [Vievis], and the next day, 29 November (11 December), to Rumshishki [Rumšiškės]. On 29 November [11 December], the main body of the Army of the Danube arrived

---

64 *Rückzug der Franzosen bis zum Niemen, Vermehrte Ausgabe*, 51. Labaume, *Relation* etc. 416-419. Labaume wrote that the cross from the bell tower of Ivan the Great was also abandoned here, but this is doubtful, because it was never found. It is much more likely that it was lost while crossing the Berezina.
65 Count Platov's report to Prince Kutuzov, dated 29 November [11 December], No. 222. Chambray, III, 131-132.
66 War Diary of the Army of the Danube, maintained by Malinovsky. In this diary it states that Chaplits liberated Vilna on 29 November [11 December] (and not 28 November [10 December]), but this statement contradicts other sources on the seizure of Vilna by Russian troops. Czaplitz, *Remarques sur la campagne de 1812*. Archive of the M.T.D. No. 44712.
67 Major General Borozdin's report to Count Wittgenstein, dated 30 November [12 December], No. 14.
68 *Général de division* Zajączek and *généraux de brigade* Guillaume de Vaudoncourt, Lefebvre, Viviès, Husson, Norman and Iwanowski.
69 Prince Kutuzov's report to Emperor Alexander I, dated 2 [14] December, No. 647.

in Vilna, to where Prince Kutuzov immediately moved our headquarters. During his career, he had twice been the military governor of this city, and often reminisced on his life there and very much loved, as he put it, 'my gracious Vilna.' The Field Marshal was quartered in the castle with his staff; there Chichagov met him in naval undress-uniform with short sword, holding his cap under his arm, and gave him a strength return on the state of his army and handed him the keys to the city. Witnesses of this meeting confirm that its conduct was extremely frosty. Chichagov knew that the Field Marshal also blamed him for imperfect operations on the Berezina, while Kutuzov knew that Chichagov had justified himself from intelligence received from Kutuzov about Napoleon's intention to move towards Igumen. It was claimed that the Field Marshal told the admiral that the carriages taken from him at Borisov with crockery and such like, had been recaptured from the French and would be returned to him, and that Chichagov answered: 'are you telling me that I have nothing from which to eat? On the contrary, I can provide you with everything in the event that you wish to host dinners.'[70]

After the strenuous labour and hardships of a winter campaign, the camp at Vilna was delightful. There, at the end of his days, great honours, the grace of the Monarch, and the respect and gratitude of the Russian people awaited Kutuzov. Around this magnificent residence and in its chambers, friends and rivals of all nations and all classes crowded. Poets praised him; in the theatre, on the stage, a brightly illuminated image of Kutuzov shone, with the inscription: 'Избавителю Отечества' [Saviour of the Fatherland].[71] This feat, eternally blessed from above, had been accomplished, but some enemy still remained within Russia; it was vital to expel, for good and all, the remnants of the formidable hordes who had imagined they could enslave our Fatherland. To that end, the Field Marshal issued the following orders:

1. 'Count Platov is to continue the pursuit of the enemy towards Kovno.
2. Admiral Chichagov is to move to Gezno[72] in order to cross the Neman there and isolate Murat if he holds in Kovno. Strong detachments from the Army of the Danube are to be sent to Olita and Merecz, where the partisan Lieutenant Colonel Davydov is also to go.
3. Count Wittgenstein to operate against MacDonald by continuing to move from Niemenczyn, along the right bank of the Viliya, to Kovno and is to cross the Neman downstream of this city and go towards Gumbinnen [Gusev, Kaliningrad *Oblast*], seeking to smash MacDonald between the Neman and Pregel, if he does not hasten his retreat.
4. General Löwis [Fëdor Fëdorovich Leviz or Friedrich von Löwis of Menar], leaving only the troops necessary to secure Riga, is to set off

---

70 'est-ce pour me dire que je n'ai pas sur quoi manger? Je puis, au contraire, vous fournir de tout dans le cas même si vous vouliez donner des diners.' Notes by Prince Golitsyn, who served under Prince Kutuzov in 1812.
71 Mikhailovsky-Danilevsky, Description of the Patriotic War of 1812, IV.
72 The village of Gezno is close to the Neman on the route between Vilna and Preny.

after MacDonald with the remainder and, after closing up to the corps under Count Wittgenstein, is to come under his command.

5. General Tormasov, having taken command of Tuchkov's corps coming up from Minsk, Essen's corps detached by Saken, Colonel Knorring's detachment stationed in Minsk and eight battalions under Lieutenant General Radt [Semën Lukich Radt or Simon Rath], who is en route from Bobruisk, it to establish communications with Saken and maintain liaison with the main army, while operating together with him [Saken] against Schwarzenberg, until he has retreated into Austria, but is not to cross the border.
6. If MacDonald succeeds in retreating to the lower Vistula, then Count Wittgenstein is to halt in order to monitor him from Allenstein [Olsztyn], while Chichagov is to march through Tykocin and Węgrów to Warsaw, to link up with the corps under Tormasov and Saken.
7. The main army is to be placed in quarters between Wiłkomierz [Ukmergė] and the upper Neman, until the stragglers and convalescents have rejoined, as well as 15 battalions from Prince Urusov's division assigned as replacements, upon the arrival of which the army will take up a central position in the vicinity of Grodno.
8. The raiding detachment under Count Ozharovsky is to move towards Belitsa, Adjutant General Vasilchikov towards Mosty, and Lieutenant Colonel Davydov, through Olita and Merecz, towards Grodno, and are to halt at these location in order to shield the quarters of the Main Army.'[73]

All these orders by Prince Kutuzov are evidence that he, having changed his previous plans, had the intention of moving relentlessly towards the Vistula with the bulk of his force. But the extreme weakening of our forces, which was an inevitable consequence of a winter campaign and the shortage of food on the march from the Berezina to Vilna, forced the Field Marshal to again change his plan of operations and entrust the pursuit of the enemy up to the Vistula to Platov's Cossack detachment and the vanguards of the Army of the Danube and the independent I Corps alone. After giving the troops a two-day rest in order to allow stragglers to rejoin and for the arrival of supplies, Admiral Chichagov and Count Wittgenstein were ordered to move up to the Neman and halt on the right bank of this river.[74]

The extraordinary loss of life in our armies was evident in the Note presented to the Tsar by Prince Kutuzov, with the following report:

> Most Merciful Sovereign! The ten-day strength returns have not been submitted to Your Imperial Majesty until now. The reason for this is that, due to incessant combat continuing over two months, the Main Army had

---

[73] Prince Kutuzov's report to the Tsar, dated 1 [13] December, No. 644. Archive of the M.T.D. No. 29,172.
[74] Prince Kutuzov's report to the Tsar, dated 2 [14] December, No. 652. Archive of the M.T.D. No. 29,172.

come to such a state from those killed by the enemy, from the wounded, and even more from the sick and stragglers from the unusually long marches, that its weakness in the number of men had to be concealed not only from the enemy, but also from the officers serving with the army themselves, and to that end, this data was collected discreetly by regiment and brigade, in order to thus calculate the total, which although not quite complete, is enclosed herewith. And this information has only been handled by Duty General Konovnitsyn and the clerk in whose hand it was written.

To this, however, such units are expected to be added soon, which until now have been unable to catch up with the army, namely: the 15 battalions under Major General Urusov's command, up to strength and well trained. Moreover, those who have recovered from various hospitals and those who dropped out along the route, have been collected, of whom I cannot determine the precise number. But I trust that at least 20,000 of these will arrive very shortly. Moreover, the governors have been ordered to search for many men hiding out in the villages; it must be said that former Belorussian and Lithuanian recruits deserted from their regiments as the Russian army retreated towards Russia, almost as far as Smolensk, but now they are being searched for.

I cannot hide from you, Most Merciful Sovereign, that such losses were not due to negligence by corps and regimental commanders, but it is also true that from Tarutino itself to Vilna there could have been no thought, but simply to chase after the fleeing enemy, and no matter how much the army was diminished, that of the enemy was almost wiped out.

I must take no less care, however, over the winter, that the army of Your Imperial Majesty becomes as terrifying in numbers as it is fearsome in valour.

Vilna, 7 [19] December, 1812.[75]

The Note on the composition of the force present in the ranks shows:

With the Main Army, that is, in III Corps, IV Corps, V Corps, VI Corps and VIII Corps, IV Cavalry Corps, Prince Golitsyn's cuirassiers and escort to the main headquarters: Infantry – 20,926 men. Cavalry – 3,496 men. Artillery – 2,617 men. Pioneers – 425 men. Total – 27,464 men, with 200 guns.

With the Western Army (formerly Army of the Danube), namely, Chaplits' vanguard, Count Langéron's and Voinov's corps and in Lanskoy's and Knorring's detachments: Infantry – 8,215 men. Cavalry – 6.898 men. Artillery – 2,201 men. Pioneers – 140 men. Total – 17,454 men, with 156 guns.

In addition, 7,034 men with 24 guns in the 15 replacement battalions of Tuchkov's corps.

Giving a grand total under Admiral Chichagov's command of 24,488 men with 180 guns.

---

75 Prince Kutuzov's letter to Emperor Alexander I, dated 7 [19] December, from Vilna. Held in the classified Archive of the General Staff Department.

Under Wittgenstein's command: Infantry – 26,257 men. Cavalry – 5,044 men. Artillery – 3,182 men. Total – 34,483 men with 177 guns.

Grand total: Infantry – 62,432 men. Cavalry and Cossacks – 15,438 men. Artillery – 8,000 men. Pioneers – 565 men. Overall total – 86,435 men with 557 guns.

(Of these guns, the Note submitted by the Field Marshal does not show 24 that were with Tuchkov's corps).

In addition, the following are not shown due to lack of data:

1. Sakens' corps.
2. The 14 replacement squadrons in Tuchkov's corps.
3. Miloradovich's vanguard, consisting of II Corps, VII Corps, II Cavalry Corps (which had absorbed III Cavalry Corps) and two light cavalry regiments.
4. Those in the independent detachments: all Cossack regiments with the Main Army, 11 infantry regiments and 1½ battalions; two cuirassier regiments and six of dragoons, three regiments and five squadrons of hussars, one regiment and one squadron of lancers, 130 artillery pieces, the entire reserve artillery and two pontoon companies.

Thus, the Main Army, which had set out from the Tarutino camp with a strength of 97,112 men and had been brought up to strength with some 102,254 recruits, upon arrival in the vicinity of Vilna two months later, counted only about 27,500 men in its ranks; there were some 6,500 in Miloradovich's vanguard, while the independent detachments, reserve artillery, and so on, had 8,500 men: consequently, in the Main Army overall there were about 42,000 men present; another 48,000 men lay sick in hospital; 12,000 had been killed in action, died of wounds or died from disease. Of the 622 guns that had been with the army at Tarutino, two hundred remained; the rest had been left behind, as a result of the loss of horses, or awaiting replenishment of the crews. Overall, the cavalry had suffered the most damage: the Cossack regiments, which had arrived at the Tarutino camp at full strength, had diminished to 150 men each; the regular cavalry had suffered even more painful losses: the strongest regiments had between 120 and 150 men, while some had no more than 60. The causes of general illness and death were: lack of food, drinking water contaminated by rotting corpses, and forced marches in the severe cold after crossing the Berezina. On this campaign, although the troops of the Main Army covered around no more than 20 *versts* a day, nevertheless, they were frequently marching through deep snow and became extremely exhausted, especially since the mobile magazines lagged behind the troops; over the entire stretch from Kopys to Vilna, for a period of about three weeks, the Main Army received only one convoy of provisions, totalling 2,000 carts sent from Bobruisk; finding forage was even more problematic: thus foraging and even requisitioning were insufficient. Our numerous and excellent cavalry was noticeably melting away. Another reason for the extraordinary losses to the force was the harshness of the season: many of our soldiers had been issued with sheepskin coats; others acquired them for themselves; put on fur-lined boots, felt boots, wore earmuffs, or wrapped themselves up in whatever was available; but in a campaign such as this, there was no time to take care of the repair of clothing and footwear. Having travelled 20 *versts* or more through deep snow, in severe frosts and blizzards, the soldiers hastened to kindle fires and cook food, if there was anything to cook, and lay down around the fires, freezing on one side and burning on the other. In such circumstances, clothing and footwear wore out in a few days, and it was impossible to replace them. The officers endured all these hardships in equal measure with the soldiers, and for that reason they were almost as badly clothed. Both they and the generals proceeded on foot to warm themselves through exercise, and yet many got frostbite on their hands and feet and were forced to stay in hospital. Chichagov's force, after crossing the Berezina, chasing quickly on the heels of the enemy, arrived in Vilna, having suffered even more damage than the Main Army.

Such was the situation of the Russian forces upon reaching Vilna. Having said that, we had achieved the aim of our operations: the *Grande Armée* no longer existed, and its miserable remnants, no longer thinking of glory and conquest, were in a hurry to escape across the borders of Russia.

44

Retreat of the remnants of the *Grande Armée* across the borders of Russia

Emperor Alexander I's thought on further operations following the liberation of Vilna. – The formation of reserves and other orders for military units. – The enemy retreat to Kovno. – The action at Kovno and the liberation of this city by Platov. – Measures taken by Prince Kutuzov for the further pursuit of the remnants of the enemy army.

The deployment of Russian forces into the Duchy of Warsaw and their entry into Prussian territory. – Appeal to the population of Prussia. – The enemy retreat to the Vistula.

Emperor Alexander's arrival in Vilna. – Manifesto of forgiveness. – The Sovereign's visit to Vilna hospitals. – Review of French historians regarding Emperor Alexander.

Emperor Alexander I, having received the report from Prince Kutuzov, dated 25 November (7 December) regarding his intention to halt the main body of the army at Vilna and pursue the enemy with the advanced detachments of Chichagov's army and the corps under Count Wittgenstein alone, did not express His consent to this plan. The Sovereign's opinions on further operations were set out in the following Supreme Rescript addressed to the Field Marshal:

Prince Mikhail Ilarionovich! Having received your report, dated 25 November [7 December], No. 593, today, I hasten to respond to it without losing a moment:

Our superiority over a disordered and weary enemy, acquired with the help of the Almighty and your skilful orders, and the current state of affairs in general, requires every effort to achieve the main objective, despite any hindrances. Time has never been so precious to us as under the present circumstances. And therefore, nothing should prevent our troops from pursuing the enemy, not even to halt for the shortest moment in Vilna. Respecting the reasons placed in your report, I find it necessary to hold only a small part of the force, more disordered than any other, in Vilna, which would round up the stragglers and convalescents, as well as the battalions under Major General Prince Urusov; while all the rest of the force, both the Main Army and the army under Admiral Chichagov and the corps under Count Wittgenstein, are to pursue the enemy without pause, taking whichever direction keeps in mind the same objective, that not only inside but also outside our borders, will sever their communications and links with their new reinforcements.

I approve of the principles adopted by you on the issue of the borders of Austria; on the subject of our deployment into Prussia, you will receive a detailed explanation from Me in due course. I remain grateful to you.

Alexander.

St Petersburg, 2 [14] December 1812.[1]

Emperor Alexander grieved over the hardships that his valiant warriors were forced to endure, continuing the offensive through the harshest of seasons, but throughout the long struggle with Napoleon, having studied the nature of his adversary, he became convinced of the need not to get euphoric at the successes gained so far, rather to complete them by persistently pursuing the remnants of the enemy army, and therefore considered the winter campaign of 1812 not to be the end-game which was to resolve the issue, but merely the conclusion of the first phase of the war: would the neighbours of France remain dependent upon Napoleon, or would they restore their political independence once more? Kutuzov and most of the personalities in our headquarters considered this question to be irrelevant to Russian interests; in contrast, Emperor Alexander was determined to continue the war and was actively preparing for a new campaign.[2]

For this purpose, the following orders were issued:

1. On 30 November (12 December), a general recruitment selection was announced, of eight men per 500 souls.[3]

---

1 Rescript dated 2 [14] December. Archive of the M.T.D. No. 29,174.
2 Bernhardi, *Denkwürdigkeiten des Grafen v. Toll*, II, 377-378. During his stay in Vilna, outlining his own plans regarding future operations, among other things, Emperor Alexander wrote: 'it seems that, in order to immediately exploit the superiority we have gained, the time has come to act, unencumbered by the usual methods and conventions of the art of war... Initiative and high tempo of operations by the military, pragmatism, striving for the common cause and a policy directed towards peace, should guide our actions.' From a letter dated 12 [24] December 1812, held in the Archive of the General Staff Department. In contrast, in one of Prince Kutuzov's private letters we find: 'Have no fear! I cannot go too far. I'm not getting any younger.'
3 The following governorates were excluded from selection: Poltava, Chernigov, Courland, Vilna, Grodno and Minsk, also Georgia and the Bialystok and Tarnopol Oblasts. A separate decree was issued for the Siberian governorates. Those noble estates which had fielded *opolchenie*, and villages in the interior governorates of the Empire which had been devastated by the enemy, were exempted from selection. Directed Decree for the Senate dated 30 November [12 December] 1812. Complete Collection of Laws, XXXII, 25,280.   Shortly beforehand there was a selection in the Livonia Governorate of one recruit per 50 souls.

2. On the occasion of the disbandment of one regiment in each of ten infantry divisions of the Main Army, Prince Lobanov-Rostovsky [Dmitry Ivanovich Lobanov-Rostovsky] was ordered to raise one more battalion for each of these regiments, over and above their previous replacements.[4]
3. For the seven divisions of the Army of the Danube, as well as for 13th Division stationed in the Crimea, Lieutenant General Essen 3rd was ordered to raise one battalion for each regiment, for a total of 48 battalions. The locations for the formation of these battalions were indicated between Chernigov and Bobruisk, and the cadres for them were to come from: replacement and recruit battalions located in Bobruisk and Kiev, and recruits recently called up to nearby depots.[5]
4. Notwithstanding the reserves formed by General Kologrivov [Andrei Semënovich Kologrivov], Major General Chalikov [Anton Stepanovich Chalikov (Shalikoshvili)?] and Colonel Gendre were ordered to form 20 squadrons in order to bring the cavalry up to strength.[6]
5. Six battalions, ten squadrons and an horse artillery half-company (battery) were to be formed in St Petersburg for the Lifeguard.[7] Overall, the reserves for the operational army consisted of 77 battalions under Prince Lobanov-Rostovsky, 24 battalions under Kleinmichel [Andrei Andreevich Kleinmichel], 48 battalions under Essen 3rd, 24 battalions under Bashutsky [Pavel Yakovlevich Bashutsky], 94 squadrons under Kologrivov, twenty squadrons under Chalikov, ten squadrons and five reserve cavalry units for the Lifeguard; a total of 173 battalions, 124 squadrons and five reserve cavalry units, numbering 173,000 infantry and 25,000 cavalry.[8]

Directed Decree for Lieutenant General Marquis Paulucci, dated 9 [21] November 1812. Complete Collection of Laws, XXXII, 25,261.

4 Rescript to General-of-Infantry Prince Lobanov-Rostovsky, dated 5 [17] December. The following regiments were disbanded: Selenginsk Infantry from 3rd Division, Minsk Infantry from 4th Division, Sofia Infantry from 7th Division, Polotsk Infantry from 11th Division, Novo Ingermanland Infantry from 12th Division, Wilmanstrand Infantry from 17th Division, Rylsk Infantry from 23rd Division, Tomsk Infantry from 24th Division, Nizhegorod Infantry from 26th Division and Tarnopol Infantry from 27th Division.

5 Supreme Orders to the Director of the Ministry of War, Lieutenant General Prince Gorchakov, dated 29 November [11 December], No. 366.

6 Supreme Orders to the Director of the Ministry of War, dated 5 [17] November, No. 294, and dated 29 November [11 December], No. 366, regarding the raising of two squadrons each for the: Mittau Dragoons, Finland Dragoons, Grodno Hussars and Poland Ulans, and eight squadrons of cuirassiers. In addition, four reserve squadrons belonging to regiments that were then in St. Petersburg from the Riga Dragoons, Kazan Dragoons, Nezhin Dragoons and Yamburg dragoons, were ordered to amalgamate in order to form two squadrons each for the Riga and Kazan regiments.

7 Supreme Orders to the Director of the Ministry of War, dated 11 [23] October, No. 198, and dated 20 October [1 November], No. 230.

8 In addition to an initial 67 battalions, Prince Lobanov-Rostovsky was ordered to raise another 12; but the raising of two grenadier battalions was subsequently cancelled. Reserve battalions were to have 1,000 men each, squadrons 190 each, and Lifeguard cavalry reserves 300 each.

6. Orders were issued to reorganise all the cavalry regiments, dependant on the number of men and horses remaining in them, into three, two or even a single squadron, while the remaining squadrons, leaving a cadre of officers, non-commissioned officers and privates in each of them, were to be sent to Starodub together with their squadron commanders, where, over the winter, they were to be reconstituted with recruits assembling in Kiev, and with horses from the Volhynia Governorate and Podolsk Governorate. Their formation was entrusted to Adjutant General Count Komarovsky [Yevgraf Fedotovich Komarovsky].[9]
7. In order to bring the artillery up to strength, the Field Marshal was ordered to designate battle-worthy companies from the entire artillery of the active army with a full complement of ammunition caissons, field officers, subalterns and crews, the best horses, harness and transport, and then to send all the remaining companies to Bryansk, for re-equipment and staffing with men and remounts over the winter.[10]

At the same time, the reserves under Prince Lobanov-Rostovsky and General Kologrivov, in order to close up to the active armies, were transferred to the vicinity of Orël and Novgorod-Seversky.[11]

In order to resupply the troops with firearms, which, despite the intensive work at our arms factories, were still insufficient, orders were issued for announcements in churches in every province where hostilities had previously been conducted, that weapons could be sold to the government with the treasury paying five roubles for each musket, or pair of pistols; those who located a gun buried in the ground or submerged in water were entitled to a reward of 50 roubles.[12] Emperor Alexander also involved himself in the commissariat department in every detail of the resupply of the troops, and his own notes on the reports and returns submitted to him serve as evidence of this.[13]

The supply of food to the army was the subject of constant attention in particular by Emperor Alexander I. On the basis of the 'Note on the methods of supplying the army during further offensive operations,' sent to the Field Marshal, with a Supreme Rescript dated 7 [19] November, Kutuzov informed the Tsar that, on the success of our armed forces and as the regions of the Empire were cleared of the enemy, the following measures had been taken:

---

9   Supreme Orders for Prince Kutuzov, dated 9 [21] November, No. 316.
10 Supreme Orders for Prince Kutuzov, dated 9 [21] November, No. 317.
11 Supreme Orders for Prince Kutuzov, dated 29 November [11 December], No. 364.
12 Supreme Orders to provincial governors, dated 23, 26 and 30 November [5, 8 and 12 December] and 24 December [5 January 1813].
13 So, for example, in one of the reports by *Kriegskommissar* General Tatishchev, the Tsar pointed out to him that some of the proposed preparations should have been done much earlier, while in a Note on the Novgorod *Opolchenie*, attached to a report by Commander-in-Chief of the 2nd *Opolchenie* District, General Meller-Zakomelsky, he wrote: 'all this is in order, except for cloth haversacks, as it was precisely instructed for them to be made of leather.' General Meller-Zakomelsky's report dated 17 [29] November, No. 682.

1. Stocks prepared at the treasury's expense or donated by private individuals located in magazines in Tver and Vyshny Volochyok, following the liberation of Smolensk, were ordered to be transported to this city, but once our army reached Vilna, then, the previous orders were cancelled and only 15,000 *Chetvert* of flour or hard-tack (with the instructed quantity of cereals), and 10,000 *Chetvert* of oats were ordered to be sent; while all the rest of the supplies from the aforementioned magazines, 70,000 *Chetvert* of flour and 39,000 *Chetvert* of oats were to be transported to Vitebsk and Belskaya wharf each. From magazines in Novgorod, 14,000 *Chetvert* of flour and 17,000 *Chetvert* of oats were sent to Sebezh and Volyntsy; the remaining portion of the supplies, 28,000 *Chetvert* of flour and 34,000 *Chetvert* of oats, were left in Novgorod, for shipping to St Petersburg next spring, and from there by sea to Riga, or to other locations. The transportation and shipping of provisions and fodder had been entrusted to the care of the Provisioning Department.
2. Two echelons of magazines have been established: the forward magazines, or closest to the location of the army, are in Schaulen [Šiauliai], Wiłkomierz, Vilna, Belitsa, Minsk, Slonim, Pinsk and Lutsk. Minsk, Belitsa and Pinsk are instructed to have 40,000 *Chetvert* of flour (with the instructed amount of cereals) and 30,000 *Chetvert* of oats, and at all other points, 20,000 *Chetvert* of flour and 15,000 *Chetvert* of oats. These magazines are to be stocked by requisition in Lithuania, from supplies collected in the Minsk, Volhynia, Chernigov, Poltava and Kursk governorates, and from provisions transported from Kiev. The rear magazines, or second echelon, are assigned in Orsha, Borisov, Mogilev, Bobruisk, Rechitsa, Mozyr, Dubna and Rogachev, each of 20,000 *Chetvert* of flour and 15,000 *Chetvert* of cereals, stocked in Orsha and Borisov from donations from the Tula and Kaluga governorates and from collections in the Smolensk Governorate; in Mogilev from the collection ordered from the Mogilev Governorate during the passage of our forces through it; in Bobruisk and Rechitsa by transport sent to the army from Trubchevsk, with which are to be the most exhausted horses; in Mozyr and Dubna partly from collections from the Volhynia Governorate; in Rogachev from stores in Sosnitsa.[14]

Upon clearing Vilna of enemy troops, the Field Marshal, fulfilling the will of Emperor Alexander I, proposed: firstly, to pursue the remnants of the *Grande Armée* beyond the Neman; secondly, exploiting MacDonald's delay in the vicinity of Riga, to cut him off from the Neman and drive him towards the sea; and thirdly, to eject the corps under Schwarzenberg and Reynier from Russian territory.[15]

---

14 Prince Kutuzov-Smolensky's report to the Tsar, dated 8 [20] December. Archive of the M.T.D. No. 46,692.
15 Prince Kutuzov's report to the Tsar, dated 1 [13] December, No. 644. Archive of the M.T.D. No. 29,172.

Meanwhile, after their departure from Vilna, the flight of the remnants of the enemy army accelerated. The distance of more than 100 *versts* from Vilna to Kovno was covered by them in three stages; while their rearguard completed it in four. Murat himself, having left on the evening of 29 November (11 December), the *Garde* and the marshals accompanying him to Rumshishki, arrived in Kovno at about midnight. There were very significant magazines and 2,500,000 francs (about 700,000 silver roubles), the evacuation of which no one had considered, because no one believed that the French army could have come to such a pass. There were no more than 1,500 newly recruited German troops and 42 guns remaining for the defence of Kovno, for which there were only horses for 25. As it was possible to cross the Neman on the ice at that time, the Kovno garrison was in danger of being enveloped from all sides by our troops. At two o'clock in the afternoon of 30 November (12 December), the *Garde* and many isolated individuals moving under their protection reached Kovno. A completely overwhelmed Murat summoned the *Chef d'état-major général*, all the marshals and Daru to a conference. From the reports of the formation commanders, it emerged that in the *Garde*, which constituted the most reliable element of the army, 1,500 men remained and even then, not all were capable of fighting. Murat, driven to despair, began to curse Napoleon in front of his associates, accusing him of an insatiable lust for power that had destroyed the army; but Davout forced him to stop his ranting, observing that a man raised to high status by Napoleon should not criticise him, and that at the present time it was essential to think about saving the troops, and not arouse their displeasure with pointless complaints. It was decided that Ney would halt at Kovno with the rearguard, in order to cover the retreat of the army, and then retreat to Königsberg and link up with MacDonald there. The remnants of the other corps would be directed to the Vistula.[16] In order to defend the position at Kovno, Murat placed nine guns at Alexoten, on the high ground that dominates the city; by evening, the *Garde* had set up in bivouacs in the same location; while at five o'clock on the morning of the following day, 1 (13) December, Murat departed from Kovno, taking the *Garde* and four guns from among those at Alexoten with him; the remaining five were left on the high ground opposite the city with little protection.

On that same day, Ney, having set off from Rumshishki before dawn in a severe frost and blizzard, arrived at Kovno at about nine o'clock in the morning. The fearless marshal, having taken over the defence of this city, demanded that General Gérard be assigned to him, which was done. Meanwhile, in the city, the greatest disorder was taking place from a crowded multitude of men; the vast magazines were being looted; soldiers, stiff from the cold, rushed into the cellars storing vodka, rolled the barrels out into the street, smashed them open and perished, drunk to the point of oblivion. Fires had broken out in many places. Such was the situation in which it was vital for Ney to organise the defence of the city. *Généraux de division* Gérard and Marchand assisted him. Several hundred German soldiers with twenty guns occupied the fortifications erected to protect the bridges on the Viliya and Neman; the rest of Loison's division, under Marchand's command, was

---

16 Chambray, *Histoire de l'expédition de Russie*, III, 133-134. Thiers, *Histoire du Consulat et de l'Empire*, XIV, Ed. de Brux. 736-738.

stationed along the banks of the Viliya and the Neman, whose ice-bound courses no longer constituted a barrier. On the following day, 2 [14] December, Platov with his Cossacks and O'Rourke with Chaplits' cavalry closed up to the city. Both of them, having pursued the enemy relentlessly from Vilna to Kovno, had captured more than 2,000 prisoners and 15 guns (the infantry from Chaplits' vanguard, on the orders of Chichagov, had been left in Vilna to rest and for ration resupply). At ten o'clock in the morning, Platov opened a cannonade on the enemy occupying Kovno from eight guns accompanying his detachment on sled runners; the raw recruits stationed at the Vilna Gate, who had never been under fire, being overcome by panicky terror, spiked their guns and threw away their muskets. It is claimed that their commanding officer shot himself in despair. Ney and Gérard themselves, dashing to this point, restrained the fugitives, while Ney's aide de camp, Rumigny [Marie-Théodore Gueilly de Rumigny], led some of the *29e régiment d'infanterie* and held back the Cossacks who were already breaking into the city.[17] Whereupon Platov, wanting to manoeuvre the French out of Kovno, sent his Cossack regiments around the city, crossing to the far side of the river. At two o'clock in the afternoon, dismounted Cossacks forced the small detachment stationed at Alexoten to retreat and occupied the high ground opposite the city. General Marchand, noticing this movement threatening to cut off the French, attacked the high ground and recaptured it, but was driven off by the Cossacks once more. The enemy, not daring to stay in the city any longer, set fire to the magazines, crossed the ice to the far side of the Neman, and some fled towards Tilsit, some towards Wilkowischken [Vilkaviškis]. The Cossacks pursued them and captured many men, mostly stragglers who had left with the rearguard.[18] Meanwhile, Ney, who had no more than 200 fighting men left, raced along the shortest route to Wilkowischken, but as almost all his soldiers had scattered in different directions, he turned to the right down the course of the Neman, and then through the Pilwiszki forest making his way to Wilkowischken on the highway leading to Gumbinnen, leaving the artillery from Loison's division, which he had evacuated from Kovno, in the forest. General Dumas [Mathieu Dumas] wrote:

> Having escaped from accursed Russia, I was resting in my quarters in Wilkowischken, when suddenly a man in a brown frock coat, with a long beard, bloodshot, glittering eyes, burst in.
> 'You do not recognise me?' he asked.
> 'No! Who are you?'
> 'I am the rearguard of the *Grande Armée*, Marshal Ney.' Indeed, by that time there was no one with him except General Gérard.[19]

On 3 (15) December, Count Platov, having entered the city of Kovno, cleared of the enemy by him and his detachment, ordered a thanksgiving service attended by the

---

17 Chambray, III, 137. Thiers, XIV, 738-739.
18 Chambray, III, 137. Count Platov's report to Chichagov, dated 3 [15] December, No. 230.
19 *Souvenirs du lieutenant-général Dumas*, III, 484. Chambray, III, 138. Chambray wrote that Ney went to Schirwindt, not to Wilkowischken.

force assembled on the square, praying on their knees. A long life to the Monarch and the Reigning House were proclaimed, and a 101 gun salute was fired. Celebratory cheers of 'Hurrah!' by our troops were repeated with feeling by the inhabitants, who had suffered ruin from their self-styled saviours, and greeted the Russians with unfeigned delight. The Catholic priest also asked Platov for permission to perform a mass, and the Jewish community also went to the square where a celebration took place, carrying their ark of the ten commandments [*Aron Kodesh*].[20]

After our troops had occupied Kovno and extinguished the fires in the city, several cannon were found (overall, 21 cannon were taken including those captured during the pursuit from Vilna), 779 ammunition caissons and some 3,000 *Chetvert* of provisions and oats. Some 5,000 prisoners had been captured by the Cossacks on the march from Vilna and in the city of Kovno.[21]

The number of fighting men from the *Grande Armée* who crossed back over the Russian border did not exceed 400 infantry of the *Vieille Garde* (the *Jeune Garde* had already been totally scattered) and 600 *cavalerie de la Garde*. In each of the other corps, only Colour parties remained, accompanied by a handful of officers and non-commissioned officers. Artillery for the entire army consisted of the nine guns evacuated from Kovno by Murat. On 7 (19) December, the *État-major général de la Grande Armée* reached Königsberg, where Heudelet's [Étienne Heudelet de Bierre] division (*11e Corps*) was expected on 10 (22) December, numbering 14,000 recruits with 20 guns.[22]

On our side, the main force under Prince Kutuzov, the vanguard under Miloradovich and the detachment formerly under Yermolov (disbanded upon the arrival of the army in Vilna), settled down in quarters between Wiłkomierz and Valozhin. Chichagov proceeded to pursue the remnants of the *Grande Armée* with his vanguard and Platov's detachment. The pursuit of MacDonald from the rear had been entrusted to the Riga garrison, while, in order to cut the enemy corps off from the Vistula, Count Wittgenstein was to move downstream along the right bank of the Neman with his corps to Kovno and then march on Gumbinnen. In addition to the force under Saken, the following were ear-marked for operations against Schwarzenberg, under the overall command of Dokhturov: Essen 3rd's Corps (detached from Saken's force), and the detachments under Tuchkov, Radt and Knorring, sent from Minsk towards Slonim, as well as the vanguard of the Main Army, under the command of General Vasilchikov, directed towards Bialystok.[23]

---

20 Count Platov's report to Chichagov, dated 3 [15] December, No. 230.
21 Count Platov's report to Chichagov, dated 3 [15] December, No. 230. War Diary of the Main Army, signed off by Prince Kutuzov.
22 Chambray, III, 138-140.
23 Prince Kutuzov's report to the Tsar, dated 7 [19] December, No. 689. The troops of the Main Army were assigned to quarters as follows: II Cavalry Corps together with Poland Ulans and Lithuania Ulans between Merecz, Jeziory and Lida; VI Corps in Wiłkomierz; VII Corps in Niemenczyn; V Corps and the headquarters in Vilna; IV Corps in Novy Troki; II Corps in Soleczniki; III Corps in Oshmyany; VIII Corps in Holszany; 1st Cuirassier Division in the area of Vilna and Sventsiany; 2nd Cuirassier Division between Svir and Naliboki. Buturlin, II, 416-417.

Postponing for the moment the description of operations by the forces directed against MacDonald and Schwarzenberg, I shall describe here only the movements by Chichagov's army and the Cossack detachment under Count Platov, which pursued the remnants of the *Grande Armée* from the Neman to the Vistula.

While Platov, following the occupation of Kovno, remained there until 17 (29) December, the main body under Chichagov, having reached the Neman on 5 (17) December, settled in cantonments in the vicinity of the town of Gezno (near Preny), where the headquarters of the Army of the Danube was located, and remained there also until 17 (29) December.

Throughout the dispersal of our troops into quarters, in order to preserve their health, it was instructed:

1. To allocate the men as much space as possible.
2. Ensure that a moderate temperature is maintained in each hut [*izba*].
3. To engage the soldiers for two hours each day with some light exercise.
4. To observe that the men have hot food every day, in particular cabbage soup with sauerkraut, and, if possible, issue a cup of vodka; do not permit water to be drunk directly from a river or from a well.
5. Sentries on duty, in severe frosts, are to have warm boots and are to smear their toes with fat.
6. The sick are to be sent to the infirmary immediately.
7. Keep the hospitals clean and try to isolate those suffering from contagious diseases from other sick men, in a dedicated *izba*.
8. With a vomit-inducing cough or mild stomach upset, give *sbiten* [a spiced honey drink with herbs, served hot] with ginger, or with vodka.[24]

After the occupation of Kovno, further pursuit of the enemy was entrusted to the vanguard under Chaplits, who, having crossed the Neman at Preny, on 5 (17) December, settled down in the vicinity of this town, in the Duchy of Warsaw; while his leading detachments, which were under the command of Count O'Rourke and Lanskoy, took up positions in cantonments from Pilwiszki to Sejny.[25] Our troops were allowed to obtain essential supplies through forage and requisitions, but without imposing any indemnities on the inhabitants of the duchy. Here the cavalry regiments were reorganised into fully manned squadrons; while the supernumerary officers were sent to Russia with cadres in order to be reconstituted with other squadrons. Thus there remained six squadrons in the Pavlograd Hussars, three in the Volhynia Ulans, and two each in the dragoon regiments. 12th Horse Artillery Company, to that same end, was returned to Vilna. Major General Lanskoy's detachment became part of the Main Army.

---

24 Admiral Chichagov's Order of the Day, for 13 [25] December, No. 168. Archive of the M.T.D. No. 36,749.
25 The composition of Chaplits' vanguard and Lanskoy's detachment, which had been assimilated into this vanguard, has been shown in Chapter XLII and in the footnotes to this chapter.

On 17 (29) December, Chichagov's army continued their offensive and on 21 December (2 January 1813) entered Prussia. Major General Count O'Rourke, sent forwards to Stallupönen [Nesterov, Kaliningrad *Oblast*], the first Prussian town that lay on the route of our forces, was greeted by the inhabitants with great joy, and when the *Bürgermeister* of the town announced the impending arrival the next day of the Russians to the population, everyone cheered in delight: 'May Emperor Alexander be our protector!' Many ran home, informing their relatives of the entry of our army into Prussia, and immediately set about preparing food and fodder for their liberators.[26] Feelings of mutual trust and friendship, nourished by the Monarchs of these neighbouring peoples, seemed to be reflected in their respective subjects. Even before the arrival of the Russians in Prussia, the following printed proclamation was intercepted from the enemy by one of the Cossack patrols, issued by an unknown person, in German:

> The Russian nation, inspired by patriotism, has triumphed.
>
> The French are on the run; if you do not believe it, just ask: where is the French army?
>
> Onwards Germans! the moment has come for you also to avenge the insults you have suffered, and to raise yourselves back to the status of a free nation.
>
> Your princes are in fetters and look to each and every one of you in particular, to set them free and avenge them.
>
> If you cannot, as one, join side by side with the brave Russians who have recently been fighting for your benefit, then at least come to us individually. We will receive you as brothers.
>
> All of us – Russians, Germans, Italians, Swiss and Spaniards are brothers, because we have a common enemy.
>
> If we join forces, the common enemy of the peace and happiness of all peoples will never raise their heads again.[27]

For our part, all possible measures were taken to protect the inhabitants of the countryside into which we were preparing to bring armed forces. Prince Kutuzov,

---

26 War Diary of the Army of the Danube (Third Army), compiled by Malinovsky.
27 '*Die russische Nation, beseelt von Vaterlandsliebe, hat gesiegt.* Die Franzosen sind auf der Flucht; wer es nicht glaubt mag nur fragen: wo ist die französische Armee? Auf Deutsche! auch euer Augenblick ist gekommen, euch, wegen der Beschimpfungen, die ihr erlitten habt, zu rächen, und euch wieder zu dem Range einer freien Nation emporzuheben. Eure Fürsten sind in Fesseln und erwarten von euch allen und von jedem insbesondere, dass ihr sie befreiet und rächet. Wenn ihr euch nicht alle zusammen, mit den braven Russen vereinigen könnet, welche noch unlängst für euer Wohl und an ihrer Seite kämpften, so kommet wenigstens einzeln zu uns. Wir werden euch als Brüder empfangen. Wir alle – Russen, Deutsche, Italiener, Schweizer und Spanier sind Brüder, denn wir haben den nehmlichen Feind. *Vereinigen wir unsere Streitkräfte, so wird der allgemeine Feind der Ruhe und Glückseligkeit aller Völker nie sein Haupt wieder erheben.*' A copy of this proclamation was attached to Count Wittgenstein's report to Prince Kutuzov, dated 12 [24] December, No. 205. Archive of the M.T.D. No. 29,172.

reminding the commanders of individual formations, instructed that, when crossing the border, the following orders be issued to the forces entrusted to them:

> Gentlemen corps and divisional commanders and unit commanders are ordered immediately to take strict measures such that peace and calm are preserved in the current quartering arrangements, and the military lower ranks do not cause any disorder; and if there are any manors or other estates nearby that are not being held by a military outpost, then issue the necessary guarantees, both to persons and to places, as may be required; and the inhabitants are to be informed that they, with their produce and other supplies, may safely trade in the towns and in any place, regarding which also the commanders are obliged to do through their appropriate orders.[28]

At the same time, an appeal to the inhabitants of Prussia was published, sent by the Tsar to Prince Kutuzov for publication in the name of the Field Marshal. In this proclamation, the views of the Russian Government were expressed in relation to every nation that wished to detach themselves from Napoleon, and especially to Prussia, which had experienced so many disasters and had the opportunity to restore the power and glory formerly bequeathed to it by Frederick the Great. In conclusion, it was announced that Russian forces, upon entering Prussian territory, had received binding orders from the Sovereign Emperor to avoid any behaviour which could give rise to a disruption of the cooperation between them and the populace, and to alleviate the suffering associated with the occupation of the country in wartime by all possible means.[29]

It must be admitted that our forces, fatigued by the winter campaign and weakened by many sick men, had an essential need for rest; but, having said that, Murat, taking advantage of the pause by our light detachments, after crossing the Neman, had rallied the scattered remnants of his corps on the Vistula: *5e Corps* in Warsaw, *6e Corps* in Plotzk [Płock], *1er Corps* and *8e Corps* in Thorn, *2e Corps* and *3e Corps* in Marienburg [Malbork] and *4e Corps* in Marienwerder [Kwidzyn]; the *Garde*, in the role of rearguard, occupied Insterburg [Chernyakovsk, Kaliningrad *Oblast*], until Heudelet's division arrived to relieve them, and then withdrew to Königsberg, where there were some 10,000 men in hospital, mostly with frostbitten hands and feet, or stricken with contagious typhus, with which almost all of them ended up suffering. The distinguishing features of this disease, which carried many thousands of men to the grave at this time, were: despondency, homesickness, loss of appetite, nausea, complete slackening of the muscular system, hot and dry skin, and unbearable thirst. This disease initially appeared in military hospitals, but then it raged among the population throughout Lithuania, and in general wherever the remnants of the French army had passed. Stimulants had been of benefit in the treatment of typhus; at the onset of the disease, emetics were sometimes given. Treatment also included quinine, camphor, sulphuric ether; mustard and Spanish fly [cantharidin] were used

---

28 Army Order of the Day, for 7 [19] December, No. 85. Archive of the M.T.D. No. 36,749.
29 Declaration sent to Prince Kutuzov, under Supreme Orders dated 6 [18] December. For the original text of the declaration (in French) see Appendix XV.

as an external application. But of those afflicted by typhus, few recovered, and even they subsequently suffered from consumption of the lungs [tuberculosis], hardening of the liver, and so on.[30] Among the victims of these infections were generals Lariboisière and Éblé, who had been constantly ill since the time of the Berezina crossing. Of the hundred pontoniers who had assisted him in the construction of the bridges, only 12 had survived. Larrey [Dominique-Jean Larrey], who spent days on end in the hospitals, fell seriously ill, but recovered.[31]

Meanwhile, as the remnants of the enemy army retreated from the Neman to the Vistula, as soon as he had received reports of the taking of Vilna by our troops, Emperor Alexander I, taking measures to continue the fight against a defeated, but still dangerous enemy, set off from St Petersburg on the night of 6 to 7 (18 to 19) December, for Prince Kutuzov's headquarters. With His Majesty were: Count Arakcheev, *Oberhofmarschall* Count Tolstoy, Adjutant General Prince Volkonsky and Baron Wintzingerode, Secretary of State Shishkov and Active Councillor of State Marchenko. The main aim of the Tsar's journey was to infuse greater tenacity into the operations by our armies. And in fact, the presence of the adored Monarch among the troops who had achieved the feat of liberating the Fatherland increased the performance of each and every one. At five o'clock in the afternoon of 11 (23) December, loud cheering by the population resounded in the streets and squares of Vilna. The Tsar, in an open touring sleigh, drawn by a team of three, galloping into the courtyard of the castle, was met at the entrance by the Field Marshal, who was waiting for Him in full dress uniform. The Emperor embraced His commander, received a strength report from him, greeted the men of the Lifeguard Semenovsky who were on guard and, taking the Field Marshal by the hand, led him to His office. It is claimed that the Tsar, in a private conversation with Kutuzov, criticised him for the inaction of the army during Napoleon's retreat. The Field Marshal, acknowledging that not everything that could have been done was done, apologised for the need to act with all possible caution against a dangerous enemy.[32] But Emperor Alexander, having frankly expressed his opinion of Kutuzov's operations, considered it fair to reward the victor. Upon the Field Marshal's exit from the Tsar's office, Count Tolstoy presented him with the Order of St George, 1st class, on a silver salver. The next morning, on Emperor Alexander's birthday, 12 (24) December, the Tsar, turning to the generals who had assembled in the palace, said to them, as representatives of the entire army: 'You have saved more than Russia alone; you have saved Europe.' This was how the views of Emperor Alexander were expressed from then on. The Tsar, on this day, dined with the Field Marshal. As they drank the health of the Emperor and a cannon salute rang out, Kutuzov told the Tsar that our gunners were burning French gunpowder from captured enemy cannon. In the evening, the Emperor attended a ball hosted by the Field Marshal, who, having received captured enemy banners shortly before from Platov, scattered them at the feet of the Tsar, at the entrance to the ballroom.[33]

---

30 Roos, *Ein Jahr aus meinem Leben*.
31 Thiers, XIV, 741-742.
32 Prince Golitsyn's notes, who was serving under Kutuzov in 1812.
33 Mikhailovsky-Danilevsky, Description of the War of 1812, IV. Shishkov's notes, 74.

On the same day, 12 (24) December, the following Supreme Manifesto was promulgated:

> In the current war with the French, the majority of the population in the former Polish, now Russian, regions and districts have remained faithful to Us, which is why they share Our gratitude and goodwill along with all Our loyal subjects. But others in various ways have incurred Our righteous wrath: some, upon the enemy invasion of the borders of Our Empire, fearing violence and coercion, or dreaming of saving their property from ruin and robbery, accepted the appointments and positions imposed upon them; others, whose numbers were smaller, but whose crime is incomparably greater, even before the invasion of their lands, became adherents to the country of a foreigner alien to them and raised up in arms against Us with them, they would rather have been their shameful slaves than Our loyal subjects. These latter should face just punishment; but seeing the wrath of God poured out on them, striking them together with those under whose dominion they treacherously submitted, and yielding to the voice of mercy and pity crying out in Us, We announce Our Most Merciful general and personal amnesty, consigning everything that has passed to eternal oblivion and deep silence, and forbidding from now on the making of any claim or investigation into these matters, in full confidence that these who have fallen away from Us will feel the magnanimity of these acts towards them and will return to their *oblasts* within two months from this date. Once thereafter, if any of them should remain in the service of Our enemies, not wanting to take advantage of this Our mercy, and continuing to remain in the same crime even after forgiveness, as complete apostates, Russia will not accept such into its bosom and all their property shall be confiscated. Prisoners taken with weapons in their hands, although they are not excluded from this universal amnesty, nevertheless, We cannot follow the urges of Our heart without insulting justice until their captivity has been resolved by the conclusion of this war. However, in due time they shall enter into the rights of this Our forgiveness to each and every one. Let all participate in the universal joy of the complete extermination and destruction of the forces of the enemies of all nations, and yes, with an unburdened heart, offer the purest thanksgiving to the Almighty! Meanwhile, we hope that this forgiveness of Ours, paternalistic and by a single act of mercy, will lead to sincere repentance by the guilty, and to all the inhabitants of these *oblasts* in general, will prove that they, as a people of a similar tongue from ancient times and of a similar tribe to the Russians, nowhere and never can one be happy and safe, except in a perfect single whole merging with powerful and magnanimous Russia.
> Alexander
> Vilna, 12 [24] December, 1812.

Upon the arrival of Emperor Alexander I in Vilna, changes to the composition of the army headquarters staff followed. The Tsar, noticing that the labours and stresses of the latter campaign had greatly weakened the health and strength of the Field Marshal, began to get involved in the administration of the armies himself, moreover, those specified personalities who were with Him, were awarded special authority by the Monarch and instructed to collect the necessary information about the state of the forces and the means to supply them with all their necessities. The closest collaborator with the Tsar was, in the appointment of Chief of the General Staff, Adjutant General Prince Volkonsky 1st, with whom the Quartermaster General was von Toll, recently promoted to major general; thereafter, Lieutenant General Yermolov was appointed Chief of Artillery for all active armies. Lieutenant General Konovnitsyn was ordered to be commander of III Corps, and Lieutenant General Prince Dolgorukov, commander of VIII Corps.[34]

During the Tsar's stay in Vilna, Supreme Orders were issued on account of the reorganisation of the cavalry and troops of the engineering department.

Based on the experience of the recent campaign, finding it necessary to make some changes in the composition of the cavalry and to re-establish mounted jägers, Emperor Alexander I ordered: firstly, the reorganisation of 18 dragoon regiments: two as cuirassiers, one as hussars, seven as lancers and eight as mounted jägers.[35] Secondly, to compose all cavalry regiments (both Lifeguard and line) of six active and one replacement squadrons.[36] Initially, the troops of the engineering department were intended to be reorganised in such a way that five companies were to be expanded to form five battalions, but subsequently were ordered to form: a Lifeguard Sapper Battalion and three regiments, one of which was to be of sappers and two of pioneers, of a three-battalion establishment.[37] Later, once the Tsar was already in Merecz, the need for the siege artillery from Riga was acknowledged, and therefore Orders were issued to inspect all the bronze guns located in the Riga fortress and, selecting those that were suitable for the formation of a siege park, to construct gun carriages for them and prepare accessories for the guns and all the necessary transport.[38]

Emperor Alexander, upon his arrival in Vilna, received a report about the disastrous state of the local hospitals, filled with enemy sick and wounded. Even before

---

34 A.P. Yermolov's notes. Supreme Orders for Prince Kutuzov, dated 17 [29] December, No. 428. For further detail of these orders, see Appendix XVI.
35 Pskov Dragoons and Starodub Dragoons became cuirassiers; Irkutsk Dragoons became hussars (the hussar regiment formed by Count Saltykov was amalgamated into its composition); Yamburg Dragoons, Orenburg Dragoons, Siberia Dragoons, Zhitomir Dragoons, Vladimir Dragoons, Taganrog Dragoons and Serpukhov Dragoons became lancers; Nezhin Dragoons, Chernigov Dragoons, Arzamas Dragoons, Livland Dragoons, Seversk Dragoons, Pereyaslavl Dragoons, Tiraspol Dragoons and Dorpat Dragoons became mounted jägers. Orders for the Director of the War Ministry, Lieutenant General Prince Gorchakov, dated 17 [29] December, No. 422.
36 Orders for the Director of the War Ministry, Lieutenant General Prince Gorchakov, dated 27 December [8 January, 1813], No. 455.
37 Order for Lieutenant General Oppermann, dated 20 December [1 January, 1813], No. 436, and Orders for the Director of the War Ministry, Lieutenant General Prince Gorchakov, dated 27 December [8 January, 1813], No. 456.
38 Orders for the inspector of artillery, Lieutenant General Baron Meller-Zakomelsky, dated 29 December [10 January 1813], No. 459.

the arrival of our army, these unfortunates were dying, deprived of proper supervision and aid. Their corpses were lying in the streets or stacked around the hospitals in great heaps. From time to time, the survivors were given some hard tack; the sick lay on the bare floors in cold, damp rooms; they had neither straw nor firewood to keep warm; no water to quench their thirsts. There they lay, covered with flies and all kinds of filth, alongside the corpses of their dead comrades. In the mornings, there were dedicated teams to throw the bodies out through doors and windows into the street, contaminating the already foul air of the sufferers' residence. Under such circumstances, the malign spread of typhus and death were inevitable. Every physician who had the misfortune to observe the course of this epidemic agrees that only a tenth of the sick recovered. Such was the fate of those incarcerated in Vilna's hospitals, which presented a true semblance of hell, when Emperor Alexander appeared there like a comforting angel. 'Such was the fate of the prisoners' wrote a French historian of the war of 1812, 'when Alexander, following the promptings of his heart alone, wished to see their situation with his own eyes; he was not afraid to visit those terrible, stinking quarters, in which the contaminated air was a destructive vehicle for disease. My God! What a spectacle was revealed to the eyes of this Sovereign, still heady from the triumph of victory! Monarch of Russia! On this day, you performed one of the kindest deeds of your life.'[39]

Grand Duke Konstantin Pavlovich competed with him in the virtuous cause. According to one of the French generals, who owed his salvation to Him, 'the Grand Duke ordered treatment of French officers found by Himself in hospitals, under his own supervision, also even in his own chambers. He visited the afflicted himself, consoling them with kindness and tenderness. He even carried one of the officers out of a burning building, while his valet was saving another; prompted by the generous tendency of his heart, he paid no attention to the deadly infections and was himself exposed to them. Many French officers, plucked from the jaws of death through his humanity, owe him their lives, myself included' wrote the author (the renowned Vaudoncourt), 'and I justly owe him a debt of gratitude.'[40]

Emperor Alexander, deeply moved by the situation of the sick and wounded prisoners, entrusted their care to one of his adjutant generals, Count Saint-Priest, who proved himself a worthy executor of the will of the benevolent Monarch. All prisoners located in Vilna received proper subsistence; in the hospitals there was no distinction between our patients and those of the enemy.[41]

If it has already been pre-destined by Eternal Providence that war must serve as the last resort (*ultima ratio*) in disagreements arising between peoples, then let Monarchs like the Blessed Alexander emerge to console the friends of humanity, and let the sounds of battle then merge with the prayers of the unfortunates for the Benefactor from their adversaries.

---

39 Chambray, III, 147.
40 Chambray, III, 148. Vaudoncourt, *Mémoires pour servir à l'histoire de la guerre entre la France et la Russie en 1812*, 324.
41 Chambray, III, 147-148.

45

The retreat of Schwarzenberg's and Reynier's Corps to the Russian frontier

The march of the Austrian corps from Kobrin to Slonim and the Saxon corps from Brest to Ruzhany. – The withdrawal of Saken's corps into Volhynia. – Inaction. – Movements against the Austro-Saxon army by Russian detachments, initially Ozharovsky's and Davydov's, and then by Tuchkov's, Radt's and Saken's corps. – Vasilchikov's and Miloradovich's offensive with elements of the Main Army. – Schwarzenberg's retreat toward Bialystok and Reynier's behind the river Lesna. – Davydov's liberation of Grodno. – Schwarzenberg's and Reynier's retreat into the Duchy of Warsaw. – Our diplomatic relations with the Austrians. – The surrender of Warsaw and the retreat by the Austrian corps to the borders of Galicia, and Reynier's to Kalisz.

On 13 (25) November, on the very day of the arrival of the headquarters of the Austrian corps in Kobrin, a dispatch was received there from the French *ministre des Relations extérieures*, Maret, regarding the need for a quick march by the Austro-Saxon army to Minsk, which forced Schwarzenberg, after resting his troops on 14 (26) November, to depart the very next day in the indicated direction. On 19 November (1 December), the Austrian corps arrived at Pruzhany, from where it moved to Slonim a few days later. While still on the march, Schwarzenberg, having received another letter from Maret, sent on 20 November (2 December), with news of Napoleon's crossing of the Berezina and his successes over Russian forces, pushed his vanguard forward, under the command of General Frimont [Johann Maria Philipp Freiherr Frimont von Palota], from Slonim to Nesvizh and sent fighting patrols towards Minsk and Slutsk, in order to operate against the Russian troops driven away from the Berezina, but accurate intelligence was delivered to him from Vilna (*sic*). Upon arrival at Slonim, Schwarzenberg was baffled by Maret's dispatch dated 22 November (4 December), in which, together with details of the alleged French victory on the Berezina, the Austrian Commander-in-Chief had been ordered, on behalf of Emperor Napoleon, 'to follow the movements of the army and manoeuvre in respect of its current location.' Since nothing was said about 'the current location of the army,' Schwarzenberg halted at Slonim, waiting for more definitive orders.[1]

Reynier's corps and Durrutte's division arrived in Brest-Litovsk on 14 (26) November, on the very day that the Austrian force halted for a rest day in Kobrin. The troops from both corps, from the very beginning of the march from Wołkowysk, had slept in bivouacs and in sheds in the snow; upon reaching Brest and Kobrin themselves, orders were given to place the men in quarters. Reynier remained in Brest until 18 (30) November, and then followed Schwarzenberg to Ruzhany and, having arrived there on 25 November (7 December), deployed his troops in the vicinity of this town.[2]

On our side, General Saken, withdrew behind the Mukhavets on the night of 11 to 12 (23 to 24) November and might have stopped there without continuing to retreat, which had brought significant losses with it, but had diverted the Austro-Saxon army towards the Bug, and had contributed to the success of our operations in the main theatre of war. In all probability, the enemy would not decisively attack the positions held by our corps on the Bug, because a victory would bring them little, and if they, having defeated Saken, pursued him further and moved into Volhynia, they would become dislocated and would be even farther from the *Grande Armée*. General Saken, recognising these factors, wanted to stay close to the enemy in order to follow all their movements relentlessly; but a shortage of rations, after the evacuation of Brest, forced him to withdraw, to get closer to the magazines established in Volhynia. Having the holding of Pinsk with at least part of his corps in mind, in order to make it difficult for Schwarzenberg to communicate with Napoleon's main body and to maintain liaison with other Russian formations as they advanced from the Berezina to Minsk and Slonim, General Saken ordered Essen 3rd to withdraw to Ratno with part of his corps stationed on the left wing of the overall deployment. The remaining troops under Saken withdrew in two columns, of which one proceeded up the Bug, and the other towards Kovel; and settled down between this town and Luboml, with the corps headquarters in the town of Dolsk, from 20 to 23 November (2 to 5 December). Meanwhile, Essen, having received orders to go to Pinsk on 18 (30) November, in Luchitsy [Luchychi, Ukraine], near Ratno, in order to liaise with Chichagov's force, could not comply with this, because the enemy had occupied Pinsk and devastated the magazines we had set up there; General Essen, having learned of this, moved along the Kovel road, to Datin, towards Kolki, on 23 November (5 December), and having arrived there, he continued in order to link up with the Army of the Danube, on Chichagov's orders, diverting via Novograd-Volynsk [Zvyahel] and Ovruch. According to Prince Kutuzov, 'as a result of this dispersal of forces, the army lost two corps for the duration of the operation, because, after Essen's secondment, Saken's corps had to retreat to Luboml due to its weakness, while Lieutenant

---

1 '… elle (sa majesté) attache la plus grande importance à ce que vous siuviez le mouvement de l'armée et que vous manoeuvriez dans le sens de la position actuelle.' Chambray, *Histoire de l'expédition de Russie*, II, 410, & III, 89-90.
2 Chambray, III, 90. Funck, *Erinnerungen aus dem Feldzuge in Russland im Jahr 1812*, 193.

General Essen's corps wasted time in pointless marches.'[3] Meanwhile, as the fate of the war was being decided between the main armies, the forces of both sides in Volhynia remained in complete inactivity. Schwarzenberg's successes were limited to occupying the sector from Wołkowysk to Brest and Kobrin; this temporary advantage had come at a high cost: the Saxon *7e Corps* had been reduced to 10,000 men, the Austrian to 20,000, and Durutte's division to 5,000; the mobilisation of the Duchy of Warsaw did not justify the hopes of our enemies. In contrast, Saken would be reinforced by the troops left in Volhynia as he retreated. Cossacks intercepted the foragers of the Austro-Saxon army, which began to lack for everything. At the same time as the arrival of Schwarzenberg in Slonim and Reynier in Ruzhany, the temperature dropped to some 28 degrees below freezing; almost no-one avoided frozen hands or feet, and among the victims of the cold were the generals including Reynier himself.[4]

After Napoleon had crossed the Berezina, the detachments under Colonel Davydov had been sent directly to the Neman as was Adjutant General Count Ozharovsky to the left of the Main Army, towards Belitsa: the latter was to monitor Schwarzenberg's corps. Following the occupation of Vilna by our forces, the following formations were sent to oppose the Austro-Saxon army (as mentioned above):

1. Tuchkov's corps (formerly Ertel's), and eight replacement battalions under Radt from Minsk via Nesvizh and Saken's corps from Kovel towards Brest, under the overall command of General Tormasov and later Dokhturov.
2. A vanguard from the Main Army, under the command of Adjutant General Vasilchikov, towards Mosty.[5]

In support of all these detachments, II Corps, IV Corps and II Cavalry Corps were assigned, under the overall command of General Miloradovich, and sent towards Grodno. Finally, the force under General Essen 3rd, who had been detached, by order of Admiral Chichagov, from Saken's corps and was marching to Novograd-Volynsk, were ordered to join Dokhturov.[6]

Subsequently, it emerged that there was no need for brute force of arms in order to induce Schwarzenberg to evacuate our territory. Staff Captain Löwenstern [Vladimir Ivanovich Levenshtern or Woldemar Hermann von Löwenstern], sent from Count Ozharovsky's detachment with a large Cossack patrol in order to reconnoitre the enemy, on 28 November (10 December), captured two Hungarian hussars and sent them to the commander of the detachment. Löwenstern went to Belitsa himself,

---

3 War Diary of General Essen 3rd's corps, archive of the M.T.D. No. 16,646. *Journal militaire de opérations du Corps sous les ordres de lieutenant-général baron de Saken*, archive of the M.T.D. No. 29,180. Prince Kutuzov's report to the Tsar, dated 10 [22] December, No. 713.
4 Funck, 192-194.
5 Vasilchikov's detachment consisted of: IV Cavalry Corps, one jäger regiment and another of Cossacks. Subsequently, on the disbandment of Count Ozharovsky's detachment, four more Cossack regiments were transferred from him to the detachment under Vasilchikov.
6 Prince Kutuzov's report to the Tsar, dated 1 [13] December, No. 644, and dated 10 [22] December, No. 713.

where the Austrian general Mohr was stationed with 3,000 men, and posing as a *parlementaire*, had a meeting with Mohr, who announced to Löwenstern that he had been ordered to hold a line on the right bank of the Neman and that he intended to remain in place so long as nobody disturbed him. 'At the same time' added Mohr, 'having learned of the approach of your troops towards me and not wanting a battle with you, I have sent a report to Prince Schwarzenberg and shall remain pending his orders.' Following these discussions, which revealed the total cooling of the Austrians towards Napoleon, Count Ozharovsky ordered a release of prisoners, and received thanks from the Field Marshal, who gave orders to continue to deal with the Austrians as gently as possible.[7] In all probability, General Mohr had been ordered to avoid engaging with our troops, because soon after the dispatch from Count Ozharovsky, the Austrian detachment began to withdraw through Rozhanka towards Grodno. The Hungarian hussars mixing with the Cossacks, called them comrades and claimed that they had been forbidden from fighting with the Russians.[8] Prince Schwarzenberg had very comprehensively realised that he could no longer be of any use to the remnants of the *Grande Armée*, which was retreating a considerable distance from him, towards Molodechno and Vilna, whereas, if he remained in Lithuania with the weakened Austro-Saxon army, he would be in danger of being attacked and overwhelmed by superior forces. Moreover, at that time he already had confirmed intelligence of the destruction of Napoleon's army, which allowed him to take a completely different course from the policy of the Viennese Court. All these circumstances forced the Austrian Commander-in-Chief to pay attention exclusively to the preservation of his force, which he could achieve only by a hasty retreat to the Duchy of Warsaw, while Reynier, who commanded a small corps, was forced to conform to the actions by Schwarzenberg. On 2 (14) December, the Austrian corps set off from Slonim towards Bialystok, covered from the left flank by Mohr's detachment, moving from Belitsa, to Mosty, also towards Bialystok, and from the right by the Saxon corps, retreating from Ruzhany to Wysokie-Litewskie. On 6 (18) December, Schwarzenberg placed the main body of his corps in quarters in the vicinity of Bialystok, between Narewka and Grodno; while, on the following day [19 December], Reynier also took up a rather extended position on the right bank of the Lesna river, between Wołczyn and Kamieniec, detaching 700 Polish troops with two guns to Brest-Litovsk. But a few days later, the enemy commanders were forced to retreat into the Duchy of Warsaw.

At the same time as Schwarzenberg was withdrawing to Bialystok, Adjutant General Count Ozharovsky, having arrived outside Grodno with his detachment, where General Fröhlich was stationed with 3,000 Austrian troops, demanded that he surrender the city, and having received a refusal, reported this to army headquarters. But when, the next day, 7 (19) December, the partisan Davydov approached Grodno with a much smaller detachment, then the matter took a completely different turn. Having captured two Austrian soldiers, Davydov, mindful of the order from the

---

7   Adjutant General Count Ozharovsky's report to Commander First Army, General Tormasov, dated 1 [13] December, No. 55, from Voronovo.
8   Adjutant General Ozharovsky's report to Duty General Konovnitsyn, dated 3 [15] December, No. 66, from Lida.

Field Marshal to deal with the Austrians as gently as possible, released the prisoners and had them inform Fröhlich of the complete annihilation of Napoleon's army, reminding him that our Government had constantly been seeking to restore the friendly relations that had long existed between Russia and Austria. General Fröhlich, visiting the outposts, expressed his readiness to avoid a hostile clash with our forces, and even agreed to surrender the city, but only if he were permitted to destroy the magazines located there. But Davydov, informing Fröhlich that such an act would show obvious hostility by the Austrians towards the Russians, convinced him to leave Grodno, leaving the magazines intact, and entered the city on 8 (20) December, from where the Austrian troops left for Bialystok.[9] In order to induce Schwarzenberg to retreat without resorting to brute force, Adjutant General Vasilchikov was ordered to get behind the left flank of the Austrian forces stationed in the vicinity of Bialystok, at Tykocin; but even before receiving this order, Vasilchikov had managed to achieve the objective of this operation. Colonel Yuzefovich, who commanded his leading detachment, having arrived at the outposts of Austrian Lieutenant Colonel Latour at Supraśl, told him that General Vasilchikov wanted to have a meeting with Prince Schwarzenberg, who, having learned of this and being acquainted with Vasilchikov from his time in the embassy in St Petersburg, invited him to come to the headquarters of the Austrian Corps. At that time Vasilchikov, having recently fallen from his horse, had injured his arm, whereupon he sent Major General Prince Shcherbatov with a letter for Schwarzenberg, who from the first words expressed a desire to resolve the matter without bloodshed. Schwarzenberg agreed to evacuate our territory, but in a conversation with Prince Shcherbatov he made it clear that the Austrian troops, having withdrawn into the Duchy of Warsaw, would go into winter quarters; in the event, however, that there was no consent on our part, he would find it necessary to meet force with force. Prince Shcherbatov replied that, as General Vasilchikov had not been authorised to make any negotiations, he could not take a decision upon himself on this matter.[10] On 13 (25) December, the Austrian corps set off from Bialystok and withdrew through Wysokie Mazowieckie towards Pultusk, where they settled in quarters, occupying outposts from Nur to Zambrów. The next day [26 December], Vasilchikov, having occupied Bialystok and received the order from Prince Kutuzov, to get behind the left flank of the Austrians, moved on to Wizna and halted there awaiting further orders from headquarters. Following this, he was instructed to halt in Wizna with the regular troops and give them a

---

9 Colonel Davydov's reports to Duty General Konovnitsyn, dated 9 and 14 December. A.P. Yermolov's notes.
10 Adjutant General Vasilchikov's report to Duty General Konovnitsyn, dated 13 [25] December, No. 183. With this report, a copy of the following letter from him to Prince Schwarzenberg was attached: '*Monsieur le maréchal! Le lieutenant-colonel Latour, ayant fait entrevoir au colonel Jozefovitch la possibilité pour moi d'avoir l'honneur de voir Votre Altesse à Souprasle, je me félicitais d'une entrevue aussi honorable. Le sort en a décidé autrement, car revenant de mes avant-postes ce matin je fis une chute de cheval et me demis un bras et bien que je me vois forcé de me servir d'une main étrangère et d'envoyer le général prince Scherbatoff prier Votre Altesse d'agréer mes excuses. Il sera l'interprète de mes sentimens et du desir que j'ai de faire tout ce qui pourrait Vous être agreable, Monsieur le maréchal, ainsi que des regrets bien sincères d'être privé pour le moment de l'honneur de vous présenter mes hommages.*'

rest, while the Cossack regiments were to shadow Schwarzenberg, restricting themselves to monitoring his movements.[11] At the same time, by Supreme Command, the diplomat Anstett [Ivan Osipovich Anstett or Johann Protasius von Anstett] was sent to Prince Schwarzenberg, with secret instructions issued by the Field Marshal, which determined the conditions under which he was permitted to conclude a truce.[12] But Anstett was unable to reach his destination before the Austrian corps had already withdrawn to Pultusk on 18 (30) December. They remained there for four weeks, sending light detachments to collect provisions and fodder as far as Różan on the Narew river and to Brok on the Bug. Reynier crossed the Bug at Drohiczyn and went into quarters to the right of the Austrian corps, at Węgrów, behind the river Liwiec, while the Polish corps under Prince Poniatowski was located in the vicinity of Warsaw. Overall, the Allied forces reached some 40,000 men.[13] Although the Saxon Government continued to raise the population of the Duchy of Warsaw in arms against Russia, nonetheless, these attempts were not successful.[14] The position of the Austrian Government at this time was ambiguous: swayed, on the one hand, by popular sympathy for the Russians and the desire to throw off the shackles imposed by Napoleon, and, on the other, by the fear that Russia might extend its borders at the expense of Austria, the Viennese Cabinet tried to put itself in a neutral position and buy the time they needed to complete their mobilisation. For our part, in order to maintain the friendly disposition of the Austrians, on several occasions their officers and soldiers taken prisoner were released. On 25 December (6 January 1813), General Saken reported to Duty General Konovnitsyn that Cossacks, having encountered an Austrian picket, had captured an officer and seven hussars, who were sent back. 'Fortunately' wrote Saken, 'nobody was killed or wounded.'[15]

Our attitude towards the Saxon force was not like that at all. The attempts of the Saxon Government to inflame an uprising against Russia in Poland, and even in Lithuania and Volhynia, produced mutual animosity between Russians and Saxons. After retreating into the duchy, Reynier, having received orders from Warsaw to confine himself to defence, wanted to open negotiations with General Saken via Prince Schwarzenberg, the pretext for which was the demand on our part to return Major Trocki, who had broken his word of honour and escaped from captivity. Reynier would not comply with this demand, offering an exchange of prisoners, but Saken would not agree to execute his request.

On our part, upon the retreat of the Austro-Saxon army beyond the Russian borders, the following orders were issued: the detachment under Adjutant General Vasilchikov was instructed to follow the force under Schwarzenberg;[16] the corps

---

11 Orders for Adjutant General Vasilchikov, dated 10 [22] December, No. 710, and dated 18 [30] December, No. 758.
12 For the secret instructions issued to Active State Councillor Anstett in full, see Appendix XVII.
13 Thiers, *Histoire du Consulat et de L'Empire*, XIV, Edit. de Brux, 743.
14 '... L'insurrection nationale ne fait guères des progrès. Les têtes sont refroidies généralement, et la manière dont notre avant-garde s'est conduite ici fait le meilleur effet.' From Active State Councillor Anstett's letter to Prince Kutuzov, dated 21 December [2 January 1813].
15 Lieutenant General Saken's letter, dated 25 December [6 January 1813], No. 1,489.
16 Orders dated 21 December [2 January 1813], No. 774, archive of the M.T.D. No. 29,172.

under Lieutenant General Saken was to halt in the town of Granne on the Bug, monitoring the retreating enemy with light detachments; the force under General Essen 3rd, which consisted (on his secondment to Bobruisk, to form 48 battalions), under the command of Lieutenant General Prince Volkonsky, who had arrived in Pinsk on 16 (28) December and were intended to arrive in Bialystok by 31 December (12 January, 1813), were ordered to move towards Brest and come under the direct command of General Saken.[17] A new vanguard was set up, under the command of Adjutant General Wintzingerode, from Tuchkov's detachment, II Corps under Prinz Eugen von Württemberg and Lanskoy's and Davydov's detachments, in total some 40 battalions, 40 squadrons, nine Cossack regiments and six batteries, numbering around 16,000 men with 69 guns.[18] The detachment under Major General Radt was left in Bialystok for the time being.[19] The main force under Prince Kutuzov, together with the headquarters, moved to the Neman and entered the Duchy of Warsaw in three columns, moving around the left flank of the Austro-Saxon army: the left column under General Miloradovich's command (which, together with Vasilchikov's detachment that had joined it, consisted of IV Corps,VII Corps and II Cavalry Corps, III Cavalry Corps and IV Cavalry Corps), went from Radziłów to the town of Przasnysz; the centre under General Dokhturov, of VI Corps and VIII Corps, through Augustów and Szczuczyn towards Chorzele; the right under General Tormasov, of III Corps and V Corps with both cuirassier divisions, through Suwałki and Lyck [Ełk], towards Willenberg [Wielbark]. Thus, our Main Army was directed at the left wing of the army of Prince Schwarzenberg, while General Saken, on the basis of the orders issued to him, was to remain facing him frontally in an over-watch position, to be ready to operate around the right flank of the Austro-Saxon army, should Schwarzenberg turn against the left wing of our Main Army.[20] In fact, militarily, the neutrality of the Austrian corps was disadvantageous for us, because we, having superiority in numbers of troops on our side, could have more quickly achieved the objective of operations through force of arms rather than by negotiation, but, having said that, Austrian neutrality, being the first step towards their acceptance of participation in the coalition against Napoleon, had a paramount influence on the course of the war.

The situation of the Austro-Saxon army became very precarious once the retreat of Napoleon's other forces enabled us to threaten Schwarzenberg with being

---

17 Orders for General Saken, dated 17 [29] December, No. 746 and dated 21 December [2 January 1813], No. 778. Orders for Essen 3rd, dated 17 [29] December, No. 748 and dated 21 December [2 January 1813], No. 776. Orders for Prince Volkonsky, dated the 21 December [2 January 1813], No. 779.
18 Orders for Lieutenant General Baron Wintzingerode, dated 24 December [5 January 1813], No. 792. For a full listing of General Wintzingerode's detachment, see Appendix XVIII.
19 Order for Major General Radt, dated 21 December [2 January 1813], No. 781, archive of the M.T.D. No. 29,172.
20 General disposition, on the occasion of the transition of the Main Army over the border, attached to the orders for General Dokhturov, dated 30 December [11 January 1813], No. 822. Orders for General Saken, dated 31 December [12 January 1813], No. 831. Orders for General Miloradovich, dated 31 December [12 January 1813], No. 833. Archive of the M.T.D. No. 29,172.

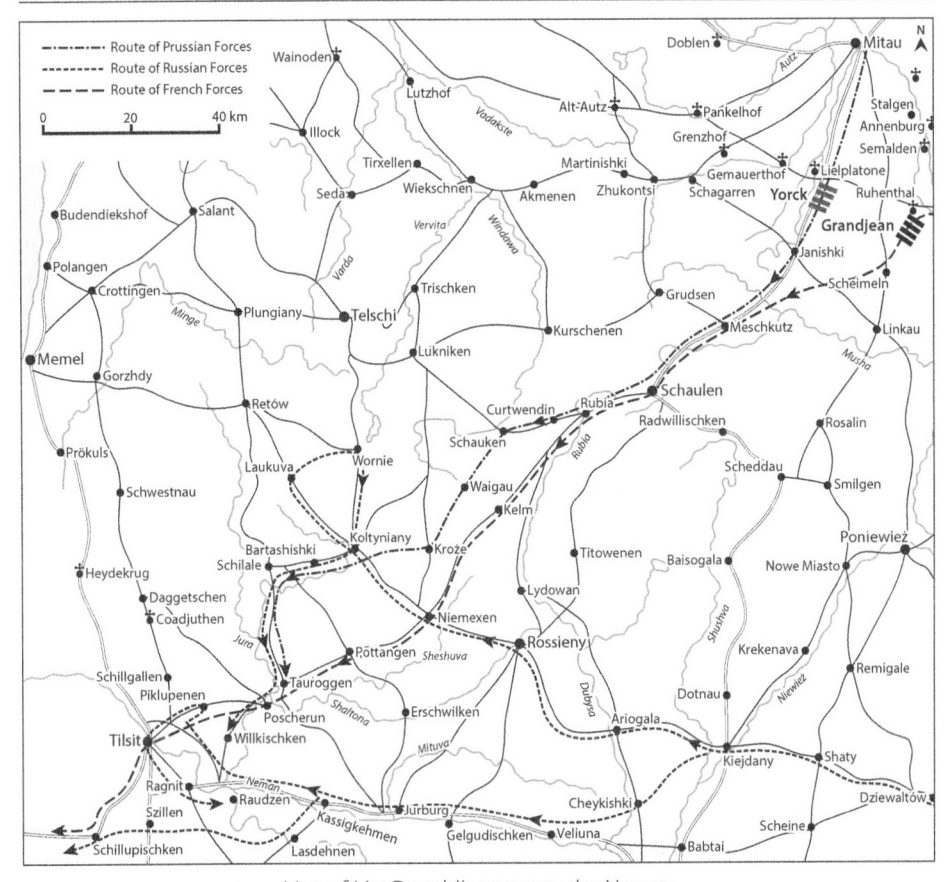

Map of MacDonald's retreat to the Neman.

enveloped from the left flank. Wanting to gain time, he opened negotiations with Anstett, and although the convention drawn up on this occasion was not approved, as agreed, by signature, however, the truce between our and the Austrian troops was observed in practice to full effect;[21] the forward outposts of both sides stood within sight of one another quite calmly, and even fraternised among themselves; Russian officers travelled to Pultusk to purchase all their necessities. Murat himself, having received reports of a truce coming into force between the Austrians and Russians, and realising its benefits exclusively in a military sense, completely approved of Schwarzenberg's orders. 'The King' Berthier wrote to him, 'would be very pleased if you manage to conclude a tacit truce (*un armistice tacite et non ecrit*), which would allow you to rest the troops, both yours and General Reynier's, without obligating you to anything, as soon as the troops operating against you turn towards some other location.' Schwarzenberg, in order to protect the Saxon force, suggested to General Saken that they be recognised as neutral, on a par with the Austrians; but

---

21 For the draft convention for an armistice between Russian and Austrian troops, see Appendix XIX.

there was no consent to this proposal on our part, and therefore the Austrians, in order to bring peace to their allies, sometimes had to shield their positions with their outposts. Under these circumstances, Reynier with the Saxon and Polish forces was forced to retreat to the Vistula, at the end of the year (10 January, 1813 new style), and then move to the left bank of the river, holding the bridgeheads at Praga and Modlin. The evacuation of Warsaw by the allied troops, as a result of orders received from Kaiser Franz by Prince Schwarzenberg, on 10 (22) January, 1813, and the occupation of this city by Russian troops on 27 January (8 February), caused a retreat by the Allies in various directions. The Austrians went to Kraków; the Poles, having left a garrison in Modlin, headed in the same direction, while the Saxons moved towards Kalisz. Thus ended the involuntary participation by the Austrian Government in Napoleon's invasion of Russia.

46

The pursuit of MacDonald's Corps by Russian forces

Count Wittgenstein's orders seeking to sever MacDonald's route. – General Paulucci's orders. – Circumstances that delayed MacDonald's departure from Courland. – His order of march. – The seizure of Memel by Paulucci's troops and further movements by Wittgenstein and his force. – MacDonald's retreat to Tilsit and General Diebitsch's situation on Yorck's line of retreat to Kołtyniany. – Action at Piklupenen.

Negotiations between our generals and Yorck. – His relationship with MacDonald. – Yorck's meeting with Diebitsch. – Movements of the detachments towards Tilsit. – The offensive by the remaining forces under Count Wittgenstein and Löwis' detachment. – The Convention of Posherun. – Yorck's letter to King Friedrich Wilhelm III. – Massenbach's defection from Macdonald. – Letters by Yorck and Massenbach to MacDonald. – MacDonald's onward retreat. – Factors preventing the severing of his route. – Action at Labiau. – The liberation of Königsberg by Russian forces. – Assimilation of the detachments under Löwis and Zhemchuzhnikov into Wittgenstein's corps. – The importance of the defection of Yorck's corps from the French.

After the rest-day granted to the main body of the independent I Corps in Rechki, on 25 November (7 December), Count Wittgenstein moved to Voistom on the following day [8 December] and advanced down the Viliya river to Chervonny Dvor, where he arrived on 1 (13) December and halted there until 5 (17) December, both in order to give the troops a rest, and to link up with detachments under Major General Novak and Colonel Pahlen, a total of 7,000 men, marching from Vitebsk and joining the corps on 3 (15) December.[1] Meanwhile, intelligence had been received at I Corps headquarters that MacDonald was still in Courland. Count Wittgenstein, hoping to sever his line of retreat, sent Borozdin's detachment, under the command of Major

---

[1] The force under Novak and Pahlen consisted of: 26th Jägers, two guns, and two groups (7th Group and 8th Group) of Novgorod *Opolchenie* from General Steinheil's corps, 2nd Marines from General Berg's corps, three groups (16th Group, 17th Group and 18th Group) of St Petersburg *Opolchenie* and 12 guns from 25th Artillery Brigade from General Foch's reserves.

General Diebitsch, to Rossieny [Raseiniai], in order to reconnoitre MacDonald's direction of travel on his return march to the Neman, and sent a detachment under Adjutant General Kutuzov, supported by Vlastov's vanguard towards Tilsit, by forced marches, in order to fix MacDonald on the right bank of the Neman until the arrival of the main body of the independent I Corps to cut across the enemy.[2]

A large part of the Riga garrison was given the mission to pursue MacDonald from behind.

Back in October, Lieutenant General Essen 1st was relieved due to illness and the Riga military governor, Adjutant General Marquis Paulucci [Filipp Osipovich Paulucci or Filippo Paulucci], was appointed in his place.[3] On the occasion of his confirmation in command over his senior in rank, Lieutenant General Löwis, Emperor Alexander honoured the latter with the following rescript:

> Lieutenant General Löwis. Due to poor health, Lieutenant General Essen 1st has been relieved of the appointment of Riga military governor, My Adjutant General, Marquis Paulucci, is appointed in his place.
>
> I am sure that you, even in this event, will not cease to show the same diligence in service, which, to My pleasure, has been noted during your time under the command of Lieutenant General Essen.
>
> Adjutant General to Myself, a title borne by Marquis Paulucci, is likewise appointed as the military governor, regardless of being subordinate to you in seniority.
>
> I shall be pleased to see, in this case, further evidence of your diligent service and to offer you proof of My goodwill towards you.

In early [mid] December, General Paulucci, having received orders from Prince Kutuzov to send Lieutenant General Löwis with his detachment to link up with Count Wittgenstein, had detached 7,000 infantry and 1,200 cavalry from the troops of the Riga garrison, who were to accompany General Löwis to Eckau [Iecava, Latvia]. Paulucci intended to move towards Memel [Klaipėda, Lithuania] himself, with 2,500 men.[4]

Meanwhile, during the retreat by Napoleon's headquarters from the Berezina to Vilna, Berthier and Murat, preoccupied with the disasters of the *Grande Armée*, neglected to notify MacDonald of their retreat. He received the first information about the troubles of the French forces from our official communiques on military operations, and although he could not immediately withdraw to the Neman on the basis of such information, they nevertheless convinced him of a rapid retreat by Napoleon's main army to Vilna, and onwards to the Neman. Under such circumstances, commanding a corps of which two-thirds consisted of Prussian troops whose allegiance to Napoleon could not be counted upon, MacDonald, awaiting orders from the headquarters, concentrated Grandjean's division [Charles Louis

---

2   *Précis des opérations du 1er Corps*, archive of the M.T.D. No. 29,200.
3   Supreme Rescript to General Essen, dated 14 [26] October.
4   Prince Kutuzov's orders for Lieutenant General Marquis Paulucci, dated 9 [21] December, No. 705. For a breakdown of Löwis' detachment, see Appendix XX.

Dieudonné Grandjean] at Bauske; Yorck [Johann David Ludwig von Yorck] held Mitau [Jelgava, Latvia] with his force, while headquarters *10e Corps* was in Stalgen [Staļģene, Latvia], on the Aa [Lielupe] river.[5] MacDonald, concerned about being cut off from the Neman, was already preparing to retreat, when, finally, on 6 (18) December, he received orders from the emperor sent to him from Vilna on 27 November (9 December). The Prussian officer who was instructed to deliver the vital dispatch about the withdrawal of *10e Corps*, Major Schenck, did not dare to take the direct route, but went via Olita and Tilsit, where, having found relatives, he stayed with them for several hours to rest. Major Lützow [Ludwig Adolf Wilhelm Freiherr von Lützow?] wrote that when MacDonald asked about the state of the *Grand Armée*, Schenck replied: 'the cavalry are without horses, the artillery without cannon and the infantry are frozen.'[6] Having received such disappointing news, on that same day, 6 (18) December, MacDonald sent all the transport along the roads leading to Tilsit and Memel, and on 7 (19) December set out to Janishki [Ioniškis] towards Schaulen with his first echelon, which consisted of Grandjean's division and part of the Prussian force, under the command of General Massenbach [Eberhard Friedrich Fabian von Massenbach];[7] another echelon, consisting of the rest of the Prussian force, under the command of generals Yorck and Kleist [Friedrich Emil Ferdinand Heinrich von Kleist], moved a day later, 8 (20) December, and followed the first at a distance of one stage.[8] Upon reaching Kołtyniany [Kaltinėnai], it was decided to continue the retreat to Tilsit in two columns: MacDonald towards Coadjuthen [Katyčiai, Lithuania] with Grandjean's and Massenbach's troops, while Yorck and Kleist headed for Tauroggen [Tauragė, Lithuania].[9]

From our side, Count Wittgenstein having departed from Chervonny Dvor on 5 (17) December, arrived in Wiłkomierz on 7 (19) December, while Diebitsch had by then reached Rossieny with his detachment. The next day, 8 (20) December, noting the retreat of MacDonald, Paulucci left his pursuit to Löwis, while he moved towards Mitau himself, ejected Yorck's rearguard and liberated the city at dawn on 9 (21) December; thereafter, he marched on Memel and entered there after the capitulation of the local commandant on 15 (27) December. Upon the seizure of Memel, 26 cannon, nine gunboats, 30 merchant ships (of which 18 were owned by residents of the city), 900 serviceable muskets, 26,000 cartridges, around 12,000 *Pud* of flour and bread, and rather significant quantities of oats, salt and colonial goods, were discovered. General Paulucci appointed a Russian commandant in Memel, as to a city conquered by force of arms; but Count Wittgenstein later countermanded this order.[10]

---

5 Chambray, *Histoire de l'expédition de Russie*, III, 148-149.
6 '*la cavalerie est sans chevaux, l'artillerie sans canons et l'infanterie gelée.*'
7 Massenbach's force consisted of: six battalions, ten squadrons and two batteries, in total, some 4,000 to 5,000 men.
8 Yorck's and Kleist's force consisted of: 13 or 14 battalions, four squadrons, and four batteries, for a total of 10,000 to 12,000 men.
9 Clausewitz, *Der Feldzug v. 1812 in Russland*, 208.
10 War Diary signed off by Prince Kutuzov. Orders from General Paulucci to the Commandant of Memel, Colonel von Ekesparre, dated 27 December [8 January 1813], No. 385.

In the meantime, the main body under Count Wittgenstein moved from Wiłkomierz, through Shaty, to Kiejdany, on 10 (22) December. Diebitsch's detachment, moving from Rossieny across MacDonald's line of communications, had passed Kołtyniany and as early as the previous day, 9 (21) December, was at Laukuva, 140 *versts* from the corps. The detachment under Adjutant General Kutuzov was approaching Tilsit on 9 (21) December; his vanguard, under the command of Lieutenant-Colonel Tettenborn, after a minor skirmish near Tilsit, occupied this town and took possession of one gun and the significant magazines. As the detachment under Vlastov, who had joined the force under Adjutant General Kutuzov, was moving away from the corps for several stages, on 11 (23) December a new vanguard was formed, numbering 3,500 infantry and 700 cavalry, with six horse artillery pieces, under the command of Major General Shepelev [Dmitry Dmitrievich Shepelev].[11] At the same time, Adjutant General Kutuzov received orders to hold the defile at Piklupenen [Piktupėnai] in order to stop MacDonald on his way to Tilsit and give time for the main body of the corps to close up. In Kiejdany, 25 guns were left behind, requiring remounts and physical repairs;[12] while two groups of St Petersburg *Opolchenie* were left as their escort.

General Diebitsch, having no intelligence about the direction taken by MacDonald, had no doubt that he had turned towards Memel, for onward movement along the [Kurische] Nehrung to Königsberg. This assumption compelled Diebitsch to continue to advance through Zhmud, in the direction of Memel, in order to accomplish his mission of cutting off MacDonald. As has already been mentioned, Diebitsch's detachment had reached Laukuva on 9 (21) December; its vanguard, under the command of Colonel Sukhozanet, was to advance at an interval of one stage, to Retów [Rietavas]. In Laukuva, Diebitsch learned of the enemy movement through Schaulen and on 10 (22) December he turned towards Wornie [Varniai]. Here intelligence was received about the location of an enemy rearguard at Waigau [Vaiguva], which prompted Diebitsch to move to Kołtyniany on 12 (24) December, in order to operate on MacDonald's flank during his onward march to the Neman. Several sutlers from Massenbach's detachment revealed that the entire force moving along this route had already passed, except for two squadrons and two jäger companies proceeding as the rearguard. On the basis of this intelligence, Diebitsch, having recalled his vanguard, stationed a detachment of 1,400 men with six guns on the line of retreat of the enemy rearguard.[13] He was completely unaware that this rearguard from the leading echelon was being followed by the entire column under Yorck and Kleist, numbering more than 10,000 men.

Indeed, this force, having set out from their location, in the vicinity of Mitau, the day after Grandjean and Massenbach, and having the heavy baggage with

---

11 Shepelev's vanguard consisted of the Tenginsk Infantry and 25th Jägers, who were to be joined by the Combined Lifeguard and the Combined Dragoon regiments also detached earlier from the main force, under the command of Colonel Albrecht; with six guns from 23rd Horse Artillery Company. *Précis de opérations du 1er Corps*.
12 Six guns from 27th Battery Artillery Company, seven guns from 9th Light Artillery Company and 12 guns from 25th Artillery Brigade. *Précis de opérations du 1er Corps*.
13 Diebitsch's detachment consisted of the Grodno Hussars, three Cossack regiments, 120 men from the 23rd Jägers and six guns from 1st Horse Artillery Company.

them, lagged behind MacDonald by two stages. Upon reaching Schaulen, *10e Corps* was directed towards Tauroggen in two columns: Grandjean's division through Kelm and Niemexen [Nemakščiai], while Massenbach's detachment, with whom MacDonald was travelling himself, was to go via Waigau and Kołtyniany; Yorck was ordered to divide the force entrusted to him into two further columns, which were to follow the movements of Grandjean's and Massenbach's to Tauroggen, where the marshal intended to concentrate his entire corps and break through by force if the Russians had forestalled him at Tilsit. But the appearance of Cossacks at Kelm forced MacDonald to abandon the concentration of force at Tauroggen, which would have required more than a day; wanting to accelerate the march to Tilsit, he decided to continue the retreat in two columns: Grandjean's directed on Tauroggen; while MacDonald would himself go to Vainuta, Coadjuthen and Rucken [Rukai] towards Tilsit, sending orders to Yorck to assemble all his and Kleist's troops at Kołtyniany and to go via Tauroggen and on to Tilsit.[14]

On 14 (26) December, just before dawn, Bachelu's brigade [Gilbert Désiré Joseph Bachelu], marching at the head of Grandjean's division, encountered Vlastov's detachment in the defile at Piklupenen, which, unable to hold the enemy back, began to retreat towards Tilsit, where the detachment under Adjutant General Kutuzov was located at the time. Prussian cavalry drove off the Finland Dragoons moving with Vlastov's rearguard, disordered a battalion of 23rd Jägers and the 9th Group, St Petersburg *Opolchenie* and captured a gun from the 11th Light Artillery Company as well as 300 prisoners. But the appearance of Cossack regiments under Ilovaisky 4th and Kuteinikov 6th and two squadrons of Izyum Hussars, sent up by Adjutant General Kutuzov, stopped the enemy cavalry and gave our troops time to cross into Tilsit on the left bank of the Neman and to retreat upstream to Raudzen [Ryadino, Kaliningrad *Oblast*].[15]

Meanwhile, as early as the previous day, 13 (25) December, as Grandjean's division was just arriving in Tauroggen, and MacDonald was in Vainuta, the force under Yorck and Kleist had arrived in Kroże [Kražiai] and were at a distance of more than 50 *versts* from MacDonald's other troops. Such was the situation of *10e Corps* at the time when Diebitsch was stationed in Kołtyniany with his detachment, believing that MacDonald's entire force had already passed this point, except for a weak rearguard. But soon intelligence was received from several Prussian stragglers taken prisoner that the detachment under the command of General Kleist, approaching Kołtyniany, had four battalions, two squadrons and a battery. There was no doubt that Diebitsch's small detachment, which had withdrawn a considerable distance from other Russian forces, could not halt the column advancing against it, but Diebitsch, knowing that the Prussian troops were reluctantly fighting against us, left his detachment across their path and decided to open negotiations with General Kleist.[16]

The disillusionment with Napoleon and the French, which prevailed at that time not only in Prussia, but throughout Germany, had become known to our army.

---

14 Chambray, III, 149-151.
15 Extracts from reports to the Tsar on military operations, archive of the M.T.D. No. 44,585.
16 Clausewitz, 210-211.

Many Prussian officers, after the conclusion of the Treaty of Tilsit, had resigned and entered Russian service and gave us hope that their comrades-in-arms would rise up against the French at the first opportunity. Prussian troops fought very bravely in every engagement with ours, fulfilling the will of their Sovereign who was completely under Napoleon's power, but the hour of the liberation of Prussia was already approaching. Back in October, just after General Paulucci had been appointed military governor of Riga to replace Essen 1st, Colonel Rapatel, a French émigré in Russian service, wrote to Marshal MacDonald and to General Yorck (who was commanding the Prussian contingent in *10e Corps* of the *Grande Armée* in place of Grawert [Julius August Reinhold von Grawert]), asking permission of the former to visit in order to inform him of very important intelligence; in the letter to Yorck, having expressed a desire to meet him, Rapatel informed Yorck of the defeats suffered by the French and let him know that things had taken such a turn that it was possible to render great service to Russia and Prussia.[17] MacDonald resolutely declined the offer made to him, while General Yorck replied that such a meeting might expose him to suspicion and be fatal to him. He wrote: 'I dare not even send you a reliable person with whom you might have the opportunity to explain yourself frankly, as long as outpost clashes continue, which, without achieving anything, produce mutual animosity.'[18] Meanwhile, General Paulucci, having taken command of the Riga garrison, forbade Rapatel from any involvement in this matter and sent a letter to Yorck himself, in which he suggested that he join his corps to the Russian force and operate against the French, or at least separate from MacDonald and retreat to Prussia.[19] A consequence of this comment was the constant correspondence between Yorck and General Paulucci. Count Wittgenstein, unaware of all this, for his part, had sent Major General Prince Repnin [Nikolai Grigorievich Repnin] to Riga, with instructions to open negotiations with Yorck. Paulucci diverted Prince Repnin from participating in this case and, having received permission from Emperor Alexander to continue relations with Yorck, tried to convince him of the need to defect from the French. But General Yorck had decided not to proceed with the execution of this plan until he learned the will of King Friedrich Wilhelm III, and to that end he sent his adjutant, Major Seydlitz [Anton Friedrich Florian von Seydlitz-Kurzbach], to Berlin.[20]

This was the situation as MacDonald's forces marched from Bauske and Mitau towards the Neman. Yorck, having run out of time waiting for the return of Seydlitz, marched behind MacDonald (as already mentioned) and had reached Kroże, in the vicinity of Kołtyniany, by 13 (25) December, on the very day that Diebitsch's detachment was located at this latter point, across the Prussian force's line of retreat. Diebitsch's situation, stationed between two enemy columns, each of which was

---

17 Colonel Rapatel's letters to Marshal MacDonald, dated 22 and 27 October new style, and to General Yorck, dated 29 October new style, are in the archive of the M.T.D. No. 46,692.
18 General Yorck's letter to Colonel Rapatel, dated 11 November new style.
19 General Paulucci's report to Emperor Alexander I, dated 2 [14] November. General Paulucci's letter to Yorck, dated 2 [14] November, in the archive of the M.T.D. No. 46,692.
20 Prince Repnin's letter to Count Wittgenstein, dated 25 November [7 December]. Yorck's letter to General Paulucci, dated 26 November (8 December). For the text of this letter, see Appendix XXI.

incomparably stronger than his detachment, exposed him to obvious danger, but he hoped that the Prussian generals would not move decisively against him, and, just in case, wanted to open negotiations with them. He sent Major von Rönne to announce to Kleist that his column had been cut off by significant Russian forces, and that General Diebitsch wished to enter into communications with him. General Kleist answered Diebitsch that he could not open any negotiations, because it was not he who commanded the force, but General Yorck, who was due to arrive in the evening, and therefore we would have to wait for his arrival: from this comment it emerged that Diebitsch's detachment had cut off not the rearguard, but the main body of the Prussian corps, from Macdonald.[21]

Thus the success of the proposed negotiations depended entirely on Yorck.

General Yorck, an experienced soldier who had repeatedly shown his skill in military matters, as well as courage, was distinguished by extraordinary resolve. Directness and honesty were combined in him with driving ambition. Under the guise of frankness, to the point of being rude, he was caustic and secretive, almost never revealing his point of view. When without hope of success in any action, he boasted in advance of his luck; but even more often he claimed fatal premonitions when he himself was sure that the impending danger was of little significance. At the commencement of the war of 1812, Napoleon wished that General Grawert, a man already of advanced years, in poor health, of limited ability and of an accommodating nature, should be appointed commander of the Prussian auxiliary corps. Friedrich Wilhelm accommodated the desire of his powerful ally. But Scharnhorst [Gerhard Johann David von Scharnhorst], who knew both the abilities of Yorck, and his hatred for the French, suggested to the king that Yorck should be given the appointment of deputy to Grawert; in reality, he was an informant monitoring Grawert. A month and a half after the opening of hostilities on the Dvina, once Grawert had been forced to hand over his command to his deputy due to illness, then disagreements arose between MacDonald and Yorck: while the division under Grandjean remained inactive, the Prussian force performed the duties of an observation detachment; Yorck complained that his corps was suffering severe shortages of provisions and fodder, and at the same time expressed an unfavourable opinion of their operations, or, rather, about MacDonald's inaction. For his part, the Marshal was convinced that horses in the Prussian corps were dying due to being over-fed. The correspondence that arose between them gave rise to bitterness and mutual reproach. Matters got to the point that in November both of them wrote to Vilna about the constant disagreements between them, the Marshal to the Duc de Bassano (Maret), and General Yorck to the Prussian resident Krusemarck [Friedrich Wilhelm Ludwig von Krusemarck].[22]

Without any doubt, not the disagreements with MacDonald, nor his deep hatred of the French, would have prompted Yorck to defect from his allies. It is true that Diebitsch, in pursuing the Prussian corps from the flank, in which there was very little cavalry, could have captured some of their transport and damaged the retreating force, and besides, General Yorck was unaware both of the small size of Diebitsch's

---

21 Clausewitz, 209-211. *Précis des opérations du 1er Corps*, archive of the M.T.D. No. 29,200.
22 Clausewitz, 214-216.

force, and of his distance from other Russian troops, but had he not been waiting for permission from Berlin to abandon MacDonald, all this, in other circumstances, would not have deterred Yorck from attempting to push his way through by brute force. In preparing for this, Yorck considered himself to have no right to continue hostilities against the Russians, who from hour to hour might transform from enemies to allies. And as soon as he and the rest of his force had closed up to Kleist's detachment, which was stationed four *versts* from Kołtyniany, he let Diebitsch know that he consented to a meeting at the outposts. Both generals arrived there at about nine o'clock in the evening. Although our troops had been concealed such that their true strength could not be discerned, nevertheless, Diebitsch did not leave Yorck deceived as to the weakness of his detachment. 'I have no intention at all to block your path' he said, 'but I shall only try to capture your transport and perhaps your artillery.' However, General Diebitsch did not attach particular importance to his operations, drawing Yorck's attention primarily to the complete annihilation of the French army, presenting Prussia with the opportunity of freeing itself from the yoke that weighed it down, and assuring him that all our generals had been ordered to deal with the commanders of Prussian forces, not as hostile, but as former allies, with whom friendly relations should not be deferred. After explaining the state of affairs, General Diebitsch offered to conclude an agreement on the neutrality of the Prussian corps with Yorck.[23]

General Yorck replied that although he was ready to conclude a treaty, in their joint honour, nevertheless, the time had not yet come for that. It was proposed that the troops of both sides remained overnight in the places they currently occupied; on the following morning, Yorck's corps were to go to Laukuva, while Diebitsch's detachment was to settle on the route to Schilale [Šilalė]. Upon his return to Kołtyniany, at ten o'clock in the evening, Diebitsch asked Lieutenant Colonel Clausewitz [Carl Philipp Gottlieb Clausewitz], who was in his detachment, what he thought of Yorck, and was told in response that General Yorck was a very secretive man, and that perhaps he intended to break through our lines at night and continue moving towards Tilsit. This forced Diebitsch to take appropriate precautions: two Cossack regiments were left facing the Prussian corps. A third took up positions facing in the direction of Shilale, while the Grodno Hussars settled down in the rather extensive village of Kołtyniany; they were ordered not to unsaddle the horses. At night, an alarm was sounded to the rear of the hussars, which, however, did not come to anything: it was a patrol sent from MacDonald's corps headquarter with a letter to Yorck, but upon encountering Cossacks, were forced to leave without fulfilling their mission.

On the following day, 14 (26) December, Diebitsch moved to Schilale, while General Yorck, instead of the agreed movement to Laukuva, marched to Bartashishki [Bartašiškė], between Kołtyniany and Schilale: by moving closer to Tilsit, he better concealed his intention to defect from the French, but aroused the suspicion of Diebitsch, who believed that Yorck wanted to play for time and rejoin MacDonald. General Diebitsch sent Clausewitz to Yorck to persuade him to halt, but Yorck would

---

23 Clausewitz, 219-220.

not agree to this proposal and continued to move in short stages towards Tilsit, while Diebitsch, at every overnight halt, stationed himself across the line of retreat of the Prussian corps. On 16 (28) December, Yorck was at Tauroggen, Macdonald was awaiting Yorck's arrival in Tilsit with Massenbach's force and with part of Grandjean's division, while Bachelu's brigade was behind the Neman, in Ragnit [Neman, Kaliningrad *Oblast*]. On our side: Diebitsch was stationed a little off the direct route to Tilsit, near Willkischken [Vilkyškiai], just 15 *versts* from Macdonald; Adjutant General Kutuzov was located near Ragnit facing Bachelu's brigade; the vanguard under Shepelev was also on the left bank of the Neman, near Lasdehnen [Krasnoznamensk, Kaliningrad *Oblast*]; the main body under Count Wittgenstein was in Jurburg [Jurbarkas]; the detachment under Löwis was in Wornie.[24]

Because the Prussian corps was 30 *versts* from MacDonald at that time and there was no obstacle to their reunion except for our weak detachment, then General Diebitsch, wanting to extract himself from the precarious position in which he had been placed by Yorck's actions, at noon on 17 (29) December, sent Clausewitz to him once more, with two dispatches that were intended to induce the Prussian commander to make a decisive response to the proposal given to him. In one of them, a letter sent to Diebitsch from General Dovre [Fëdor Filippovich Dovre or Friedrich August Philipp Anton Dovre], following a reproach for the slow progress of negotiations with Yorck, news was reported of the imminent arrival of Shepelev's vanguard in Schillupischken [Novokolkhoznoe, Kaliningrad *Oblast*] on 19 (31) December, on the road leading from Tilsit to Königsberg, and the main body under Count Wittgenstein at Sommerau [Zagorskoe, Kaliningrad *Oblast*], at a distance of no more than 12 *versts* from the aforementioned road. In Dovre's letter to Diebitsch, he was ordered to announce to Yorck that if he did not abandon MacDonald with his corps, then he would be dealt with as an enemy, and that in this event there could be no question of any arrangement.

The other document, a letter from Macdonald to the Duc de Bassano, contained complaints about the morale of the Prussian troops, mentioned the need to remove some officers, and so on. This might embitter Yorck further against the French, but what prompted him most to abandon MacDonald was the return of Major Seydlitz from Berlin, who had reached the Prussian corps via Königsberg and Riga. Although he did not deliver any orders to General Yorck that would exonerate him from responsibility for splitting with the French, he nevertheless informed him that the king had decided to break the alliance, which had already been repeatedly violated by Napoleon, as soon as the political relations of the state had become clearer. On passing through Berlin, Seydlitz witnessed the complete collapse of the French army and learned from General Bülow [Friedrich Wilhelm von Bülow] of French distrust towards the Austrians, who were retreating to the borders of the Duchy of Warsaw offering no resistance. Having considered all these factors, General Yorck was convinced that it was necessary to change the policy of Prussia and it was now, or never, but he was still reluctant to proceed with the execution of his bold plan, and even told Clausewitz that he did not want to continue negotiations that might

---

24 Chambray, III, 152. Clausewitz, 247. *Précis des opérations du 1er Corps*, archive of the M.T.D. No. 29,200.

ruin him. But when his Chief of Staff, Colonel Räder, read aloud the dispatches in his presence, Yorck, after thinking for a minute, turned to Clausewitz with a question: 'Is it really possible to believe General Dovre that Wittgenstein's forces will be at the aforementioned locations by 31 December? Can you be honest about that?'

'I can vouch for the truth of everything stated in the letter, it is in accord with the directness of Dovre and other personalities known to me in Count Wittgenstein's headquarters' answered Clausewitz. 'As to whether the planned operations will be executed, you know in war that planned operations are not always carried out precisely.'

Whereupon General Yorck, after thinking for a few more minutes, said: 'You have me there (*Ihr habt mich*). Tell General Diebitsch that we shall meet each other tomorrow morning at the Poscherun Mill [Požerūnai], and that I have now made up my mind to abandon the French.'

It was planned to arrive at eight o'clock in the morning. Then Yorck added: 'I shall finish this business; Massenbach shall accompany me' and ordering the officer who had come to him for orders from Massenbach, to enter his room, he asked: 'So, what about your regiments?' The officer, knowing what was going on, began to talk passionately about the desire of each and every man to break free from the alliance with the French. 'It is good that you understand young men; while my old man's head shakes on his shoulders' answered Yorck.[25]

On the following day, 18 (30) December, Diebitsch arrived at the rendezvous for the meeting, accompanied by Count Dohna ([Friedrich Karl Emil Burggraf und Graf zu Dohna-Schlobitten] a Prussian national who was in Russian service) and Lieutenant Colonel Clausewitz, while General Yorck, who had the Chief of Staff of the Prussian corps, Colonel Räder, and his aide de camp, Major Seydlitz with him.[26] On the basis of the convention drawn up by Colonel Räder and Lieutenant Colonel Clausewitz, and signed by Generals Yorck and Diebitsch, it was agreed that the Prussian corps was to occupy a sector on Prussian territory bounded by a line from Memel and Nimmersatt [Nemirseta] to the road leading from Vainuta to Tilsit, and onwards from Tilsit, via Mehlauken [Zalesie, Kaliningrad *Oblast*], to Labiau [Polessk, Kaliningrad *Oblast*]. This area was to be recognised as neutral for as long as it was occupied by Prussian troops. The Russians could pass through it, but they were not supposed to spread out in quarters in the towns of this district. In the event that Emperor Alexander I, or King Friedrich Wilhelm, did not approve this agreement, the Prussian corps had the right to go wherever it might be directed by the king, but pledged not to fight against Russian forces for two months from the date of the conclusion of the convention. If the instructions from General Yorck reach General Massenbach in time, the latter's force may also be included in this convention, and so on.[27]

---

25 Clausewitz, 224-228.
26 Count Dohna had been sent from St Petersburg to Riga under the alias of Count Nordenburg, from where, by order of General Paulucci, he attended the negotiations with Yorck. Lieutenant General Marquis Paulucci's report to the Tsar, dated 23 November [5 December].
27 Convention concluded at Poscherun Mill, near Tauroggen, on 18 (30) December, archive of the M.T.D. No. 29,172. Book of acts concluded in December 1812.

As early as 14 (26) December, General Yorck had sent *Flügeladjutant* Major Count Henckel ([Wilhelm Ludwig Viktor Graf Henckel von Donnersmarck] who was with the force at the time) from Schilale, to Berlin, in order to inform the king in advance of the situation in which the corps found itself. At the conclusion of the Poscherun Convention, Major von Thiele of the General Staff was sent with a report.

At the conclusion of his report to the king, General Yorck wrote:

> I would lay my head at Your Majesty's feet, if I am found to have erred; I would die with the joyful reassurance that at least I had not failed as a loyal subject and a true Prussian. The time is now or never for Your Majesty to tear Yourself away from the overbearing demands of an ally whose plans for Prussia would have shrouded her in justifiably alarming oblivion, had fortune been in his favour. This view has been my guide, heaven grant that it leads to the salvation of the fatherland.

On that same day, 18 (30) December, Yorck sent an officer to Massenbach in Tilsit, with an invitation to return to Tauroggen, expressed in the form of a direct order (which obliged Massenbach to act), and with a letter to MacDonald, which Massenbach was to forward, once he had executed the orders just issued to him. Most of his detachment was in Tilsit, where there were no French troops at all. During the night of 18 to 19 (30 to 31) December, Heudelet's division was expected to arrive from Königsberg, as was Bachelu's brigade from Ragnit, but this did not prevent Massenbach from crossing the Neman without any resistance and he set off at eight o'clock in the morning on 19 (31) December, with six battalions and three squadrons, to link up with the Russian forces; the remaining seven squadrons and some of the artillery from the Prussian corps, stationed at Ragnit together with Bachelu's brigade, went to the village of Raudzen and there they joined the detachment under Adjutant General Kutuzov.[28] Upon leaving Tilsit, Massenbach made an announcement to his force regarding the treaty concluded at the Poscherun Mill. The soldiers greeted this news with joyful cheers, quickened their pace and linked up with the column under Diebitsch at Piklupenen, and then with Yorck's force in Tauroggen. Thus the French lost the assistance of 19 battalions and 14 squadrons, numbering 16,000 men with 48 guns.[29]

Meanwhile, MacDonald, having reached Tilsit on 16 (28) December, halted there to await the arrival of Yorck's column, and waited for him in vain on 17 and 18 (29 and 30) December; none of the orderlies or scouts sent to him returned, and therefore the marshal, remaining completely in the dark about the Prussian corps, was in an awkward situation: if he retreated and the troops under Yorck had been cut off by superior forces, then he could be accused of abandoning his allies as prey to the enemy: staying longer at Tilsit exposed MacDonald to the danger of losing the only line of retreat to Königsberg himself. Under these circumstances, eventually

---

28 *Précis des opérations du 1er Corps*. Clausewitz, 229.
29 Major General Diebitsch's report to Count Wittgenstein, dated 18 [30] December, No. 57, from Willkischken. Clausewitz, 230. In *Précis des opérations du 1er Corps*, it states that there were 18,000 men in the Prussian corps.

deciding to retreat, he assembled his forces in Tilsit, on the night of 18 to 19 (30 to 31) December.

Following this, intelligence arrived that Massenbach had crossed the Neman with his Prussian troops, and the letter from Yorck forwarded by Massenbach was received, with the following content:

> Following very arduous marches, it has not been possible for me to continue them without being attacked on my flanks and rear; this is what has delayed the junction with your Excellency, also having to choose between the alternative of losing the greater part of my force and all the transport which, alone, ensured my subsistence, or of saving the whole, I thought it my duty to arrange a convention by which a concentration of Prussian troops must take place in that part of Eastern Prussia, which, following the retreat of the French army, is under the power of the Russian army.
>
> The Prussian force shall form a neutral corps, and shall not permit themselves hostilities towards any party; imminent events, the result of negotiations which must take place between the belligerent powers, will decide their future fate.
>
> I hasten to inform Your Excellency of a step to which I have been forced by major circumstances.
>
> Whatever judgment the world shall pass on my conduct, I am little worried; the duty towards my troops and the most mature reflection dictate it to me; etcetera.[30]

Thereafter Massenbach wrote to Macdonald that he was leaving him, obeying orders received, and that he had not personally informed the marshal about this, in order to avoid painful emotions that might be aroused by such an announcement. In conclusion of his comment, Massenbach entrusted the inhabitants of Tilsit to the mercy of the marshal.[31] MacDonald not only protected them from the vengeance of his troops, but very graciously released his Prussian Lieutenant Korff [Peter Anton von Korff], who was at the corps headquarters, with thirty dragoons.

Emperor Alexander I, having received the report on the convention concluded with General Yorck, wrote to him:

> I hasten, General, to express my gratitude to you. From now on, two nations, mutually united by feelings of respect and friendship, shall no longer destroy one another for the sake of the insatiable lust for power of the oppressor of Europe. My devotion to the king remains unchanged, while my active cooperation with the Prussian Monarchy has strengthened further. I enclose a letter to the King, which is most important, and I ask you to forward it with a reliable officer.

---

30 Chambray, III, 154-155. For the original text of this letter in French, see Appendix XXII.
31 For the original text of this letter in French, see Appendix XXIII.

Together with this, I ask you, General, to be sure of My respect for you and for the valiant troops under your command, to whom I ask you to convey My sentiments.[32]

As soon as the troops from Grandjean's division had managed to assemble in Tilsit, numbering 7,000 or 8,000 men with 12 guns, MacDonald immediately set out, on the morning of 19 (31) December, along the Königsberg road. Meanwhile, Count Wittgenstein, having already marched close to Jurburg on 16 (28) December, moved to intercept MacDonald, but being delayed by poor road conditions, he was forced to halt in Gerskullen [Gannovka, Kaliningrad *Oblast*] on 18 (30) December, waiting for the artillery to catch up with his force. General Shepelev's vanguard was ordered to march towards the village of Schillupischken, reinforced with some of Berg's and Steinheil's cavalry, in order to block MacDonald's path on the Königsberg road, but Shepelev, having arrived at Sommerau before dawn on 19 (31) December, remained there until evening, waiting for a march route from the corps headquarters,[33] and then, moving in the direction of Wanniglauken, he encountered significant delays crossing flooded streams such that he was forced to turn towards Schillupischken and arrived at this location just after the enemy had passed through and moved on.[34] Thus, there were only four Cossack regiments available to detain MacDonald along the route to Königsberg, under the command of Colonel Yagodin, sent by Platov to assist Count Wittgenstein and attached to the vanguard under General Shepelev. These regiments, unable to stop the much stronger enemy, kept themselves off to the sides of the Königsberg road. Taking advantage of the weakness of our pursuit, MacDonald had ejected the Cossack observation post from Schillupischken and, moving almost without pause, arrived in the village of Mehlauken, lying at a distance of more than 40 *versts* from Tilsit, at three o'clock in the morning of 20 December (1 January 1813). The detachment under Diebitsch and Yagodin's Cossacks caught up with the enemy at Skaisgirren [Bolshakovo, Kaliningrad *Oblast*] and, pursuing them further, captured some 500 men.[35]

General Heudelet, who was in Königsberg with his division (*11e Corps*), numbering 8,000 men, marched from there to Tapiau [Gvardeysk, Kaliningrad *Oblast*] in order to shield MacDonald's retreat. Count Wittgenstein, having received intelligence on this, changed the composition of his leading detachments, which, on 21 December (2 January, 1813), were assembled in Skaisgirren: Adjutant General Kutuzov was directed towards Wehlau [Znamensk, Kaliningrad *Oblast*] to oppose Heudelet, with 4,000 regular cavalry and Cossacks, supported by the corps under Count Steinheil; Major General Shepelev was ordered to pursue MacDonald along the road leading to Labiau and on to Königsberg, with his vanguard reinforced by Vlastov's infantry

---

32 *Copie d'une lettre de S.M. L'Empereur au général Iorck, en date de Vilna, le 25 decembre 1812* (new style), archive of the Ministry of Foreign Affairs.
33 Major General Shepelev's reports, dated 18 [30] December, archive of the M.T.D. No. 44,585 (log of incoming documents, No. 840, No. 844 & No. 845).
34 Shepelev's report, dated 20 December [1 January 1813], archive of the M.T.D. No. 44,585 (log of incoming documents, No. 849).
35 Chambray, III, 159. Relevant extracts from reports to the Tsar on military operations.

and some of Diebitsch's cavalry, numbering 6,000 infantry and 1,500 cavalry, with 18 guns; General Sivers [Karl Karlovich Sivers or Carl Gustav von Sievers] was to advance in the interval between the detachments under Kutuzov and Shepelev, with 1,200 cavalry. On 22 December (3 January 1813), Shepelev attacked Bachelu's brigade, which had been holding the town of Labiau, and enveloping them around the flanks, forced them to retreat with the loss of 500 men taken prisoner alone, and three guns; on our side, the casualties reached 350 men.[36] On that same day [3 January], Heudelet evacuated Wehlau without offering resistance; Adjutant General Kutuzov, having crossed the Pregel [Pregolya] here, moved along the left bank of the river towards Königsberg, while Sivers liberated Tapiau.

Upon the arrival of Admiral Chichagov in Gumbinnen with his main body, on 24 December (5 January 1813), Count Wittgenstein, having been subordinated to him by Prince Kutuzov, was ordered to drive the enemy through Königsberg, towards Marienburg and Marienwerder. In the meantime, Murat had set out from Königsberg on 21 December (2 January 1813) and the next day [3 January] moved his headquarters to Elbing [Elbląg]. On 23 December [4 January 1813], MacDonald withdrew into Königsberg, where the troops from Heudelet's division, which had retreated from Wehlau, and the newly arrived cavalry brigade under Cavaignac [Jacques-Marie Cavaignac] were located. Some 20,000 French and allied troops had been assembled there, but most of them were in a most miserable condition. On the evening of 23 December (4 January), the detachment under Adjutant General Kutuzov was closing in on Königsberg along the left bank of the Pregel, while the detachment under Sivers and the cavalry of Shepelev's vanguard were on the right. As soon as the Cossacks appeared, the enemy, having dumped a significant number of guns underwater, evacuated the city on the night of 23 to 24 December (4 to 5 January 1813) and retreated towards Elbing and Danzig; a few days later, on 30 December (11 January), Murat moved the headquarters of his army to Poznań.[37]

On 24 December (5 January), The vanguard under General Shepelev liberated Königsberg, where 1,300 men were taken prisoner, not including 8,000 stragglers and sick, while the Russian officers and soldiers captured in the action at Piklupenen were released. Vast enemy magazines were found in the city. On that same day, Count Wittgenstein's corps was reinforced by six reserve battalions under Colonel Zhemchuzhnikov, numbering 3,000 men who joined the force under General Berg, and the detachment under General Löwis, numbering 6,500 infantry and 1,200 cavalry, included in the vanguard under Löwis, under the command of Colonel Galatte [Iosif Nikolaevich Galatte], who had joined Diebitsch's detachment whilst they were in Kołtyniany.[38]

Yorck's defection from Macdonald was subjected to many differing opinions, but later the French themselves admitted that he acted with extraordinary self-sacrifice, fulfilling what offended national pride and love of his fatherland demanded of him.[39] His actions had very important consequences for Prussia and for the whole

---

36 Chambray, III, 159. Relevant extracts from reports to the Tsar on military operations.
37 Chambray, III, 164.
38 *Précis des opérations du 1er Corps*, archive of the M.T.D. No. 29,200.
39 Chambray, III, 157-158. Thiers, XIV, *Édit. de Brux.* 209.

of Germany in general. If Yorck had not split from MacDonald, then Murat could have assembled more than 40,000 men on the Pregel.[40] On our side, in the forces under Chichagov, Count Wittgenstein and Count Platov, directed towards the lower Vistula, there were some 50,000 men, namely; with Count Wittgenstein 30,000, in the Western (formerly Danube) Army 14,000 and in Platov's Cossack detachment between 6,000 and 7,000 men:[41] consequently, although there was superiority in numbers on the Russian side, the disparity was not so much in numbers as in the quality of the troops. Still more important was the effect of Yorck's actions on his compatriots. For a long time Germany had already been harbouring feelings of resentment and hatred for the French, suppressed by force, but threatening to explode at the first opportunity. Secret societies had formed in every German region, whose goal was to liberate their fatherland from the yoke imposed by Napoleon. Many Prussian subjects, renowned for their talents and strength of character, had sought refuge after the Peace of Tilsit in Russia and Britain, waiting for the desired moment of vengeance… It arrived with the destruction of Napoleon's half-million strong army. The most famous of the self-imposed exiles, the former Prussian minister, Stein [Heinrich Friedrich Karl vom und zum Stein], petitioned Emperor Alexander I for permission to form a Russo-German legion from captured German soldiers. At his own suggestion, from the first steps of Russian forces across the borders into Germany, appeals were published calling on each and every person to arm themselves against their common oppressor. A national uprising, embittered from many years of catastrophe, was already being prepared; all that remained was for an example to be set, and the bold Yorck, setting it at a time when the Prussian government could not yet reveal its intentions, hastened the start of the deadly struggle for the independence of Germany. Yorck's actions generated profound sympathy in the hearts of his countrymen. But in Berlin, although the need for a breach with France was recognised, they were nevertheless amazed at this decisive step, which seemed inopportune to many. As soon as the Chancellor of State, Baron Hardenberg [Karl August von Hardenberg] received the news of the defection of the Prussian corps on 4 January (new style), from the French resident Saint-Marsan [Antoine Marie Philippe Asinari de Saint-Marsan] in the company of Marshal Augereau, expressing displeasure and annoyance at Yorck, he immediately went to the king to report this emergency. Neither the king, nor his minister, were fully aware of how immense the losses to the *Grande Armée* had been, and therefore could not assess what consequences might be expected from the defection of Yorck's corps from the French ranks. No one could have known at that time about the impending retreat of the Austrian corps; finally, who could have foreseen the extent to which the passions of the Prussian people would reach? At this time, the main forces of the Russian army were halted in Vilna, almost every Prussian region with all the most important fortresses were occupied by the French, the capital of the kingdom and the king himself were under their power. Under such circumstances, there was nothing left but to placate the French government for the time being, avoiding a clear breach with Napoleon. The king did not ratify the convention on

---

40 For a breakdown of French forces on 5 January, new style, see Appendix XXIV.
41 For a breakdown of Wittgenstein's force on 31 December [12 January], see Appendix XXV.

the neutrality of the Prussian corps, removed Yorck from command over his forces and ordered his arrest and investigation; Major General Kleist, who was thereupon promoted to lieutenant general, was entrusted with the command of the corps and ordered to be at the disposal of the Emperor of the French or his deputy, the King of Naples. *Flügeladjutant* Lieutenant Colonel Natzmer [Oldwig Anton Leopold von Natzmer], took these orders to the Prussian corps; at the same time, Prince Hatzfeldt [Franz Ludwig Fürst von Hatzfeld zu Trachenberg] was sent to Napoleon in Paris, to convince him that the king had not given any grounds for Yorck's unauthorised actions. He was also instructed to offer the accession to Napoleon's army of an auxiliary Prussian corps, stronger than the one set up originally, which would serve as a pretext for the Prussians to recruit troops without violating the agreement concluded on 24 February, 1812 (new style).[42]

In order to remove General Yorck from command of the forces, Lieutenant Colonel Natzmer had to hand him the king's orders; but since the Prussian corps was behind Russian lines, Natzmer, having been detained at our outposts and escorted to Wittgenstein, asked that he be allowed to pass through to Yorck. Count Wittgenstein asked him what his mission was, and received in reply that he had been ordered to deliver the king's orders to Yorck, that Kleist had been appointed in his stead.

'Oh! If that is so, you shall not pass to him! Have you no other orders?' continued the count.

'I have a letter from the king to your Tsar,' replied Natzmer.

'I shall grant you the opportunity to deliver it with the greatest pleasure,' said Wittgenstein.

Lieutenant Colonel Natzmer was thereupon directed to Vilna, escorted by an officer of the *Feldjäger* [courier] corps.[43] On 7 (19) January 1813, an announcement from the Prussian government appeared in the Berlin newspapers regarding the dismissal of Yorck and the appointment of Kleist in his place. But on 15 (27) January, Yorck announced in the Königsberg newspapers that neither he nor General Kleist had received any orders to that effect, and as there had never been any precedent of royal commands being announced to the force commanders via newspapers, on the basis of the decree of 20 December, 1812 (new style), he did not consider himself entitled to abandon the command of his corps. General Kleist, for his part, announced that he could not take the place of General Yorck, as he was an equal participant in the defection from the French:[44] thus Yorck continued to command the Prussian corps. In the meantime, the situation was becoming clearer day by day. The destruction of Napoleon's army was no longer in doubt, while the friendly persuasion of Emperor Alexander and the solemn assurance by Him to restore the independence of Prussia prompted King Friedrich Wilhelm to renew the alliance with Russia, and the first step towards this was his departure from Potsdam to Breslau [Wrocław] on 10 (22) January, where he could reign completely independently of French influence; with his Person were: Chancellor of State Baron Hardenberg; French ambassador,

---

42 Sporschil, *Die große Chronik*, Part 1, Vol. 1, 43-44.
43 Clausewitz, 235-236.
44 *Das Leben des Ministers Freiherrn v. Stein*, III, 275-276.

Saint-Marsan; Scharnhorst, who was the soul of all the preparations by Prussia for the coming struggle; Blücher [Gebhard Leberecht von Blücher], hero of the Prussian army, and Gneisenau [August Wilhelm Anton Neidhardt von Gneisenau].[45] Shortly thereafter, General Yorck was acquitted, and, as a mark of the king's goodwill towards him, the troops under General Bülow were subordinated to him, in addition to his corps.[46]

---

45 Sporschil, *Die große Chronik*, Part 1, Vol. 1, 45.
46 Army Order of the Day, from 11 March, new style.

47

Conclusions

Consequences of the Patriotic War. – The *Grande Armée's* losses. – The composition and quality of enemy forces. – The problems of providing them with re-supply. – The Russian army's losses.

Analysis of operations. – The start of hostilities. – The advance to the Dvina and Dnieper. – Losses of both sides upon reaching Smolensk. – The battles at Smolensk and Valutina Gora. – The battle of Borodino. – Would it have been more advantageous for Napoleon to stop at Smolensk? – His casualties on the advance from Smolensk to Moscow. – Napoleon's stay in Moscow. – His movement towards Maloyaroslavets. – The indecision of both commanders. – Napoleon's retreat. – The inaction of Prince Kutuzov at Krasny. – Napoleon's crossing of the Berezina. – General conclusions on operations by Napoleon in 1812. – Memorials of this war. – Construction of the Cathedral of Christ the Saviour in Moscow. – Medals. – Annual Mass. – Proposal for the building of a monument to Emperor Alexander I. – His comments on these events.

The war of 1812 had hugely important consequences. The 600,000 strong army, led by the greatest military genius of our age and his renowned subordinates, no longer existed. Of the enemy forces that had crossed the borders of Russia, the auxiliary corps, Prussian, Austrian and Saxon, had returned behind the Neman and the Bug, but both of the former had already abandoned Napoleon, and the latter, weakened to less than half strength, would soon suffer complete defeat at Kalisz. Of the Polish forces, at the end of the campaign, only 5,000 men remained with MacDonald, who had taken refuge in Danzig, and several thousand under Poniatowski, who had retreated from Warsaw to Kraków. As for the French and other allied corps that were part of the *Grande Armée*, then, despite the eloquent claims about their condition at the end of 1812, there is not the slightest doubt that all these formations were almost completely wiped out. Chambray, the most reliable of French historians, confesses that, on the return crossing of the Nemen, at Kovno, the number of men under arms in the French army did not exceed 1,000 men,[1] and that, by the end of December and the beginning of January, around 11,500 officers and lower ranks

---

1   Chambray, *Histoire de l'expédition de Russie*, III, 138.

had managed to assemble on the Vistula from the *Garde* and four infantry corps, *1er Corps*, *2e Corps*, *3e Corps* and *4e Corps*, among whom there were only 7,000 to 8,000 men fit to fight.[2] Fezensac believes that no more than 10,000 men re-crossed the Vistula from the formations of the *Grande Armée*, and even those were sick or exhausted in the extreme.[3] In contrast, Gourgaud asserts that 36,000 men crossed back over the Neman at Kovno,[4] which, although obviously exaggerated, does not in the least change the outcome or the consequences of the war of 1812.

Taking into account that the number of Napoleon's troops that entered Russia extended to some 600,000 men overall,[5] and about 80,000 returned across the Vistula,[6] it emerges that the losses of the *Grande Armée* were no fewer than 500,000 overall. Almost all the field artillery, more than 1,200 guns, and the entire baggage train were lost. Such huge losses and the moral impact of this sudden failure, experienced after the formidable invasion of Russia by the *Grande Armée*, dealt a mortal blow to the power of Napoleon and presaged his downfall. Only a few wars have had such a decisive influence on the fate of nations, and therefore it is not surprising that our Patriotic War, as a great world event, has attracted the attention not only of Russians but has also been subjected to contradictory assessments: many, drawing conclusions on the merits of operations according to their consequences, expressed the opinion that Napoleon's entire campaign against Russia was a series of gross errors; others, carried away by a similarly uncritical respect for a brilliant commander, could not allow the thought that he could be defeated by force of arms, but attributed his failures solely to the influence of hunger and cold, or betrayal. And therefore, only an impartial study of all the circumstances of this war can explain to what extent both personalities and the elements had a part in the course and consequences of events.

In describing Napoleon's preparations for the war of 1812, I have calculated the huge forces of the army that invaded Russia on the basis of available sources. Napoleon, already in his sixth year of war in Spain at the time, which was gradually sapping French strength, was forced to form half of his *Grande Armée* from foreigners. Of the 604 battalions of which it consisted, there were 297 French and 307 foreign.[7] Excluding foot artillery crews and service support troops, the entire infantry consisted of some 453,000 men, including about 224,000 French and

---

2 Chambray, III, 162-163.
3 Fezensac, *Journal de la campagne de Russie en 1812*, 178.
4 Gourgaud, *Examen de l'ouvrage de Ségur, Livre XII*, Chap. IV.
5 Entered Russia in June: Under Napoleon's direct command – 218,000 men. Under the command of the Viceroy – 80,000 men. Under the command of the King of Westphalia – 79,000 men. MacDonald's corps – 32,000 men. Schwarzenberg's corps – 34,000 men. From August: Victor's corps – 30,000 men. From November: Loison's and Durutte's divisions; newly recruited Polish forces – 27,000 men. At various times: siege parks, train troops, march battalions, etc. – 80,000 men. In total: 580,000 men.
6 Returned back from Russia: Grandjean's division from MacDonald's corps – 5,000 men. Yorck's corps – 16,000 men. Schwarzenberg's corps – 20,000 men. Reynier's corps and Durutte's division – 15,000 men. Poniatowski's corps – 15,000 men. Various corps, around – 10,000 men. In total: 81,000 men.
7 Schreckenstein also shows 299 French and 306 foreign battalions, *Die Kavalerie in der Schlacht an der Moskwa*.

230,000 foreigners.[8] One could not expect from them either discipline, or increased enthusiasm for the success of this enterprise conceived by the conqueror with such a force composition. Such a diverse army might win victories under the leadership of a great commander, but was unable to endure the labours and hardships of a difficult campaign. This twenty-nation force, when obeying the will of Napoleon, comprised a well-shaped whole, but in extreme situations the enforced unity that linked them was destroyed, and this formidable intermixture turned into mobs of rogues and looters. Napoleon incessantly issued orders to the army to maintain order and discipline, but the formation commanders had no means of doing so: initially the foreign corps became disorderly, then the French, and eventually the *Garde* themselves. The corps under Oudinot and Victor, linking up with the remnants of the main army during the retreat to the Berezina, also diminished over the course of a few days. Napoleon's closest associates, tired of campaigning and seeing no end to the incessant wars waged by their ruler, thought more about rest and peace than about new victories.

The infantry of the *Grande Armée* was generally good and consisted for the most part of experienced veterans; but, according to claims by Napoleon and Saint-Cyr, the soldiers of the German auxiliaries were inferior to the French in their ability to endure fatigue and hunger.

It was necessary to have a lot of cavalry with the huge army assigned to invade Russia, both for proportionality in numbers with the infantry, and to counteract the numerous Russian cavalry. Of the 530 squadrons that were calculated to be in the *Grande Armée*, there were 276 foreign, and only 254 French.[9] Overall, excluding horse artillery crews and service support troops, the cavalry consisted of some 80,000 men, numbering 38,000 French and 42,000 foreigners.[10] The latter, together with the French cuirassiers and dragoons, made up the most reliable part of the cavalry: there were many recruits and young horses who could not endure a long campaign in the remainder of similar French regiments.[11]

The artillery, despite the large number of guns that were with the army, being partly made up of four-pounder calibre pieces, did not have sufficient power to counter the Russian artillery. The horses were quite poor in many batteries; this had been no great disadvantage in the earlier campaigns carried out in Germany, where the French had managed to find remounts for their artillery through the resources in country. But the occupation of Russian *Oblasts* by the enemy would provide them with almost no resources for remounts for the artillery and cavalry, and therefore both of these arms of service lost many horses and were noticeably weakened from the very opening of hostilities.[12] As the infantry and cavalry were losing many men at the same time, the number of guns became disproportionate to the strength of

---

8 Schreckenstein also shows 484,000 infantry, calculating each battalion at 800 men, *Die Kavalerie in der Schlacht an der Moskwa*.
9 In Schreckenstein: 287 foreign and 247 French squadrons, *Die Kavalerie in der Schlacht an der Moskwa*.
10 In Schreckenstein: 34,580 Frenchmen and 40,183 foreigners, calculating each squadron at 140 men, *Die Kavalerie in der Schlacht an der Moskwa*.
11 Chambray, I, 162.
12 Chambray, I, 162 & 345. Saint-Cyr, *Mémoires*, VII, 240.

other arms of service, which forced the French to leave artillery behind from their very first steps into Russia, as they could not keep up with the formations.

This multitude of war horses and draught horses with the army required a quantity of fodder that the countryside that served as the theatre of war was incapable of delivering. With the rapid advances by the formations, just as it was pointless to hope that the necessary supplies might always be found on the spot, so it was bringing up provisions, uniforms, and so on from behind the army, the formations being given an enormous train, which, in turn, required a significant amount of fodder, and made it much harder to resupply the army, rather than easier. The roads to the rear of the formations were congested with military and peasant carts; the Vistula, Vistula Lagoon [Frisches Haff], Pregel and Neman were covered with vessels on which provisions and fodder were to be shipped after the army; while the troops endured shortages of every necessity. Some believe that Napoleon should have resorted to contractors to deliver supplies, instead of an excessive increase in military transport, but one can hardly agree with this opinion.[13] Transportation by means of contractors does indeed simplify the organisation of subsistence for the troops and can in some circumstances bring undoubted advantages; but in the war of 1812, the French would hardly have been able to find contractors who would dare to deliver provisions and fodder to the troops, most especially after our partisans began blockading the French army from all sides. Everyone knows that the poorer and more sparsely populated the country serving as a theatre of operations, the more difficult it is to feed a large army within it, no matter what means are used for this. Despite the fact that we fought this war close to the sources of our strength and resources, and despite the general readiness of each and every person to contribute to the common cause, manning and providing our army with supplies required extraordinary efforts and was associated with heavy losses. Throughout the course of the campaign, some 134,000 recruits and warriors were conscripted to replenish our Main Army,[14] which had comprised only about 280,000 men under arms in both Western Armies at the start of the war, yet when we reached Vilna, in December, 70,000 remained in the army under Prince Kutuzov and in Wittgenstein's corps overall: consequently, the losses to our Main Army (including the sick in hospital) amounted to 210,000 men. As at least 40,000 sick returned to the ranks of the army, then, having accepted them in exchange for the probable losses to the forces under Tormasov, Chichagov, Ertel, Platov and the Riga garrison, it is almost possible to precisely calculate the total losses to our forces throughout the campaigns of 1812, as some 200,000 men. Notwithstanding such huge losses, we would have an advantage in strength at the end of the campaign, not only in numbers, but also in quality of troops, despite having started the war with an army only one third the size of the enemy's.

Napoleon is criticised for having commenced operations in mid-June, instead of the beginning of May, thus losing six weeks, and as a result, he lost the opportunity

---

13 Chambray, I, 347-348.
14 For a breakdown of reinforcements joining the Main Army during the war of 1812, see Appendix XXVI.

to finish the job in a single campaign.[15] But it should be noted that the reason for such a late start in the campaign, in all probability, was to wait for the emergence of the pasture necessary for the many draught horses and oxen that would proceed with the army. So, if Napoleon had occupied Moscow in mid-July, having set out from Prussia and Poland six weeks earlier, what advantages would he have gained as a result? The ability to retreat back across the Neman without exposing the army to the disasters of a winter campaign? This perverse objective could have been achieved even after Moscow was occupied in early September, had Napoleon not stayed there for more than a month and had not lost another whole week in a fruitless offensive towards Maloyaroslavets. If, however, we assume that, after capturing Moscow in mid-July, he would march on St Petersburg and, by conquering our northern capital, might induce Emperor Alexander to sue for peace, then in this case our main army would have pursued the enemy, while Wittgenstein's corps would have operated against his flank. But Napoleon would have encountered an even greater difficulty on this march due to the impossibility of feeding a force moving through sparsely populated country, where the magazines we had established would have been destroyed without fail once the enemy appeared. Even assuming that he might succeed with a campaign from Moscow to St Petersburg, and overcome our forces, and supply his army with everything necessary, the question remains: what advantage would he gain by seizing our northern capital? Without any doubt, the occupation of St Petersburg by the French would have increased the losses suffered by Russia in the war of 1812, but would not have brought any significant benefits to Napoleon: Emperor Alexander had not started the war, but being compelled to meet force with force, He had decided to continue the fight, even if he had to fight on the banks of the Volga; upon their Monarch's call, the Russian people, sparing nothing to defend the independence, honour and glory of the Fatherland, realised their strength: under such circumstances, neither the occupation of our *Oblasts*, nor the capture of both capitals, would help Napoleon to achieve his war aims.

Napoleon, with his characteristic shrewdness, realising that the Russians, waging war in their own country, would have an advantage in numbers, tried from the very beginning of hostilities to entice us into a decisive battle. In the words of Machiavelli [Niccolò di Bernardo dei Machiavelli]; 'victory rectifies every error.' Napoleon was convinced by his own experience: success in battle had got him out of the most difficult of situations on more than one occasion. Our commanders saw the need to retreat, but were overwhelmed by the instinctive desire to put a stop to the enemy invasion; as a result there was a marked hesitancy in our operations; but the influence of Barclay de Tolly [Mikhail Bogdanovich Barclay de Tolly or Michael Andreas Barclay de Tolly] saved our army from defeat and prevented Napoleon from winning the laurels of victory with his first steps into Russia. Having been unable to catch the Russians by surprise, he halted in Vilna, with his *Garde* and various other troops, for almost three weeks. One cannot but agree that such prolonged inactivity by Napoleon reduced the tenacity of the corps sent to pursue our forces. But while acknowledging the validity of this comment, it is unreasonable to blame Napoleon

---

15 Saint-Cyr, VII, 243.

for the forced marches, which, allegedly, were made by the French when advancing on Drissa and Vitebsk. These stages were very moderate; but the French troops, finding themselves marching under the influence of unfavourable circumstances, shortage of food, torrential rain ruining the roads and subsequently intense heat, lost many men and, upon reaching the Dvina, had been significantly weakened. The stages made at that time by our troops, and especially by Second Army, were incomparably more painful, and in spite of them, Prince Bagration was unable to link up with Barclay, neither via Minsk, when only 6,000 men from Davout's vanguard were engaged, nor via Mogilev, in front of which, at Saltanovka, the marshal was stationed with only part of his force. It is highly probable that Bagration could have linked up with Barclay, by moving non-stop through Minsk, or driving Davout off by using his entire force at Saltanovka. The lack of accurate intelligence on the enemy, prevented our commander from operating decisively and compelled him to detour towards Smolensk.

During the retreat of our armies to the Dvina and the Dnieper, there were several rearguard actions, in which we, for the most part, were successful, applying our knowledge of the ground which served as the field of action, while the French were forced to feel their way. These actions, boosting the morale and vigour of our troops, gradually drew Napoleon on with the elusive spectre of a decisive engagement. The further the French army advanced, the more difficult it was to supply the troops with all that they needed and the faster their casualties increased. Despite the large number officials from the provisioning and commissariat departments who accompanied the army, it was impossible to maintain any efficiency in supplying the troops with provisions, clothing and footwear, and therefore the enemy army was in need of everything, and the huge warehouses prepared in Lithuania and Belorussia were subsequently plundered by their marauders, or fell into the hands of our forces.

Meanwhile, as Napoleon's army, having invaded our *oblasts*, was noticeably dissipating, Emperor Alexander I mobilised the population of both capitals and the 16 governorates closest to them. The sacrifices made on the altar of the Fatherland by all classes in Russia were incalculable. Aside from the conscription classes, some 300,000 warriors and Cossacks were called up and some 100,000,000 in paper roubles were gifted voluntarily. The national *opolchenie*, whenever they had a chance to measure themselves against the enemy, fought bravely; but the St Petersburg groups distinguished themselves as predominant in organisation and tactical training. According to Prince Bagration, experienced in combat and one of the main organisers of our *Zemstvo* [territorial] forces, Count Tolstoy, such militias did not bear comparison alongside regular troops, but they could do useful service simply by being attached to regiments, or being incorporated into them, alongside properly trained soldiers. At the present time, when the individual training of men in the army has been brought to a higher degree than before, national mobilisation on a large scale, like the militia of 1807 and the *opolchenie* of 1812 and 1855, cannot be of any benefit, because, although requiring food supply on a par with regular troops, they are far inferior to them in combat power.

Simultaneously with the beginnings of the national *opolchenie*, the Western Armies, despite Napoleon's efforts to separate them, managed to link up at Smolensk. The movements made by them, while retreating from the borders of the Empire to this city, required an extraordinary effort; the campaign was particularly painful for Second Army, which in 45 days covered about 750 *versts*. Overall, the losses to both our armies had reached 34,000 men.[16] The casualties in the main French army, not including the corps detached from it or Dąbrowski's detachment, were at least 100,000 men.[17] Consequently, in the period from the beginning of the war to the arrival at Smolensk, the losses to the enemy army, not only in absolute terms, but also as a proportion of the number of troops, were greater than ours, and this was not as a result of forced marches, but from a lack of food and its consequences; a decline in discipline and marauding.

In the battle of Smolensk, by storming the fortified city, Napoleon had hoped to draw us into a general engagement; Barclay, going against popular opinion that demanded a continued defence of Smolensk, retreated, undertaking a very complicated manoeuvre in order to avoid moving along the banks of the Dnieper and withdrew along country roads toward the Moscow highway, but Napoleon did not take advantage of this mistake, and was not even present at Valutina Gora where a very bitter action took place.

Despite Barclay de Tolly's undoubted skill during the Patriotic War, the situation demanded the appointment of a new Commander-in-Chief in his place. His successor Kutuzov, who until that time had won fame almost exclusively in wars with the Turks, but invested with the trust of the people, justified this by completing the work begun by Barclay. It was unthinkable to give up Moscow without a fight: Barclay, in all probability, would not have refused to fight in defence of the capital. Even Kutuzov, submitting to necessity, accepted battle, in which the courage of the troops and the diligence of unit commanders made up for the inequality in numbers and rectified the errors in the initial dispositions of the army. The casualties on both sides were enormous, but we had the resources to replenish our forces more quickly than the enemy who were a long way from their depots. In addition, the battle of Borodino had a very beneficial effect on the morale of the Russian people and troops: the cunning Kutuzov, reporting on the outcome of the battle, depicted it in the form of a victory won by our forces. The guileless Barclay would have behaved differently, and the news of the defeat of our army, together with the equally fatal news of the loss of Moscow, upon reaching every part of Russia, would have sown

---

16 At the opening of hostilities, in both Western Armies, with the exception of the corps under Count Wittgenstein, there were 125,000 men. Joined on the march and upon arrival at Smolensk, by 28,600 men. Giving a total of 153,600 men. Upon arrival in Smolensk, 120,000 men remained. Therefore, net losses were 33,600 men

17 At the opening of hostilities, the forces coming under Napoleon's personal direction, calculated their strength as: 47,000 in the *Garde*, 72,000 in Davout's corps, 40,000 in Ney's corps, 47,000 in the Viceroy's corps (including the Bavarian contingent), 24,000 in Poniatowski's corps (excluding Dąbrowski), 18,000 in Vandamme's corps (later Junot's) and 30,000 in the *réserve de cavalerie* (Nansouty, Montbrun and Grouchy, less Doumerc), giving a total of 278,000. Upon arrival at Smolensk, 180,000 remained, giving a net loss of 100,000 men. Of these 100,000 men, some 8,000 or 9,000 had been left in Kovno, Vilna, Minsk, etc. and therefore the actual losses in Napoleon's army, on the march from the Neman to Smolensk and in the actions at Mir, Saltanovka, Ostrovno and Vitebsk, reached 90,000 men.

despondency among the population and could have weakened the enthusiasm for our preparations for the defence of the state.

Napoleon, having won an indecisive victory at Borodino, marched on Moscow. Until 1812, in every war waged by him, having defeated the enemy army, he raced towards the capital of the hostile state and, having seized it, dictated peace terms to the enemy. Only in Spain did the occupation of the capital and several resounding victories fail to lead to a successful conclusion to the bloody struggle, and therefore Napoleon, attributing this failure to errors by his marshals and based on the exploits accomplished by his forces in Germany and Italy, after winning a victory at Borodino and seizing Moscow, believed he had conquered Russia.

It is pointless to imagine that Napoleon would certainly have succeeded in his gigantic enterprise, if, after reaching Smolensk, instead of a continuous march on Moscow, he had arranged for his army to rest until the following spring, announced the restoration of Poland, produced a significant mobilisation in Lithuania, arranged magazines to the rear of the army and provided them with fortifications.[18] The following should be noted: firstly, judging by the insignificance of the Lithuanian mobilisation and the cooling towards the French by the population there, that it was impossible to rely on the success of a national militia in Lithuania. And could Napoleon have even proclaimed the restoration of Poland to its former borders without arousing the hostility of the Austrian government, which he prized as part of his alliance, both because of his kinship with the House of Habsburg, and in accordance with political calculations. Secondly, had Napoleon halted on the Dnieper, what methods could he have adopted to situate his troops for the winter? If the army had remained concentrated in bivouacs, then the French forces would have undergone the same disasters that befell them on the return march to the Neman; if, however, they were dispersed into quarters, then, upon being surrounded everywhere by our partisans and attacked by the main forces, they could not have avoided a defeat that would have had equally disastrous consequences. In any event, criticising Napoleon both for inaction (for the short-term pauses for the troops) and for forced marches, with their associated heavy losses not so much from the pace of movements as from a lack of food and disorder among the troops, is rather odd.

The victory at Borodino and the march on Moscow cost Napoleon dearly: at Smolensk, he had some 200,000, but when he arrived at Moscow, barely 100,000 men. The advantage in numbers was still on his side: but significant reserves were hastening to join our Main Army, and the time was fast approaching when superiority in troop numbers would come over to our side. Napoleon wanted to prevent the reinforcement of our army by concluding peace on terms that he hoped to impose upon Russia. It was this hope that had prompted him to go to Moscow; hope also forced him to stay for a whole month in the ruins of our ancient capital, in anticipation of success in the negotiations he had begun. But the days passed; the Russian army in the Tarutino camp was constantly being strengthened; partisans and civilian groups surrounded the enemy and inflicted significant losses on them. Numerous *opolchenie* were set up in the 16 governorates closest to the theatre of

---

18 Saint-Cyr, *Mémoires*, VII, 259-260.

war, which, of course, could not compare with regular troops in tactical training, but were not inferior to them in courage, and could be useful without costing the Government anything. All of Russia was turned into a vast military camp, threatening to engulf the daring conqueror who had breached the age-old inviolability of our borders. Already the enemy corps, left to the rear of the *Grande Armée*, were under pressure from our forces and could not hold them in check. Napoleon, losing hope of concluding peace little by little, remained in Moscow only in order not to reveal his impotence to a Germany ever more hostile to him.

Having finally decided to retreat, Napoleon moved around the Tarutino camp, onto the new Kaluga road, towards Maloyaroslavets. Had he dashed to this location with his usual speed, he would probably have forestalled Kutuzov in Maloyaroslavets but, even with his slow movement, he almost succeeded. Subsequent operations by both sides can only be explained by the inopportune caution of both commanders: Napoleon, having placed himself in a hopeless situation, remote from access to his resources, did not want to abandon himself and his army to chance in a decisive battle and preferred to preserve his forces in good order for the retreat; while Kutuzov avoided engaging Napoleon and tried to weaken and destroy his army without entering into a pitched battle.

As soon as our commander closed up to Maloyaroslavets with the main body of the army, then the advantages of the position he had taken were on his side, as was superiority in numbers: the enemy could attack our army only by extricating their columns from a town engulfed in flames and forming up for battle under fire from our powerful batteries, battering the entire space ahead of them under cross fire. Despite these advantages, however, the Russian troops retreated for a whole stage along the Kaluga road, and had Napoleon pursued them, then, in all likelihood, Kutuzov, unable to find a suitable position at Detchino and Goncharovo, would have retreated behind the Oka, which would have allowed Napoleon not only to seize Kaluga, but also to head towards Smolensk along the shortest and as yet untouched road, to Yelnya. The retreat back to Borovsk, however, and onwards to Mozhaisk, deprived him of these benefits and had a detrimental effect on the morale of his troops, believing that he no longer dared to give battle.

Kutuzov directed his army very skilfully along side roads in order to cut off the enemy; but moving slowly, he could not take advantage of his position: only light detachments pursued the French to Mozhaisk and Gzhatsk; the main body, however, only came level with the enemy at Vyazma; Davout's force, having been indecisively attacked there by the vanguard of the Main Army, were rescued by the Viceroy and continued their onward retreat towards Smolensk. On the route from Gzhatsk to Vyazma, all the stores carried with the French army had already been depleted; the shortage of rations and the long marches had exhausted the troops. The first snow fell after the enemy departure from Vyazma, and on the night of 25 to 26 October (6 to 7 November) freezing weather set in, reaching 18 degrees or more of frost and lasting six days, until the French troops had assembled at Smolensk. The combined effects of hunger, cold and fatigue, together with the tenacious pursuit by Platov's Cossack detachment and partisans, disordered and weakened the enemy army; the hope of finding rest and food in Smolensk was in vain. Although the cold became more tolerable after their departure from there, the slush and damp were no less disastrous for the ragged, barefoot, hungry French. To crown their desperate situation, Napoleon split his army into several echelons, exiting from Smolensk at one day intervals. Kutuzov, continuing the pursuit from the flank, had the opportunity to cut off and break up the enemy army in detail, and was only five *versts* from the main road with his main body, at the time when the corps under Davout and Ney had not yet managed to pass along it beyond his army; but by acting with his usual caution, he missed the opportunity to inflict a total defeat on Napoleon. All this notwithstanding, however, the actions at Krasny, having completed the disordering of the enemy, in all fairness, may be considered the end of the existence of a force under Napoleon's direct command.

The onward retreat by the remnants of the enemy army towards the Berezina, executed with unusual speed out of necessity, greatly exhausted and weakened them. Prince Kutuzov has been wrongly criticised for granting the main body a rest in Kopys: was it really necessary to chase after the enemy and pointlessly disperse his army through forced marches, just as Napoleon's force had been dispersed? I say, pointlessly, because on the Berezina we had no shortage of troops, but of coordination of operations: Kutuzov should not have been in Kopys by then, but where the final blow to the enemy was supposed to be delivered. Chichagov was deceived by Napoleon, but if Napoleon had known how far our army was lagging behind him, and taking advantage of that, had crossed downstream of Borisov, he could have been strengthened by significant reinforcements and his position would have been incomparably better than during the retreat through Studyanka and Zembin. Consequently, both Chichagov and our other generals quite reasonably assumed (although they were mistaken in their assessment) that Napoleon had to seek a crossing point downstream of Borisov.

In general, mistakes are inevitable in military matters, because it is only on rare occasions that a commander's assessments can be based on confirmed intelligence. And on our part, as on the part of Napoleon, many mistakes were made, which became obvious, for the most part, only once they could no longer be rectified. Napoleon's enterprise collapsed not so much as a result of his mistakes in the military sense, but from an incorrect assessment of the relative attitudes of both belligerents. Having the armed forces not only of France, but also of other states, at the beginning of the war he had a decisive advantage in troop numbers on his side; but, as he pushed into Russia, his army weakened with increasing speed, not so much from combat losses, as from campaign labours and hardships. It emerged, but only once it was already too late, that it was almost impossible to provide rations for a 200,000 strong army moving en masse, in such a sparsely populated country as our *oblasts*, which served as the theatre of operations in 1812; especially with the hostile nature of the population, who set fire to their homes and left when the French appeared. When undertaking an invasion of Russia, it is necessary to take pains to collect intelligence about the country and its population, and Napoleon did not lose sight of this, but evidently there were few traitors in our Fatherland, while immigrant informants brought such intelligence about Russia and the Russians, that nowadays may be encountered in the statements of French tourists. Napoleon was bound to fall, and actually fell, into a delusion about the nature of our country, and this was one of his most important mistakes. But his understanding of the character of Emperor Alexander I was even more mistaken: Napoleon's blindness extended to the point that at the beginning of the war he expected that his seizure of Vilna would induce the Russian Government to agree to all his persistent demands. Having been disabused of this wishful thinking, in spite of this, he was sure that stationing his victorious army in the ruins of Moscow would force our Tsar to be more accommodating than previously. But neither the retreat of our army after the battle of Borodino, nor the occupation of the ancient Russian capital, could shake the resolve of Emperor Alexander: for the Russians, the war had just begun.

Napoleon had a no less false notion of our people, hoping for a revolt by the peasants and of finding sympathy for his viewpoint in Russia. Had Napoleon fully appreciated both the willpower of Emperor Alexander I, and the excellent character of the people, constant in their faith in God, devoted to their Tsar and with love for their homeland, then he would not have violated the peace with Russia. But Almighty Providence decreed that our Fatherland would make countless sacrifices in defence of its own independence and, after a hard test, brightened with new glory, would contribute to the liberation of the oppressed nations.

The war of 1812 left the mark of devastation in the areas traversed by the enemy for a long time: wealthy cities had been razed; their inhabitants became impoverished, or lost all their property; there were heaps of debris and ashes on the sites of flourishing villages; the population had decreased markedly. But, on the other hand, a sense of self-confidence settled in the Russians for a long time after the Patriotic War, appropriate to a great people. It is not fortresses that protect our borders from enemy invasion: their most faithful defence is the remembrance of the struggle we sustained against a huge army led by a military genius, the like of which had not been seen for centuries.

Emperor Alexander I, wishing to commemorate the Patriotic War, decided to build a cathedral to Christ the Saviour and minted silver medals with the image of the All-Seeing Eye, which were issued to every man who had taken part in the war, from general to soldier.[19] Similar bronze medals were issued to the nobility in commemoration of their service and donations made by them. The words inscribed on the medals were: 'не намъ не намъ, а имени Твоему' [not us, not us, but in Your name] testifying that the main author of success, putting aside arrogant thoughts, had turned with a plea of gratitude to his source of strength, who had protected Russia with His mantle. In addition, it was intended to erect a monument from the guns captured from the enemy.[20] The Orthodox Church celebrates the deliverance of our Fatherland from the invasion by the French and the 20 nations that accompanied them, annually on the day of the Nativity of Christ.

Upon the complete ending of the war, grateful Russia, in the persons of the highest dignitaries of the Empire, proposed that Emperor Alexander I add to His Name the title 'the Blessed,' as was stated in the petition; 'all the more befitting to the modesty and pious humility of the Sovereign Emperor, that His great deeds are obviously marked by the patronage of Almighty Providence.' At the same time, it was intended

---

19 For the full texts of the documents relating to the cathedral and issue of medals, see Appendix XXVII.
20 For the full text of the document relating to the monument, see Appendix XXVIII.

to strike a medal and erect a monument in St Petersburg with the inscription: 'Александру Благословенному, Императору Всероссійскому, великодушному державъ возстановителю, отъ признательныя Россіи' [Alexander the Blessed, Emperor of All Russia, magnanimous restorer of rights, from a grateful Russia], having collected the necessary amount from voluntary donations.

On this occasion, the resulting comment, which expressed the very high spiritual qualities of Emperor Alexander I, was decreed: 'To the Holy Governing Synod, the Council of State and the Governing Senate.

Having listened to the petition sent to Me from the Holy Synod, the Council of State and the Governing Senate, about a monument erected to Me in the capital city and the adoption of the title the Blessed, I could not but feel the greatest pleasure in the depths of my soul, having seen on the one hand the blessings of God that have actually been laid upon us, while on the other, the feelings of the Russian state classes, bringing to Me a most flattering title for Myself, since every effort and thought from My soul strives to call upon Himself and on the people entrusted to Me divine blessings through heartfelt prayers, and to be blessed by My loyal subjects, so dear to Me, and from the entire human race. This is the height of My desires and My welfare! But with all My striving to achieve this, I cannot allow Myself, as a man, the boldness to think that I have already reached the point where I can boldly accept and bear this title. All the more, I honour it with the principles and way of thinking of My opposition, that directing My faithful subjects to feelings of modesty and humility of spirit always and everywhere, I myself should not be the first to set an example that does not correspond to this. For the sake of this, and expressing my perfect gratitude, I urge the state classes to leave this unfulfilled. May a monument be built to Me with your sentiments, as it is built in My sentiments for you! May My people bless Me in their hearts, as I bless them in My heart! May Russia prosper, and may the blessings of God be upon Me and upon Her!'

Appendix I

A return showing the approximate strength of Napoleon's force prior to the departure from Moscow

Corps	Infantry	Cavalry	Guns	Carts	Remarks
Garde	17,871	4,609	112	275	According to returns dated 3 (15) October.
1er Corps	27,449	1,500	144	633	2e & 4e division according to returns dated 8 (20) September; 1er, 3e & 5e dated 28 September (10 October), light cavalry estimated.
3e Corps	9,597	901	71	186	According to returns dated 10 October (new style).
4e Corps	23,963	1,661	92	450	According to returns dated 10 October (new style).
5e Corps	4,844	868	49	239	According to returns dated 9 (21) October.
8e Corps	1,916	775	34	130	According to returns dated 4 (16) October.
Dismounted cavalry Bde	4,000				Estimate as at 6 (18) October.
1er, 2e, 3e & 4e Corps de cavalerie		5,000	67	157	Estimate following the action on the Chernishnya.
TOTAL:	89,640	15,314	569	2,070	

From the cavalry totals for *1er Corps*, *3e Corps* and *4e Corps* shown in this return, 1,000 who were in action on the Chernishnya, according to Chambray, should be excluded, therefore, the strength of the French army, upon departing from Moscow, reached 104,000, and together with the gendarmes, troops of the engineering department and service support troops, were some 116,000 men. Chambray, II, 314-315. Bernhardi very convincingly puts the number of combatants in the French army at 107,000, from the fact that in Chambray the strength of the Westphalian *8e Corps* is erroneously shown as 3,000 men fewer than the actual number of troops therein. *Denkwürdigkeiten des Grafen v. Toll*, II, 233.

Appendix II

Prince Kutuzov's report to the Tsar, dated 16 (28) October 1812

The enemy, having very favourable high ground on the left bank of the Luzha river facing Maloyaroslavets, could always conveniently reinforce his attacks on this town, and if one wished to hold this location, which was so disadvantageous to us, then, in addition to the 3,000 men that we have already lost from the front line through seven assaults, even greater losses would have been incurred, and this place has been abandoned for that reason.

On 13 [25] October, the enemy remained on the left bank of the Luzha, while our army occupied the high ground on the right bank of this river. Meanwhile, our light troops, extending themselves to the road to Medyn, along which the enemy could still make their way to Kaluga, began to give notice simultaneously that their corps were pushing along this road. This appeared all the more likely because there was already fighting between our light troops and enemy detachments on it.

It was also obvious that the enemy intention was to outflank us to Kaluga by whatever means, and therefore the army, leaving a strong vanguard under the command of General Miloradovich, moved to the village of Detchino on 14 [26] October. On that day the enemy remained in contact with our vanguard without any activity all day. On the night of 14 to 15 [26 to 27] October the enemy retreated to Borovsk. Our light troops caught up with them six *versts* from Maloyaroslavets and shadowed them to Borovsk itself. The intelligence that the enemy was on the march from Vereya and Borovsk to Medyn prompted me to detach 23rd Division to the Medyn road in advance, and to make a flanking march towards this road with the army, and therefore, set out from the village of Detchino on the night of 15 to 16 [27 to 28] October and moved towards Polotnyanye Zavody; the vanguard moved towards Medyn, leaving an infantry brigade with three Cossack regiments in Maloyaroslavets, to where Major General Paskevich was moving from Polotnyanye Zavody with 26th Division to link up with them. The military Ataman Platov, with 15 regiments, excluding all the individual patrols, observed the enemy movements in the vicinity, having strong patrols in the direction of Vereya.

Intelligence recently received confirmed that the enemy is near Vereya and Borovsk, that they are sending their sick and transport back along the Smolensk road. As a result, although it could be concluded that the enemy no longer has the intent to operate towards Kaluga, and will take the direction to Smolensk via Mozhaisk, nevertheless, I shall remain on the Medyn road for the time being. While, in order to totally harass their retreat march, the partisans operating in this direction have been reinforced, over and above this, a raiding corps has been established, consisting of newly arrived Poltava Cossacks, amalgamated with the Don Cossacks, with two regiments of infantry, under the command of Adjutant General Ozharovsky, for operations directly towards Smolensk. Field Marshal, Prince G-Kutuzov.

Followed by Prince Kutuzov's handwritten postscript:

Moscow has, of course, been abandoned by the enemy, but none of my messengers have yet returned, and therefore I have yet to report officially.

Appendix III

The Viceroy's intercepted dispatches

Prince! J'ai l'honneur de rendre compte à Votre Altesse que je me suis mis en mouvement ce matin à 4 heures; mais les difficultés du terrain et le verglas ont mis tant d'obstacles à la marche de mon Corps d'armée que la tête seule a pu arriver ici à 6 heures du soir et que la queue n'a pu prendre position qu'à près de deux lieues en arrière.

De deux à 5 heures l'ennemi s'est presenté sur ma droite. Il a attaqué presqu'en même temps la tête, le centre et la queue avec l'artillerie, des cosaques et des dragons. A la tête il a trouvé une lacune dont il a profité pour faire une houra et enlever deux pièces regimentaires qui se trouvaient dans une rampe trés roide et éloignées de leurs escorts. Le 9e Regim. d'infanterie est acouru, mais les pièces étaient déjà emmenées.

A l'arrière-garde l'ennemi a fait feu avec quatre pièces de canon, et le général Ornano croit, sans l'aflirmer, avoir vu de l'infanterie. Sur chacun des autres points il avait 2 pièces.

Votre Altesse jugera facilement qu'embarassé par mes gros équipages que l'on m'a rendus, et par une nombreuse artillerie, dont plus de 400 chevaux, sans éxageration, sont morts aujourd'hui, ma position est assez critique. Neanmoins je continuerai mon mouvement demain de très grand matin pour arriver à Pologhi. De là j'enverrai aux nouvelles et suivant ce qu'elles m'apprendront je me déterminerai à me rendre à Douchovtschina ou à Pnewa.

Je ne dois pas dissimuler à Votre Altesse qu'après avoir employé tous les moyens, je me vois maintenant dans l'impossibilité de trainer mon artillerie et qu'elle doit s'attendre, sous ce rapport, à de très grands sacrifices. Dès aujourd'hui plusieurs pièces ont été enclouées et enterrées.

Je renouvelle à Votre Altesse l'assurance de tous mes sentimens.
Signé: Eugéne Napoléon.
Zasélié, ce 7-9-bre 1812.

Prince! J'adresse si-incluse à Votre Altesse, une lettre que je lui ai écrite hier, mais qui ne lui est pas parvenue, l'officier qui en était porteur ayant été egaré par son guide.

Votre Altesse sera surprise de ne me savoir encore que sur le Vop. Je n'en suis pas moins parti ce matin de Zasélié à 5 heures, mais la route est tellement coupée de ravins qu'il a fallu des efforts inouis pour arriver jusqu'ici. C'est avec douleur que je me vois dans la dure necessité de lui avouer les sacrifices que nous avons faits pour accelerer notre marche. Ces trois journées ont couté les deux tiers de l'artillerie du corps d'armée. Hier il est mort environ 400 chevaux et aujourd'hui il en est peri peut-être le double, non compris la grande quantité de chevaux qu j'ai fait ajouter par les equipages militaires et particuliers. Des attelages entiers perissoient en même temps; plusieurs ont été renouvellés jusqu'à trois fois.

Aujourd'hui le corps d'armée n'a point été inquieté dans sa marche. Il a apperçu seulement quelques cosaques, sans artillerie, ce qui ne me parait pas naturel, et s'il faut en croire le rapport d'un voltigeur envoyé à la maraude il s'ensuivroit, qu'une colonne d'infanterie, d'artillerie et de cavalerie, suivrait la même direction que nous, c'est-à-dire sur Douchovtschina. Cette nuit j'envoie une forte reconnaissance sur Douchovtschina où je compte être rendu demain si l'ennemi ne m'oppose pas une resistance sérieuse, car, je ne dois pas le cacher à Votre Altesse, ces trois jours de souffrance ont tellement abattu l'esprit du soldat que je le crois dans ce moment bien peu susceptible de faire quelque effort. Beaucoup d'hommes sont morts de faim ou de froid et d'autres desesperés ont été se faire prendre par l'ennemi.

Je renouvelle à Votre Altesse l'assurance de mes sentimens.
Signé: Eugéne Napoléon.
Passage du Vop. le 8 – 9-bre, 1812.

Appendix IV

The strength of the French army between 8 to 14 November new style

	Infantry	Cavalry	Remarks
Infanterie de la Garde	14,000		Including Claparède's division and 1,000 men who joined at Smolensk.
Cavalerie de la Garde		2,000	
1er Corps	10,000		Including 1,565 men who joined at Smolensk.
3e Corps	6,000		Including two regiments and 500 men who joined at Smolensk.
4e Corps	5,000		
5e Corps	800		
8e Corps	700		
Dismounted cavalrymen	500		
Latour-Maubourg's cavalry		1,900	
Light cavalry attached to the corps		1,200	
Total:	**37,000**	**5,100**	

In addition, artillerymen, engineering troops and gendarmes 7,000 men.

It is rather difficult to determine precisely the enemy losses in artillery. A return, signed by Prince Kutuzov, shows in general the number of guns we recovered from the enemy, before the occupation of Smolensk by our troops, as 209; but this number includes 71 guns (eight taken by us at Borodino, 26 found in Moscow and 37 captured in the Chernishnya action) lost by the *Grande Armée* before Napoleon's departure from Moscow. *Sotnik* Nazkin found 112 guns abandoned by the enemy during the retreat, on the first stage from Smolensk; in addition, many guns were abandoned on the last stage to Krasny, and even buried in the ground in various places, or pushed into lakes and rivers.

Appendix V

Prince Kutuzov's report to Emperor Alexander I, dated 7 [19] November, No. 464

Most Merciful Tsar! From my report, of today's date, Your Imperial Majesty, if you please, may see what was achieved at Krasny, towards which the enemy were directing all their strength; all this had not been done before, along the Smolensk road, for many reasons.

From the very moment the enemy decided to leave Moscow following the defeat of the 6th of last month, I had to consider the cutting of our communications with Kaluga and preventing them from reaching it, through which they intended to pass into the Orël Governorate and then into Malorussia, so as not to to endure those shortages, which have now brought their army to such a disastrous state; many of the captured generals confirmed to me that this was their intention, and therefore it was necessary to force them back along the Smolensk road, on which (as we knew) they had not prepared provisions; these reasons compelled me, upon leaving Maloyaroslavets, to move across to the road leading from Borovsk to Kaluga via Medyn, where an enemy corps was already located; from this movement of mine, the enemy, abandoning their intention, had to return via Vereya to the Smolensk road; while I went via Medyn to Borovsk in order to close up to and, if necessary, link up with my vanguard. General Miloradovich had II Corps and IV Corps and a sufficient number of cavalry under his command, but being deceived by false intelligence, believed them to be close to Medyn along the Borovsk road; but having learned of the recent enemy march from Borovsk to Vereya, he went after them, but nevertheless lost a whole march and went off in the wake of the enemy onto the Smolensk road; the main army went via side roads towards Vyazma. It happened that, for about three days, I could not get intelligence from the vanguard, because the fleeing enemy had scattered along either side of the route, and finally an incorrect report came that General Miloradovich had been forced to retreat after a battle with the enemy, before reaching Vyazma; these circumstances delayed me for eight hours and the army could not move closer to Vyazma, having made a 40 *verst* march that day, and arrived no earlier than midnight; while only 40 squadrons of cuirassiers with horse artillery had been able to keep up, under the command of Adjutant General Uvarov, who contributed to General Miloradovich's defeat of the enemy near Vyazma; the enemy could not hold on to the city into which they had been forced and part of their force was broken; that evening, having passed through

Vyazma, they did not dare to halt and retired along the Smolensk road before the army could close with them.

These are the reasons that prevented us from inflicting such a telling blow on the enemy at Vyazma, as was dealt to them at Krasny; Moreover, it must be said that at Vyazma they were not yet in such a state of disarray, they still had almost all their artillery, and those notable losses in men had not yet occurred, which they were to suffer on the retreat to Smolensk. Mistakes, due to occasional false intelligence being received, are unavoidable; the development of military operations cannot always be based on evidence, but sometimes on conjectures and rumours; the false intelligence, which I mentioned above, came from the Cossacks themselves, but they too fell into this misunderstanding in a blameless manner.

From Vyazma I undertook a diagonal march via Yelnya towards Krasny, where I caught up with the enemy.

Most Merciful Tsar, from Your Imperial Majesty's most humble Prince Mikhail G. Kutuzov. Near Krasny, in the village of Dobryanka [Dobraya].

Appendix VI

Captain Seslavin's report, dated 8 [20] November

Captain Seslavin's report, dated 8 [20] November (Log of Incoming Documents. No. 580):

> I am informing Your Excellency for a third time that an enemy depot, under the command of Major Blancard, remains in Gorki. I am forwarding to you an intercepted letter from Orsha to Gorki. They have been ordered to cross the Dnieper. Send infantry, cavalry and horse artillery, and this depot will be in our hands. Let me know when you have sent them and I shall also assist there.

The intercepted document reads as follows:

> *Orsza. Le 19 novembre, 1812, à 10 heures du soir. Monsieur le major Blancard, j'envoie un juif au devant de Vous. Je vous ai ordonné plusieurs fois de Vous rendre avec votre dépôt sur le Dnieper. Accelerez votre marche le plus qu'il vous sera possible. Signé: Le prince de Neuchatel.*

(Major Blancard, I am sending a Jew to meet You. I have ordered you several times to withdraw beyond the Dnieper with your depot. Speed up your departure as much as possible).

The state of this depot may be judged from a report by Blancard, also intercepted by the Cossacks, in which he wrote among other things:

> *... la position des dépôts devient de jour en jour plus critique: isolés et ayant une retraite très longue à faire avant de pouvoir être secourus, embarassés d'équipages, de malades et hommes désarmés, ils ne feraient probablement qu'une faible résistance et perdraient, dans tous les cas, beaucoup de monde s'ils étaient attaqués: ils manquent de cartouches. Voyant qu'il n'était pas possible de les rassembler, j'ai voulu faire entrer dans les dépôt les hommes des bataillons formés à Moscou, qui se trouvent ici; quelques uns ont obei, d'autres se sont en allés pour leur compte sur Orsza. D'ailleurs, les hommes de ces bataillons, qui devraient nous défendre, désorganisés, et démoralisés, ne feraient que nous gêner: la plupart ont jeté non seulement leurs fusils ou*

carabines, mais encore leur sabre. Plusieurs de leurs officiers (dont quelques uns sont aussi pour leur compte à Orsza), sont d'une insouciance, je dirai même d'une mauvaise volonté très coupable...

(the situation in the depot becomes more critical by the day: isolated and having a very long retreat to make before the possibility of relief, encumbered with carriages, sick and unarmed men, they would probably only put up a weak resistance and in any case, would lose many men if they were attacked: they lack cartridges. Seeing as it was not possible to assemble them, I wanted to bring the men of the battalions formed in Moscow, who are here, into the depot; some obeyed, others went to Orsha of their own accord. Moreover, the men of these battalions, who should be defending us, are disorganised and demoralised, and would only hinder us: most of them have discarded not only their muskets or carbines, but also their sabres. Several of their officers (some of whom also went to Orsha on their own authority) are recklessly, I would even say very culpably, ill-willed). Major Blancard's report to *chef d'état-major* Berthier, dated 18 November new style.

Appendix VII

Order of battle for the forces under Chichagov and Saken

The forces under Chichagov and Saken, as extracted from the returns placed in the War Diary of the Army of the Danube, following its renaming as Third Army, in 1812, compiled by Lieutenant Colonel Malinovsky of the Suite of His Imperial Majesty's Quartermaster's Department, and War Diary of General Saken's Corps in 1812, 1813 and 1814, compiled by Lieutenant Colonel Gotovsky. In Chichagov's Notes, Saken's, together with Essen's corps, are shown with 27,000 men, while 25,000 men are shown in Chichagov's army, which moved from the Bug to the Berezina, which, in all probability, is lower than the actual number of troops.

Attached are the above-mentioned returns:

Troops under the direct command of Admiral Chichagov:
Vanguard:
 14th Jägers – 2 Bns.
 27th Jägers – 3 Bns.
 38th Jägers – 2 Bns.
 Tatar Ulans – 8 Sqns.
 Alexandria Hussars – 8 Sqns.
 Starodub Dragoons – 4 Sqns.
 Zhitomir Dragoons – 4 Sqns.
 Arzamas Dragoons – 4 Sqns.
 Grekov 8th's Cossacks.
 Grekov 11th's Cossacks.
 Melnikov 5th's Cossacks.
 Barabanshchikov 9th's Cossacks.
 Yevpatoria Tatars.
 11th Horse Artillery Company.
 12th Horse Artillery Company.
 Total for the vanguard: seven battalions, 28 squadrons, five Cossack regiments and two artillery companies.

Corps under the command of General-of-Infantry Count Langéron:
Lieutenant General Voinov's Corps:
    Vladimir Infantry – 2 Bns.
    Tambov Infantry – 2 Bns.
    Dnieper Infantry – 2 Bns.
    Kostroma Infantry – 2 Bns.
    Nasheburg Infantry – 2 Bns.
    Apsheron Infantry – 2 Bns.
    Ryazhsk Infantry – 2 Bns.
    Yakutsk Infantry – Bns.
    10th Jägers – 2 Bns.
    St Petersburg Dragoons – 4 Sqns.
    Livland Dragoons – 4 Sqns.
    Seversk Dragoons – 4 Sqns.
    Belorussia Hussars – 8 Sqns.
    Kireev 2nd's Cossacks.
    3rd Ural Cossack Regiment.
    9th Battery Artillery Company.
    18th Battery Artillery Company.
    34th Light Artillery Company.
    35th Light Artillery Company.
    16th Light Artillery Company.
    17th Light Artillery Company.
    Captain Kanatchikov's Pioneer Company.
    Total for Voinov's Corps: 18 battalions, 20 squadrons, two Cossack regiments, six artillery companies and one pioneer company.

Reserve, under Lieutenant General Sabaneev's command:
    Kolyvan Infantry – 2 Bns.
    Kurin Infantry – 2 Bns.
    Vitebsk Infantry – 2 Bns.
    Kozlov Infantry – 2 Bns.
    13th Jägers – 2 Bns.
    7th Jägers – 3 Bns.
    12th Jägers – 2 Bns.
    Saratov Infantry – 2 Bns.
    Combined battalions – 6 Bns.
    Dorpat Dragoons – 4 Sqns.
    Kinburn Dragoons – 4 Sqns.
    Olviopol Hussars – 8 Sqns.
    Lukovkin's Cossacks.
    Panteleev's Cossacks.
    Melnikov's Cossacks.
    38th Battery Artillery Company.
    39th Battery Artillery Company.
    34th Battery Artillery Company.

25th Light Artillery Company.
50th Light Artillery Company.
16th Horse Artillery Company.
Total for Sabaneev's Corps: 23 battalions, 16 squadrons, three Cossack regiments and six artillery companies.

Troops under Lieutenant General Saken's command:
Lieutenant General Essen 3rd's Corps:
Schlüsselburg Infantry – 2 Bns.
Staro Ingermanland Infantry – 2 Bns.
Arkhangelogorod Infantry – 2 Bns.
Ukraine Infantry – 2 Bns.
Olonets Infantry – 3 Bns.
37th Jägers – 3 Bns.
Serpukhov Dragoons – 4 Sqns.
Vladimir Dragoons – 3 Sqns.
Tver Dragoons – 1 Sqn.
Lubny Hussars – 8 Sqns.
2nd Bashkir Regiment.
1st Kalmyk Regiment.
4th Ural Cossack Regiment.
Chikilev's Cossacks.
8th Battery Artillery Company.
14th Light Artillery Company.
15th Light Artillery Company.
15th Horse Artillery Company.
Lieutenant Colonel Gebener's Pioneer half-company.
Total for Essen 3rd's Corps: 14 battalions, 16 squadrons, four Cossack regiments, four artillery companies and a pioneer half-company.

Major General Bulatov's Corps:
Vyatka Infantry – 3 Bns.
Vyborg Infantry – 2 Bns.
Staro Oskol Infantry – 3 Bns.
Okhotsk Infantry – 2 Bns.
Mingrelia Infantry – 2 Bns.
Galits Infantry – 2 Bns.
Kamchatka Infantry – 1 Bn.
45th Jägers – 1 Bn.
29th Jägers – 2 Bns.
Pereyaslavl Dragoons – 4 Sqns.
Smolensk Dragoons – 4 Sqns.
Chuguev Ulans – 8 Sqns.
Vlasov's Cossacks.
2nd Kalmyk Regiment.
22nd Battery Artillery Company.

41st Light Artillery Company.
Lieutenant Colonel Gebener's Pioneer half-company.
Total for Bulatov's Corps: 18 battalions, 16 squadrons, two Cossack regiments, two artillery companies, and a pioneer half-company.

Reserve, under Major General Lieven's command:
Yaroslavl Infantry – 2 Bns.
Crimea Infantry – 3 Bns.
Vyborg Infantry – 2 Bns.
Bialystok Infantry – 3 Bns.
8th Jägers – 3 Bns.
39th Jägers – 2 Bns.
Vladimir Dragoons – 3 Sqns.
Tver Dragoons – 1 Sqn.
10th Battery Artillery Company.
18th Light Artillery Company.
Total for Count Lieven's Corps: 15 battalions, four squadrons and two artillery companies.

Appendix VIII

Situation de la place de Minsk à l'époque du 12 novembre (new style) *1812*

	Men	Horses
Württemberg *Infanterie-Regiment Nr. 7*	709	96
Convalescent Depot	502	
22e régiment d'infanterie légère	26	1
9e régiment d'artillerie à pied	44	13
Gendarmes	37	41
Depot of the Grand Duchy of Warsaw	162	
Cavalry Depot	266	32
Duchy of Warsaw *18 Pułk Ułanów*	17	22
Régiment d'Illyrie	95	13
Depot *6e bataillon, 46e régiment d'infanterie de ligne*	9	
Depot *93e régiment d'infanterie de ligne*	59	20
Cavalry Depot of the *Grande Armée*	133	145
Cavalry Depot of *2e Corps* and *6e Corps*	84	86
33e régiment d'infanterie de ligne	25	9
Total:	1,996	475

A calculation of the number of newly recruited Lithuanian troops is included in Chambray, *Histoire de l'expédition de Russie en 1812*, II, 403.

Appendix IX

Details of Ertel's inaction

Lieutenant General Ertel, having received orders from Admiral Chichagov, dated 17 [29] October, to set out from Mozyr to Minsk, responded to Chichagov with a report dated 24 October [5 November], that it was impossible to follow the issued march-route, because all the bridges along the route were broken, and besides, he could not abandon Mozyr, where there were a large amount of provisions.

Meanwhile, Field Marshal Prince Kutuzov, having ordered the governor of Volhynia to send all the provisions purchased in Mozyr to the Bobruisk fortress, on 16 [28] October, ordered Ertel to ensure that provisions from Mozyr were transported to Bobruisk. Having received these orders, Ertel informed Chichagov of this in a report dated 25 October [6 November], asking for permission on precisely how many troops should be ordered to be left in Mozyr in order to protect the convoy.

On 29 October [10 November], Chichagov ordered Ertel to set out as quickly as possible to the rendezvous point, without waiting for the arrival of the reserve squadrons from Zhitomir, which could follow later, along with the reserve battalions. In response to this command, Ertel reported on 2 [14] November, that he had issued all the orders for their departure; but the next day, 3 [15] November, he ordered Lieutenant Colonel Palageyka [Anton Lavrovich Palageyka?], who was stationed in Slutsk with a detachment, to remain there, due to heavy ice floes on the river, and to inform Admiral Chichagov that General Ertel would hardly be able to cross the river. Also on 3 [15] November, Ertel received instructions from Prince Kutuzov and from Chichagov: the former wrote that Ertel, if he had not received a specific mission from Chichagov, was to move to Bobruisk with his corps, to assist the Main Army, while Chichagov sent orders to go to Igumen without fail, finding that the reasons given by Ertel in his report dated 24 October [5 November] did not warrant the slightest concern. In response to these orders, Ertel, in a report to Chichagov, also dated 3 [15] November, explained that in the admiral's orders he had received earlier, it stated: 'to depart for Minsk if you do not encounter significant obstacles' and that, moreover, in Chichagov's own handwriting: 'be careful to operate without taking great risks.' Furthermore, Ertel wrote that 'there are also 2,000 sick in this corps, that about 25,000 *Chetvert* of grain and 100,000 *Pud* of hay had been collected in Mozyr, and that he had orders from the Field Marshal to send convoys of provisions to Bobruisk, while General Ignatiev had demanded that 5,000 *Chetvert* of bread be sent to him.' Under these circumstances, with the hostility of the population in the countryside towards us and cases of cattle, he did not dare to leave Mozyr; but if he was mistaken, he asked for forgiveness and for orders on where to go following the orders received from the Field Marshal to go to Bobruisk and what to do about the convoys? Further on, the report by General Ertel mentions the obstacles facing him due to a lack of bridges over the rivers on the route assigned to him.

Two days later, in a report dated 5 [17] November, General Ertel reported to the admiral that, despite all the obstacles encountered, he had laid bridges across the Pripyat and would arrive in Yakimovskaya Sloboda on 13 [25] November, where he would await orders.

On 6 [18] November, General Ertel received two sets of orders from Admiral Chichagov: in the first, dated 1 [13] November, he was ordered to act, notwithstanding any obstacles, because he must not upset the execution of the general plan of operations based on personal considerations. At the same time, it was made clear to him that the orders issued by him to the reserve squadrons – to halt in Ovruch [Owrucz] – also had negative consequences. In the second orders, as permission for Ertel's report dated 24 October [5 November], he was ordered to leave two battalions and four squadrons in Mozyr and to go to Igumen immediately with all other troops. On 7 [19] November, General Ertel reported on the execution of these orders and on the arrival in Mozyr of the squadrons left in Ovruch.

Appendix X

Yermolov's report to Wittgenstein, dated 11 [23] November, from Pogost

Sir, General-of-Cavalry, Commander I Corps and Chevalier, Count Wittgenstein. From Chief-of-Staff, First Army, Major General Yermolov. I report:

Today I am in the village of Pogost, moving in the direction of Kokhanovo with a vanguard assigned to reinforce the troops under General Count Platov. Count Platov is already far ahead, as the enemy is retreating in extreme haste. No doubt His Grace's courier might find Your Excellency in Smolny [Smoliyantsy?]. It is reasonable to assume that Marshal Victor is retreating to link up with the *Grande Armée*, unless their direction is not towards Borisov, but rather towards Kholopenichi and Dokshitsy. Our army is proceeding somewhat hastily, and therefore I conclude that His Grace is minded that the troops who have the honour to serve under the command of Your Excellency, are also in hot pursuit. For the resolution of which I have been honoured with orders to humbly request that I be notified of the location of the main body of your force. Tomorrow I shall be moving on and will hurry as quickly as possible. I lost a day and a half while crossing the Dnieper, in which time I was forced to lose contact with the enemy. As yet, the direction of the enemy army has not been determined, because if Minsk is already held by our troops, then it is doubtful that they would head there rather, of course, than to press on and link up with Victor. In any case, whether our troops are located in Minsk having caught up or lightened their load, or if they have not arrived there yet, the situation allows Your Excellency, by pursuing, to force the enemy to hasten their retreat, this alone would seal their doom and deprive them of all their heavy equipment and also an incredible amount of artillery.

Count Platov is proceeding close to the highway towards Borisov with the entire force from the Don. If it pleases Your Excellency to notify me of your progress, via this means if possible, as tomorrow we may already have communications with you.

Chief-of-Staff, First Army, Major General Yermolov.

No. 510.

11 [23] November 1812, from Pogost.

Appendix XI

The strength of Napoleon's forces

The strength of Napoleon's forces, as given in:

Chambray On the morning of 26th November	Men	Fain 28th November	Men
Vieille Garde	3,500	*Vieille Garde*	4,500
Jeune Garde	1,500	*Jeune Garde*	2,200
cavalerie de la Garde	1,400	*cavalerie de la Garde* dismounted cavalry	200 180
2e Corps – Oudinot	9,300	*2e Corps* – Oudinot	7,000
3e Corps – Ney	5,400	*3e Corps* – Ney	4,000
1er Corps – Davout	1,200	*1er Corps* – Davout	}
4e Corps – the Viceroy	1,200	*4e Corps* – the Viceroy	} 9,000
8e Corps – Junot (disbanded)		*8e Corps* – Junot	}
9e Corps – Victor	10,800	*9e Corps* – Victor (less Partouneaux)	10,000
Réserve de cavalerie	100		
Total:	30,000	Total:	40,780
Including 26,700 infantry and 4,000 cavalry.		In addition, some 45,000 to 50,000 stragglers and unarmed men.	

There were some 250 artillery pieces. Chambray, III, 50. Fain, II, 334. According to Sołtyk, Napoleon had 50,000 armed men with 250 guns and as many again of marauders and unarmed men. *Napoléon en 1812*, 441-442. Fezensac wrote that there were 50,000 men under arms in Napoleon's army at the Berezina, of whom 5,000 were cavalry, and there was much artillery. *Journal de la campagne de Russie en 1812*, 126.

Appendix XII

Excerpts from General Bennigsen's letters to Emperor Alexander I

Sire! Il n'est pas douteux, que Votre Majesté Imperiale a été informé du peu d'intelligence, qui depuis quelque tems a regné entre Mr. le Maréchal et moi. J'en appelle aux temoignages de toute l'armée si c'est moi qui en suis la cause, et j'en appelle à la conscience du Prince lui-même, si je ne lui ai pas proposé de servir comme il voulait et même avec les cosaques. Jamais, Sire, V.M.I. le sçait, je n'ai brigué de commandement en chef; je suis convaincu qu'il faut un nom russe à la tête des armées, et il se trouve toujours assez de gloire à recueillir, quand on remplit strictement les devoirs qu'imposent l'amour de son Souverain, celui de l'état et celui de son metier. Ce sont ces mêmes devoirs qui me forcent de ne point cacher à V.M.I. que le mal-entendu qui a eu lieu et les desagremens de tous les genres, que j'ai eu à endurer, ont leur source dans la conduite du colonel Toll, qui se croit lésé quand il doit servir sous ma direction. – Le colonel Toll a assurement la routine qu'un long travail à un dépôt de cartes donné à un officier, mais il ne faut point exiger de lui plus que de diriger la marche de quelques colonnes. Faute d'expérience, ses connaissances ne vont pas encore plus loin...
Romanowa, le 9 [21]. Novembre 1812.

Sire! J'ai l'honneur de soumettre ci-joint à V.M.I. l'ordre que je viens de recevoir de la part de Mr. le Maréchal Prince Koutousoff. J'en aurais été etonné, Sire, si je n'avais dû penser que les affaires militaires tirant à leur fin, on a voulu éloigner un homme qui se trouve ordinairement à l'avant-garde.
Krougloe, le 16 [28] Novembre 1812.

In the original, the following order from Prince Kutuzov was attached to this letter:

Sir, General-of-Cavalry, Baron Bennigsen. Due to your painful seizures, if you please, Your Excellency, upon receipt of this, you are to go to Kaluga, where you will await your future assignment from His Imperial Majesty.
15 [27] November 1812. Headquarters, village of Krugloe.

Appendix XIII

The composition of Chaplits' vanguard

Infantry:
Major General Kornilov's Brigade: 7th Jägers, 14th Jägers, 28th Jägers.
Major General Meshcherinov's Brigade: 10th Jägers, 32nd Jägers, 38th Jägers.
Colonel Poltoratsky's [Konstantin Markovich Poltoratsky] Brigade: 27th Jägers, Nasheburg Infantry.

Cavalry – under Major General Count O'Rourke's command:
Colonel Prince Zhevakhov's [Spiridon Yurastovich Zhevakhov] Brigade: Pavlograd Hussars, Volhynia Ulans.
Major General Umanets' Brigade: Kinburn Dragoons, Tver Dragoons.

Irregular cavalry regiments:
Colonel Dyachkin's [Grigory Andreevich Dyachkin] Brigade: Dyachkin's Cossacks, Kireev 2nd's Cossacks.
Major General Grekov 8th's Brigade: Grekov 8th's Cossacks, Isaev 2nd's Cossacks.
Colonel Melnikov 5th's Brigade: Melnikov 5th's Cossacks, Grekov 4th's Cossacks.
Colonel Lukovkin 2nd's Brigade: Lukovkin 2nd's Cossacks, Barabanshchikov 2nd's Cossacks.

Artillery:
11th Horse Artillery Company, 12th Horse Artillery Company, 13th Horse Artillery Company.
War Diary of the Army of the Danube (Third Army), compiled by Malinovsky.

Appendix XIV

The composition of the detachments at Berezina

The composition of the detachments were as follows:

Adjutant General Kutuzov's: five Cossack regiments, including the Lifeguard Cossacks, one Kalmuk regiment and another of Tatars, the Izyum Hussars and part of the Kazan Dragoon Regiment, with two horse artillery pieces, for a total of 3,300 men.

Major General Novak's (formerly Adjutant General Prince Volkonsky's), on the march from Vitebsk to rejoin the corps: 2nd Marine Regiment, three groups of the St Petersburg *Opolchenie*, two groups of the Novgorod *Opolchenie*, three Bashkir regiments, of whom one remained in Vitebsk, one light company from 25th Artillery Brigade, for a total of 6,000 men with 12 guns.

Colonel Zhemchuzhnikov's, also on the march to rejoin the corps: six replacement battalions, totalling 3,000 men.

Colonel Pahlen's, marching from Vitebsk towards Niemenczyn: 26th Jäger regiment with two guns, for a total of some 1,000 men.

Guarding magazines in Volyntsy and Sebezh: around 1,000 men.

Appendix XV

Declaration sent to Prince Kutuzov, under Supreme Orders, dated 6 [18] December 1812

Au moment de faire franchir aux armées que je commande les frontières de la Russie, L'Empereur mon Maître me charge de déclarer, que cette mesure ne doit être envisagée que comme une suite inévitable des opérations militaires. Fidèle au principe qui La fait agir dans tous les tems, S.M.I. n'est guidée par aucune vue de conquête. Les sentiments de modération qui ont constamment caractérisé sa politique sont encore les mêmes après les succés decisifs par les quels la Providence Divine a béni ses efforts légitimes. L'indépendance et la paix en seront les résultats. S.M. les offre avec son assistance à tous les peuples qui entrainés aujourd'hui contre Elle, abandonneront la cause de Napoléon, pour ne suivre que celle de leurs vrais intérêts. Je les invite à profiter des chances heureuses que les armées russes leur ont ménagées et de se rallier à Elle dans la poursuite d'un ennemi, dont la fuite précipitée leur montre i'impuissance. C'est surtout à la Prusse que j'adresse cette invitation. L'intention de S.M. L'Empereur est de faire cesser les malheurs qui l'accablent, de donner au Roi des preuves de l'amitié qu Il Lui conserve, de rendre à la Monarchie de Frédéric son éclat et son étendue. Il espère que Sa M. Prussienne animée des sentiments que cette déclaration franche doit faire naitre en Elle, ne prendra en ces circonstances d'autre parti que celui, que réclament l'intérêt de ses Etats et les voeux de ses peuples. Dans cette conviction L'Empereur mon Maitre m'a envoyé l'ordre positif de ne point traiter en pays ennemi les provinces de la Prusse où Ses armées vont entrer, et d'adoucir en autant que l'état de guerre peut le permettre les maux qui resulteraient de cette occupation.

Appendix XVI

Correspondence Regarding the Appointment of Chief of Artillery for all armies

Supreme Orders for Prince Kutuzov, dated 17 (29) December 1812.

> Prince Mikhail Ilarionovich! For better and more consistent control of the artillery attached to the armies, which, under the current circumstances, requires a larger establishment in terms of the administrative element, I find it necessary for Lieutenant General Yermolov to be the Chief of Artillery for all armies.

At the same time, Supreme Orders were issued to Count Wittgenstein, in which the Tsar, informing him of the appointment of Yermolov as Chief of Artillery for all armies, wrote:

> And as Lieutenant General Prince Iashvili is senior to him, I consider it necessary to inform you, in order to announce to Prince Iashvili, that I could not entrust this assignment to him in respect of his service for the most part in command of a vanguard, and so that the corps entrusted to you is not deprived of such a general. But so that he does not consider himself subordinate to Yermolov, he may select a colonel as the head of the corps artillery, having him and the artillery under his direction; while you are not to neglect Prince Iashvili himself from being used to command a force with the status of general.
>
> Supreme Orders dated 18 [30] December, No. 432 (Archive of the M.T.D. No. 46, 692).

Prince Dolgorukov was appointed commander of VIII Corps, in place of Lieutenant General Borozdin 1st, who was sent by the Field Marshal to round up stragglers and to restore order in the army rear areas. Prince Kutuzov's orders for General Borozdin 1st, dated 17 [29] November, No. 924 (Archive of the M.T.D. No. 46,692). Prince Kutuzov's Army Orders of the Day, for 11 and 19 [23 and 31] December (Archive of the M.T.D. No. 36,749).

Appendix XVII

Kutuzov's secret instructions regarding Schwarzenberg

The line that the Austrian army under Prince Schwarzenberg is to occupy must be drawn in such a manner that it does not hamper our operations, and therefore mutual benefit requires that we do not encounter it during the onward movement of our forces. In the event of an armistice, you are empowered to extend it for up to three months.

And therefore, it will be necessary, firstly, to propose a demarcation line along the San river, having occupied which, the Austrian corps are to close up to their natural borders and at the same time remain in eastern Galicia, located along the left bank of this river as far as its confluence with the Vistula.

If this proposal, which you must defend by every possible means, is not accepted, then it is left to you to agree that the Austrian troops occupy a line running from Zawichost, through Janów and Tarnogóra, to Hrubieszów.

Finally, as a last resort, you may agree to the occupation of Lublin by our troops in conjunction with the Austrians and to the designation of a demarcation line along the postal road going from this city to Kraków.

If, against all expectations, Prince Schwarzenberg wishes to agree only to a withdrawal, without concluding a truce, then he should determine the duration of this movement, in accordance with the present season, assuming stages of three *Meilen* and a rest day every two stages.

Prince K. Smolensky.
In the archive of the Foreign Ministry.

Appendix XVIII
Listing of General Wintzingerode's detachment

From 12th Division: one replacement battalion each from Smolensk Infantry, Narva Infantry, Alexopol Infantry, Novo Ingermanland Infantry, 6th Jägers and 41st Jägers, for a total of 1,030 men.

From 15th Division: one battalion each from Kozlov Infantry, Kolyvan Infantry, Kura Infantry, 13th Jägers and 14th Jägers, for a total of 1,389 men.

From 18th Division: one battalion each from Vladimir Infantry, Tambov Infantry, Dnieper Infantry, Kostroma Infantry and 32nd Jägers, for a total of 1,091 men.

From 26th Division: one battalion each from Poltava Infantry and 5th Jägers, for a total of 496 men.

From 9th Division: two battalions from Ryazhsk Infantry, for a total of 567 men.

One recruit battalion each from Arkhangelogorod Infantry, Staro Ingermanland Infantry, Ukraine Infantry and 37th Jägers, for a total of 1,094 men.

75th Ship's Company with 294 men.

Two replacement squadrons each from Sumy Hussars, Akhtyrka Hussars and Lithuania Ulans.

One replacement squadron each from Irkutsk Hussars, Chernigov Mounted Jägers, Courland Dragoons, Kharkov Dragoons, Kiev Dragoons and Novorossia Dragoons.

Eight squadrons of Tatar Ulans, for a total of 1,582 regular cavalry.

Grekov 9th's Don Cossacks, Semenchikov's Don Cossacks.

Elements of Grekov 21st's Don Cossacks, Isaev 2nd's Don Cossacks, Yevpatoria Cossacks and Forest Rangers, for a total of 1,123 irregular cavalry.

33rd Battery Artillery Company from 4th Reserve Artillery Brigade.

Half of 16th Light Artillery Company from 9th Artillery Brigade.

Two guns from 4th Light Artillery Company from 11th Artillery Brigade.

One captured Austrian gun, for a total of 21 guns and 315 artillerymen.

II Corps under Prince Eugen von Württemberg's command:

From 3rd Division: two battalions each of Murom Infantry, Reval Infantry, Chernigov Infantry and 20th Jägers.

From 4th Division: two battalions each of Tobolsk Infantry, Volhynia Infantry, Kremenchug Infantry and 4th Jägers, for a total of 2,500 infantry.

One light artillery company from 3rd Artillery Brigade, one battery artillery company and one light artillery company from 4th Artillery Brigade, Colonel Nikitin's horse artillery company.

Two Don Cossack regiments from General Miloradovich's vanguard, totalling 400 men.

Major General Lanskoy's detachment:
Eight squadrons each of Alexandria Hussars and Belorussia Hussars, four squadrons of Livland Mounted Jägers, for a total of 1,527 regular cavalry.
1st Ukraine Cossack Regiment and 3rd Ukraine Cossack Regiment, for a total of 1,812 irregular cavalry.

Colonel Davydov's detachment:
Two Cossack regiments and an hussar sub-unit, for a total of 550 men.

Thus, in General Wintzingerode's corps:
40 infantry battalions with 8,461 men.
40 cavalry squadrons, nine Cossack regiments and four sub-units, with 6,994 men.
Five companies of artillery and nine guns, with 1,000 men.
Grand total of 16,455 men with 69 guns.
From the archive of the M.T.D. No. 29,172.

Appendix XIX

Draft convention for an armistice between the Russian and Austrian forces

The onset of the harsh season and other considerations no less important prompt the Commanders-in-Chief of the armies of His Majesty the Emperor of All Russia and His Majesty the Emperor of Austria, King of Hungary and Bohemia, to agree to a cessation of hostilities, on the basis of this secret convention, which, being signed by each of them separately (*unilatéralement*) and exchanged between them, should be considered fully binding on both contracting parties.

1. The armistice is concluded for an indefinite period, and neither side has the right to renew hostilities until 15 days have elapsed from the announcement of the termination of the armistice.
2. The plans for the conduct of the withdrawal of the Austrian army, as approved by both sides, is binding on each of them, with regard to the direction and timing, the proposed movements, and the line of demarcation that the Austrian army will occupy.

Willenberg, 16 (28) January, 1813.

Held in the archive of the Foreign Ministry.
With regard to the direction and timing of the movements of the Austrian corps, the following plans were made at the headquarters of Prince Schwarzenberg:

Wyszków, 12 January 1813.
If we set out from the banks of the Narew in five days, then on 22 January (3 February) we will be beyond the Vistula. On 23 or 24 January (4 or 5 February), Warsaw may be surrendered, whereupon we shall withdraw in a direction leading beyond the Pilica.

Thus, after eight days, i.e. on 1 (13) February, the force will be behind the Pilica.

Beyond this river and on the line formed by the road leading from Petrikau [Piotrków] to Breslau to the Silesian border, if we halt for six days in order to evacuate our hospitals and stores, then we shall set out on 7 (19) February from Petrikau and Nowe Miasto.

And therefore, having accepted as a demarcation line the line running from Józefowo along the Kamenny river and onward, through Kunov and Małogoszcz, it will take another eight days to withdraw: therefore, we shall occupy this line by 15 (27) February.

Held in the archive of the Foreign Ministry.

Appendix XX

Composition of Löwis' detachment

1st Brigade – Major General Velyaminov [Ivan Alexandrovich Velyaminov]:
1st Combined Infantry Regiment – 1,168 men.
2nd Combined Infantry Regiment- 1,170 men.
3rd Combined Infantry Regiment- 1,144 men.
From the Grodno Hussars – 160 men.
From Selivanov's Don Cossacks – 144 men.
Yakhontov's Cossacks – 420 men.
10th Light Artillery Company and 57th Light Artillery Company – 343 men.

2nd Brigade – Major General Gorbuntsov [Yegor Sergeevich Gorbuntsov].
Bryansk Infantry Regiment – 1,255 men.
44th Jäger Regiment – 1,149 men.
4th Combined Infantry Regiment – 1,227 men.
Replacement squadrons from Riga Dragoons, Kazan Dragoons & Finland Dragoons – 178 men.
From Selivanov's Don Cossacks – 141 men.
Baron Boda's Cossack Regiment – 370 men.
von Nieroth's Volunteers – 33 men.
40th Light Artillery Company from 21st Artillery Brigade – 183 men.
Infantry total: 7,113 men.
Cavalry total: 1,446 men.
Artillerymen: 526.
Grand total for the detachment: 9,085 men.

Extracted from a strength return, dated 7 [19] December, submitted with Löwis' report to Prince Kutuzov (archive of the M.T.D. No. 29,172).

Appendix XXI

Yorck's letter to General Paulucci, dated 26 November (8 December)

Dear General! Your Excellency should be convinced of my opinion that unilateral action and any private interference in matters of state are inconsistent both with my views and with my character.

I have sent my aide de camp, in whom I have full confidence, to Berlin, and am expecting his return hour by hour. I beg the pardon of Your Excellency for not sharing your views on the importance of the present situation. What influence can a corps of 12,000 or 13,000 now have at such a considerable distance from the line of operations of the *Grande Armée*? Judging by recent events, it is no longer possible to block their retreat beyond the Neman, or beyond the Vistula. Perhaps Napoleon wants to place Prussia in an ambiguous position himself in order to deal with us as with a conquered country. One misstep of mine might remove the King from his throne; our forces would be divided; we would have no time to concentrate them: in a word, the state would perish. The time is already approaching when we shall have to act as one with all our strength. Having recognised the astuteness of a statesman in you, I dare to ask you not to consider possible that which only appears so.

Notwithstanding my desire to explain myself entirely to you personally, I find this impossible. I am under strict surveillance as they would very much want to make sure of my guilt. It is no less difficult for me to communicate with you through one of the persons in whom I could confide myself. The only one of my aides de camp in whom I would dare to rely in such a delicate matter is currently in Berlin. And as I have already had the honour to bring to the attention of Your Excellency, I cannot do anything by myself, independently of others. Distrust of me has been aroused once more; it has almost been decided to replace me, and I remain in anticipation of my successor.

Archive of the M.T.D. No. 46,692. Correspondence on relations with General Yorck.

Appendix XXII

Yorck's letter to MacDonald

Taurogen, le 30 decembre (new style) *1812.*

Monsigneur. Après des marches très-pénibles, il ne m'a pas été possible de les continuer sans être entamé sur mes flancs et mes derrières; c'est ce qui a retardé la jonction avec votre excellence, et devant opter entre l'alternative de perdre la plus grande partie de mes troupes et tout le matériel qui, seul, assurait ma subsistance, ou de sauver le tout, j'ai cru de mon devoir de faire une convention par la quelle le rassemblement des troupes prussiennes doit avoir lieu dans une partie de la Prusse orientale, qui se trouve, par la retraite de l'armée française, au pouvoir de l'armée russe.

Les troupes prussiennes formeront un corps neutre, et ne se permettront pas d'hostilités envers aucun parti; les événemens à venir, suite de négociations qui doivent avoir lieu entre les puissances belligérantes, décideront sur leur sort futur.

Je m'empresse d'informer V.E. d'une démarche à la quelle j'ai été forcé par les circonstances majeures.

Quelque jugement que le monde portera de ma conduite, j'en suis peu inquiet; le devoir envers mes troupes et la réflexion la plus mûre me la dictent; les motifs les plus purs, quelles que soient les apparences, me guident. En Vous faisant, Monseigneur, cette déclaration, je m'acquitte des obligations envers vous, et vous prie d'agréer l'assurance du plus profond respect, avec le quel j'ai l'honneur d'être, de votre excellence le très-humble serviteur,

le lieutenant-général
d'Iork.

Appendix XXIII

Massenbach's letter to MacDonald

Tilsit, le 31 decembre (new style) *1812.*

Monseigneur. La lettre du général Iork aura déjà prévenu votre excellence que ma dernière démarche m'est prescrite, et que je n'en pourrais changer rien, parceque les mesures de prevoyance, que V.E. fit prendre cette nuit, me parurent suspectes de vouloir peutêtre me retenir par force, ou désarmer mes troupes dans le cas présent.

Il me fallut prendre ce parti, dont je me suis servi pour joindre mes troupes, à la convention que le général commandant a signée, et dont-il me donne l'avis et l'instruction ce matin.

Votre excellence pardonne que je ne suis venu moi-même pour l'avertir du procédé; c'était pour m'épargner une sensation très pénible à mon coeur, parceque les sentimens de respect et d'estime pour la personne de V.E. que je conserverai jusqu'à la fin de mes jours, m'auraient empêché de faire mon devoir.

Je connais le coeur de votre excellence; elle ne permettra pas que les pauvres habitans de Tilsit, qui ont déjà tant souffert pendant cette malheureuse guerre, ne soient encore rendus plus malheureux par les troupes qui sont dans ce moment sous les ordres de votre excellence.

Daignez recevoir l'assurance de ma pure estime et de la plus haute considération,
le lieutenant-général
Massenbach.

Appendix XXIV

French forces on 5 January (new style)

According to French strength returns dated 5 January 1813, new style, there were:

In MacDonald's corps – 26,000 men.
In Heudelet's division – 8,000 men.
In Detrès' division in Danzig – 6,000 men.
In Marchand's division (formerly Loison's) reinforced with several march battalions – 2,400 men.
In Cavaignac's brigade – 1,600 men.
Total: 44,000 men.

In the *Garde* and *1er Corps*, *2e Corps*, *3e Corps* and *4e Corps*, 13,467 men had been among the people who rejoined them on the way back from the Neman, of whom about 7,000 were fit to fight. Among them, the officers alone numbered:
In the *Garde* – 437.
In *1er Corps* – 996.
In *2e Corps* – not known.
In *3e Corps* – 358.
In *4e Corps* – 668.
Numbering: 2,459.

Appendix XXV

Listing of troops under Count Wittgenstein, dated 31 December [12 January, 1813]

5th Division	Perm Infantry	2 battalions
	Sevsk Infantry	2 battalions
	Mogilev Infantry	2 battalions
	Kaluga Infantry	2 battalions
	23rd Jägers	2 battalions
	24th Jägers	2 battalions
	Combined Grenadiers	2 battalions
6th Division	Azov Infantry	2 battalions
	Nizov Infantry	2 battalions
	3rd Jägers	2 battalions
14th Division	Tula Infantry	2 battalions
	Tenginsk Infantry	2 battalions
	Navaginsk Infantry	2 battalions
	Estland Infantry	2 battalions
	25th Jägers	2 battalions
	26th Jägers	2 battalions
	Combined Grenadiers	2 battalions
21st Division	Neva Infantry	2 battalions
	Petrovsk Infantry	2 battalions
	Lithuania Infantry	2 battalions
	2nd Jägers	2 battalions
25th Division	Voronezh Infantry	2 battalions
	1st Marines	2 battalions
	2nd Marines	2 battalions
	1st Combined Infantry	4 battalions
	2nd Combined Infantry	4 battalions
	Combined Jägers	3 battalions

APPENDIX XXV

General Löwis' Detachment (infantry)	1st Combined Infantry	2 battalions
	2nd Combined Infantry	2 battalions
	3rd Combined Infantry	2 battalions
	4th Combined Infantry	2 battalions
	44th Jägers	2 battalions
	Total:	69 battalions
	Numbering:	21,000 men
Combined Dragoons		3 squadrons
Riga Dragoons		3 squadrons
Yamburg Dragoons		4 squadrons
Mittau Dragoons		4 squadrons
Finland Dragoons (one squadron of which from Löwis' Detachment)		4 squadrons
One sub-unit of Kazan Dragoons		
Poland Ulans		2 squadrons
Combined Hussars		4 squadrons
Grodno Hussars (one squadron of which from Löwis' Detachment)		9 squadrons
One sub-unit of Izyum Hussars		
Total:		33 squadrons
Numbering:		3,200 men
Platov 4th's Cossacks		
Rodionov 2nd's Cossacks		
Loshchinin's Cossacks		
Panteleev's Cossacks		
Ilovaisky 4th's Cossacks		
Ilovaisky 12th's Cossacks		
Chernozubov 8th's Cossacks		
Denisov 7th's Cossacks		
Kashkin's Cossacks		
Gorin's Cossacks		
Yagodin's Cossacks		
Stavropol Kalmyks		
Tatars		
Selivanov 2nd's Cossacks	from Löwis' Detachment	
Yakhontov's Mounted Petersburg Opolchenie		
Body's Mounted Petersburg Opolchenie		
Total:		16 regiments
Numbering:		3,700 men
5th Battery Artillery Company		12 guns
6th Battery Artillery Company		12 guns

14th Battery Artillery Company	12 guns
21st Battery Artillery Company	12 guns
28th Battery Artillery Company	10 guns
11th Light Artillery Company	12 guns
26th Light Artillery Company	12 guns
27th Light Artillery Company	12 guns
10th Light Artillery Company	12 guns
40th Light Artillery Company	12 guns
57th Light Artillery Company	12 guns
1st Horse Artillery Company	10 guns
3rd Horse Artillery Company	12 guns
23rd Horse Artillery Company	12 guns
Total:	164 guns
Numbering:	2,500 men

Précis des opérations du 1er Corps, archive of the M.T.D. No. 29,200.

Appendix XXVI

Schedule of reinforcements joining the Russian Main Armies throughout the war of 1812

To First Army in the Drissa camp, 19 battalions and 20 squadrons – 10,000 men.
To Second Army in Nesvizh, 27th Division – 8,500 men.
To Second Army in Bobruisk and on the march to Saltanovka, nine reserve battalions – 3,000 men.
To both Western armies in Smolensk, 17 battalions and four artillery companies – 7,000 men.
To both Western armies in Gzhatsk and before Borodino, Miloradovich's force – 15,589 men.[1]
To both armies, on the river Mocha – 7,690 men.
In the Tarutino camp, recruits – about 33,000 men.
Opolchenie warriors – 5,489 men.
On the march from Tarutino to Vilna, recruits – 5,142 men.
To the independent I Corps between the first and second battles of Polotsk – 17,600 men.
Steinheil's corps – 9,000 men.
After the Berezina crossing, Adjutant General Kutuzov's, Major General Novak's and Colonel Zhemchuzhnikov's forces – 12,300 men.
In total: 134,419 men.

---

[1] In addition, several thousand men joined the army during the retreat from Borodino to Moscow.

Appendix XXVII

Collection of Supreme Manifestos, Decrees and Rescripts. St Petersburg, 1816

Collection of Supreme Manifestos, Decrees and Rescripts. St Petersburg, 1816, page 103:

> The salvation of Russia from foes, as numerous in strength as they were evil and ferocious in intent and deed, the annihilation of every one of them within six months, such that even with the most rapid flight, only the smallest number of them could get beyond Our borders, is clearly the grace of God poured out upon us, and is a truly memorable incident that the passage of centuries shall not erase from history. In order to preserve the eternal memory of that unparalleled diligence, loyalty and love for Faith and for Fatherland, with which the Russian people exalted themselves in these difficult times, and in commemoration of OUR gratitude to the providence of God, which saved Russia from the ruin that threatened her, WE set out to create a church in the name of Christ the Saviour in OUR capital city of Moscow, a detailed decree about which shall be announced in due course. May the Almighty bless OUR undertaking! May it be done! May this cathedral stand for many centuries, and let the censer of gratitude be smoked in it before the Holy Throne of God for later generations, along with love for and emulation of the deeds of their ancestors.
> Vilna, 25 December 1812 [6 January 1813].

Collection of Supreme Manifestos, Decrees and Rescripts. St Petersburg, 1816, page 113:

> To OUR forces. Soldiers! It has been a glorious and memorable year in which you have struck and punished a ferocious and powerful enemy in an unheard of and exemplary manner, who had dared to enter our Fatherland, this glorious year has ended; but your resounding feats and your deeds shall not pass away and shall not be silenced. Future generations shall keep them in their memory. You have redeemed the Fatherland from the many nations and kingdoms united against it with your blood. Through your labours, patience and wounds you have gained the gratitude of your own and the respect of foreign powers. Through your valour and courage you

have shown the world that where God and Faith are in the hearts of the people, even if enemy forces were as waves of the ocean, yet all of them, as their fortresses, just as a solid unshakable mountain, shall crumble and lament! From all their fury and ferocity only their groans and the rattle of death shall remain. Soldiers! In commemoration of these your unforgettable deeds, WE have commanded the striking and consecration of a silver medal, with the inscription 1812 upon it, the most memorable past year, which is to be worn on a blue ribbon upon the insurmountable shield of the fatherland, your chests. Each of you is worthy to wear this honourable token, as evidence of your labours, courage and participation in glory; for you have all borne the same burdens and drawn breath with unanimous courage. You may be justly proud of this token: it marks you out as true sons of the Fatherland blessed by God. May your enemies shudder, seeing it upon your chest, knowing that beneath it courage burns, based not on fear or greed but on love of faith and Fatherland and is therefore invincible.

Kłodawa, 5 [17] February 1813. Alexander.

Appendix XXVIII

Collection of Supreme Manifestos, Decrees and Rescripts. St Petersburg, 1816, page 69

To the Gentleman Commander-in-Chief of Moscow, General-of-Infantry Count Rostopchin. Although the enemy expelled from Moscow was there for just a short while, and although they entered not by overcoming the defenders facing them, and not by the power of siege weapons, but through indecent actions shameful for a warrior, arson, looting and demolition, they have inflicted grave harm upon her, nevertheless, it has not stopped them being arrogant and boastful. In order to humble and dim this arrogance of theirs, WE have ordered General Field Marshal Prince Kutuzov to forward all the artillery captured by him in various battles to Moscow, where a pillar crowned with laurels is to be erected in memory of the multiple victories and complete annihilation of all the enemy forces that dared to enter Russia, from the very guns taken from them. Let this monument testify not to the shameless and predatory deeds of contemptible arsonists, but to the glorious renowned feats of the brave nation and troops, who know how to scourge the enemy and punish fiends on the field of battle. As a result of this, you are to issue proper orders for the reception and storage of this artillery, and as it is delivered, bring it to OUR knowledge.

St Petersburg, 14 [26] November 1812.

Appendix XXIX

Ivan Liprandi's opinions on Clausewitz as Bogdanovich's 'reliable source' and an officer

Indeed, it may very well be that Clausewitz has a truthful outlook, but definitely from a German point of view. However, one cannot argue about taste, and therefore, the metaphysics and Clausewitz's bragging are tasteful even in the opinion of General Bogdanovich, but why did he refer to his personal-German only 29 times, while others presenting the dubious truth, much more, as will be seen later?

In 1812, during the retreat, I saw Clausewitz, as a colleague, daily, sometimes even several times a day, on the march, when taking up positions, and so on, especially because he often spent the night in our corps headquarters, where there was also a Prussian officer, Captain Lützow, a relative or, apparently, in close friendly relations with him, who had been admitted to our General Staff at the very opening of the campaign. I was serving as Chief Quartermaster and Lützow, who, like Clausewitz, did not know any Russian, would stay with me overnight. I do not know why or by whom exactly Clausewitz was dubbed the metaphysician, the nickname by which he was known to everyone. There was no arrogance in him at all; this appeared later, in his writing, and occasionally to a high degree. Appropriately, with regard to him here, in the History Of The Patriotic War, the author, through his transformations, turns Clausewitz into a kind of Vishnu, the Indian deity. Thus, at Smolensk, General Bogdanovich has promoted him without precedent, as Chief of Staff of III Cavalry Corps, under Count Pahlen. A few days later, he was already (also without precedent) only Chief Quartermaster of the corps yet at the same time not of the latter, but only of I Cavalry Corps! It is a shame that the honourable Professor has not revealed the catastrophe that overwhelmed Clausewitz, as they say, from Priest to Deacon, and then from Deacon to Sexton. By such meticulous editing of the book, another might possibly think that these were three namesakes and find it difficult to decide which of them, as General Bogdanovich has referred to one of them, was renowned? Yet it turns out that these are one and the same, only in three persons at once, like [the magician] Pinetti, who appeared in various appointments. In this History, such cases are not uncommon even with persons senior to Clausewitz. The fluctuations by the author of the History of The Patriotic War in determining the significance of Clausewitz in 1812 is all the more remarkable because, apparently, for General Bogdanovich he constitutes something enigmatic, something mythical. The influx of a number of foreigners, especially Prussian officers, to us, and mainly into the General Staff, fell into two periods. The first between one to three years before the war of 1812. Among the personalities from this period I was with two of them, Lieutenant Baron von Diest (later a Lieutenant General in Prussian Service), my colleague in Finland, especially from an infamous duel, where his name is visible after mine in Swedish periodicals and Åbo newspapers (restored in 1861, once more), and Captain Hoffmann, with whom I became close in early 1812, as a result of his duel in Dubno with Baron von Nolken, aide de camp to General Dokhturov, who fell at Borodino. The second period was from the beginning of the campaign of 1812. A few days before the battle of Smolensk, Captain Lützow was seconded to VI Corps and arrived in the army with Clausewitz, both of brilliant courage. Clausewitz took refuge with Count Pahlen, whose corps was permanently attached to VI Corps; Count Pahlen had Staff Captain Dannenberg in the appointment of Chief Quartermaster (Clausewitz could only dream of being Chief of Staff). At Borodino, Count Pahlen was ill, and Clausewitz, as a semi-volunteer, as he had no permanent duties, went to Uvarov, commander of I Cavalry Corps, during the action and was with him for about an hour during the fighting. He asked to be transferred to the corps under Count Wittgenstein from Tarutino. He invented the fairy tale of his conversation with Barclay, and so on. I shall expand elsewhere on Clausewitz and other volunteers like him who were in our army at the time.

Sources for the History of the War of 1812[1]

It would be impossible to list every manuscript and printed book that contains information about the events of the Patriotic War of 1812, and therefore I shall limit myself to a list of the main works that may serve as a guide for a thorough study of this war. For convenience, sources are listed systematically, all documents being grouped under three headings:
1. Official documents.
2. Official and private correspondence.
3. Memoirs.

Published works are generally grouped under two headings:
1. Books exclusively comprising a description of the war of 1812.
2. Books that contain information about operations by only a few elements of the forces, or about any single event of the Patriotic War.

---

1 [Liprandi comments: 'This is what P. Glebov had to say about this (in Artillery Journal, 1861, No. 6, in an article titled: A Few Words In Defence Of The Memory Of Gavril Alexandrovich Ignatiev): 'In conclusion, let us make one more remark: the title page of General Bogdanovich's work reads: History Of The Patriotic War Of 1812, According To Reliable Sources. At the end of the third volume, a detailed listing of sources is attached, and from this list it emerges that most of them are far from reliable. As evidence, let us cite the opinions of the author himself on the main sources that he used.' Whereupon P. Glebov briefly describes the reviews made about them and continues: 'Thus, apart from the famous Clausewitz and the marquis de Chambray, according to General Bogdanovich not a single work that contains a complete description of the war of 1812 is exempt from a misrepresentation of facts. Let us assume that such universal condemnation is justified, but why does the honourable author shore up his own statements and assessments for the most part with references to works that he himself recognises as tainted by extreme bias? Saying nothing of Danilevsky and Buturlin, the endnotes to all three volumes are filled with references to Bernhardi, Fain, Labaume, Thiers, and, according to General Bogdanovich, such other biased writers who did not care about the truth in the least. Consequently, is it possible to agree that the History Of The Patriotic War Of 1812, by General Bogdanovich, was compiled according to reliable sources? In any event, this title contradicts what the honourable author himself has written about the reliability of the sources used as the basis for his extensive and, for most readers, very curious work'].

Official Documents

1. Brief War Diary for Second Army from the time of the enemy forces' crossing of the Neman to the retreat of First Army to the Dvina, compiled by Major General Mukhin (Archive of the M.T.D. No. 29,180).
2. Brief War Diary for First Army from the entrenched camp at Drissa to the city of Smolensk and its continuation following the unification with Second Army. Compiled by Quartermaster General Colonel Toll in 1812 (brought up to the arrival of the army in Moscow. It is complemented by descriptions of the battles at Smolensk, Lubino and Borodino, also compiled by Colonel Toll). Archive of the M.T.D. No. 29,180.
3. Brief War Diary of the movements by Second Army in 1812 (brought up to the unification of both western armies at Smolensk). Archive of the M.T.D. No. 29,180.
4. War Diary from 1 [13] September to 31 December 1812 [12 January 1813] (archive of the M.T.D. No. 29,179). A copy of this diary and its continuation has been signed off by Prince Kutuzov (archive of the M.T.D. No. 46,692, folio No. 18).

    All four of these diaries, despite their brevity, provided the essential material for describing operations by our Main Army.
5. Historical Journal of Operations by I Corps (Independent) during the French war of 1812, compiled by Colonel Parensov (from the opening of hostilities to 9 [21] August). Archive of the M.T.D. No. 44,585, folio No. 8.
6. Brief description of military operations by I Corps (Independent) from 18 [30] June to 18 [30] October (archive of the M.T.D. No. 29,200).
7. *Précis des opérations du 1er Corps de la 1er armée d'Occident pendant l'année 1812*. Compiled, in all probability, by Diebitsch. It contains a concise but clear description of operations by Count Wittgenstein from the beginning of the war to 31 December 1812 [12 January 1813] (archive of the M.T.D. No. 29,200).
8. Selected Extracts From Reports To Emperor Alexander I, from 16 [28] June 1812 to 24 March [5 April 1813] (archive of the M.T.D. No. 44,585, folio No. 5).

    Of the sources mentioned above, describing operations by I Corps (Independent), *Précis des opérations du 1er Corps* and the Selected Extracts are particularly noteworthy.
9. Diary of the vanguard of Third Army (archive of the M.T.D. No. 32,417).
10. Diary of the erstwhile Army of the Danube, renamed Third Army, under the direction of Admiral Chichagov. Compiled by Lieutenant Colonel (later Lieutenant General) Malinovsky (archive of the M.T.D. No. 32,417).
11. Diary of Essen 3rd's corps, compiled by Lieutenant Colonel Freigang (from the day of their departure from Bucharest to their arrival in Paris). Archive of the M.T.D. No. 46,646.
12. Diary of military operations by General Saken's corps in 1812, 1813 and 1814, compiled by Colonel Gotovsky (archive of the M.T.D. No. 16,643).
13. *Journal militaire des opérations du corps sous les ordres de lieutenant-général baron de Saken depuis sa formation en date du 11 [23] octobre 1812 jusqu'à sa dissolution en fevrier 1813.*

The diary of the vanguard of Third Army may serve as a source for describing operations by Tormasov; of the others, the diary compiled by Malinovsky deserves particular attention for its clarity and completeness.

14. Brief notes on military operations by Finland Corps (archive of the M.T.D. No. 15,302).
15. General information on the movements and operations of the Imperial Russian forces and their allies in the war against the French, 1812, 1813 and 1814 (archive of the M.T.D. No. 37,640). Compiled by Lieutenant General Khatov. This daily account of the movements of each of the corps and detachments operating against Napoleon, with the addition of very good maps, may serve as a guide to studying the history of the above mentioned wars.
16. Log of Outgoing Directed Imperial Decrees and Rescripts by Emperor Alexander I, from 21 June [3 July] to 31 December 1812 [12 January 1813] (archive of the M.T.D. No. 46,692, folio No. 4).
17. Log of Outgoing Supreme Orders, as announced by Count Arakcheev in 1812 from the opening of hostilities (archive of the M.T.D. No. 46,692, folios No. 5 & No. 6).

Both of these logs constitute an essential source for obtaining information about the orders of Emperor Alexander I in the war of 1812.

18. Classified Rescripts from Emperor Alexander I to Prince Kutuzov, 1811 and 1812 (archive of the M.T.D. No. 32,416).
19. Emperor Alexander I's rescripts to Prince Kutuzov (archive of the M.T.D. No. 29,174).
20. Original Army Orders, under Prince Kutuzov's signature, from 18 [30] August to 31 December 1812 [12 January 1813] (archive of the M.T.D. No. 36,749).
21. Original Orders by Admiral Chichagov, from 17 [29] November 1812 to 2 [14] February 1813 (archive of the M.T.D. No. 36,749).
22. Log of outgoing documents from the Main Army, from 9 [21] September to 31 December 1812 [12 January 1813] (archive of the M.T.D. No. 29,172, folio No. 2).
23. Log of incoming documents to the Main Army, from 9 [21] September to 31 December 1812 [12 January 1813] (archive of the M.T.D. No. 29,172, folio No. 2).
24. Incoming documents to the Main Army for September, October, November and December 1812 (archive of the M.T.D. No. 29,172).
25. Incoming documents to Count Wittgenstein's Independent I Corps, from the outbreak of war to 31 December 1812 [12 January 1813] (archive of the M.T.D. No. 44,585).
26. Incoming business from August 1812 to 1 [13] January, 1813 (archive of the M.T.D. No. 46,692, folio No. 2).
27. Reports on the movements and operations by formations under: Barclay de Tolly, Prince Bagration, Admiral Chichagov, General Tormasov, Count Wittgenstein, adjutants general Wintzingerode and Kutuzov, General Yermolov, Adjutant General Prince Volkonsky, General Ertel, Colonel Chernyshev, lieutenant generals Essen 1st, Count Steinheil, Marquis Paulucci, etc. (archive of the M.T.D. No. 46,692, folio No. 3).

Correspondence

1. Correspondence between Emperor Alexander I and the Crown Prince of Sweden (archive of the Foreign Ministry [A.F.M.]).
2. Handwritten letters and notes from Emperor Alexander I to Barclay de Tolly, 1811 and 1812 (28 in total). Copies are held in the Classified Archive of the Department of the General Staff.
3. Handwritten letters from Emperor Alexander I to Barclay de Tolly, Chichagov and Rostopchin. Stored in the marble colonnade of the General Staff Library.
4. Letters, rescripts and other documents by Emperor Alexander I to various persons (36 in total). Copies are held in the Classified Archive of the Department of the General Staff.
5. Reports and letters to Emperor Alexander I from Barclay de Tolly. Copies are held in the Classified Archive of the Department of the General Staff.
6. Letters to Emperor Alexander I from General Paulucci (from July 1812) on various subjects relating to the organisation of the army. Copies are held in the Classified Archive of the Department of the General Staff.
7. Letters to Emperor Alexander I from Count Saint-Priest. Copies are held in the Classified Archive of the Department of the General Staff.
8. Letters to Emperor Alexander I and to Count Arakcheev from General Bennigsen. Copies are held in the Classified Archive of the Department of the General Staff.
9. Letters to Emperor Alexander I from Admiral Chichagov. Copies are held in the Classified Archive of the Department of the General Staff.
10. Letters to Emperor Alexander I from Count Rostopchin. Copies are held in the Classified Archive of the Department of the General Staff.
11. Letters from Prince Bagration to Count Arakcheev. Copies are held in the Classified Archive of the Department of the General Staff.
12. Letters from the army, held in the archives of the Chancellery of the Ministry of War.
13. Correspondence between Prince Kutuzov and Count Rostopchin. Archive of the M.T.D. No. 47,352.
14. General Raevsky's letter to General Jomini (notes on various events of the war of 1812).
15. Correspondence between Prince Kurakin and Count Nesselrode from the office of Count Rumyantsev, and the French *ministère des Affaires étrangères (A.F.M.)*.
16. Letters from Flügel Adjutant Chernyshev to Count Rumyantsev (A.F.M.).
17. Reports to Emperor Alexander I from Count Sukhtelen (A.F.M.).
18. Correspondence with General Yorck (archive of the M.T.D. No. 46,692).
19. Intercepted enemy dispatches and letters (A.F.M.).
20. Intercepted Orders to *2e régiment de grenadiers from Napoleon's Grande Armée* (archive of the M.T.D. No. 47,352). The original is held in the Imperial Public Library.

Memoirs

1. General Yermolov's notes. Some of these fascinating notes, relating to the description of the war of 1812, were handed to me by A.P. Yermolov. In general, it should be noted that copies of this manuscript in circulation, among which is one copy in the Imperial Public Library titled 'Notes on the War of 1812, A.P.Ye.' are for the most part fakes.
2. A depiction of military operations by First Army, compiled by Barclay de Tolly. These notes, submitted to Emperor Alexander I by Barclay, upon his departure from the army, contain a justification for all his actions during the campaign of 1812 as well as complaints against Prince Bagration, Kutuzov and other personalities who were in the headquarters of the army. Although the assessments by Barclay de Tolly are not entirely unbiased, they may nevertheless serve to explain the state of affairs at that time, and in particular Barclay's situation and the factors that influenced him. This manuscript in (German) original, corrected by Barclay de Tolly's own hand, is in the archive of the M.T.D. A Russian translation is in the Classified Archive of the Department of the General Staff.
3. Original notes by Count Toll (descriptions of the battles of Smolensk and Borodino).
4. *Extrait de mon journal militaire des campagnes de 1812, 1813 et 1814. Par le prince Eugène de Würtemberg (manuscript),* archive of the M.T.D. No. 47,344.
5. Benkendorf's notes on the war of 1812, archive of the M.T.D. No. 47,352.
6. Major General Löwenstern's notes, archive of the M.T.D. No. 47,352.
7. A.A. Shcherbinin's notes. The author, who served in His Majesty's Suite of the quartermaster's department (of the general staff), compiled very fascinating notes, which were a source for much of Bernhardi's work: Denkwürdigkeiten des Grafen v. Toll.
8. Maevsky's notes, formerly adjutant general in Second Army in 1812 and director of Prince Kutuzov's chancellery.
9. General Chichagov's notes (Remarques sur la campagne de 1812), archive of the M.T.D. No. 44,712.
10. Description of the action at Dziewałtów and Kulnev's advance to Yakubovo. From I.O. Sukhozanet's notes.
11. Description of operations by the Lifeguard Artillery in the battle of Borodino, extracted from the history of Russian artillery compiled by V.F. Ratch.
12. General Arnoldi's notes regarding the Berezina crossing.
13. Leslie's notes on the part played by the Leslie family in the opolchenie in 1812.
14. Admiral Lermontov's notes on the Lifeguard Ship's Company in 1812.
15. *Mémoire concernant les opérations de la 17me division sous les ordres du général de division Dombrowsky* [Dąbrowski], archive of the M.T.D. No. 32,417.

Published Works

Books exclusively comprising a description of the war of 1812
Napoleon's downfall, giving free rein to French war historians to discuss his actions, was the catalyst for many works on the war of 1812. It is quite natural that a world event that had such a huge impact on the fate of nations could not be discussed dispassionately by his contemporaries: many historians blamed Napoleon for the failure of this war, not taking into account the extraordinary difficulties that he had to overcome; others, in defending him, cannot admit that he might have made any mistakes, do not want to admit that the Russians somehow beat his hordes, victorious for so many years, and attributed the demise of the Grande Armée solely to the influence of climate and season.

Among the works hostile to Napoleon were books by: comte Ségur, Ker-Porter, Labaume, etc. Among those favourable towards him were: Vaudoncourt, Baron Fain, Gourgaud. Chambray's work is more unbiased than any other. The description of the war of 1812, in volume XIV of the *Histoire du Consulat et de l'Empire* by Thiers, despite every desire by the author to preserve historical truth, he very often sins with incorrect presentations of the facts.

Comte Ségur's work: *Histoire de Napoléon et de la grande armée pendant l'année 1812* was a great success and aroused conflicting opinions: many praised it, comparing its significance to that of the Iliad; Marshal Marmont, one of the most erudite military men in France, considered Ségur's book to be among the best sources for studying contemporaneous Military History. Others, denying any historical merit in this work by Count Ségur, compared it to a novel. In reality, however, this work is distinguished by a liveliness of style, the graphic depiction of the scenes of action, the entertaining presentation, which comes from the author's ability to present events in a dramatic manner. But these undoubted virtues of the *'History of Napoleon and the Grande Armée'* are marred by a complete absence of historical rigour: alongside the most important events, the author very extensively describes all the gossip that reached him from headquarters, not caring at all about the truth. It goes without saying that one can form neither a correct idea of the numbers and locations of the forces of both sides from such a work, nor a clear indication of movements by both sides out of contact or in battle. On almost every page, instead of a simple description of events devoid of artistic license, the author resorts to rhetorical devices and captivates the imagination but does not convince the intellect. Despite the respect expressed by Count Ségur for Napoleon, and the patriotism with which his book is filled, the errors by the Emperor of the French and the failings of the management of the Grande Armée are depicted with pedantic severity.[2] This compelled General Gourgaud to make a critical analysis of Ségur's book *(Examen critique de l'ouvrage du comte de Ségur)* in which, in refuting his testimony, Gourgaud, in turn, falls into hyperbole and often distorts the truth.[3]

---

2 [Liprandi comments: 'Here the author accuses Ségur of patriotism in the same way as he does Danilevsky. This sacred sentiment seems only to be permitted to the Germans'].
3 [Liprandi comments: '*Despite such an assessment, however, General Bogdanovich resorts to Ségur's testimony 24 times and, of course, only when whatever this comte wrote was to the taste*

Ker-Porter's work: *Narrative of the campaign of 1812*, in English, which appeared shortly after the fall of Napoleon, is very biased. Many of the author's statements are inaccurate, and in general his book is of little merit.[4]

Relation circonstanciée de la campagne de Russie en 1812, is by Eugène Labaume, who took part in this campaign. Although the author is sometimes carried away by anger towards Napoleon and, giving free rein to the imagination, delivers some very dubious statements, nevertheless he presents the events related to the actions of the Grande Armée, and especially 4e Corps, in vivid colours and in satisfactory detail.[5]

The work by General Vaudoncourt: *Mémoires pour servir à l'histoire de la guerre entre la France et la Russie en 1812*, reveals the military intelligence of the author, renowned in the academic world for his work Campagnes d'Annibal. His notes on the war of 1812 were compiled on the basis of official documents and information that he was able to collect in St Petersburg when he was a prisoner of war there as well as those later received from Admiral Chichagov and other Russians. Thus Vaudoncourt's book contains a less one-sided account of operations than many other books on the war of 1812. But this undoubted merit in Vaudoncourt's composition is overshadowed by his extreme predilection for his countrymen and hatred for the Russians. These sentiments, so inconsistent with the dignity of History, are expressed on almost every page of his book. He seeks to prove that Napoleon acted faultlessly everywhere and that the French constantly surpassed the Russians in courage and resourcefulness, and to that end he resorts to distorting the truth, often also misinterpreting the meaning of documents that served as sources for his narrative.[6]

Baron Fain, who was in Napoleon's retinue, could not help but be subjected to the charismatic influence of his master. For this very reason, impartiality cannot be expected from him: and indeed, his work Manuscrit de 1812 is the work of a man utterly devoted to Napoleon. But despite the author's bias, his book is one of the best sources for obtaining information about Napoleon's orders and everything that happened in the État-major général de la Grande Armée. The many official documents collected by the author have exalted the quality of this work.[7]

---

of the author of this History, likewise there are 17 references to Gourgaud'].

4 [Liprandi comments: '*Of course, on this basis, the honourable author made only three references to him. Perhaps borrowing from him (but without a reference) the tale of the wounding of Prince Vorontsov*'].

5 [Liprandi comments: '*And after counting the score, it turns out that this author, who gives free rein to the imagination, delivers some very dubious statements, is called 22 times as a witness to events selected by the author such that he is sometimes given more credibility than statements from Russians who were participants in the events described.*' Adding: '*But why, I repeat, are his statements about the capture of the central battery not shown?*'].

6 [Liprandi comments: '*This narrator only deserved to be referenced three times*'].

7 [Liprandi comments: '*This is also quite a wonderful juxtaposition of contradictions: 'impartiality cannot be expected from him' and yet this book is one of the best! If this latter is true, then why does he condemn Danilevsky for limiting himself to Fain and Chambray only, whom Bogdanovich himself considers to be the best? Fain, distrusted by our gentleman historian, was selected along with Chambray because of the unsuitability of Danilevsky's Description, nevertheless caught the attention of General Bogdanovich, who refers to his statements 56 times*'].

The best of all French compositions on the war of 1812, in all fairness, is: *Histoire de l'expédition de Russie* by marquis de Chambray. It is distinguished by its measured, impartial presentation of the subject matter. The author's comments reveal a thorough knowledge of military matters; his descriptions of events are concise but clear; his statements are based on official documents from both sides. His appendices contain very important documents. To all this must be added the fact that Chambray knew how to avoid outbursts inconsistent with the dignity of History.8

More recently, a work by Thiers has been published and gained great fame: *Histoire du Consulat et de l'Empire,* in which volume XIV contains the history of the war of 1812. This famous writer and publicist cannot compete with either Chambray or Vaudoncourt in describing military operations, but, on the other hand, his work is very entertaining and conveys an image painted by the hand of a master. In relation to the politics of the belligerent Powers and their neighbouring states, he is fairly impartial, in everything else he very often deviates from the truth:[9] for example, according to his statements, French forces were undefeated in all of the battles of the war of 1812.

Of the works in German containing full descriptions of our Patriotic War, the most noteworthy are:
1. *Der russiche Feldzug von 1812,* by General Clausewitz.
2. *Denkwürdigkeiten des Grafen v. Toll,* by Bernhardi.

This work by the renowned Clausewitz is distinguished by; knowledge of the business of war, impartiality and a critically accurate view of the events described.[10] Bernhardi's book also has great merit. In the first two volumes of this work we find many facts about the war of 1812 that had hitherto remained completely unknown, or at least were unexplained. In addition to Toll's own notes, the author's sources were written and verbal statements from participants in Napoleon's gigantic struggle with Russia. One must do justice to Bernhardi in that he has used these sources most skilfully, combining engaging presentation with a clear indication of the composition and numbers of troops, the times and places of events, and other factors to which previous historians of the war of 1812 have not given due attention. Unfortunately, the author, like many German writers wanting to repay their heavy debt of gratitude to Russia by diminishing our military glory, does not recognise the contributions of any of the Russians, and is especially unjust towards Kutuzov.[11]

---

8 [Liprandi comments: '*Chambray has been referenced 219 times! It is a pity, however, that this figure is low; as the author of the History Of The Patriotic War published few of the events of the sack of Moscow and the violence that Chambray had witnessed*'].
9 [Liprandi comments: 'Although '*he very often deviates from the truth*' Thiers *is used as a reference 47 times, that is more than Vaudoncourt, with whom Thiers 'cannot compete' by a factor of 16*'].
10 [For Liprandi's opinions on Clausewitz, see Appendix XXIX.]
11 [Liprandi comments: 'Most skilfully, however, everywhere, in our Patriotic War, it is his contributions that are brought to the fore. But here is what I do not understand: why are Toll's *Denkwürdigkeiten* mostly referred to as Bernhardi's and presented under the name of the latter? This man was merely the editor, he added his remarks, but all the same, these are Toll's *Denkwürdigkeiten*, and Bernhardi was the editor. In any case, one should acknowledge just

All other full descriptions of the war of 1812, by Germans, are no better than more or less successful compilations, in which there is no independent critical opinion, nor clear explanation of the facts. Such are the works by: Liebenstein: *Der Krieg Napoleons gegen Russland in den Jahren 1812 und 1813;* Kosegarten: *Darstellung der französische-russischen Vernichtungs-Krieges im Jahr 1812;* Mortonval: *Histoire de la guerre de Russie en 1812;* Beitzke: *Geschichte des russischen Krieges im Jahre 1812;* an anonymous author: *Das Buch vom Jahr 1812, oder Napoleon in Russland; etc.* Of these, Liebenstein's work deserves the most attention, but it, like the others, was written on the basis of rather dubious sources.[12]

As for *Das Buch vom Jahr 1812*, the author of this work has not limited themselves to extracts from Chambray, Gourgaud and Clausewitz, and sets out his own impressions as an eyewitness to the events described; but these notes, which could have been of interest and instructive, unfortunately, are not distinguished either by sound historical critique or impartiality.

The following descriptions of the war of 1812 have appeared in Russian: in 1819, by Akhsharumov; in 1823, by Buturlin, and in 1839, by Mikhailovsky-Danilevsky.

Akhsharumov, a former aide-de-camp to General Konovnitsyn, at his request, was commissioned to compile a *History of the War of 1812*. Being Minister of War, Konovnitsyn not only delivered much source material to Akhsharumov, but requested that he be seconded to Vorontsov's corps, then stationed in France, in order to collect information on operations by French forces. But Akhsharumov, being insufficiently prepared for employment as a military historian, did not make good use of the resources given to him and wrote a book that deserves attention only because it was the first Russian work on the war of 1812.[13]

---

the one: Toll, or Bernhardi. *But be that as it may, these Germans, are referenced 98 times for various events! The quotes are accepted as valid, despite the fact that they are so suspect! General Bogdanovich, as someone who did not participate in the war, cannot identify one as true, another as a lie, without strict critical analysis of the contradictions encountered in the depiction of paramount events, yet in these cases his criticism is not apparent and whatever is said according to statements by Bernhardi is confirmed by almost a hundred references to him! And what kind of deceit is this from General Bogdanovich himself, taking the side of Kutuzov here, when he himself has criticised him and condemned him on the basis of these same Germans?'*].

12 [Liprandi comments: 'Kosegarten first described this war from St Petersburg, and therefore, strictly speaking, this work is not foreign, although it is written in German. It must be assumed that the Frenchman Mortonval has been misplaced among the Germans. But, after all that, none of the listed German works have an independent viewpoint, nor a clear explanation of the facts; and therefore, what are we to understand here that from among them, Liebenstein mainly deserves attention; that is, that he is no worse than all the others, or more tolerable? Talking of successful compilations: after all, this book is nothing but a compilation, only less successful: he did not participate in the war, and therefore he cannot bear witness himself, but Liebenstein, Müller participated and could describe what they saw, just as well as any others'].

13 [Liprandi comments: 'Had Akhsharumov not been sufficiently prepared for employment as a military historian, then, of course, the enlightened Konovnitsyn, who appreciated Akhsharumov, would not have entrusted him with this assignment, as another could have done it. Therefore, the mention of an official request is completely misplaced. Whether he made good use of the resources given to him or not, can only be judged once those resources are known. I saw Akhsharumov every day when I travelled from Rethel to Maubeuge, which happened several times that year, and I know very well that these resources were very limited;

A.P. Buturlin was not only a participant in the events of 1812, he also studied them thoroughly. Unfortunately, this study is one-dimensional: the author was an ardent follower of Jomini's strategic theory, which dominates his work. Every event is discussed within it on the basis of the thoughts of General Jomini, which puts extreme limits on the vision of his critical conclusions. It is also impossible to ignore that Buturlin, having the opportunity to explore all the treasures of our state archives, left very important sources unused. Thus, for example, when describing operations by Count Wittgenstein, he was content almost everywhere with extracting quotes from *Précis historique des opérations du 1er Corps,* without comparing them with reports by unit commanders available in the archive of the Military Topographic Department and constituting one of the best sources for a History of the War of 1812. Nevertheless, everything related to troop movements and operations is set out quite clearly in this work by General Buturlin; but anyone beginning to look for an explanation of the nature and personal characteristics of the main actors, the intentions and decisions of the military commanders from proceedings in the councils of war, the influence of counter-measures taken by the enemy, the morale of the people and troops, the situation of the army in various phases of the war, will search in it in vain: in a word, the influence of human factors is absent. As a result, the narration itself by the author, despite the enthralling nature of the subject, is dry, lifeless, devoid of everything that distinguishes the beauty of creation, it is like a skeleton.

Buturlin's work, having been written in French, and therefore soon becoming well known in France, gave rise to French historians confirming many biases in their statements and assessments using quotations from this book by our compatriot. To that end, remaining silent about everything that might show the Russians in a positive light, they limit themselves to extracts in which their countrymen are praised, and refer to Buturlin as justification for what was said.[14]

---

as at that time our records had not yet been collected in one place, while many of the works by foreigners had yet to be published. Akhsharumov completed his History in 1817 and sent it to St Petersburg, where it was undoubtedly reviewed by Konovnitsyn, and perhaps even by other participants in the war. In Maubeuge, Count Vorontsov, read the chapters as they were being prepared. Akhsharumov was so conscientious that he did not neglect any clarification and wrote accurately. If he did not go into various details, then, as I have noted, there were not yet enough resources for that. With regard to the speculation with which modern military works abound, he was too enlightened to give his opinions or try to show off his conclusions, and too noble for flattery or libel. He has described events accurately, as an eyewitness, and in my opinion, an eyewitness is in the lead when it comes to describing what happened within their sight, ahead of those who have only heard about it or read about it. I cannot hide my surprise that the honourable author of this History did not find anything worthy of attention in the work by Akhsharumov, and spoke of him so cuttingly that he 'wrote a book that deserves attention only because it was the first Russian work on the war of 1812.' But does it not deserve attention due to the simple fact that it contains no self-contradictions, and this proves that its author understood logic, and was not writing at random?'].

14 [Liprandi comments: '*Buturlin accurately describes the movements and operations of the forces, but did not want to indulge in metaphysics or a description of the characters of certain individuals, which, nevertheless, he could have done more easily and more accurately than General Bogdanovich, knowing the actors personally of course, but limited himself only to presenting their deeds. The honourable author of this History forgot to add one thing, that in the History by Buturlin there is not a single self-contradiction*'].

General Okunev's work: *Considerations sur les grandes opérations de la campagne de 1812 en Russie*, may be classed as a doctrinal rather than historical book. The author, having assumed the role of a professor, instructs his readers, presenting the conclusions he has made on the basis of the theories of General Jomini in the form of indisputable principles. It is impossible to ignore that the disciples of Jomini, forgetting that his most important gift was the liberation of inquisitive military minds from the one-dimensional theories that constrained them, follow principles that he himself did not recognise as undisputed. From this, a narrow critical view of military operations emerges, which is epitomised by Mack, Weyrother, Pfuel and pedants like them. Such wisdom, which hampers freedom of thought, is as harmful as ignorance.[15]

The latest of the complete works in Russian was: *Description Of The Patriotic War Of 1812*, by General Mikhailovsky-Danilevsky. During the compilation of this book, the author had access to the entire state archives. Danilevsky's encyclopaedic knowledge and literary abilities helped him write a work, which, thanks to the lightness of his style and the fascination of the subject, became popular yet was condemned by foreign historians. The author stated, in the Preface to his book: 'A critical military history was not my objective. Let us leave that to military academics, devotees of strategy and tactics. Rather, my aim was to present as accurate a representation of events as possible' and so on. These few lines are sufficient to indicate the author's concept of Military History in general and the direction he intended to follow in describing the Patriotic War of 1812. He proceeds, in his own words: firstly, that he not only doubted the usefulness of military-historical criticism, but left that to the pedants, in denial of strategy and tactics... But is it possible to write, let alone fully understand, any military work without a thorough knowledge of these sciences?[16] Secondly, the author stated that he had another aim in mind: the truth... Is historical criticism opposed to the truth? All the greatest historical works are notable for sound, unbiased criticism, and it can even be said that there is not a single good military-historical or historical book in general that does not contain critical assessments. And the History of the Patriotic War by General Danilevsky itself is not free of them, no doubt despite the will of the author. His rebellion against strategy and tactics was also in vain. A closer acquaintance with the military sciences would have protected him from some of the errors that are found in his book, such as, for example, Engelhardt's detachment using red-hot round shot on an open battlefield at Brest, and so on.[17] And is it even possible to

---

15 [Liprandi comments: '*What sort of review is this? I simply thought that while Okunev was not stretching a point by featuring the deeds of a Lieutenant with two guns, then at least he was developing the concepts of strategic theory. But no, there is no pleasing the priest of truth*'].
16 [Liprandi comments: '*I do not see from Danilevsky's words that he doubted the usefulness of military-historical criticism or was in denial of strategy and tactics; he left it to others, limiting his account to events. It is difficult to please Bogdanovich, who, it seems, has made it an indispensable principle to reject everything that has been written by others about the war of 1812. He is dissatisfied with Buturlin and Okunev because they embarked on a discussion of strategy, and he is indignant at Danilevsky for leaving these discussions to academics, or, as the author refers to them, to pedants*'].
17 [Liprandi comments that this was in fact Chichagov's error as Danilevsky was quoting from: '*the disposition issued by Admiral Chichagov for an attack on Schwarzenberg at Brest, having*

rebel against historical criticism at the present time, following the works of Smith, Höpfner, Bernhardi, Charras and Milyutin?

Overall, the author began to compose his book without giving himself a clear calculation of the direction he intended to follow: in refusing to be critical, he often expresses his own opinions, for which he would be thanked if his conclusions had been impartial. But, unfortunately, it sometimes happens that he lavishes praise or reproaches, guided more by personal relationships than truth. Such as, among other things, a description of active participation allegedly from Prince Kutuzov during the battle of Borodino, while witnesses of this action confirm that the Field Marshal, throughout the entire battle, did not leave the location taken up by him in the morning at Gorki;[18] such was the desire to present Napoleon as outmoded, Napoleon, who amazed every military personality with the speed and decisiveness of his actions in the campaign of 1814. Even more common in the work by General Danilevsky is the deliberate omission of memorable acts, towering exploits: not a word was mentioned of the participation by General Yermolov and Colonel Toll in the action at Lubino; about the participation of Toll in the battle at Tarutino, as well as on Yermolov's orders in the battle of Maloyaroslavets, also not a word; Gaverdovsky, one of the most outstanding officers of our general staff, is not mentioned at all.[19] The author speaks several times of the merits of the flank pursuit from Mozhaisk to Vyazma and beyond, but is silent regarding the active participation of General Yermolov in pursuit of the enemy. The actions of Barclay are barely noticeable in the *Description of the Patriotic War of 1812*.[20]

---

indicated the axis of each column, it was added that Engelhardt's detachment, located at Pryluky, had orders 'to attack Brest from the left bank of the Mukhavets and, upon observing the success of our forces, to set fire to the town with red-hot (misspelled) round shot'].

18 [Liprandi comments: '*General Bogdanovich should have named all the witnesses to this false statement, which he cannot do; as, in writing about this, he referred only to Hoffmann, who was in our General Staff and during the battle of Borodino was at Utitsa, that is, at the extremity of our left flank, therefore, a few versts from Gorki. This source has been accepted by General Bogdanovich as the testament of all! Unfathomable! In any case, Danilevsky, who was accompanying the Field Marshal, would serve as a better authority than Hoffmann, who might have been sent from Utitsa to Kutuzov and found him in Gorki. Kutuzov rode up to Gorki for a very brief visit in the morning and hurried to the place behind VI Corps which he had assigned for himself in accordance with the disposition; thereafter he revisited Gorki at around noon, and returned once more. As for Kutuzov taking an active part in the battle of Borodino, then, of course, Danilevsky had no wish to infer with these words that Kutuzov led attacks in person, indeed, even General Bogdanovich himself states, as has been noted above, that all his orders during the battle were sound and so on. What more can be demanded of a Commander-in-Chief on the day of battle?*'].

19 [Liprandi comments on the exclusion of Gaverdovsky: '*a particular feat is needed in order to give special mention to a field officer killed in a battle such as Borodino, in which hundreds of field officers fell, which, unfortunately, he did not have the opportunity to perform. P. Glebov, in discussing the inappropriate criticism of Mikhailovsky-Danilevsky, among other things, adds that: 'Gaverdovsky's entire fame in the action at Borodino lies merely in the act of Konovnitsyn notifying his wife of this*'].

20 [Liprandi gives two examples where Danilevsky richly praises Barclay, concluding: '*Danilevsky would have kept silent about all this, or mentioned it in passing if he had any intention not to reveal Barclay's virtues*'].

Inaccuracy of information is also found in the presentation of events: the author does not pay due attention to the composition or troop numbers, to the times and places of events; Often, when describing a battle, he substitutes banalities for the most important factors, so that a definitive concept of the features of the described battle are not presented at all.

But these shortcomings are partly compensated by the clarity of the style[21] and the quality of the sources, which, having been skilfully assembled by the author, give great fascination to the work. All of Russia has read his book, and this circumstance makes one regret even more that truth and impartiality did not always guide the pen of this eloquent historian.

Partial histories

Of the French works relating to the war of 1812, the following are noteworthy: *Mémoires pour servir à l'histoire militaire sous le directoire, le consulat et l'empire*, by Marshal Gouvion-Saint-Cyr (its seventh volume contains a description of operations in 1812 by Napoleon's corps detached to the Dvina). Marshal Saint-Cyr, one of the most skilful associates of the crowned head, described all the events that he witnessed very informatively and quite impartially. Actions in other theatres of war are described by him briefly.

A very good source for studying operations by the Bavarian corps is also provided in the German work by Völderndorff und Waradein, under the title: *Kriegsgeschichte von Bayern unter König Maximilian-Joseph*.

Journal de la campagne de Russie en 1812, by General Fezensac, contains a description of operations by Marshal Ney's 3e Corps. It is remarkably unbiased.

Denniée's Itinéraire de l'empereur Napoléon pendant la campagne de 1812 is a listing of the dates of all the most important events of this campaign.

Puybusque's *Lettres sur la guerre de Russie en 1812* is a work, hostile to Napoleon, that contains fascinating details about the logistic units of the French force and, in general, about everything that happened in the rear areas of the Grande Armée.

Bourgeois' *Tableau de la campagne de Moscou en 1812* is a work by one of the doctors from the Grande Armée, characterised by a concise but clear presentation of the state of the troops at various stages of the war of 1812.

There are similar works in German: firstly, Doctor Roos' *Ein Jahr aus meinem Leben, oder der Reise von den westlichen Ufer der Donau an die Nara, südlich von Moskwa, und zurück an die Beresina mit der grossen Armee Napoleons im Jahre 1812*. Secondly, Lemazurier's *Medicinische Geschichte des Russischen Feldzuges von 1812*. The work by Roos is particularly noteworthy; it presents a clear picture of the state of the troops and the main diseases that prevailed at various stages of the campaign.

Lettres sur l'incendie de Moscou by Abbot Surrugue, is an eyewitness account of events during the occupation of Moscow by the French.

---

21 [Liprandi comments: 'it seems to me that if a military book with such errors is so inaccurate, as is the Description Of The War published by Danilevsky, in the opinion of the Gentleman Professor, then style is no compensation for the major failings of such a book'].

La vérité sur l'incendie de Moscou is a work by Count Rostopchin.

Histoire de la déstruction de Moscou en 1812 et des évènemens qui ont precedé, accompagné et suivi ce desastre, par A.F. de B...ch ancien officier au service de Russie.

Sołtyk's *Napoléon en 1812* is a work comprising a presentation of operations by the Grande Armée, and in particular the Polish forces. It is very biased.

The most noteworthy works in German are:

Miller's *Darstellung des Feldzuges der franzosischen verbündeten Armee gegen die Russen im Jahr 1812*. Operations by the Grande Armée are briefly described. Operations by the Württemberg contingent, who were in Ney's 3e Corps, are described in some detail.

Funck's *Erinnerungen aus dem Felzuge in Russland im Jahr 1812* details operations by the Saxon contingent.

Beitrag zu der Geschichte des neunten Korps der französischen verbündeten Armee im Feldzug gegen Russland 1812, mit einem Anhang in besonderer Beziehung auf die Geschichte der grosherzoglich badenschen Truppen in diesem Feldzuge is an article that was published in the *Oestreichische militärische Zeitschrift, 1821*, in three parts.

Seydlitz. *Tagebuch des K. Preussischen Armee-corps im Feldzuge 1812.*

Wolzogen Memoiren. Are worthy of little credibility, according to contemporaries of the war of 1812.

Denkwürdigkeiten eines Livländers (aus den Jahren 1790-1815), Herausgegeben von Fr. v. Smitt. These notes, compiled by the famous partisan Major General Löwenstern, provide many interesting details about operations in 1812 and subsequent years.

Erinnerungen aus dem Feldzuge des Jahres 1812 in Russland, by the Prince von Württemberg, who in the Patriotic War, initially commanded 4th Division, and later II Corps. The author clearly and impartially explains the operations in which he happened to be a participant (the battle of Smolensk, the action at Gedeonovo, the battle of Borodino, on the Chernishnya river, at Maloyaroslavets, Vyazma and Krasny).

Die Schlacht von Borodino mit einer Uebersicht des Feldzuges von 1812, by General Hofmann, formerly Chief of Staff in Prinz Eugen von Württemberg's corps during the campaigns of 1813 and 1814. One of the best descriptions of the Battle of Borodino.

Die Kavallerie in der Schlacht an der Moskwa, by the Prussian General Roth von Schreckenstein. A detailed and thorough description of the part played by cavalry in the battle of Borodino.

Bataille de la Moskowa. Extrait des mémoires inédits du général Pelet sur la guerre de Russie en 1812. Entry in volume VII of the *French Bibliotheque historique et militaire.*

Ruckzug der Franzosen bis zum Niemen. An outline of the war of 1812, containing some interesting detail.

Notes sur la campagne de 1812, recueillies sur les champs de bataille de la Russie, par M. Georges de Pimodan. An article published in the periodical: *Spectateur militaire, 1856, Janvier.*

Mémoires inédits de l'amiral Tchitchagoff. These include: I. The Turkish affair of 1812. A planned diversion against Napoleon. II. The campaign against Schwarzenberg. III. The seizure of the Borisov bridgehead. IV. The Berezina crossing. V. Pursuit of the French army by Russian forces. The contents of this book are most intriguing, but, unfortunately, the author does not always keep to the truth about troop numbers, the timing of events mentioned, and so on.

Mémoires pour servir à l'histoire de la campagne de 1812 en Russie, suivis des lettres de Napoléon au roi de Westphalie pendant la campagne de 1813, is a work by Captain du Casse of the general staff. The author tries to justify King Jérôme's tardiness in operations by his army at the start of the 1812 campaign.

Observations sur la retraite du prince Bagration, by Colonel Chapuis. Extremely one-sided. No less biased are the author's comments on works by historians of the war of 1812 (*Observations sur les historiens de la campagne de Russie*) in volume VII of the *Bibliotheque historique et militaire.*

Puissance de la Russie, Wilson.

Notes by S.N. Glinka.

Memoires of the campaigns of 1812, 1813 and 1814, Prince N.B. Golitsyn.

Campaign notes of an artilleryman from 1812 to 1816, Lieutenant Colonel Radozhitsky.

Brief Notes by Admiral Shishkov.

Practise and theory of partisan operations and excerpts from the diary of a partisan, by D.V. Davydov.

A brief narrative of the French occupation of Moscow. Korbeletsky's work.

Notes on the St Petersburg Opolchenie. R. Zotov.

Ueber die Militär-Oeconomie. Count Kankrin's work. This contains information about the food supply of the Russian forces in the war of 1812.

Index

Adamovskoe; 44, 50.
Albrecht, Alexander Ivanovich; 123, 131, 185.
Alekseev, Ilya Ivanovich; 118, 120, 126, 130, 132, 139-140, 144, 147
Alexeevo; 70,77.
Alexoten; 238-239.
Amey, François-Pierre Joseph; 124-125, 129.
Anstett, Ivan Osipovich; 253, 255.
Arakcheev, Alexey Andreevich; 203, 244, 331-332.
Aristovo; 15-17.
Arnoldi, Ivan Karlovich; 196-197, 333.
Aubry de La Boucharderie, Claude Charles; 126, 180-182.
Augereau, Charles Pierre François; 159, 218, 271.
Augereau, Jean-Pierre; 70-72
Austria, Empire of; contingent of the Grande Armée; 110, 151-153, 155-157, 174, 218-219, 248-256, 265, 271, 274, 310, 313.

Babinovichi; 81, 113, 134, 171.
Bachelu, Gilbert Désiré Joseph; 261, 265, 267, 270.
Baden, Grand Duchy of; contingent of the Grande Armée; 143, 190, 195, 342.
Bagration, Pëtr Ivanovich; 49, 279, 331-333, 343.
Balk, Mikhail Dmitrievich; 120-122, 124, 127.
Baraguey d'Hilliers, Louis; 54, 66, 68, 71.
Barany; 111, 185.
Barclay de Tolly, Mikhail Bogdanovich; 278-280, 328, 331-333, 340.
Bavaria, Kingdom of, contingent of the Grande Armée; 74, 120, 122, 124-126, 128-132, 134, 140-141, 180, 195, 213, 215, 223-224, 341.
Beauharnais, Eugène Rose de (Viceroy of Italy); 7-11, 13, 16, 20, 28-31, 33-34, 36, 38, 40, 49, 55, 57-61, 63, 65, 68, 70, 72-76, 80, 82, 84-88, 91-92, 97, 103, 107, 111, 170, 172, 190, 195, 200, 204-205, 218, 224-225, 282, 289-290, 304.
Begichev, Ivan Matveevich; 118, 120-121, 123.
Beloe; 120-121, 125, 143.
Belorussia; 67, 105-106, 213, 230, 279
Bely; 51, 142.
Belitsa; 229, 237, 250-251.
Benitsa; 216, 218, 222.
Benkendorf, Alexander Khristoforovich; 20, 22, 24, 333.
Bennigsen, Leonty Leontevich; 36, 203, 305, 332.
Berezina river; 80-81, 108, 111, 113, 115, 141, 148, 149-151, 153, 158-160, 163-169, 170-185, 186-187, 189-191, 194-196, 198-199, 201-202, 204-208, 210-218, 228-229, 231-232, 244, 248-250, 258, 276, 283, 296, 304, 307, 323, 333, 343.
Berg, Grand Duchy of; contingent of the Grande Armée; 134, 195. *2e régiment chevau-légers de Berg*; 178.
Berg, Grigory Maksimovich; 118, 120, 123, 133, 136-138, 144, 146, 191, 193, 197-198, 269-270.
Berlin; 262, 264-265, 267, 271-272, 316.
Berthemy, Pierre-Augustin; 8-9.
Berthier, Louis-Alexandre (prince de Neuchâtel, *chef d'etat-major*); 8-9, 14, 36, 38, 45-47, 67, 92, 113, 159, 172, 190, 218-219, 222, 224-225, 238, 255, 258, 294-295.
Beshankovichi [Bieszenkowicze]; 67, 120, 135-136, 138, 140-141, 146.
Bessières, Jean-Baptiste; 36-37, 225.
Beurmann, Frédéric Auguste de; 11.
Biała; 149, 151.
Białowieża; 153, 155-156.
Bistrom, Karl Ivanovich; 77.
Bobr; 114, 168, 170-171, 173, 175-176, 178-179, 206.

Bobruisk; 67, 159, 162, 164, 167, 174, 181, 206, 212-213, 229, 231, 235, 237, 254, 301-302, 323.
Bocheikovo; 136, 140, 143.
Bogdanov, Nikolay Ivanovich; 66.
Bologovsky, Dmitry Nikolaevich; 15, 17.
Boltutino; 70-71, 77.
Borodino; 48, Battle of; 103, 280-281, 284, 291, 323, 328, 330, 333, 340, 342.
Borisov; 67, 103, 108, 111-115, 139, 141, 148, 162-168, 170-178, 180-185, 186, 188-198, 204, 206-207, 211, 213, 228, 237, 283, 303, 343.
Borovsk; 12, 14-18, 29, 36-38, 40, 42-45, 48, 50, 282, 287-288, 292.
Borozdin 1st, Mikhail Mikhailovich; 34, 96, 309.
Borozdin 2nd, Nikolai Mikhailovich; 90, 95, 109, 112, 216, 224, 227, 257.
Boyare; 140, 144, 148.
Brest-Litovsk; 148, 149-151, 156-157, 163, 173, 218, 249-251, 254, 339.
Brili; 177, 181, 183-185, 188, 196, 202.
Bronikowski-Oppeln, Mikolaj Deodatus Kajetan; 108, 159-160, 162, 165, 175.
Broussier, Jean-Baptiste; 7, 13-14, 29-31, 73-75, 82, 84, 87.
Bryansk; 9, 236.
Bug river; 150-151, 157, 249, 253-254, 274, 296.
Bulatov, Mikhail Leontievich; 150-151, 154-155, 298-299.
Bulletins de la Grande Armée; 216-218, 222.
Bülow, Friedrich Wilhelm von; 265, 273.
Bychi; 181, 197.
Bykhalov 1st, Vasily Andreevich; 35, 38, 72.
Bykovo; 57, 64-66, 70.

Candras, Jacques Lazare Savettier de; 124, 199.
Carrière de Beaumont, Louis Chrétien; 9.
Castex, Bertrand Pierre; 176-177, 190.
Caulaincourt, Armand Augustin Louis de, (duc de Vicence); 45-46, 219-220.
Cavaignac, Jacques-Marie; 270, 319.
Chambray, Georges de; 202, 274, 286, 300, 304, 334, 336-337.
Chaplits, Yefim Ignatievich; 150, 158-159, 164, 168, 175, 177, 183-185, 187-191, 196-197, 204, 207, 210, 215-216, 222-223, 227, 230, 239, 241, 306.

Charpentier, Henri François Marie; 54, 83.
Chashniki; 132-133, 143-144, 147-148, 171. Battle of; 67, 108, 135-141.
Chasseloup-Laubat, François Charles Louis de; 173, 182, 184.
Chechensky, Alexander Nikolaevich; 25, 71.
Chereya; 111, 114, 143-144, 146-147, 171, 174, 177-178, 182, 206.
Chernigov; 213, 235, 237.
Chernishnya river, action on the; 8, 286, 291, 342.
Chernyshev, Alexander Ivanovich; 152, 331-332.
Chervonoe; 77, 82.
Chichagov, Pavel Vasilevich; 53-54, 64, 67, 80-81, 113-115, 139, 141-142, 147-148, 149-153, 157, 161-164, 168-169, 173-180, 182-184, 188, 190-191, 194-197, 204-208, 210-213, 216, 222-223, 228-229, 231-232, 233-234, 239-242, 249-250, 270-271, 277, 283, 296, 301-302, 330-333, 335.
Choglokov, Pavel Nikolaevich; 62.
Claparède, Michel Marie; 13, 36, 38, 40, 82-83, 91, 173, 189, 197, 291.
Clausewitz, Carl Philipp Gottlieb; 264-266, 327-328, 336-337.
Colbert-Chabanais, Édouard Pierre David de; 11, 13.
Compans, Jean Dominique; 33.
Confederation of the Rhine; 46, 219. contingent of the Grande Armée; *Rheinbund Regiment Nr. 4*; 220.
Corbineau, Jean-Baptiste Juvénal; 120, 125, 129, 132, 180, 187, 190.
Courland; 214, 221, 257.

Dąbrowski, Jan Henryk; 108, 159-161, 163-165, 167-168, 171, 176, 184-185, 187, 197, 280, 333.
Daendels, Herman Willem; 134, 135-136, 178, 190, 195.
Danzig [Gdańsk]; 159, 218, 225, 270, 274, 319.
Daru, Pierre-Antoine-Noël-Mathieu Bruno; 225, 238.
Davout, Louis Nicolas (prince d'Eckmühl); 7-11, 13-14, 16, 32-34, 36, 38, 40, 44, 47-50, 54-55, 57-62, 64-65, 68, 82-84, 88, 90-97, 103, 107, 111, 170, 190, 195, 200, 204-205, 223-225, 238, 279, 282-283, 304.

Davydov, Denis Vasilevich; 25, 50, 52, 70-71, 85, 109, 113, 171, 212, 228-229, 250-252, 254, 312, 343.
Davydov, Nikolai Vladimirovich; 87.
Delaborde, Henri François; 9, 82, 84.
Delaitre, Antoine Charles Bernard; 189-190, 193-194.
Delfanti, Cosimo Damiano; 73, 87.
Delzons, Alexis Joseph; 7, 13, 20, 29-31.
Delzons, Benoît; 30.
Denisov 7th, Vasily Timofeevich; 22, 98, 204, 321.
Detchino; 42-44, 282, 287.
Diebitsch, Wilhelm Friedrich von; 142.
Diebitsch und Narten, Hans Karl von; 118, 120-121, 124-125, 258-267, 269-270, 330.
Disna [Dzisna]; 118, 120, 122, 124-126, 130-131.
Dmitrov; 7, 20.
Dnieper river; 11, 54, 66-69, 73-77, 81-82, 84, 91, 94-95, 97-98, 100-102, 105, 109-114, 159, 171, 178, 202-203, 205, 279-281, 294, 303.
Dobroe; 90, 94-96, 102.
Dode de la Brunerie, Guillaume; 119, 172.
Dokhturov, Dmitry Sergeevich; 14-17, 29-30, 32-34, 44, 240, 250, 254, 328.
Dokshitsy [Dokšycy]; 67, 81, 143, 180, 210, 213, 216, 303.
Dolginov; 215-216, 224.
Dolgorukov, Sergei Nikolaievich; 96, 246, 309.
Dorogobuzh; 39, 54, 65-70, 73, 76.
Dorokhov, Ivan Semënovich; 14, 29, 35.
Doumerc, Jean-Pierre; 120, 187, 190, 196.
Dovre, Fëdor Filippovich; 265-266.
Drissa; 120, 279, 323, 330.
Drohiczyn; 149-151, 253.
Druya; 131, 143.
Dubna; 237.
Dubrovo; 57, 146, 152.
Dubrowna; 85, 95, 107-112, 171.
Dufour, François Marie; 13.
Duka, Ilya Mikhailovich; 93-94.
Dukhovshchina; 68-70, 73-75, 78.
Durutte, Pierre François Joseph; 150-151, 154, 159, 250.
Dvina [Daugava]; 51, 53-54, 67-68, 75-76, 81, 110, 117-122, 124-131, 134, 140, 143, 147-148, 179, 217, 263, 279, 330, 341.

Eagle; 87, 100, 103, 168, 178, 216, 222.

Éblé, Jean-Baptiste; 173, 182, 184, 187, 199-200, 244.
Emmanuel, Georgy Arsenievich; 60.
Ertel, Fëdor Fëdorovich; 67, 150, 159, 162-163, 173, 212, 250, 277, 301-302, 331.
Essen 1st, Ivan Nikolaevich; 258, 262, 331.
Essen 3rd, Pëtr Kirillovich; 150-151, 155, 157, 163, 235, 240, 249-250, 254, 298, 330.
État-major général; 11, 13, 15, 38, 45, 48, 57, 65, 67-69, 75-77, 82, 92, 103, 108-109, 112, 171, 173, 179, 181, 200, 215, 218, 225, 240, 335.
Evers, Charles Joseph; 13, 40, 48, 55.

Fain, Agathon Jean François; 201-202, 304, 334-335.
Fedorovskoe; 57-58.
Ferrier, Gratien; 47.
Fezensac, Raymond Aymeric Philippe Joseph de Montesquiou-; 63, 99, 202, 275, 304, 341.
Figner, Alexander Samoilovich; 14, 50, 52, 62, 70-72.
Foch, Alexander Borisovich; 133, 143-144, 197-198.
Fominskoe; 7, 13-15.
Fontainebleau; 39.
Fontane, Jacques; 33.
Fournier-Sarlovèze, François Louis; 134, 139, 190, 195, 198-199.
French contingent of the Grande Armée:
 1er régiment de chevau-légers lanciers polonais de la Garde; 219. *1er régiment de Voltigeurs de la Garde*; 93-94. *2e régiment de chevau-légers lanciers de la Garde*; 85. *3e régiment croates*; 124, 199. *3e régiment de grenadiers à pied de la Garde*; 93. *4e régiment d'infanterie de ligne*; 69, 99. *7e régiment de cuirassiers*; 125. *9e régiment d'artillerie à pied*; 300. *9e régiment d'infanterie*; 289. *18e régiment d'infanterie de ligne*; 69, 99. *19e régiment d'infanterie de ligne*; 123. *22e régiment d'infanterie légère*; 159, 300. *26e régiment d'infanterie légère*; 123. *29e régiment d'infanterie*; 239. *33e régiment d'infanterie légère*; 95. *33e régiment d'infanterie de ligne*; 300. *35e régiment d'infanterie de ligne*; 87. *46e régiment d'infanterie de ligne*; 159, 300. *56e régiment d'infanterie de ligne*; 123. *93e*

régiment d'infanterie de ligne; 159, 300. *106e régiment d'infanterie*; 75. *113e régiment d'infanterie de ligne*; 220. *126e régiment d'infanterie de ligne*; 178. *artillerie à cheval de la Garde*; 92. *artillerie de la Garde*; 12, 37, 82, 195, 198-199. *cavalerie de la Garde*; 8, 11, 37, 39, 91, 112, 178, 224, 240, 291, 304. *Chasseurs à cheval de la Garde*; 37. *Garde impériale*; 8, 13, 15, 32, 34, 36-38, 40, 45, 47-49, 55, 57, 65, 68, 76, 82-86, 88, 91, 95-96, 107-109, 170, 179, 181, 185, 187-188, 196, 199, 201, 204-205, 215, 224-226, 238, 243, 275-276, 278, 286, 319. *Infanterie de la Garde*; 291. *Jeune Garde*; 9, 11, 20-21, 49, 65, 82, 84, 91-94, 107, 189-190, 199, 240, 304. *régiment d'Illyrie*; 99, 300. *Vieille Garde*; 7, 11, 13, 48, 65, 82, 84, 91-94, 107-108, 189-190, 199, 240, 304.
Friant, Louis; 82.
Friederichs, Jean-Parfait; 13, 94-95.
Friedrich Wilhelm III, King of Prussia; 262-263, 266, 272
Fröhlich, Franz von; 155, 251-252.

Gajna river; 181, 188, 201, 206, 214-215.
Galicia; 157, 310.
Gamen, Alexey Yuryevich; 123, 127.
Gendarmes; 21, 45-46, 152, 286, 291, 300.
Gérard, Étienne Maurice; 33, 38, 146, 190, 195, 199, 238-239.
Gerngross, Rodion (Ilarion) Fëdorovich; 138, 141, 178, 198.
Girardin d'Ermenonville, Alexandre Louis Robert de; 11.
Glubokoe; 132, 140-141, 143, 172.
Gniezna; 154-155.
Gogel, Fëdor Grigorievich; 83.
Golenishchev-Kutuzov, Mikhail Illarionovich; 8-9, 14-15, 17-19, 32, 34-36, 40-42, 44-48, 50-53, 57, 64-67, 70, 76-78, 80-81, 84-85, 87-88, 90-91, 93, 96, 102-105, 109, 114-115, 139, 147, 163, 169, 171-174, 178-179, 182-183, 189, 202-203, 205-208, 211, 216, 223, 228-229, 233-234, 236, 240, 242-244, 249, 252, 254, 258, 270, 277, 280, 282-283, 287-288, 291, 292-293, 301, 305, 308, 309, 310, 315, 326, 330-333, 336, 340.
Golenishchev-Kutuzov, Pavel Vasilyevich; 52, 73-74, 78, 110, 113, 171, 210-211, 215-216, 224, 227, 258, 260-261, 265, 267, 269-270, 307, 323, 331.
Golitsyn, Boris Andreevich; 45.
Golitsyn, Dmitry Vladimirovich; 44, 90-96, 102, 230.
Golitsyn, Nikolai Borisovich; 343.
Goncharovo; 42-44, 282
Gorikhvostov, Alexander Zakharievich; 98.
Göring, P.Kh.; 86.
Gorki; 84, 109, 113, 170-171, 294, 340.
Gorodnya; 36-38.
Gorodok; 118, 120.
Gourgaud, Gaspard; 36, 64, 103, 111, 202, 275, 334, 337.
Goryany; 118, 121, 125, 171.
Grabbe, Pavel Khristoforovich; 62.
Grande Armée:
   Corps: *1er Corps*; 8, 11, 13, 33-34, 38, 40, 47, 55, 58, 63, 83, 243, 275, 286, 291, 304, 319. *1er corps de cavalerie*; 40, 55, 286. *2e Corps*; 119, 121, 125, 130-134, 135-136, 138-139, 142-143, 172, 180, 184, 187-188, 190, 243, 275, 300, 304, 319. *2e corps de cavalerie*; 40, 55, 65, 286. *3e Corps*; 7-8, 11, 13, 40, 55, 58, 63, 83, 243, 275, 286, 291, 304, 319, 341-342. *3e corps de cavalerie*; 40, 55, 286. *4e Corps*; 7-8, 13, 20, 28, 30-31, 33-34, 38, 40, 55, 58, 61, 63, 68, 72, 74, 84, 88, 103, 243, 275, 286, 291, 304, 319, 335. *4e corps de cavalerie*; 13, 40, 55, 65, 286. *5e Corps*; 13, 38, 42, 45, 55, 58, 77, 81, 218, 243, 286, 291. *6e Corps*; 108, 119-120, 129, 131-132, 140-141, 218, 243, 300. *7e Corps*; 250. *8e Corps*; 8, 12, 38, 48-49, 218, 243, 286, 291, 304. *9e Corps*; 75, 133-134, 135-136, 139, 142, 144, 190, 215, 304. *10e Corps*; 259, 261-262. *11e Corps*; 150, 159, 218, 240, 269. *Réserve de cavalerie*; 34, 48, 57, 60, 178, 304.
   Divisions: *1er Division*; 286. *2e Division*; 286. *3e Division*; 33, 286. *3e division de cuirassiers*; 120, 187. *4e Division*; 286. *5e Division*; 33, 286. *13e Division*; 87. *14e Division*; 87. *15e Division*; 75, 87. *17e Division*; 333.
Grandjean, Charles Louis Dieudonné; 258-261, 263, 265, 269.
Grawert, Julius August Reinhold von; 262-263.

Grodno; 151-152, 159, 218, 229, 250-252.
Gromy; 122, 125.
Grekov 1st, Dmitry Yevdokimovich; 70, 77, 98.
Grekov 8th, Pëtr Matveevich; 161, 296, 306.
Gridnevo; 49, 51, 53.
Gudovich, Nikolay Vasilievich; 67, 110, 213.
Guilleminot, Armand Charles; 30-31.
Gumbinnen [Gusev]; 228, 239-240, 270.
Gundius, Vilim Antonovich; 100.
Guyon, Claude-Raymond; 86.
Gzhatsk [Gagarin]; 22, 40, 45, 48-55, 74, 159, 282, 323.

Hardenberg, Karl August von; 271-272.
Harpe, Vasily Ivanovich; 132, 140-142, 147-148, 178.
Helffreich, Bogdan Borisovich; 124-125, 127, 131, 144.
Hessen-Darmstadt: contingent of the Grande Armée; 93, 195.
Heudelet de Bierre, Étienne; 240, 243, 267, 269-270, 319.
Heyligers, Ghisbert Martin Cort; 87.
Hospitals; 8, 10, 13, 22, 48, 53, 62, 69, 83, 97, 120, 143, 204, 227, 230-232, 241, 243-244, 246-247, 277, 313.

Iashvili, Levan Mikhailovich; 118-122, 124-126, 132, 136-138, 144-146, 309.
Iashvili, Vladimir Mikhailovich; 70.
Ignatiev, Gavriil Alexandrovich; 162, 212, 301.
Igumen [Chervyen]; 114, 162-165, 174, 182-183, 206, 228, 301-302.
Ilovaisky 3rd, Alexey Vasilievich; 37.
Ilovaisky 4th, Ivan Dmitryevich; 20, 22, 45, 47, 261, 321.
Ilovaisky 5th, Nikolai Vasilevich; 57, 226.
Ilovaisky 9th, Grigory Dmitryevich; 35, 38, 41, 44.
Ilovaisky 12th, Vasily Dmitryevich; 22, 73-74, 321.
Italy, Kingdom of: contingent of the Grande Armée; 219. *cavalleria de la Guardia Reale*; 7. *Guardia Reale*; 29, 31-32, 73-75, 82, 84. *Reggimento Granatieri*; 31.
Ivashev, Pëtr Nikiforovich; 18.
Izabelin; 152-155.

Jomini, Antoine Henri de; 172-173, 332, 338-339.
Junot, Jean-Andoche (duc d'Abrantès); 8, 12, 38-40, 48, 82, 85, 107, 170, 173, 185, 190, 195, 304.
Jurburg [Jurbarkas]; 265, 269.

Kabluchi; 131-132.
Kaidanovo [Dzerzhinsk]; 160-161.
Kaisarov, Paisy Sergeevich; 50, 96-97, 112, 222.
Kakhovsky, Mikhail Ivanovich; 121.
Kaluga; 7-10, 13, 15, 17-19, 22, 28-29, 33, 35-38, 40-42, 54, 70, 203, 237, 282, 287-288, 292, 305.
Kamen; 143, 152, 204, 211, 215.
Kamieniec; 149, 156, 251.
Karpenko, Moisey Ivanovich; 77.
Karpov, Akim Akimovich; 18, 42, 50, 70.
Kaverin, Pavel Nikitich; 17.
Khalyapin, Vasily Mikhailovich; 30-31.
Kholopenichi; 141, 178, 303.
Khrapovitsky, Yason Semënovich; 25, 189.
Kiev [Kyiv]; 235-237.
Kiselev, Pavel Dmitryevich; 18.
Kleist, Friedrich Emil Ferdinand Heinrich von; 259-261, 263-264, 272.
Kleszczele; 151, 153.
Knorring, Karl Bogdanovich; 158, 160-161, 164, 174, 182, 206, 213, 229-230, 240.
Kobrin; 156-157, 248-250.
Kobyzevo; 78, 82, 85, 96.
Kokhanovo; 111, 171, 303.
Kologrivov, Andrei Semënovich; 235-236.
Kolotsk Monastery; 13, 48, 51.
Kołtyniany [Kaltinėnai]; 259-262, 264, 270.
Königsberg [Kaliningrad]; 159, 218-219, 225, 238, 240, 243, 260, 265, 267, 269-270, 272.
Konovnitsyn, Pëtr Petrovich; 32, 34, 51, 64, 90, 101, 230, 246, 253, 337.
Kopys; 109-110, 113-114, 171, 178, 185, 189, 202-203, 207, 212, 231, 283.
Korf, Fëdor Karlovich; 56, 58, 60-61.
Korff, Peter Anton von; 268.
Kornilov, Pëtr Yakovlevich; 183, 185, 187, 196.
Korytnya; 82, 91, 98.
Kosiecki [Kossecki], Franciszek Ksawery; 160-162, 168.
Kotovo; 13-15.
Kovel; 157, 249-250.

Kovno [Kaunas]; 133, 212, 218, 221, 225-226, 228, 238-241, 274-275.
Kozen, Pëtr Andreevich; 33.
Kozyany; 118, 120.
Kraków; 256, 274, 310.
Krapivna; 58, 62.
Krasny; 42, 66-67, 78, 81-85, 88-92, 94-100, 103-105, 107-110, 114, 169, 171, 217-218, 283, 291, 292-293, 342.
Krasovsky, Afanasy Ivanovich; 160, 167, 196.
Kremenskoe; 38, 44, 50-51.
Kremlin (Moscow); 8-12, 15, 20-21, 23-24.
Kretov, Nikolai Vasilievich; 95.
Krugloe; 203, 206, 305.
Kudashev, Nikolay Danilovich; 18, 50, 86, 226.
Kuteinikov 2nd, Dmitry Yefimovich; 37, 57, 97, 226.
Kutkovo; 82, 84, 90.
Kutuzov (see Golenishchev-Kutuzov)

Labiau [Polessk]; 266, 269-270.
Lambert, Karl Osipovich de; 150-151, 158-168, 174.
Lanchantin, Louis François; 100.
Langéron, Alexander Fëdorovich; 163-164, 168, 175, 183-184, 190-191, 207, 230, 297.
Lanniki; 110, 113, 171, 206.
Lanskoy, Sergei Nikolaevich; 204, 210, 227, 230, 241, 254, 312.
Lariboisière, Jean Ambroise Baston de; 10-11, 244.
Latour-Maubourg, Marie Victor Nicolas de Faÿ de; 13, 76, 84, 91-92, 111- 112, 178, 291.
Lanskoy, Sergei Nikolaevich; 204, 210, 227, 230, 241, 254, 312.
Lanskoy, Vasily Sergeevich; 34.
Laskin, Alexei Andreevich; 224, 227.
Laukuva; 260, 264.
Lauriston, Jacques Jean Alexandre Bernard Law, marquis de; 9, 45, 190.
Ledru des Essarts, François Roch; 69, 100.
Lefebvre, François Joseph; 225.
Lefebvre-Desnouettes, Charles; 38.
Legrand, Claude Juste Alexandre Louis; 121-123, 126, 128-131, 135-139, 143, 197.
Lepel [Lyepyel]; 67, 81, 132, 140-144, 147-148, 152, 172-174, 181, 210.
Letashevka [Letashovo]; 18-19.
Levié, Joseph Marie; 31.
Lhéritier de Chézelles, Samuel François; 125.

Liders, Nikolai Ivanovich; 150, 162-163.
Lieven, Ivan Andreevich; 150-151, 155, 299
Lithuania; 52, 54, 76, 108, 159, 217, 224, 237, 243, 251, 253, 279, 281 contingent of the Grande Armée; 159-161, 218, 230, 281, 300.
Lizogub, Alexander Ivanovich; 72.
Lobanov-Rostovsky, Dmitry Ivanovich; 235-236.
Loison, Louis-Henri; 159, 218-220, 223, 225, 238-239, 319.
Loshnitsa; 175-176, 179-181, 183, 185, 189-190.
Losmina river [Losvinka]; 92-94, 96, 98-99, 101.
Lossberg, Friedrich Wilhelm von; 82.
Löwenstern, Woldemar Hermann von; 250-251, 333, 342
Löwis of Menar, Friedrich von; 229, 258-259, 265, 270, 315, 321.
Lyuboml; 157, 249.
Lukomka river; 135-140, 144-146.
Lukoml; 143-144.
Lukovkin 2nd, Gavriil Amvrosievich; 164, 168, 175, 177, 297, 306
Luzha river; 16, 28-30, 32-33, 36-38, 40, 44, 50, 287.
Luzhki; 143, 147.
Lyady; 83, 85, 88, 91, 94-95, 107, 109.
Lyakhovo; 71-72, 77.
Lyubavichi; 81, 101-102.

MacDonald, Étienne Jacques-Joseph-Alexandre; 131, 143, 212-213, 225, 228-229, 237-238, 240-241, 257-265, 267-271, 274, 317, 318, 319.
Maison, Nicolas-Joseph; 120-122, 126, 135-136.
Malet, Claude-François de; 68, 219.
Maloyaroslavets; 14-19, 28-45, 52, 55, 103-104, 278, 282, 287, 292, 340, 342.
Marauders; 21-22, 68, 74, 76, 97, 102, 111, 118, 193, 226, 279, 304.
Marchand, Jean Gabriel; 36, 38-39, 99, 238-239, 319.
Maret, Hugues-Bernard, duc de Bassano; 53, 157, 220-221, 248, 263, 265.
Martynov, Andrei Dmitrievich; 96.
Massenbach, Eberhard Friedrich; 259-261, 265-268, 318.
Medniki; 218, 220, 222-223.

Medyn; 28-29, 35-36, 38, 41-42, 44, 50-51, 55, 287-288, 292.
Melissino, Alexey Petrovich; 151, 153-156.
Meller-Zakomelsky, Yegor Ivanovich; 14, 16, 84.
Memel [Klaipėda]; 258-260, 266.
Merecz [Merkinė]; 218, 228-229, 246.
Merle, Pierre Hugues Victoire; 121, 124, 126, 131, 135-136.
Merlino; 85, 87.
Meshcherinov, Vasily Dmitrievich; 196, 306.
Miloradovich, Mikhail Andreevich; 17-18, 34, 42-45, 50-51, 54-62, 66-67, 69-70, 77-78, 82-87, 90-93, 96, 99-100, 102, 105, 110, 114, 171, 178, 185, 189, 204, 207, 211-212, 216, 223, 231, 240, 250, 254, 287, 292, 312, 323.
Minsk; 67, 81, 108, 110, 114, 133, 139, 150, 152, 157-165, 169, 172, 174, 182-183, 204-206, 210, 212-213, 217, 224, 229, 237, 240, 248-250, 279, 300, 301, 303.
Mitau [Jelgava]; 259-260, 262.
Mocha river; 13, 323.
Mogilev; 54, 66, 77, 81, 105, 107, 109-110, 113, 159, 170-171, 185, 189, 237, 279.
Mohr, Johann Friedrich von; 152, 251.
Molodechno; 181, 215-216, 218, 222, 251.
Monthion, François Gédéon Bailly de; 46.
Morand, Charles Antoine Louis Alexis; 11, 13.
Mortier, Adolphe Édouard Casimir Joseph; 9, 11-12, 15, 18, 20-22, 38-40, 45, 48, 82, 91, 107, 172, 190, 225.
Moscow; 7-12, 15, 17-18, 20-25, 38-41, 45-46, 48-50, 52, 54-55, 73-74, 80, 111, 113, 141, 157, 159-160, 172, 179, 199-201, 213-214, 218, 221, 224, 278, 280-282, 284, 286, 288, 291, 292, 295, 324, 326, 330, 341, 343.
Mosty; 152, 229, 250-251.
Mouton, Georges, comte de Lobau; 36-37, 219.
Mozhaisk; 7-8, 11-15, 22, 29, 37-38, 40-42, 47, 49-50, 282, 288, 340.
Mozyr; 67, 150, 159, 162-164, 237, 301-302.
Mstislavl; 66, 77, 80, 84, 91, 134.
Mukhavets river; 156, 249.
Murat, Joachim (King of Naples); 8, 13-14, 18, 36-37, 45, 48, 172, 184, 190, 218-219, 221-223, 225-226, 228, 238, 240, 243, 255, 258, 270-272.
Myasoedovo; 58-60.

Naples, Kingdom of, contingent of the Grande Armée; *Veliti della Guardia Reale*; 220.
Nara river; 13-15, 18, 341.
Narbonne-Lara, Louis-Marie-Jacques-Amalric de; 46.
Narew river; 151, 153, 156, 253, 313.
Naryshkin, Lev Alexandrovich; 20-21, 45-47, 152.
Nashchokin, Fëdor Alexandrovich; 113.
Natzmer, Oldwig Anton Leopold von; 272.
Neman river; 37, 65, 131, 133-134, 152, 158, 160, 205, 213, 218, 228-229, 237-241, 243-244, 250-251, 254, 258-262, 265, 267-268, 274-275, 277-278, 281, 316, 319, 330, 342.
Nesvizh; 158, 160, 163, 206, 248, 250, 323.
Ney, Michel; 7-11, 13, 36, 38, 40, 48, 55, 57-58, 61-63, 65, 69, 76-77, 80, 82-85, 88, 90, 92, 96-103, 111, 170, 185, 189-190, 195-196, 199, 201, 204-205, 223-226, 238-239, 283, 304, 341-342.
Niemenczyn; 204, 210, 212, 224, 228, 307.
Nikitin, Alexey Petrovich; 14, 16, 31, 93-94, 312.
Nikolskoe; 20, 51.
Nizhny-Berezino; 162, 164, 177, 183, 185, 188, 206.
Novak, Ivan Ivanovich; 142, 211, 257, 307, 323.
Novgorod; 142, 169, 237.
Novogrudok; 152, 158, 212.
Novoselki; 85, 90.
Novy-Sverzhen; 158, 160-161, 174, 206.

Obol river; 118.
Oka river; 41, 282.
Olita [Alytus]; 218, 225, 228-229, 259.
Olsufiev, Zakhar Dmitryevich; 58.
Opperman, Karl Ivanovich; 101.
Order of St George; 105, 244.
Orlov, Mikhail Fëdorovich; 114, 174, 182.
Orlov-Denisov, Vasily Vasilevich; 32, 44, 50-52, 57, 70-72, 77, 211, 216, 226.
Ornano, Philippe Antoine d'; 87, 289.
O'Rourke, Iosif Kornilovich; 158, 160, 162, 175, 177, 183, 185, 188-189, 196, 204, 239, 241-242, 306.
Orsha; 66-67, 80-82, 85, 90-91, 93-94, 96, 100-104, 107-114, 139, 143, 147-148, 168, 170-172, 174-176, 178, 185, 187, 191, 213, 222, 237, 294-295.

Oshmyany; 213, 218-220, 222-224.
Osterman-Tolstoy, Alexander Ivanovich; 58, 78, 82-83, 85, 91, 96.
Oudinot, Nicolas Charles Marie; 108, 112, 114, 134, 135-136, 143-144, 146, 148, 171-174, 176, 179-182, 184-185, 187-190, 195-197, 199, 204, 214, 276, 304.
Ozharovsky, Adam Petrovich; 50, 52, 70-71, 78, 82, 84-85, 88, 91, 95, 109-110, 113, 171, 185, 189, 211-212, 229, 250-251, 288.

Pahlen 1st, Pëtr Petrovich; 327-328.
Pahlen 2nd, Pavel Petrovich; 175-176, 178, 196.
Pahlen, Matvei Ivanovich; 141, 211, 257, 307.
Pakosz, Czesław Karol; 165, 167.
Paris; 21, 68, 141, 216, 218-219, 221-222, 272, 330.
Parlementaire; 20, 47, 72, 86, 99, 193, 251.
Partisans; 8, 11, 15, 18, 25, 34, 45, 50, 52, 62, 70-72, 88, 109-111, 115, 142, 169, 171, 174, 191, 193, 206, 212, 222, 228, 251, 277, 281-282, 288, 342-343.
Partouneaux, Louis de; 134, 144, 190-191, 193-194, 197-199, 304.
Paskevich, Ivan Fëdorovich; 44, 50, 54, 56-58, 61-62, 86-87, 98-99, 287.
Paulucci, Filipp Osipovich; 258-259, 262, 316, 331-332.
Pelleport, Pierre de; 100.
Pelletier, Jean-Baptiste; 62.
Perrin, Claude-Victor, duc de Bellune; 38, 53-54, 67, 76, 98, 107-108, 111, 114, 130, 133-134, 135-136, 138-139, 143, 146-148, 159, 164, 171-174, 177-180, 182, 185, 189-190, 193-195, 197-201, 204, 214-217, 222-223, 276, 303, 304.
Piklupenen [Piktupėnai]; 260-261, 267, 270.
Pino, Domenico; 29, 31.
Pinsk; 150, 157, 159, 162-163, 237, 249, 254.
Platov, Matvey Ivanovich (Don *Ataman*); 16-18, 35, 37, 44-45, 50-52, 54-55, 57-58, 61-62, 66, 69-70, 73-77, 81-82, 85, 96, 98, 101-103, 105, 109-112, 114, 171, 178, 185, 189, 191, 194-195, 204, 207, 210, 212, 215-216, 224, 226-229, 239-241, 244, 269, 271, 277, 282, 287, 303.
Platov 4th; 119, 132, 321.
Pleshchenitsa [Pliešcanicy]; 115, 204, 215.
Pochaevitsy; 144, 146-147.

Pogost; 178, 189, 206, 303.
Poitevin de Maureilhan, Jean Étienne Casimir; 73.
Poll, Ivan Lavrentievich; 87.
Polota river; 119, 121-122, 124-127.
Polotnyanye Zavody; 44-45, 50-51, 287.
Polotsk; 53, 67, 117-121, 125-132, 134, 139-140, 143, 180, 217, 323.
Poltava; 172, 213, 237.
Ponary hills [Aukštieji Paneriai]; 226-227.
Poniatowski, Józef Antoni; 13, 15, 29, 38-42, 45, 49, 57-58, 60-61, 65, 77, 81, 185, 253, 274.
Pontoniers; 173, 182, 187, 199, 244.
Pontoons; 10, 18, 111, 118, 125, 172, 177-178, 187, 194, 204, 210, 231.
Porozów; 153, 155-156.
Poscherun Mill [Požerūnai]; 266-267.
Pouget, François René Cailloux, *dit*; 72, 141.
Pregel [Pregolya] river; 228, 270-271, 277.
Pripyat river; 162-163, 302.
Prismenitsa manor; 121, 124.
Protva river; 16-19, 32.
Prussia, Kingdom of; 205, 222-223, 234, 242-243, 261-262, 264-266, 268, 270-273, 278, 316. contingent of the Grande Armée; 258-259, 261-268, 271-273, 274.
Pruzhany; 151, 156-157, 248.
Pultusk; 252-253, 255.
Puybusque, Louis-Guillaume de; 113, 341.

Radoszkowicze; 152, 162, 212, 223.
Radt, Semën Lukich; 229, 240, 250, 254.
Raevsky, Nikolai Nikolaevich; 32-33, 57, 100, 332.
Rapp, Jean; 45-46.
Ratno; 157, 249.
Razout, Louis-Nicolas de; 61, 69, 99-100.
Razumovsky, Lev Kirillovich; 12.
Rechki; 222-223, 257.
Rennenkampf, Astafy Astafievich; 99.
Reynier, Jean-Louis-Ébénézer; 149-151, 153-155, 157, 159, 172, 237, 249-251, 253, 255-256.
Ricard, Étienne Pierre Sylvestre; 82, 97-99.
Riga; 121, 229, 237, 240, 246, 258, 262, 265, 277.
Rogachev; 163, 212, 237.
Roguet, François; 11, 13, 82, 84.
Romanovo; 110, 171.
Roos, Heinrich Ulrich Ludwig von; 66, 341.

Rosen, Major General, Baron; 90, 92, 95, 109.
Roslavl; 66, 70, 77, 85, 91.
Rossieny [Raseiniai]; 258-260.
Rostopchin, Fëdor Vasilievich; 12, 326, 332, 342.
Roth, Loggin Osipovich; 122-123, 127.
Rüdiger, Fëdor Vasilievich; 122-123, 126, 130-132, 143-144, 146-147.
Rudnia; 153, 156.
Rudzevich, Alexander Yakovlevich; 188, 190, 196.
Rumshishki [Rumšiškės]; 228, 238.
Russian Army Formations:
  Armies: Army of the Danube (Third Army); 108, 149-150, 152-153, 157, 159-160, 162-163, 168-169, 172-173, 177-179, 184-185, 188-189, 194-195, 206-207, 210, 213, 215-216, 223-224, 228-230, 235, 241, 249, 271, 296, 306, 330-331. First Army; 303, 323, 330, 333. Second Army; 279-280, 323, 330, 333. United (Western) Armies; 277, 279, 323, 330.
  Corps: I Cavalry Corps; 14, 44, 77, 83, 90, 96, 99, 171, 327-328. I Corps; 125, 132, 140, 142, 148, 198, 206, 210-211, 215-216, 229, 257-258, 303, 323, 330-331. II Cavalry Corps; 42, 56-58, 77-78, 82-83, 85, 90, 96, 99, 110, 114, 171, 185, 231, 250, 254. II Corps; 18, 34, 42, 70, 77, 83, 86, 90, 92, 96, 99, 110, 114, 171, 185, 211, 231, 250, 254, 292, 311, 342. III Cavalry Corps; 91, 231, 254, 327. III Corps; 34, 44, 77, 83, 85, 90, 93, 96, 99, 171, 202, 230, 246, 254. IV Cavalry Corps; 57-58, 77-78, 85, 96, 171, 204, 230, 254. IV Corps; 18, 34, 42, 58, 61-62, 70, 77, 85, 91, 96, 171, 230, 250, 254, 292. V Corps; 34, 44, 77, 90, 92, 171, 230, 254. VI Corps; 14-15, 29, 32, 34, 44, 77, 85, 90, 92, 109, 171, 230, 254, 328. VII Corps; 32, 34, 44, 77-78, 83, 90, 96, 99, 110, 114, 171, 185, 211, 231, 254. VIII Corps; 34, 44, 77, 85, 90, 92, 96, 171, 230, 246, 254, 309. Finland Corps; 125-126, 128-130, 331.
  Divisions: 1st Cuirassier Division; 85, 90, 92. 1st Grenadier Division; 96, 99. 2nd Cuirassier Division; 18, 85, 90, 96, 99. 2nd Grenadier Division; 96. 3rd Division; 34, 93, 96, 311. 4th Division; 44, 54, 56, 58, 61, 69, 83, 86, 96, 311, 342. 5th Division; 119, 121, 133, 320. 9th Division; 196, 311. 11th Division; 58, 62, 78, 82. 12th Division; 32, 44, 86, 98, 311. 13th Division; 235. 14th Division; 119, 123, 133, 144, 320. 17th Division; 58-62, 96. 18th Division; 196, 311. 23rd Division; 61-62, 78, 287. 26th Division; 32, 44, 51, 54, 56-57, 60-62, 86-87, 98, 287, 311.
Russian Army Units:
  Artillery: 1st Horse Company; 140, 197-198, 132, 322. 3rd Horse Company; 121-122, 133, 138, 144, 146, 322. 4th Light Company; 311. 5th Battery Company; 122, 133, 138, 321. 6th Battery Company; 132, 138, 144, 146, 321. 7th Battery Company; 34. 8th Battery Company; 298. 9th Battery Company; 297. 9th Light Company; 193, 198. 10th Battery Company; 299. 10th Light Company; 315, 322. 11th Horse Company; 165, 168, 198, 296, 306. 11th Light Company; 133, 144, 261, 322. 12th Horse Company; 167, 177, 241, 296, 306. 13th Horse Company; 196, 306. 14th Battery Company; 132-133, 138, 144, 198, 322. 14th Light Company, 298. 15th Horse Company; 151, 298. 15th Light Company; 156, 298. 16th Horse Company, 298. 16th Light Company; 297, 311. 17th Light Company; 297. 18th Battery Company; 297. 18th Light Company; 299. 21st Battery Company; 133, 322. 22nd Battery Company; 298. 23rd Horse Company; 118, 133, 198, 322. 25th Light Company; 298. 26th Light Company; 132, 138, 322. 27th Battery Company; 132, 193, 198. 27th Light Company; 122-123, 133, 138, 322. 28th Battery Company; 133, 322. 33rd Battery Company; 311. 34th Battery Company; 163, 165, 297. 34th Light Company; 297. 35th Light Company; 121, 132, 297. 38th Battery Company; 184, 297. 39th Battery Company; 297. 40th Light Company; 315, 322. 41st Light Company; 299. 49th Light Company; 118, 122. 50th Light

Company; 298. 57th Light Company; 132, 315, 322. Don Horse; 17, 57, 226.
Cavalry (irregular): 1st Kalmyks; 298. 2nd Kalmyks; 298. Bashkirs; 189, 211, 298. Ataman's Cossacks; 226. Barabanshchikov's Cossacks; 158, 161, 296, 306. Boda's Cossacks; 315, 321. Bug Cossacks; 25. Chechensky's Cossacks; 71. Chernozubov 8th's Cossacks; 22, 191, 194, 321. Chikilev's Cossacks; 151, 153, 298. Denisov's Cossacks; 204, 321. Dyachkin's Cossacks; 306. Gorin's Cossacks; 321. Grekov 4th's Cossacks; 306. Grekov 8th's Cossacks; 161, 296, 306. Grekov 9th's Cossacks; 311. Grekov 11th's Cossacks; 161, 296. Grekov 21st's Cossacks; 311. Ilovaisky 4th's Cossacks; 22, 321. Ilovaisky 11th's Cossacks; 35. Ilovaisky 12th's Cossacks; 321. Isaev 2nd's Cossacks; 306, 311. Kashkin's Cossacks; 321. Kireev 2nd's Cossacks; 162, 297, 306. Loshchilin's Cossacks; 178, 321. Lukovkin 2nd's Cossacks; 164, 297, 306. Melnikov 5th's Cossacks; 184, 224, 296, 306. Nieroth's Volunteers; 315. Panteleev's Cossacks; 152, 178, 296, 321. Perekop Tatars; 22. Platov 4th's Cossacks; 119, 132, 321. Poltava Cossacks; 113, 288. Popov 13th's Cossacks; 71. Rodionov 2nd's Cossacks; 118, 122, 130, 132, 147, 197-198, 321. Selivanov's Cossacks; 315, 321. Semenchikov's Cossacks; 311. Shamshev's Cossacks; 113. Stavropol Kalmyks; 20, 321. Teptyar Cossacks; 131. Ukrainian Cossacks; 150, 156-157, 312. Ural Cossacks; 142, 153, 156, 204, 297-298. Vlasov's Cossacks; 298. Yagodin's Cossacks; 269, 321. Yakhontov's Cossacks; 315, 321. Yevpatoria Tatars; 161, 296, 311.
Cavalry (regular): Akhtyrka Hussars; 60, 72, 311. Alexandria Hussars; 158, 161, 167-168, 204, 296, 312. Arzamas Dragoons; 160, 167-168, 226, 296. Belorussia Hussars; 204, 297, 312. Chernigov Dragoons/Mounted Jägers; 70, 97, 311. Chuguev Ulans; 298. Combined Cuirassiers; 123-124, 133, 198. Combined Dragoons; 132, 138, 321. Combined Hussars; 118, 138, 140-141, 178, 197-198, 321. Courland Dragoons; 60, 311. Dorpat Dragoons; 297. Finland Dragoons; 261, 315, 321. Grodno Hussars; 122-124, 130, 132, 138-139, 193, 264, 315, 321. Her Majesty's Cuirassiers; 90, 109. His Majesty's Cuirassiers; 77, 90, 109. Irkutsk Hussars; 311. Izyum Hussars; 20, 22, 47, 152, 261, 307, 321. Kargopol Dragoons; 61, 82, 87. Kazan Dragoons; 20, 22, 307, 315, 321. Kharkov Dragoons; 60, 311. Kiev Dragoons; 60, 311. Kinburn Dragoons; 183, 297, 306. Lithuania Ulans; 72, 311. Livland Dragoons/Mounted Jägers; 162, 204, 297, 312. Lubny Hussars; 151, 155-156, 298. Malorussia Cuirassiers; 93-94. Mariupol Hussars; 50. Military Order Cuirassiers; 95. Mittau Dragoons; 118, 132, 144, 321. Moscow Dragoons; 77, 87. Nezhin Dragoons; 44, 71-72. Novgorod Cuirassiers; 93-94. Novorossia Dragoons; 70, 97, 311. Olviopol Hussars; 226, 297. Pavlograd Hussars; 197, 241, 306. Pereyaslavl Dragoons; 298. Poland Ulans; 82, 140-141, 321. Pskov Dragoons; 72, 82. Riga Dragoons; 124, 132, 140-141, 315, 321. Saint Petersburg Dragoons; 297. Serpukhov Dragoons; 155-156, 298. Seversk Dragoons; 297. Smolensk Dragoons; 298. Starodub Dragoons; 158, 161, 296. Sumy Hussars; 83, 311. Tatar Ulans; 158, 160-161, 164, 296, 311. Tver Dragoons; 156, 298-299, 306. Vladimir Dragoons; 151, 298-299. Volhynia Ulans; 177, 224, 241, 306. Yamburg Dragoons; 133, 140, 143, 321. Yekaterinoslav Cuirassiers; 95. Yelisavetgrad Hussars; 69, 83. Zhitomir Dragoons; 158, 161, 226, 296.
Infantry: 1st Marines; 118, 133, 198, 320. 2nd Marines; 142, 307, 320. Alexopol Infantry; 311. Apsheron Infantry; 297. Arkhangelogorod Infantry; 298, 311. Azov Infantry; 133, 193, 320. Belozersk Infantry; 62. Bialystok Infantry; 151, 299. Bryansk Infantry; 315. Chernigov Infantry; 92-93, 311. Combined Grenadiers; 121, 123, 133, 320. Combined Infantry; 118, 315,

320-321. Crimea Infantry; 299. Dnieper Infantry, 297, 311. Estland Infantry; 132, 138, 144, 320. Galits Infantry; 298. Kaluga Infantry; 122-123, 133, 320. Kamchatka Infantry; 298. Kexholm Infantry; 62, 122-123. Kolyvan Infantry; 297, 311. Kostroma Infantry; 297, 311. Kozlov Infantry; 297, 311. Kremenchug Infantry; 61, 86, 311. Kura Infantry; 297, 311. Leib Grenadiers; 123. Libau Infantry; 30. Lithuania Infantry; 132, 146, 320. Narva Infantry; 311. Navaginsk Infantry; 132, 140, 144, 193, 320. Mingrelia Infantry; 298. Mogilev Infantry; 122-123, 132, 144, 198, 320. Murom Infantry; 93-94, 311. Nasheburg Infantry; 297, 306. Neva Infantry; 132, 144, 320. Nizov Infantry; 133, 198, 320. Novo-Ingermanland Infantry; 311. Okhotsk Infantry; 298. Olonets Infantry; 298. Orël Infantry; 32, 99. Pavlov Grenadiers; 99, 123, 198. Perm Infantry; 122-123, 133, 198, 320. Pernov Infantry; 62. Petrovsk Infantry; 132, 320. Podolsk Infantry; 144, 211. Polotsk Infantry; 132. Poltava Infantry; 311. Reval Infantry; 93-94, 311. Ryazhsk Infantry; 297, 311. Saint Petersburg Grenadiers; 123, 127. Saratov Infantry; 297. Schlüsselburg Infantry; 156, 298. Selenginsk Infantry; 93. Sevsk Infantry; 122, 133, 146, 198, 320. Smolensk Infantry; 99, 311. Sofia Infantry; 30-31. Staro-Ingermanland Infantry; 298, 311. Staro-Oskol Infantry; 154, 298. Tambov Infantry; 297, 311. Tauride Grenadiers; 123, 127. Tenginsk Infantry; 132, 138, 144, 320. Tobolsk Infantry; 61, 311. Tula Infantry; 132, 138, 144, 320. Ukraine Infantry; 298, 311. Vitebsk Infantry; 163, 167, 297. Vladimir Infantry; 297, 311. Volhynia Infantry; 61, 86, 311. Voronezh Infantry; 132, 144, 146, 198, 320. Vyatka Infantry; 154, 298. Vyborg Infantry; 298-299. Wilmanstrand Infantry; 32. Yakutsk Infantry; 297. Yaroslavl Infantry; 299. Yekaterinoslav Grenadiers; 123.
Lifeguard: Artillery; 90, 333. Chevalier Guard; 62, 198. Combined Cavalry; 122-124, 133. Cossacks; 20, 22, 307. Dragoons; 123. *Équipage*; 17. Finland; 90, 95, 109. Horse; 62, 189, 198. Horse Artillery; 14, 33, 57. Hussars; 83, 100, 113, 123. Jägers; 77, 90, 95, 109. Preobrazhensky; 96. Sappers; 246. Semenovsky; 244. Ulans; 62, 99-100.
Light infantry: 1st Jägers; 69, 70, 77, 97-98, 110. 2nd Jägers; 130, 132, 136, 320. 3rd Jägers; 130, 132, 136, 320. 4th Jägers; 69, 311. 5th Jägers; 83, 87, 99, 311. 6th Jägers; 14, 29, 87, 311. 7th Jägers; 158, 165, 167, 176, 297, 306. 8th Jägers; 299. 10th Jägers; 158, 160, 297, 306. 11th Jägers; 29, 32. 12th Jägers; 297. 13th Jägers; 163, 167, 297, 311. 14th Jägers; 158, 160, 164-165, 167-168, 176, 296, 306, 311. 19th Jägers; 29, 50. 20th Jägers; 35, 37, 70-71, 96, 98, 212, 311. 23rd Jägers; 121, 132, 136, 261, 320. 24th Jägers; 121, 198, 320. 25th Jägers; 122-123, 132, 144, 193, 320. 26th Jägers; 121-122, 132, 138, 140-141, 307, 320. 27th Jägers; 164, 296, 306. 28th Jägers; 183, 227, 306. 29th Jägers; 154, 298. 30th Jägers; 69. 32nd Jägers; 227, 306, 311. 33rd Jägers; 14, 29, 204. 37th Jägers; 151, 156, 298, 311. 38th Jägers; 158, 165, 167, 176, 296, 306. 39th Jägers; 153-154, 299. 41st Jägers; 311. 44th Jägers; 315, 321. 45th Jägers; 154, 298. 48th Jägers; 69. Combined Jägers; 133, 320.
Opolchenie: 19, 37, 279, 281, 323, 333. Bely; 142. Chernigov; 67. Kaluga; 66, 70, 110, 213. Malorussia; 110, 213. Moscow; 213. Novgorod; 131, 142, 189, 193, 307. Poltava; 67. Ryazan; 213. Smolensk; 66-67, 213. Saint Petersburg; 117-121, 123-124, 127-128, 132-133, 136, 139-140, 142, 198, 211, 260-261, 307, 321, 343. Sychyovka; 142. Toropets; 142. Tula; 14, 66, 213. Tver; 22. Vladimir; 45, 213.
Ruzhany; 249-251.
Rzhavets; 61-62.
Rzhavka; 78, 83-85.
Rzhevsky, Pavel Alexeevich; 113.

Sabaneev, Ivan Vasilievich; 150-151, 196, 297-298.
Saint-Cyr, Laurent de Gouvion; 53-54, 67, 119-128, 130-132, 134, 139, 159, 217, 276, 341.

Saint Petersburg; 10, 18, 46-47, 82, 121, 128, 142, 203, 224, 234-235, 237, 244, 252, 278, 285, 324, 326, 335.
Saint-Priest, Guillaume Emmanuel Guignard de; 52, 247, 332.
Saken, Fabian Wilhelmovich Osten-; 150-151, 153-157, 163, 229, 231, 240, 249-250, 253-255, 296, 298, 330.
Saltanovka; 279, 323.
Sanson, Nicolas-Antoine; 38, 42, 73.
Sappers; 9, 73, 99, 128, 173, 187, 246.
Saxony, Kingdom of; contingent of the Grande Armée; 151-157, 159, 219, 248-251, 253-256, 274, 342.
Sazonov, Ivan Terentyevich; 124, 130-132
Scharnhorst, Gerhard Johann David von; 263, 273.
Schaulen [Šiauliai]; 237, 259-261.
Schilale [Šilalė]; 264, 267.
Schillupischken [Novokolkhoznoe]; 265, 269.
Schwarzenberg, Karl Philipp; 54, 67, 110, 149-158, 172, 174, 206, 212-213, 218, 222-223, 225, 229, 237, 240-241, 248-256, 310, 313, 343.
Sebezh; 124, 126, 143, 237, 307.
Ségur, Philippe Paul de; 57, 202, 334.
Semlevo; 25, 57, 65, 69.
Senno; 67, 81, 139-140, 142, 144.
Seredinskoe; 44, 50.
Seslavin, Alexander Nikitich; 14-15, 50, 52, 62, 70-72, 77, 85, 88, 109, 113, 191, 193-194, 207, 212, 219, 223-225, 294.
Seydlitz-Kurzbach, Anton Friedrich Florian von; 262, 265-266, 342.
Shabashevichi; 168, 175, 183-185, 188, 191, 206.
Shakhovsky, Alexander Alexandrovich; 22.
Shakhovsky, Ivan Leontevich; 34, 93-94.
Shakhovsky, Pëtr Ivanovich; 143.
Shchelkanovo; 77, 85.
Shcherbatov, Alexei Grigorievich; 176-177, 197, 252.
Shepelev, Dmitry Dmitrievich; 260, 265, 269-270.
Shepelev, Vasily Fëdorovich; 110.
Sheremetev, Nikolai Petrovich; 22.
Shilovo; 85, 90.
Shulman, Fëdor Maksimovich; 138, 146.
Sicard, Joseph Victorien; 20.
Sierawski, Jan Kanty Julian; 167-168.

Sievers, Karl Karlovich; 270.
Sievers, Yegor Karlovich; 118, 120, 128, 131.
Sivoshina; 118, 120, 125.
Slavkovo; 65.
Slidzy; 143-144.
Slonim; 150-151, 153-154, 157-159, 237, 240, 248-251.
Slutsk; 159, 248, 301.
Smolensk; 8, 10, 13, 20-21, 28, 37-38, 40, 42, 45, 47-52, 53-54, 57, 62, 64-73, 75-78, 80-85, 87, 90-92, 96-98, 100, 103-105, 130, 133, 141-142, 147, 152, 206, 212-213, 217, 224, 230, 237, 279-283, 288, 291, 292-293, 323, 327-328, 330, 333, 342.
Smoliyantsy; 108, 136, 138-139, 144-147.
Smorgon; 172, 174, 204, 206, 210, 213, 216, 218-219, 222-223.
Sołtyk, Roman; 199, 304, 342.
Solovieva; 67-70, 76-77.
Spasskoe [Spas-Zagorye]; 16, 18-19, 29, 32.
Stakhov; 174, 180-181, 185, 188, 190-191, 196-197, 204, 207.
Steinheil, Fabian Gotthard von; 67, 117-118, 121, 125-126, 128-129, 130-132, 136-138, 144, 146, 181, 191, 193, 197-198, 269, 323, 331.
Stolypin, Nikolai Alekseevich; 121, 124, 140-141, 147.
Stragglers; 39, 49, 55, 60-61, 63, 68, 83, 88, 97-98, 100, 190-191, 194, 199-200, 202, 204, 223, 226, 229-230, 234, 239, 261, 270, 304, 309.
Stroganov, Pavel Alexandrovich; 93, 96.
Strunya; 121-122, 126, 130.
Studyanka; 180-182, 184-185, 186-187, 189-193, 195, 197-201, 204, 206-207, 210, 283.
Sukhozanet 1st, Ivan Onufrievich; 197, 227, 260, 333.
Sukhozanet 2nd, Nikolai Onufrievich; 140.
Svislach; 159, 174, 205, 207.
Switzerland, contingent of the Grande Armée; 199. *1er régiment suisse*; 121, 124. *2e régiment suisse*; 124, 129. *4e régiment suisse*; 124.
Sychyovka; 51-52, 142.
Syrokorenie; 101-102.
Sysoev, Vasily Alexeevich; 16.

Talyzin, Fëdor Ianovich; 30.

Tarutino; 14, 17-19, 25, 28, 33, 78, 230-231, 281-282, 323, 328, 340.
Taube, Karl Karlovich; 93.
Tauroggen [Tauragė]; 259, 261, 265, 267.
Teste, François Antoine; 13.
Tettenborn, Friedrich Karl von; 215, 227, 260.
Tilsit [Sovetsk, Kaliningrad Oblast]; 133, 225, 239, 258-262, 264-269, 271, 318.
Toll, Karl Wilhelm von; 35-36, 42, 64, 66, 90, 203, 246, 305, 330, 333, 336, 340.
Tolochin [Tołoczyn]; 112, 114, 178, 185, 206.
Tormasov, Alexander Petrovich; 34, 90, 92-96, 223, 229, 250, 254, 277, 331.
Troitskoe; 11, 13.
Tsarevo-Zaimishche; 52, 54-57.
Tuchkov 2nd, Sergei Alekseevich; 163, 212, 229-231, 240, 250, 254.
Tula; 9, 18, 66, 237.
Turchaninov, Andrey Petrovich; 129-130.
Tutolmin, Ivan Akinfievich; 22.
Tver; 23, 105, 169, 237.
Typhus; 243-244, 247.
Tyszkiewicz, Tadeusz; 38, 45.

Ukholoda; 180-181, 206.
Ulla river; 125, 130, 134-136, 139, 144, 148, 205-206.
Umanets, Andrei Semënovich; 183, 306.
Urusov, Alexander Petrovich; 212, 223, 229-230, 234.
Ushacha river; 125, 129-130.
Uvarov, Fëdor Petrovich; 57, 62, 65, 292, 328.
Uvarovo; 90, 92-94, 96, 99.

Vadbolsky, Ivan Mikhailovich; 60.
Valova lake; 122-124.
Valutina Gora; 77, 280.
Vasilchikov 1st, Ilarion Vasilevich; 58, 60-61, 204, 229, 240, 250, 252-254.
Vasilchikov 2nd, Dmitry Vasilevich; 70.
Vaudoncourt, Guillaume de; 247, 334-336.
Vereya; 12-13, 29, 38, 40, 44-45, 50, 287-288, 292.
Veselovo; 165, 173-174, 180, 183-185, 191, 193, 206.
Victor (See Perrin)
Vileyka [Wilejka]; 115, 195, 212-213, 216.
Viliya [Neris] river; 195, 228, 238-239, 257.
Vilna [Vilnius]; 53, 108, 115, 120, 131-133, 139, 148, 152, 157, 159, 162, 168, 172, 174, 181, 183, 188, 204-206, 210-211, 213-216, 218-221, 223-232, 233, 237-241, 244-248, 250-251, 258-259, 263, 271-272, 277-278, 284, 323, 324.
Vistula river; 133, 229, 238, 240-241, 243-244, 256, 271, 275, 277, 310, 313, 316.
Vitebsk; 54, 68, 72, 75-76, 81, 107, 122, 134, 139-142, 148, 211, 237, 257, 279, 307.
Vivandières; 10, 125.
Vladimir; 203.
Vladimir [Volodymyr]; 150.
Vlastov, Yegor Ivanovich; 120-121, 124, 126, 131-132, 143, 147, 152, 178, 185, 189, 191, 193, 197-198, 204, 210, 215, 258, 260-261, 269.
Voinov, Alexander Lvovich; 150-151, 158, 164, 168, 230, 297.
Volhynia; 114, 150-151, 156-157, 213, 236-237, 249-250, 253, 301.
Volkonsky, Pëtr Mikhailovich, Prince; 9, 142, 244, 246, 254, 307, 331.
Volkovo; 78, 82-83.
Vop river; 72-75, 289-290.
Voronovo; 14, 18.
Vuich, Nikolai Vasilevich; 29.
Vyazma; 13, 22, 25, 38-41, 48-51, 53-55, 57-65, 69, 78, 103-105, 217, 282, 292-293, 340, 342.
Vyshny Volochyok; 105, 142, 237.

Warsaw; 149-150, 217-219, 221, 229, 243, 253, 256, 274, 313.
Warsaw, Duchy of; 220, 222, 225, 241, 250-254, 265; (Polish) contingent of the Grande Armée; 15, 77, 81-83, 85, 113, 159, 164-165, 167, 177, 195, 199, 225, 251, 253, 256, 274, 300, 342; *1 Pułk Piechoty*; 165; *2 Pułk Ułanów*; 176; *6 Pułk Piechoty*; 167; *7 Pułk Ułanów*; 176; *14 Pułk Piechoty*; 159; *15 Pułk Ułanów*; 159; *17 Pułk Piechoty*; 159; *18 Pułk Ułanów*; 300.
Wehlau [Znamensk]; 269-270.
Westphalia, Kingdom of, contingent of the Grande Armée; 12, 25, 48-49, 55, 57, 65, 82-83, 85, 286, 343; *8e régiment d'infanterie de ligne*; 55.
Willoughby, Nesbit Josiah; 130.
Wiłkomierz [Ukmergė]; 229, 237, 240, 259-260.
Wilkowischken [Vilkaviškis]; 239.
Wilson, Robert Thomas; 104, 343.

Wintzingerode, Ferdinand Fëdorovich; 18, 20-22, 45-47, 52, 74, 152, 244, 254, 311-312, 331.
Witt, Ivan Osipovich de; 150, 156-157.
Wittgenstein-Berleburg, Ludwig Adolf Peter zu Sayn-; 45, 54, 64, 67, 76, 80-81, 110, 114-115, 117-134, 136, 138-144, 147-148, 152, 164, 169, 171-175, 177-180, 182-185, 189-191, 193-195, 197-198, 200-201, 204-208, 210-212, 215-216, 222-223, 228-229, 231, 233-234, 240, 257-260, 262, 265-266, 269-272, 277-278, 303, 309, 320, 328, 330-331, 338.
Wołczyn; 151, 153, 251.
Wołkowysk; 151-157, 249-250.
Wrede, Carl Philipp von; 120, 128-132, 143, 180, 195, 213, 215, 223, 225.
Württemberg, contingent of the *Grande Armée*; 36, 99, 164, 342; *Infanterie-Regiment Nr. 7*; 159, 300.
Württemberg, Friedrich Eugen Carl Paul Ludwig von; 44, 54, 56, 58, 60-61, 69, 83, 86, 92, 96, 104, 254, 311, 333, 342.
Wysokie Litewskie; 151, 153, 251.

Yefremov, Ivan Yefremovich; 50, 52.
Yegorievskoe; 40, 50-51.

Yelnya; 28, 38, 42, 50, 52, 66-71, 77, 96, 282, 293.
Yermolov, Alexey Petrovich; 14-16, 30-32, 42, 51, 57-58, 60, 62, 64, 83, 87, 109, 112, 114, 171, 178, 185, 189, 194-195, 207, 216, 240, 246, 303, 309, 331, 333, 340.
Yorck, Johann David Ludwig von; 259-268, 270-273, 316, 317, 332.
Yukhnov; 13, 25, 28, 38, 40, 42, 50-51, 57, 64.
Yukhnovka; 163-164.
Yurkovsky, Anastasy Antonovich; 69-70, 76-77, 83.
Yurovichi; 118, 121, 125.
Yurovo; 78, 83.
Yushkovichi; 167, 177, 183.
Yuzefovich, Dmitry Mikhailovich; 60, 252.

Zajączek, Józef; 77, 81-83, 85, 107, 170, 173, 197.
Zembin; 115, 164, 167-168, 175, 177, 180-181, 183-185, 188, 195, 200-201, 204, 210, 215, 283.
Zhartsy; 120-121.
Zhemchuzhnikov, Apollon Sepanovich; 211, 270, 307, 323.
Zvenigorod; 22, 74.

From Reason to Revolution – Warfare 1721-1815
http://www.helion.co.uk/series/from-reason-to-revolution-1721-1815.php

The 'From Reason to Revolution' series covers the period of military history 1721–1815, an era in which fortress-based strategy and linear battles gave way to the nation-in-arms and the beginnings of total war.

This era saw the evolution and growth of light troops of all arms, and of increasingly flexible command systems to cope with the growing armies fielded by nations able to mobilise far greater proportions of their manpower than ever before. Many of these developments were fired by the great political upheavals of the era, with revolutions in America and France bringing about social change which in turn fed back into the military sphere as whole nations readied themselves for war. Only in the closing years of the period, as the reactionary powers began to regain the upper hand, did a military synthesis of the best of the old and the new become possible.

The series examines the military and naval history of the period in a greater degree of detail than has hitherto been attempted, and has a very wide brief, with the intention of covering all aspects from the battles, campaigns, logistics, and tactics, to the personalities, armies, uniforms, and equipment.

Submissions
The publishers would be pleased to receive submissions for this series. Please email reasontorevolution@helion.co.uk, or write to Helion & Company Limited, Unit 8 Amherst Business Centre, Budbrooke Road, Warwick, CV34 5WE

You may also be interested in:

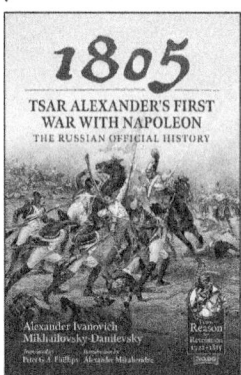

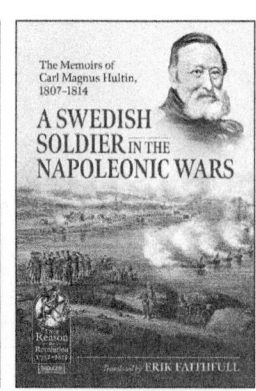

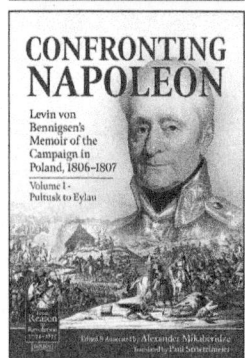

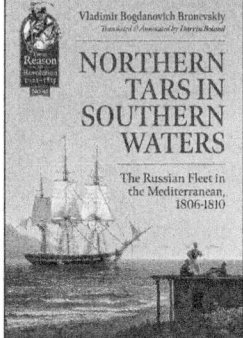

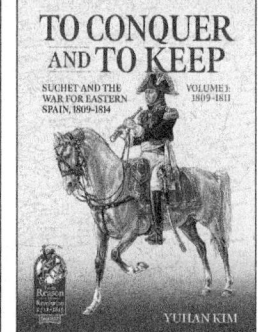